American and English Popular Entertainment

PERFORMING ARTS INFORMATION GUIDE SERIES

Series Editor: Louis A. Rachow, Librarian, The Walter Hampden-Edwin Booth Theatre Collection and Memorial Library, New York

Also in this series:

ACTORS AND ACTING—*Edited by Stephen M. Archer**

THE AMERICAN STAGE TO WORLD WAR I—*Edited by Don B. Wilmeth*

THE AMERICAN STAGE FROM WORLD WAR I TO THE 1970S—*Edited by Don B. Wilmeth**

BUSINESS OF THE THEATRE, FILMS, AND BROADCASTING—*Edited by J. Kline Hobbs**

GUIDE TO DANCE IN FILM—*Edited by David Parker and Esther Siegel*

LAW OF THE THEATRE, FILMS, AND BROADCASTING—*Edited by Daniel Jon Strehl**

PERFORMING ARTS RESEARCH—*Edited by Marion K. Whalon*

STAGE SCENERY, MACHINERY, AND LIGHTING—*Edited by Richard Stoddard*

THEATRE AND CINEMA ARCHITECTURE—*Edited by Richard Stoddard*

THEATRICAL COSTUME—*Edited by Jackson Kesler*

*in preparation

The above series is part of the
GALE INFORMATION GUIDE LIBRARY

The Library consists of a number of separate series of guides covering major areas in the social sciences, humanities, and current affairs.

General Editor: Paul Wasserman, Professor and former Dean, School of Library and Information Services, University of Maryland

Managing Editor: Denise Allard Adzigian, Gale Research Company

American and English Popular Entertainment

A GUIDE TO INFORMATION SOURCES

Volume 7 in the Performing Arts Information Guide Series

Don B. Wilmeth

Professor of Theatre Arts and English
and
Chairman of the Department of Theatre Arts
Brown University
Providence, Rhode Island

Foreword by Brooks McNamara

Professor of Theatre (Graduate)
New York University
and
Curator, The Shubert Archives
New York City

Gale Research Company
Book Tower, Detroit, Michigan 48226

Library of Congress Cataloging in Publication Data

Wilmeth, Don B
    American and English popular entertainment.

    (Performing arts information guide series ; v. 7)
(Gale information guide library)
    Includes indexes.
    1. Amusement—United States—Bibliography. 2. Amuse-
ment—Great Britain—Bibliography. 3. Performing Arts—
United States—Bibliography. 4. Performing Arts—Great Britain—
Bibliography. 5. Popular Culture—United States—Bibliography.
6. Popular Culture—Great Britain—Bibliography. I. Title.
II. Series.
Z7511.W53   [GB1815]   016.79   79-22869
ISBN 0-8103-1454-1

VITA

Don B. Wilmeth (Ph.D., University of Illinois) teaches theatre history and directs theatre productions at Brown University, where he is now professor of theatre and English and chairman of the Department of Theatre Arts. He has published articles in such journals as THEATRE NOTEBOOK, THEATRE SURVEY, CHOICE, EDUCATIONAL THEATRE JOURNAL, and THE JOURNAL OF THE ILLINOIS STATE HISTORICAL SOCIETY. He is the contributor of two chapters on aspects of American popular entertainment in A HANDBOOK OF AMERICAN POPULAR CULTURE. He has served as book review editor for the THEATRE JOURNAL (formerly EDUCATIONAL THEATRE JOURNAL), columnist for USA TODAY, advisory editor for NINETEENTH CENTURY THEATRE RESEARCH, and has been on the board of directors of the American Society for Theatre Research, the Theatre Library Association (in his capacity as chairman of the George Freedley and TLA book award committees), and the Society for the Advancement of Education. He is editor of THE AMERICAN STAGE TO WORLD WAR I, volume 4 in the Gale Performing Arts Information Guide Series, author of a recently published critical biography of the eighteenth-century actor George Frederick Cooke, and is currently completing a glossary of popular entertainment terminology and slang to be published by Greenwood Press.

CONTENTS

Foreword ix

Preface xi

Acknowledgments xvii

Part I.   General Sources on Popular Entertainment
   Chapter 1.   European Origins, Early Forms, Major
                References, and Surveys. 3
   Chapter 2.   American Historical, Social, and Cultural
                Background 21
   Chapter 3.   General Sources on Popular Entertainment 31
           A.   American Forms 31
           B.   English Forms 51

Part II. Popular Entertainment Forms: Predominantly American
   Chapter 4.   The Circus and Wild West Exhibitions 67
           A.   Circus Histories and Surveys 67
           B.   Animal Acts and Performance Specialists 91
           C.   Early Circus Clowns and Major Surveys 97
           D.   Wild West Exhibitions and William F. Cody
                ("Buffalo Bill") 101
   Chapter 5.   Outdoor Amusements and Environmental
                Entertainments 121
           A.   Fairs, Exhibitions, and Pleasure Gardens 121
           B.   Dime Museums, P.T. Barnum, Freaks, and
                Wax Museums 126
           C.   Carnivals 140
           D.   Amusement Parks, Theme Parks, and Seaside
                Resorts 145
   Chapter 6.   Variety Forms 153
           A.   Medicine Shows and Patent Medicines 153
           B.   The Minstrel Show 160
           C.   Early Variety and Vaudeville 171
           D.   Burlesque and Striptease 196
           E.   Lyceum and Chautauqua 203

Contents

Chapter 7. Optical and Mechanical Entertainments, Stage
            Magic, Puppetry, and Toy Theatres 209
   A. Stage Magic 209
        1. Bibliographies 209
        2. General Histories, Reference, and Autobiography
            and Biography 211
   B. Puppetry and Toy Theatres (Juvenile Drama) 221
   C. Stage Illusions, Panorama and Diorama, and Early
            Optical and Mechanical Entertainments 227
Chapter 8. Early Musical Theatre and Revues 237
Chapter 9. Major Sources on Principal English Forms 263
   A. Pantomime 263
   B. Music Hall: Principal and Recent Sources 274

Part III. Popular Theatre: English and American
Chapter 10. Popular Theatre: General Sources, United
             States 295
Chapter 11. Popular Theatre: General Select Sources,
             Great Britain 311
Chapter 12. Major Dramatic Genres and Forms: English
             and American 323
Chapter 13. Native American Types from the Yankee to
             Toby 335
Chapter 14. American Small-Town and Provincial
             Operations 343
Chapter 15. The American Showboat (Floating Theatres) 359

Appendixes
Appendix A. Selected Periodicals and Serials 365
             Periodicals and Serials 365
Appendix B. Specialized Collections and Museums 375
             Collections and Museums 375
Appendix C. Concerned Organizations 383

Indexes
Author Index 389
Title Index 411
Subject Index 431

FOREWORD

About a dozen years ago I began work on what was for the time a somewhat eccentric and academically suspect project, a history of the American medicine show. As penalty for my hubris, I found myself involved with research problems of a sort that I had never encountered before. It soon became clear that medicine showmen had not been much inclined to write about their exploits, except in a mellow old age, when the main events of their careers often took on a somewhat romantic glow. In fact, all of the early books and articles on the shows, I discovered, were the most casual sort of journalism, relentlessly anecdotal and fanciful in the extreme. Yet, often they contained all there was to be found about some event or personality central to my research. I began to use what I found quite warily, largely out of desperation, and soon discovered to my delight that by careful cross checking it could often be turned into revealing source material about both the facts and the spirit of a long-vanished American theatre form. Serious research about the medicine show, in fact, began to seem quite possible.

This piece of serendipity was more than offset, however, by the great difficulty I experienced in simply determining the titles of these early works. Aside from portions of Raymond Toole-Stott's great CIRCUS AND ALLIED ARTS: A WORLD BIBLIOGRAPHY, which did not bear very much on my project, I soon found that there were no useful bibliographies in the field of popular entertainment-- and, in fact, not even much agreement about the definition of the field. The result was that my research was drawn out for months and, I suspect, years longer than it ought to have taken, as I discovered a reference to some obscure book or pamphlet--usually by accident--and painfully tracked down a copy, only to find that it had no real connection with my work.

Many times the curious research problems connected with popular entertainment seemed insurmountable, and I often thought about abandoning my project for something less colorful and more conventionally documented. But I did not. I had become genuinely interested in the medicine show and I was growing increasingly attracted to the whole elusive field of popular entertainment. Soon I found that I was not alone in my interest in popular performance as a subject for serious study. Important and sometimes classic research, I discovered,

Foreword

was being done in spite of all difficulties by Sybil Rosenfeld, Michael Booth, George Speaight, Ralph Allen, A.H. Saxon, Robert Toll, and David Mayer, among others.

The amount of serious work in the field was small, but it seemed to be growing steadily. In fact, by the mid-seventies, it was apparent that the study of popular entertainment was starting to emerge as a viable part of theatre history. As old biases broke down, such forms as circus, vaudeville, and burlesque were coming to be seen not merely as parts of some primitive substratum of theatre, but as significant kinds of cultural expression, well worth the time and trouble required for close investigation. Conferences on various facets of popular performance were held in England at the University of Manchester and the University of Kent, and in this country at Ohio State University and, under the co-sponsorship of the American Society for Theatre Research and the Theatre Library Association, at Lincoln Center. Issues of THEATRE QUARTERLY, JOURNAL OF POPULAR CULTURE, and EDUCATIONAL THEATRE JOURNAL were devoted to discussion of popular material, and John Towsen and I attempted to sketch out the dimensions of the emerging field in a 1974 issue of THE DRAMA REVIEW.

Towsen appended to the issue a brief list of source materials in an attempt to provide readers with references to at least a few standard works. "Since there has been little scholarly research in the field of popular entertainment," he wrote, "there are no comprehensive bibliographies in such areas as vaudeville, melodrama, carnivals, etc. In such cases, the bibliographies provided in the standard works on the subject are usually of most use to the reader." To this day, aside from Toole-Stott's brilliant but specialized volumes, there are no bibliographies on the subject of popular entertainment beyond those contained in books devoted to one or another aspect of the field. There is a certain irony in the fact that many of the basic bibliographic problems which I first encountered in the sixties remain for the student and scholar in a field which now is generally acknowledged to offer immense scholarly opportunity.

Some of these problems, I believe, are built into the study of popular literature and will probably always exist. But at least one major difficulty--the lack of a useful general bibliography of works on American and British popular entertainment--has now been surmounted by Professor Don B. Wilmeth. In the work that follows, Professor Wilmeth offers us a systematically organized and painstakingly researched survey of the materials available to the historian of popular entertainment. It is clearly a valuable research tool. But it is perhaps more valuable in terms of the stimulus which it will surely offer young historians to seek new intellectual connections among the various forms of popular entertainment and between those forms and the culture which surrounds them. With this work, I think, a new field of theatre research finally has begun to come of age.

Brooks McNamara
New York University

PREFACE

To the best of my knowledge, this is the first attempt to assemble in one volume sources on all major forms of American and English popular entertainment (including a selective section on "popular theatre"). "Popular entertainment" is tricky nomenclature; its meaning has been used in this guide in a fairly specific way but with both limitations, restrictions, and some flexibility. In general, popular entertainment in the context of this guide refers to live amusements created by professional showmen for profit and aimed at broad, relatively unsophisticated audiences. A small section is devoted to precinematic optical entertainments, which, although not "live," did depend on the ingenuity of showmen and represents the transition from popular culture in the entertainment business to mass culture.

Prior to the late eighteenth century, popular entertainments could not appeal to large audiences, for a more concentrated society and the incorporation of the majority of the population into that society was necessary in order to foster popular entertainment. In this country, for example, with the rise of technology and the expansion of the frontier during the nineteenth century, Americans found increased time for leisure activities and developed a need for entertainment to fill their often empty lives. As urban centers developed, a huge market for entertainment was created; whereas rural America depended upon the traveling troupe in the form of a circus, a Wild West show, a repertoire or a variety company.

Popular entertainment, then, as defined above, flourished during the nineteenth century, although vestiges of some forms still remain and others continue to flourish, such as the amusement park. Others began their evolutions prior to the nineteenth century but flourished during that century. The focus throughout this guide is, therefore, on the nineteenth century, although selected sources are included on antecedents of the various forms and their early origins. Likewise, forms such as the circus or musical theatre have continued their evolutions with unbroken lines of development. For these forms, major survey sources which cover their entire histories have been included.

Most popular entertainment forms lack a strong literary base and depend more significantly on the performer and the audience than a written text. I have chosen to exclude most of the textual sources and have instead concentrated on sources which provide a comprehensive history or analysis of individual forms. A section on popular theatre has been included but is quite selective. This is one area, or perhaps even a separate category, of popular entertainment that offers great difficulties in terms of definition because of its scripted nature and its overlap with mainstream theatre forms. Virtually all theatre histories deal with various aspects of popular theatre. This guide lists the more specialized and major sources and excludes most general histories. The user of the guide is encouraged to consider this section as a complement to other major references on American and English theatre (see items 18 and 93). In order to include as many specific sources as possible on popular entertainment, I have excluded most general reference materials as well. The user should, therefore, consult item 89 for additional reference sources.

Somewhat arbitrarily, because of the emphasis on live entertainment, this guide ends with the advent of the motion picture, although sources have been included that carry a given form to its demise or to the present, in many cases stretching well beyond the establishment of the motion picture.

In devising categories for this guide I have been influenced in part by the amount of material available on specific forms. The user of the guide should be aware that throughout history popular forms have appeared, merged, mutated, disappeared, and, in some cases, reappeared in new guises. A number of sources that touch on several forms but are most useful for one specific form have been placed where in my judgment they offer the greatest usefulness. In order to avoid too many subdivisions, the sources are arranged alphabetically and not chronologically, although in a very general way the entire guide is so arranged as to suggest the overall evolution of popular entertainment. Subheadings, likewise, are kept to a minimum. The overlapping nature of the forms suggests a great deal of cross-listing. This too, however, has been kept minimal, although major sources are in some instances cross-listed. To do this throughout would have necessitated the elimination of too many other sources. Instead, the user is well advised to survey a section thoroughly, as well as related sections, and the indexes.

This is not meant to be an exhaustive listing, indeed, this would have been impossible. As explained below, some sections are more selective than others because of the availability of a few excellent specialized bibliographies. Each chapter has demanded different criteria and judgments. Specialists may find certain sections or chapters highly selective. Selectivity became a necessity in order to be as comprehensive in coverage as possible. I have examined, or attempted to examine, several thousand sources other than those listed. The choices made have not been done so in a capricious manner, but I must admit to some personal preferences, bias in certain highly selective chapters, and lack of accessibility, or ignorance. Some rather mediocre sources are included in order to warn the user or because of a lack of excellence in that area. Ultimately, my aim has been to make available a balanced guide with a historical overview. In each section major, standard, or recent sources have been stressed, although more specialized, older, or popular sources have not been avoided. In my quest for balance, I have undoubtedly omitted or overlooked some important source or gem of information. Users of this guide who note such omissions are encouraged to make these lapses known to the editor.

A number of areas included in this guide, in particular the circus and magic, already have received detailed treatment by bibliographers. Others are beginning to receive similar treatment. Consequently, one major goal of this guide is to help stimulate more detailed and specialized guides to specific forms of popular entertainment and to encourage research in those areas that have yet received only nominal attention.

This guide is most concerned with American forms of popular entertainment. Because of parallels or similar developments in England, frequent exchanges of performers and performances between the United States and Great Britain, and early English influences on American forms (and, in some cases, American influences on English forms, e.g., minstrelsy), a secondary focus has been placed on English examples and, in the case of British pantomine and music hall, major stress. Throughout the guide the user will find sources as well that cover forms outside of these two countries. Most of these will be found in the first chapter; it seemed only logical to include some of these major or recent sources. Furthermore, a limited number of sources in French and Italian, too important to exclude, will be found, although the majority of sources are in English. Only very select items have been included from specialized periodicals, such as BILLBOARD and VARIETY, or the various periodicals and serials itemized in appendix A. These, however, are extremely important sources to information and the serious student of popular entertainment must examine these thoroughly. Selected doctoral dissertations have been included, which, when possible, were first examined before inclusion. All sources, with the exception of a few that need no explanation or have no truly significant features, have been annotated. Most annotations are descriptive, although a few have been evaluative as well in order to indicate excellence or degree of usefulness. Each item has been numbered (2478 plus total items), since some sources are listed more than once and others are included in annotations, it is advisable to consult the indexes for locations within the guide. All relevant bibliographical information has been provided for each source. Although a few have been added since May 1978, most were chosen from available material prior to that date.

The guide is divided into four parts: 1) general sources on popular entertainment, 2) popular entertainment forms (predominantly American), 3) popular theatre, and 4) three appendixes.

The major section of the guide is part II (popular entertainment forms). Chapters 4 through 8 are arranged generally in terms of evolution of forms; the subdivisions of each of these chapters, with the exception of chapters 8 (early musical theatre and revues) and 9 (English forms), also suggest the order of the development of forms within larger categories. As indicated previously, however, it should not be forgotten that there is much overlapping of forms and their spans of existence. Within each subdivision there has been no attempt to arrange sources in terms of evolution and development. Annotations will indicate the scope and focus of each individual source. In chapter 4, sources on both the English and the American circus are included (plus a limited number of sources on the European circus). Not only are there obvious parallels between the English and American circus, especially in their early years, but the early English circus and equestrian displays (covered primarily in part III) serve as early prototypes of the early American circus. Chapter 5 (outdoor amusements and environmental entertainments) likewise includes American and English examples, especially in subdivision "A" (fairs, exhibitions, and pleasure gardens) and "D" (amusement parks, seaside resorts, and theme parks). The contributions of Phineas Taylor Barnum, normally associated with the American circus, are included in subdivision "B" because of his more significant contribution to the dime museum tradition and the exhibition of human oddities (both real and artificial). Obviously in dealing with Barnum sources on the circus must be consulted as well. Any serious inquirer into the circus, it should be noted, should not depend totally on chapter 4 of this guide but must consult Toole-Stott (item 81) and other bibliographical sources on the subject. Chapter 6 (variety forms) deals exclusively with American forms, with the exception of "A" (medicine shows). Chapter 7 (optical and mechanical entertainments, and so forth) is the least restrictive of all the chapters. The forms included in this chapter were or are the most universally transportable and depend the least on language barriers. Again, however, when possible the emphasis is on the American and English examples. Like the circus, stage magic, included in chapter 7, has received considerable attention from bibliographers, so much so, in fact, that a separate listing of bibliographies has been included in subdivision "A" of this chapter. Chapter 8 (early musical theatre and revues) includes major survey histories up to the present but focuses on the early development of American and English musical theatre forms, plus the phenomenon of the revue. The one major exclusion in this chapter has been the work of Gilbert and Sullivan, for two reasons: 1) the body of material is so enormous as to over-shadow other forms of musical theatre, and 2) the work of Gilbert and Sullivan virtually stands untouched as a genre and has not evolved into other musical forms (see item 18 for select sources on Gilbert and Sullivan). For much the same reason, the work of Noel Coward has been limited to his own major auto-biographical writings.

Chapter 9 (principal English forms) focuses on the two major and uniquely English forms, pantomine and music hall. In the former instance, the few examples of American pantomine, in particular the work of George L. Fox, is included in this chapter. In both subdivisions only the most important and recent sources have been cited.

Part I (general sources on popular entertainment) includes selected sources on European origins (e.g., the commedia dell'arte), early forms (e.g., the mounte-bank, jester, and itinerant entertainers prior to the nineteenth century), major reference works (in many cases referred to elsewhere in the guide), and surveys or sources that do not limit themselves to subsequent chapter headings. Chapter 2 is included in order to provide adequate historical, social, and cultural background for the study of American popular entertainment and to help place specific forms in their proper context. Rather than an inclusive list of background sources, an effort has been made to give a balanced guide to sources covering the time span through the depression years. Similar sources on England are included in chapter 3, "B" on general sources on English forms of popular entertainment. Because of the major focus on American forms, a separate subdivision is included on general sources on American popular entertainment forms as well (chapter 3, "A").

Part III (popular theatre), the most selective in this guide, includes chapters that focus exclusively on either general sources of popular theatre of the United States or England, plus a chapter that deals more generally with major dramatic genres and forms, English and American. Three additional chapters are devoted exclusively to aspects of American popular theatre. Chapter 13 provides sources on native American type characters from the stage Yankee to the rural character of Toby and includes items on such types as the Indian, the city low-life character, the frontiersman, and the stage Negro. A major aspect of American popular theatre is that of theatre in small-town America, where versions of most of the popular plays of the day were presented in town halls, concert halls, opera houses, and ultimately theatre tents. Chapter 14 deals specifically with this area. One part of this movement might be considered the traveling chautauqua; this topic, however, is dealt with under Chapter 6 (variety forms). Chapter 15 (showboats) concludes part III. Few sources on specific playwrights of popular fare are included. Conolly and Wearing (item 18) should be consulted for sources on English authors and Walter Meserve's AMERICAN DRAMA TO 1900 (American Literature, English Literature, and World Literatures in English Information Guide Series, vol. 28. Detroit: Gale Research Co., 1980) should provide resources on American authors and plays. For specific performers, my guide to the American stage to World War I (item 93) and Stephen Archer's guide to American actors, forthcoming in this series, should be consulted.

The fourth section of this guide contains three appendixes that list selected periodicals and serials, specialized collections and museums, and concerned organizations. Data included in this section is the most recent available, although it should be cautioned that addresses and titles might change in the future.

Brief explanations of the nature of most chapters have been included throughout the guide in order to better prepare the user for the focus and scope of each individual chapter or subdivision.

ACKNOWLEDGMENTS

Without the assistance, advice, and guidance of a large number of people, this volume would have not been possible. The enormous efforts made by E.G. Coogan and her student assistant Barbara R. Myles in the Brown University Interlibrary Loan Department rank high on my list of acknowledgments. In addition, the staffs of the Rockefeller Library and the Harris Collection of American Drama at Brown graciously gave me their assistance and helped me track down the answers to some rather strange and obscure inquiries. During my search for sources I was privileged to work in a number of public and private collections. Robert L. Parkinson of the Circus World Museum Library in Baraboo, Wisconsin, was most helpful, as were the staffs at the Performing Arts Collection at Lincoln Center, the Dallas Public Library (Texas Collection), and the various branches and central library of the Providence Public Library. A special word of thanks must go to Louis A. Rachow, curator and librarian of the Walter Hampden-Edwin Booth Theatre Collection and Memorial Library, and editor of the Gale Performing Arts Series. He was a continuing support in this project and made available to me the marvelous collection at The Players in New York. H. Adrian Smith, the country's outstanding magic bibliophile, not only opened his collection to me but made me feel very much a part of his home for several days. Liz Fugate, drama librarian at the University of Washington, Seattle, went above and beyond the call of duty in helping to locate a number of items on the Wild West exhibition. My good friend and an acknowledged authority on popular entertainment, Brooks McNamara, not only offered suggestions on the organization of this guide, but made me aware of a number of important sources that I had been unfamiliar with and provided me with material from his own private collection. My appreciation for the foreword contributed to this volume by Professor McNamara is great, indeed its addition to this guide is considerable.

In assembling this volume I have been heavily dependent on the authority of others and the advice of many. The following were most generous with their advice and suggestions: Ralph G. Allen and William Green on American burlesque; Robert C. Toll on minstrelsy; Richard W. Flint and Robert Parkinson on the circus; A.H. Saxon on the circus and equestrian drama; Laurence Senelick and Ellis Ashton on British music hall; Marcello Truzzi on the carnival and the circus; Trish Sandberg on burlesque and striptease; Mrs. Neil Schaffner on tent, folk, and repertoire theatre; Max Morath on vaudeville and early

Acknowledgments

popular music; Attilio Favorini for information on the burlesque collection of Pittsburgh; and Julian Olf on magic. Students in my popular entertainment course have discovered a number of the sources included in this guide. Virginia Clark, an editor of CHOICE, gave me the opportunity to do a bibliographical essay for that periodical (see item 92) that helped get this project started, and she has supplied me with appropriate review assignments that have been invaluable in my efforts to keep abreast of the most current publications on popular entertainment. Many others along the way have offered suggestions, and I apologize if their names are excluded from this list.

If it were not for the interlibrary loan service and member libraries, many sources could not have been examined with such ease and convenience. I owe a special word of thanks to the following libraries: the universities of North Carolina at Chapel Hill, Arizona State at Tempe, Delaware, Ohio, Georgia, North Carolina State, New Hampshire, Texas at Austin, Maryland, Wisconsin-Milwaukee, Arizona, Illinois, Hofstra, South Florida, Colorado, Connecticut, Rhode Island, Ohio Dayton, Old Dominion, Wayne State, Temple, Roosevelt, Vermont, Cornell, Harvard, Cleveland State, Pennsylvania, Virginia, Rutgers, Case Western Reserve, Toledo, Louisville, Louisiana State, Rochester, Arkansas at Little Rock, New Mexico State, Alabama at Birmingham, Abilene Christian, Northwestern, Florida Atlantic, Massachusetts-Amherst, Florida, Kent State, Southern Illinois-Edwardsville and Carbondale, Tulane, Duke, Miami, Tennessee, North Carolina at Greensboro, Duke, Wake Forest, and Clark. Also the state universities of New York at Brockport, Oneonta, and Binghamton; the Cleveland Public Library; Washington University; Orlando Public Library; Oberlin College; Seattle Public Library; Jacksonville Florida Public Library; Hartford Public Library; Urbana College in Ohio; Swarthmore College; Chicago Public Library; the George L. Chindahl Collection at the State Historical Society of Wisconsin; Slippery Rock State College; Mt. Vernon Nazarene College; Dartmouth College; Bowdoin College; William & Mary College; Montgomery County Community College (Pennsylvania); Allegheny College; Kirkland College; and Hamilton College.

Throughout a large portion of the research period, my job was made far easier because of the effort and eagerness of my volunteer research assistant, Ann Costelloe. To her I owe a great debt of gratitude.

Part I

GENERAL SOURCES ON

POPULAR ENTERTAINMENT

Chapter 1

EUROPEAN ORIGINS, EARLY FORMS,

MAJOR REFERENCES, AND SURVEYS

See the preface for an explanation of the contents of this and subsequent chapters in part I. Bibliographies on stage magic are included in chapter 7.

1   Altick, Richard D. THE SHOWS OF LONDON. For full entry and annotation see item 279.

2   Appignanesi, Lisa. THE CABARET. New York: Universe Books, 1976. 192 p. Illus., index, bibliog.

> The best English-language history of the cabaret from its Parisian beginnings to the present; a clear delineation of cabaret's unique hybrid form, combining aspects of the carnival, the variety show, and the music hall.

3   Arnott, James Fullarton, and Robinson, John William. ENGLISH THEATRICAL LITERATURE 1559-1900; INCORPORATING ROBERT W. LOWE'S A BIBLIOGRAPHICAL ACCOUNT OF ENGLISH THEATRICAL LITERATURE PUBLISHED IN 1888. London: Society for Theatre Research, 1970. xxii, 486 p. Indexes (author and title).

> Arranged by general topics, bibliographical data, and location.

4   Bader, Arno Lehman. "The Italian Commedia Dell' Arte in England, 1660-1700." Ph.D. dissertation, University of Michigan, 1933.

5   Baker, Roger. DRAG: A HISTORY OF FEMALE IMPERSONATION ON THE STAGE. London: Triton Books, 1968. 256 p. Illus., index, bibliog.

> Surveys history of female impersonation, particularly in England, from its beginnings in the thirteenth and fourteenth centuries, through the golden ages of the Elizabethan era and the Restoration, up to the dawn of the twentieth century. Only the latter is dealt with in detail, in England and else-

where. For the purpose of this guide, Baker's sections on the dame in English pantomime, glamor girls in vaudeville and variety (one chapter is devoted to Julian Eltinge and American impersonators), and "Guys and Dolls" are the most important. Some coverage of performers, such as Vesta Tilley who wore men's clothing for acts in music hall.

6   Baskervill, Charles Read. THE ELIZABETHAN JIG AND RELATED SONG DRAMA. Chicago: University of Chicago Press, 1929. x, 642 p. Index.

Documented study of the ballad and the most significant beliefs embedded in balladry. Traces the history of dramatic song and dance specialities both in popular pastimes and on stage. It covers the history of dramatic song and ballad and operatic farce in England during the sixteen and seventeenth centuries. Texts of thirty-six songs are included.

7   Bristol, Michael. "Acting Out Utopia, The Politics of Carnival." PERFORMANCE 1 (May–June 1973): 13–28. Illus.

Focus on the traditional "carnival" of the Middle Ages and the Renaissance as "an old and persistent way of acting out Utopia." Modern examples are discussed as well (Mardi Gras, the modern amusement park, Montreal's "Man and His World," and so forth).

8   Browne, Walter, and Koch, E. De Roy, eds. WHO'S WHO ON THE STAGE, 1908. THE DRAMATIC REFERENCE BOOK AND BIOGRAPHICAL DICTIONARY OF THE THEATRE. CONTAINING CAREERS OF ACTORS, ACTRESSES, MANAGERS AND PLAYWRIGHTS OF THE AMERICAN STAGE. New York: B.W. Dodge, 1908. 467 p. Illus.

Contains numerous entries relevant to popular entertainment and entertainers.

9   Brownstein, Oscar. "The Popularity of Baiting in England Before 1600: A Study in Social and Theatrical History." EDUCATIONAL THEATRE JOURNAL 21 (October 1969): 237–50. Illus.

9a   Burke, Peter. POPULAR CULTURE IN EARLY MODERN EUROPE. New York: New York University Press, 1978. xiii, 365 p. Illus., index, bibliog., notes.

Survey of popular culture of preindustrial Europe (1500–1800) as a whole, with reasonably good coverage of professional entertainers--minstrels, fools, jugglers, charlatans, strolling players, and so forth. Superb bibliography.

10   Castaigne, Andre. "Strolling Mountebanks." HARPER'S MONTHLY

MAGAZINE 103 (November 1901): 841-51.

"Modern" day American circuses and fairs related to early
origins and the world at large.

11 Cautero, Gerard Salvatore. "Studies in the Influence of the Commedia
Dell' Arte on English Drama, 1650-1800." Ph.D. dissertation, University of Southern California, 1962. 262 p.

The influence during the latter half of the seventeenth century
and through the eighteenth on farce, ballad opera, and bourgeois comedy.

12 Chambers, E.K. THE MEDIEVAL STAGE. London: Oxford University
Press, 1903. Reprint. 2 vols. London: Oxford University Press, 1963.
Index, appendixes.

Dated and frequently incorrect but still a standard source on
early forms of popular entertainment.

13 Claflin, Edward, and Sheridan, Jeff. STREET MAGIC. AN ILLUS-
TRATED HISTORY OF WANDERING MAGICIANS AND THEIR CONJUR-
ING ARTS. Garden City, N.Y.: Doubleday and Co. (Dolphin Books),
1977. xiii, 156 p. Illus., index, bibliog. (annotated). Paper.

Deals with the entire history of the street entertainer from the
earliest forms, e.g., the medieval jongleur, to the modern
New York street magician. See also item 1330.

14 Cochran, Charles B. COCK-A-DOODLE-DO. London: J.M. Dent and
Sons, 1941. xv, 376 [8] p. Illus., index.

Memoirs of the English theatrical producer. See below.

15 _____. SHOWMAN LOOKS ON. London: J.M. Dent and Sons,
1945. viii, 324 p. Illus., index, bibliog.

Observations by the English theatrical producer, known primarily for his musical comedies and revues, of entertainment
in England, the United States, and France. This book contains his final reminiscences. Earlier volumes were SECRETS
OF A SHOWMAN (1925), I HAD ALMOST FORGOTTEN
(1932), and COCK-A-DOODLE-DO (1941). See above.

16 Cockton, Henry. THE LIFE AND ADVENTURES OF VALENTINE VOX,
THE VENTRILOQUIST. London: Robert Tyas, 1840. xx, 620 p. Illus.

Fictional but useful account of an early ventriloquist-magician.

17 Compardon, Emile. LES SPECTACLES DE LA FOIRE. 2 vols. Paris,
1877. Reprint. 2 vols. in one. Geneva: Slatkine, 1970. Index.

Fairground development in the area of Paris (1595-1791) and the factors that sent several important performers to England between 1699 and 1710. In French.

18   Conolly, L.W., and Wearing, J.P., eds. ENGLISH DRAMA AND THEATRE, 1800-1900. American Literature, English Literature, and World Literatures in English Information Guide Series, vol. 12. Detroit: Gale Research Co., 1978. xix, 508 p. Index (general).

Lists and annotates 3,234 sources. Emphasis is on drama and specific authors but good sections are provided on contemporary and modern histories and chapters on "The Theatres" and "Acting and Management." Excellent supplement on British popular theatre to this guide.

19   Cox, Harvey G. THE FEAST OF FOOLS. Cambridge, Mass.: Harvard University Press, 1969. xii, 204 p. Index, notes.

Theological study of the meaning of Christianity in the Middle Ages and modern times with a useful essay on festivity and fantasy.

20   Croce, Benedetto. "Commedia Dell' Arte." THEATRE ARTS MONTHLY 17 (December 1933): 929-39.

Analysis of the commedia as a professional or industrial conception.

21   Damase, Jacques. LES FOLIES DU MUSIC-HALL: A HISTORY OF THE MUSIC-HALL IN PARIS. Foreword by Noel Coward. New York and London: Spring Book, 1970. 190 p. Illus., bibliog.

History from 1914 of "music hall" in Paris; some coverage of postwar variety. Both French and international stars mentioned and pictured (over two hundred illustrations).

22   Derval, Paul. THE FOLIES BERGERE. Translated by Lucienne Hill. Preface by Maurice Chevalier. London: Methuen and Co., 1955. ix, 147 p. Illus.

A sketchy history by the director of the Folies from the 1890s, with major chapters on Josephine Baker, Mistinguett, and Chevalier.

23   Dexter, T.F.G. THE PAGAN ORIGIN OF FAIRS. Perranporth, Cornwall: New Knowledge Press, 1930. 44 p. Illus., bibliog.

Study of the earliest origins of the fair tradition. See also item 741.

24   Disher, M[aurice].Willson. CLOWNS AND PANTOMIMES. London:
        Constable and Co., 1925. Reprint. New York and London: Benjamin
        Blom, 1968. xix, 344 p. Ilius., index.

>   Informal history of the clown from antiquity to nineteenth-
>   century pantomime, burlesque, and extravaganza. Chapters
>   on music hall comedians and circus clowns (especially Grock).

25   Doran, John. THE HISTORY OF COURT FOOLS. 1858. Reprint.
        New York: Haskell House, 1968. 389 p.

>   Though dated, still a useful history, especially good on English
>   minstrels, jesters, and court fools. Not limited, however, to
>   England. France, Northern courts of Europe, Spain, Germany,
>   Italy, and Eastern fools are covered.

26   Ducharte, Pierre Louis. THE ITALIAN COMEDY. London: G.G.
        Harrap, 1929. Reprint. New York: Dover Publications, 1965. 366 p.
        Illus., index, bibliog. Paper.

>   Long unavailable, this reprint makes available one of the more
>   invaluable histories. Ducharte traces the beginnings, growth,
>   and influence of the commedia and describes the improvisations,
>   staging, masks, scenarios, acting troupes, and characters of
>   the commedia. Features 217 illustrations.

27   ENCICLOPEDIA DELLO SPETTACOLO. 9 vols. Rome: Casa Editrice
        Le Maschere, 1954–62. Illus. Supplement, 1955–65 (1966); Index
        volume (1968).

>   Useful survey essays on many forms of popular entertainment
>   plus entries on individuals. For example, there is a good
>   survey of burlesque by William Green and one on the circus
>   by Henry Thetard. In Italian. Sources indicated after each
>   entry.

28   Erenstein, Robert L. "Satire and the Commedia dell'Arte." In
        WESTERN POPULAR THEATRE, edited by David Mayer and Kenneth
        Richards, pp. 29–47. London: Methuen and Co., 1977.

>   An examination of the satiric dimension of the commedia dell'
>   arte in the period from 1560 to 1640.

29   Esslin, Martin, general ed. THE ENCYCLOPEDIA OF WORLD THEATRE.
        New York: Charles Scribner's Sons, 1977. 320 p. Illus., index (play
        titles).

>   Based on FRIEDRICHS THEATERLEXIKON (1969) by Kark Gronig
>   and Werner Kliess. Although not at all exhaustive in its
>   coverage, this one–volume encyclopedia does include entries on
>   most popular entertainment forms and many performers. It is
>   very uneven in its coverage.

30   Falk, Heinrich Richard. "Conventions of Popular Entertainment: Frame-
      work for a Methodology." JOURNAL OF POPULAR CULTURE 9 (Fall
      1975): 480/128-481/129.

      Suggestion that popular entertainment be approached in terms
      of "conventions" frequently used in traditional theatre studies,
      i.e.: 1) nature of the performer(s)-presentor(s), 2) manner of
      presentation, 3) nature of the spectator, 4) manner of atten-
      dance to or reception of the presentation, and 5) material be-
      ing presented (the least germane for many forms).

31   Faral, Edmond. LES JONGLEURS EN FRANCE AU MOYEN AGE.
      Paris: H. Champion, 1910. Reprint. New York: Burt Franklin, 1970.
      x, 339 p.

      Along with Chambers (item 12), Nicoll (item 59), and Wickham
      (item 90), one of the more valuable sources on medieval popu-
      lar entertainment. Chapters on origin, church hostility,
      eighteenth-century prosperity of the jongleur, classifications,
      minstrels. Text in French.

32   Flint, Richard W. "A Selected Guide to Source Material on the Ameri-
      can Circus." JOURNAL OF POPULAR CULTURE 6 (Winter 1972): 615-
      19.

      Good basic guide; especially useful for his classification of
      types of circusiana.

33   Frost, Thomas. THE OLD SHOWMEN AND THE OLD LONDON FAIRS.
      1881. Reprint. Ann Arbor, Mich.: Gryphon Books, 1971. 388 p.
      Index.

      A standard source on early fairground entertainment in England.
      See also item 745.

34   Goldsmith, Robert. WISE FOOLS IN SHAKESPEARE. East Lansing:
      Michigan State University Press, 1955. x, 123 p. Index, notes.

      Good general study on the fool in the plays of Shakespeare
      and his contemporaries with a review of the popular and
      literary traditions of the fool.

35   Gorham, Maurice [Anthony Coneys]. SHOWMEN AND SUCKERS: AN
      EXCURSION ON THE CRAZY FRINGE OF THE ENTERTAINMENT
      WORLD. Illustrated by Edward Ardizzone. London: Percival Marshall,
      1951. ix, 262 p. Illus.

      Explores the relationship between the showman and sucker
      (author admits to being the latter), discusses the skill of a
      showman, slapstick comedy and melodrama, magicians, freaks
      and fakes, the circus and its dangers, burlesque and the strip-

tease, English pantomime, fairs, and Punch and Judy. Not a scholarly study but insightful first-hand observation of popular entertainment in England, United States, and elsewhere.

36   Hartnoll, Phyllis, ed. THE OXFORD COMPANION TO THE THEATRE. 3d ed. London: Oxford University Press, 1967. xv, 1,088 p., 176 pls.

Summary essays on most popular entertainment forms by noted authorities, strongest entries on English forms.

37   Hotson, Leslie. SHAKESPEARE'S MOTLEY. New York: Oxford University Press, 1952; London: Rupert-Hart Davis, 1952. ix, 133 p. Illus.

Study of Shakespeare's fools; chapters on their dress (costume, color, shape, or form), Will Sommer (fool of Henry VIII), and Robert Armin (Shakespeare's fool-actor).

38   [Hunt, Brampton, ed.]. THE GREEN ROOM BOOK: OR WHO'S WHO ON THE STAGE. New York: F. Warne and Co., 1906-9. Illus., index.

An annual biographical record of the dramatic, variety, and musical world (mostly American).

39   Jacques-Charles. CENT ANS DE MUSIC-HALL. Paris: Editions Jeheber, 1956. 318 p. Illus., index.

General history of "music hall" in England, France, and the United States. Topics include: English music hall (and types of performers); ventriloquists and magicians; ballet and revue in England; French variety and revue; American vaudeville, minstrelsy, burlesque, revue; and French cabaret. Text in French.

40   Katz, Herbert, and Katz, Marjorie. MUSEUMS, U.S.A. For full entry and annotation, see item 820.

41   Kennard, Joseph Spencer. MASKS AND MARIONETTES. New York: Macmillan Co., 1935. Reprint. Port Washington, N.Y.: Kennikat Press, 1967. 129 p. Illus., index.

Ninety-six pages devoted to the commedia dell' arte, its origin, development, famous players and companies, structure of the scenario, and the adaptations of Goldoni and Gozzi. Also contains a section on Italian marionettes.

42   Kirby, E.T. "The Shamanistic Origins of Popular Entertainment." DRAMA REVIEW 18 (March 1974): 1-9.

An attempt to relate and trace back many popular entertain-

ment to the rituals of shamanism, "which were functional
rituals of similar pattern that operated within a metaphysical
systems."

43   Lagerkvist, Par. THE DWARF. London: Chatto and Windus, 1967.
        175 p.

        Fictional work about a dwarf and his relationship with his
        Renaissance master. Good atmosphere and background.

44   Lea, Kathleen. ITALIAN POPULAR COMEDY. A STUDY IN THE
        COMMEDIA DELL'ARTE, 1560-1620. 2 vols. London: Oxford Univer-
        sity Press, 1934. Index, bibliog.

        A dated but still standard work with a focus on the English
        stage. Volume 2 contains seven appendixes dealing with
        performers, plays connected with the commedia, and scenarios.

45   Le Roux, Hughes, and Garnier, Jules. ACROBATS AND MOUNTEBANKS.
        Translated by A.P. Morton. London: Chapman and Hall, 1890. xii,
        336 p. Illus., index.

        Early study of fairs, booth theatres, and permanent shows or
        "entresorts," plus chapters on animal trainers, tamers, eques-
        trians, the Parisian Hippodrome, equilibrists, gymnasts, clowns,
        and the private circus. Examples mostly French.

46   Litto, Fredric M. AMERICAN DISSERTATIONS ON THE DRAMA AND
        THE THEATRE. Kent, Ohio: Kent State University Press, 1969. ix,
        519 p.

        Useful guide to American and Canadian dissertations up to
        1965.

47   McDowell, John H. "Some Pictorial Aspects of Early Mountebank
        Stages." PUBLICATION OF THE MODERN LANGUAGE ASSOCIATION
        61 (1945): 84-96. Illus.

        Examination of iconographic evidence from the sixteenth to the
        early eighteenth centuries. Based on his 1937 Ph.D. disserta-
        tion ("An Iconographical Study of the Early Commedia Dell-
        Arte (1560-1650)," Yale University).

48   McKechnie, Samuel. POPULAR ENTERTAINMENTS THROUGH THE
        AGES. London: Sampson Low, Marston, 1931. Reprint. New York:
        Benjamin Blom, 1969. xvi, 240 p. Illus., index.

        Although apparently dated, this is actually one of the few
        good surveys of popular entertainment available and is highly
        recommended. Forms covered include mimes, minstrels, stroll-

ing players, fairs, commedia dell'arte, Punch and Judy, pantomime, music hall, circus, and cinematograph. Basically limited to English forms and early European origins.

49   McNamara, Brooks. "The Scenography of Popular Entertainments." DRAMA REVIEW 18 (March 1974): 16-25.

A brief but useful survey of the architecture and design of traditional popular entertainments, including 1) the street booth and the mobile entertainer, 2) improvised theatres, 3) variety entertainment, 4) popular theatre, 5) spectacle theatres, 6) processional forms, and 7) entertainment environments.

50   _____. "'Scavengers of the Amusement World': Popular Entertainment and the Birth of the Movies." In AMERICAN PASTIMES, pp. 17-19. Brockton, Mass.: Brockton Art Center, 1976. Paper.

The indebtedness of early cinema to popular entertainment forms and their use as a resource until the rising popularity of film led directly to the decline and fall of the old popular forms which had given it birth. For other sources on optical entertainment, see chapter 7.

51   Madden, David. HARLEQUIN'S STICK, CHARLIE'S CANE: A COMPARATIVE STUDY OF COMMEDIA DELL'ARTE AND SILENT SLAPSTICK COMEDY. Bowling Green, Ohio: Bowling Green University Press, 1975. 174 p. Illus., bibliog.

Disappointing comparison of the commedia and silent comedy (in terms of technique, characters, origin, and operation). Limited text but interesting for comparative illustrations of commedia actors and silent comedic performers.

52   Matlaw, Myron, ed. PROCEEDINGS OF THE CONFERENCE ON THE HISTORY OF AMERICAN POPULAR ENTERTAINMENT. Westport, Conn.: Greenwood Press, forthcoming (1979).

Papers delivered at the first major conference on American popular entertainment at Lincoln Center of the Performing Arts, November 1977. Essays on vaudeville, burlesque, minstrelsy, G.L. Fox and pantomime, Yiddish vaudeville, tent repertoire, circus, Wild West, medicine shows, and dance as popular entertainment.

53   Mayer, David. "Towards a Definition of Popular Theatre." In WESTERN POPULAR THEATRE, edited by David Mayer and Kenneth Richards, pp. 257-77. London: Methuen and Co., 1977.

An attempt to present criteria for the classification of theatrical forms as "popular." Less a definition than a posing of questions and possibilities but nonetheless useful and stimulating for further attempts at defining what is so large and amorphous a category of forms.

54   Mistinguett [Jeanne-Marie Bourgeois]. MISTINGUETT. QUEEN OF THE PARIS NIGHT. Translated by Lucienne Hill. London: Paul Elek, 1954. [8], 248 p. Illus.

      The story of the queen of French revue, born Jeanne Bourgeois in 1875.

55   Morley, Henry. MEMORIES OF BARTHOLOMEW FAIR. 1857. 2d ed. 1874. 3d ed. 1880. Reprint. Detroit: Singing Tree Press, 1969. xxi, 404 p. Illus., index.

      First serious history of an English fair. See also item 749.

56   Moynet, Georges. LA MACHINERIE THEATRALE: TRUCS ET DECORS. Paris: Libraire Illustree, 1893. 408 p. Illus.

      French text but a valuable source on theatrical effects in the popular theatre, in particular in France but by extension applies to much of the trick work in English and American forms, such as pantomime.

57   Moynet, Jean-Pierre. L'ENVERS DU THEATRE. 2d ed. Paris: Hackette et Cie, 1874. Translated and augmented by Allan S. Jackson and M. Glen Wilson as FRENCH THEATRICAL PRODUCTION IN THE NINETEENTH CENTURY. American Theatre Association, Rare Books of the Theatre Series, no. 10. Binghamton, N.Y.: Max Reinhardt Foundation with the Center for Modern Theater Research, 1976. xiv, 239 p. Illus., index, bibliog.

      Important source on theatrical practice during the nineteenth century; good for popular theatre production and effects.

58   Mulholland, John. THE EARLY MAGIC SHOWS. New York: By the author, 1945. 18 p. Illus. Paper.

      Discusses early mountebanks and travelling performers. See also item 1371.

59   Nicoll, Allardyce. MASKS, MIMES AND MIRACLES: STUDIES IN THE POPULAR THEATRE. New York: Cooper Square, 1963. 408 p. Illus., index.

      Nicoll's subtitle suggests his intent; one of the first major studies in English and covers early mime and pantomime in Greece and Rome, popular theatre during the Middle Ages, and the commedia dell' arte. There are 226 illustrations.

60 _____. THE WORLD OF HARLEQUIN. London: Cambridge University Press, 1963. xiv [v], 242 [3] p. Illus., index, bibliog.

> Good study of the commedia dell' arte with a useful evaluation of sources as of 1963.

61 Niklaus, Thelma. HARLEQUIN. New York: George Braziller, 1956. 259 p. Illus., index, bibliog.

> One of the less useful studies of the commedia dell' arte, focusing on the various forms of Harlequin (Arlecchino, Arlequin, Harlequin). Approximately half of the study concentrates on the development and decline of English pantomime.

62 Oreglia, Giacomo. THE COMMEDIA DELL 'ARTE. Translated by Lovett F. Edwards. Introduction by Evert Sprinchorn. New York: Hill and Wang, 1968. 158 p. Illus., index, bibliog.

> A concise but adequate description of the origins and history of the commedia with examples of scenarios and separate chapters on each of the main "masks" or types. Well illustrated.

63 Papich, Stephen. REMEMBERING JOSEPHINE: A BIOGRAPHY OF JOSEPHINE BAKER. Indianapolis and New York: Bobbs-Merrill Co., 1976. xviii, 237 p. Illus., index.

> Story of the legendary black entertainer, star of cabaret and revue and an immortal in the history of the Folies Bergere in Paris.

64 "People's Theatre." THEATRE QUARTERLY 1 (October-December 1971): Entire issue.

> Issue devoted to popular theatre, including sections on "People's Theatre in Nineteenth Century Britain" and "Popular and Political Theatre in America."

65 "Popular Entertainments." DRAMA REVIEW 18 (March 1974): Entire issue.

> Essays on the Shamanistic origins of popular entertainment (E.T. Kirby, see item 42); popular scenography (Brooks McNamara, see item 49); Boulevard theatre in France (Marvin Carlson); Grand Guignol (Frantisek Deak); commedia and the actor (Carlo Mazzone-Clementi); classification of circus technique (Hovey Burgess, see item 542); and a section on "Popular Entertainments and the Avant-Garde."

66 "Popular Theatre." EDUCATIONAL THEATRE JOURNAL 27 (October 1975): Entire issue.

Issue devoted to essays on popular entertainment, including circus (A.H. Saxon); buskers or street entertainers (Brook McNamara, see item 1393); early American musical theatre (Roger Allan Hall, see item 1556); burlesque (Steve Mills and Trish Sandberg, see item 1248 and 1254); vaudeville (Kate Davy, see item 1089); revue (Margaret M. Knapp, see item 1580); and several essays on folk theatre, outside the scope of this guide.

67   Pyke, E.J. A BIOGRAPHICAL DICTIONARY OF WAX MODELLERS. For full entry and annotation, see item 835.

68   Rust, Brian, with Debus, Allen G. THE COMPLETE ENTERTAINMENT DISCOGRAPHY FROM THE MID-1890S TO 1942. New Rochelle, N.Y.: Arlington House, 1973. 677 p.

Over five thousand entertainers—minstrel, music hall, and vaudeville performers; actors and actresses; show business singers, comics, and so forth. Recordings arranged alphabetically according to artists.

69   Sand, Maurice. THE HISTORY OF THE HARLEQUINADE. 2 vols. London: M. Secker, 1915. Reprint. Bronx, N.Y.: Benjamin Blom, 1967. Illus., index.

Translation of MASQUES ET BOUFFONS with questionable material on the commedia; not a reliable source.

70   Scala, Flaminio. SCENARIOS OF THE COMMEDIA DELL'ARTE. Translated by Henry F. Salerno. New York: New York University Press, 1967. xxxii, 413 p.

The first major English translation of the only significant comprehensive collection of scenarios used by the commedia dell' arte (Flaminio Scala's IL TEATRO DELLE FAVOLE RAPPRESENTA-TIVE, published in 1611). Fifty plot summaries included, plus in an appendix a discussion of analogues suggesting the extent to which the repertory of the commedia companies pervaded the theatres of England and France during the sixteenth and seventeenth centuries. The latter section is based, in part, on the author's Ph.D. dissertation, "The Elizabethan Drama and the Commedia Del Arte" (University of Illinois, 1956).

71   Scott, Virginia P. "The Jeu and the Role: Analysis of the Appeals of the Italian Comedy in France in the Time of Arlequin-Dominque." In WESTERN POPULAR THEATRE, edited by David Mayer and Kenneth Richards, pp. 1-27. London: Methuen and Co., 1977.

Essay defends the assertion "that the Italian comedies performed in France by the company known as the ancien theatre italien between 1660 and 1688 can best be understood and accounted for by analysis of their audience appeals, that popular theatre yields to such structural analysis, and that the Italian companies are most profitably classified as popular theatre." Excellent essay, although largely outside the major scope of this guide.

72   Seldes, Gilbert. THE 7 LIVELY ARTS. Rev. ed. New York: Sagamore Press, 1957. 306 p.

First attempt by an American to justify and defend popular entertainment; still stimulating and strongly recommended.

73   Sergel, Sherman Louis, ed. THE LANGUAGE OF SHOW BIZ. Chicago: Dramatic Publishing Co., 1973. xliii, 254 p. Illus.

A dictionary of show business terminology, with special consideration given to circus, vaudeville, burlesque, carnival, and Toby shows. Not at all exhaustive.

74   Smith, Horatio. FESTIVALS, GAMES AND AMUSEMENTS, ANCIENT AND MODERN. London: Colburn and Bentley, 1831; New York: J.J. Harper, 1831. x, 355 p. Illus.

Eight chapters devoted to festivals, games, and amusements of the Greeks and Romans; the remainder on dances, jugglers, festivals, bull fights, animal baiting, theatre, and so forth in England. An appendix by Samuel Woodworth covers early American festivals, games, and amusements.

75   Smith, Winifred. THE COMMEDIA DELL' ARTE. New York: Columbia University Press, 1912. xv, 290 p. Illus., index, bibliog., appendixes.

A standard study of the commedia: definitions, origins, typical scenarios, commedia in foreign countries (France, Germany, Austria, Spain, England), and the transformation of the commedia from the seventeenth to the nineteenth century. Two appendixes: (A) "Scenarios" (list of printed and manuscript collections of scenarios and plays, and (B) the influence of Italian comedy in England.

76   _____. "Harlequin Dances." THEATRE ARTS MONTHLY 12 (August 1928): 551–53. Illus.

French and Italian dancers' influence on early English Harlequins. Illustrated with designs by Le Rousseau with music and notations for movement. Based on R.A. Feuillet's CHOREOGRAPHIE.

77   Sokan, Robert. A DESCRIPTIVE AND BIBLIOGRAPHIC CATALOG OF

THE CIRCUS & RELATED ARTS COLLECTION AT ILLINOIS STATE UNI-VERSITY, NORMAL, ILLINOIS. Bloomington, Ill.: Scarlet Ibis Press, 1975. [6], 176 p. Illus., 32 pls.

> Limited edition of four hundred copies. Details of 1,373 items. Books already described in Toole-Stott (see item 81) and the Amsterdam University Library's catalog are noted but not detailed.

78   Speaight, George. "The Entertainment of the Streets." In THE SATUR-DAY BOOK 31, edited by John Hadfield, pp. 10-31. New York: Clarkson N. Potter, 1971. Illus.

> Survey of various types of street entertainers through the ages.

79   Swain, Barbara. FOOLS AND FOLLY DURING THE MIDDLE AGES AND THE RENAISSANCE. New York: Columbia University Press, 1962. [4], 234 p.

> Study of fools and jesters; based on her Columbia thesis.

80   Thompson, C[harles]. J[ohn]. S[amuel]. THE QUACKS OF OLD LONDON. New York, London, and Paris: Brentano's, 1928. xvii [19], 356 p. Illus., index.

> Includes a discussion of early mountebanks, clowns, and quacks. See also item 964.

81   Toole-Stott, Raymond. CIRCUS AND ALLIED ARTS, A WORLD BIBLIOG-RAPHY. 4 vols. Derby, Engl.: Harpur, 1958-71. Illus.

> Contains over fifteen thousand entries drawn from works in thirteen languages. Books and other materials are annotated and include material from several notable public and private collections. Especially strong on the English circus. Volume 1: Foreword by M. Willson Disher. Sections of William Cody, Adah Menken, P.T. Barnum, and Philip Astley. Volume 2: Foreword by D.L. Murray. Especially strong on pantomime and equestrian drama. Volume 3: Foreword by Antony D. Hippisley Coxe. Section on periodicals; list of one hundred best circus books. Index. Volume 4: Foreword by A.H. Saxon. Index.

82   _____. A BIBLIOGRAPHY OF THE BOOKS ON THE CIRCUS IN ENGLISH FROM 1773 TO 1964. Derby, Engl.: Harpur, 1964. [8], 80 p.

> Selective list of major circus books.

83   Towsen, John H. "Sources in Popular Entertainment." THE DRAMA REVIEW 18 (March 1974): 118-22.

Good general guide to sources, including a list of basic
research tools, libraries and museums, organizations, performer
training, and a select bibliography.

84 _____. CLOWNS. New York: Hawthorn Books, 1976. xiii, 400 p.
Illus., index, bibliog.

Despite some limitations and weaknesses, this is the only full
survey of the clown in all its various forms; fools and jesters,
medieval mimes, jongleurs and minstrels, Pueblo Indian delight makers, Harlequins and Pierrots, circus clowns, and so
forth. Its greatest weakness may be, indeed, its comprehen-
siveness.

85 Underwood, Peter. LIFE'S A DRAG! DANNY LA RUE AND THE
DRAG SCENE. London: Leslie Frewin, 1974. 192 p. Illus., index.
Paper.

Life and career of the highest paid drag performer in the world
today with limited insights into his contributions to revue and
pantomime.

86 Vardac, A. Nicholas. STAGE AND SCREEN: THEATRICAL METHOD
FROM GARRICK TO GRIFFITH. Cambridge, Mass.: Harvard University
Press, 1949. xxvi, 283 p. Illus., index, notes.

Study of the transition of popular theatre into film and the
death of certain stage forms due to the pressure of melodrama,
stage spectacle, pantomime, and the birth of the film from
1895 to 1902. Deals in detail with the melodrama and
spectacle of Henry Irving, David Belasco, and Steele MacKaye,
which the author calls "The Photographic Ideal." Notes supply
a guide to other related sources.

87 Veinstein, Andre, et al. BIBLIOTHEQUE ET MUSEES DES ARTS DU
SPECTACLE DANS LE MONDE [PERFORMING ARTS COLLECTIONS:
AN INTERNATIONAL HANDBOOK]. Compiled for the International
Federation of Library Associations. Paris: Editions du Centre National
de la Recherche Scientifique, 1967. 801 p. Index.

Guide to collections in general libraries, museums, and special
collections in thirty-seven countries, including most major
American collections. Text in French and English.

88 Welsford, Enid. THE FOOL: HIS SOCIAL AND LITERARY HISTORY.
London: Faber and Faber, 1935. xv, 374 p. Illus., index, bibliog.

Traces the social history of the fool and relates it to the fool
figure in literature. Chapter on Harlequin and the Harlequinade. Good bibliography and documentation.

89   Whalon, Marion K., ed. PERFORMING ARTS RESEARCH: A GUIDE
      TO INFORMATION SOURCES. Performing Arts Information Guide
      Series, vol. 1. Detroit: Gale Research Co., 1976. xi, 280 p.
      Index.

      With the exclusion of most reference material from this guide,
      this volume fills that gap together with items 18 and 93.

90   Wickham, Glynne. EARLY ENGLISH STAGES 1300 to 1600. VOL.
      ONE: 1300 TO 1576. New York: Columbia University Press, 1959.
      xliv, 428 p. Illus., index, bibliog., notes, appendixes.

      A seminal work on early English theatre and an excellent
      source for early forms of popular entertainment in Great
      Britain and origins of later, more structured forms in England
      and the United States. Sections on "Open-Air Entertainments
      of the Middle Ages" (tournament, pageant theatres of the
      street, and miracle plays) and on "Indoor Entertainments"
      (minstrelsy; indoor theatres and entertainers; mummings, dis-
      guisings, and masks; and morals and interludes).

91   Willeford, William. THE FOOL AND HIS SCEPTER: A STUDY IN
      CLOWNS AND JESTERS AND THEIR AUDIENCES. Evanston, Ill.:
      Northwestern University Press, 1969. xxii, 265 p. Illus., index, notes.

      Theoretical study of the fool's appeal by a practicing psycho-
      therapist from ritual clowning of primitive societies, "fool
      literature" and court jesters of the Middle Ages and Renais-
      sance, Shakespearean tragedy, to comic turns and vaudeville
      sketches, circus, stage, and screen.

92   Wilmeth, Don B. "American Popular Entertainment: A Historical
      Perspective." CHOICE 14 (October 1977): 987-1004.

      Assessment of major sources on popular entertainment; check-
      list of 235 sources.

93   _____, ed. THE AMERICAN STAGE TO WORLD WAR I: A GUIDE
      TO INFORMATION SOURCES. Performing Arts Information Guide
      Series, vol. 4. Detroit: Gale Research Co., 1978. 269 p. Indexes
      (author, title, subject).

      Annotated guide to 1,461 sources on all aspects of the Ameri-
      can theatre. Useful supplement to this guide for American
      popular theatre.

94   Winter, Marian Hannah. THE THEATRE OF MARVELS. Preface by
      Marcel Marceau. Translated by Charles Meldon. New York: Benjamin
      Blom, 1964. 208 p. Illus., indexes (ballets and plays, names), bibliog.,
      notes.

Originally published in a French edition by Olivier Perrin, Paris, in 1962. The English version contains some incorrect captions. The text deals with pantomime, automata, acrobats, ballet dancers, equestrians and animal trainers, stage designers, and magicians. A good history, although the focus is primarily on France with a chapter on America, 1790-1860.

95 _____. "Popular Theatre and Popular Art." In WESTERN POPULAR THEATRE, edited by David Mayer and Kenneth Richards, pp. 203-19. Illus. London: Methuen and Co., 1977.

An informal account of the relationship between "popular theatre" and the rise of popular art in the form of advertising posters and other souvenir illustrative materials during the eighteenth and nineteenth centuries.

96 Wright, Richardson. HAWKERS AND WALKERS IN EARLY AMERICA. Philadelphia: J.B. Lippincott, 1927. Reprint. New York: Frederick Ungar Publishing Co., 1965. [6], 317 p. Illus., index, bibliog.

Strolling pedlars, preachers, lawyers, doctors, players, and others, from the beginning to the Civil War. Although inaccurate in fact, this is a reasonably good survey of early itinerant performers, including early medicine shows, menageries, puppet and peep shows, automatons, panoramas, minstrel and concert troupes, freaks, and early troupers.

97 Young, William C. AMERICAN THEATRICAL ARTS: A GUIDE TO MANUSCRIPTS AND SPECIAL COLLECTIONS IN THE UNITED STATES AND CANADA. Chicago: American Library Association, 1972. 166 p. Index.

Guide to collections in 138 institutions. Inconsistent in coverage.

Chapter 2

AMERICAN HISTORICAL, SOCIAL, AND
CULTURAL BACKGROUND

98   Allen, Frederick Lewis. THE BIG CHANGE, 1900-1950. New York:
      Harper and Row, 1952. xi, 308 p. Index, bibliog.

      Major changes in the first half of the century; little specific
      mention of entertainment but useful for background.

99   Asbury, Herbert. THE GANGS OF NEW YORK. New York and
      London: Alfred A. Knopf, 1928. Bibliog.

      An informal history of the underworld chronicles the more
      spectacular exploits of the refractory citizen who was a dan-
      gerous nuisance in New York for almost one hundred years.
      Atmosphere of the Bowery and the origin of Mose the Bowery
      B'hoy is provided.

100   Atherton, Lewis. MAINSTREET ON THE MIDDLE BORDER. Blooming-
      ton: Indiana University Press, 1954. xix, 423 p. Illus., index,
      appendixes, notes.

      On life in the midwest from the mid-nineteenth century to the
      early twentieth century. Includes considerable mention of
      popular entertainments: minstrel and medicine shows, circuses,
      opera houses, traveling tent shows and carnivals, and chau-
      tauqua, among other topics.

101   Baral, Robert. TURN WEST ON 23RD; A TOAST TO NEW YORK'S
      OLD CHELSEA. New York: Fleet Publishing Corp., 1965. 128 p.
      Illus., index.

      History of the area in New York from Fifth Avenue to the
      Hudson and from Fourteenth Street to Thirty-fourth Street.
      Includes coverage of vaudeville-variety, the Eden Musee, and
      Florenz Ziegfeld. Good handling of atmosphere of nineteenth-
      century New York.

102   Barrett, Marvin. THE JAZZ AGE. New York: G.P. Putnam's Sons,

1959. 208 p. Index, bibliog.

The years 1919–29 recreated in text and pictures, including the entertainment of the age.

103   Beaumont, Charles. REMEMBER? REMEMBER? New York: Macmillan Co., 1963. 248 p.

Background on the era of vaudeville, early film, and radio.

104   Beer, Thomas. THE MAUVE DECADE. New York: Alfred A. Knopf, 1926. 268 p.

A study of American life at the end of the nineteenth century. Limited theatrical allusions.

105   Bendiner, Robert. JUST AROUND THE CORNER. New York: Harper and Brothers, 1967. xiv, 268 p. Illus., index.

A history of the social and political atmosphere in the 1930s with a chapter included on the Roosevelt government's patronage of the arts under the Works' Progress Administration.

106   Bier, Jesse. THE RISE AND FALL OF AMERICAN HUMOR. New York: Holt, Rinehart, and Winston, 1968. xii, 506 p. Illus., bibliog.

On nineteenth-century popular culture.

107   Blair, Walter. NATIVE AMERICAN HUMOR (1800-1900). New York: American Book Co., 1937. xv, 573 p. Index, bibliog.

107a   Boardman, Fon W., Jr. THE THIRTIES. AMERICA AND THE GREAT DEPRESSION. New York: Harry Z. Walck, 1967. 152 p. Index, bibliog.

Perspective on the depression era; entertainment discussed in the context of the period.

108   Bode, Carl. THE ANATOMY OF AMERICAN POPULAR CULTURE, 1840-1861. Berkeley and Los Angeles: University of California Press, 1959. xv, 292 p. Illus., index, note on sources.

Attempt to suggest how the American character may have revealed itself through its cultural preferences.

109   Botkin, B.A., ed. A TREASURY OF AMERICAN FOLKLORE. New York: Crown Publishers, 1949. xxvii, 932 p. Index.

Collection of stories, ballads, and traditions from American folklore; a veritable encyclopedia, including material on

Buffalo Bill, Wild Bill Hickok, and music often heard in the popular theatre.

110   Bowen, Ezra, ed. THIS FABULOUS CENTURY. PRELUDE, 1870–1900. New York: Time-Life Books, 1970. 290 p. Illus., index, bibliog.

Largely pictorial retrospective look at American life prior to the twentieth century. Chapter entitled "Entertainment" (pp. 248–69) offers an overview of popular theatre, sports, minstrelsy, circus, and Cody's Wild West. Excellent colored reproductions of lithographs for various types of attractions.

111   Calkins, Earnest Elmo. THEY BROKE THE PRAIRIE. New York: Charles Scribner's Sons, 1937. xi, 451 p. Illus., bibliog.

Ostensibly the history of Galesburg, Illinois, and Knox College, but also a useful picture is created of a small town in the Upper-Mississippi Valley and the various forms of entertainment seen there in the nineteenth century.

112   Churchill, Allen. REMEMBER WHEN. New York: Golden Press, 1967. 288 p. Illus.

Illustrated study of American culture, 1900–1942, with frequent references to all forms of entertainment. Good section on vaudeville.

113   Congdon, Don, ed. THE THIRTIES--A TIME TO REMEMBER. New York: Simon and Schuster, 1962. 625 p.

A portrait of the '30s as a time of unprecedented social reform, artistic ferment, and imaginative leadership as drawn by the editor and selected writers of the time. A section on the theatre includes essays by Harold Clurman, Ward Morehouse, and Guy Bolton on musicals.

114   Crouse, Russell. IT SEEMS LIKE YESTERDAY; WITH NUMEROUS ILLUSTRATIONS FROM CONTEMPORARY SOURCES. Garden City, N.Y.: Doubleday Co., 1931. ix [12], 192 p. Illus.

Essay on passing types from the American scene, e.g., the matinee idol (with numerous examples, both male and female), the stagedoor Johnny and the appeal of the chorus girl in the late nineteenth century, the minstrel, and the international beauty (such as Lillie Langtry).

115   Crowder, Richard. THOSE INNOCENT YEARS. Indianapolis: Bobbs-Merrill Co., 1957. 288 p. Index, bibliog. ("authorities").

Biography of the American poet James Whitcomb Riley (1849–

1916), his life story includes a great deal on other artists of the time, particularly on literary and performing artists.

116   Dallas, Sandra. NO MORE THAN FIVE IN A BED: COLORADO HOTELS IN THE OLD DAYS. Norman: University of Oklahoma, 1967. xiv, 208 p. Illus., index.

History of hotels in Colorado from the mid-nineteenth century, including information on concert saloon entertainment and brief mention of other assorted forms of amusement. Principal value is in the background provided on transient living in the West of the nineteenth century.

117   Denney, Reuel. THE ASTONISHED MUSE: POPULAR CULTURE IN AMERICA. Chicago: University of Chicago, 1957; New York: Universal Library, 1964. x, 273 p.

Essays on mass communications and spectator sports; little on early forms of popular entertainment.

118   Dorson, Richard M. AMERICAN FOLKLORE AND THE HISTORIAN. Chicago: University of Chicago Press, 1959. xii, 239 p. Index, bibliog.

Relationship between folklore and antebellum popular culture.

119   _____. "The Question of Folklore in a New Nation." In FOLKLORE AND SOCIETY, edited by Bruce Jackson, pp. 21-33. Hatboro, Pa.: Folklore Associates, 1966.

Discusses early America's need for and creation of popular folk heroes and demigods. Dorson also deals with the folk heroes created for and found in prominence on the early American stage, e.g., Mike Fink, Davy Crockett, and Sam Patch. The subject of Sam Patch is a favorite one of Dorson; for other more detailed essays see "Sam Patch, Jumping Hero" in NEW YORK FOLKLORE QUARTERLY 1 [1945]: 133-51, and "The Wonderful Leaps of Sam Patch" in AMERICAN HERITAGE 18 [December 1966]: 12-19.

120   Dulles, Foster Rhea. AMERICA LEARNS TO PLAY. A HISTORY OF POPULAR RECREATION 1607-1940. New York: Appleton-Century, 1940. xviii, 441 p. Illus., index, bibliog.

One of the better general introductions to early American popular entertainment and its cultural background. Includes much more than show business in its coverage of how Americans made use of their leisure time. Specific forms covered include minstrelsy, variety, and the circus. A second edition appeared in 1965 but adds little.

121 Earle, Alice Morse. STAGE-COACH AND TAVERN DAYS. 1900.
Reprint. New York and London: Benjamin Blom, 1969. xvi, 449 p.
Index.

> On the nature and importance of the tavern in early America
> as a meeting place for townspeople and rest for travellers.
> Also deals with the development of public roads in America
> and the consequences of stage coach travel. The types of
> entertainments and attractions offered at these taverns is co-
> vered on pages 200-222.

122 Ellis, Edward Robb. A NATION IN TORMENT. New York: Coward,
McCann and Geoghegan, 1970. 576 p. Index, bibliog.

> Study of the American Depression, 1929-39. Focus is on the
> effect of the period on the people, with little specifically on
> the entertainment other than the WPA Theatre Project.

123 Hall, Stuart, and Whannel, Paddy. THE POPULAR ARTS. New York:
Pantheon Books, 1965. 480 p. Illus., index.

> Social and cultural aspects of mass media and some mention
> of early forms.

124 Harris, Neil, ed. THE AMERICAN CULTURE. 8 vols. New York:
George Braziller, 1970-73. Illus., bibliog.

> All aspects of American culture dealt with by a variety of
> authors provides excellent background for a study of popular
> entertainment.

125 Hecht, Ben. A CHILD OF THE CENTURY. New York: Simon and
Schuster, 1954. 654 p. Illus., index.

> Autobiography of the author, dramatist, and veteran newspaper
> man for the Chicago DAILY NEWS. Especially good insights
> into the period up to the 1930s, with frequent reference to
> entertainment of the time.

126 Hunt, Gaillard. LIFE IN AMERICA ONE HUNDRED YEARS AGO.
New York: Harper and Brothers, 1914. x [11] p. Illus., index,
bibliog.

> Outline of the life and manner of the United States in 1814.
> Chapter 11, "Plays and Songs," provides a brief survey.

126a Inge, M. Thomas, ed. HANDBOOK OF AMERICAN POPULAR CUL-
TURE. Vol. 1. Westport, Conn.: Greenwood Press, 1978. x, 404 p.
Index, bibliog.

> Volume 2 is scheduled for publication in 1980.

127   Jensen, Oliver, ed. THE NINETIES. New York: American Heritage
       Publishing Co., 1967. 144 p. Illus.

       The decade of the 1890s as a dividing line between an older,
       isolated America and a new urban society. Recreates an ex-
       cellent sense of the time through text, photographs, lithographs,
       paintings, and other visual material. Good essay by Heywood
       Hale Broun, "Innocent Merriment (More or Less)," on enter-
       tainment.

128   Jones, Howard Mumford. THE PURSUIT OF HAPPINESS. Cambridge,
       Mass.: Harvard University Press, 1953. Reprint. Ithaca, N.Y.:
       Cornell University Press, 1966. ix, 168 p.

       Although only indirectly concerned with entertainment, Jones's
       essay offers a penetrating survey of the origins, interpretations,
       and mutations in the meaning of the phrase "the pursuit of
       happiness."

129   Kaplan, Max. LEISURE IN AMERICA: A SOCIAL INQUIRY. New
       York: John Wiley and Sons, 1960. xii, 350 p. Index, notes.

       Exploration and analysis of leisure activity, trends, and so
       forth in modern America. Chapter 15, "Art as Leisure," re-
       lates all arts to modern American leisure, their functions,
       relations to work, community, and the like. Not a major
       source for popular entertainment but a good look at subsequent
       periods.

130   Keats, John. YOU MIGHT AS WELL LIVE. New York: Simon and
       Schuster, 1970. 319 p. Illus., index, bibliog.

       The life and times of Dorothy Parker (1893-1967); good re-
       creation of an era.

131   Leighton, Isabel, ed. THE ASPIRIN AGE, 1919-1941. New York:
       Simon and Schuster, 1949; New York: Clarion paperback, 1968. ix,
       491 p.

       Collection of essays on America between two wars, told in
       terms of significant or typical events. Background material
       only.

132   Leuchtenburg, William E. THE PERILS OF PROSPERITY, 1914-32.
       Chicago: University of Chicago Press, 1958. ix, 313 p. Index,
       bibliog.

       Period between America's entrance into World War I and the
       end of postwar prosperity placed in the full context of Ameri-
       can history. Little specific mention of entertainment; good
       essay on "suggested reading."

133   Lord, Walter. THE GOOD YEARS. FROM 1900 TO THE FIRST WORLD
        WAR. New York: Harper and Brothers, 1960. ix, 369 p. Illus.,
        index, note on sources.

        Social history of peacetime years; some reference to entertain-
        ment but extremely limited.

134   Minnigerode, Meade. THE FABULOUS FORTIES, 1840-1850, A PRE-
        SENTATION OF PRIVATE LIFE. New York: G.P. Putnam's Sons,
        1924. xvi, 345 p. Illus.

        Private and civic life of America in the 1840s, with a focus
        largely on New York City. Good chapter on popular theatre,
        "Tonight at Seven," and dioramas and panoramas, exhibitions,
        garden amusements, museums (Barnum's), child prodigies, and
        minstrels ("Prodigies and Tambourines").

135   Morris, Lloyd. POSTSCRIPT TO YESTERDAY. AMERICA: THE LAST
        FIFTY YEARS. New York: Random House, 1947. xxvi, 475 p.
        Index, bibliog.

        Secondhand account, sometimes penetrating, often superficial;
        excellent introduction to the turn of the century and the time
        of trolley parks, midways, variety and vaudeville, minstrels,
        legit, and troupers.

136   _____. INCREDIBLE NEW YORK. For full entry and annotation, see
        item 1177.

137   Mumford, Lewis. THE BROWN DECADES: A STUDY OF THE ARTS IN
        AMERICA, 1865-1895. New York: Harcourt, Brace and Co., 1931.
        2d ed. New York: Dover Publications, 1955. xii, 266 p. Illus.,
        index, bibliog.

        Promise, achievement, and influence of this period on the
        contemporary scene. Does not deal with popular live enter-
        tainment but instead, architecture, engineering, landscape
        design, and painting.

138   Nye, Russel B. THE CULTURAL LIFE OF THE NEW NATION, 1776-
        1830. New York: Harper and Brothers, 1960. xii, 324 p. Illus.,
        index, bibliog.

        General survey, including a brief glimpse at the theatre.

139   _____. "The Juvenile Approach to American Culture, 1870-1930."
        In NEW VOICES IN AMERICAN STUDIES, edited by Ray B. Browne,
        pp. 7-84. Lafayette, Ind.: Purdue University Studies, 1966.

        The dime novel is the subject of this essay with a good look
        at how books were used to introduce young people to their
        culture and to instill virtue. Only of peripheral interest.

140 _____. THE UNEMBARRASSED MUSE: THE POPULAR ARTS IN AMERICA. New York: Dial Press, 1970. 497 p. Index, bibliog.

Excellent general introduction of the popular arts in America by an acknowledged authority with good section on "popular theatre" (including musical theatre).

141 Partridge, Bellamy, and Bettmann, Otto. AS WE WERE: FAMILY LIFE IN AMERICA, 1850-1900. New York and London: Whittlesey House, 1946. 184 p. Index.

The final chapter, "Sports and Amusements," covers spectator sports, concert saloons, legitimate theatres, opera, minstrel shows, Barnum's Museum, amusement resorts, and so forth. Text is relatively insignificant but lithographs and photographs from the Bettmann archive are of interest.

142 Phillips, Cabell. FROM THE CRASH TO THE BLITZ, 1929-1939. New York: Macmillan and Co., 1969. [xii], 596 p. Index.

A "journalist's reprise" of the decade from the stock market crash of 1929 to the onset of World War II in 1939. Includes chapters entitled "Popular Culture-Highbrow" and "Popular Culture-Middlebrow," covering legitimate theatre and film, radio, and popular music.

143 Rosenberg, Bernard, and White, David Manning, eds. MASS CULTURE: THE POPULAR ARTS IN AMERICA. Glencoe, Ill.: Falcon's Wing Press, 1959. x, 561 p.

Collection of essays on mass culture, including a section entitled "Perspectives of Mass Culture," with essays by Alexis De Tocqueville, Walt Whitman, Jose Ortega Y Gasset, Leo Lowenthal, Dwight MacDonald, Gilbert Seldes, and Clement Greenberg offered as background to mass culture.

144 Rourke, Constance. AMERICAN HUMOUR: A STUDY OF THE NATIONAL CHARACTER. New York: Harcourt, Brace and Co., 1931. x, 324 p. Index, bibliog., notes.

Excellent discussion of American comic stereotypes in the nineteenth century, including the Yankee, frontiersman, and Negro. See also below.

145 _____. THE ROOTS OF AMERICAN CULTURE. Edited by Van Wyck Brooks. New York: Harcourt, Brace and Co., 1942. xii, 305 p.

Rise of theatricals and early American music.

146 Schlesinger, Arthur M. THE RISE OF THE CITY, 1878-1898. New York:

Macmillan and Co., 1933. xvi, 494 p. Illus., index, bibliog.

History of American civilization between two worlds, one rural
and agricultural, the other urban and industrial. Includes
coverage of all major entertainment forms--burlesque, vaudeville, circus, chautauqua, minstrelsy, Wild West shows, and so
forth, in context of the times.

147   Schoener, Allon, ed. PORTAL TO AMERICA: THE LOWER EAST SIDE
1870-1925. New York: Holt, Rinehart, and Winston, 1967. 256 p.
Illus.

Life on the lower East Side in photographs and New York
newspaper essays and articles. Focus is on the Jewish immigrant. Good photographs of automatic one-cent vaudeville on
Fourteenth Street, the Grand Theater, and the Thalia Theater.

148   Shaw, Arnold. THE STREET THAT NEVER SLEPT. New York: Coward,
McCann and Geoghegan, 1971. xiv, [9] 378 p. Illus., index.

Biography of New York's 52d Street, including its association
with Tin Pan Alley.

149   Silverman, Kenneth. A CULTURAL HISTORY OF THE AMERICAN
REVOLUTION. New York: Thomas Y. Crowell Co., 1976. xvii,
699 p. Illus., index, bibliog., notes.

A superb cultural history with frequent details on entertainment
during the years 1763-89.

150   Smith, Matthew Hale. SUNSHINE AND SHADOW IN NEW YORK.
Hartford, Conn.: J.B. Burr and Co., 1869. 718 p. Illus.

Good sense of what New York was like as popular entertainment was on the verge of raising its head.

151   Still, Bayrd. MIRROR FOR GOTHAM. New York: New York University Press, 1956. xix, 417 p. Illus., index, bibliog.

New York as described by contemporaries through the years,
from its beginnings to 1950s, with frequent reference to all
forms of entertainment. Extensive bibliography.

152   Sullivan, Mark. OUR TIMES, THE TURN OF THE CENTURY. New
York and London: Charles Scribner's Sons, 1926. xviii, 610 p. Index.

Chapter 10, "The Nineties," covers all forms of amusement
with other references scattered throughout the text.

153   Tandy, Jennette. CRACKERBOX PHILOSOPHERS IN AMERICAN HUMOR

AND SATIRE. New York: Columbia University Press, 1925. xi, 181 p. Index, bibliog.

Tandy discusses popular American folk heroes from 1775 to 1925, whose colloquilized and often comical philosophy and blatant political satire are indicative of popular attitudes in each period covered. Includes many excerpts from plays, popular songs, and poems, all dealing with the American folk tradition.

Chapter 3

GENERAL SOURCES ON POPULAR ENTERTAINMENT

The user should also consult sources listed in chapters 1 and 2 and "General Sources" in part III, "Popular Theatre."

A. AMERICAN FORMS

154   Abbott, George. MISTER ABBOTT. For full entry and annotation, see item 1852.

155   AMERICAN PASTIMES. Brockton, Mass.: Brockton Art Center, 1976. 44 p. Illus., bibliog. Paper.

Catalog of an exhibit on American pastimes. Essays by Neil Harris ("Pastimes: From Threat to Therapy"), David Winslow ("Children and Pastimes"), Brooks McNamara ("'Scavengers of the Amusement World': Popular Entertainment and the Birth of the Movies." See item 50).

156   Anderson, John. THE AMERICAN THEATRE. New York: Dial Press, 1938. vii, 430 p. Illus., index, bibliog.

General history of American stage with frequent allusion to popular forms.

157   Appel, Livia. "Early Drama in Minneapolis." MINNESOTA HISTORY BULLETIN 5 (February 1923): 43-45.

Deals principally with popular theatre and amusements in the 1860s.

158   Atkinson, Brooks. BROADWAY. Rev. ed. New York: Macmillan and Co., 1974. ix, 564 p. Illus., index.

Copiously illustrated history of Broadway from 1900 to 1974. Section 1 is the most relevant to popular entertainment.

159 Bandelier, Adolf F. THE DELIGHT MAKERS. 2d ed. 1890. Reprint. New York: Dodd, Mead and Co., 1954. xvii, 490 p. Illus.

> Manners, customs, rites of the Pueblo Indians of New Mexico; a classic work and good for early native entertainment with ritual implications.

160 Bennett, Joan. THE BENNETT PLAYBILL. New York: Holt, Rinehart and Winston, 1970. xi, 332 p. Illus.

> Five generations of theatrical families, the Morrisons, Woods, and Bennetts, including early American grass roots careers. Also covers careers of family as strolling players at English fairs and pantomime performers at Drury Lane.

161 Blesh, Rudi, and Janis, Harriet. THEY ALL PLAYED RAGTIME. For full entry and annotation, see item 976.

162 Blumenthal, George, as told to Arthur H. Menkin. MY SIXTY YEARS IN SHOW BUSINESS. New York: Frederick C. Osberg, 1936. xiv, 336 p. Illus.

> Covers the period 1874 to 1934; sixty years behind the scenes association with Oscar Hammerstein. Covers the legitimate stage, vaudeville, light opera, and grand opera.

163 Bond, Frederick W. THE NEGRO AND THE DRAMA. College Park, Md.: McGrath, 1940. x, 213 p. Indix, bibliog.

> Discusses Negro involvement in legitimate theatre, dramatic music, dance, and many forms of popular entertainment, including minstrelsy, burlesque, melodrama and musical comedy, night clubs, and movies and radio.

164 Bowen, Elbert R. THEATRICAL ENTERTAINMENT IN RURAL MISSOURI BEFORE THE CIVIL WAR. Columbia: University of Missouri, 1959. xiii, 140 p. Illus., bibliog. Paper.

> Most useful for coverage of paratheatrical forms, i.e., wagon shows, circus boats, and minstrels.

165 Brady, William A. SHOWMAN. New York: E.P. Dutton, 1937. 278 p.

> Autobiography of actor-entertainer and material on late nineteenth- , early twentieth-century theatrical figures and popular entertainments. Appeared first in condensed form in SATURDAY EVENING POST (11 January-7 April 1936).

166 Briggs, Harold E. "Entertainment and Amusement in Cairo, 1848-1858."

JOURNAL OF THE ILLINOIS STATE HISTORICAL SOCIETY 47 (Autumn 1954): 231-51. Illus.

Circuses and showboats surveyed.

167   Brown, Daniel J. "Footlight Favorites Forty Years Ago: A Stroll up Old Broadway." In VALENTINE'S MANUAL OF OLD NEW YORK, edited by Henry Collins Brown, pp. 133-66. New York: Valentine's Manual, 1922. Illus.

An imaginary walking tour of New York theatres in the 1860s.

168   Brown, Henry Collins, ed. VALENTINE'S MANUAL, 1927: NEW YORK IN THE ELEGANT EIGHTIES. Hastings-on-Hudson, N.Y.: Valentine's Manual, [1927]. Illus.

Summary of New York theatres in the 1880s (pp. 272-324).

169   _____. IN THE GOLDEN NINETIES. Hastings-on-Hudson, N.Y.: Valentine's Manual, 1928. Illus.

New York in the 1890s, including popular theatre attractions-- circus, Coney Island, and the introduction of movies (pp. 105-41).

170   Brown, John Mason. TWO ON THE AISLE. New York: W.W. Norton, 1938. ix [12], 321 p. Index.

Covers the period 1929-38; collection of reviews, including Brown's comments on revues, Ed Wynn, Beatrice Lillie, Gypsy Rose Lee, Bert Lahr, and plays-musicals of the popular variety.

171   Brown, T. Allston. HISTORY OF THE NEW YORK STAGE, FROM THE FIRST PERFORMANCE IN 1732 TO 1901 IN ENCYCLOPEDIC FORM. 3 vols. New York: Dodd, Mead and Co., 1903. Reprint. New York: Benjamin Blom, 1963. Index (in Vol 3).

Contains histories of over four hundred New York theatres, opera houses, music halls, and circuses, with a separate entry on each.

172   Browne, Ray B. "Shakespeare in American Vaudeville and Negro Minstrelsy." AMERICAN QUARTERLY 12 (Fall 1960): 374-91.

Examples of how Shakespeare's name and works permeated popular entertainment in the nineteenth century, especially minstrelsy and vaudeville.

173   Burton, Jack. IN MEMORIUM--OLDTIME SHOW BIZ. New York: Vantage Press, 1965. 102 p.

Reminiscences of a pop song and theatre buff for almost eighty
years; Burton was a newspaperman, magazine editor, and radio
program producer. Essays on minstrelsy, the opera house, the
road show, one-night stands, circuses, burlesque, vaudeville,
and follies and revues. Most useful on vaudeville and burlesque.

174   Cahn, William. THE LAUGH MAKERS: A PICTORIAL HISTORY OF
      AMERICAN COMEDIANS. New York: Bramhall House, 1957. 192 p.
      Illus., index.

      From Thomas Wignell (1787 in THE CONTRAST) to TV comics
      of the '50s. Covers native types, clowns (minstrelsy and
      circus), vaudeville, and revues. Ignores burlesque altogether.

175   Cantor, Eddie. THE WAY I SEE IT. Edited by Phyllis Rosenteur.
      Englewood Cliffs, N.J.: Prentice-Hall, 1959. viii, 204 p.

      At the age of sixty-seven years after a heart attack, Cantor
      looks back at his life in show business. In chapter 15 he
      catalogs his choices for "All-time Greats in Show Business":
      George M. Cohan, Ed Wynn, Charlie Chaplin, Al Jolson,
      Noel Coward, Jack Benny, Jimmy Durante, Groucho Marx,
      Will Rogers, Bert Williams, George Jessel, and other notables
      of the popular entertainment world.

176   _____. AS I REMEMBER THEM. New York: Duell, Sloan and
      Pearce, 1963. 144 p. Illus.

      Reminiscences of Jack Benny, W.C. Fields, Bea Lillie,
      Groucho Marx, Al Jolson, Greta Garbo, Judy Garland, James
      Cagney, Red Skelton, Jimmy Durante, Fanny Brice, Gus
      Edwards, Florenz Ziegfeld, Bert Williams, George M. Cohan,
      Ted Lewis, Milton Berle, Will Rogers, The Palace Theatre,
      Atlantic City and Grossinger's, and "freak" acts in vaudeville.
      Very anecdotal and inexact. Each portrait very brief.

177   Cantor, Norman I., and Werthman, Michael S., eds. THE HISTORY
      OF POPULAR CULTURE. New York: Macmillan and Co., 1968.
      xxxviii, 788 p.

      Includes a section of reprinted essays on "Popular Entertain-
      ments and Recreation" (pp. 446-79) by such authorities as
      Foster Rhea Dulles, Earl Chapin May, and James H. Young.

178   Carson, Gerald. MEN, BEASTS, AND GODS. New York: Charles
      Scribner's Sons, 1972. x, 268 p. Illus., index, bibliog., notes.

      The relationships that have existed between mankind and the
      lower animals from prehistoric eras to the present time. Con-
      cerned primarily with the protection of animals. Most useful

for its extensive documentation and references to P.T. Barnum, the circus, and a major chapter on the rodeo.

179   Carson, Jane. COLONIAL VIRGINIANS AT PLAY. Williamsburg: Colonial Williamsburg. Distributed by the University Press of Virginia, Charlottesville, 1965. xv, 326 p. Illus., index, bibliog., appendixes.

Survey of Colonial entertainments in Williamsburg (primarily), including games, sports, theatres, exhibitions, concerts, and tavern clubs.

180   Charters, Samuel B., and Kunstadt, Leonard. JAZZ: A HISTORY OF THE NEW YORK SCENE. Garden City, N.Y.: Doubleday and Co., 1962. 382 p. Index, bibliog.

Covers period 1900–1930. Includes mention of Pastor's, Weber and Fields's, and other variety houses and music halls, as well as pavilions and resorts such as Coney Island and Manhattan Beach. A definitive study of the black entertainer in New York and the rise of jazz.

181   Chase, Gilbert. AMERICA'S MUSIC. For full entry and annotation, see Item 981.

182   Churchill, Allen. THE GREAT WHITE WAY. New York: E.P. Dutton, 1962. 310 p. Illus., index, bibliog.

Broadway from 1900 to 1919, good chapter on vaudeville and frequent allusions to popular theatre.

183   _____. THE THEATRICAL TWENTIES. New York: McGraw-Hill, 1975. 326 p. Illus., index, bibliog.

Fascinating year-by-year account of the American theatre from 1920 through 1929. Being the age of the revue, there is considerable coverage of the Ziegfeld Follies, George White's Scandals, Earl Carroll's Vanities, Charlot's Revue, Passing Shows and Artists and Models (the Shuberts), as well as more legitimate forms of popular theatre and the personalities associated with the various forms. Excellent illustrations throughout.

184   Clapp, William W., Jr. A RECORD OF THE BOSTON STAGE. Boston, James Monroe and Co., 1853. Reprint. New York: Benjamin Blom, 1968. xiii, 479 p.

Standard history of Boston theatre through the 1840s with frequent mention of popular forms, including an account of early circuses. For an index to this work see THEATRE DOCUMENTATION 1 (Fall 1968): 35–68.

185   Davis, A.W. "Past Days of Minstrelsy, Variety, Circus and Side Show."
       AMERICANA 8 (June 1912): 529-47.

       Retrospective survey and nostalgic glance backwards.

186   Davis, Michael Marks, Jr. THE EXPLOITATION OF PLEASURE. A
       STUDY OF COMMERCIAL RECREATIONS IN NEW YORK CITY. New
       York: Department of Child Hygiene of the Russell Sage Foundation,
       1911. 61 p. Paper.

       Survey of early twentieth-century entertainment in New York,
       including penny arcades, dancing academies and dance halls,
       burlesque, vaudeville, legitimate theatre and motion picture.
       Looks at their status, offers statistical data, comparable tables
       to illustrate attendance and money spent; discusses laws, need
       to elevate vaudeville, morals, education, and question of
       censorship.

187   Dillon, William A. LIFE DOUBLES IN BRASS. Ithaca, N.Y.: House
       of Nollid, 1944. x, 239 p. Illus., appendix.

       Memoirs of a theatre song writer's carrer includes information
       on one-night stands, medicine shows, minstrel shows, theatre
       repertory, and vaudeville. Inexact in details and lacking in
       dates and specifics but interesting firsthand account. Songs
       by Dillon are listed in an appendix.

188   Dimmick, Ruth Crosby. OUT THEATRES TO-DAY AND YESTERDAY.
       New York: H.K. Fly Co., 1913. 97, x p. Illus., index.

       Anecdotal account of the growth of the amusement industry in
       New York, 1732-1913, including the circus, THE BLACK
       CROOK, literary burlesque, Barnum's Museum and others,
       Castle Garden, homes of popular theatre (i.e., the Bowery),
       minstrel theatre, the Hippodrome, Roof Garden, summer "Lot
       Shows," cabarets, and the like. Sketchy and not always
       reliable.

189   Durang, John. THE MEMOIR OF JOHN DURANG (AMERICAN ACTOR,
       1785-1816). Edited by Alan S. Downer. Pittsburgh: University of
       Pittsburgh Press, 1966. xix, 176 p. Illus., index, bibliog.

       Well-edited autobiography of the early American actor pub-
       lished for the Historical Society of York County, Pennsylvania,
       and the American Society for Theatre Research. Especially
       important for Durang's memoirs of Ricketts's Circus and his
       work as a circus clown and puppeteer, as well as actor and
       producer in the circuit covering the Eastern states and Canada.
       A significant source on all early forms of American popular
       entertainment.

190   Edgar, Randolph. "Early Minnesota Theatres." MINNESOTA HISTORY
       9 (March 1928): 31–38.

       Dime museums, opera houses, and variety theatres from 1850s
       to the 1890s.

191   Edwards, Richard Henry. POPULAR AMUSEMENTS. New York and
       London: Association Press, 1915. 239 p.

       Includes in its broad examination of amusements, popular
       theatre in its various forms, vaudeville, cafes with amusement
       features, commercial amusement parks, circuses, and fairs.
       Basically a social and moralistic investigation with solutions
       offered for community action.

192   Estavan, Lawrence, ed. "San Francisco Theatre Research." 20 vols.
       San Francisco: WPA, 1938–42. Illus., index, bibliog. Paper.
       Mimeographed.

       Volumes 13 and 14 are the most relevant (minstrelsy and
       burlesque). Other volumes useful as well for popular theatre
       in San Francisco in the nineteenth century.

193   Fields, W.C. W.C. FIELDS BY HIMSELF. HIS INTENDED AUTO-
       BIOGRAPHY WITH HITHERTO UNPUBLISHED LETTERS, NOTES, SCRIPTS
       AND ARTICLES. Commentary by Ronald J. Fields. Englewood Cliffs,
       N.J.: Prentice-Hall, 1973. xiv, 510 p. Illus., index.

       Over one hundred photographs, drawings, and posters help to
       illustrate Fields as he perceived himself; extensive section
       contains heretofore unpublished vaudeville scripts (many ex-
       panded later into film scripts) covering the period of the
       1920s and '30s, during which time he appeared in the Ziegfeld
       Follies and Earl Carroll's Vanities.

194   Flint, Richard W. STEP RIGHT UP! AMUSEMENT FOR ALL. SHOW
       BUSINESS AT THE TURN OF THE CENTURY. Rochester, N.Y.:
       Margaret Woodbury Strong Museum, 1977. [21] p. Illus. Paper.

       Magnificently illustrated exhibition catalog for an exhibition
       at the Memorial Art Gallery in Rochester. Contains a good
       general survey, though brief, of live entertainment around the
       turn of the century with a selected essay and illustrated sec-
       tions on carnival, amusement parks, circus, theatre, and
       vaudeville. Illustrated with artifacts from the Margaret
       Woodbury Strong Museum (see item 2432).

195   Fyles, Franklin. THE THEATRE AND ITS PEOPLE. For full entry and
       annotation, see item 1887.

196   Gilbert, Douglas. LOST CHORDS: THE DIVERTING STORY OF
       AMERICAN POPULAR SONGS. Garden City, N.Y.: Doubleday,
       Doran and Co., 1942. xii, 377 p.

       Good on songs written for vaudeville, but less useful for
       other forms.

197   Gilder, Rosamond. "In the Service of Comedy." THEATRE ARTS
       MONTHLY 22 (September 1938): 637-46.

       Gilder's evaluation of successful comic ingredients in all
       forms of comedy, including musical comedy, vaudeville,
       revues, and high comedy.

198   Gordon, Max, and Funke, Lewis. MAX GORDON PRESENTS. New
       York: Bernard Geis Associates, 1963. vi, 314 p. Illus., index.

       Autobiography of one of Broadway's leading producers. Refer-
       ences to vaudeville, revue, Florenz Ziegfeld, Jerome Kern,
       George M. Cohan, Noel Coward, Eddie Foy, Sr., George
       White's Scandals, Al Lewis, and more.

199   Granlund, Nils Thor; with Feder, Sid; and Hancock, Ralph. BLONDES,
       BRUNETTES, AND BULLETS. New York: David McKay Co., 1957.
       300 p.

       Autobiography of a press agent, radio broadcaster, vaudeville
       impresario, and producer of nightclub shows from Texas
       Guinan's bistro to the Flamingo in Las Vegas. Granlund also
       served as talent scout for Ziegfeld and Earl Carroll. Career
       began in Providence, Rhode Island as a press agent in 1912.

200   Grau, Robert. THE STAGE IN THE TWENTIETH CENTURY. New York:
       Broadway Publishing Co., 1912. xxvii, 360 p. Illus.

       Volume 3 in a series of books by Grau (see also items 1114
       and 1117). Chapters on "The Vaudeville Situation" (ca. 1911),
       vaudeville managers (B.F. Keith, Jacob Litt, Alexander
       Pantages, E.F. Albee), a plea for opera comique, early film,
       and other topics relevant to popular entertainment. Essay on
       "The Twentieth Century Stage, Mechanically" by the machin-
       ist, Claude L. Hagen, included. An important source.

201   Green, Abel. THE SPICE OF VARIETY. New York: Henry Holt and
       Co., 1952. viii, 277 p.

       Collection of essays by contributors to VARIETY covering all
       aspects of "show biz." Especially good on vaudeville informa-
       tion and insights. Authors include such notables as Joey
       Adams, Fred Allen, Jack Benny, Eddie Cantor, Charles B.

Cochran, Mrs. Gus Edwards, George Jessel, Arthur Kober, Joe Laurie, Jr., Gypsy Rose Lee, Groucho Marx, Benny Rubin, Phil Silvers, Joe Smith, and Charles Dale.

202   Green, Abel, and Laurie, Joe, Jr. SHOW BIZ FROM VAUDE TO VIDEO. For full entury and annotation, see item 1122.

203   Handlin, Oscar. "Comments on Mass and Popular Culture." In CULTURE FOR THE MILLIONS, edited by Norman Jacobs, pp. 63-71. Princeton, N.J.: D. Van Nostrand and Co., 1961.

Good analysis of popular theatre and vaudeville in order to reveal significant elements in the difference between popular culture of that period and mass media of today.

204   Handy, W[illiam]. C[hristopher]. NEGRO AUTHORS AND COMPOSERS OF THE UNITED STATES. New York: Handy Brothers Music Co., [ca. 1938]. 24 p. Paper.

Guide to black authors and composers, focuses on those published by the Handy Brothers.

205   Harper, Robert D. "Theatrical Entertainment in Early Omaha." NEBRASKA HISTORY 36 (June 1955): 93-104. Illus.

Musical and variety shows from the 1850s to 1867.

206   Harris, Neil, ed. THE LAND OF CONTRASTS: 1880-1901. New York: George Braziller, 1970. xii, 365 p. Illus., bibliog.

Includes section on "Amusements" (pp. 159-90) with Edwin Royle's 1899 essay on vaudeville from SCRIBNER'S (see item 1195), John Corbin on East Side Italian theatre from HARPER'S (1898), and other essays. Part of series: THE AMERICAN CULTURE (see item 124).

207   Hartley, Marsden. ADVENTURES IN THE ARTS. Introduction by Waldo Frank. New York: Boni and Liveright Publishers, 1921. Reprint. New York: Hacker Art Books, 1972. xviii, 254 p.

Part two (pp. 155-88) is concerned with various forms of show business. The author bemoans the passing of the acrobat, especially the wandering street entertainer, essays on vaudeville and the equestrienne of interest.

208   Hartt, Rollin Lynde. THE PEOPLE AT PLAY; EXCURSIONS IN THE HUMOR AND PHILOSOPHY OF POPULAR AMUSEMENTS. Boston and New York: Houghton Mifflin Co., 1909. vii, 316 [7] p. Illus.

Chapters on the Folly Theatre, "The Home of Burlesque," and

a delineation of a typical series of acts; "The Amusement
Park" and its evolution; "The Dime Museum" and its wonders;
the biograph show ("The World in Motion"); "Melodrama,"
plus mention of other minor forms of popular entertainment as
they existed in 1909. Fairly useful introduction.

209　　Henderson, Mary C. THE CITY AND THE THEATRE. Clifton, N.J.:
James T. White, 1973. xiv, 323 p. Illus., index, bibliog., notes.

Useful background on New York and its places of entertainment from 1700. Presented in five stages of development.

210　　Hopper, DeWolf, written in collaboration with Stout, Wesley Winans.
ONCE A CLOWN, ALWAYS A CLOWN. Boston: Little, Brown and
Co., 1927. x, 238 p. Illus.

Reminiscences of the comic-singer's career as a travelling
trouper, a performer in Gilbert and Sullivan and in early
films.

211　　Horton, Judge [William E.]. ABOUT STAGE FOLKS. Detroit:　Free
Press Printing Co., 1902. 151 p. Illus.

Chapters on Tony Pastor, "Polite" vaudeville, popular theatre,
circus, theatrical slang, song and dance men, and similarly
related topics.

212　　＿＿＿＿. DRIFTWOOD OF THE STAGE. Detroit: Press of Winn and
Hammond, 1904. 383 p. Illus., index.

Miscellaneous essays on all aspects of nineteenth-century
American entertainment, including circus, minstrelsy, music,
and vaudeville. A very personal account but generally
reliable.

213　　Hughes, Langston, and Meltzer, Milton. BLACK MAGIC, A PICTORIAL
HISTORY OF THE NEGRO IN AMERICAN ENTERTAINMENT. Englewood Cliffs, N.J.: Prentice-Hall, 1967. [6], 375 p. Illus., index.

A major survey from sixteenth-century minstrels, with coverage
of such topics as UNCLE TOM'S CABIN, Ira Aldridge, early
musicals, Bert Williams, Barnum, carnivals, side shows, Negro
vaudeville circuit, jazz, and so forth.

214　　Hutton, Laurence. CURIOSITIES OF THE AMERICAN STAGE. New
York: For full entry and annotation, see item 1900.

215　　Ireland, Joseph N. RECORDS OF THE NEW YORK STAGE FROM
1750 TO 1860. For full entry and annotation, see item 1901.

216   Isaacs, Edith J.R. THE NEGRO IN THE AMERICAN THEATRE. New
       York: Theatre Arts Books, 1947. 143 p. Illus.

       Historical survey through the early 1940s.

217   James, Reese D. CRADLE OF CULTURE, 1800-1810: THE PHILADEL-
       PHIA STAGE. Philadelphia: University of Pennsylvania Press, 1957.
       156 p. Illus., index, note on sources.

       Good for lists of popular entertainments during the early nine-
       teenth century.

218   Janis, Elsie. SO FAR, SO GOOD: AN AUTOBIOGRAPHY OF ELSIE
       JANIS. New York: E.P. Dutton and Co., 1932. 344 p. Illus.

       Memoirs of the famous impersonator's rise from a child vaude-
       villian to star stints with the Orpheum Circuit, Ziegfeld,
       New York variety, the legitimate stage, and in films.

219   [Jeffrey, John B., ed.]. JNO. B. JEFFREY'S GUIDE AND DIRECTORY
       TO THE OPERA HOUSES, THEATRES, PUBLIC HALLS, BILL POSTERS,
       ETC. OF THE CITIES AND TOWNS OF AMERICA. Chicago: Jno. B.
       Jeffrey, 1887. xxxvi, 365 p.

       Publication intended primarily for amusement managers and
       agents and theatre proprietors. Useful information on enter-
       tainment in the 1880s and practices of the time. Contains
       lists of critics, circuses, and a directory by state of useful
       information to the theatrical profession.

220   Jenkins, Stephen. THE GREATEST STREET IN THE WORLD--BROADWAY.
       New York: G.P. Putnam's Sons, 1911. xxii, 509 p. Illus., index,
       bibliog.

       A useful history of Broadway's development, changes, and
       characteristics, including a chapter on "Places of Amusement
       Below Union Square." Discusses the progression of theatre
       Uptown and includes most major centers of amusement, i.e.,
       Barnum's Museum, Niblo's Garden, Harrigan and Hart's New
       Theatre Comique, and Buckley's Hall (minstrel house), and
       most major performers of the late nineteenth century.

220a   Jennings, John J. THEATRICAL AND CIRCUS LIFE; OR, SECRETS OF
       THE STAGE, GREENROOM AND SAWDUST ARENA. St. Louis: Herbert
       and Cole, 1882. 608 p. Illus.

       A compendium of popular entertainment, including American
       pantomime (G.L. Fox), Variety Theatre, concert saloons,
       dime museums, circuses, minstrelsy, and magic. An excellent
       period source with several hundred illustrations.

221   Jessel, George. ELEGY IN MANHATTAN. Foreword by Ben Hecht.
       New York: Holt, Rinehart, and Winston, 1961. xv, 198 p. Index.

       A bizarre little volume; anthology of verses in the style of
       Masters's SPOON RIVER ANTHOLOGY in which fifty-seven
       performers, institutions, and managers from the past speak
       their epitaphs. Notables include Eva Tanquay, Bill Robinson,
       P.T. Barnum, Oscar Hammerstein I, Florenz Ziegfeld, George
       M. Cohan, Earl Carroll, Julian Eltinge, Fred Allen, Vernon
       Castle, Will Rogers, Al Jolson, Lillian Russell, Anna Held,
       and other known politicians, managers, entrepreneurs, vaude-
       villians, actors, comics, musicians, and sports figures.

222   Jones, LeRoi. BLUES PEOPLE: NEGRO MUSIC IN WHITE AMERICA.
       For full entry and annotation, see item 1007.

223   JULIUS CAHN'S OFFICIAL THEATRICAL GUIDE. New York: Empire
       Theatre Building Publication Office, 1895-- . Indexes.

       A series of information guides on theatres and attractions in
       the United States, Canada, Mexico, and Cuba for "members
       of the dramatic profession" and "travelling men." Indexes to
       illustrations, theatres, railroad maps, advertisers, and so forth.

224   King, Donald C. "A Historical Survey of the Theatres of Boston."
       MARQUEE 6 (3d quarter, 1974): 5-22. Illus.

       Survey of physical theatres in Boston, including vaudeville
       houses, dime museums, and burlesque houses (The Howard).

225   Kirstein, Lincoln. "Eccentric Dancing." THEATRE ARTS MONTHLY
       24 (June 1940): 443-49. Illus.

       Essay assessing the eccentric dancer as essentially a dancing
       clown. Examples include Ray Bolger, Fred Astaire, Buddy
       Ebsen, Hal Sherman, Buster West, and Jack Buchanan. Traces
       eccentric art from the antics of Phlyax vases through the
       commedia dell' arte to Broadway's dancing fools.

226   Lahr, John. NOTES ON A COWARDLY LION. New York: Alfred A.
       Knopf, 1969. x, 394 p. Illus., index, appendixes.

       Biography of Bert Lahr, one of America's great clowns. Covers
       his career in burlesque, vaudeville, the Ziegfeld Follies,
       George White's Scandals, and his later career on stage and in
       films. Includes a "Dramatic Chronology" of Lahr's career and
       seven appendixes: a "Kid Act" based on the Avon Comedy
       Four by Joe Smith and Charlie Dale (ca. 1900); "Flugel
       Street" burlesque routine (ca. 1918); "Beach Babies," a comic
       afterpiece (ca. 1924); "Chin Up" by David Freedman (1934);

a comic sketch; the "If I Were King of the Forest" from THE
WIZARD OF OZ (1939); "The Baseball Sketch" (1951) by Abe
Burrows; and "Hostility" (1959) by Arnold B. Horwitt and
Aaron Ruben.

227   Leavitt, M[ichael]. B[ennett].   FIFTY YEARS IN THEATRICAL MAN-
       AGEMENT, 1859-1909.   For full entry and annotation, see item 1160.

228   Leonard, Eddie [Lemuel Toney].   WHAT A LIFE I'M TELLING YOU.
       New York: Eddie Leonard, 1934. xv [17], 240 p. Illus.

       Rambling and poorly written autobiography of Leonard, known
       as Eddie Leonard the Minstrel, in latter-day minstrelsy and
       vaudeville.

229   Logan, Olive.   APROPOS OF WOMEN AND THEATRE.   New York:
       Carleton Publishers, 1869.   240 p.

       In part, her protests against the early girlie show with chap-
       ters such as "About the Leg Business" and "About Nudity in
       Theatres," and chapters on other aspects of morality in the
       theatre (i.e., "About the Drunken Drama" in which she con-
       demns "Moral" drama).   See also items 1244 and 1245.

230   McCabe, James D., Jr.   LIGHTS AND SHADOWS OF NEW YORK
       LIFE; OR, SIGHTS AND SENSATIONS OF THE GREAT CITY.   Phila-
       delphia, Cincinnati, Chicago, and St. Louis: National Publishing Co.,
       1872.   850 p.   Illus.

       Chapters on street musicians; theatres and minor amusement
       (minstrels, concerts, lectures, circus); beer gardens, concert
       saloons, and dance halls.

231   Maney, Richard.   FANFARE: THE CONFESSIONS OF A PRESS AGENT.
       New York: Harper and Brothers, 1957.   viii, 374 p.   Illus., index.

       Thirty-three year career in New York and the author's contact
       with all forms of popular entertainment, as well as legitimate
       theatre.

232   Marcuse, Maxwell F.   TIN PAN ALLEY IN GASLIGHT.   Watkins Glen,
       N.Y.: Century House, 1959.   448 p.   Illus., index.

       Music of the Gay '90s (1880s up to 1910).   A year-by-year
       account.   Some mention of stage entertainment, in particular
       the work of Harrigan and Hart and Charles H. Hoyt.

233   Marks, Edward Bennett, as told to Liebling, Abbott J.   THEY ALL
       SANG: FROM TONY PASTOR TO RUDY VALLEE.   New York: Viking
       Press, 1934.   xi, 321 p.   Illus., index (names and subjects, songs),
       appendixes.

Covers fifty years (1880s to 1930s) in American musical history
and deals with nearly every important popular entertainment
figure of the time. Includes lyrics and music of numerous
popular songs, plus excellent illustrations of photographs, playbills, and sheet music covers. Very good source.

234 _____. THEY ALL HAD GLAMOUR: FROM THE SWEDISH NIGHTIN-
GALE TO THE NAKED LADY. New York: J. Messner, 1944. xvii,
448 p. Illus., index, glossary.

Lesser remembered theatre and musical artists from: THE
BLACK CROOK (1866) to the end of the nineteenth century.
Useful chapters on G.L. Fox, Lola Montez, Adah Isaacs
Menken, plus brief biographical sketches of performers and
others up to the 1940s, mostly still living in 1944, such as
Ethel Barrymore, Blanche Bates, Rose Coghlan, Henry E.
Dixey, Daniel Frohman, Julia Marlowe. Good glossary of
"Old-Time Colloquialisms" (pp. 431-38).

235 Martin, Pete. PETE MARTIN CALLS ON. New York: Simon and
Schuster, 1962. 510 p.

Essays on Groucho Marx, Phil Silvers, and other show business
personalities.

236 Matlaw, Myron, ed. PROCEEDINGS OF THE CONFERENCE ON THE
HISTORY OF AMERICAN POPULAR ENTERTAINMENT. For full entry
and annotation, see item 52.

237 Matthews, Brander. A BOOK ABOUT THE THEATRE. New York:
Charles Scribner's Sons, 1916. xii, 334 p.

Useful perspective on popular entertainments by the early
American theatre historian. Includes essays on toy theatres,
pantomime, circus, minstrelsy, variety, magic, and Punch
and Judy. Variety is seen as a not-so-new novelty and
comparisons are made to various other forms and countries.

238 Moody, Richard. AMERICA TAKES THE STAGE. For full entry and
annotation, see item 1925.

239 _____. DRAMAS FROM THE AMERICAN THEATRE, 1762-1909. For
full entry and annotation, see item 1926.

240 Morehouse, Ward. MATINEE TOMORROW. New York: Whittlesey
House (McGraw-Hill), 1949. xii, 340 p. Illus., index.

Informal history of New York theatre from 1900; from the days
of Lillian Russell to Mary Martin. Chapter titles include:
"1898--and Before," "Belasco, Fitch, Gillette, and C.F.,"

"Turn of the Century," "The Early 1900s," "The stock Company Craze," and "Frenzy of the Twenties." The panoramic treatment is good on popular legitimate theatre but treats in some detail as well vaudeville, revue, and early musicals. An entertaining book.

241 Morosco, Helen M., and Dugger, Leonard P. LIFE OF OLIVER MOROSCO; THE ORACLE OF BROADWAY, WRITTEN FROM HIS OWN NOTES AND COMMENTS, BY HELEN M. MORASCO AND LEONARD PAUL DUGGER. Caldwell, Idaho: Caxton Printers, 1944. 391 p. Illus., index.

Career of the producer from his beginnings in a California circus to Broadway.

242 Nathan, George Jean. THE POPULAR THEATRE. New York: Alfred A. Knopf, 1918. 2d ed. 1923. Reprint. Rutherford, N.J.: Fairleigh Dickinson University Press, 1971. 236 p.

Chapters on popular theatre and vaudeville (both "Big Time" and "Small Time"), musical shows and revue, and the motion picture. Musical shows should not try to be intelligent or artistic, says Nathan; their function is to provide sensual entertainment. Ziegfeld, he felt, was the embodiment of this ideal.

243 _____. THE THEATRE, THE DRAMA, THE GIRLS. New York: Alfred A. Knopf, 1921. 261 p.

Nathan's comments on just about every aspect of the theatre and individuals at that time. As usual, witty, insightful, entertaining, and highly opinionated.

244 _____. THE WORLD IN FALSEFACE. New York: Alfred A. Knopf, 1923. xxix, 326 p.

Nathan expresses his opinion that melodrama is the blood of the stage, explains how to test a real comedian, expounds on the superior aspects of Ziegfeld's Follies, analyzes Cohan's theatre, condemns UNCLE TOM'S CABIN as the worst "persistent popular play ever produced," catalogs music show comedians, and touches on a score of other topics relevant to popular entertainments of the 1920s.

245 _____. ENCYCLOPAEDIA OF THE THEATRE. New York: Alfred A. Knopf, 1940. ix, 449 p.

Entries on all aspects of the theatre and entertainment, many tongue in cheek, including paragraphs on "Dancing Girls," "Intelligence in Musical Shows," "Morality and Burlesque," "Musical Shows," and "Vaudeville."

246 _____. THE WORLD OF GEORGE JEAN NATHAN. Edited by
Charles Angoff. New York: Alfred A. Knopf, 1952. xxviii, 489 p.
Bibliog.

> Anthology of Nathan's essays in all their various facets. In-
> cludes essays on musical comedies, striptease, vaudeville,
> Ziegfeld, melodrama, and other similar topics. Volumes in-
> cludes a chronology and bibliography of Nathan's life and work.

247 Northall, William Knight. BEFORE AND BEHIND THE CURTAIN, OR
FIFTEEN YEARS' OBSERVATION AMONG THE THEATRES OF NEW
YORK. New York: W.F. Burgess, 1851. 229 p.

> Chapters on most of the major homes of popular entertainment
> and theatre in the nineteenth century, including Barnum's
> Museum, the National Theatre, Mitchell's, Burton's, the
> Olympic Theatre, Niblo's Gardens, and others.

248 Odell, George C.D. ANNALS OF THE NEW YORK STAGE. 15 vols.
New York: Columbia University Press, 1927-49. Illus., indexes.

> Standard work on the New York stage through the 1893-94
> season and a must for the student-scholar of popular entertain-
> ment and theatre, since Odell includes all forms of entertain-
> ment. Especially good on minstrelsy, variety, vaudeville, and
> circus.

249 Oppenheimer, George, ed. THE PASSIONATE PLAYGOER. New
York: Viking Press, 1958. xiv, 623 p. Illus., index.

> Anthology of more than one hundred selections by more than
> ninety contributors on all aspects of American theatre and
> entertainment, e.g., Edna Ferber on audiences on a show
> boat, Aston Stevens's "Bert Williams' Last Interview," Gypsy
> Rose Lee's "June Havoc's Sister," Heywood Broun on the
> Hippodrome, and Percy Hammond on the Ziegfeld Follies.

250 Pancoast, C[halmers]. L[owell]. TRAIL BLAZERS OF ADVERTISING.
New York: Frederick H. Hitchcock, 1926. Reprint. New York:
Arno Press, 1976. xiv, 269 p. Illus.

> Excellent study of advertising techniques in show business.
> Chapters on P.T. Barnum, Buffalo Bill Cody, circuses and
> shows, UNCLE TOM'S CABIN, medicine shows, wax figures,
> Ballyhoo artists, and other relevant topics. A pioneer work.

251 Provol, W[illiam]. Lee. THE PACK PEDDLER. Chicago, Philadelphia,
Toronto: John C. Winston Co., 1937. xii, 254 p. Illus. (one sketch).

> Although extremely jingoistic, this is an interesting memoir of
> a Polish emigrant, son of a pack peddler, and his varied

experiences during the late nineteenth century. Especially vivid are his memories of the circus, the Cardiff giant, medicine shows, Hubert's dime museum, and Cody's Wild West.

252   Richman, Harry, with Gehman, Richard. A HELL OF A LIFE. New York: Duell, Sloan, and Pearce, 1966. xii, 242 p. Illus.

Career of a song and dance man in the '20s and '30s in night clubs, on Broadway (Earl Carroll's Varieties and George White's Scandals), and as proprietor of his own club.

253   Schafer, William J., and Riedel, Johannes. THE ART OF RAGTIME. Baton Rouge: Louisiana State University Press, 1973. xix, 249 p. Illus., index, bibliog.

Complete study of ragtime, an important phase in black music and related to other popular entertainment forms. Extensive bibliography on all aspects of ragtime.

254   Schiffman, Jack. UPTOWN, THE STORY OF HARLEM'S APOLLO THEATRE. New York: Cowles Book Co., 1971. xii, 210 p. Illus., index.

Story of the Apollo Theatre, the fountainhead of black entertainment during the 1930s, as told by the son of coowner, Frank Schiffman. Prior to becoming the Apollo, the theatre was the Lafayette and then the Harlem Opera House. Book focuses on the 1940s and '50s.

255   Seldes, Gilbert. "Bunk and Hokum on the Stage." THEATRE MAGAZINE 39 (May 1924): 10, 68.

"Hokum is Honorable. Bunk is a Nuisance. They identify two theatres, miles apart." Seldes explains that "bunk" is found in serious theatre; "hokum" is found in vaudeville, musical comedies, and revues.

256   Sobel, Bernard. BROADWAY HEARTBEAT: MEMOIRS OF A PRESS AGENT. New York: Hermitage House, 1953. 352 p. Index.

Good coverage of the revue, vaudeville, and burlesque, plus chapters on Earl Carroll and Ziegfeld.

257   Sobol, Louis. THE LONGEST STREET. Foreword by Jim Bishop. New York: Crown Publishers, 1968. 448 p. Illus., index.

Memoirs of the Broadway columnist; covers the speakeasy era and the last days of vaudeville and burlesque.

258   Spaeth, Sigmund. A HISTORY OF POPULAR MUSIC IN AMERICA.

New York: Random House, 1948. xv, 729 p. Index, bibliog., appendix.

History up to the 1940s includes music of minstrelsy, vaudeville, and early musical comedy. Appendix: "Additional Music From Colonial Times to the Present."

259   Stearns, Marshall, and Stearns, Jean. JAZZ DANCE. New York: Macmillan and Co., 1968. xvi, 464 p. Illus., index, bibliog.

Black dance and dancers in American show business. Good documented source for general history of blacks in show business. Includes minstrelsy, medicine shows and gillies, carnivals, circuses, revues, and early musicals. A selected list of films and kinescopes; analysis and notation of basic Afro-American movements (Labanotation).

260   Steiner, Jesse Frederick. AMERICANS AT PLAY. New York and London: McGraw-Hill, 1933. xiv, 201 p. Index.

Trends in recreation and leisure time activities in the 1930s. Includes a chapter on commercial amusement--drama, dance halls, cabarets, night clubs, roadhouses, amusement parks, traveling chautauqua, and radio broadcasting.

261   Stoddart, Dayton. LORD BROADWAY. VARIETY'S SIME. New York: Wilfred Funk, 1941. 385 p. Illus., index.

Biography of the founding editor of VARIETY, Sime Silverman.

262   Stone, Fred. ROLLING STONE. New York: Whittlesey House, 1945. vi, 246 p. Illus.

Autobiography of a would-be boy acrobat who became a major Broadway star (the original scarecrow in WIZARD OF OZ). Good look at the impact of the circus on children throughout the country. Stone's career included stints with various small and large circuses, Dr. Wait's Kickapoo Indian Medicine Show, traveling troupes in the West, vaudeville (Stone and Montgomery), and musical comedy.

263   Taylor, Robert Lewis. W.C. FIELDS, HIS FOLLIES AND FORTUNES. Garden City, N.Y.: Doubleday and Co., 1949. 340 p. Illus.

Life of Fields; good coverage of his career in vaudeville, variety in Europe, the Folies Bergere, and in revues.

264   _____. THE RUNNING PIANIST. Garden City, N.Y.: Doubleday and Co., 1950. 340 p.

Collection of essays, most of which appeared originally in the

NEW YORKER, including essays on the comic Bobby Clark
and the vaudeville team of Clark and McCullough, the Flying
Concellos (an aerial-trapeze act), Dr. Samuel J. Crumbine's
work in public health and crusades against patent medicine,
and Gargantua (the Ringling Brothers and Barnum and Bailey
gorilla).

265   Toll, Robert C. ON WITH THE SHOW: THE FIRST CENTURY OF
SHOW BUSINESS IN AMERICA. New York: Oxford University Press,
1976. 361 p. Illus., index, bibliog. essay.

The only recent attempt to chronicle American forms of popular
entertainment and, despite organization and emphases problems,
this oversized volume is generally an excellent introduction to
major American forms. Although it is not specifically documented, excellent bibliographical essays for each chapter are
appended. Toll includes a useful comparative chronology
showing the parallel between the evolution of American society
and American show business. Recommended.

266   Treadwell, Bill. 50 YEARS OF AMERICAN COMEDY. New York:
Exposition Press, 1951. 241 p.

Somewhat superficial study of the ingredients of American
comedy through the lives, careers, and personal styles of the
famous comics from 1900 to 1950. Chapters on vaudeville
and frequent allusion to burlesque.

267   Urban, Joseph. THEATRES. New York: Theatre Arts, 1929. 48 p.
Illus. (one in color).

Urban discusses six popular theatres of the time and how each
is structurally suited to the type of entertainment given there--
legitimate theatre, opera, and revue. Focus is on the theatres'
architecture and decoration; of special interest is the Ziegfeld
Theatre in New York.

268   Vallee, Rudy, with McKean, Gil. MY TIME IS YOUR TIME: THE
STORY OF RUDY VALLEE. New York: Ivan Obolensky, 1962. viii,
244 p. Illus.

Autobiography of Vallee. Chapter on George White and his
Scandals beginning in 1931 is somewhat useful.

269   _____. LET THE CHIPS FALL. Harrisburg, Pa.: Stackpole Books,
1975. 320 p. Illus., index.

More memoirs of fifty years in show business, including the
end of vaudeville and the revue era. Focuses throughout on
individuals. Less an autobiography and more a gossip excur-
sion.

270   Waters, Ethel, with Samuels, Charles. HIS EYE IS ON THE SPARROW.
        New York: Doubleday and Co., 1951; London: W.H. Allen, 1958.
        278 p.

> Rise from ghetto poverty through the black entertainment cir-
> cuits to big-time show business.

271   Wilson, Francis. FRANCIS WILSON'S LIFE OF HIMSELF. Boston and
        New York: Houghton Mifflin Co., 1924. 463 p. Illus., index.

> Charming autobiography by the first president of Actor's Equity
> and a famous American actor in musical and straight comedies,
> recognized first in his role of Cadeaux in ERMINIE in 1886
> at the Casino. Good on this period of early musicals.

272   Wilson, Garff B. THREE HUNDRED YEARS OF AMERICAN DRAMA
        AND THEATRE. Englewood Cliffs, N.J.: Prentice-Hall, 1973. viii,
        536 p. Illus., index, bibliog.

> Wilson's survey history contains a useful summary chapter ("The
> Popular Theatre Grows Up--and Captivates the Crowd," pp.
> 181-200) that discusses vaudeville, minstrelsy, burlesque,
> musical entertainment, circus, Edward Harrigan, the "Tom
> Shows," chatauqua and lyceum. There are several chapters
> on melodrama.

273   Young, Miriam. MOTHER WORE TIGHTS. New York: Whittlesey
        House, 1944. 255 p. Illus.

> The life of a "Floradora" girl (Myrtle McKinley) at the turn
> of the century. Episodes in dime museums and barrooms on
> her way up to being a headliner. Behind-the-scenes glimpses
> at vaudeville and revue.

274   Young, William C. FAMOUS ACTORS AND ACTRESSES ON THE
        AMERICAN STAGE. 2 vols. New York and London: Bowker, 1975.
        Illus., indexes, bibliog.

> Although intended as reference, not recommended in this respect
> except for Young's bibliography which lead the user to other
> valuable sources. Basically, a selection of essays, alphabeti-
> cally arranged, by or about 225 actors (and their performances
> and theories). Focus is on the eighteenth- and nineteenth-
> century performer, including many known primarily for their
> work in popular forms. In many ways a disappointment but
> still of limited use. Stephen M. Archer's guide to American
> actors, forthcoming in this series, promises to be more exhaus-
> tive in its coverage and listing of sources.

275   Zolotow, Maurice. NO PEOPLE LIKE SHOW PEOPLE. Introduction
        by Brooks Atkinson. New York: Random House, 1951. xii, 305 p.

Portraits of eight show business greats, including their early careers in vaudeville and other popular forms (Tallulah Bankhead, Jimmy Durante, Oscar Levant, Jack Benny, Frank Fay, Jed Harris, Fred Allen, and Ethel Merman).

B. ENGLISH FORMS

The sources in this section are highly selective, since an exhaustive or even highly representative listing was not possible. There has been an effort, however, to include the more significant sources of a general nature, as well as a select number of more specialized and scholarly items of general interest. Chapter 11 of part III should be consulted for additional relevant sources.

276   Agate, James. IMMOMENT TOYS. A SURVEY OF LIGHT ENTERTAIN-
       MENT ON THE LONDON STAGE, 1920–1943. London: Jonathan
       Cape, 1945. 264 p.

       Agate's reviews of musicals, plays, revues, and pantomimes,
       plus portraits of music hall and vaudeville artists: (Pelissier,
       Fred Emney, Griffiths Brothers, Harry Lauder, George Carney,
       Vesta Tilley, Marie Lloyd, Grock, Kate Carney, Toto, Nora
       Bayes, Will Fyffe, Billy Bennett, Gracie Fields, George Robey,
       Sophie Tucker, and Nervo and Knox.

277   _____. THOSE WERE THE NIGHTS. London: Hutchinson, [1946].
       xi, 145 p.

       Anthology of theatrical reviews and essays from 1887 to 1906.

278   Aline, Mackenzie Taylor. "Sights and Monsters and Gulliver's Voyage
       to Brobdingnag." TULANE STUDIES IN ENGLISH 7 (1957): 29–82.

       Similarities between Gulliver's public exhibition by the farmer
       in chapter 2 and part of 3 in THE VOYAGE TO BROBDING-
       NAG to practices of eighteenth-century showmen in England.

279   Altick, Richard D. THE SHOWS OF LONDON: A PANORAMIC
       HISTORY OF EXHIBITIONS, 1600–1862. Cambridge and London:
       Belknap Press of Harvard University Press, 1978. 553 p. Illus., index,
       notes.

       Social history of exhibitions from the Elizabethan era to the
       mid-Victorian period (Crystal Palace of 1851); from the display
       of relics in pre-Reformation churches, through collections of
       eighteenth-century virtuosi, to the first science museums and
       public art galleries. Includes a history of panoramas and
       dioramas (as nineteenth-century popular art), and touches on
       such diverse topics as the Eidophusikon, Madame Tussaud's

Wax Museum, the Egyptian Hall, Bartholomew Fair, optical, mechanical, and spectral exhibits, freaks, and so on. Extensive notes should be consulted for additional sources. Highly recommended.

280   Arundell, Dennis. THE STORY OF SADLER'S WELLS, 1683-1964. London: Hamish Hamilton, 1965. xiv, 306 p. Illus., index. THE STORY OF SADLER'S WELLS, 1683-1977. London and North Pomfret, Vt.: David and Charles, 1978. xvi, 352 p. Illus., index, appendix.

Historical survey that contains information on Joseph Grimaldi's connections with and benefit for the Wells and its early history as a music house; also covers the associations of the Charles Dibdins (Junior and Senior) with the Wells.

281   Baker, H. Barton. HISTORY OF THE LONDON STAGE AND ITS FAMOUS PLAYERS (1576-1903). London: Routledge, 1904. Reprint. New York and London: Benjamin Blom, 1969. xiv, 557 p. Illus., index.

A good early history of the London stage, useful for the author's treatment of all forms of popular entertainment up to 1903.

282   Barker, Kathleen. BRISTOL AT PLAY: FIVE CENTURIES OF LIVE ENTERTAINMENT. Bradford-on-Avon, Wiltshire, Engl.: Moonraker Press, 1976. vi, 65 p. Illus., index, bibliog.

Survey of popular entertainment and popular theatre in Bristol up to 1975.

283   _____. "Bristol at Play 1801-53: A Typical Picture of the English Provinces?" In WESTERN POPULAR THEATRE, edited by David Mayer and Kenneth Richards, pp. 91-103. London: Methuen and Co., 1977.

A survey of popular entertainment in Bristol.

284   Beerbohm, Max. MORE. London: John Lane the Bodley Head, 1899. 201 p.

The London critic's essays on Madame Tussaud's, music hall (bemoans the passing of the "hall's" heyday), and other topics of interest.

285   _____. MAINLY ON THE AIR. New York: Alfred A. Knopf, 1958. vii, 212 p.

Six broadcasts and six essays, including "Music Halls of My Youth," "Nat Goodwin--and Another [Hall Caine]," "Marie Lloyd," and other topics from the Victorian-Edwardian era.

286   _____. AROUND THEATRES. New York: Taplinger Publishing Co.,
1969. xvi, 583 p. Index.

287   _____. MORE THEATRES. Introduction by Rupert Hart-Davis. London: Rupert Hart-Davis, 1969. 624 p. Index.

Reviews 1898-1903; popular theatre, music hall, and pantomimes.

288   Binder, Pearl. THE PEARLIES. A SOCIAL RECORD. London: Jupiter
Books, 1975. 160 p. Illus.

Story of the Costers, or street traders, in London's East End.
Good for background of East End life, including a section
"East London Entertainment" (pp. 48-50).

289   Birks, Reginald. CIVIC THEATRES AND ENTERTAINMENTS DIRECTORY.
Harlow, Essex: National Council for Civic Theatres, 1971. 149 p.

Revision of council's 1966 THEATRE AND ENTERTAINMENTS
FACILITIES DIRECTORY. Good for existing halls and civic
theatres throughout Great Britain. A contemporary "who's
who" of the entertainment world. Historically, not as useful
as Howard (item 324) or Mander and Mitchenson (items 331
and 332).

290   Booth, J[ohn]. B[ennion]. OLD PINK 'UN DAYS. London: Grant
Richards, 1924. New York: Dodd, Mead and Co., 1925. 413 p.
Illus.

Booth was a writer-reporter for SPORTING TIME, better known
as "Pink 'Un," under John Corlett. His various books (see
below) are excellent sources on virtually every form of popular
entertainment in England during the late nineteenth century
and early twentieth. He comments on such topics as circus,
exhibitions, popular theatre (especially melodrama), musical
comedy, the music hall, and showmen in all forms. Recommended.

291   _____. "MASTER" AND MEN, PINK 'UN YESTERDAYS. London:
T. Werner Laurie, 1926. 380 p. Illus., index.

292   _____. LONDON TOWN. London: T. Werner Laurie, 1929. 324 p.
Illus.

293   _____. PINK PARADE. London: Thornton Butterworth; New York:
E.P. Dutton, 1933. 317 p. Illus.

294   _____. A "PINK 'UN" REMEMBERS. London: T. Werner Laurie,
1937. xx, 286 p. Illus.

295 _____. SPORTING TIMES, THE "PINK 'UN" WORLD. London: T. Werner Laurie, 1938. xx, 284 p. Illus.

296 _____. THE DAYS WE KNEW. London: T. Werner Laurie, 1943. xvi, 256 p. Illus.

297 Burke, Thomas. LONDON IN MY TIME. New York: Loring and Mussey, 1934. 256 p. Index.

Contains a useful chapter on entertainment (pp. 133-200) in which the author discusses popular forms from the nineteenth century through the 1920s and explains the passing of the music halls in terms of the passing of nineteenth-century political naivete and the passing of "popular entertainment" from the hands of the people to those of commercial exploiters.

298 Burnand, Sir Francis C. RECORDS AND REMINISCENCES, PERSONAL AND GENERAL. 2 vols. London: Methuen and Co., 1904. Illus.

Rambling memoirs which include numerous allusions to nineteenth-century forms, places of entertainment, and performers, e.g., Madame Vestris, Vauxhall Garden, Cremorne, Crystal Palace, the Cider Cellars, Lola Montez, Lydia Thompson, Adah Isaacs Menken, Astley's, MAZEPPA, and so forth.

299 Chancellor, Edwin Beresford. THE PLEASURE HAUNTS OF LONDON DURING FOUR CENTURIES. London, Boston, and New York: 1925. Reprint. New York: Benjamin Blom, 1969. ix, 466 p. Illus., index.

Covers a span from the Tudors to the twentieth century and includes virtually every form of entertainment, from pleasure gardens to minor theatre, fairs, dioramas, and panoramas.

300 Chaplin, Charles. MY AUTOBIOGRAPHY. New York: Simon and Schuster, 1964. 512 p. Illus., index.

Although not detailed, Chaplin's early career in pantomime, music hall, and variety is recounted.

301 _____. MY LIFE IN PICTURES. Introduction by Francis Wyndham. New York: Grosset and Dunlap Publishers, 1975. 320 p. Illus.

Largely illustrated biography with small section on Chaplin's English stage career.

302 Cheshire, David. "Male Impersonators." In THE SATURDAY BOOK 29, edited by John Hadfield, pp. 245-52. New York: Clarkson N. Potter, 1969. Illus.

Summary survey of male impersonators on stage and in films
(mostly English examples), including those in extravaganzas
(Madame Vestris), music hall (Vesta Tilley), and pantomime.

303   Clinton-Baddeley, V.C. ALL RIGHT ON THE NIGHT. London:
Putnam, 1954. 243 p. Illus., index, notes.

Entertaining study of the Georgian theatre, especially audience
behavior, including frequent reference to popular entertainment
and theatre, especially pantomime.

304   Cook, Dutton. A BOOK OF THE PLAY: STUDIES AND ILLUSTRA-
TIONS OF HISTRIONIC STORY, LIFE, AND CHARACTER. 2d ed.
2 vols. London: Sampson, Low, Marston, Searle, and Rivington, 1876.

Volume 2 contains chapters on equestrian drama, pantomime,
and other topics related to popular entertainment and popular
theatre.

305   De Courville, Albert. I TELL YOU. London: Chapman and Hall,
1928. x, 249 p. Illus., index.

Autobiography; good perspective on some of the more popular
entertainments of his time: revues, variety, and the London
Hippodrome, and so forth.

306   Delgado, Alan. VICTORIAN ENTERTAINMENT. New York: American
Heritage Press, 1971. 112 p. Illus., index, bibliog.

Largely pictorial survey of English Victorian entertainment;
includes buskers, pleasure gardens, music hall (song and supper
rooms), magic lanterns, diorama, popular theatre, pantomime,
fairs and circuses (and equestrian drama), and the 1851 Exhibition at the Crystal Palace. Brief text but useful overview.

307   Dickens, Charles. THE DICKENS THEATRICAL READER. Edited by
Edgar and Eleanor Johnson. Boston: Little, Brown and Co., 1964.
xiv, 370 p.

Selected writings of Dickens on the theatre addressed to the
general reader. Includes all the SKETCHES BY BOZ devoted
to entertainment; scenes from his novels; dramatic criticism;
articles on popular theatre; comments on cabarets and minstrel
shows, pantomime, magicians, circus, and similar topics.

308   Disher, Maurice Willson. CLOWNS AND PANTOMIMES. London:
Constable and Co., 1925. Reprint. New York and London: Benjamin
Blom, 1968. xix, 344 p. Illus., index.

Useful and fairly reliable source on various forms of popular entertainment in England, especially pantomime (from its origins to its twentieth-century forms). See also item 24.

309 _____. FAIRS, CIRCUSES AND MUSIC HALLS. Britain in Pictures. London: William Collins, 1942. 47[8] p. Illus.

Brief but informative illustrated essay on English fairs and early circus; little on music hall. Includes nine color plates. Nineteenth-century forms emphasized.

310 _____. PLEASURES OF LONDON. London: Hale, 1950. 346 p. Illus., 43 pls.

Information of London's music halls, theatres, circuses, fairs, and other places of entertainment.

311 _____. VICTORIAN SONG: FROM DIVE TO DRAWING ROOM. London: Phoenix House, 1955. 256 p. Illus. (31 photos of music covers).

Study of Victorian songs, decorated with "Fronts" from ballads and piano pieces; covers minstrels, coster songs and Albert Chevalier, songs of Gus Elen, George Formby and others, Christmas pantomime, and mid-Victorian music hall.

312 _____. PHAROAH'S FOOL. Melbourne, London, and Toronto: William Heinemann, 1957. viii, 251 [2] p. Illus., index.

Early chapters deal with Giovanni Battista Belzoni's career as a giant, strongman, conjuror, actor-performer at fairs, in pantomime and plays. Fairly good though undocumented account of his association with Sadler's Wells. Good illustrations. See also item 332.

313 Elsom, John. EROTIC THEATRE. Introduction by John Trevelyan. London: Secker and Warburg, 1973; New York: Taplinger Publishing Co., 1974. xv, 269 p. Illus., index.

Contrast of social sexual attitudes of 1890 to 1910 with those of 1950 to 1972 as reflected in entertainment, including strip clubs, music hall (poses plastiques, living statuary, and so forth), popular theatre. Mostly English examples, but some from the United States.

314 Fiske, Roger. ENGLISH THEATRE MUSIC IN THE EIGHTEENTH CENTURY. London: Oxford University Press, 1973. xiv, 684 p. Illus., indexes, bibliog.

Analysis of the musical and theatrical genres which influenced the first century of English pantomime. Also good on ballad opera, burlesque, and pleasure gardens.

315   Flanagan, Bud. MY CRAZY LIFE. London: Frederick Muller, 1961.
       207 p. Illus., index.

       Autobiography of the English comic (b. 1896), member of the
       group called "The Crazy Gang," and his experiences in En-
       glish variety, musical revue, and films.

316   Glasstone, Victor. VICTORIAN & EDWARDIAN THEATRES. Cambridge,
       Mass.: Harvard University Press, 1975. 136 p. Illus. (210; 8 in color),
       index, bibliog.

       An architectural and social survey. Good section of music
       hall architecture.

317   Glover, Jimmy. JIMMY GLOVER--HIS BOOK. London: Methuen
       and Co., 1911. xv, 299 p. Illus.

       This and the following two reminiscences and autobiographies
       by James M. Glover (b. 1861), "The Master of Music" at
       Drury Lane, provide firsthand information on pantomime,
       minstrelsy, and latter-day music hall.

318   _____ . JIMMY GLOVER AND HIS FRIENDS. London: Chatto and
       Windus, 1913. xi, 325 p. Illus., index.

       See above.

319   _____ . HIMS ANCIENT AND MODERN. London: T. Fisher Unwin,
       1926. 256 p. Illus., index.

       The third of Glover's reminiscences is written in the form of
       letters to "Tommy" from his apocryphal uncle, Sir Affable
       Hawk.

320   Graves, Charles. THE COCHRAN STORY. London: W.H. Allen,
       [1951]. xii, 281 [2] p. Illus., index.

       Biography of the showman-impresario (1872-1951), written
       shortly after his death. See Heppner, below.

321   Heppner, Sam. 'COCKIE'. London: Leslie Frewin, 1969. 288 p.
       Illus., index.

       Although not documented, this is the best of the several
       biographies of Charles Cochran. See Graves, above.

322   Hicks, Seymour. VINTAGE YEARS WHEN KING EDWARD THE
       SEVENTH WAS PRINCE OF WALES. London: Cassell and Co., 1943.
       184 p. Index.

Rambling but atmospheric memoris of the 1890s in London with numerous references to the music hall, the Gaiety, and other popular entertainment subjects.

323   Howard, Diana. LONDON THEATRES AND MUSIC HALLS 1850-1950. For full entry and annotation, see item 1781.

324   Jones, Barbara. THE UNSOPHISTICATED ARTS. [London]: Architectural Press, 1951. 192 p. Illus. (184; some in color), index.

"About the things that people make for themselves or that are manufactured in their taste." Covers such topics as fairs (roundabouts-carousels), English seaside resorts and their architectures, tattooing, automata and simulacre (including Madame Tussaud's), and amusement arcades.

325   Kennedy, David. ENTERTAINMENT. London: B.T. Batsford, 1969. 96 p. Illus., index, bibliog.

Superficial and undocumented survey of popular entertainment in England from medieval times to television in the late 1960s. Includes tournaments, minstrels, fairs and festivities, pageants, baitings and cock fighting, pleasure gardens, spas and seaside resorts, street showmen, circus, pub entertainment, peep-show men, magic lantern, music hall, and popular forms of theatre. Good illustrations.

326   Laver, James. BETWEEN THE WARS. Boston: Houghton Mifflin Co., 1961. 236 p. (plus 4 p. index). Illus.

Picture of life in England from 1918 to 1939, good for background.

327   Macqueen-Pope, W. CARRIAGES AT ELEVEN. THE STORY OF THE EDWARDIAN THEATRE. London and New York: Hutchinson and Co., 1947. 232 p. Illus., index.

Survey of theatre and music hall with chapters on Daly's, Old Drury, Charles Frohman, the Gaiety, and the Haymarket. Not very reliable.

328   _____. GHOSTS AND GREASEPAINT. A STORY OF THE DAYS THAT WERE. London: Robert Hale, 1951. 334 p. Illus., index.

A nostalgic retrospective glance at the West End of London including information on the music hall and its performers, pantomime, melodrama, the circus, burlesques, revue, opera bouffe, exhibitions at Earl's Court, and other topics of interest.

329   Malcolmson, Robert W. POPULAR RECREATIONS IN ENGLISH SOCIETY,

1700-1850. Cambridge: Cambridge University Press, 1973. x, 188 p.
Illus., index, bibliog., appendix.

Useful study of popular leisure activities in eighteenth- and
early nineteenth-century England, including many forms of
popular entertainment. Focus throughout is on the social
context of these and other period amusements that, in some
cases, contributed to the decline of many entertainments.
Good bibliography.

330   Mander, Raymond, and Mitchenson, Joe. THE THEATRES OF LONDON.
Illustrated by Timothy Birdsal. 2d ed. London: Rupert Hart-Davis,
1963. 292 p. Appendixes: chronological list of the theatres of London and lists of architects.

Useful companion and sequel to their LOST THEATRES (below).
A major reference source.

331   _____. THE LOST THEATRES OF LONDON. New York: Taplinger
Publishing Co., 1968. 572 p. Illus. (108, including a map), alphabetical lists of theatres and architects.

Excellent source of information on eighteenth- and nineteenth-
century places of amusement, the Alhambra Theatre, the
Gaiety Theatre (Strand Musick Hall), the Holborn Empire, the
Royal Aquarium Theatre, the Oxford, the San Souci, and
Maskelyne's Theatre of Mystery. Twenty-eight places are
treated in detail, including all changes of name of building.

332   Mayes, Stanley. THE GREAT BELZONI. London: Putnam, 1959.
344 p. Illus., index, bibliog., notes, appendixes.

The best of the modern biographies of Giovanni Battista Belzoni
(1778-1824), giant, strongman, and conjuror. See also item
312.

333   Mayhew, Henry. LONDON LABOUR AND THE LONDON POOR.
3 vols. London: Charles Griffin and Co., 1864. Illus. Reprint.
4 vols. New York: A.M. Kelly, 1967. Reprint. 4 vols. New
York: Dover Publications, 1968.

Excellent primary source on street entertainers and their
economic plight in nineteenth-century London. Volumes 2
and 3 are the most valuable. See also item 351.

334   Minney, R.J. THE EDWARDIAN AGE. Boston and Toronto: Little,
Brown and Co., 1964. Illus., index, bibliog.

Reasonably good introduction to the age with frequent references to entertainment, especially music hall and its performers.

335   Morley, Henry. JOURNAL OF A LONDON PLAYGOER, FROM 1851
       TO 1866. London: George Routledge, 1891. 320 p. Index.

       Chronological account including observations on pantomime,
       magic, popular theatre, and literary burlesque.

336   Oulton, W.C. A HISTORY OF THE THEATRES OF LONDON, CON-
       TAINING AN ANNUAL REGISTER OF NEW PIECES, REVIVALS,
       PANTOMIMES, &C WITH OCCASIONAL NOTES AND ANECDOTES.
       BEING A CONTINUATION OF VICTOR'S & OULTON'S HISTORIES,
       FROM THE YEAR 1795 TO 1817 INCLUSIVE. 3 vols. London: C.
       Chapple, W. Simpkin and R. Marshall, 1818.

       Review of productions at Covent Garden, Drury Lane, Hay-
       market, and the English Opera House, in addition to some
       summaries of each season's affairs and other miscellaneous in-
       formation, including coverage of early pantomimes.

337   Pearl, Cyril. THE GIRL WITH THE SWANSDOWN SEAT. Indianapolis
       and New York: Bobbs-Merrill Co., 1955. 263 p. Illus., index.

       Account of mock trials held in "night cellars" (pre-music hall)
       in Regency London and various other elicit forms of entertain-
       ment. See especially chapter 5 (pp. 167-203), "London Amuses
       Itself."

338   Priestley, J.B. THE EDWARDIANS. New York and Evanston: Harper
       and Row, 1970. 302 p. Illus., index, select bibliog.

       Copiously illustrated (many in color) introduction to the Ed-
       wardian Age, with chapters on the theatre and music hall and
       vaudeville. A vivid, though not scholarly, assessment of the
       period.

339   _____. PARTICULAR PLEASURES. BEING A PERSONAL RECORD OF
       SOME VARIED ARTS AND MANY DIFFERENT ARTISTS. New York:
       Stein and Day, 1975. 192 p. Illus.

       Priestley's glimpses at some of his favorite entertainers and
       entertainment forms, including performers of the circus, vaude-
       ville, and music hall, e.g., Little Tich, Harry Tate, George
       Robey and Robb Wilton, the Marx Brothers, Grock, the
       Fratellini, and others. A charming and entertaining book.

340   Ritchie, J[ames]. Ewing. NIGHT SIDE OF LONDON. London:
       William Tweedie, 1857. 236 p.

       Fascinating expose of the underside of London life at mid-
       century. Tells the story of the Cider Cellars from the days
       of Marlowe and Kean to the residence of the "Sam Hall"
       singers and bemoans the development of the music halls into

vulgar variety houses. Chapters on the "Cyder Cellars," the Cave of Harmony, the Canterbury Hall, the Southwark Music Hall, the Eagle Tavern, Cremorne, and costermongers's entertainments.

341 Rowell, George. VICTORIAN DRAMATIC CRITICISM. London: Methuen and Co., 1971. Distributed in the United States by Barnes and Noble. xxv, 372 p.

Good introduction to popular theatre and entertainment of the Victorian age and the critics of the time, plus biographical notes on each critic represented in the anthology. Contains a useful section on "Pantomime and Music Hall" with criticisms of Bernard Shaw and Max Beerbohm.

342 Scott, Clement. THE DRAMA OF YESTERDAY AND TODAY. 2 vols. London: Macmillan and Co., 1899. Illus., index.

On nearly every aspect of British theatre from the 1840s to 1899. Volume 2 is most useful for popular entertainment.

343 Sherson, Erroll. LONDON'S LOST THEATRES OF THE NINETEENTH CENTURY, WITH NOTES ON PLAYS AND PLAYERS SEEN THERE. London: John Lane the Bodley Head, 1925 [5], 392 p. Illus., indexes (places and general, plays, persons).

Dated but still valuable survey of theatres and performers from the past, including chapters on Astley's, the Grecian Theatre (melodrama and pantomime), Old Strand (and burlesque), and other places of popular fare. Coverage is generally good on music hall, equestrian drama, pantomime, melodrama, as well as saloons and minor theatres, Richardson's show and other booth theatres.

344 Short, Ernest, and Compton-Rickett, Arthur. RING UP THE CURTAIN, BEING A PAGEANT OF ENGLISH ENTERTAINMENT COVERING HALF A CENTURY. London: Herbert Jenkins, 1938. 319 p. Illus., index.

Survey of popular entertainments in England from J.R. Planche and Madame Vestris to the cabarets of the 1920s and '30s. Coverage includes Gaiety burlesque, music hall, Gilbert and Sullivan, early musical comedy, Daly's, comic opera, pantomime, revue, and cabaret.

345 Smith, Charles Manby. CURIOSITIES OF LONDON LIFE. London: A.W. Bennett, 1853. Reprint. Preface by Anne Humphreys. London: Frank Cass and Co., 1972. vi (preface), xi, 408 p.

Amusements of the working class in Victorian London, including sketches of various types of buskers.

346   Southern, Richard. CHANGEABLE SCENERY: ITS ORIGIN AND
        DEVELOPMENT IN THE BRITISH THEATRE. London: Faber and Faber,
        1951. 411 p. Illus., index.

        A major source on the use and tradition of stage scenery in
        Britain from the Restoration to the New Art Movement of the
        early twentieth century. A useful book for background mate-
        rial on all forms of theatre and staged entertainment in England.

347   _____. THE VICTORIAN THEATRE. Newton Abbot, Devon, Engl.:
        David and Charles, 1970. 112 p. Illus., index, bibliog.

        Though not specifically concerned with minor theatres or popu-
        lar entertainment, this pictorial survey is a useful source of
        visual materials on staging and machinery during the Victorian
        period. Some of his facts are incorrect, especially on the
        Hanlon-Lees. See also item 2041 and 2042.

348   Stedman-Jones, Gareth. "Working Class Culture and Working Class
        Politics in London, 1870-1900: Notes on the Remaking of a Working
        Class." JOURNAL OF SOCIAL HISTORY 7 (Summer 1974): 460-508.

        Conditions affecting the emergence of a new working-class
        culture in London and its characteristic institutions and ideol-
        ogy. Good for background plus comments on the music hall.

349   Strutt, Joseph. THE SPORTS AND PASTIMES OF THE PEOPLE OF
        ENGLAND. 1876. New ed. London: Chatto and Windus, 1898.
        Reprint. Detroit: Singing Tree Press, 1968. xii, 530 p. Illus.,
        index.

        From the invasion of the Romans to the end of the seventeenth
        century--tournaments, jousts, military sports, seventeenth-
        century recreations (pageants and morris dancing), rope danc-
        ing, trained animals, puppet shows, minstrels, bell ringing,
        and so forth.

350   Thompson, Edward Palmer, and Yeo, Eileen, eds. THE UNKNOWN
        MAYHEW. London: Merlin Press; New York: Pantheon Books, 1971.
        489 p. Illus.

        Selections by Henry Mayhew from THE MORNING CHRONICLE,
        1849-1850. See also item 334.

351   Timbs, John. CURIOSITIES OF LONDON. New ed. London: J.S.
        Virtue, 1885. vii, 871 p. Illus., index.

        First published in 1855; study of "the amusements of the People,
        and their sights and shows." A mammoth encyclopedic work
        enumerating all types of exhibits and places of interest--
        archeological, historical, and topographical sites--arranged,

for the most part, alphabetically. Section on "Amusements"
is the most relevant (equestrian, fairs, puppet shows, and
gardens).

352 _____. THE ROMANCE OF LONDON. SUPERNATURAL STORIES,
SIGHTS AND SHOWS, STRANGE ADVENTURES AND REMARKABLE
PERSONS. London and New York: Frederick Warne and Co., [1880s?].
xii, 473 p. Index.

> Potpourri of information on such subjects as quack doctors
> (Dr. Graham), Punch and Judy, Mrs. Salmon's waxworks,
> freaks, pleasure gardens, conjurors, fairs, popular theatre,
> and Philip Astley the equestrian.

353 _____. ENGLISH ECCENTRICS AND ECCENTRICITIES. London:
1875. New ed. London: Chatto and Windus, 1898. xvi, 578 p.
Illus., index.

> Bizarre assortment of examples of English oddities throughout
> history, including some pertinent to popular entertainment,
> such as Joseph Grimaldi, freaks, quacks, and so forth. Less
> useful than items 351 and 352.

354 Wilson, A[lbert]. E[dward]. EAST END ENTERTAINMENT. London:
Arthur Barker, 1954. 240 p. Illus.

> Undocumented account of minor theatres, e.g., the Pavilion,
> City, Garrick (Whitechapel), City of London, Effingham
> Saloon, Britannia Saloon, Queen's, Theatre Royal (Stratford
> East), Dalston, and Borough.

Part II

POPULAR ENTERTAINMENT FORMS:

PREDOMINANTLY AMERICAN

Chapter 4

THE CIRCUS AND WILD WEST EXHIBITIONS

The following highly selective list emphasizes the American circus; major sources on the English circus, however, are included as well, in addition to a few sources on European circuses. Additional sources on the circus can be found in the sections on the carnival (chapter 5), popular theatre (especially equestrian drama in chapter 12), showboats (chapter 15), and in chapters 3, 5, and 6. Toole-Stott's CIRCUS AND ALLIED ARTS (item 81) should be consulted for a more definitive and exhaustive listing of sources, although this present guide is more current in its listings.

A. CIRCUS HISTORIES AND SURVEYS

355   Amidon, C.H. "Inside Ricketts' Circus with John Durang." BAND-
       WAGON 19 (May-June 1975): 15-17. Illus. (drawings).

       Reconstruction of Ricketts's eighteenth-century circus based on
       the memoirs of John Durang (see item 189).

356   Aronson, Boris. "The Circus." THEATRE ARTS MONTHLY 21 (March
       1937): 216-26. Illus.

       A portfolio of circus drawings by Aronson with an introduction
       to Ringling Brothers-Barnum and Bailey Circus and statistics on
       the 1937 edition of this circus.

357   Ballantine, Bill. "Circus Talk." AMERICAN MERCURY 76 (June 1953):
       21-25.

       Good general discussion of circus terminology; see also his
       book WILD TIGERS AND TAME FLEAS (item 535).

358   Barton, Bob, as told to Thomas, G. Ernest. OLD COVERED WAGON
       SHOW DAYS. New York: E.P. Dutton and Co., 1939. 238 p.
       Illus.

       The traveling circus in the 1890s, told in narrative form with few precise details. Touches on other traveling forms as well, in particular the medicine show. All aspects of the circus mentioned: animals, magic, aerial performers, and freaks. Gives a good sense of circus atmosphere and the Cole Brothers Wagon Show in particular.

359   Bayly, Charles, Jr. "The Circus: Say, Pa, Which Cage Is Barnum In?" THEATRE ARTS MONTHLY 15 (August 1931): 655-58, 671-86, 691-99. Illus.

Part of an issue largely devoted to the circus, including a good portfolio of circus paintings. Bayly traces the circus from Rome to the present in a brief summary and deals with the current (1931) status of the circus in America.

360   Bateman, Dr. E.J. "The Origin of the Barnum and Bailey Circus." BANDWAGON 6 (September 1956): 7-9.

Brief history of the early years of Barnum and Bailey, from 1871.

361   Beal, George Brinton. THROUGH THE BACK DOOR OF THE CIRCUS. Springfield, Mass.: McLoughlin and Reilly Co., 1938. xii, 308 p. Illus.

Impressionistic history and memoir.

362   Bernard, Charles. HALF CENTURY REVIEWS AND RED WAGON STO-RIES. N.p.: By the author, 1930. 111 p. Paper.

Very personal glimpses of the circus, fairs, and Wild West shows. Still useful, however.

363   Bostock, E[dward]. H[enry]. MENAGERIES, CIRCUSES AND THEATRES. London: Chapman and Hall, 1927. Reprint. New York: Benjamin Blom, 1972. vii, 305 p. Illus.

Life and career of the "Barnum of British Circuses."

364   Bouissac, Paul. CIRCUS & CULTURE: A SEMIOTIC APPROACH. Bloomington and London: Indiana University Press, 1976. xiii, 206 p. Illus., index, notes.

Although this recent work uses European circuses as examples, Bouissac presents a unique method of examining the phenomenon of the circus. Basically, an application of sign systems to the one-ring European circus is presented. The circus is seen as "a complex medium of mass communication."

365   Bowen, Elbert R. "The Circus in Early Rural Missouri." MISSOURI

HISTORICAL REVIEW 47 (October 1952): 1-17.

> Record of sixty-one circuses and menageries under thirty-one different managements that toured rural Missouri before the Civil War. Expanded into book form (see item 164).

366 _____. "The Circus in Early Rural Missouri." BANDWAGON 9 (September-October 1965): 12-17. Illus.

> Documented account, similar to other writings. See above.

367 Bowman, Harry P. AS TOLD ON A SUNDAY RUN. Flint, Mich.: Circus Research Foundation, 1942. 31 p. Paper.

> Compilation of circus facts (firsts, circus wrecks and accidents, and an extensive list of circuses and tent shows with dates).

368 Braathen, Sverre O., and Braathen, Faye O. "Circus Monarchs." BANDWAGON 14 (March-April 1970): 4-17: 14 (May-June): 11-24. Illus.

> Biographies of Wm. Cameron Coup, P.T. Barnum, James A. Bailey, and the Ringling Brothers.

369 Bradbury, Joseph T. "Tom Mix Curcus 1936 Coast to Coast Tour." BANDWAGON 7 (April-May 1952): 5-8.

> First transcontinental tour of a motorized show. Note that volume numbers of BANDWAGON varies and is not consistent.

370 _____. "The Coop & Lent Circus." BANDWAGON 3 (May-June 1959): 3-14.

> For this rather informal publication, this is a fairly detailed account of the Coop and Lent Circus from 1916 to 1918 when it became a fully motorized circus and the first large scale attempt to transport a circus entirely by trucks.

371 _____. "Campbell-Bailey-Hutchinson Circus." BANDWAGON 4 (May-June 1960): 3-9, 12-17.

> History of this circus from 1919 to 1922 with the complete routes.

372 _____. "The Rhoda Royal Circus, 1919-1922." BANDWAGON 5 (May-June 1961): 3-19.

> Historical survey.

373 _____. A History of the Cole Bros. Circus 1935-40." BANDWAGON

9 (May-June 1965): 4-19; (July-August): 9-19; (September-October): 4-11; (November-December): 30-35; 10 (January-February 1966): 15-25; 11 (March-April 1967): 17-29; (July-August): 20-22; (September-October): 16-30; (November-December): 9-11. Illus.

Useful historical survey with routes indicated.

374 Bradna, Fred, as told to Spence, Hartzell. THE BIG TOP: MY 40 YEARS WITH THE GREATEST SHOW ON EARTH. New York: Simon and Schuster, 1952. xv, 332 p. (plus a portfolio of photographs), index.

Career of Bradna from 1903, first as a performer, then as "equestrian director," or stage manager, includes "A Circus Hall of Fame."

375 Carver, Gordon M. "Sells-Floto Circus 1906-1910." BANDWAGON 18 (July-August 1974): 4-13; ". . . 1910 to 1913." 19 (July-August 1975): 4-12; ". . . 1914-1915." 19 (November-December): 22-29. ". . . 1916-1918." 20 (May-June 1976): 4-12. Illus.

Season-by-season survey.

376 Chindahl, George L. HISTORY OF THE CIRCUS IN AMERICA. Caldwell, Idaho: Caxton Printers, 1959. xvi, 279 p. Illus., bibliog., appendix.

Especially good on nineteenth-century American circus, although the author also deals with Canadian and Mexican circuses and Wild West show. Organized in seven sections: early circus, circus takes form, Civil War, rise of the railroad circus, the golden age, decline of the railroad and the growth of motorized circus, and indoor circus. Chapters on the types of entertainment, performers, horsemanship, clowning, music, and so forth. Appendix: partial list of American circuses and menageries, ca. 1771-1956. Good annotated bibliography.

377 Chipman, Bert J. HEY RUBE. Hollywood: Hollywood Print Shop, 1933. 203 p. Illus., glossary.

Miscellaneous stories on the circus includes routes of major circuses, roster of staffs of major circuses (1900-1915), and a glossary of lot terms.

378 CIRCUS! Introduction by Charles Fox. New York: Hawthorn Books, 1964. 64 p. Illus.

Lovely collection of photographs, many in color; limited text.

379   Clapp, William W., Jr.   A RECORD OF THE BOSTON STAGE.
Boston, 1853. Reprint. New York: Benjamin Blom, 1968. xiii,
479 p.

Contains an account of the early circuses in America. See
also item 184.

380   Clarke, John S.   CIRCUS PARADE. New York: Charles Scribner's
Sons, 1936. viii, 170 p. Illus., index.

Circus lore based on Clarke's thirty-five years with the circus
as roughrider and animal trainer. Illustrated from old prints
and pictures and modern photographs (138 illustrations).

381   Clement, Herb.   THE CIRCUS, BIGGER AND BETTER THAN EVER?
South Brunswick, N.J.: A.S. Barnes; London: Thomas Yoseloff, 1974.
146 p. Illus., index.

An account of the author's involvements with several circuses,
principally of the smaller variety (i.e., Circus Bartok, Sells
and Gray, Hoxie Brothers, and King Brothers), accompanied by
over one hundred photographs.

382   Conklin, George.   THE WAYS OF THE CIRCUS, BEING THE MEMORIES
AND ADVENTURES OF GEORGE CONKLIN, TAMER OF LIONS. New
York: Harper and Bros., 1921. xix, 209 p. Illus.

Autobiography of the lion tamer but most useful on circus life
in the forty years after the Civil War.

383   Conover, R[ichard].E.   TELESCOPING TABLEAUX. Xenia, Ohio:
By the author, 1956. 16 p. Illus. Paper.

Historical note on the big circus parade wagons of the 1870s.

384   _____.   THE AFFAIRS OF JAMES A. BAILEY. Xenia, Ohio: By the
author, 1957. 17 p. Illus., bibliog. Paper.

Pamphlet concerned primarily with Bailey's business relationships with James E. Cooper, P.T. Barnum, William Cody,
W.W. Cole, the Sells Brothers, the Adam Forepaugh Show,
and Barnum and Bailey.

385   _____.   THE GREAT FOREPAUGH SHOW. Xenia, Ohio: By the
author, 1959. 17 p. Illus. Paper.

Brief history of America's largest circus (1864-94).

386   _____.   "The European Influence on the American Circus Parade."
BANDWAGON 5 (July-August 1961): 3-9.

Historical survey from the importation of the first tableau wagons from England in 1864.

387 _____. GIVE 'EM A JOHN ROBINSON. Xenia, Ohio: By the author, 1965. 96 p. Illus., bibliog.

Factual history of the John Robinson Circus.

388 _____. THE CIRCUS, WISCONSIN'S UNIQUE HERITAGE. Baraboo, Wis.: Circus World Museum, 1967. 48 p. Illus. Paper.

389 _____. THE FIELDING BAND CHARIOTS. Xenia, Ohio: By the author, 1969. 64 p. Illus. Paper.

Circus wagons built by the Fielding firm, 1866 into the early 1870s.

390 Cooper, Courtney Ryley. "The Big Show." CENTURY MAGAZINE 107 (December 1923): 182-94. Illus. (woodcuts).

Analysis of circus operations in the 1920s.

391 _____. UNDER THE BIG TOP. Boston: Little, Brown and Co., 1929. 238 p. Illus.

Impressions of circus life.

392 _____. CIRCUS DAY. New York: Farrar and Rinehart, 1931. 263 p. Illus.

Typical Cooper rambling and inexact prose, still, good impressions of circus life during the first half of the century.

393 Coplan, Maxwell Frederick, and Kelley, F. Beverly. PINK LEMONADE. New York: McGraw-Hill, 1945. [130 p.]. Illus.

Illustrated essay on contemporary American circus.

394 Coup, W[illiam]. C. SAWDUST AND SPANGLES: STORIES AND SECRETS OF THE CIRCUS. Chicago: H.S. Stone and Co., 1901. xv, 262 p. Illus.

Undocumented account. Coup died in 1895 and the actual author or editor is not given.

395 Cowell, Joseph. THIRTY YEARS PASSED AMONG THE PLAYERS IN ENGLAND AND AMERICA. New York: Harper and Co., 1844. Reprint. Hamden, Conn.: Shoestring Press, 1979. 103 p.

Cowell (1792-1863) provides important commentary on the early American circus in part 2 (devoted to America).

396   Coxe, Antony D. Hippisley. A SEAT AT THE CIRCUS. London:
        Evans Brothers, 1951. 252 p. Illus., index, bibliog., glossary.

        One of the better books in English on the circus; typical
        circus performance described, including various acts and what
        to look for. History of acts and circus in general is re-
        counted

397   _____. "The Lesser-Known Circuses of London." THEATRE NOTE-
        BOOK 13 (Spring 1959): 89-100. Illus.

        Good survey of circus buildings or sites which were patronized
        during the late eighteenth and nineteenth centuries, including
        pleasure gardens and theatres.

398   _____. "Historical Research and the Circus." THEATRE NOTEBOOK
        21 (Autumn 1966): 40-42.

        Recent discoveries and research projects in the area of the
        circus, in particular the English circus.

399   Croft-Cooke, Rupert. THE CIRCUS BOOK. London: S. Low, Marston,
        [1948]. xiii, 192 p.

        General introduction to the circus.

400   _____. THE CIRCUS HAS NO HOME. London, 1941. New ed.,
        rev. and augmented. London: Falcon Press, 1950. 255 p. Illus.

        On Rasaire's circus and zoo.

401   Croft-Cooke, Rupert, and Cotes, Peter. CIRCUS: A WORLD HISTORY.
        New York: Macmillan Co., 1976. 192 p. Illus., index, bibliog.

        Not truly a world history but a survey of circus highlights,
        primarily in England, to a lesser extent in the United States.
        Illustrations are superb, however, and authors attempt, some-
        what unsuccessfully, to prove a continuous tradition from the
        Roman "circus" to the present. Short list of circus slang and
        list of circus music, films, and plays.

402   Croft-Cooke, Rupert, and Meadmore, W.S. THE SAWDUST RING.
        London: Odhams Press, 1951. 159 p. Illus.

        Basic circus history.

403   Cushing, Charles Phelps. "Behind the Scenes at the Circus." INDE-
        PENDENT 99 (2 August 1919): 156-58, 164-65. Illus.

        Author describes a typical week with the traveling circus.

404 Daum, Paul Alexander. "The Royal Circus 1782-1809: An Analysis of Equestrian Entertainments." Ph.D. dissertation, Ohio State University, 1973. 268 p.

Development of a significant minor form of entertainment during the late eighteenth century and one of the two early major English circuses.

405 Davies, Ayres. "Wisconsin, Incubator of the American Circus." WISCONSIN MAGAZINE OF HISTORY 25 (March 1942): 283-96. Illus.

Summary of Wisconsin's strong association with the circus up to ca. 1938.

406 Davis, Hartley. "The Business Side of the Circus." EVERYBODY'S 23 (June 1910): 118-28.

On moving the tent city.

407 Decastro, Jacob. THE MEMOIRS OF THE LIFE OF J. DECASTRO, COMEDIAN. Edited by R. Humphreys. London: Sherwood, Jones and Co., 1824. xx, 279 p. Illus., index.

Pages 115-65 contain Decastro's THE HISTORY OF THE ROYAL CIRCUS, an important source on early circus in England and listed by some circus historians as a separate work.

408 Delavoye, Will [William Lambert]. SHOW LIFE IN AMERICA. East Point, Ga.: By the author, 1925. 318 p. Illus.

Circus history with a focus on the illegal methods used by some traveling shows. Based on forty years as a performer. Not very reliable, but an interesting and unusual source.

409 Denier, Tony. HOW TO JOIN A CIRCUS. New York: Dick and Fitzgerald, 1877. 103 p. Illus. Paper.

Brief history of the American circus and secrets of acrobatics by a circus and pantomime clown.

410 Disher, M[aurice]. Willson. GREATEST SHOW ON EARTH. ASTLEY'S --AFTERWARDS SANGER'S--ROYAL AMPHITHEATRE OF ARTS, WEST-MINSTER BRIDGE ROAD. London: Bell, 1937. Reprint. New York: Benjamin Blom, 1969. xvi, 306 p. Illus.

Disher is one of the few authors, other than A.H. Saxon (see items 499 and 2127), to have written at any length on equestrian drama (see also item 526). This book, both informative and amusing, contains a number of Disher's earlier articles on the subject (portions of which first appeared in the SAWDUST RING, formerly the official organ of the Circus Fans Association of Great Britain).

411   Dodd, William G. "Theatrical Entertainment in Early Florida."
       FLORIDA HISTORICAL QUARTERLY 25 (October 1946): 121-74.

       Principally a survey of early Florida theatre but contains use-
       ful information on the early circus there as well.

412   Dressler, Albert, ed. CALIFORNIA'S PIONEER CIRCUS, JOSEPH
       ROWE, FOUNDER. MEMOIRS AND PERSONAL CORRESPONDENCE
       RELATIVE TO THE CIRCUS BUSINESS THROUGH THE GOLD COUNTRY
       IN THE 50'S. San Francisco: H.S. Crocker Co., 1926. [3], 98 p.
       illus., notes.

       Memoirs of the Western circus pioneer (1819-87).

413   Durang, John. THE MEMOIR OF JOHN DURANG. (AMERICAN
       ACTOR, 1795-1816). Edited by Alan D. Downer. Pittsburgh: Univer-
       sity of Pittsburgh Press, 1966, xix, 176 p. Illus., index, bibliog.

       Good first-hand account of Ricketts's circus. See also item
       189.

414   Durant, John, and Durant, Alice. PICTORIAL HISTORY OF THE
       AMERICAN CIRCUS. New York: A.S. Barnes and Co., 1957. vii,
       328 p. Illus., index.

       Sumptuously illustrated history, some in color; good on the
       nineteenth century. Useful list of circuses compiled by Tom
       Parkinson, then circus editor of BILLBOARD.

415   Edmonds, Walter D. CHAD HANNA. Boston: Little, Brown and Co.,
       1940. xi, 548 p. Illus.

       Fictional circus account but good for atmosphere. Appeared
       originally in serial form in SATURDAY EVENING POST under
       the title "Red Wheels Rolling."

416   Eipper, Paul. CIRCUS: MEN, BEASTS, AND JOYS OF THE ROAD.
       Translated by Frederick H. Martens. New York: Viking Press, 1931.
       213 p. Illus.

       Survey of the circus in Sweden covers twenty days of one tour.

417   Elbirn, William L. "Austin Bros. 3 Ring Circus and Real Wild West."
       BANDWAGON 6 (January-February 1962): 12-17. Illus.

       Evolution of the 1945 show with a complete route record.

418   Fawcett, Claire H. WE FELL IN LOVE WITH THE CIRCUS. New
       York: H.L. Lindquist, 1949. 198 p. Illus.

       Circus impressions by an artist and writer of children's stories;
       good illustrations.

419   Fawcett, James Waldo. "The Circus in Washington [D.C.]." RECORDS
       OF THE COLUMBIA SOCIETY 50 (1948-50): 265-72.

       Brief survey and review of the literature on the early circus in
       Washington, D.C.

420   Fellows, Dexter W., and Freeman, Andrew A. THIS WAY TO THE
       BIG SHOW: THE LIFE OF DEXTER FELLOWS. New York: Viking
       Press, 1936. 362 p. Illus., Index, appendix.

       Life story of press agent for Ringling Brothers and Barnum and
       Bailey Circus, who traveled with the show for forty years.
       Also contains considerable information on Buffalo Bill and the
       Wild West as part of the circus. Appendix: excerpts from
       Wild West diary of 1896 kept by M.B. Bailey, the show's
       superintendent of electric lights. Illustrates obstacles, daily
       life of personnel, accidents, sickness, and so forth.

421   Fenner, Mildred S., and Fenner, Wolcott, eds. and comps. THE
       CIRCUS: LURE AND LEGEND. Englewood Cliffs, N.J.: Prentice-
       Hall, 1970. 208 p. Illus.

       Collection of essays on the circus covering the entire gamut
       of circus literature. Good introduction for the uninitiated
       Excellent illustrations.

422   Field, Al[fred]. G[riffith]. WATCH YOURSELF GO BY. Illustrated
       by Ben W. Warden. Columbus, Ohio: Spaar and Glenn, 1912. [2],
       537 p.

       Reminiscences of circus life in the nineteenth century. See
       also item 994.

423   FitzGerald, William G. "Side-Shows." STRAND MAGAZINE 13
       (March 1897): 318-28; 14 (April 1897): 407-16; (May 1897): 521-28;
       14 (June 1897): 774-80; 14 (July 1897): 92-97; 14 (August 1897);
       152-57. Illus.

       More than a study of freaks, these illustrated essays survey side-
       show and circus attractions in the late nineteenth century, in-
       cluding fat babies, skeleton men, contortionists, armless wonders,
       albinos, midgets, dogfaced men, to balancing acts, living
       statues, sharpshooters, snake charmers, ventriloquists, magicians,
       performing geese, human claw hammers, jugglers, and the like.

424   Flint, Richard W. "Rufus Welch: America's Pioneer Circus Showman."
       BANDWAGON 14 (September-October 1970): 4-11. Illus.

       Most current biography of the early nineteenth century circus
       showman. See item 32 for Flint's guide to circus sources.

425   Fowler, Gene. TIMBER LINE. For full entry and annotation, see item 648.

426   Fox, Charles Philip. CIRCUS PARADES: A PICTORIAL HISTORY OF AMERICA'S PAGEANT. Watkins Glen, N.Y.: Century House, 1953. 180 p. Illus.

       Circus wagons and parades, especially during its heyday, 1880-1920. Excellent illustrations, many in color.

427   _____. A TICKET TO THE CIRCUS. New York: Bramhall House, 1959. 184 p. Illus.

       Primarily a pictorial history of Ringling Brothers Circus from 1884 to 1958; touches on such topics as circus parades, trains, cook tents, and sideshows. Good illustrations.

428   _____. A PICTORIAL HISTORY OF PERFORMING HORSES. New York: Bramhall House, 1960. 168 p. Illus.

       Covers most phases of the performing horse, including circus, Wild West shows, equestrian acts, rodeo, and early history from drawings made by Cro-Magnon men to the mid-eighteenth century. Scant text but good illustrations; includes glossary of terms.

429   Fox, Charles Philip, and Kelley, F. Beverly. THE GREAT CIRCUS STREET PARADE IN PICTURES. New York: Dover Publications, 1978. viii, 127 p. Illus. Paper.

       Features 183 rare and unusual photographs and posters (ten in color) that illustrate the history and development of the circus parade. Excellent re-creation, with good captions for the illustrations, of the excitement, exotic flavor, and sense of wonder and joy of a unique form of advertisement that has disappeared from American life.

430   Fox, C[harles]. P[hilip]., and Parkinson, Tom. CIRCUS IN AMERICA. Waukesha, Wis.: Country Beautiful, 1969. 289 p. Illus., index, bibliog.

       Large number of colored illustrations, mostly from period lithographs; good coverage of the circus in its heyday, including history of circus acts, organization, parades, trains, and the like. Fairly extensive bibliography with a brief chapter on Wild West shows.

431   Freedman, Jill. CIRCUS DAYS. New York: Crown Publishers (Harmony Books), 1975. 128 p. Illus. Paper.

Pictorial essay on the Beatty-Cole Circus; about fifteen pages of text.

432   Frost, Thomas. CIRCUS LIFE AND CIRCUS CELEBRITIES. 1875. Reprint. Detroit: Singing Tree Press, 1970. xvi, 328 p. Index.

Classic study of the early English circus, from tumblers and performing horses of the Middle Ages to Barnum and the Sangers.

433   Gerson, Walter M. "The Circus: A Mobile Total Institution." In his SOCIAL PROBLEMS IN A CHANGING WORLD: A COMPARATIVE READER, pp. 262-63. New York: Thomas Y. Crowell Co., 1969.

Sociological view of the modern circus.

434   Gollmar, Robert H. MY FATHER OWNED A CIRCUS. Caldwell, Idaho: Caxton Printers, 1965. 205 p. Illus.

History of the Gollmar Brothers Circus, a major competitor to Ringling Brothers early in the century. By 1916 they were the fourth largest railroad show in America.

435   LE GRAND LIVRE DUE CIRQUE. Edited by Monica J. Renevey. 2 vols. Geneva: Edito-Servize, 1977. Illus. (5,000, many in color).

International history of the circus with contributions by circus authorities from many countries, including a concise history of the American circus by A.H. Saxon.

436   GREAT DAYS OF THE CIRCUS. New York: American Heritage Publishing Co., 1962. 153 p. Index, bibliog.

Text insignificant but illustrations good.

437   Greenwood, Isaac J. THE CIRCUS: ITS ORIGIN AND GROWTH PRIOR TO 1835. WITH A SKETCH ON NEGRO MINSTRELSY. New York: Dunlap Society, 1898. 2d ed. with additions. New York: William Abbatt, 1909. 136 p. Illus.

Brief undocumented survey with focus on the American circus. Although it contains some errors, it is still a useful older source.

438   Hallock, E.S. "The American Circus." CENTURY MAGAZINE 70 (August 1905): 568-85. Illus.

The author traces the origin of the American circus to English shows and then outlines the history of the American circus up to the period 1875 to 1900.

439 Hamid, George A., as told to his son Hamid, George A., Jr. CIRCUS. New York: Sterling Publishing Co., 1950. 253 p.

Life of a circus family and circus proprietor.

440 Harlow, Alvin F. THE RINGLINGS--WIZARDS OF THE CIRCUS. New York: Julian Messner, 1951. v, 181 p. Illus., index.

Undocumented life and career of the Ringling Brothers.

441 Harriman, Karl Edwin. "Social Side of the Circus." COSMOPOLI-TAN 41 (July 1906): 309-18. Illus.

Pastimes of circus people other than professional responsibilities.

442 Hensey, Donald L. "The Circus and the American Short Story." BANDWAGON 18 (July-August 1974): 14-15.

Circus as depicted in the short story; includes a bibliography of forty-one short stories.

443 "How the Circus Dodges the Railroad Blockade." LITERARY DIGEST 57 (16 March 1918): 87-88.

Methods of travel used in circumventing contractual and governmental difficulties with the railroad.

444 Hunt, Charles T., Sr., as told to Cloutman, John C. THE STORY OF MR. CIRCUS. Rochester, N.H.: Record Press, 1954. vii, 252 p. Illus. (24 p.), index.

Annals of the author's circus enterprise of over sixty-one years.

445 Inciardi, James A., and Petersen, David M. "Gaff Joints and Shell Games: A Century of Circus Grift." JOURNAL OF POPULAR CUL-TURE 6 (Winter 1972): 591-606.

"Short-changing and varieties of sure-thing" gambling in the American circus. Well documented.

446 Jennings, John J. THEATRICAL AND CIRCUS LIFE. For complete entry and annotation, see item 220a.

447 Jensen, Dean. THE BIGGEST, THE SMALLEST, THE LONGEST, THE SHORTEST. Madison: Wisconsin House Book Publishers, 1975. [8] 205 p. Index, glossary.

History of Wisconsin's circus; excellent illustrations, many in color. Glossary of terms and list of Wisconsin circuses.

448   Kelley, Francis Beverly.   "The Land of Sawdust and Spangles--A World in Miniature."   NATIONAL GEOGRAPHIC 60 (October 1931): 463-516. Illus.

Excellent essay with photographs (some in color) on circus operations in 1930.

449   _____. "The Wonder City That Moves by Night." NATIONAL GEOGRAPHIC 93 (March 1948): 289-305. Illus.

Status and operation of the circus (Ringling Bros.). Following this essay is a good portfolio of circus photographs with text by Harold E. Edgerton (pp. 305-24).

450   _____. DENVER BROWN AND THE TRAVELING TOWN. New York: Exposition Press, 1966. 169 p.

Undistinguished but accurate fictional account of an American traveling circus. By an authority on the circus and coauthor and author of six or more books.

451   Kirk, Rhina. CIRCUS HEROES AND HEROINES. [Maplewood, N.J.]: Hammond, 1972. 93 p. Illus., index, bibliog., glossary.

Brief profiles of famous circus personalities: P.T. Barnum, Clyde Beatty, Annie Oakley, Ringling Brothers, Dan Rice, William Cody, Lillian Leitzel, May Wirth, Merle Evans, various famous clowns, the Wallendas, and so forth, plus a short history of the origins of the circus.

452   Knight, Laura. OIL PAINT AND GREASE PAINT. London: Ivor Nicholson and Watson, 1936. x, 397 p. Illus., index.

Autobiography of an English artist, closely associated with the circus and theatre in her work of the 1920s and '30s.

453   Kober, A.H. CIRCUS NIGHTS AND CIRCUS DAYS. London: Sampson, Low, Marston; New York: Morrow, 1931. xi, 240 p. Illus.

Life of a German circus entrepreneur and animal trainer. International tours discussed.

454   Koford, William. "Old Time Billing Wars." BANDWAGON 2 (May-June 1958): 7.

The job of an advance man and the rivalry in 1920 of the John Robinson Circus and the Sells-Floto Circus in Kansas City.

455   Kunzog, John C. "Dan Rice Leger Reveals Circus Conditions in 1870."

BANDWAGON 5 (June 1954): 6-9.

Contents of 1870 ledger sheds light on 1870 circus.

456 _____. TANBARK AND TINSEL. Jamestown, N.Y.: John C. Kunzog, 1970. xi, 179 p. Illus.

Stories of the circus told by an avid amateur historian.

457 Lathrop, West. RIVER CIRCUS. New York: Random House, 1953. 252 p.

Fictional story of a riverboat circus.

458 Lee, Albert. "The Moving of a Modern Caravan." Illustrated by W.A. Rogers. HARPER'S WEEKLY 39 (25 May 1895): 493-95.

The process of moving the circus during the period of tent-wagons.

459 Lukens, John. THE SANGER STORY. London: Hodder and Stoughton, 1956. 256 p. Illus., index, appendixes.

Story of George Sanger Coleman and his grandfather "Lord" George Sanger. Based on Coleman's manuscript and reminiscences placed in Lukens's hands. Appendixes: "Lord" Sanger's route, 1886, and his will. See item 496.

460 Maloney, Tom. CIRCUS DAYS AND WHAT GOES ON BACK OF THE BIG TOP. Philadelphia: Edward Stern, 1934. Unpaged. Cardboard covers.

Pictorial study of the circus in the 1930s.

461 Marcosson, Isaac F. "Sawdust and the Gold Dust, the Earnings of the Circus People." BOOKMAN 31 (June 1910): 402-10.

Review of circus wages from the early period to the current 1910 situation.

462 Maurer, David W. "Carnival Cant: Glossary of Circus and Carnival Slang." For full entry and annotation, see item 875.

463 May, Earl Chapin. THE CIRCUS FROM ROME TO RINGLING. New York: Duffield and Green, 1932. Reprint. New York: Dover Publications, 1963. xii, 332 p. Illus.

Considered by many circus authorities the best single-volume history of the circus. The American circus receives the most detailed attention.

464 Middleton, George, as told to and written by his wife. CIRCUS MEMORIES. Los Angeles: Geo. Rice and Sons, 1913. 118 p. Illus.

Personal insights on turn-of-the-century American circus life.

465 Milburn, George. "Circus Words." AMERICAN MERCURY 24 (November 1931): 351-54.

A glossary of terms gleaned from conversation with H.L. Johnson, a veteran circus man.

466 Miller, H.E. "The Sanitation of a Large Circus." AMERICAN JOURNAL OF PUBLIC HEALTH 26 (November 1936): 1106-12.

Results of a survey in 1934 by the Public Health Service on sanitary equipment and practices and subsequent measures instituted.

467 Moy, James S. "John B. Ricketts' Circus 1793-1800." Ph.D. dissertation, University of Illinois, 1977. 134 p.

In-depth treatment of Ricketts's travels. Ricketts is credited with having introduced the first large scale multiact circus to America.

468 _____. "Entertainments at John B. Ricketts's Circus, 1793-1800." EDUCATIONAL THEATRE JOURNAL 30 (May 1978): 186-202. Illus.

Based, in part, on his dissertation (above). Examines the development of Ricketts's entertainments, how they were popular, and what effect their acceptance had on the established theatres of the day.

469 Murray, Charles Theodore. "In Advance of the Circus." McCLURE'S 3 (August 1894): 252-60. Illus.

Routines of an advance man.

470 _____. On the Road with the Big Show." COSMOPOLITAN 29 (June 1900): 115-28. Illus.

Brief history and assessment of circus operations in 1900.

471 Murray, Marian. CIRCUS! FROM ROME TO RINGLING. New York: Appleton, Century, Crofts, 1956. 354 p. Illus., index, bibliog.

Popular history focusing on early period of European and American circus. Useful but not definitive; not to be confused with Earl May's superior book of the same title (see item 463). Glossary of circus terms from WHITE TOPS (see item 2408).

472   North, Henry Ringling, and Hatch, Alden. THE CIRCUS KINGS.
        Garden City, N.Y.: Doubleday and Co., 1960. 383 p. Illus.

        Story of the famous Ringling family.

473   O'Brien, Esse F. CIRCUS: CINDERS TO SAWDUST. San Antonio:
        Naylor, 1959. xxxii, 268 p. Illus., index, bibliog., glossary.

        Hodgepodge of circus history, lore, and anecdotes. Primarily
        useful on nineteenth-century circus; good glossary of lot lingo.

474   "Old Days of Sawdust and Spangles." LITERARY DIGEST 55 (18 August
        1917): 50, 53.

        Discussion of pre-1900 methods of training animals, the early
        American clown (the refined "jester"), and accidents in the
        ring.

475   Otis, James. TOBY TYLER; OR, TEN WEEKS WITH A CIRCUS. New
        York: Harper Brothers, 1881. 265 p. Illus.

        A classic fictional account of the nineteenth-century American
        circus; the illustrations alone give a good sense of the travel-
        ing circus. The novel has been reprinted often in numerous
        editions. Otis wrote a number of sequels, the first being
        MR. STUBB'S BROTHER (Harper and Row, 1883), and other
        fictional works on the circus.

476   Papp, John. THOSE GOLDEN YEARS--THE CIRCUS. Schenectady,
        N.Y.: John Papp, 1971. 36 p. Illus. Paper.

        Brief, introductory pamphlet to the circus includes list of
        circus museums and public collections.

477   Parkinson, Bob. "Circus Balloon Ascensions." BANDWAGON 5
        (March-April 1961): 3-6. Illus.

        From 1871 through ca. 1894, balloon feats rivaled the free
        street parade as a circus free attraction.

477a   _____. "John Robinson Circus." BANDWAGON 6 (March-April
        1962): 4-8. Illus.

        Survey of the circus that bore Robinson's name from ca.
        1836 to 1938.

478   _____. "The Circus and the Press." BANDWAGON 7 (March-April
        1963): 3-9. Illus.

        Survey of the part played by newspapers in advertising.

479   Pfening, Fred D., Jr. "Circus Couriers of the Late 1800s." BAND-WAGON 3 (January–February 1959): 3–4. Illus.

      Essay on advertising booklets issued by circuses in the latter half of the nineteenth century.

480   _____. "Circus Songsters." BANDWAGON 7 (November–December 1963): 10–12. Illus.

      On published songsters from ca. 1869; information provided on the clown Dan Rice.

481   _____. "The Big Show of the World--Sells Brothers Enormous United Shows." BANDWAGON 8 (January–February 1964): 4–15. Illus.

      History of the Sells Circus, 1871–1935.

482   _____. "Buck Jones Wild West and Round Up Days." BANDWAGON. For full entry and annotation, see item 692.

483   _____. "The Frontier and the Circus." BANDWAGON 15 (September–October 1971): 16–20. Illus.

      Attempt to place the evolution of the early American circus in historical perspective.

484   Pfening, Fred D. III. "The Circus in Fiction: An Interpretation." BANDWAGON 16 (March–April 1972): 14–19.

      Survey of best-known fictional treatments of the circus and their depiction of the circus.

485   Plowden, Gene. THOSE AMAZING RINGLINGS AND THEIR CIRCUS. New York: Bonanza Books, 1967. [7], 302 p. (plus 8 p. index), illus.

      Story of the five Ringling brothers and their circus which began in the 1880s. This study, the most complete history of the Ringling Brothers' Circus is, unfortunately, not documented. Includes an eight-page index.

486   _____. MERLE EVANS, MAESTRO OF THE CIRCUS. Miami, Fla.: E.A. Seemann Publishing, 1971. 154 p. Illus.

      Biography of a circus conductor. Evans's career (1919–69) included stints with show boats, the 101 Ranch Wild West, and Ringling Brothers.

487   Polacsek, John F. "The Circus in New Orleans 1861–1865." BAND-WAGON 20 (September–October 1976): 4–7. Illus.

Historical survey; includes details on such circuses as the Dan Rice Circus, Spalding and Rogers Circus, Bailey (George F.) Circus, and Howes Circus.

488   Powledge, Fred. MUD SHOW: A CIRCUS SEASON. New York and London: Harcourt Brace Jovanovich, 1975. 374 p. Illus.

Fascinating glimpse of a third-rate traveling circus during the 1974 season (the Hoxie Brothers Circus).

489   Rennert, Jack. 100 YEARS OF CIRCUS POSTERS. New York: Darien House, 1974. 112 p. Illus.

Introduction to American circus and posters plus an excellent collection, many in color, of American and European circus posters. Oversized volume.

490   Reynolds, Chang. PIONEER CIRCUSES OF THE WEST. Los Angeles: Westernlore Press, 1966. 212 p. Illus., index, bibliog.

Efforts of circus proprietors in the area between the Rocky Mountains and the Pacific Ocean between 1849 and 1900. Generally reliable source.

491   Ringling, Alf[red]. T. LIFE STORY OF THE RINGLING BROS. Chicago: R.R. Donnelley and Sons, 1900. 242 p. Illus.

Published ostensibly for Ringling Brothers' promotion.

492   Robeson, Dave. AL G. BARNES, MASTER SHOWMAN, AS TOLD BY AL G. BARNES. Caldwell, Idaho: Caxton Printers, 1935. 460 p. Illus.

History of the Al G. Barnes Circus and biography of Barnes; plus a list of Barnes's personnel.

493   Robinson, C.O. "Tom Mix Was My Boss." FRONTIER TIMES. For full entry and annotation, see item 699.

494   Robinson, Gil. "The Circus Life in the Early Days." BILLBOARD (9 December 1911): 22, 72.

Expanded in his book, below.

495   _____. OLD WAGON SHOW DAYS. Cincinnati: Brockwell Publishers, 1925. 250 p.

Author's recollections and family tradition concerning the John Robinson Circus. Includes list of traveling shows for 1865-89 and list of crews 1857-93.

496   Sanger, "Lord" George. SEVENTY YEARS A SHOWMAN. New York:
        E.P. Dutton; London and Toronto: J.M. Dent, 1926. xxx, 249 p.
        Illus.

        Life of the English circus impresario; apparently Sanger was not
        able to write himself and it has been suggested that his biog-
        raphy was ghostwritten by the Victorian journalist and melo-
        drama writer George Robert Sims. See item 459.

497   Saxon, A.H. ENTER FOOT AND HORSE: A HISTORY OF HIPPO-
        DRAMA IN ENGLAND AND FRANCE. For full entry and annotation,
        see item 2127.

498   _____. "A Franconi in America: The New York Hippodrome of 1853."
        BANDWAGON 19 (September-October 1975): 13-17. Illus.

        Reprinted from LE CIRQUE DANS L'UNIVERS. Equestrian
        performance in nineteenth-century America. Documented.

499   _____. THE LIFE AND ART OF ANDREW DUCROW & THE ROMANTIC
        AGE OF THE ENGLISH CIRCUS. Hamden, Conn.: Shoe String Press,
        1978. 511 p. Illus. (93, with 5 in color), index, bibliog, appendixes.

        The first full-length study of the English circus's most famous
        nineteenth-century performer, Andrew Ducrow (1793-1842).
        Great detail; two appendixes: "The Ducrow Apocrypha" and
        "The Ducrow Iconography." Saxon is currently preparing a
        biography of the equestrian performer and impresario Philip
        Astley. For other essays by Saxon on related topics, see the
        author index.

500   Schlicher, J.J. "On the Trail of the Ringlings." WISCONSIN
        MAGAZINE OF HISTORY 26 (September 1942): 8-22. Illus.

        The wanderings and fortunes of August Ringling and his family
        before the Ringling circus.

501   Seago, Edward. CIRCUS COMPANY. LIFE ON THE ROAD WITH THE
        TRAVELLING SHOW. London: Putnam, 1933. xv, 295 p. Illus.,
        glossary.

        Impressionistic view of English circus life, illustrated by the
        author.

502   Speaight, George. "Some Comic Circus Entrees." THEATRE NOTE-
        BOOK 32, no. 1 (1978): 24-27. Illus.

        History and description of nineteenth-century unscripted comic
        sketches featuring horses in English and American circuses
        (i.e.: THE TAILOR TO BRENTFORD, THE GRANDMOTHER

AND THE MILLER, THE METAMORPHOSIS OF A SACK, and
THE CLOWN'S WAISTCOAT, and versions thereof).

503   Stow, Charles. "The Pioneers of 'the American Circus.'" THEATRE
       MAGAZINE 5 (August 1905): 192-94. Illus.

       The author lists prominent managers and actors who began in
       the circus and then reviews the careers of early pioneers--
       John Robinson, Dan Rice, the Melville family (James and
       Frank most prominently), Mme. Dockrill, and Alice Lake.

504   Sturtevant, Col. C.G. "Opposition in Circus Press Writing." WHITE
       TOPS 18 (November-December 1945): 5-9.

       Nineteenth-century rivalries, especially between "Old Flat-
       foot shows" and "Zoological Institute Menageries" expressed
       in press releases, with several examples.

505   _____. "The Circus in Philadelphia." WHITE TOPS 22 (November-
       December 1949): 3-9. Illus.

       History of early circus in Philadelphia from 1700s to late
       nineteenth century.

506   Sutton, Felix. THE BIG SHOW: A HISTORY OF THE CIRCUS.
       Garden City, N.Y.: Doubleday and Co., 1971. viii, 176 p. Illus.,
       index.

       Unsatisfactory history, generally to be avoided.

507   Sweet, Robert C. "The Circus: An Institution in Continuity and
       Change." Ph.D. dissertation, University of Missouri, 1970. 307 p.

       Documented scholarly study of the circus and the changes it
       has undergone in the United States.

508   Sweet, Robert C., and Habenstein, Robert W. "Some Perspective on
       the Circus in Transition." JOURNAL OF POPULAR CULTURE 6 (Winter
       1972): 583-90.

       Part of a special issue on circuses, carnivals, and fairs, it
       deals with changes in the circus since 1920.

509   Taber, Bob. "Ringling and Sells-Floto Battles." BANDWAGON 3
       (March-April 1959): 13.

       Rivalry from 1909 through the next eight years or so.

510   Taylor, Robert Lewis. "Talker." NEW YORKER 34 (19 April 1958):
       47-; 34 (26 April 1958): 39-.

       On Nate Eagle, a sideshow talker. See also item 884.

511   Tedford, Harold C. "Circuses in Northwest Arkansas Before the Civil War." ARKANSAS HISTORICAL QUARTERLY 26 (Autumn 1967): 244-56.

General survey with listing of circuses, 1838-64.

512   Thayer, Stuart. "Tom Mix Circus and Wild West." For full entry and annotation, see item 715.

513   _____. "The Geography of Early Show Movements." BANDWAGON 17 (January-February 1973): 12-13.

Growth of early American circus and its relationship to geographical development.

514   _____. "The Anti-Circus Laws in Connecticut 1773-1840." BANDWAGON 20 (January-February 1976): 18-20. Illus.

Historical survey; limited documentation.

515   _____. "P.T. Barnum's Great Travelling Museum, Menagerie, Caravan and Hippodrome." BANDWAGON 20 (July-August 1976): 4-9. Illus.

Barnum's early circus involvement with W.C. Coup and the circus's attractions.

516   _____. ANNALS OF THE AMERICAN CIRCUS 1793-1829. Manchester, Mich.: Rymack Printing Co., 1976. iii, 241 p. Illus., index, list of newspaper sources. Paper.

Despite its modest appearance and an edition limited to two hundred copies, this is the most scholarly and best documented history of the early American circus to date. Although it is not well written, Thayer does an excellent job of separating myth (of which circus lore abounds) from fact. Includes thirteen-page index.

517   THEATRE ARTS MONTHLY 15 (August 1931): entire issue. Illus., 26 pls.

Issue devoted mainly to the circus; chapters by Charles Bayly (see item 359), Margaret Shedd, and Carl Carmer; numerous reproductions of circus pictures.

518   Thetard, Henry. LA MERVEILLEUSE HISTOIRE DU CIRQUE. 2 vols. Paris: Prisma, 1947.

Although this is in French and generally would be excluded from this almost exclusively English-language guide, this set is quite possibly the most comprehensive and authoritative

history of world circus to date (certainly among the best).
Five hundred sets were accompanied by a slender third volume
devoted to the Fratellini clown family.

519 Thomas, Richard. JOHN RINGLING. New York: Pageant Press,
1960. 268 p.

Undistinguished biography of the circus impresario and art
patron.

520 Thompson, William C. ON THE ROAD WITH A CIRCUS. N.p.:
Goldmann, 1903. 259 p. Illus.

Author's experiences as press agent with the Forepaugh Circus,
ca. 1900; also with Pawnee Bill's Wild West Show.

521 Truzzi, Marcello. "The American Circus as a Source of Folklore: An
Introduction." SOUTHERN FOLKLORE QUARTERLY 30 (December 1966):
289-300.

An introduction by a sociologist with a circus background, to
the traditions of the circus transmitted through and tradition,
"encompassing many variants, and traceable through several
centuries." Outlines four general categories of circus folklore: 1) the techniques involved in circus production (the
knowledge of the various skills involved in such areas as
tumbling, juggling, and animal control); 2) the special language of the circus; 3) the tales and legends of the circus;
and 4) the music and songs of the circus.

522 _____. "Folksongs of the American Circus." NEW YORK FOLKLORE
QUARTERLY 24 (September 1968): 163-75.

Article outlining folksongs emenating from the circus with
numerous examples.

523 _____. The Decline of the American Circus: The Shrinkage of an
Institution." In SOCIOLOGY AND EVERYDAY LIFE, edited by
Marcello Truzzi, pp. 314-22. Englewood Cliffs, N.J.: Prentice-Hall,
1968.

Sociologist and expert on the circus investigates the reasons
for the demise of the traditional American circus; perceptive
and penetrating analysis. Recommended.

524 _____, ed. "Circuses, Carnivals and Fairs in America." JOURNAL
OF POPULAR CULTURE 6 (Winter 1972): 531-619.

Special section of this issue devoted to these forms. Eight
useful essays.

525   Truzzi, Marcello, with Truzzi, Massimiliano. "Notes Toward a History
       of Juggling." BANDWAGON 18 (March-April 1974): 4-7. Illus.

       Brief attempt to salvage the history of juggling. Excellent
       explanation of specialized terms and good outline of data on
       key events and performers.

526   Tuttle, George Palliser. "The History of the Royal Circus, Equestrian
       and Philharmonic Academy, 1782-1816, St. George's Fields, Surrey,
       England." Ph.D. dissertation, Tufts University, 1972. 416 p.

       Covers the management of many popular theatre names, Charles
       Dibdin the Elder, Charles Hughes, Thomas Read, John Palmer,
       Thomas Dibdin, and others. Discusses the theatre's competition
       with Astley's Amphitheatre, and the battle with the patent
       theatres, and so forth, until 1816 when Thomas Dibdin took
       over as its manager, changing its name to the Surrey Theatre
       and initiating a totally new type of theatrical venture.

527   Tyrwhitt-Drake, Sir Garrard. THE ENGLISH CIRCUS AND FAIR
       GROUND. London: Methuen and Co., 1946. xiv, 215 p. Illus.
       (16 plates and 10 line drawings in the text), index.

       All but one chapter deals with the English circus with chapters
       covering the history of the circus in England, circus habits
       and customs, circus acts, clowns, performing animals, traveling
       manageries, and sideshows.

528   Vail, R[obert]. W[illiam]. G[lenroie]. "The Early Circus in America."
       PROCEEDINGS OF THE AMERICAN ANTIQUARIAN SOCIETY, N.S.
       43 (April 1933): 116-85. Reprint. Barre, Mass.: Barre Gazette,
       1956. x, 92 p.

       Good outline of circus history (1720 to mid-nineteenth century).
       Drawn from standard sources and the collection of the American
       Antiquarian Society. Headings include: "Animals," "Trained
       Animals," "The Menageries," "Acrobats," "Freaks," "Indians,"
       "Equestrians," and "The Circus." For sequel, see next entry.

529   _____ . "This Way to the Big Top." NEW YORK HISTORICAL
       SOCIETY BULLETIN 29 (July 1945): 137-59. Reprint. New York:
       New York Historical Society, 1953. 24 p. Illus. Paper.

       Supplement and update of Vail's earlier work on early American
       circus. See entry above.

530   Verney, Peter. HERE COMES THE CIRCUS. New York and London:
       Paddington Press. Distributed in the United States by Grosset and
       Dunlap, New York. 1978. 287 p. Illus., index.

       A history of the circus which focuses principally on the English and American circus traditions with chapters on most aspects of the circus plus Wild West shows and sideshows. Over two hundred excellent illustrations adorn this generally reliable but undocumented study.

531   Westervelt, Leonidas. THE CIRCUS IN LITERATURE: AN OUTLINE OF ITS DEVELOPMENT AND A BIBLIOGRAPHY WITH NOTES. New York: Privately printed, 1931. 88 p. Illus. (one).

Edition limited to three hundred copies; thirty-eight page history of the circus followed by a checklist of books in the author's collection. The checklist is divided into several divisions, with the most prominent and useful on P.T. Barnum and publications relating to him. Also includes route books, circus in foreign languages, freaks, fiction, juvenile books, animals, and clowns.

532   Winter, Marian Hannah. "The Prices--An Anglo-Continental Theatrical Dynasty." THEATRE NOTEBOOK 28, no. 3 (1974): 117-23. Illus.

Essay chronicling the lives of a theatrical family, including questrian and circus performers, from the eighteenth century to the present.

B. ANIMAL ACTS AND PERFORMANCE SPECIALISTS

533   Allen, Edward, and Kelley, F. Beverly. FUN BY THE TON. New York: Hastings House, 1941. ix, 116 p. Illus.

Relates one hundred fifty years of elephants in the American circus and the experiences of trainer Edward Allen, with the Cole Brothers and Clyde Beatty Circus.

534   Bailey, Olga. MOLLIE BAILEY, THE CIRCUS QUEEN OF THE SOUTH-WEST. Dallas: Harben-Spotts Co., 1943. 160 p.

Undocumented biography by the daughter-in-law of Mollie Bailey.

535   Ballantine, Bill. WILD TIGERS AND TAME FLEAS. New York and Toronto: Holt Rinehart and Winston, 1958. 344 p. Illus., index, glossary.

Good study and history of animals in the circus. Contains glossary of terms relating to the circus. See also item 358.

536   Banks, G[eorge]. L[innaeus]. BLONDIN, HIS LIFE AND PERFOR-MANCES. London and New York: Routledge, Warne and Routledge, 1862. 128 p. Illus.

Life of the famous tightrope walker.

537   Bateman, Dr. E.J. "Trouping in the Early Days." BANDWAGON
       4 (March–April 1960): 1–2, 14. Illus.

       Career of the early nineteenth-century equestrian, John H.
       Glenroy. See also item 550.

538   Baumann, Charly, with Stevens, Leonard A. TIGER TIGER--MY 25
       YEARS WITH THE BIG CATS. Chicago: Playboy Press, 1975. vi,
       279 p. Illus.

       Life of the Ringling Brothers and Barnum and Bailey cat
       trainer.

539   Beatty, Clyde, with Anthony, Edward. THE BIG CAGE. New York:
       Century Co., 1933. 408 p. Illus.

       Beatty's experiences as a wild animal trainer.

540   Bostock, Frank. THE TRAINING OF WILD ANIMALS. New York:
       Century Co., 1903. xvii, 256 p. Illus.

       Good on early circus methods of animal training.

541   Bouissac, Paul A. "Myths vs. Rites: A Study of 'Wild' Animal Dis-
       plays in Circuses and Zoos." JOURNAL OF POPULAR CULTURE 6
       (Winter 1972): 607–14.

       Brief essay on animals in the circus, limited to twentieth-
       century examples.

542   Burgess, Hovey. "The Classification of Circus Technique." THE
       DRAMA REVIEW 18 (March 1974): 65–70.

       Divisioning of circus techniques into three broad categories:
       juggling, equilibrium, and vaulting. These classifications are
       illustrated in his instructional book (below).

543   _____. CIRCUS TECHNIQUES. New York: Drama Book Specialists,
       1976. [5], 154 p. Illus.

       See above.

544   Clausen, Connie. I LOVE YOU HONEY, BUT THE SEASON IS OVER.
       New York: Holt, Rinehart and Winston, 1961. ix, 240 p.

       Memoirs of a circus performer with Ringling Brothers.

545   Cooper, Courtney Ryley. LIONS 'N' TIGERS 'N' EVERYTHING.
       Boston: Little, Brown and Co., 1924. xix, 260 p. Illus.

       On circus animal acts.

546 _____. WITH THE CIRCUS. Boston: Little, Brown and Co., 1930. 212 p. Illus.

Focus is on animals in this survey of circus life.

547 Court, Alfred. WILD CIRCUS ANIMALS. London: Burke, 1954. viii, 192 p. Illus.

Life of a wild cat tamer; see below.

548 _____. MY LIFE WITH THE BIG CATS. New York: Simon and Schuster, 1955. viii, 178 p.

Performer with Ringling Brothers as well as owner of his own circus relates his memoirs; see above.

549 Dhotre, Damoo G., as told to Taplinger, Richard. WILD ANIMAL MAN. Boston: Little, Brown and Co., 1961. 154 p. Illus.

Autobiography of an animal trainer.

550 Glenroy, John H. INS & OUTS OF CIRCUS LIFE. Compiled by Stephen S. Stanford. Boston: M.M. Wing, 1885. 190 p.

Wealth of useful information on career of the bareback rider for forty-two years and his tours through the United States, Canada, South America, and Cuba. See also item 537.

551 Hagenbeck, Lorenz. ANIMALS ARE MY LIFE. Translated by Alec Brown. London: Bodley Head, 1956. 254 p. Illus.

Life of the German-born animal trainer.

552 Haley, James L. "The Colossus of His Kind." AMERICAN HERITAGE 24 (August 1973): 62-68, 82-85. Illus.

About Jumbo, the elephant owned by Barnum; from the animal's acquisition in England in 1882 to his death in 1883, and the display of both bones and skin; the former at the American Museum of Natural History and the latter at Tufts University (the building containing these bones has since been destroyed by fire). See also items 574 and 771.

553 Hediger, H[einrich]. STUDIES OF THE PSYCHOLOGY AND BEHAVIOR OF CAPTIVE ANIMALS IN ZOOS AND CIRCUSES. London: Butterworth Scientific Publications; New York: Criterion Books, 1955. vii, 166 p. Illus., index, bibliog.

Important study of animal psychology. Chapter 9 (pp. 117-32) investigates the behavior of animals in the circus and the effects of their close connection with men.

554   Henderson, J.Y., as told to Taplinger, Richard. CIRCUS DOCTOR. Boston: Little, Brown and Co., 1952. 238 p. Illus.

       Career of the chief veterinarian of the Ringling Brothers and Barnum and Bailey Circus.

555   Hubler, Richard. THE CRISTIANIS. London: Jerrolds, 1967; Boston: Little, Brown and Co., 1966. x, 319 p. Illus.

       Story of an important acrobatic and bareback riding family and their circus.

556   Keller, George. HERE, KELLER--TRAIN THIS! London: Jerrolds, 1962; New York: Random House, 1961. 190 p. Illus.

       Autobiography of a tamer of big cats.

557   Kerr, Alex. NO BAR BETWEEN. LION TAMER TO BERTRAM MILLS CIRCUS. Foreword by Bernard Mills. New York: Appleton-Century-Crofts, 1957. 215 p. Illus.

       Life of the English lion tamer.

558   Lano, David. A WANDERING SHOWMAN. East Lansing: Michigan State University Press, 1957. viii, 290 p.

       Life of a marionette impresario, 1887 to 1935, on the road with circuses and on his own.

559   Logan, Herschel C. BUCKSKIN AND SATIN. Harrisburg, Pa.: Stackpole Co., 1954. xiv, 218 p. Illus., index, bibliog.

       Life of Texas Jack (J.B. Omohundro) and his wife Mlle. Morlacchi. See also item 636.

560   Millette, Ernest Schlee, as told to Wyndham, Robert. THE CIRCUS THAT WAS. Philadelphia: Dorrance and Co., 1971. 180 p. Illus.

       Autobiography of an acrobat with Ringling Brothers and other circuses.

561   Moffett, Cleveland. CAREERS OF DANGER AND DARING. New York: Century Co., 1906. xiv, 419 p. Illus.

       Chapters on the aerial acrobat and the wild beast tamer.

562   Norwood, Edwin P. THE OTHER SIDE OF THE CIRCUS. Garden City, N.Y.: Doubleday and Co., 1926. xiii, 276 p. Illus.

       Good accurate source on circus animals, although written in narrative form.

563   _____. THE CIRCUS MENAGERIE. Garden City, N.Y.: 1929. xii, 230 p. Illus.

Descriptive account of circus animals; accurate and detailed.

564   Pfening, Fred [D.] III. "William P. Hall." MISSOURI HISTORICAL REVIEW 42 (April 1968): 286-313. Illus.

Reprinted, in part, from the November-December 1966 issue of BANDWAGON. Twenty-eight-year career of a major supplier of circus and Wild West animals and equipment, operating out of his farm in Lancaster, Missouri. Well-documented account.

565   Plowden, Gene. GARGANTUA, CIRCUS STAR OF THE CENTURY. New York: Bonanza, 1972. 96 p. Illus., index.

The story of one of the circus's greatest attractions, the gorilla called Gargantua the Great, including behind the scene stories of the people involved in the gorilla's life (owners, keepers, and vets). Gargantua died in 1949.

566   Pond, Irving K. A DAY UNDER THE BIG TOP: A STUDY IN LIFE AND ART. Chicago: Chicago Literary Club, 1934. 39 p. Paper.

Artistic interpretation of circus acts, with diagrams illustrating rhythm and movements of acrobatics. See below.

567   _____. BIG TOP RHYTHMS. New York: Willet, Clark and Co., 1937. 229 p. Illus.

Analysis of circus acts in terms of rhythmical patterns and forms. An expansion of the previous source.

568   Posey, Jake. LAST OF THE FORTY HORSE DRIVERS. New York: Vantage Press, 1959. 90 p. Illus.

Autobiography of a horse driver with Van Amberg and other circuses in the 1880s; Forepaugh, Robinson, and Barnum and Bailey in the 1890s; Barnum and Bailey in Europe, 1898-1902; with Buffalo Bill, 1903-6; and on the road in the United States, 1910-37.

569   Proske, Roman. LIONS, TIGERS AND ME. New York: Henry Holt and Co., 1956. 317 p. Illus.

The techniques and perils of a wild animal trainer in the circus and theatres; principally in America.

570   Riker, Ben. PONY WAGON TOWN, ALONG U.S. 1890. Indianapolis: Bobbs-Merrill Co., 1948. 312 p. Illus.

Description of small wagons used by dog and pony shows built by the author's father (see especially pp. 68-85, 184).

571   Robeson, Dave. LOUIS ROTH; FORTY YEARS WITH JUNGLE KILLERS. Caldwell, Idaho: Caxton Printers, 1941. 241 p. Illus.

Roth's experiences as a trainer of wild animals.

572   Robinson, Josephine DeMott. THE CIRCUS LADY. New York: Thomas Y. Crowell Co., 1925. xii, 304 p. Illus.

Autobiography of an equestrienne.

573   Rowe, J.A. CALIFORNIA'S PIONEER CIRCUS. Edited by Albert Dressler. San Francisco: H.S. Crocker and Co., 1926. 98 p. Illus.

Edition limited to 1,250 copies; memoirs of an equestrian and horse trainer in California (born in 1819).

574   Scott, Matthew. AUTOBIOGRAPHY OF JUMBO'S KEEPER AND JUMBO'S BIOGRAPHY. Bridgeport, Conn.: Matthew Scott and Thomas E. Lowe, 1885. 96 p.

Story of Jumbo, the elephant. See also items 552 and 771.

575   Sherlock, Charles R. "Risking Life for Entertainment." COSMOPOLI-TAN 35 (October 1903): 613-26.

Surveys wide range of death-defying circus acts.

576   Sturtevant, Col. C.G. "The Flying Act and Its Technique." WHITE TOPS 6 (May 1932): 4, 6.

Early but good analysis of the aerialist's rigging and techniques of the flyer.

577   Taylor, Robert Lewis. CENTER RING. Garden City, N.Y.: Double-day and Co., 1956. 250 p.

Collection of essays on circus people, most of which were previously published in NEW YORKER.

578   Thetard, Henry. LES DOMTEURS, OU LA MENAGERIE DES ORIGINES A NOS JOURS. Paris: Librairie Gallimard, 1928. 348 p. Illus., notes. Paper.

History of animal trainers by the French circus performer-historian. International in scope, this volume contains information on such trainers as Henri Martin, Isaac Van Amburgh, George Wombwell, James Carter, Huguet de Massilia and

Charles James Crockett, Hermann, Thomas Batty, Frank
Bostock, The Pezons (Jean, Baptiste, Theodore, and so forth),
Upilio Faimali, Francois Bidel, Carl Hagenbeck, and others.

579   Thomas, Lowell. MEN OF DARING. New York: Grosset and Dunlap
Publishers, 1936. 289 p.

Chapter 3 is on acrobats and lion tamers.

580   Watson, William R. MY DESIRE. Toronto: Macmillan and Co., of
Canada, 1935. 85 p. Illus.

Autobiography of an armless performer.

581   Zora, Lucia. SAWDUST AND SOLITUDE. Edited by Courtney Ryley
Cooper. Boston: Little, Brown and Co., 1928. x, 230 p. Illus.

Life of an elephant trainer and performer.

C. EARLY CIRCUS CLOWNS AND MAJOR SURVEYS

There is a large literature on the clown, including important books on European
clowns, such as Grock, and notable French sources by Tristan Remy (two of
which are included in this list). An excellent list of sources can be found in
the notes to John Towsen's CLOWNS (see item 84) and in Toole-Stott's bibliographies (see items 81 and 82). Even a representative list would be far too
extensive for this guide. The word "clown" is an ambiguous one and sources
in the broadest sense can be found in chapters 1, 6, and 9. There is a useful
chapter (with sources noted) on early American clowns in Toll (item 265).

582   Bishop, George. THE WORLD OF CLOWNS. Los Angeles: Brooke
House Publishers, 1976. xii, 184 p. Illus., select bibliog.

Undistinguished but well-illustrated (including paintings of
clowns by Dyer Reynolds) study of clowns with an emphasis
throughout on American clowns and routines.

583   Bouissac, Paul A.R. "Clown Performances as Metasemiotic Texts."
LANGUAGE SCIENCES no. 19 (February 1972): 1-7.

Linguistic analysis of clown performances.

584   Brown, Maria Ward. THE LIFE OF DAN RICE. London Branch, N.Y.:
By the author, 1901. ix, 501 p. Illus.

Although very little documentation is included in this source,
it is nonetheless a full and lengthy biography of the early
American clown.

585   Charles, Lucille Horner. "The Clown's Function." JOURNAL OF AMERICAN FOLKLORE 58 (January-March 1945): 25-34.

>A fair review of dated literature and offers a documented summary of a study based upon the Cross-Cultural Survey of the Institute of Human Relations, Yale University, with commentary. Focus is on the "primitive clown."

586   Coco the Clown [Nicholai Poliakoff]. BEHIND MY GREASEPAINT. London and New York: Hutchinson and Co., 1950. 176 p. Illus.

>Autobiography of the international clown-star.

587   Cook, Gladys Emerson. CIRCUS CLOWNS ON PARADE. New York: Franklin Watts, 1956. 62 [3] p. Illus. (by the author).

>Ostensibly a book for children on circus clowns, including brief sections on clowns' makeup, circus terminology, and sketches of twenty-three specific clowns, e.g., Emmett Kelly, Felix Adler, Lou Jacobs, Paul Jung, Billy Rice, and Otto Griebling. Not a particularly notable book for specialists or older readers but a good introduction for young readers.

588   Gillette, Don Carle. HE MADE LINCOLN LAUGH: THE STORY OF DAN RICE. New York: Exposition Press, 1967. 170 p. Illus.

>Biography of the early American clown; less exacting than items 584 or 591.

589   Grock. [Adrian Wettach]. LIFE'S A LARK. Edited by E. Behrens. Translated by Madge Pemberton. London: W. Heinemann, 1931. viii, 276 p. Illus.

>English version of ICHE LEBEGERN! Autobiography of internationally renowned clown.

590   Kelly, Emmett, with Kelley, F. Beverly. CLOWN. New York: Prentice-Hall, 1954. 271 p. Illus.

>Life and circus career of Emmett Kelly, known as "Willie" the Clown, from trapeze artist to clown. Interesting treatment of the evolution of the famous clown costume and makeup in photographs and text.

591   Kunzog, John C. THE ONE-HORSE SHOW. THE LIFE AND TIMES OF DAN RICE. Jamestown, N.Y.: By the author, 1962. xiv, 434 p. Illus.

>Fairly reliable and well-illustrated biography of the early American clown. See also items 584 and 588.

592   Loeffler, Dr. Robert J. "Biographies of Some of the Early Singing Clowns." BANDWAGON 13 (September-October 1969): 16-23.

        Useful minibiographies of William Ethelbert Burke (b. 1845), Peter Conlin (b. 1842), John Davenport, John Lowlow, and others.

593   _____. "The Clowns of Yesteryear." BANDWAGON 18 (September-October 1974): 19-22.

        Brief biographies of two nineteenth-century clowns, Johnny Patterson and Joe Pentland.

594   Marcosson, Isaac F., [ed.]. AUTOBIOGRAPHY OF A CLOWN [Jules Turnour]. Foreword by Alfred T. Ringling. New York: Moffatt, Yard and Co., 1910. xii, 102 p. Illus.

        Superficial autobiography of the once senior clown in Ringling Brothers and Barnum and Bailey Combined Shows.

595   Matthews, Brander. "The Clown in History, Romance and Drama." MENTOR 12 (December 1924): 3-17. Illus.

        Survey history of clowns of which commedia dell'arte, Shakespearean clown, Punch, minstrel clown, and George L. Fox are principally discussed.

596   Morley, Christopher. PIPEFULS. New York: Doubleday and Co., 1924. x, 274 p. Illus.

        "First Lessons in Clowning" (pp. 194-202) provides an account of Ringling circus clowns at Madison Square Garden--an impressionistic essay.

598   Newton, Douglas. CLOWNS. New York: Franklin Watts, 1957. 215 p. Illus.

        General survey; not a significant study.

599   Pitzer, F.P. "Gay Carusos of the Circus." ETUDE (October 1942): 676, 707.

        Survey of the early singing clowns.

600   Remy, Tristan. LES CLOWNS. Paris: Bernard Grasset, 1945. 484 p. Illus., index. Paper.

        A classic work on clowns; recommended.

601   _____. ENTREES CLOWNESQUE. Paris: L'ARCHIE, 1962. 370 p.

        Sequel to above.

602   Senelick, Laurence, and Venne, Bill. A CAVALCADE OF CLOWNS. San Francisco: Bellerophon Books, 1977. [48] p. Illus. (by Venne). Paper.

> Although ostensibly written and illustrated for a youthful reader, this is still a good, succinct introduction to major clowns from the Middle Ages to Emmett Kelly. Superb drawings of each of the twenty-four clowns represented.

603   Sherwood, Robert Edmund. HERE WE ARE AGAIN; RECOLLECTIONS OF AN OLD CIRCUS CLOWN. Indianapolis: Bobbs-Merrill Co., 1926. 293 p. Illus.

> Autobiography of an early American clown who joined the circus in the 1870s.

604   _____. HOLD YER HOSSES! THE ELEPHANTS ARE COMING. New York: Macmillan Co., 1932. xxi, 361 p. Illus.

> Further reminiscences of a Barnum clown who served his apprenticeship under Dan Rice. Includes a section on circus language.

605   Sutton, Felix. THE BOOK OF CLOWNS. New York: Grosset and Dunlap, [1966]. 30 p. Illus.

> Small book for juvenile readers; describes different types of clowns, their costumes and makeup, and their particular roles on the stage and in the circus.

606   Swortzell, Lowell. HERE COMES THE CLOWNS: A CAVALCADE OF COMEDY FROM ANTIQUITY TO THE PRESENT. Illustrated by C. Walter Hodges. New York: Viking Press, 1978. 245 p. Illus., index, bibliog.

> Survey study of the personalities and performing styles of some of the great clowns from their origins in the ritual of tribal societies to the comic stars of the stage, films, and television. Most of the major circus figures are included, with some notable exclusions. Useful though selective bibliography.

607   Towsen, John H. CLOWNS. New York: Hawthorn Books, 1976. xiii, 400 p. Illus., index, bibliog.

> One of the more complete and important studies of the clown in its many forms. See also item 84.

608   Tyron, John. THE OLD CLOWN'S HISTORY. New York: Torrey Bros., 1872. 242 p.

> An early history of well-known clowns and showmen.

609   Wallett, William F. THE PUBLIC LIFE OF W.F. WALLETT, THE
       QUEEN'S JESTER. Edited by John Luntley. London: Bemrose and
       Sons, 1870. xvi, 188 p. One portrait.

       Autobiography of the nineteenth-century talking clown, re-
       nowned in England, the United States, Canada, South
       America, Mexico, the West Indies, and elsewhere.

D. WILD WEST EXHIBITIONS AND WILLIAM F. CODY ("BUFFALO BILL")

See also sources under "Circus Histories and Surveys" (section A) and Cody in
index.

610   Beitz, Lester U. "The Original Deadwood Stage." FRONTIER TIMES
       40 (January 1966): 41, 58. Illus.

       An attempt to reconstruct the actual stagecoach and contrast
       it to the one used in Buffalo Bill's Wild West shows.

611   Bentley, James M. "William F. Cody, Buffalo Bill, An Iowa-Born
       Folk Hero." ANNALS OF IOWA 39 (Winter 1968): 161-68. Illus.

       Summary of his life and description of the Buffalo Bill Museum
       in LeClaire, Iowa.

612   Bradbury, Joseph T. "Tompkins Wild West Show 1913-17." BAND-
       WAGON 15 (March-April 1971): 4-14; 15 (May-June): 30-31; 15
       (November-December): 26-28. Illus.

       Historical survey.

613   _____. "Buck Jones Wild West Shows and Round Up Days." BAND-
       WAGON 16 (March-April 1972): 20-23; 16 (July-August): 11-16.
       Illus.

       Supplement to essay in December 1965 issue of BANDWAGON.
       See item 692. Photographs and details supplied.

614   Brasmer, William. "The Wild West Exhibitions and the Drama of
       Civilization." In WESTERN POPULAR THEATRE, edited by David
       Mayer and Kenneth Richards, pp. 133-56. London: Methuen and Co.,
       1977. Illus.

       Brasmer views the 'Wild West' "with its stereotype of the
       American Indian and its blatant disregard for his life and
       poverty" as cultural genocide. Generally accurate historical
       survey of the origin and development of the Wild West show,
       Cody's career in melodrama, and Steele MacKaye's production
       of THE DRAMA OF CIVILIZATION at Madison Square Garden
       in 1887.

615   Buel, J.W. HEROES OF THE PLAINS. Philadelphia: West Philadel-
       phia Publishing Co., 1891. 612 p. Illus. (drawings).

       History of such "plain heroes" as Buffalo Bill, Wild Bill
       Hickok, California Joe, and Kit Carson. Unabashed admira-
       tion for the adventurers represented.

616   BUFFALO BILL'S WILD WEST. Hartford, Conn.: Calhoun Printing Co.,
       1884. [28] p. Illus. Paper.

       One of the numerous programs for "America's National Enter-
       tainment." Of interest is the "salutory" by John M. Burke,
       who describes the fascination of the frontier and assures the
       reader that the "Wild West" is not a circus. Useful blurbs
       on the stars and officials of the show, with information on
       such topics as bison hunting, the Deadwood stage, cowboys,
       horses, and Indians. See below.

617   BUFFALO BILL'S WILD WEST AND CONGRESS OF ROUGH RIDERS OF
       THE WORLD: HISTORICAL SKETCHES AND PROGRAMME, GREATER
       NEW YORK. New York: Fless and Ridge Printing Co., 1897. xvi,
       64 p. Illus. (map). Paper.

       A later program than the above item but also a rich treasure-
       house of such material as biographies of performers, the show's
       international travels, Indian lore, celebrated events of the
       Western frontier, and the origin of cowboys and gauchos.
       Contains colored map showing worldwide travels of the show
       and advertisements.

618   Burke, John. BUFFALO BILL, THE NOBLEST WHITESKIN. New York:
       G.P. Putnam's Sons, 1973. 320 p. Illus., index, bibliog.

       Popularized biography of Cody the man and the legend and
       his "Wild West show. Though not definitive, readable and
       essentially correct.

619   Cheney, Louise. "Lucile Mulhall, Fabulous Cowgirl." REAL WEST 12
       (March 1969): 13-15, 58-59, 73.

       Born in 1885, by the age of thirteen Mulhall, the daughter
       of a famous rancher and showman, was a top hand who was
       responsible for the term "cowgirl" and took part in the first
       rodeos; also appeared in her father's Wild West show.

620   _____. "Mr. Rodeo Himself: Milt Hinkle." REAL WEST 12 (June
       1969): 22-24, 58-59, 64, 74. Illus.

       Career of one of the greatest of the cowboys and a performer
       with numerous Wild West shows. Born in 1881, Hinkle worked

seven years with Cody, knew and played with Will Rogers, and was the first white man to bulldog a steer. See also items 657-67.

621 Clancy, Foghorn. MY FIFTY YEARS IN RODEO. San Antonio: Naylor Co., 1952. ix, 285 p. Illus.

Life of a famous rodeo cowboy who also worked as a talker or barker in carnivals and medicine shows. The book centers on rodeo but includes allusions to Wild Wild shows, in particular the small shows after the turn of the century.

622 Clemens, Samuel L. [Mark Twain]. "A Horse's Tale." HARPER'S MONTHLY 113 (August 1906): 328-42; (September): 539-49.

Fictional story about Buffalo Bill told from the point of view of his horse. Pre-Wild West setting.

623 Coburn, Walt. "The Inimitable Breeze Cox." TRUE WEST 15 (September 1967): 14-17, 54-57.

Life of an "uncouth" cowboy at the turn of the century who performed in rodeos and stampedes.

624 _____. "Tom Mix's Last Sundown." FRONTIER TIMES 42 (August-September 1968): 6-11, 48. Illus.

Essay on Tom Mix by a man who spent an evening reminiscing with him in October 1940, shortly before the cowboy star's death.

625 Cody, Louisa Frederici, in collaboration with Cooper, Courtney Ryley. MEMORIES OF BUFFALO BILL. New York: Appleton, 1919. 326 p. Illus. (one).

Details of a great love affair. Must be read skeptically, however, as the marriage was apparently an unhappy one. Permeated by the sadness of a wife who outlived all her children and husband.

626 Cody, William Frederick. LIFE AND ADVENTURES OF BUFFALO BILL. Chicago: John R. Stanton Co., 1917. xiii [15], 352 p. Illus.

One of the many autobiographies of Buffalo Bill told in Cody's fanciful and exaggerated prose. This edition incorporated the original 1879 autobiography and additions from the 1888 edition, plus a final chapter on Cody's death by Col. William Lightfoot Visscher.

627 Collier, Edmund. THE STORY OF BUFFALO BILL. New York: Grosset

and Dunlap, 1952. 182 p.

A biography for younger readers.

628 _____. THE STORY OF ANNIE OAKLEY. Illustrated by Leon Gregori. New York: Grosset and Dunlap, 1956. viii, 181 p.

Popular biography for younger readers.

629 Collings, Ellsworth, and England, Alma Miller. THE 101 RANCH. Foreword by Glenn Shirley. Norman: University of Oklahoma Press, 1971. xxx, 255 p. Illus., index.

Documented history of the Miller Brothers' 101 Ranch of Oklahoma and its Wild West and Great Far East shows. The definitive source. Originally issued in 1937.

630 Cooper, Courtney Ryley. ANNIE OAKLEY, WOMAN AT ARMS. New York: Duffield and Co., 1927. 271 p. Illus.

Popularized, undocumented biography of Annie Oakley, including a major portion on her involvement with the Wild West show of Buffalo Bill.

631 Cooper, Frank C. STIRRING LIVES OF BUFFALO BILL AND PAWNEE BILL. New York: S.L. Parsons and Co., 1912. 224 p. Illus.

Biography of the two western heroes plus a final chapter entitled "Story of Buffalo Bill's and Pawnee Bill's Great Exhibitions." Very superficial treatment.

632 Cooper, Tex. "I Knew Buffalo Bill." FRONTIER TIMES 33 (Spring 1959): 19.

Brief memoirs of Cody by a member of the Wild West show from 1892 through the next forty-five years. Reveals that Cody was in a patent-medicine show with Frank Powell for three years before he went on the stage in 1872. See also item 656.

633 Courtney, W.B. "The Prairie Prince." COLLIER'S WEEKLY 81 (14 April 1928): 12-13, 50-52; 81 (21 April): 16-17, 47; 81 (28 April): 24-26, 44; 81 (5 May): 13-14, 26, 28; 81 (12 May): 18-20, 59, 60-61; 81 (19 May): 22-24, 44-45. Illus.

Biography of Buffalo Bill Cody; the 19 May issue deals with the Wild West show.

634 Crawford, Captain Jack. THE POET SCOUT. New York: Funk and Wagnalls, 1886. xiii [15], 181 p. Illus.

Biographical sketch of Crawford by Leigh Irvine (pp. v–xiii) followed by a collection of songs and stories by the "Poet Scout." Includes a poem entitled "Farewell to Our Chief," written 24 August 1876, the day Cody bade farewell to the command as chief of scouts.

635   Croft-Cooke, Rupert, and Meadmore, W.S. BUFFALO BILL: THE LEGEND, THE MAN OF ACTION, THE SHOWMAN. London: Sidgwick and Jackson, 1952. 239 p. Illus., bibliog.

A sympathetic treatment of Cody, stressing the fact the Wild West show was a true projection of the man's life. Both are viewed as exciting, adventurous, and heroic.

636   Croy, Homer. "Texas Jack." THE WESTERNERS NEW YORK POSSE BRAND BOOK 2, no. 2 (1955): 29.

Brief sketches of three western characters called Texas Jack, including John B. Omohundro and an American showman in South Africa (the only one from Texas; see item 1243). The third was a train robber and lecturer who died in 1950.

637   Deahl, William E., Jr. "Nebraska's Unique Contribution to the Entertainment World." NEBRASKA HISTORY 49 (Autumn 1968): 283-97. Illus.

Essay on William F. Cody and the beginning of his Wild West show in 1883.

638   _____. "Buffalo Bill's Rival Dr. Carver. BANDWAGON 17 (November-December 1973): 40, 42-43. Illus.

Rivalry of Cody and William F. Carver briefly outlined.

639   _____. "Buffalo Bill's Wild West Show in New Orleans." LOUISIANA HISTORY 16 (Summer 1975): 289-98. Illus.

Well-documented study of the appearance of the Wild West show in New Orleans for the 1884 World's Industrial and Cotton Exposition. Corrects previous accounts.

640   De Wolff, J.H. PAWNEE BILL (MAJOR GORDON W. LILLIE): HIS EXPERIENCE AND ADVENTURE ON THE WESTERN PLAINS. N.p.: Pawnee Bill's Historic Wild West Co., 1902. 108 p. Illus.

Romanticized life of Pawnee Bill sold to customers of his Wild West show. Although the author claims historical accuracy and factual precision, this is doubtful.

641   Dunn, Roy Sylvan. "Buffalo Bill's Bronc Fighter." MONTANA 7

(April 1957): 2-11. Illus.

Memories of Cody and the Wild West show as told to the author by Ed Botsford, a show ring cowboy.

642   Elbirn, William L. "Austin Bros. 3 Ring Circus and Real Wild West." For full entry and annotation, see item 417.

643   Erskine, Gladys Shaw. BRONCHO CHARLIE, A SAGA OF THE SADDLE. New York: Thomas Y. Crowell Co., 1934. xiv, 316 p. Illus.

Life of Broncho Charlie Miller, "The Last of the Pony Express Riders," associated with Buffalo Bill's Wild West show and Pawnee Bill's show in the 1880s.

644   Fellows, Dexter W., and Freeman, Andrew A. THIS WAY TO THE BIG SHOW: THE LIFE OF DEXTER FELLOWS. New York: Viking Press, 1936. 362 p. Illus., index, appendix.

Contains excerpts from M.B. Bailey's Wild West diary of 1896. See also item 420.

645   Fielder, Mildred. WILD BILL AND DEADWOOD. Seattle: Superior Publishing Co., 1965. 160 p. Illus., bibliog.

Documented, pictorial life of Hickok, including a chapter entitled "Peace Officer and Showman," which discusses his brief time in a Wild West show and in the melodrama SCOUTS OF THE PLAINS. Confuses the latter with a Wild West show.

646   Foote, Stella Adelyne. LETTERS FROM BUFFALO BILL. Billings, Mont.: Foote Publishing Co., 1954. 80 p. Illus.

Letters written by Cody from 1873-1916, plus a brief biography.

647   Foreman, Carolyn Thomas. INDIANS ABROAD. Norman: University of Oklahoma Press, 1943. xxiii, 248 p. Index, bibliog.

History of the foreign travel of Indians. Chapter 19 is devoted to "Buffalo Bill and the 'Wild West'," and other Wild West and circus aggregates abroad with Indians. Extensive bibliography.

648   Fowler, Gene. TIMBER LINE. New York: Covici Friede Publishers, 1933. 480 p.

The story of Harry Hege Tammen and Frederick Gilmer Bonfils, publishers and owners of the Denver EVENING POST. Good portrait of Cody in the 1880s to 1913 Curio (Museum) business in Denver and Tammen's and Bonfils's involvement in the circus world (Sells-Floto Show) and warfare with Ringling Brothers-- especially their skullduggery to obtain Buffalo Bill's Wild West show, and Pawnee Bill's concern in 1913.

649 _____. A SOLO IN TOM-TOMS. New York: Viking Press, 1946. x, 390 p.

Autobiography of the journalist's early life and career in Colorado; interesting episode surrounding his encounter with Buffalo Bill in 1899.

650 Gipson, Fred. FABULOUS EMPIRE. COLONEL JACK MILLER'S STORY. Boston: Houghton Mifflin Co., 1946. ix, 411 p.

Story of the 101 Ranch in Oklahoma and of the Wild West show it sponsored told through the biography of Col. Zack Miller, one of the Miller brothers. The lack of an index and illustrations is unfortunate.

651 Grant, H. Roger. "An Iowan with Buffalo Bill: Charles Eldridge Griffin in Europe, 1903-1906." PALIMPSET 54 (January-February 1973): 2-15. Illus.

Life of the only author of a book-length commentary on Buffalo Bill's second great tour of Europe and his experiences with Cody. Griffin died in 1914; excerpts included from Griffin's book of 1895 on how to be a fire-eater and a sword swallower. See below.

652 Griffin, Charles Eldridge. FOUR YEARS IN EUROPE WITH BUFFALO BILL. Albia, Iowa: Stage Publishing Co., 1908. 94 p. Illus.

Edition limited to five hundred copies. Reviews 1903-7 seasons; a rare source of firsthand observations. See above.

653 Harvey, R.M. "Some Inside Facts About Buffalo Bill's Wild West." BANDWAGON 3 (January-February 1959): 13-14.

Personal reminiscences of Buffalo Bill during his latter years by one of his publicists.

654 Havighurst, Walter. ANNIE OAKLEY OF THE WILD WEST. New York: Macmillan and Co., 1954. viii, 246 p. Illus., index.

Popular account of "Little Sure Shot" and the Wild West show with which she was closely associated all of her working life. Generally well researched, although not specifically documented.

655 _____ . BUFFALO BILL'S GREAT WILD WEST SHOW. New York: Random House, 1957. 183 p. Illus., index.

Life of Cody and the Wild West show written for young readers.

656 Hebberd, Mary Hardgrove. "Notes on Dr. David Franklin Powell, Known as 'White Beaver.'" WISCONSIN MAGAZINE OF HISTORY 35 (Summer 1952): 306-9. Illus.

Career of Powell, from LaCrosse, Wisconsin, who, as a marksman, was associated with Cody, traveling with Cody's show circuit, speculating with Cody on real estate projects, and in the manufacture of patent medicines. See item 632.

657 Hinkle, Milt. "The Dusky Demon." TRUE WEST 8 (July-August 1961): 30-31, 55-57. Illus.

Career of Bill Pickett, a famous black Wild West performer, who worked for the Miller Brothers and 101 Ranch. Died in 1932.

658 _____ . "Cowboy!" TRUE WEST 8 (September-October 1961): 38-39. 62.

Origin and evolution of the term "cowboy" as related by the former cowboy and authority on the West.

659 _____ . "Kit Carson's Buffalo Ranch Wild West Big Three Ring Wild West Circus." BANDWAGON 7 (September-October 1963): 4-9; 7 (November-December): 17-21. Illus.

Four-year history of this show (1911-15) as told by a trouper. See below.

660 _____ . "The Kit Carson Wild West Show." FRONTIER TIMES 38 (May 1964): 6-11, 57-58. Illus.

Good account of the Kit Carson Buffalo Ranch Wild West Show in 1911 by one of the participants. See above.

661 _____ . "A Texan Hits the Pampas." OLD WEST 2 (Fall 1965): 2-11, 40-41, 44-45, 48. Illus.

Hinkle's account of the 101 Ranch show tour of South America, 1 November 1913 to 1 November 1914. A very full and informative essay.

662 _____ . "Circuses and Contests." OLD WEST 3 (Fall 1966): 24-28. Illus.

Hinkle's experiences with various Wild West shows, circuses,

wagon shows, and rodeo exhibitions during the early twentieth
century.

663　　　　. "Milt Blew His Show in Chicago." FRONTIER TIMES 42
(February–March 1968): 30–31, 52–54.

The Star Ten Ranch Wild West Show in Chicago in 1933 and
Hinkle's association and confrontation with Zack Miller of the
101 Ranch Wild West.

664　　　　. "Winning or Losing." FRONTIER TIMES 42 (August–September
1968): 26–28, 48.

Experiences of Mildred and Milt Hinkle on the rodeo circuit.

665　　　　. "Memoirs of My Rodeo Days." REAL WEST 11 (September
1968): 35–37, 65. Illus.

Memoirs, including Hinkle's stint with Cody's Wild West show
and other "show biz" enterprises.

666　　　　. "The Way a Wild West Show Operated." FRONTIER TIMES
43 (March 1969): 20–23, 50–52.

Useful summary of the Wild West show operation by a member
of numerous shows, including Buffalo Bill's Wild West, the
101 Ranch Real Wild West, the Irwin Bros. Wild West, Kit
Carson's Wild West, the Two Bills Wild West Show, and
others.

667　Hinkle, Milt, and Elder, Mildred. "Suicide Ted Elder." TRUE WEST
41 (June 1969): 40–42, 72.

Career of an outstanding horseman, who, in addition to rodeo
appearances, played with Ringling Brothers and Barnum and
Bailey Circus and the 101 Ranch Show.

668　Holbrook, Stewart H. LITTLE ANNIE OAKLEY AND OTHER RUGGED
PEOPLE. New York: Macmillan and Co., 1948. x, 238 p.

Previously published essays collected in book form. The essay
on Oakley originally appeared in LIFE and is a brief summary
of her life and career with the Wild West show. Also includes chapters on Ned Buntline, Buffalo Bill, and Boston's
Temple of Burlesque (the Howard).

669　Holm, Don. "Were There Two Buffalo Bills?" FRONTIER TIMES 39
August–September 1965): 35, 61. Illus.

Essay on Dr. William DeVeny, a pioneer chiropodist, Buffalo

Bill look-alike, lifelong friend of Cody, and impersonator or double for Cody, who died in 1913.

670   Holm, Ed. "Gertrude Kasabier's Indian Portraits." AMERICAN WEST 10 (July 1973): 38-41. Illus.

Photographic portraits of four Indians that appeared with Cody's Wild West show in either 1900 or 1901, and probably photographed while the show was at Madison Square Garden. Brief text.

671   Inman, Henry, and Cody, William F. THE GREAT SALT LAKE TRAIL. Minneapolis: Ross and Haines, 1966. 529 p. Illus., index.

Edition limited to fifteen hundred copies. Originally published in 1897; one of the numerous books in which Cody had a hand. Includes biographical material on Cody's adventures on the Great Salt Lake Trail in the 1850s, including the "First Scalp for Custer." Includes frontispiece of collaborators.

672   Jerrard, Leigh. "Rosa Bonheur Revealed as a Painter of Westerns." WESTERNERS BRAND BOOK 10 (August 1953): 41-42.

Brief essay on the French artist who depicted scenes from Buffalo Bill's Wild West show; includes list of illustrations.

673   Johannsen, Albert. THE HOUSE OF BEADLE AND ADAMS. 3 vols. Norman: University of Oklahoma Press, 1950, 1962. Illus., index (titles, localities, general; songs indexed in vol. 3), bibliog.

Definitive reference source to the major publisher of dime novels with extensive coverage of Buffalo Bill and stories about him. Background material and bibliographical listings are quite valuable.

674   Jones, John Bush. "Impersonation and Authenticity: The Theatre as Metaphor in Kopit's INDIANS." QUARTERLY JOURNAL OF SPEECH 59 (December 1973): 443-451.

"Kopit has structured his play on a series of theatrical images, thereby conveying his theme of impersonation versus authenticity in myth-making through visualizations and dramatizations of impersonation in the theatrical event itself." A useful and perceptive analysis of the play by Arthur Kopit on Buffalo Bill and his Wild West show.

675   Katigan, Madelon B. "The Fabulous 101." TRUE WEST 8 (September-October 1960): 6-12, 50-51. Illus.

History of the famous ranch and the three Miller brothers

(George L., Zack T., and Joseph C.) and their "Real Wild West Show." Although lacking in documentation, this is one of the better accounts of this important organizations.

676   Kreps, Bonnie. "Annie Oakley's Untold Love Story." MS 5 (January 1977): 8, 12-13. Illus.

Superficial effort to reestablish the true relationship of Annie Oakley and Frank Butler and correct the mystique created by the musical ANNIE GET YOUR GUN, especially the film version. Butler's devotion to Oakley and her exceptional ability to shoot are underscored.

677   Leonard, Elizabeth Jane, and Goodman, Julia Cody. BUFFALO BILL, KING OF THE OLD WEST. Edited by James William Hoffman. New York: Library Publishers, 1955. 320 p. Illus., index, bibliog.

Biography by Cody's sister, billed as the first true history of the family. Book was actually written before her death in 1928 and is a reasonably accurate picture of Cody. See also items 702 and 727.

678   McCracken, Harold, and Frost, Richard I. THE BUFFALO BILL STORY-- A BRIEF ACCOUNT. Cody, Wyo.: Buffalo Bill Historical Center, n.d. 16 p. Illus. Paper.

Introduction to the life and career of Cody; brief section on the Wild West show. Description of the Historical Center is included. Photographs and reproductions in sepia; cover is a color reproduction of Rosa Bonheur's 1889 painting of Cody.

679   McCreight, M.I. "Buffalo Bill as I Knew Him." TRUE WEST 4 (July-August 1957): 25, 41-42.

Memoirs of Cody by a ninety-two-year-old veteran of the west who first met Buffalo Bill in 1887-88. At that time McCreight was living in Dubois, Pennsylvania. Earlier he had been a buyer and seller of buffalo bones on the plains. McCreight last saw Cody in 1916.

680   McDaniel, Ruel. "Requiem for the Wild West Shows." FRONTIER TIMES 36 (Winter 1961): 22-23, 40. Illus.

The life and career of Glenn Kischko, born in 1882 in one of Buffalo Bill's show wagons and a witness to the glory and death of the spectacles of the Wild West show. Kischko was also with the 101 Ranch show.

681   Mann, E.B. "Little Sure Shot." AMERICAN RIFLEMAN 96 (April 1948): 41-44.

Biographical sketch of Annie Oakley, her association with Buffalo Bill, and an estimation of her shooting skills.

682   Mark, Frederick A. "Last of the Old West Artists--R. Farrington Elwell." MONTANA 7 (January 1957): 58-63.

Elwell's chance meeting with Cody in 1890 and their subsequent association. Elwell's drawings and paintings illustrate the essay.

683   Mix, Olive Stokes, with Heath, Eric. THE FABULOUS TOM MIX. Englewood Cliffs, N.J.: Prentice-Hall, 1957. 177 p. Illus.

Chatty and rather undistinguished biography of the cowboy star with surprisingly little on his career in the circus and with Wild West shows. See below.

684   Mix, Paul E. THE LIFE AND LEGEND OF TOM MIX. New York and South Brunswick, N.J.: A.S. Barnes and Co., 1972. 206 p. Illus., index.

The best biography of Mix with good coverage of his Wild West career.

685   Monaghan, Jay. THE GREAT RASCAL: THE LIFE AND ADVENTURES OF NED BUNTLINE. New York: Bonanza Books, 1951. 353 p. Illus., index, notes, bibliog.

Biography of Edward Zane Carroll Judson (Buntline); good coverage on Buntline's association with William Cody, their theatrical tour, and the Wild West show. Extensive bibliography.

686   Muller, Dan. MY LIFE WITH BUFFALO BILL. Chicago: Reilly and Lee Co., 1948. 303 p. Illus. (drawn by the author).

A young man's experiences with Cody; not very significant in terms of the Wild West show.

687   Mundis, Jerrold J. "He Took the Bull by the Horns." AMERICAN HERITAGE 19 (December 1967): 50-55. Illus.

In the early days of the century, Bill Rickett, a sometime Wild West performer, roused audiences on two continents by giving the fledgling sport of rodeo the event called bulldogging. Includes mention of Will Rogers, Tom Mix, the Millers' 101 Ranch Wild West.

688   Nordin, Charles R. "Dr. W.F. Carver." NEBRASKA HISTORY 10 (October-December 1927): 344-51. Illus.

Brief summary of Carver's career as "The Wizard Rifle Shot of the World," written on the occasion of his death, 31 August 1927.

689   O'Brien, Esse Forrester. THE FIRST BULLDOGGER. San Antonio: Naylor Co., 1961   xi, 58 p.   Illus.

Life of Bill Pickett and his career with the 101 Wild West Show.

690   A PEEP AT BUFFALO BILL'S WILD WEST. New York: McLoughlin Bros., 1887. [18] p. Illus.

Children's poem on the life and times of Buffalo Bill, including the Wild West show. Illustrated with colored lithographs.

691   Pfening, Fred D., Jr. COL. TIM McCOY'S REAL WILD WEST AND ROUGH RIDERS OF THE WORLD. Columbus, Ohio: Pfening and Snyder, 1955. 63 p. Illus., Paper.

Biography of Tim McCoy and the history of his Wild West show in 1938, with speculations as to its failure. Some documentation.

692   _____. "Buck Jones Wild West and Round Up Day." BANDWAGON 9 (November-December 1965): 25-28. Illus.

Western motion picture personalities who have been featured with or owned circuses and Wild West shows are spotlighted in this essay, e.g., Tom Mix, Ken Maynard, Tim McCoy, Buck Owens, Jack Hoxie, and Buck Jones, with details on the latter.

693   Posey, Jake. "With Buffalo Bill in Europe." BANDWAGON (October 1953): 4-6.

Brief reminiscences of 1902-7 European tour by a "boss hostler."

694   Pouska, Frank J. "Young Buffalo Wild West Show." BANDWAGON 3 (May-June 1959): 15-16, 18.

The history and evolution of this show from 1908 to 1914, with memoirs of Joe R. Smith, the prominent "Young Buffalo."

695   Remington, Frederick, illus. "Behind the 'Wild West' Scenes." Text by Julian Ralph. HARPER'S WEEKLY 38 (18 August 1894): 775-76.

An illustrated visit to Buffalo Bill's camp in Brooklyn in 1894 with a full page of drawings by Remington.

696   Rennert, Jack. 100 POSTERS OF BUFFALO BILL'S WILD WEST. Poster Art Library. New York: Darien House, 1976. 112 p.

> Contains an introduction to Cody, the lithographers, and detailed explanations for each poster. An excellent collection; the volume (11 inches by 15 1/2 inches) contains many full-page posters and two pull-out posters.

697   Reynolds, Chang. "101 Ranch Wild West Show, 1907-1916." BANDWAGON 13 (January-February 1969): 4-21. Illus.

> Historical survey. See below.

698   _____. "Miller Brothers 101 Ranch Wild West Shows." BANDWAGON 19 (March-April 1975): 3-13; 19 (May-June): 3-14. Illus.

> Survey of this show from 1925 to 1931. See above.

699   Robinson, C.O. "Tom Mix Was My Boss." FRONTIER TIMES 43 (June-July 1969): 18-20, 42-43. Illus.

> A musician reminisces about his experiences with Tom Mix's circus beginning in 1934.

700   Rosa, Joseph G. THEY CALLED HIM WILD BILL. Norman: University of Oklahoma Press, 1964. xxi, 377 p. Illus., index, bibliog.

> Life of James Butler Hickok; includes chapter, "A Wild West Show," covering his brief show business career in the 1870s.

701   Russell, Don. THE LIVES AND LEGENDS OF BUFFALO BILL. Norman: University of Oklahoma Press, 1960. x, 514 p. Illus. (photographs, map), index, bibliog.

> Well-researched biography which attempts to separate the man from myth and place the Wild West show in proper perspective within Cody's life. Noteworthy for its investigation of Buffalo Bill's scouting career and for elucidating the truths that lay behind the legends exploited in dime novels, stage plays, and Wild West exhibitions. Includes an extensive list of dime novels signed by Buffalo Bill or about him. Extensive bibliography. Recommended.

702   _____, ed. "Julia Cody Goodman's Memoirs of Buffalo Bill." KANSAS STATE HISTORICAL QUARTERLY 28 (Winter 1962): 442-96. Illus.

> Memoirs by Cody's elder sister, written, says a family tradition, to correct errors made by her sister Helen Cody Wetmore in LAST OF THE GREAT SCOUTS (see item 727). Well edited and illustrated by Russell.

703   . THE WILD WEST OR, A HISTORY OF THE WILD WEST SHOWS. Fort Worth: Amon Carter Museum of Western Art, 1970. vi, 149 p. Illus. (13 in color), index, bibliog.

> The only book-length history of traveling Wild West shows of the late nineteenth and early twentieth centuries. Extensive bibliography; checklist of 119 Wild West shows. Highly recommended.

704   . "Cody, Kings, and Cornets." AMERICAN WEST 7 (July 1970): 4-10, 62.

> Adapted from his book (above). The first ten years of Buffalo Bill's Wild West (1883 to 1893) marked the golden era of the Wild West show in America, according to Russell.

705   . "The Golden Age of Wild West Shows." BANDWAGON 15 (September-October 1971): 21-27. Illus.

> Good summation of the Wild West show's history based on a speech given in 1970.

706 Sayers, Isabelle. RIFLE QUEEN, ANNIE OAKLEY. Ostrander, Ohio: By the author, 1973. 39 p. Illus. Paper.

> Brief biography of Oakley. Good illustrations.

707 Schwartz, Joseph. "The Wild West Show; 'Everything Genuine.'" JOURNAL OF POPULAR CULTURE 3 (Spring 1970): 656-66.

> Brief history and analysis of the Wild West show's appeal.

708 Secrest, William B. "Bill Hickok's Girl on the Flying Trapeze." OLD WEST 4 (Winter 1967): 26-30, 68. Illus.

> Agnes Lake (d. 1907), wife of Wild Bill Hickok, and her career with circuses and Wild West shows; also the careers of other members of the Lake family (Lake was the name of her first husband), as equestriennes, especially her daughter, Emma Lake, who was with Cody.

709   . "'Indian' John Nelson." OLD WEST 5 (Spring 1969): 24-27, 60-63. Illus.

> On John Young Nelson, frontiersman, and his participation in Cody's Wild West show.

710 Sell, Henry Blackman, and Weybright, Victor. BUFFALO BILL AND THE WILD WEST. New York: Oxford University Press, 1955. x, 278 p. Illus., index, bibliog.

Life of Cody and his association with Wild West presentations.
Highly readable; deals knowledgeably with both the man and
the legend. Annotated bibliography.

711   Shirley, Glenn. PAWNEEE BILL: A BIOGRAPHY OF MAJOR GORDON
       W. LILLIE. Lincoln: University of Nebraska Press, 1958. 256 p.
       Illus., index, bibliog.

       Contains a great deal on Cody, who is credited with stimulat-
       ing Lillie's experiences on the western frontier. Informative
       history of the Wild West show in general and valuable data
       on the association between the shows of Cody and Pawnee Bill.
       Extensive bibliography.

712   _____, ed. BUCKSKIN JOE. Lincoln: University of Nebraska Press,
       1966. xii, 194 p. Illus., index.

       Memoirs of Edward Jonathan Hoyt, hunter-trapper, scout,
       soldier, showman, frontiersman, and friend of the Indian,
       1840-1918. Compiled from his original manuscript and notes.
       In 1892 Hoyt ran his own "Buckskin Joe Wild West Show."

713   Spring, Agnes Wright. BUFFALO BILL AND HIS HORSES. Denver:
       Bradford-Robinson Printing Co., 1968. Reprinted from the 1948 LIVE-
       STOCK ANNUAL OF WESTERN FARM LIFE, Denver, 24 p. Illus.,
       bibliog.

       Good coverage of Cody's favorite mounts and his relationship
       with them. Horses were an essential element in Cody's career;
       this historian presents him as the superb horseman he actually
       was.

714   Swartwout, Annie Fern. MISSIE. Blanchester, Ohio: Brown Publishing
       Co., 1947. vii, 298 p. Illus.

       Biography of Annie Oakley by her niece.

715   Thayer, Stuart. "Tom Mix Circus and Wild West." BANDWAGON 15
       (March-April 1971): 18-23, 15 (May-June): 4-11: Illus.

       Survey covering the years 1934-38.

716   Thompson, William C. ON THE ROAD WITH A CIRCUS. N.p.:
       Goldmann, 1903. 259 p. Illus.

       On Pawnee Bill's Wild West show. See also item 520.

717   Thorp, N. Howard (Jack), and Clark, Neil M. PARDNER OF THE
       WIND. Caldwell, Idaho: Caxton Printers, 1945. 309 p. Illus.,
       index.

Excellent firsthand account of the west at the turn of the century by a cowboy, cattleman, and top rider; known for his systematic study and collection of cowboy songs and range ballads. This volume is a vivid account of a South-western cowboy during the days of round ups, Wild West shows, and other precursors of the rodeo. A good comparison of the modern rodeo to actual work done on cow ranches is included, plus an appendix of rangeland words and phrases.

718   Thorp, Raymond W. SPIRIT GUN OF THE WEST. THE STORY OF DOC W.F. CARVER. Glendale, Calif.: Arthur H. Clark Co., 1957. 266 p. Illus., index, bibliog.

The most definitive and best-documented life of the plainsman, trapper, buffalo hunter, medicine chief of the Santee Sioux, world's champion marksman, and, according to Thorp, origina-tor of the American Wild West show--a fact not agreed upon by other authorities. Fair treatment of his career in Wild West shows and his controversial association with Cody.

719   Tompkins, Charles H. "Gabriel Brothers Wild West Show." WESTERNERS BRAND BOOK 13 (October 1956): 64.

Information and undocumented account of a small-time Wild West show in the early twentieth century.

720   Towne, Charles Wayland. "Preacher's Son on the Loose with Buffalo Bill Cody." MONTANA, THE MAGAZINE OF WESTERN HISTORY 18 (Autumn 1968): 40-55.

A newspaperman's account of Cody and the Wild West show, plus Cody's enterprises in Wyoming.

721   Vestal, Stanley [Walter S. Campbell]. SITTING BULL, CHAMPION OF THE SIOUX. Boston: Houghton Mifflin Co., 1932. New ed. Normal: University of Oklahoma Press, 1957. xxi, 349 p. Illus., index.

Life of Sitting Bull. Chapter 32, "White Hair," is a brief chronicle of Sitting Bull's stint with Cody's wild west show in 1885. Their subsequent associations are included as well. Good bibliographical essay.

722   Walsh, Richard J., in collaboration with Salsbury, Milton S. THE MAKING OF BUFFALO BILL. Indianapolis: Bobbs-Merrill Co., 1928. vii [14], 391 p. Illus., index, bibliog.

A study of the process by which Cody became a semi-legendary figure and how Buffalo Bill was the subject of the deliberate and infinitely skillful use of publicity. Includes lists of books by Cody and fiction about him.

723   Watson, Elmo Scott. "The Photographs of Sitting Bull." WESTERNERS
       BRAND BOOK 6 (August 1949): 43, 47-48.

       Checklist of pictures of Sitting Bull, including a number made
       while with Buffalo Bill's Wild West exhibition.

724   Webb, Harry E. "My Years with Buffalo Bill's Wild West Show."
       REAL WEST 13 (January 1970): 12-14, 52-55. Illus.

       Memoirs of a cowhand with Cody's show beginning in 1910;
       although very imprecise in details, some interesting insights
       into the operation of the Wild West show are presented.

725   THE WESTERNERS BRAND BOOK 1945-46. Chicago: Westerners, 1947.
       166 p. Index.

       Papers presented during the second year of THE WESTERNERS
       (1945-46), together with some original papers "rescued from
       manuscripts and ephemera." On pp. 25-45 is "The Truth
       About Buffalo Bill: A Symposium," with the following partici-
       pants: Edgar F. Medary, David Magowan, James Sharpe, Don
       Russell, Lt. Commander Frank Martinek, Will M. Maupin, and
       E.A. Brininstool.

726   THE WEST OF BUFFALO BILL. Introduction by Harold McCracken.
       New York: Harry N. Abrams, n.d. 289 p. Illus.

       Collection of Frontier Art, Indian crafts, and memorabilia
       from the Buffalo Bill Historical Center. Illustrated life of
       Cody and the Wild West show (pp. 29-84) with color plates
       of paintings and lithographs and black and white photographs
       is quite good; superb illustrations of the Wild West show, in-
       cluding numerous participants.

727   Wetmore, Helen Cody. LAST OF THE GREAT SCOUTS. Duluth:
       Duluth Press Publishing Co., 1899. xiii, 267 p. Illus.

       Biography of William F. Cody written by his sister. Six brief
       chapters are devoted to the Wild West show. Corrected, in
       part, by Cody's elder sister (see items 625 and 702).

728   Wilstach, John. "Buffalo Bill's Last Stands." ESQUIRE 21 (June 1944):
       46-47, 126.

       Popularized telling of Cody's last days.

729   Winch, Frank. THRILLING LIVES OF BUFFALO BILL AND PAWNEE
       BILL. New York: S.L. Parsons and Co., 1911. 224 p. Illus.

       Written by a hero worshipper of Cody, who regarded Pawnee
       Bill as his only legitimate successor. Sentimental treatment of

Cody's life, with useful information nonetheless on Pawnee
Bill. Includes good coverage of the origin and history of
the Wild West show, based on data furnished by Louis E.
Cooke, who was associated with many of the big time shows
for thirty-five years.

730   Yellow Rob, Chauncey. "The Menance of the Wild West Show."
QUARTERLY JOURNAL OF THE SOCIETY OF AMERICAN INDIANS.
2 (July-September 1914): 224-28.

Deals with the effect of Wild West shows on the American Indian.

Chapter 5

OUTDOOR AMUSEMENTS AND

ENVIRONMENTAL ENTERTAINMENTS

The following sections stress American forms, although in several parts, notably sections A, B, and D, sources on English forms are included as well, but more selectively. Sources in part I, "General Sources on Popular Entertainment," also should be consulted.

A. FAIRS, EXHIBITIONS, AND PLEASURE GARDENS

731   Addison, William. ENGLISH FAIRS AND MARKETS. London: B.T. Batsford, 1953. viii, 199 p. Illus., index, bibliog.

Focus on one aspect of England's social and commercial history as seen in fairs and markets. Includes chapters on the origin of fairs and some reference to entertainments at the early fairs (especially Bartholomew Fair).

732   Altick, Richard D. THE SHOWS OF LONDON. For full entry and annotation, see item 279.

733   THE ARTISTIC GUIDE TO CHICAGO AND THE WORLD'S COLUMBIAN EXPOSITION. [Chicago]: Columbian Art Co., 1892 [1]. 421 p. Illus.

History of Chicago and a detailed guide to the Exposition.

734   Austin, E.L., and Hauser, Odell. THE SEQUI-CENTENNIAL INTERNATIONAL EXPOSITION. Philadelphia: Current Publications, 1929. Reprint. New York: Arno Press, 1976. 520 p. Illus., appendix.

Guide to the 1926 Exposition; chapter on "The Gladway [the name for the general amusement section], Amusements, and Concessions."

735   Beaver, Patrick. THE CRYSTAL PALACE 1851-1936: A PORTRAIT OF VICTORIAN ENTERPRISE. London: Hugh Evelyn, 1970. 151 p. Illus., appendixes.

From the 1851 Exhibition to the move to Sydenham and the final destruction by fire in 1936. Most notable for its illustrations; documentation minimal.

736 Bird, Anthony. PAXTON'S PALACE. London: Cassell, 1976. xi, 179 p. Illus., index, bibliog.

Study of Sir Joseph Paxton and the building of the 1851 Crystal Palace.

737 Braithwaite, David. FAIRGROUND ARCHITECTURE: THE WORLD OF AMUSEMENT PARKS, CARNIVALS, AND FAIRS. New York: Frederick A. Praeger, 1968. xi[13], 195 p. Illus., index, bibliog., appendixes.

Excellent study by an English architect on the diverse elements that form the physical environment of the fairground; descriptions and commentaries upon the side shows and rides and the development of the ingenious machines. Includes a brief historical survey of the English fair. Especially valuable for its numerous illustrations. Appendixes: glossary of terms of the traveling English fair, biographical notes, and calendar of fairs in the British Isles.

738 Burg, David F. CHICAGO'S WHITE CITY OF 1893. Lexington: University Press of Kentucky, 1976. xv [16], 381 [2] p. Illus., index, notes.

Probably the most thorough history of the World's Columbian Exposition (Chicago's World Fair) to date; perceptive commentary on the meaning of the Exposition and a lengthy chapter on the exhibits and entertainment.

739 Cook, Olive. "Fairground Baroque." In THE SATURDAY BOOK 31, edited by John Hadfield, pp. 73-86. New York: Clarkson N. Potter, 1971. Illus.

Influences that shaped the "merry-go-round, booth and caravan." Superb illustrations.

740 Dallas, Duncan. THE TRAVELLING PEOPLE. London: Macmillan and Co., 1971. 182 p. Illus., glossary.

On the English fair; brief historical survey followed by chapters on specific aspects of traveling carnivals and fairs--the rides, the showmen, show booths (sideshows), stalls for food and games of skill.

741 Dexter, T.F.G. THE PAGAN ORIGIN OF FAIRS. Perranporth, Cornwall: New Knowledge Press, 1930. 44 p. Illus., bibliog.

A documented monograph that concludes that the theory of the Christian origin of fairs does not rest on evidence but that rather gods or semimythical beings presided over fairs in Britain, just as they did in Ireland and elsewhere.

742   Doenecke, Justus D.   "Myths, Machines and Markets: The Columbian Exposition of 1893."   JOURNAL OF POPULAR CULTURE 6 (Winter 1972): 533-49.

An outline of some of the significant thematic elements in this historic exposition.

743   Eustis, Morton.   "Big Show in Flushing Meadows."   THEATRE ARTS MONTHLY 23 (August 1939): 566-77.

"World of Tomorrow" Fair analyzed as a form of theatre, focusing on the work of Norman Bel Geddes and Walter Dorwin Teague, as well as C. Richard Wooten's "The Biggest Little Show on Earch," a mammoth mechanical circus.

744   "Exhibition Architecture: 16 Designs for the New York World's Fair." ARCHITECTURAL FORUM 119 (August 1963): 33-41.   Illus.

744a   ffrench, Yvonne. THE GREAT EXHIBITION: 1851.   London: Harvill Press, [1950].   297 p.   Illus., index, bibliog.

Commentary on the Crystal Palace and the exhibition of 1851, from its inception to ultimate fruition.

745   Frost, Thomas.   THE OLD SHOWMEN AND THE OLD LONDON FAIRS. 1881.   Reprint.   Ann Arbor, Mich.: Gryphon Books, 1971.   388 p. Index.

Survey of the fairground entertainers of England, during its early period; detailed historical facts and anecdotes.   A standard source.

746   Garrett, Thomas M.   "A History of Pleasure Gardens in New York City, 1700-1865."   Ph.D. dissertation, New York University, 1978.   661 p.

Survey of forty-eight pleasure gardens from 1700 to 1865.

747   Jackson, Joseph.   "Vauxhall Garden."   PENNSYLVANIA MAGAZINE OF HISTORY AND BIOGRAPHY 57, no. 4 (1933): 289-98.

History of summer amusement resort (1814-24), including theatrical performances.

748   McCullough, Edo.   WORLD'S FAIR MIDWAY: AN AFFECTIONATE

ACCOUNT OF AMERICAN AMUSEMENT AREAS FROM THE CRYSTAL PALACE TO THE CRYSTAL BALL. New York: Exposition Press, 1966. Reprint. New York: Arno Press, 1976. 190 p. Illus., bibliog.

> Fascinating history of major American fairs from the first World's Fair in 1853 to New York's 1964 World's Fair. Indicates the strong influence that midways exert on the entire realm of "public entertainment."

749 Morley, Henry. MEMOIRS OF BARTHOLOMEW FAIR. 1857. 2d ed. 1874. 3d ed. 1880. Reprint. Detroit: Singing Tree Press, 1969. xvi, 404 p. Illus., index.

> First serious history of an English fair; although dated, still an important source on the fair and its entertainments.

750 Moses, John, and Selby, Paul. THE WHITE CITY. THE HISTORICAL, BIOGRAPHICAL AND PHILANTHROPICAL RECORD OF ILLINOIS. Chicago: Chicago World Book Co., 1895. xv, [468] p. Illus., index.

> Divided into three parts, each with its own pagination. Part 3 (166 p.) is on the Columbian Exposition of 1893, which includes details on fair officials, transactions of the World's Columbian Commission, and a section on Illinois exhibits at the fair. Drawings of various buildings at the fair (not limited to Illinois) and advertisements from around the world which related to each exposition hall, including an advertisement for Cody's Wild West exhibition (p. 152), are featured. Map index of Illinois.

751 Muncey, R.W. OUR OLD ENGLISH FAIRS. London: Sheldon Press, 1936. x, 174 p. Illus., index.

> Although a brief study, the author covers a large number of topics germane to the English fair, its origin, legislation, and history. Specific chapters are devoted to the following fairs: Sturbridge, Bartholomew, Southwark, May Fair, Fairlop, Charlton "Horn Fair," Winchester, Rothwell (Northants), Oxford, Chester, St. Ives, Boston, Frost, Bury St. Edmunds, Northampton, Stagshawbank, and Doncaster. A final chapter is entitled "Interesting and Curious Customs Relating to Fairs."

752 Ritchey, David. "Columbia Garden: Baltimore's First Pleasure Garden." SOUTHERN SPEECH COMMUNICATION JOURNAL 39 (Spring 1974): 241-47.

> Interesting aspect of outdoor entertainment by an authority on Baltimore theatre.

753 Rosenfeld, Sybil. THE THEATRE OF THE LONDON FAIRS IN THE EIGHTEENTH CENTURY. For full entry and annotation, see item 2027.

754   Sands, Mollie. INVITATION TO RANELAGH, 1742-1803. London: John Westhouse, 1946. 244 p. Illus., index, bibliog.

> History of Ranelagh Gardens--its music, social life, and customs.

755   Scott, W[alter]. S[idney]. GREEN RETREATS, THE STORY OF VAUX-HALL GARDENS, 1661-1859. London: Odhams Press, 1955. 128 p. Illus., index, select bibliog.

> Full history of Vauxhall from its restoration, pastoral beginnings, its heyday in the Georgian period, and to the late nineteenth century when it had sunk to a "Place of entertainment for the rowdy and the raffish," and its final period of decline and decay.

756   Scott-Stewart, Dick, and Williams, Mark. FAIRGROUND SNAPS. London: Gordon Fraser Books, 1974. 84 p. Illus.

> One hundred fifty color and black-and-white photographs of contemporary English fairground art.

757   Sonneck, O.G. EARLY CONCERT LIFE IN AMERICA (1731-1800). Leipzig: Breitkopf and Hartel, 1907. 338 p. Index.

> Sonneck devotes about one-third of this study to concerts performed at pleasure gardens in New York City and elsewhere.

758   Southworth, James Granville. VAUXHALL GARDENS--A CHAPTER IN THE SOCIAL HISTORY OF ENGLAND. New York: Columbia University Press, 1944. viii[20], 199 p. Illus., index, bibliog.

> Probably the best study of Vauxhall in its heyday (the Georgian period). Good chapters on entertainments, singers, and composers.

759   Starsmore, Ian. ENGLISH FAIRS. N. Village Green, Levittown, N.Y.: Transatlantic Arts, 1976; London: Thames and Hudson, 1975. 128 p. Illus., index.

> Covers the evolution of the fair over the past two hundred years; focus is on the changes brought about by mechanization. Contains a list of English fairs, locations, and dates.

760   Thanet, Octave. "The Trans-Mississippi Exposition." COSMOPOLITAN 25 (October 1898): 598-614. Illus.

> Overview of the 1898 exposition in Omaha, including a description of the midway. Interesting comparison to the Columbian Exposition.

761   Truman, Ben[jamin] C. HISTORY OF THE WORLD'S FAIR BEING A
       COMPLETE AND AUTHENTIC DESCRIPTION OF THE COLUMBIAN
       EXPOSITION FROM ITS INCEPTION. Philadelphia: H.W. Kelley,
       1893. Reprint. New York: Arno Press, 1976. 610 p. Illus.

       A thorough history of the Columbian exposition. Part II
       (pp. 549-91) focuses on the Midway Plaisance and especially
       its "Street of Nations."

762   Walford, Cornelius. FAIRS, PAST AND PRESENT. 1883. Reprint.
       New York: A.M. Kelley, 1968. vii, 318 p. Index.

       Chronological history; focus on commerce. Primarily English
       but a section on the more notable fairs of France is included.

763   Waters, H.W. HISTORY OF FAIRS AND EXPOSITIONS. London,
       Ontario: Reid Bros. and Co., 1939. 158 p. Illus., index (iv p.).

       Study of the classification, function, and values of fairs and
       expositions, plus a history and economic study. Chapters on
       international or world's fairs, trade fairs, annual fairs, exhi-
       bitions or expositions, agricultural fairs, and aspects of each.

764   Wroth, Warwick. CREMORNE AND THE LATER LONDON GARDENS.
       London: Elliot Stock, 1907. xii, 102 p. Illus., index.

       Nineteenth-century open-air resorts frequented by the lower
       and middle classes. Twenty typical examples are described
       and illustrated with good contemporary lithographs. Provides
       an interesting contrast to the grander pleasure gardens de-
       scribed in the source above.

765   Wroth, Warwick, and Wroth, Arthur Edgar. THE LONDON PLEASURE
       GARDENS IN THE EIGHTEENTH CENTURY. London: Macmillan and
       Co., 1896. Reprint. Foreword by A.H. Saxon. Hamden, Conn.:
       Shoestring Press, 1979. xviii, 335 p. Illus.

       Early but still a major study of the prominent pleasure gardens
       such as Vauxhall and Ranelagh.

766   Yates, Edmund. THE BUSINESS OF PLEASURE. 2 vols. London:
       Chapman and Hall, 1865.

       Volume I contains good material on Cremorne Gardens.

B. DIME MUSEUMS, P.T. BARNUM, FREAKS, AND WAX MUSEUMS

Rather than include Phineas T. Barnum under the circus, it has been decided
to place sources on the showman under this section, stressing his more important
contributions to the museum tradition. Most histories of the circus, however,

do include material on Barnum and should be consulted. Likewise, volume one of Toole-Stott (item 81) contains numerous sources on Barnum. Those items listed in this section are principally on American examples, although important sources on English exhibition museums and human oddities of international prominence are included as well. For a definitive study of English exhibitions and early museums, see Richard D. Altick's THE SHOWS OF LONDON (item 279).

767 Abrahams, Aleck. "The Egyptian Hall, Piccadilly, 1813-1873." ANTIQUARY 42 (1906): 61-64, 139-44, 225-30.

> Good summary of the history of this famous London museum and exhibition hall.

768 Alden, W[illiam]. L[ivingston]. AMONG THE FREAKS. London, New York, and Bombay: Longmans, Green, and Co., 1896. vii, 195 p. Illus.

> An early investigation into freaks, including mermaids, bearded women, the Wildman of Borneo, fat women, and other similar attractions. Although imprecise and fictional in approach, a good sense of nineteenth-century dime museums is communicated.

769 Altick, Richard D. "Snake was Fake but Egyptian Hall Wowed London." SMITHSONIAN 8 (April 1978): 68-72, 74, 76. Illus.

> Adapted from his book (item 279); on William Bullock and the Egyptian Hall.

770 Appleton, William W. "The Marvelous Museum of P.T. Barnum." REVUE D'HISTOIRE DU THEATRE 15 (January-March 1963): 57-62.

> Barnum's museum as a curious example of the genre, "marvellous," as defined by Marian Hannah Winter (see item 94), i.e., the lure of the wonderful with examples and a brief history of the museum.

771 Ardman, H[arvey]. A. "Phineas T. Barnum's Charming Beast." NATURAL HISTORY 82 (February 1973): 46-50, 55-57. Illus.

> The life and times and the sad end of Jumbo. Deals with the dispute between England and America over Barnum's acquisition of the famous elephant. One color lithograph. See also Haley (item 552) and Scott (item 574).

772 Avery, S.P. THE LIFE AND GENIUS OF JENNY LIND, WITH BEAUTI-FUL ENGRAVINGS. New York: W.F. Burgess, 1850. 48 p. Illus.

> Detailed account of Barnum and Jenny Lind's appearance at Castle Garden.

773   Bacon, Gertrude. "The Story of the Egyptian Hall." ENGLISH
       ILLUSTRATED MAGAZINE 23 (1902-03): 298-308. Illus.

       Exhibits at the famous Piccadilly Museum (1813-73).

774   Barnum, Phineas T. THE HUMBUGS OF THE WORLD. 1865.   Reprint.
       Detroit: Singing Tree Press, 1970. vi, 315 p.

       Barnum "exposes" several of the chief hoaxes of the world
       in his own humbug style; includes spiritualists, trade and
       business impositions, money manias, medicine and quacks,
       ghosts and witchcraft, adventurers, religious humbugs, and
       other hoaxes.

775   _____. STRUGGLES AND TRIUMPHS; OR, THE LIFE OF P.T. BARNUM,
       WRITTEN BY HIMSELF. Hartford, Conn.: J.B. Burr and Co., 1869.
       New York: Arno Press, 1970. xxiv, 780 p.

       Barnum's autobiography underwent many editions and revisions.
       His style is bombastic and his facts are unreliable but this
       remains an important source. The first edition focuses primarily
       on his museum career.

776   _____. DOLLARS AND SENSE, OR HOW TO GET ON. THE
       WHOLE SECRET IN A NUT SHELL. TO WHICH IS ADDED SKETCHES
       OF THE LIVES OF SUCCESSFUL MEN, WHO ROSE FROM THE RANKS,
       AND FROM THE MOST HUMBLE STARTING POINT ACHIEVED HONOR-
       ABLE FAME (BY HENRY M. HUNT). AND AN APPENDIX CONTAIN-
       ING "MONEY! WHERE IT COMES FROM AND WHERE IT GOES TO,
       BEING A CONCISE HISTORY OF MONEY, BANKS AND BANKING"
       (BY SHELDON R. HOPKINS). Boston: Eastern Publishing Co., 1890.
       xv [17], 488 p.

       Contains excerpts from Barnum's autobiography and lectures;
       virtually the same material as in THE ART OF MONEY-
       GETTING, OR HINTS AND HELPS TO MAKE A FORTUNE
       (New York: J.S. Ogilvie and Co., 1882) and HOW I MADE
       MILLIONS, THE LIFE OF P.T. BARNUM, WRITTEN BY HIM-
       SELF, TO WHICH IS ADDED THE ART OF MONEY-GETTING
       (New York: G.W. Dillingham, 1888). There are various
       other similar editions.

777   Benet, Laura. ENCHANTING JENNY LIND. New York: Dodd,
       Mead, and Co., 1940. ix, 452 p. Illus.

       Popularized biography of the "Swedish Nightingale" and
       Barnum attraction.

778   Benton, Joel. LIFE OF PHINEAS T. BARNUM. New York: Edgewood
       Publishing Co., 1891. 621 p. Illus.

Basically a rewriting of Barnum's own autobiography with a
shift from the first person to the third.

779 _____. "P.T. Barnum, Showman and Humorist." THE CENTURY MAGA-
ZINE 64 (August 1902): 580-92. Illus.

Barnum, "the Majordomo or Lord of Laughter and Fun, the
protean Dispenser of Amusement." Essay on his life and
career.

780 Betts, John Rickards. "P.T. Barnum and the Popularization of Natural
History." JOURNAL OF THE HISTORY OF IDEAS 20 (June-September
1959): 353-68.

Critical perspective on Barnum's contribution to the popularization of natural history through the curiosity museum and the
circus. Good assessment of Barnum's recognition of the appeal
of both science and religion to men and women of the Victorian age and the moral overtones of natural history that were
always stressed.

781 Bodin, Walter, and Hershey, Burnet. IT'S A SMALL WORLD. ALL
ABOUT MIDGETS. New York: Coward-McCann, 1934. 312 p. Illus.

Covers virtually all aspects of the midget: life, sex, what is
a midget, famous midgets (e.g., Tom Thumb), and the history
of midgets.

782 Boxell, Paul J. "P.T. Barnum's Lectures for Londoners." QUARTERLY
JOURNAL OF SPEECH 54 (April 1968): 140-46.

Barnum's lecture in London (1858-59) on "The Art of Money-
Getting." See item 776.

783 Bradford, Gamaliel. "Phineas Taylor Barnum." ATLANTIC MONTHLY
130 (July 1922): 82-92.

Exploration of Barnum's business acumen and his motivations.
Deals with advertising and his resilience. Good on Barnum's
ability to laugh at himself and his knack of creating entertainment no matter what he did. Not a biography although there
are references to Barnum's autobiography.

784 Brayley, Arthur W. "Woods' Boston Museum." BOSTONIAN 2 (May
1895): 125-30.

Also known as the Market Museum; discloses evidence discovered when structure was razed and discusses earlier museums
than this 1804 operation.

785 Bryan, J. III. THE WORLD'S GREATEST SHOWMAN. THE LIFE OF

P.T. BARNUM. New York: Random House, 1956. 182 p. Illus., index.

A biography for younger readers.

786 Buckland F.T. CURIOSITIES OF NATURAL HISTORY. 4 vols. London: Richard Bentley and Sons, 1890. Illus., index.

Volume 4 concerns itself with human curiosities: giants, the so-called mummy of Julia Pastrama, the Australian Fat Boy, fire-eaters, Barnum's freaks, the living skeleton, performing fleas, Blondin and his leap, and similar topics of interest.

787 A CABINET OF CURIOSITIES: FIVE EPISODES IN THE EVOLUTION OF AMERICAN MUSEUMS. Introduction by Walter Muir Whitehill. Charlottesville: University Press of Virginia, 1967. xii, 166 p. Illus.

Essays by Whitfield J. Bell, Jr.; Clifford K. Shipton; John C. Ewers; Louis Leonard Tucker; and Wilcomb E. Washburn. Proceedings at the Washington meeting of the American Historical Association, 28 December 1964. Especially relevant to dime museums are essays on "William Clark's Indian Museum in St. Louis: 1818-1838" by Ewers and "Ohio Show-Shop: The Western Museum of Cincinnati, 1820-1867" by Tucker. Documented.

788 Carmichael, Bill. INCREDIBLE COLLECTORS, WEIRD ANTIQUES, AND ODD HOBBIES. Englewood Cliffs, N.J.: Prentice-Hall, 1971. iv, 282 p. Illus.

On strange collections and collectors. Includes a chapter "Hi, Ho, Come to the Fair" (pp. 189-208) about collectors of world fair memorabilia and "Kid Show" (pp. 253-78) about Edward G. Malone, a collector of photographs of freaks. Author discusses various types of human oddities.

789 Carrington, Richard. "The Natural History of the Giant." In THE SATURDAY BOOK 17, edited by John Hadfield, pp. 261-68. New York: Macmillan and Co., 1957. Illus.

Survey of famous giants.

790 Cavanah, Frances. JENNY LIND'S AMERICA. New York: Chilton Book Co., 1969. x, 226 p. Illus.

Fair treatment of Lind's dealings with Barnum and a chronology of her subsequent experiences in America.

791 Cavin, Lee. THERE WERE GIANTS ON THE EARTH. Seville, Ohio: Chronicle, 1959. 41 p. Illus.

Story of Capt. and Mrs. Martin Van Buren Bates, the giants of Seville.

792   Clair, Colin. HUMAN CURIOSITIES. New York: Abelard-Schuman, 1968. [2], 183 p. Illus.

Chapter 8: "Raree Shows and Eighteenth-Century Marvels" on exhibition of curiosities at English fairs and elsewhere. Includes a discussion of Tom Thumb and Commodore Nutt, famous giants in history (including Chang, the Chinese Giant, and the Nova Scotia Giantess (the latter exhibited by Barnum), strongmen (including Sandow, exhibited in the United States by Ziegfeld), and other assorted curiosities. Explores the insatiable desire to see such people by the masses.

793   Collins, Pete. NO PEOPLE LIKE SHOW PEOPLE. London: Frederick Muller, 1957. 258 p. Illus.

Amusing memoirs of offbeat artists, including sword swallowers, strong women, alligator wrestlers, giants, and the like.

794   Cottrell, Leonard. MADAME TUSSAUD. London: Evans Brothers, 1951. 194 p. Illus., index.

Includes a chronology of Madame Tussaud's travels, 1803-35. Text covers the origins of wax modeling, the exhibit of Tussaud's uncle in Paris, her childhood and early life in Paris, and her life and career from her arrival in England in 1803 to her death in 1850. The last section of the book describes how the exhibition developed after her death. The best study to date of Madame Tussaud's. Illustrations from the Wax Museum. See item 844.

795   Delcourt, Marie. HERMAPHRODITE. MYTHS AND RITES ON THE BISEXUAL FIGURE IN CLASSICAL ANTIQUITY. Translated by Jennifer Nicholson. London: Studio Books, 1961. xiii, 109 p. Bibliog.

Useful for background information only.

796   Desmond, Alice Curtis. BARNUM PRESENTS GENERAL TOM THUMB. New York: Macmillan Co., 1954. vii, 236 p. Illus.

Popularized biography of Charles Sherwood Stratton (1838-83), better known as Tom Thumb. Sixteen pages of illustrations.

797   Dingwall, Eric John. SOME HUMAN ODDITIES. London: Home and Van Thal, 1947. 198 p. Illus., bibliog.

Studies in the queer, the uncanny, and the fanatical. Portraits, with limited documentation, of six unusual individuals. Not directly concerned with side show attractions or freaks as such and, therefore, of peripheral interest only.

798   Drimmer, Frederick. VERY SPECIAL PEOPLE: THE STRUGGLES, LOVES AND TRIUMPHS OF HUMAN ODDITIES. New York: Amjon Publishers, 1973. Reprint. New York: Bantam Books, 1976. xix, 357 p. Illus., bibliog. Paper (Bantam).

Popularized study of the strange history and accomplishments of human oddities which the author prefers not to call freaks but very special people.

799   Edwards, Frank. STRANGE PEOPLE. New York: Lyle Stuart, 1961. 287 p.

Deals with all forms of unexplained and unexplainable experience, only a small portion of which relate to freaks, i.e., the monkey girl, giants and midgets, fat-men, the Elephant Boy, the Dog-Faced Boy, freaks with extra limbs, and several individuals with psychic powers.

800   Fadner, Frederick, assisted by Wadlow, Harold F. THE GENTLEMAN GIANT. Boston: Bruce Humphries, 1944. 206 p. Illus.

Biography of the American giant, Robert Pershing Wadlow.

801   Ferris, Helen. HERE COMES BARNUM. New York: Harcourt, Brace and Co., 1932. xiii, 368 p.

Life of Barnum collected from his various writings with a useful introduction by Ferris.

802   Fiedler, Leslie. "The Fascination of Freaks." PSYCHOLOGY TODAY 11 (August 1977): 56-59, 80-82.

Based on the literary critic's book (see below). Explores the notion that the appeal of human oddities responds to our basic insecurities about scale, sexuality, our status as more than beasts, and our tenuous individuality.

803   _____. FREAKS: MYTHS & IMAGES OF THE SECRET SELF. New York: Simon and Schuster, 1978. 367 p. Illus., index, bibliog.

A stimulating and provocative study of the freak from classical times to the present era of film and pop-culture "freaking out." The most thorough and thoughtful study of the topic to date. Fiedler leaves virtually no aspect of the "other" unexamined, from the freak as a holy figure, a living good-luck charm, a kind of household pet, to a showpiece and a source of entertainment, object of pity and scorn, a symbol of the human condition, and a symbol for the future possibilities of man. Fiedler examines the freak in all its forms, both natural and unnatural, and looks at the subject in literature, film, and art, as well as mythology. Well illustrated with an excellent bibliography. Recommended.

804   FitzGerald, William G. "Side-Shows." For full entry and annotation, see item 424.

805   Fitzsimons, Raymond. BARNUM IN LONDON. London: Geoffrey Books, 1969. [3], 180 p. Illus., index, bibliog.

Barnum's visit in 1844 (until February 1847) and the phenomenal effect of his sojourn on the British, including Queen Victoria, who was especially fond of Tom Thumb, is the topic of this study. Brief review of his return to London in 1858-59 and his lectures on "The Art of Money-Getting." Major section on Tom Thumb's encounter with the artist Benj. Robert Haydon.

806   Fowler, Gene, and Meredyth, Bess. THE MIGHTY BARNUM. New York: Covici-Friede, 1935. xvi, 240 p. Illus.

Screenplay of the 1935 film with Wallace Beery as Barnum; the first shooting script to be published in book form.

807   Franco, Barbar. "The Cardiff Giant; A Hundred Year Old Hoax." NEW YORK HISTORY 50 (October 1969): [420]-40. Illus.

On the "Cardiff Giant," the 10 1/2 foot stone giant "discovered" on a farm outside Cardiff, N.Y. in 1869. Tells of its "conception, discovery, and exploitation."

808   Futcher, Palmer Howard. GIANTS AND DWARFS: A STUDY OF THE ANTERIOR LOBE OF THE HYPOPHYSIS. Cambridge, Mass.: Harvard University Press, 1933. 80 p. Illus., bibliog.

Scientific investigation into giantism and dwarfism with some historical observation.

809   "Gallery: A Leaf from P.T. Barnum's Album." LIFE 68 (17 April 1970): 8.

An interesting composite photo of P.T. Barnum and his family (taken in 1875 on his sixty-fifth birthday).

810   Gould, George M., and Pyle, Walter L. ANOMALIES AND CURIOSITIES OF MEDICINE. New York: Bell Publishing Co., 1896. Reprint. New York: Julian Press, 1956. 968 p. Illus., index, bibliog.

Medical history with early findings on giantism, dwarfism, and virtually every other anomaly known. Encyclopedic in scope.

811   Haberly, Loyd. "The American Museum from Baker to Barnum." NEW YORK HISTORICAL SOCIETY QUARTERLY 43 (July 1959): 273-87. Illus.

Useful survey of American "Museums" from Gardiner Baker's Tommany Museum (late 1790s) to Barnum's acquisition of the American Museum (early 1850s). Includes a good deal of information on John Scudder's museum ventures.

812   Haines, George W. PLAYS, PLAYERS & PLAYGOERS! BEING REMINISCENCES OF P.T. BARNUM AND HIS MUSEUMS. New York: Bruce, Haines and Co., 1874. 114 p. Illus.

Cursory history of Barnum's Museum written by Barnum's special advertising agent for public relations, including remarks on Tom Thumb, Jenny Lind, Grizzly Adams, and other notable attractions; the merger with Van Amburgh Menagerie Company; Barnum's competitor, Wood's Museum and Metropolitan Theatre; Barnum's association with W.C. Coup and his traveling museum and menagerie (in 1871); and subsequent circus enterprises. The building of the Great Roman Hippodrome in 1873 and other topics are related.

813   Harris, Neil. HUMBUG: THE ART OF P.T. BARNUM. Boston: Little, Brown and Co., 1973. xiv, 337 p. Illus., index, notes, bibliog, essay.

The best-documented study of Barnum's career; especially strong on analyzing Barnum's career in its social, economic, entertainment, and intellectual context. Fair on the development of dime museums in general. Harris's notes and bibliographical essay contain good sources not listed in this guide and should be consulted by serious students of Barnum and popular culture.

814   Honour, Hugh. "Curiosities of the Egyptian Hall." COUNTRY LIFE 115 (1954): 38-39.

On exhibits at the famous London museum.

815   Hume, Ruth. "Selling the Swedish Nightingale. Jenny Lind and P.T. Barnum." AMERICAN HERITAGE 28 (October 1977): 98-107. Illus. (some in color).

Barnum's exploitation of Jenny Lind at the Castle Garden (1850) and her independent tour in 1851-52 after withdrawing from Barnum's control. A portion of this essay was reprinted in VARIETY (4 January 1978).

816   Hunter, Kay. DUET FOR A LIFETIME. New York: Coward-McCann, 1964. 127 p. Illus., index, bibliog.

The story of the original Siamese Twins, Chang and Eng. Superficial and undocumented account; one brief chapter devoted to their association with Barnum, which was itself brief. See item 846.

817   AN ILLUSTRATED CATALOGUE AND GUIDE BOOK TO BARNUM'S AMERICAN MUSEUM. New York: Published by Barnum, n.d. [ca. 1860]. 112 p. Illus. Paper.

One of many such guides. Contains description and illustrations of the various curiosities and displays at Barnum's. Includes brief history, list of attractions in the seven "Saloons," and provides a description of "The Lecture Room" and its live attractions, including Tom Thumb.

818   James, Theodore, Jr. "Tom Thumb's Giant Wedding." SMITHSONIAN 4 (September 1973): 56–62. Illus.

The marriage in 1863 of Tom Thumb (Charles Stratton) and Lavinia Warren.

819   Juliani, Giovanni. FREAKS: A COLLECTOR'S EDITION OF NATURE'S HUMAN ODDITIES, PAST AND PRESENT. Montreal: By the author, n.d. 33 p. Illus. Paper.

Photograph collection of freaks.

820   Katz, Herbert, and Katz, Marjorie. MUSEUMS, U.S.A. Garden City, N.Y.: Doubleday and Co., 1965. x, 395 p. Illus., index, bibliog., appendix.

Excellent introductory chapter provides background on the history of the American museum and places museums as entertainment centers, such as Barnum's and the Boston Museum, in relationship to the evolution of "serious" repositories. Appendix lists museums and data for each state. Useful as a reference source as well.

821   Lee, Polly J. GIANT: THE PICTORIAL HISTORY OF THE HUMAN COLOSSUS. South Brunswick and New York: A.S. Barnes and Co., 1970. 148 p. Illus., index, bibliog.

History of giants, legend and fact, told largely through pictures, and an investigation into the condition of giantism.

Discusses giants for exhibit, including a chapter on dime
museums, sideshows, and circuses. Although limited documentation, not a scholarly work and rife with careless error and
distortion.

822   Lewiston, Harry, as told to Holtman, Jerry. FREAK SHOW MAN.
Los Angeles: Holloway House, 1968. 327 p. Paper.

Lewiston's (1900-1965) amusement park and carnival sideshow
memoirs.

823   Luckhurst, Kenneth W. THE STORY OF EXHIBITIONS. London and
New York: Studio Publications, 1951. 221 p. Illus., bibliog.

History of national and international exhibitions.

824   McClung, Robert M., and McClung, Gale S. "Tammany's Remarkable
Gardiner Baker." NEW YORK HISTORICAL SOCIETY QUARTERLY 42
(April 1958): 143-69. Illus.

Life of New York's first museum proprietor, menagerie keeper,
and promoter extraordinary, including a history of Tammany
Society's American Museum (1790s to 1860s). Also mentions
of Charles Willson Peale (his predecessor), John Scudder (his
successor), and P.T. Barnum. Useful history prior to Barnum.

825   McNamara, Brooks. "'A Congress of Wonders': The Rise and Fall of
the Dime Museum." EMERSON SOCIETY QUARTERLY 20 (3d quarter
1974): 216-32. Illus.

Excellent survey of the dime museum and its history. The
dime museum according to the author was a "lively, influential and uniquely American brand of popular entertainment."

826   _____. STEP RIGHT UP: AN ILLUSTRATED HISTORY OF THE AMERI-
CAN MEDICINE SHOW. Garden City, N.Y.: Doubleday and Co.,
1976. xviii, [20], 233 p. Illus., index, bibliog., notes, appendixes.

Numerous references to dime museums and other forms of early
museums of entertainment and curiosity interest. See also
item 949.

827   Mannix, Daniel. WE WHO ARE NOT AS OTHERS. New York:
Pocket Books, 1976. 176 p. Illus. Paper.

Although documented only in passing and written for a popular
audience, Mannix, a former carnie, brings understanding and
first-hand observation to this survey of freaks. Deals with
most categories plus those who have made themselves into
human oddities by choice. See also his book on carnivals
(item 874).

828   Mitchell, Joseph. McSORLEY'S WONDERFUL SALOON. New York:
Eagle Book. Distributed by Duell, Sloan and Pearce, 1943. Reprint.
New York: Grosset, 1959. 253 p.

Stories from the NEW YORKER (principally from the 1930s)
in slightly altered form. Portraits of the characters who fre-
quented McSorley's and were known in the Bowery district,
including Charles Eugene Cassell, who ran Captain Charley's
Private Museum for Intelligent People, and Jane Barnell, a
bearded lady.

829   Money, John. SEX ERRORS OF THE BODY. Baltimore: Johns Hopkins
University Press, 1968. xiv, 145 p. Illus., index, bibliog.

Medical study of transsexuals, hermaphroditism, and other
physical anomalies. Good introductory background.

830   Montagu, Ashley, and Treves, Frederick. ELEPHANT MAN. New
York: Outerbridge and Dienstfrey, 1971. x, 140 p. Illus.

Documented and well-illustrated investigation into the life of
John Merrick, "The Elephant Man," and his association with
Dr. Frederick Treves in the 1880s. Includes reprint of
Treves's account of Merrick from: THE ELEPHANT MAN AND
OTHER REMINISCENCES (1923) and ten appendixes of official
reports and accounts of the Elephant Man, plus an article by
Laurence M. Solomon, "Quasimodo's Diagnosis" from JOUR-
NAL OF THE AMERICAN MEDICAL ASSOCIATION 204 (1958):
190-91.

831   Mullens, W.H. "William Bullock's London Museum." MUSEUMS JOUR-
NAL 17 (1917-18): 51-56, 132-37, 180-87.

Early history of the Egyptian Hall.

832   Neafie, Nelle. A P.T. BARNUM BIBLIOGRAPHY. Lexington: University of Kentucky, 1965. 55 p. Multilith.

Guide to the Barnum Collection in the Bridgeport Public Library. Fairly exhaustive listing, especially of correspondence
and books.

833   Northall, William Knight. BEFORE AND BEHIND THE CURTAIN, OR
FIFTEEN YEARS' OBSERVATION AMONG THE THEATRES OF NEW
YORK. New York: W.F. Burgess, 1851. 229 p.

Barnum's Museum and some of the leading events in the life of
the showman. See also item 247.

834   Parry, Albert. TATTOO: SECRETS OF A STRANGE ART. New York:
Simon and Schuster, 1933. Reprint. New York: Macmillan Co., 1971.
xii, 171 p. Illus., index, bibliog. Paper.

Parry's early work covers all aspects of tattooing--its history, motivation, famous tattooers and tattooees, and so forth. Chapter 4: "The Circus," discusses tattooees as freaks in side shows and dime museums and gives a brief history of the phenomenon in the United States.

835   Pyke, E.J. A BIOGRAPHICAL DICTIONARY OF WAX MODELLERS. Oxford: Oxford University Press, 1973. lxvi, 216 p. (text) plus 79 p. (plates). Illus., index, bibliog.

Definitive reference and bibliographical work on wax modellers. Superb bibliography. Includes a list of public and private collections, including those of the Tussaud's dating from the nineteenth century.

836   Romaine, Mertie E. GENERAL TOM THUMB AND HIS LADY. Taunton, Mass.: William S. Sullwold Publishing, 1976. 94 p. Illus.

Romaine has lived in Lavinia Warren's hometown most of her life and knew Mrs. Tom Thumb. This is the story of Charles S. Stratton (Tom Thumb) and his wife.

837   Root, Harvey W. THE UNKNOWN BARNUM. New York: Harper and Bros., 1927. vii, 376 p.

Traits and abilities of Barnum that set him apart.

838   Rosenberg, C.G. JENNY LIND: HER LIFE, HER STRUGGLES AND HER TRIUMPHS. New York: Stringer and Townsend, 1850. 82 p.

Her tour in America, partially under Barnum's auspices.

839   Rourke, Constance. TRUMPETS OF JUBILEE. New York: Harcourt, Brace and Co., 1927. xiv, 445 p. Illus., index, note on sources.

Chapter on Barnum (pp. 369-426), contemporary of Harriet Beecher Stowe, Henry Ward Beecher, Horace Greeley, and other subjects of the book. Good treatment of the myth and the portion of "The American Legend" around Barnum; focus on his new England background and his use of the popular medium of language in superabundance.

840   Saxon, A.H. "Waxworks as a Source of Theatrical Iconography: Madame Tussaud's and the Nineteenth-Century British Stage." THEATRE NOTEBOOK 30, no. 2 (1976): 52-57. Illus. (1 pl.).

Madame Tussaud's as a repository "for a small and generally select collection of notable performers who graced the British stage" in the nineteenth century.

841 _____, ed. THE AUTOBIOGRAPHY OF MRS. TOM THUMB. Hamden, Conn.: Shoe String Press, forthcoming.

This volume is part of a new series on popular entertainment under the general editorship of So:.on.

842 Thompson, C[harles]. J[ohn]. S[amuel]. THE MYSTERY AND LORE OF MONSTERS. WITH ACCOUNTS OF SOME GIANTS, DWARFS, AND PRODIGIES Hyde Park, N.Y.: University Books, 1968. Reprint. New York: Citadel Press, 1970. 256 p. Illus., index, bibliog.

Thompson, who died in 1943, presents here a full history from Greek and Egyptian mythology to the early 1900s. Includes a chapter on General Tom Thumb and one on dwarfs at Bartholomew Fair in 1825 and at Barnum's Museum. One of the more complete and authoritative studies of freaks; good listing of older sources.

843 Truzzi, Marcello. "Lilliputians in Gulliver's Land: The Social Role of the Dwarf." In his SOCIOLOGY AND EVERYDAY LIFE, pp. 197-211. Englewood Cliffs, N.J.: Prentice-Hall, 1968.

The problems of the dwarf reveal that they share many of the social difficulties and problems of self-preservation found among other stigmatized minority groups.

844 Tussaud, John T. THE ROMANCE OF MADAME TUSSAUD'S. London: Odhams Press, 1921. 314 p. Illus., index.

History of Madame Tussaud's waxworks. Largely superseded by Cottrell, item 794.

845 Wallace, Irving. THE FABULOUS SHOWMAN. New York: Alfred A. Knopf, 1959. vii, 279 p. Illus., index, bibliog.

Although a popularized account of Barnum's career, still useful and generally reliable; fairly extensive bibliography.

846 Wallace, Irving, and Wallace, Amy. THE TWO: THE STORY OF THE ORIGINAL SIAMESE TWINS. New York: Simon and Schuster, 1978. 352 p. Illus., index, bibliog.

The definitive full-length biographical study of Eng and Chang, born in Siam in 1811 (they were actually Chinese). Exhibited by, among others, P.T. Barnum. Excellent list of sources. See Hunter, item 816.

847 Wells, Helen. BARNUM, SHOWMAN OF AMERICA. New York: David McKay Co., 1957. ix, 239 p. Illus. (drawings), index, bibliog.

Life of Barnum based largely on his autobiography.

848   Werner, M.R. BARNUM. New York: Harcourt, Brace and Co.,
       1923. viii, 381 p. Illus., index.

       Standard biography of Barnum.

849   Westervelt, Leonidas. THE CIRCUS IN LITERATURE. For full entry
       and annotation, see item 531.

850   Wood, Edward J. GIANTS AND DWARFS. London: Richard Bentley,
       1868. xii, 472 p. Index.

       Although dated, still a major source book. From biblical
       giants and dwarfs up to the most recent examples of the mid-
       nineteenth century.

C. CARNIVALS

Related sources can be found in sections B and D.

851   Bakner, Andrew J. "Side Show Attractions." BANDWAGON 17
       (November-December 1973): 35-38. Illus.

       Brief history; focus on major attractions.

852   Boles, Don. THE MIDWAY SHOWMAN. Atlanta: Pinchpenny Press,
       1967. 61 p.

       A guide to building a show and an excellent, albeit brief,
       collection of tips for the carnival hopeful--equipment needed,
       booking a show, setting it up, animal shows (including
       specific examples), geek or wildman shows, mouse circuses,
       exhibit shows (mechanical shows, headless woman, cannibals),
       and so forth.

853   Braithwaite, David. FAIRGROUND ARCHITECTURE. For full entry and
       annotation, see item 737.

854   Carrington, Hereward. SIDESHOW AND ANIMAL TRICKS. Kansas
       City: A.M. Wilson, 1913. Reprint. Atlanta, Ga.: Pinchpenny
       Press, 1973. 66 p. Illus. Paper.

       Author reveals tricks of the side show performer: animal
       tricks, gamblers's tricks, juggling secrets, stage effects, and
       the like.

855   Crews, Harry. "Carny." PLAYBOY 23 (September 1976): 96, 98, 195,

196, 200, 201-204.

A journalist looks at the carnival in rather exploitative terms. Still, useful for behind-the-scenes atmosphere and terminology of the carnival.

856　Dadswell, Jack. HEY THERE SUCKER. Boston: Bruce Humphries, 1946. 256 p. Illus.

Veteran carnival press agent's inside story of the carnival. Covers topics such as how a show operates, carnival language, American fairs, flea circus, freaks, lion tamer, midway machinery, and various types of midway performers.

857　DeBelle, Starr. WEBSTER WAS A SUCKER: DICTIONARY OF MIDWAY SLANG. [Cincinnati: Billboard Publications, 1946. 12 p.]. Paper.

Dictionary of carnival terms in a 4 by 5 1/2 inch pamphlet.

858　Dembroski, Theodore M. "Hanky Panks and Group Games versus Alibis and Flats: The Legitimate and Illegitimate of the Carnival's Front End." JOURNAL OF POPULAR CULTURE 6 (Winter 1972): 567-82.

Descriptive overview of one major segment of the carnival, the front end: the game, food, and straight sale concession area. Deals with the social significance of this area versus the back end (shows) and the rides. Very useful.

859　Easto, Patrick C., and Truzzi, Marcello. "Carnivals, Roadshows, and Freaks." SOCIETY 9 (March 1972): 26-34.

A knowledgeable and perceptive analysis, including distinctions between circus and carnival, carnival history, the carnival social system, and an explanation of terminology. Reprinted in ANNUAL EDITIONS: READINGS IN SOCIOLOGY '72-'73, pp. 297-305. Guilford, Conn.: Dushkin, 1972; and in SOCIOLOGICAL REALITIES II, edited by I.L. Horowitz and C. Nanry. New York: Harper and Row, 1975.

860　_____. "Towards an Ethnography of the Carnival Social System." JOURNAL OF POPULAR CULTURE 6 (Winter 1972): 550-66.

Review of available literature and an introduction of the carnival to the social scientist and a suggestion that the carnival is a testing ground for notions about subcultures and total institutions. Good definition of carnival given and an excellent evaluation of the literature. Reprinted in ANTHROPOLOGY IN AMERICAN LIFE, edited by Marcello Truzzi and Joseph G. Jorgensen. Englewood Cliffs, N.J.: Prentice-Hall, 1974.

861   Gibson, Walter. THE BUNCO BOOK. Holyoke, Mass.: Sidney H. Radner, 1946. 96 p. Illus.

Methods of the bunco man--from the carnival worker and his games of chance to more sophisticated techniques of the confidence man.

862   Gresham, William Lindsay. NIGHTMARE ALLEY. New York and Toronto: Rinehart and Co., 1946. 275 p.

Well-known fictional story with a carnival background.

863   _____. "The World of Mirth." LIFE 25 (13 September 1948): 142-44, 146, 149-50, 152, 154, 156. Illus.

Essay on Frank Bergen, owner of "The World of Mirth" carnival and forty-one years a carnival man; covers all aspects of carnival life and practice.

864   _____. MONSTER MIDWAY. New York: Rinehart and Co., 1953. 309 p. Bibliog., glossary.

Nature and history of the carnival business; deals with history, mechanics, and stars of the carnival. Generally recommended.

865   _____. "Its Magic is the Magic of Life." NEW YORK TIMES BOOK REVIEWS 65 (13 March 1960): 34-35.

Review with insights of AND WHERE IT STOPS NOBODY KNOWS by David Mark (New York: Doubleday and Co., 1960), a novel with a carnival setting.

866   "Hey Rube." NATION 129 (6 November 1929): 513.

Why "the road" was declining; based on a survey made by BILLBOARD. Cause: Shady business methods and the treatment of patrons.

867   "I'll Gyp You Every Time." SATURDAY EVENING POST 222 (17 September 1949): 24+. Illus.

A carnival sharpie tells how he clips the chumps who gamble on the midway's games of skill.

868   Irwin, Will. THE CONFESSIONS OF A CON MAN. New York: B.W. Huebsch, 1909. 182 p. Illus.

A circus and carnival gambler reveals his secrets--up to a point. Good on three-card monte.

869 Klein, Frederick C. "Step Right Up: How 'Heels' Shapiro Makes a Tidy Living Off a Carnival Game." WALL STREET JOURNAL 174 (30 September 1969): 1, 21.

> Journalistic essay on Sam "Heels" Shapiro and the appeal of his "razzle" game at carnivals. Good description of current carnival practice and life on a Southern circuit.

870 Kobler, J. "World's Biggest Show: Royal American Shows." COSMOPOLITAN 135 (November 1953): 78-83. Illus.

> Survey of this major carnival organization.

871 Krassowski, Wittold. "Social Structure and Professionalization in the Occupation of the Carnival Worker." M.A. thesis, Purdue University, 1954.

> An important study of the sociological implications of the carnival worker.

872 Lewis, Arthur H. CARNIVAL. New York: Trident Press, 1970. 320 p.

> A journalistic study of the carnival; authoritative in tone but its total credibility is somewhat doubtful. Nonetheless, one of few full-length treatments of carnival life. It should be noted, however, that a number of old-time show people dismiss Lewis's book summarily.

873 McKennon, Joe. A PICTORIAL HISTORY OF THE AMERICAN CARNIVAL. Sarasota, Fla.: Carnival Publishers of Sarasota, distributed by Popular Press, 1972. 192 p. Illus., index, glossary.

> An excellent source; includes essays on European roots, American roots, the World's Columbian Exposition (1893), and a chronological breakdown to the present. Copiously illustrated.

874 Mannix, Dan[iel]. STEP RIGHT UP. New York: Harper and Bros., 1950. 270 p. Illus. (pen and ink sketches).

> Same as MEMOIRS OF A SWORD SWALLOWER. Mannix's memoirs of carnival life and the performers of the sideshows. A highly entertaining book and fairly reliable.

875 Maurer, David W. "Carnival Cant: A Glossary of Circus and Carnival Slang." AMERICAN SPEECH 6 (June 1931): 327-37.

> Brief introductory essay on the evolution of circus and carnival slang followed by a very useful, though not inclusive, glossary of terms. By a recognized authority on American slang, in particular the con artist.

876   Meiselas, Susan. CARNIVAL STRIPPERS. For full entry and annotation, see 1247.

877   Millstein, Gilbert. "Carnie Biz--Bigger Than Ever." NEW YORK TIMES MAGAZINE (May 18, 1952): 22-23, 58-59. Illus.

> The James E. Strates Shows and Dr. Serge Urling, trainmaker; a journalistic portrait of the carnival and carnies.

878   Mockridge, Norton. "Carnival." AMERICAN WAY [American Airlines]. (May 1970): 8-21. Illus.

> On the contemporary carnival business.

879   Nathe, Patricia A. "Carnivals, Also Fairs, Circuses, and Amusement Parks: A Historical Perspective." M.A. thesis, University of California, Berkeley, 1969.

> The criminal element in these forms (their games) in perspective. Most useful on carnivals.

880   "No More Rubes." TIME 72 (29 September 1958): 41-42.

> Colonel Lew Alter, talker on the Gratz Midway, and other carnies discuss the diminishing number of suckers at the carnival.

881   Poling, James. "Sawdust in Their Shoes." SATURDAY EVENING POST 225 (11 April 1953): 32-33, 102-103, 105, 107. Illus.

> The life of a carnie in the James E. Strates Shows.

882   Scarne, John. "Carnival, Fair, Bazaar, Arcade and Amusement Park Games." In his SCARNE'S COMPLETE GUIDE TO GAMBLING. Rev. ed., pp. 556-624. New York: Simon and Schuster, 1974. Illus., index, glossary.

> Excellent exposure and explanation of carnival games, with illustrations. Some of the games discussed are hanky-panks, percentage games, wheels of fortune, one-ball game, mouse game, carnival dice games, penny pitch, six-ball roll-down, razzle dazzle, three-marble tivoli, pin stores and peek joints, dart games, devil's bowling alley, milk bottles, string game, and three-shell game--and, the ever popular, three-card monte. Includes a glossary of carnival terms and technical idioms.

883   Sidenberg, Sid. "Pitchdom Forty Years Ago and Today." AMUSEMENT BUSINESS (31 December 1969): 153.

> Good retrospective comparison.

884   Taylor, Robert Lewis. "Talker." NEW YORKER 34 (19 April 1958):
        47 ; 34 (26 April): 39 .

> Nate Eagle, manager of the Ringling Brothers and Barnum and
> Bailey Sideshow, last of the great carnival "talkers" remembers
> his past life; an in-depth portrait with much on carnivals and
> the circus.

885   Truzzi, Marcello, ed. "Circuses, Carnivals and Fairs in America."
        JOURNAL OF POPULAR CULTURE 6 (Winter 1972): 531-619.

> Special section of this issue devoted to these forms. Eight
> useful essays. Recommended.

886   Truzzi, Marcello, and Easto, Patrick C. "The Carnival as a Marginally
        Legal Work Activity: The Typological Approach to Work Systems." In
        DEVIANT BEHAVIOR: OCCUPATIONAL AND ORGANIZATIONAL
        BASES, edited by Clifton D. Bryant, pp. 336-53. Chicago: Rand
        McNally, 1974.

> An introduction of the carnival for students of work and de-
> viant behavior. Includes a definition and scope of carnivals,
> a history, carnival work organization, the carnival as a
> marginally legal work system, and a selected additional bib-
> liography on the American carnival.

887   Zincser, William K. "A Lot of Quarters." LOOK 31 (5 September
        1967): 18.

> The James E. Strates Show and the trend in carnivals toward
> "uplift" and gentility, except in the games.

D. AMUSEMENT PARKS, THEME PARKS, AND SEASIDE RESORTS

888   Albert, Frank L. "The Future of the Amusement Park in America."
        BILLBOARD (19 March 1910): 20, 21, 86.

> Early twentieth-century prediction of interest from a retrospec-
> tive standpoint.

889   Aronson, Arnold. "The Total Theatrical Environment: Impression Man-
        agement in the Parks." THEATRE CRAFTS 11 (September 1977): [34],
        35, 72-74, 76. Illus.

> A look at the environmental theatre aspects of current parks;
> focus on "Six Flags Over Texas."

890   Barrett, Richmond. GOOD OLD SUMMER DAYS. Introduction by
        Mary Lasswell. Boston: Houghton Mifflin Co., 1952. xiii, 338 p.

Illus., index, note on sources.

History of five American resorts ("watering places"): Newport and Narragansett Pier, Rhode Island; Saratoga, New York; Long Branch, N.J.; and Bar Harbor, Maine.

891 Baxter, Sylvester. "The Trolley in Rural Parks." HARPER'S MONTHLY 97 (June 1898): 60–69.

The phenomenon of the recreation grounds run by street–railway companies providing all sorts of attractions in rural parks.

892 Braithwaite, David. FAIRGROUND ARCHITECTURE. For full entry and annotation, see item 737.

893 Charles, Barbara F. "Mix antique charm and artistry, add children and spin." SMITHSONIAN 3 (July 1972): 41–47. Illus. (in color).

Excellent illustrations of merry–go–round carvings. Brief historical text and description of Smithsonian collection.

894 Cuber, John F. "Patrons of Amusement Parks." SOCIOLOGY AND SOCIAL RESEARCH 24 (September–October 1939): 63–8.

Based on one hundred interviews with amusement park patrons in the Cleveland metropolitan area, Cuber analyzes the patron as to age, sex, occupation, the motives for attendance, and how often they attend and with whom. Also sheds some light on the amusement park as an urban recreational pattern.

895 Cummings, E.E. "Coney Island." In E.E. CUMMINGS: A MISCEL-LANY REVISED, edited by George J. Firmage, pp. 149–53. New York: October House, 1965.

Reprinted from VANITY FAIR (June 1926); the poet's appreciation of the famous "pleasure park." Interesting comparison of its appeal as opposed to the theatre and the circus. See Cummings's play HIM (1946).

896 Davidson, Randall. "Buckle Up: Safety in the Parks." THEATRE CRAFTS 11 (September 1977): 54, 96, 98.

Potential hazards and guidelines for safety in the theme parks discussed by the president of the International Safety Institute.

897 "Disneyland and Disney World." THEATRE CRAFTS 11 (September 1977): 28–31.

Illustrated tour through Disneyland (opened 1955) and Disney World (opened 1971).

898 Fause, Kenneth. "Surround Sound; Guidelines for Background Entertainment and Ride Sound Systems." THEATRE CRAFTS 11 (September 1977): 53, 88, 90-92, 94-95.

>Audio expert analyzes the engineering of theme park sound systems for background music, live entertainment, and rides.

899 Fried, Frederick A. PICTORIAL HISTORY OF THE CAROUSEL. London: Thomas Yoseloff; New York: A.S. Barnes and Co., 1964. 230 p. Illus., index, bibliog., appendixes.

>Generally well-researched and superbly illustrated history of the carousel, both in England and America. Chapters on carousel makers, carvers, band organs and makers, and figures made by carvers. Six appendixes: 1) "Chronological List of Great Amusement Park Fires," 2) "Some Locations of Spillman Carousels," 3) "Caravans That Featured C.W. Parker Carry-Us-Alls," 4) "Carousels Built by the Philadelphia Toboggan Company," 5) "Lists of Personnel," and 6) "Band Organ Manufacturers."

900 Funnell, Charles F. BY THE BEAUTIFUL SEA. THE RISE AND HIGH TIMES OF THAT GREAT AMERICAN RESORT, ATLANTIC CITY. New York: Alfred A. Knopf, 1975. xi, 199 p. plus Illus., (32 p.), index, (8 p.), bibliog., notes.

>The only detailed study of Atlantic City that discusses its entertainments, e.g., rolling chairs, horse-powered merry-go-rounds, performing pigs, the first multiple ferris wheel, and so forth. Includes thirty-two pages of illustrations, and an eight-page index.

901 Green, Benny. I'VE LOST MY LITTLE WILLIE. A CELEBRATION OF COMIC POSTCARDS. London: Elmtree Books-Arrow Books, 1976. 159 p. Illus. Paper.

>Entertaining and informative study of English seaside resorts as seen through the postcard. Superb illustrations, many in color.

902 "A Greeting from Coney Island." AMERICAN HERITAGE 26 (February 1975): 49-55. Illus.

>Excellent collection of postcards (from the Richard F. Snow Collection) of the days of the Luna, Dreamland, and Steeplechase at Coney Island.

903 Griffin, Al. "STEP RIGHT UP FOLKS!" Chicago: Henry Regnery Co., 1974. xii, 257 p. Illus., index.

>Survey of American amusement parks, including brief history and a rating of parks for each section of the country. Chap-

ters on "Kiddie Lands" and theme parks, entertainments, re-
freshments and concessions, and types of rides. Appendix:
"Recently Defunct Amusement Parks." Terms explained in
text.

904   Hartt, Rollin Lynde. "The Amusement Park." ATLANTIC MONTHLY
      99 (May 1907): 667-77.

      Evolution of the American amusement park and an analysis of
      the institution seen as "an artificial distraction for an artificial
      life."

905   Hutton, James S. "The Amusement Park: American Institution." BILL-
      BOARD (19 March 1910): 25, 84.

      An early twentieth-century appraisal.

906   Kyriazi, Gary. THE GREAT AMERICAN AMUSEMENT PARKS. Secaucus,
      N.J.: Citadel Press, 1976. 256 p. Illus., index.

      Pictorial history of the American amusement park (and European
      antecedents) from the early nineteenth-century picnic groves
      and beer gardens. Most detailed section is a history of Coney
      Island from its early days as a seaside resort for the rich to
      its great days with its Luna Park, Dreamland, and Steeple-
      chase Park, to its decline in recent years. Not a distin-
      guished study but good for its illustrations. Chapters on
      American amusement parks, "East to West," Disneyland and
      the theme parks, and list of America's top one hundred parks.
      Minimal documentation.

907   Lindley, Kenneth. SEASIDE ARCHITECTURE. Excursions into Architec-
      ture Series. London: Hugh Evelyn, 1973. 160 p. Illus.

      Useful general survey of the architecture and design of the
      English seaside resort. A chapter is devoted to the design
      aspects of seaside amusements.

908   Lines, Harry. "From Cyclone to Scream Machine: Approaches to Ride
      Themeing." THEATRE CRAFTS 11 (September 1977): 41, 100-103.
      Illus.

      Discussion of the heritage of modern day rides and various
      approaches to ride themeing, with a retrospective glance at
      Coney Island. On pages 43-44 there is a portfolio of photo-
      graphs of the cyclone and similar rides.

909   Lyon, Peter. "The Master Showman of Coney Island." AMERICAN
      HERITAGE 9 (June 1958): 14-20, 92-95. Illus.

      George Tilyou, the man who in 1897 installed the Steeplechase

Horses as the principal attraction of his prototypal carnival (amusement park) grounds--his life and career. Essay is based on McCullough's GOOD OLD CONEY ISLAND (see below). Excellent illustrations, several in color. Also covers Luna Park and Dreamland in addition to Tilyou's Steeplechase Park.

910 McCullough, Edo. GOOD OLD CONEY ISLAND. New York: Charles Scribner's Sons, 1957. viii, 344 p. Illus., index, glossary.

A definitive study and history of Coney Island up to 1956. Glossary of carnival jargon and underworld cant.

911 MacKay, Patricia. "Theme Parks: USA." THEATRE CRAFTS 11 (September 1977): 27, 56, 65-69.

Survey of the growth and expansion of theme parks today.

912 McNamara, Brooks. "Come on Over: The Rise and Fall of the American Amusement Park." THEATRE CRAFTS 11 (September 1977): 33, 84-86. Illus.

Brief but useful summary of the American park's history.

913 Mangels, William F. THE OUTDOOR ENTERTAINMENT BUSINESS. New York: Vantage Press, 1952. 206 p. Illus.

One of the better histories of the amusement park in its various forms. Includes a list of American Outdoor Amusement Associations, publications (throughout the world), and amusement trade associations in foreign countries.

914 Manley, Seon, and Manley, Robert. BEACHES: THEIR LIVES, LEGENDS, AND LORE. Philadelphia, New York, and London: Chilton Book Co., 1968. xi, 383 p. Illus., index, bibliog.

Chapter twelve (pp. 224-32): "Broadwalks and Promenades of the Beach: The Beach Resort" is the most useful. History of broadwalks from Atlantic City in 1870; also English examples.

915 Manning-Sanders, Ruth SEASIDE ENGLAND. London: B.T. Batsford, 1951. viii, 151 p. Illus.

Brief study of English seaside resorts.

916 Marsden, Christopher. THE ENGLISH AT THE SEASIDE. Britain in Pictures. London: Collins, 1947. 47 p. Illus.

Brief survey of English summer resorts.

917 "The Mechanical Joys of Coney Island." SCIENTIFIC AMERICAN 19

(15 August 1908): 101, 108-10. Illus.

Useful essay on the mechanisms behind the various rides.

918   Mellor, G.J. POMS-POMS AND RUFFLES. THE STORY OF NORTH-
       ERN SEASIDE ENTERTAINMENT. Clapham, Lancaster, Engl.: Dales-
       man Publishing Co., 1966. 72 p. Illus. Paper.

       Account of the traditional English seaside Pierrots, usually
       performed on makeshift stages on the beaches or in small
       theatres at the end of amusement piers.

919   Metcalf, Francis. SIDE SHOW STUDIES. Illustrated by Oliver Herford.
       New York: Outing Publishing Co., 1906. 232 p.

       Partially fictionalized stories of the Dreamland Arena at Coney
       Island and its various acts, many of the animal variety. Good
       sense of turn of the century "sideshows."

920   Middleton, William D. "Gems of Symmetry and Convenience." AMERI-
       CAN HERITAGE 24 (February 1973): 23-37, 99. Illus.

       History of the electric trolley and its effect on the develop-
       ment of the American city in the 1880s. Touches on trolleys
       as a source of pleasure travel and entertainment. Illustrated
       with color postcards.

921   Onosko, Tim. FUN LAND U.S.A. New York: Ballantine Books,
       1978. [4], 296 p. Illus., index. Paper.

       Guide book to one hundred major amusement and theme parks
       in the United States, plus a brief history and several other in-
       formative and impressionistic essays. Intended more for the
       tourist than the serious student-scholar.

922   Pilat, Oliver, and Ranson, Jo. SODOM BY THE SEA: AN AFFEC-
       TIONATE HISTORY OF CONEY ISLAND. Garden City, N.Y.: Double-
       day, Doran and Co., 1941. ix, 334 p. Illus.

       History of Coney Island as a summer resort and amusement park
       from 1829. Chapters on "Trident of Entertainment" (singing,
       dancing cabaret, and refreshments), 1870s-1900; "Amusement
       Parks" (from 1897); "Side Shows" (from ca. 1905). Other
       forms of entertainment are included as well. The chapter on
       sideshows is exceptionally good.

923   Snow, Robert E., and Wright, David E. "Coney Island: A Case Study
       in Popular Culture and Technical Change." JOURNAL OF POPULAR
       CULTURE 9 (Spring 1976): 960-75. Illus. (map).

       Study of Coney Island as America's first and probably still
       most symbolic commitment to mechanized leisure.

924   "That's Live Entertainment: On Stage in the Parks." THEATRE CRAFTS
        11 (September 1977): 46-51, 76-78, 80-82, 84. Illus.

        Essay on various kinds of live entertainment, from trained
        animals and puppet shows to musical revues, in today's theme
        parks. Focus on Opryland's Production Center, the GHOST
        OF THE GLOBE at Busch's Old Country, and an Aniforms
        puppet show for the Six Flags chain. Technical information
        included.

925   "Theme Parks." THEATRE CRAFTS 11 (September 1977): Entire issue.
        Illus.

        Special issue containing ten essays on the theme park, one
        focusing on the rise and fall of the American amusement park
        (see item 912). In addition to specifically authored essays,
        there are pictorial essays on Marriotts's Great America (Santa
        Clara, California and Gurnee, Illinois), Busch Gardens (Wil-
        liamsburg, Virginia and Tampa, Florida).

926   Willey, Day Allen. "The Trolley-Park." COSMOPOLITAN 33 (July
        1902): 265-72.

        On the phenomenon brought about by the increase in trolley
        travel for pleasure.

927   _____. "The Open-Air Amusement Park." THEATRE MAGAZINE 10
        (July 1909): 18-19. Illus.

        The nature of amusement parks of that period: "large scale
        outdoor recreation for the masses." Describes mainly the "Luna
        Park" and "Dreamland" amusement parks and the various attrac-
        tions to be found there at the time on Coney Island.

Chapter 6
VARIETY FORMS

A. MEDICINE SHOWS AND PATENT MEDICINES

928   Barton, Bob. OLD COVERED WAGON SHOW DAYS. For full entry and annotation, see item 359.

929   [Brand, Jean]. "Picturesque Medicine Shows Combined Entertainment with Salesmanship." MISSOURI HISTORICAL REVIEW 45 (July 1951): 374-76.

        Brief sketch of medicine shows in Missouri in the late nineteenth century and attempts to control medicine showmen by licensing laws.

930   Burt, William P. "Back Stage with a Medicine Show Fifty Years Ago." COLORADO MAGAZINE (July 1942): 127-36.

        Information on John Austin Hamlin and Hamlin's Wizard Oil and his show during the Civil War.

931   Camp, John. "The Golden Age of Quackery." BRITISH HISTORY ILLUSTRATED 5 (June-July 1978): 54-61. Illus.

        Useful summary survey of eighteenth-century quackery in England (with a passing mention of American examples), with the few decades preceding and following it. Camp is the author of a number of full-length studies on medical history in England.

932   Carson, Gerald. ONE FOR A MAN, TWO FOR A HORSE: A PICTORIAL HISTORY, GRAVE AND COMIC, OF PATENT MEDICINES. Garden City, N.Y.: Doubleday and Co., 1961. 128 p. Illus., index, bibliog.

        Eleven pages focus on medicine shows but the entire book provides excellent background on the topic with illustrations on all aspects of patent medicine from the early nineteenth century to Hadacol in the 1950s. Fair bibliography. Illustrations in color and black and white.

933 _____. "Sweet Extract of Hokum." AMERICAN HERITAGE 22 (June 1971): 19-27, 108-10. Illus.

Story of Lydia Pinkham's original 35.8 proof vegetable compound and other patent medicines of the late 1800s and early 1900s. Excellent illustrations of medicine-trade cards. Brief mention of medicine shows (John E. Healy and Kickapoo Indian Medicine Co., Madame DuBois, Princess Iola, Little Lotus Blossom, and others on the gasoline-torn circuit). Covers up to Geritol in the 1950s.

934 Clifford, F.J. "The Medicine Show." FRONTIER TIMES (December 1930): 92-96.

Brief and superficial survey.

935 Donovan, Richard, and Whitney, Dwight. "Painless Parker--Last of America's Tooth Plumbers." COLLIER'S 129 (5 January 1952): 7-9, 54-55; 129 (12 January): 20, 43-45; 129 (19 January): 26, 27, 38-40. Illus. (some in color).

A dental medicine showman's life and career of fifty-nine years, during which time he used acrobats, dancing girls, and a circus to attract patients. An entertaining and vivid series.

936 Douglas, W.A.S. "Pitch Doctors." AMERICAN MERCURY 10 (February 1927): 222-26.

Medicine shows in the 1920s and the survival of tent shows despite laws governing medical practice. Information on two ends of the mainline: Chicago and Oklahoma City.

937 Edstrom, David. "Medicine Men of the '80s." READERS DIGEST 32 (June 1938): 77-78.

Good condensation of the author's THE TESTAMENT OF CALIBAN (New York: Funk and Wagnalls, 1937). Outline of Dr. Lamereux's Indian Medicine Show.

938 Francesco, Grete de. THE POWER OF THE CHARLATAN. Translated by Miriam Beard. New Haven: Yale University Press, 1939. viii, 288 p. Illus., index, bibliog.

Classic work on quacks and charlatans between the sixteenth and the nineteenth centuries. Beard contributes sections on American quackery.

939   Freeman, Graydon La Verne. THE MEDICINE SHOWMAN. Watkins
       Glen, N.Y.: Century House, 1957. 100 p. Illus. Paper.

       Lore of the old peddler of nostrums, his advertisements, wagons,
       and tent shows. Includes a listing of the "Bitters" and marked
       proprietary medicine bottles that are now collector's items.
       Written by the son of a medicine show operator whose show
       was modeled after the Kickapoo Indian Show. Actual text is
       only six pages; the balance is on proprietary medicines sold
       by showmen up to 1900.

940   Hebberd, Mary Hardgrove. "Notes on Dr. David Franklin Powell."
       For full entry and annotation, see item 656.

941   Hechtlinger, Adelaide. THE GREAT PATENT MEDICINE ERA. New
       York: Grosset and Dunlap, 1970. 248 p. Illus.

       Virtually nothing on medicine shows but an intriguing collec-
       tion of illustrations and texts of books, advertisements, and
       the like on patent medicine.

942   Holbrook, Stewart H. THE GOLDEN AGE OF QUACKERY. New
       York: Macmillan Co., 1959. viii, 302 p. Index, bibliog.

       The fight against patent medicine leading to the 1906 Pure
       Food and Drug Act and a history of patent medicine from
       1790. Two parts on medicine shows. ("Masters of the Mon-
       ster Pitch" and "The World of Medicine Shows." See espe-
       cially pages 187-215 on Mrs. Violet Blossom, methods of a
       pitchman, Oregon Indian Medicine Company, and Kickapoo
       Medicine Show [Healy and Bigelow]).

943   Jameson, Eric. THE NATURAL HISTORY OF QUACKERY. London:
       Michael Joseph; Springfield, Ill.: Charles C. Thomas, 1961. 224 p.
       Illus., index, bibliog.

       History of cures and nostrums from the sixteenth century.

944   Johnston, Winifred. "Medicine Show." SOUTHWEST REVIEW 21 (July
       1936): 390-99.

       Brief history of medicine shows from the Middle Ages with a
       section on traveling medicine shows in Texas and Mississippi
       around 1886 and Oklahoma in the 1930s (Albert Yoder and
       Little Doc Roberts's Tay-Joy Show). Good for atmosphere,
       practices, and entertainment of a medicine show.

945   Kelley, Thomas P., Jr. THE FABULOUS KELLEY: HE WAS KING OF
       THE MEDICINE MEN. New York: Pocket Books; Richmond Hill, On-
       tario: Simon and Schuster of Canada, 1968. 208 p. Illus.

As told by his son, the fifty-year career of Doc Kelley
(1865-1931) as a medicine show entrepreneur in thirty-seven
states and every province in Canada.

946   LeBlanc, Thomas J. "The Medicine Show." AMERICAN MERCURY 5
(June 1925): 232-37.

Reminiscences of the medicine show's yearly visit to a small
American town. Explores the entertainment methods and selling procedures.

947   McNamara, Brooks. "The Indian Medicine Show." EDUCATIONAL
THEATRE JOURNAL 23 (December 1971): 431-45.

The traveling medicine show which flourished at the end of
the nineteenth century, expanded in his book, STEP RIGHT
UP (see item 949).

948   _____. "Medicine Shows: American Vaudeville in the Marketplace."
THEATRE QUARTERLY 4 (May-July 1974): 19-30. Illus.

Succinct history of this unique American form of popular entertainment.

949   _____. STEP RIGHT UP: AN ILLUSTRATED HISTORY OF THE AMERI-
CAN MEDICINE SHOW. Garden City, N.Y.: Doubleday and Co.,
1976. xviii [20], 233 p. Illus.

The definitive history of the American medicine show in all its
forms and permutations, from the earliest European mountebank
and charlatan to the demise of the form in the 1960s. In
addition to a large number of black-and-white illustrations,
there is a portfolio of colored reproductions of trade and advertising cards from the William Helfand Collection. Appendixes A-D provide examples of a medicine show bit and three
acts, appendix E is a glossary of pitchmen's terms. For additional sources on medicine shows, McNamara's bibliography is
useful.

950   McNeal, Violet. FOUR WHITE HORSES AND A BRASS BAND. New
York: Doubleday and Co., 1947. 267 p.

Life of one of the few female medicine show operators (Princess
Lotus Blossom) during the early twentieth century. One of the
better first-hand accounts and good on the caste system among
medicine shows: "high pitch" (prestigious performers) to "low
pitch" ("jamb workers" and sheer frauds).

951   Miller, Doc Art. "Medicine Show Tonight!" BANDWAGON 16
(July-August 1972): 20-22. Illus.

A medicine showman's reminiscences; describes wagon and show structure.

952   Nathan, George Jean. "The Medicine Men." HARPER'S WEEKLY 55 (9 September 1911): 24.

A medicine show, selling "Indian Sagwa," is outlined and methods are explored.

953   Nebel, Long John. "The Pitchman." HARPER'S 222 (May 1961): 50-54.

Radio and television advertising and the pitchman; an approach that has not altered in fifty years. Written by a former pitchman with one of the last medicine shows, it explains the process and the terminology.

954   Noell, Mae. "Some Memories of a Medicine Show Performer." THEATRE QUARTERLY 4 (May-July 1974): 25-30. Illus.

Recollections of the best-loved "bits" and life on the rural circuits. Sketches by the author show a typical setup of a medicine show in the twentieth century.

955   Oliver, N.T., as told to Stout, Wesley Winans. "Med Show." SATURDAY EVENING POST 202 (14 September 1929): 12, 166, 169, 173-74.

Good first-hand observations of Nevada Ned, a big-time showman and his summation of the ingredients of a medicine show. Also information on the Healy and Bigelow operation.

956   _____. "Alagazam, The Story of Pitchmen, High and Low." SATURDAY EVENING POST 202 (19 October 1929): 12+.

On the medicine show caste system. See preceding entry and item 950.

957   Petersen, William J. "Patent Medicine Advertising Cards." PALIMP-SEST 50 (June 1969): 317-31. Illus.

Claims and advertisements; illustrated with colored advertising cards. This is part of an issue entitled "Devils, Drugs, and Doctors" (pp. 305-68). On pages 359-62 is an 1861 account of a patent medicine man's visit to the editorial office of the IOWA VALLEY DEMOCRAT at Marengo.

958   Pickard, Madge E., and Buley, R. Caryle. THE MIDWEST PIONEER, HIS ILLS, CURES, AND DOCTORS. New York: Henry Schuman, 1946;

Crawfordsville, Ind.: R.E. Banta, 1945. 339 p. Index, bibliog., notes.

Brief mention of medicine show techniques in the Midwest but a good treatment of quackery, in general, in the nineteenth century.

959 Reeves, Dorothea D. "Come All for the Cure-all: Patent Medicines; Nineteenth Century Bonanza." HARVARD LIBRARY BULLETIN 15 (July 1967): 253-72. Illus. (16 pls.).

History of American patent medicine business; discusses itinerant medicine shows briefly. Note on trade cards.

960 Rose, Will. THE VANISHING VILLAGE. New York: Citadel Press, 1963. 350 p.

Partially fictionalized story set in Woodstock Valley, New York, between 1896 and 1903. "The Medicine Show" (pp. 130-41) deals with the visit of a medicine show. Minimal usefulness.

961 Sappington, Joe. "The Passing of the Medicine Show." FRONTIER TIMES (February 1930): 229-30.

Retrospective analysis.

962 Shafer, Henry B. THE AMERICAN MEDICAL PROFESSION, 1783 TO 1850. New York: Columbia University Press, 1937. 271 p.

Background on the allopathic physician and the effects of quacks and patent medicine on regular medicine.

963 Taylor, Robert Lewis. A JOURNEY TO MATECUMB. New York: McGraw-Hill, 1961. 424 p. Bibliog.

Fictional tale, based in part on fact, of a Dr. Ewing T. Snodgrass and his medicine showboat on the Mississippi.

964 Thompson, C[harles]. J[ohn]. S[amuel]. THE QUACKS OF OLD LONDON. New York, London, and Paris: Brentano's, 1928. xvii [19], 356 p. Illus., index.

Although virtually lacking in documentation, still an important source on the history of the mountebank. See also item 80.

965 Tully, Jim. "The Giver of Life." AMERICAN MERCURY 14 (June 1928): 154-60.

On Jonathon Maloney (Brother Jonathon) who called himself "the Giver of Life" and toured with his medicine show (which included a vaudeville act and an afterpiece) from one carnival to the next. Good description of medicine show pitches.

966   Webber, Malcolm. MEDICINE SHOW. Caldwell, Idaho: Caxton Printers, 1941. 265 p. Illus.

Fictionalized reminiscences of a traveling medicine show in the 1900s. Color frontispiece depicts Dr. J.W. Wellington and his Ton-Ko-Ko Medicine Show (tent and railroad car) illustrated by L.P. Harting.

967   Wilson, Harry Leon. PROFESSOR HOW COULD YOU? New York: Grosset and Dunlap, 1924. 340 p.

Novel by the author of RUGGLES OF RED GAP and MERTON OF THE MOVIES. A respectable professor joins a traveling medicine show. His toils, tribulations, and adventures are narrated. Chapter 6 gives a good account of medicine show structure and audience reaction.

968   Young, James Harvey. "The Hadacol Phenomenon." EMORY UNIVERSITY QUARTERLY 7 (June 1951): 72-86.

Story of this patent medicine and its promoter, Dudley J. LeBlanc.

969   _____. "Patent Medicines: The Early Post-Frontier Phase." ILLINOIS STATE HISTORICAL JOURNAL 46 (Autumn 1953): 254-64.

Background material on patent medicine in the West and the development of the medicine show.

970   _____. "American Medical Quackery in the Age of the Common Man." MISSISSIPPI VALLEY HISTORICAL REVIEW 47 (March 1961): 579-93.

"Conflicting trends in the age of the common man both accelerated a patent medicine boom and, at the same time, exposed the hazards inherent in medical quackery." Nothing specifically on medicine shows.

971   _____. "Patent Medicines and Indians." EMORY UNIVERSITY QUARTERLY 17 (Summer 1961): 86-92.

Significant role of the Indian as a promotional symbol for patent medicines from the 1820s, and the Kickapoo Indian Sagwa of the 1880s.

972   _____. THE TOADSTOOL MILLIONAIRES, A SOCIAL HISTORY OF PATENT MEDICINES IN AMERICA BEFORE FEDERAL REGULATION. Princeton, N.J.: Princeton University Press, 1961. xii, 282 p. Illus. index, note on sources.

On early American patent medicines; chapter 12 "Medicine Show" is a good documented account of the phenomenon covering such topics as charlatans in colonial America, variety in the late nineteenth century, small medicine shows, the nature of entertainment, pitches, demonstrations, and the sale of medicines. See also item 974.

973 _____. "The Patent Medicine Almanac." WISCONSIN MAGAZINE OF HISTORY 45 (Spring 1962): 159-63.

Focus on the almanac's advertising and use as a textbook, beginning in the 1840s.

974 _____. THE MEDICAL MESSIAHS. Princeton, N.J.: Princeton University Press, 1967. xiv, 460 p. Index, note on sources.

Sequel to THE TOADSTOOL MILLIONAIRES (see item 972). Whereas the first study is a criticism of patent medicines in America from the importation of British brands during the colonial days to the enactment in 1906 of the first restraining statute, the sequel deals with the rise in the twentieth century of modern medical science and of pseudomedical nonsense. "Medicine Show Impresario" (pp. 316-32) is concerned with Hadacol and Dudley LeBlanc.

B. THE MINSTREL SHOW

See also sources in Chapters 3 (A), 8, 10, and 13.

975 Belcher, Horace G. "Mr. Tambo and Mr. Bones; Rhode Island in Negro Minstrelsy." RHODE ISLAND HISTORY 8 (October 1949): 47-110.

Minstrel performers or managers either from Providence or prominent on the Providence stage up to 1917. Includes Billy Ashcroft, Denman Thompson, Ira D. Sankey, Charles H. Duprez, Lew Benedict, "Big Dic" Melville, Ben Cotton, Noah D. Payne, Sam Sharpley, and Tony Hart.

976 Blesh, Rudi, and Janis, Harriet. THEY ALL PLAYED RAGTIME. New York: Alfred A. Knopf, 1950. xviii, 338 [xviii, index] p.

Standard work on evolution of ragtime with surprisingly little on minstrelsy. Chronology of important ragtime dates, list of musical compositions by important composers, and a selected list of phonograph records and player piano rolls.

977 Bowen, Elbert R. "Negro Minstrels in Early Rural Missouri." MISSOURI

HISTORICAL REVIEW 47 (January 1953): 103-9.

Survey from 1830 to 1860 with information on J.D. Rice,
minstrel format, and the minstrels' association with the circus.

978   Brown, T. Allston. "The Origin of Negro Minstrelsy." In FUN IN
BLACK, OR SKETCHES OF MINSTREL LIFE, edited by Charles H. Day,
pp. 5-10. New York: Robert M. DeWitt, 1874. Illus. Paper.

Brown's essay, an important early account of minstrelsy's
origin (which he dates from 1799), is more important than the
series of anecdotal stories on minstrelsy by Day, a minstrel
with Arlington Minstrels, 1868-69.

979   Browne, Ray B. "Shakespeare in American Vaudeville and Negro
Minstrelsy." For full entry and annotation, see item 172.

980   Burleigh, H[enry]. T. NEGRO MINSTREL MELODIES. Preface by
W.J. Henderson. New York: G. Shirmer, 1910. vi, 52 p.

Collection of twenty-one songs with piano arrangements by
Stephen Foster, James E. Stewart, Will S. Hays, B.R. Hanby,
Henry C. Work, James A. Bland, Luke Schoolcraft, and S.S.
Steele. Useful preface on the music of negro minstrelsy.

981   Chase, Gilbert. AMERICA'S MUSIC FROM THE PILGRIMS TO THE
PRESENT. New York: McGraw-Hill, 1955. xxiii, 733 p. Index,
bibliog.

Good general history of American music and three informative
chapters on minstrelsy (pp. 232-300). Extensive bibliography.

982   Daly, John Jay. A SONG IN HIS HEART. Illustrated by Marian L.
Larer. Philadelphia and Toronto: John C. Winston Co., 1951. ix,
102 p. Illus.

Life of James Bland, composer of "Carry Me Back to Old
Virginny," and his career as a minstrel performer. Rather
undistinguished biography with words and music to his best
known songs.

983   Damon, Foster S. "The Negro in Early American Songsters." PAPERS
OF THE BIBLIOGRAPHICAL SOCIETY OF AMERICA 28 (1934): 132-63.

Preminstrel to blues; an investigation into the songsters and
their origins. Includes a bibliography of songsters in the
Harris Collection at Brown University. See item 2422.

984   Davenport, Francis Garvin. CULTURAL LIFE IN NASHVILLE ON THE
EVE OF THE CIVIL WAR. Chapel Hill: University of North Carolina

Press, 1941. x, 232 p. Index, bibliog.

Social history of the antebellum period, with a section on concerts and minstrels, 1850–60.

985   Davidson, Frank C. "The Rise, Development, Decline, and Influence of the American Minstrel Show." Ph.D. dissertation, New York University, 1952. 268 p.

Study of the background, development, and decline of the minstrel show and its influence on subsequent entertainment forms. Concludes that "the minstrel show is the only indigenous American contribution to the drama, and that the melodies the negro minstrel inspired are America's only approach to 'national music.'"

986   Day, Charles H. FUN IN BLACK, OR SKETCHES OF MINSTREL LIFE. For full entry and annotation, see item 978.

987   Demarest, Michael. "Music to Which the Gold Rushed." OPERA AND CONCERT 15 (1950): 9–11, 15–16.

Minstrel shows and balladry in San Francisco (1849–1902).

988   Dormon, James H. "The Strange Career of Jim Crow Rice." JOURNAL OF SOCIAL HISTORY 3 (Winter 1969–70): 109–22.

Documented biographical essay on Rice's life and career and his contributions to the Negro stereotype.

989   Eaton, W[alter]. P[richard]. "Dramatic Evolution and the Popular Theatre: Playhouse Roots of Our Drama." AMERICAN SCHOLAR 4 (Spring 1935): 148–59.

Eaton believed that native characters and Negro minstrels were important in the story of America's changing drama and the evolution of public taste. This essay gives a good indication of the influence of minstrelsy in the American theatre by a perceptive critic.

990   Edwall, Harry R. "The Golden Era of Minstrelsy in Memphis: A Reconstruction." WEST TENNESSEE HISTORICAL SOCIETY PAPERS no. 9 (1955): 29–47.

Useful survey.

991   Ellison, Ralph. "Change the Joke and Slip the Yoke." In his SHADOW AND ACT, pp. 45–59. New York: Vintage Books, 1954. xxiii, 317 p.

A series of essays spanning Ellison's writing career, including this one on the Negro folk tradition and a discussion of the minstrel show and the Negro image projected through that entertainment form.

992   Engle, Gary D. THIS GROTESQUE ESSENCE: PLAYS FROM THE AMERICAN MINSTREL SHOW. Baton Rouge and London: Louisiana State University Press, 1978. xxix, 200 p. Illus., bibliog.

Collection of twenty-two minstrel afterpieces from 1833 to 1871, with useful prefaces to each and a general introduction to minstrelsy entitled "American Minstrelsy and Democratic Art."

993   Epstein, Dena J. SINFUL TUNES AND SPIRITUALS: BLACK FOLK MUSIC TO THE CIVIL WAR. Urbana, Chicago, and London: University of Illinois Press, 1977. xix, 433 p. Illus., index, bibliog.

Excellent survey with brief reference to black minstrelsy. Extensive bibliography on all aspects of black music, including minstrelsy.

994   Field, Al [fred]. G [riffith]. WATCH YOURSELF GO BY. Illustrated by Ben W. Warden. Columbus, Ohio: Spahr and Glenn, 1912. [2], 537 p.

Minstrel and circus reminiscences of the nineteenth century.

995   Fletcher, Tom. 100 YEARS OF THE NEGRO IN SHOW BUSINESS. New York: Burdge and Co., 1954. 337 p. Illus.

Good coverage of minstrelsy with a focus on individual performers or composers of the more notable minstrels, such as Billy Kerstand, Sam Lucas, and James Bland. Fletcher joined Howard's Novelty Colored Minstrels in 1888.

996   Gaul, Harvey B. "The Minstrel of the Alleghenies." THE WESTERN PENNSYLVANIA HISTORY MAGAZINE 34 (March 1951): 1-22; 34 (June 1951): 97-118; 34 (September 1951): 168-84; 34 (December 1951): 239-60. Reprint. Pittsburgh: Friends of Harvey Gaul, n.d. 86 p. Paper.

Minstrelsy in Pennsylvania with a focus on the Foster family and the life of the ninth son, Stephen (1826-64), mostly in Pittsburgh.

997   Green, Alan W.C. "'Jim Crow,' 'Zip Coon'; The Northern Origins of Negro Minstrelsy." MASSACHUSETTS REVIEW 11 (Spring 1970): 385-97.

Green discusses first, pre-1800 stage Negroes in American

plays which had begun to reflect white American attitudes toward "real" Negroes, and, then "Negro" dances and songs as special acts on the American stage, which, by the end of the eighteenth century were a standard part of theatre repertory. Green then turns to more immediate events, George Washington Dixon and J.D. Rice, and a general discussion of the full-fledged minstrel show. An excellent essay.

998   Greenwood, Isaac J. THE CIRCUS: ITS ORIGIN AND GROWTH PRIOR TO 1835. WITH A SKETCH ON NEGRO MINSTRELSY. For full entry and annotation, see item 437.

999   Handy, W[illiam]. C[hristopher]. FATHER OF THE BLUES. Edited by Arna Bontemps. New York: Macmillan Co., 1941. xiv, 317 p. Index.

Reminiscences of the black minstrel and blues composer. Includes a list of his compositions and books.

1000   Haverly, Jack. NEGRO MINSTRELS: A COMPLETE GUIDE. Chicago: Frederick J. Drake and Co., 1902. 129 p. Paper. Reprint. Boston: Gregg Press, 1969.

An interesting "how to" book by a successful minstrel manager.

1001   Haywood, Charles. A BIBLIOGRAPHY OF NORTH AMERICAN FOLK-LORE AND FOLKSONG. New York: Greenberg, 1951. xxx, 1,292 p. Index; 2d rev. ed. 2 vols. New York: Dover Publications, 1961.

Contains the best bibliography of minstrel songsters (1st ed., pp. 522-41), but not definitive.

1002   _____. "Negro Minstrelsy and Shakespearean Burlesque." In FOLK-LORE AND SOCIETY, edited by Bruce Jackson, pp. 77-92. Hatboro, Pa.: Folklore Associates, 1966.

Good discussion of the exploitation of Shakespeare for burlesque and comic opera travesty. Information on "Ethiopian Extravaganzas" during their heyday, 1850 to 1870.

1003   Howard, John Trasker. STEPHEN FOSTER: AMERICA'S TROUBADOUR. Rev. ed. New York: Thomas Y. Crowell Co., 1954. xv, 433 p. Illus., index.

The definitive, documented biography of Foster, which includes a chronological outline, published works of Foster, and a list of the authors of words to songs for which Foster wrote the music.

1004   Huggins, Nathan. HARLEM RENAISSANCE. New York: Oxford
University Press, 1971. xi, 343 p. Index, notes.

On pages 244-302, Huggins closely examines the role of the
Negro in the history of American entertainment from a liberal,
contemporary black perspective. After having been misrepre-
sented on the American stage for so long (e.g., in minstrel
shows), black Americans, he states, were still struggling to
establish their own ethnic theatre at the time this book was
written. "Black identity has been, too often, the projection
of white vision and white needs," he concludes.

1005   Hutton, Laurence. "The Negro on the Stage." HARPER'S MAGAZINE
79 (June-November 1889): 131-45.

Hutton traces the origin of minstrelsy to a Mr. Graupner in
1799 and touches on other early manifestations leading up to
T.D. Rice. Includes most major minstrel companies and
performers in his essay in which he makes little or no distinc-
tion between real black and blackface performers.

1006   Johnson, James Weldon. BLACK MANHATTAN. For full entry and
annotation, see item 1573.

1007   Jones, LeRoi. BLUES PEOPLE: NEGRO MUSIC IN WHITE AMERICA.
New York: William Morrow and Co., 1963. xii, 244 p. Index.

Perspective on the black blues singer and bands in black
minstrel shows, vaudeville shows, carnivals, and circuses.
Insight into black minstrelsy (pp. 82-166) especially useful.
Serviceable as a general theoretical introduction to Negro
music in the United States.

1008   Kaufmann, Helen L. FROM JEHOVAH TO JAZZ. New York: Dodd
Mead, and Co., 1937. xii, 303 p.

Includes a chapter on minstrels (pp. 221-39), which, other
than its focus on the music, adds little to a basic understanding of the form.

1009   Keeler, Ralph. "Three Years a Negro Minstrel." ATLANTIC MONTHLY
24 (July 1869): 71-85.

An account of the author's stint with Spaulding and Rogers's
"Floating Circus Palace" and other experiences as a minstrel
during its early years (1860s). Interesting and often insightful. See below.

1010   _____ . VAGABOND ADVENTURES. Boston: Fields, Osgood and
Co., 1870. viii, [11] 274 p.

Book 2 (pp. 101-220) covers his three years as a traveling minstrel in the Booker Troupe, "The Mitchells," and finally, Dr. Spaulding's Floating Palace. See above.

1011   Kendall, John Smith. "New Orleans Negro Minstrels." LOUISIANA HISTORICAL QUARTERLY 30 (January 1947): 128-48.

New Orleans' contributions to minstrelsy in the nineteenth century; specific information is provided on such minstrel performers as Geo. Washington Dixon, Luke Schoolcraft, James C. Fulton, Barry Maxwell, Bill Payne, Ed. H. Banker, Billy Carter, Wash Norton, and John Queen. The manager Charles H. Duprez is included also.

1012   Kinnard, J. "Who Are Our National Poets?" KNICKERBOCKER MAGAZINE 26 (October 1845): 331-41.

Proposes that America's truly original poets of the period (slave performers on the plantation) had their work corrupted and burlesqued from the ranks of minstrelsy. Examples are cited and discussed.

1013   Kmen, Henry A. "Old Corn Meal: A Forgotten Urban Negro Folk-singer." JOURNAL OF AMERICAN FOLKLORE 75 (January-March 1962): 29-34.

Theatrical career of a Negro vendor and singer in the late 1830s and '40s, alleged to be the first appearance of a Negro on the white stage in New Orleans (St. Charles Theatre) and perhaps the United States. Author suggests that Corn Meal was a direct influence on the minstrel show and presents the sketchy evidence.

1014   Leavitt, M[ichael]. B[ennett]. FIFTY YEARS IN THEATRICAL MANAGEMENT, 1859-1909. For full entry and annotation, see item 1160.

1015   Leonard, Eddie [Lemuel Toney]. WHAT A LIFE I'M TELLING YOU. For full entry and annotation, see item 228.

1016   Locke, Alain. THE NEGRO AND HIS MUSIC & NEGRO ART: PAST AND PRESENT. Washington, D.C.: Associates in Negro Folk Education, 1936. Reprint. 2 booklets in 1. New York: Arno Press, 1969. 122 p. Bibliog.

The former includes interesting chapters on "The First Age of Minstrelsy, 1850-1875," "The Second Age of Minstrelsy, 1875-1895," and "Ragtime and Negro Musical Comedy, 1895-1925." Locke was the first Negro to be awarded a Rhodes Scholarship and was professor of philosophy at Howard University.

1017   Logan, Olive. "The Ancestry of Brudder Bones." HARPER'S MONTHLY
        58 (April 1879): 687-98.

    Logan discusses George Christy and Dan Bryant, and attempts
    to show parallels between American minstrelsy and medieval
    bas-reliefs of musicians, as well as similarities to instruments
    used by ancient civilizations and those of the minstrels,
    bones, banjo, and so forth.

1018   Matthews, Brander. "The Rise and Fall of Negro Minstrelsy." SCRIB-
        NER'S MAGAZINE 57 (January-June 1915): 754-59.

    Mathews traces the rise of minstrelsy from T.D. Rice, its
    evolution and form, and its decline as it began to turn to
    spectacular elaboration of the original entertainment. A fair
    summary.

1019   "Melodies and Soft Shoes in Blackface." MISSOURI HISTORICAL RE-
        VIEW 38 (January 1944): 192-95.

    Cursory survey of minstrelsy in Missouri in the nineteenth
    century.

1020   Miller, Kelly. "The Negro 'Stephen Foster'." ETUDE 57 (July 1939):
        431-32, 472. Illus.

    Sketchy biography of James A. Bland, written by an educator
    born a slave in South Carolina.

1021   Moody, Richard. "Negro Minstrelsy." QUARTERLY JOURNAL OF
        SPEECH 30 (October 1944): 321-28.

    Good appraisal of minstrelsy, largely as a romantic invention
    of Northern whites, with a historical summary.

1022   _____. AMERICA TAKES THE STAGE. For full entry and annotation,
        see item 1925.

1023   _____. DRAMAS FROM THE AMERICAN THEATRE, 1762-1909. For
        full entry and annotation, see item 1926.

1024   Nathan, Hans. "The First Negro Minstrel Band and Its Origins."
        SOUTHERN FOLKLORE QUARTERLY 16 (June 1952): 132-44.

    The formation of the Virginia Minstrels in 1843 is explored.

1025   _____. DAN EMMETT AND THE RISE OF EARLY NEGRO MINSTRELSY.
        Norman: University of Oklahoma Press, 1962. xiv, 496 p. Illus.,
        index, bibliog., notes.

Life of the minstrel and the early period of minstrelsy from the point of view of a musicologist. Includes a bibliography of Emmett's work (pp. 290-306).

1026 Nathanson, Y.S. "Negro Minstrelsy--Ancient and Modern." In MAGA PAPERS, pp. 277-96. New York: G.P. Putnam and Son, 1867.

Evolution of minstrelsy from "Jim Crow" song and dance beginnings and the difference between songs of African minstrelsy and Northern white imitations. See item 1045.

1027 Nevin, R.P. "Stephen C. Foster and Negro Minstrelsy." ATLANTIC MONTHLY 20 (November 1867): 608-16.

Life and career of Foster. Extensive coverage of T.D. Rice, mistakenly called W.D. Rice.

1028 Paskman, Dailey, [and Spaeth, Sigmund]. "GENTLEMEN, BE SEATED!" A PARADE OF THE OLD-TIME MINSTRELS. Garden, N.Y.: Doubleday, Doran, 1928. Rev. ed. New York: Clarkson N. Potter, 1976. xiv, 253 p. Illus., index.

A romanticized history and study of minstrelsy with music, sample minstrel routines, and good illustrations (photographs and prints). New edition is updated (mostly by way of illustration) to include Judy Garland, Mickey Rooney, Scott Joplin, and Ben Vereen.

1029 Patterson, Cecil L. "A Different Drummer: The Image of the Negro in Nineteenth Century Popular Song Books." Ph.D. dissertation, University of Pennsylvania, 1961. 1,161 p.

A study of nineteenth-century popular song books and other writings showing the attitudes reflected in America toward the nineteenth-century black American.

1030 _____. "A Different Drummer: The Image of the Negro in Nineteenth Century Songsters." CALIFORNIA LANGUAGE ASSOCIATION 8 (September 1964): 44-50.

Essay based on his dissertation; see above.

1031 Patterson, Lindsay, ed. THE NEGRO IN MUSIC AND ART. 2d rev. ed. New York: Publishers Co. under the auspices of the Association for the Study of Negro Life and History, 1970. xvi, 304 p. Illus., index, bibliog.

Anthology of essays on music and art, including Locke's essay on minstrelsy (see item 1016) and other useful background essays on Negro music.

1032   Ramshaw, Molly Niederlander. "Jump, Jim Crow! A Biographical
       Sketch of Thomas D. Rice." THEATRE ANNUAL 17 (1960): 36-47.

       The life of T.D. Rice, the first blackface comedian.

1033   Rehin, George F. "The Darker Image: American Negro Minstrelsy
       through the Historian's Lens." JOURNAL OF AMERICAN STUDIES 9
       (December 1975): 365-73.

       Trends in scholarly studies of minstrelsy reviewed; ostensibly
       a review of Toll's BLACKING UP (see item 1042).

1034   _____. "Harlequin Jim Crow: Continuity and Convergence in Black-
       face Clowning." JOURNAL OF POPULAR CULTURE 9 (Winter 1975):
       682-701.

       Useful as a review of the literature of blackface minstrelsy.
       The author then attempts to explain minstrelsy in something
       other than American terms, essentially through a study of the
       adoption of the minstrel mode in Britain, and to show through
       other European traditions the kindred spirit of Jim Crow to
       harlequin, clown, and others.

1035   Reynolds, Harry. MINSTREL MEMORIES; THE STORY OF BURNT CORK
       MINSTRELSY IN GREAT BRITAIN FROM 1836-1927. London: Alston
       Rivers, 1928. 256 p. Illus.

       Development of minstrelsy in Great Britain, its originators
       there, where it stood in relation to other popular entertain-
       ment forms of the time, location of minstrel shows, and the
       content of such shows. Also a section on the major British
       minstrel troupes and their leaders. Well illustrated; reprint
       of numerous songs.

1036   Rice, Edward LeRoy. MONARCHS OF MINSTRELSY FROM "DADDY"
       RICE TO DATE. New York: Kenny Publishing Co., 1911. 366 p.
       Illus., index (10 p.).

       Sketch of minstrelsy in America and minstrel specialists; index
       of minstrels and a list of organizations. Good for general
       reference; photographs of most performers accompany the text.
       Includes ten-page index.

1037   Sawyer, E.T. "Old-Time Minstrels of San Francisco. Recollections of
       a Pioneer." OVERLAND MONTHLY 81 (October 1923): 5-7.

       Ben Cotton, Joe Murphy, Dan Bryant, Lew Rattler, Harry
       Hank, Billy Emerson, Sam Rickey, Billy Courtright, Charley
       Rhoades, and other minstrel favorites of the 1860s are remem-
       bered.

1038 Simond, Ike. OLD SLACKS'S REMINISCENCES AND POCKET HISTORY OF THE COLORED PROFESSION FROM 1865 TO 1891. Edited by Robert C. Toll and Francis Lee Utley. Bowling Green, Ohio: Popular Press, 1974. xxxiv, 123 p. Illus., index, bibliog.

> Knowledgeable account of nineteenth-century black performers; lists over a thousand names. Excellent preface by Utley and introduction by Toll. Originally published ca. 1892, it is a precious, although limited resource.

1039 Spinney, Frank Oakman. "A New Hampshire Minstrel Tours the Coast." CALIFORNIA HISTORICAL SOCIETY QUARTERLY 20 (September 1941): 243-58.

> Rhodolphus Hall, "Plough-Boy of '44" and "New Hampshire Minstrel," and his tour of California in the mid-1860s. Includes six edited letters written by Hall from California during his tour.

1040 Stoutamire, Albert. MUSIC OF THE OLD SOUTH: COLONY TO CONFEDERACY. Rutherford, Madison, and Teaneck, N.J.: Fairleigh Dickinson University Press, 1972. 349 p. Illus., index, bibliog.

> A history of music in Richmond, Virginia, with frequent references to minstrel entertainment.

1041 Suthern, Orrin Clayton II. "Minstrelsy and Popular Culture." JOURNAL OF POPULAR CULTURE 4 (Winter 1971): 658-73.

> Contributors to popular shows of the nineteenth century are examined, plus offshoots of the minstrel show.

1042 Toll, Robert C. BLACKING UP: THE MINSTREL SHOW IN NINETEENTH CENTURY AMERICA. New York: Oxford University Press, 1974. x, 310 p. Illus., index, bibliog.

> The most comprehensive history and analysis of the minstrel show to date; portrays minstrelsy as an institution that spoke for and to huge numbers of common Americans. Chronological list of real black minstrel troupes, 1855-90, is provided in an appendix. Superb bibliography. A paperback edition appeared in 1977 (Oxford). See below and item 265.

1043 _____. "Behind the Blackface: Minstrel Men and Minstrel Myths." AMERICAN HERITAGE 29 (April-May 1978): 93-105. Illus. (9 in color).

> A summary of Toll's work on minstrelsy, drawn from BLACKING UP (above) and ON WITH THE SHOW (item 265).

1044 Trotter, James Monroe. MUSIC AND SOME HIGHLY MUSICAL

PEOPLE. Boston: Lee and Shepard; New York: Charles T. Dillingham, 1881. Reprint. New York: Johnson Reprint, 1968. 152 p.

Classic work on black musicians of the nineteenth century. Chapter 20, "The Georgia Minstrels," is especially useful. Trotter bemoans the fact that present minstrelsy has "deviated from the refined, the brilliant practices of their predecessors."

1045   Trux, J.J.   "Negro Minstrelsy--Ancient and Modern."   PUTNAM'S MONTHLY 5 (1885): 72-79.

Dated essay which focuses on minstrel music. Contrasts Negro slave songs to white Northern minstrel imitations after 1841. See item 1026.

1046   White, Newman.   "The White Man in the Woodpile."   AMERICAN SPEECH 4 (February 1929): 207-15.

Blackface minstrel influences on Negro secular folk-songs.

1047   White, Stanley.   "The Burnt-Cork Illusion of the 1920s in America: A Study in Nostalgia."   JOURNAL OF POPULAR CULTURE 5 (Winter 1971): 530-50.

Extensions of the minstrel mode are analyzed, such as Al Jolson, Amos 'n' Andy, and other examples from the 1920s.

1048   Winter, Marian Hannah.   "Juba and American Minstrelsy."   DANCE INDEX 6 (1947): 28-47.

Career of William Henry "Juba" Lane perceptively discussed. Demonstrates the impact of Afro-American dance on the minstrel show.

1049   Wittke, Carl.   TAMBO AND BONES. A HISTORY OF THE MINSTREL SHOW. Durham, N.C.: Duke University Press, 1930. Reprint. Westport, Conn.: Greenwood Press, 1968. ix, 269 p. Index.

Though dated, still an excellent basic history and explanation of minstrelsy form but without an analysis of its implications.

1050   Zanger, Jules.   "The Minstrel Show as Theater of Misrule."   QUARTERLY JOURNAL OF SPEECH 60 (February 1974): 33-38.

Analysis of the minstrel show that revals it had as its target the pieties of genteel culture, education, and art.

C. EARLY VARIETY AND VAUDEVILLE

1051   Adams, Franklin P.   "Olympic Days."   SATURDAY EVENING POST

201 (22 June 1929): 18, 123, 126.

Vaudeville during the first ten years of the nineteenth century; "the Rainbow Decade" recalled.

1052 Adams, Joey, with Tobias, Henry. THE BORSCHT BELT. New York, Indianapolis, and Kansas City: Bobbs-Merrill Co., 1959.

In the 1930s and '40s, resorts in the Catskills became a haven for comics and training ground for entertainers formerly weaned in vaudeville; indeed, the Borscht Belt became a new kind of vaudeville circuit. This is the story of this phenomenon by comic, Joey Adams.

1053 Adamson, Joe. GROUCHO, HARPO, CHICO--AND SOMETIMES ZEPPO. A HISTORY OF THE MARX BROTHERS AND A SATIRE ON THE REST OF THE WORLD. New York: Simon and Schuster, 1973. 464 p. Illus., index, bibliog.

One chapter, "Antiquity," concerns their stage and vaudeville career from ca. 1907 to 1919.

1054 Albee, Edward F. "Twenty Years of Vaudeville." THEATRE MAGAZINE 31 (May 1920): 408, 450.

Biased evaluation of the progress of vaudeville over the preceding twenty years by the president of the B.F. Keith circuit.

1055 "The Apotheosis of Vaudeville." CURRENT LITERATURE 33 (November 1902): 523

Editorial comment on the transformation of vaudeville into respectability.

1056 Bakshy, Alexander. "Vaudeville Must Be Saved." NATION 129 (24 July 1929): 98, 100.

Plea for the revival of good vaudeville, original and inventive, with real talent, unity, and coherence in the performance as a whole. Interesting retrospective look at the decline of vaudeville.

1057 _____. "Vaudeville's Prestige." NATION 129 (4 Sptember 1929): 258.

"Vaudeville has lost 'class' as an art form, and this is only one step removed from ultimately losing itself." Good analysis of ills.

1058 Barber, W. Charles. A Great Show Town: Golden Age of Elmira's Theaters, Movies." CHEMUNG HISTORICAL JOURNAL 7 (June 1962): 975-82.

Vaudeville in a small New York town.

1059   Bayes, Nora. "Holding My Audience." THEATRE MAGAZINE 26 (September 1917): 128.

       Analysis by the vaudeville performer of her techniques for winning an audience.

1060   Bell, Archie. A LITTLE JOURNEY TO B.F. KEITH PALACE, CLEVE-LAND. Cleveland: N.p., n.d. 46 p. Paper.

       Romanticized description of the vaudeville house built by E.F. Albee at Euclid Avenue and East Seventeenth Street in Cleveland, Ohio.

1061   Beuick, Marshall D. "The Vaudeville Philosopher." DRAMA 16 (December 1925): 92-93, 116.

       The reflection in vaudeville of a common, limited, and not too optimistic view of life is discussed.

1062   Blesh, Rudi. KEATON. New York: Macmillan Co., 1966. xii, 395 p. Illus., index.

       The life of Joseph Frank "Buster Keaton" written with the subject's cooperation. Excellent coverage of Keaton's stage career beginning with the medicine shows in 1897 and moving into the golden years of vaudeville.

1063   Brady, Cyrus T. "A Vaudeville Turn." SCRIBNER'S MAGAZINE 30 (September 1901): 351-55.

       Reveals the use of plants in audiences (example: small girl on stage, discovered by "Papa" in house and a tear-jerking story about mother running away and having not seen Nellie for two years).

1064   Briggs, Harold E. "Early Variety Theatres in the Trans-Mississippi West." MID-AMERICA 34 (July 1952): 188-202.

       Survey of early variety in mid-America with interesting images.

1065   Bristow, Eugene Kerr. "Look Out for Saturday Night: A Social History of Professional Variety Theatre in Memphis, Tennessee, 1859-1880." Ph.D. dissertation, University of Iowa, 1957. 241 p.

       Covers the progress and decline of variety theatres from 1859-80 focusing on one American city. Study sought to clarify the meaning and range of the term "Variety Theatre." Considers the managers, variety personnel, program fare, and audiences. Extremely useful for early variety.

1066   _____. "The Low Varieties Program in Memphis, 1865-1873." QUAR-

TERLY JOURNAL OF SPEECH 44 (December 1958): 423-27.

Adapted in part from preceding source. History of variety in Memphis during a period that emphasized the female performer, a wine room, and pretty waitresses.

1067 _____. Variety Theatre in Memphis, 1859-1862." WEST TENNESSEE HISTORICAL SOCIETY PAPERS 13 (1959): 117-27.

Historical survey of the period preceding the above source.

1068 _____. "Charley Broom, Variety Manager in Memphis, Tennessee, 1866-1872." SOUTHERN SPEECH JOURNAL 25 (Fall 1959): 11-20.

Career of Charles H.H. Broom and the history of Memphis low varieties.

1069 Brock, H.I. "Vaudeville Still the Same--and Still Going Strong." NEW YORK TIMES MAGAZINE (16 January 1944): 16-17. Illus.

Contends that vaudeville reached a new level of popularity when Bob Hope began entertaining servicemen abroad. The war created a strong need for entertainment on American soil as well.

1070 Brown, T. Allston, and Day, Charles H. FUN IN BLACK, OR SKETCHES OF MINSTREL LIFE. New York: Robert M. DeWitt, 1874. 70 p. Illus. Paper.

Contains brief references to Tony Pastor. See also item 978.

1071 Browne, Ray B. "Shakespeare in American Vaudeville and Negro Minstrelsy." For full entry and annotation, see item 172.

1072 "Browsing the Vaudeville Talent." THEATRE 20 (December 1914): 281-82, 295.

Role of the browsing agent and how talent is located.

1073 Caffin, Caroline, and Zayas, Malins de. VAUDEVILLE. New York: Mitchell Kemerley, 1914. 231 p. Index.

Series of critical essays on vaudeville as seen by a member of the audience.

1074 Canfield, Mary C. "The Great American Art." NEW REPUBLIC 32 (22 November 1922): 334-35.

The American art is vaudeville.

1075   Cantor, Eddie, as told to Freedman, David. MY LIFE IS IN YOUR
        HANDS. Foreword by Will Rogers. New York: Blue Ribbon Books,
        1932. xiv, 309 p. Illus.

>   Cantor's life up to age thirty-six. Deals with his experiences
>   with Gus Edwards's "Kid Kabaret" and Georgie Jessel in
>   vaudeville and his later career in Ziegfeld's revues. Very
>   personal and informal.

1076   Carrillo, Leo. THE CALIFORNIA I LOVE. Englewood Cliffs, N.J.:
        Prentice-Hall, 1961. 280 p.

>   Although remembered for his Mexican roles in films, Carrillo
>   was also a monologist in vaudeville and his first appearance
>   performing before an audience of Sioux Indians in Chicago
>   is a classic "show biz" story.

1077   Carson, Saul. "Theatre: Vaudeville." NEW REPUBLIC 120 (13 June
        1949): 19-20.

>   On the attempt to revive vaudeville at the Palace Theatre and
>   the inevitability of its failure.

1078   Cohen, Octavus Roy. "Vaudeville." COLLIER'S 79 (12 February 1927):
        24.

>   Short story based on a big-time vaudevillian.

1079   Collins, Sewell. "Breaking Into Vaudeville." COLLIER'S 42 (20 March
        1909): 20, 28.

>   Humorous essay on the "genial art" of writing one-act playlets
>   for vaudeville.

1080   Copley, Frank B. "The Story of a Great Vaudeville Manager, E.F.
        Albee." AMERICAN MAGAZINE 94 (December 1922): 46-47, 152-
        53, 154-55. Illus.

>   Unabashedly biased and flattering account of Albee's life and
>   contributions to vaudeville.

1081   Crane, Warren E. "Alexander Pantages." SYSTEM 37 (March 1920):
        501-3.

>   Career of the vaudeville impresario.

1082   Cressy, Will M. CONTINUOUS VAUDEVILLE. Boston: Richard G.
        Badger, 1914. 181 p. Illus.

>   All aspects of vaudeville, especially small-time, are touched
>   upon in this vaudevillian's disjointed, anecdotal memoir; door-

man, one-night stand orchestras, types of acts, vaudeville
versus legit, and so forth.

1083   Crichton, Kyle. THE MARX BROTHERS. Garden City, N.Y.: Doubleday and Co., 1950. viii, 310 p. Illus.

Career of Harpo, Chico, Groucho, Zeppo, and Gummo, with
and emphasis on their early escapades in vaudeville.

1084   David, John Russell. "The Genesis of the Variety Theatre: The Black
Crook Comes to St. Louis." MISSOURI HISTORICAL REVIEW 64 (January 1970): 133-49. Illus.

The development of variety at Deagle's Varieties Theatre in
St. Louis and the import of THE BLACK CROOK in 1867.

1085   Davis, Hartley. "In Vaudeville." EVERYBODY'S MAGAZINE 13
(August 1905): 231-40.

Traces the development from variety to vaudeville, including
discussions of the most popular types of acts.

1086   _____. The Business Side of Vaudeville." EVERYBODY'S MAGA-
ZINE 17 (October 1907): 527-37.

On the structure of vaudeville.

1087   _____. "Tabloid Drama." EVERYBODY'S MAGAZINE 21 (August
1909): 249-57. Illus.

On the lack of one-act plays ("tabloid dramas") produced in
"first-class" American theatres of the time. Such dramas were,
however, to be found in vaudeville houses. Discusses vaudeville and the types of tabloid dramas to be found there,
vaudeville's advancing standards, and predictions for the future of tabloid drama in vaudeville houses.

1088   Davis, Sammy, Jr.; Boyar, Jane; and Boyak, Burt. YES I CAN: THE
STORY OF SAMMY DAVIS, JR. New York: Farrar, Straus and Giroux,
1965. 630 p. Illus.

Autobiography of one of the top entertainers of today who began his career in vaudeville.

1089   Davy, Kate. "An Interview with George Burns." EDUCATIONAL
THEATRE JOURNAL 27 (October 1975): 345-55.

Some interesting insights into Burns's career in vaudeville,
especially with his wife, Gracie Allen. Burns and Allen
played the top vaudeville houses until 1933 when they began

their radio show. This interview occurred during the period in 1974 in which Burns was promoting his movie based (in part) on the vaudeville team of Smith and Dale, Neil Simon's THE SUNSHINE BOYS. This is more useful than Burns's various memoirs which are excluded from this guide.

1090 "The Decay of Vaudeville." AMERICAN MAGAZINE 69 (April 1910): 840-48. Illus.

Develops the premise that "no refined or gentle person can visit a vaudeville house without running the risk of encountering the ribaldry and atmosphere of the corner barroom."

1091 "Decline of Vaudeville." HARPER'S MONTHLY 106 (April 1903): 811-15.

A familiar theme at the turn of the century is rehashed.

1092 DeLeon, Walter. "The Wow Finish." SATURDAY EVENING POST 197 (14 February 1925): 16, 44, 47-48. Illus.

On how to form a vaudeville act with various examples.

1093 DiMeglio, John E. "New York vs. Rural America . . . Who Ruled Vaudeville?" MANKATO STATE COLLEGE TODAY 2 (Fall 1970): 8-9.

Vaudeville outside of New York City; developed more fully in next source.

1094 _____. VAUDEVILLE U.S.A. Bowling Green, Ohio: Bowling Green University Popular Press, 1973. 259 p. Illus., index, bibliog.

The best-documented single-volume history of vaudeville and its role in the nation's development; extensive notes and bibliography. Highly recommended.

1095 Distler, Paul A. "The Rise and Fall of the Racial Comics in American Vaudeville." Ph.D. dissertation, Tulane University, 1963. 226 p.

Investigation into the emergence, popularity, decline, and eventual disappearance of the Irish, Dutch, and Jewish vaudeville comic. Includes representative monologue, sketches, and song lyrics of famous racial comics, e.g., Weber and Fields, Julian Rose, J.W. Kelly, and Harrigan and Hart.

1096 _____. "Exit the Racial Comics." EDUCATIONAL THEATRE JOURNAL 18 (October 1966): 247-54.

Adapted from his dissertation, above, the racial comic who ruled the comic realm of variety from the 1880s through the early years of this century was a thing of the past by the 1920s. A recent paper delivered at the Conference on the History of Popular Entertainment on the same topic is to be published soon. See item 52.

1097   Douglas, W.A.S. "The Passing of Vaudeville." AMERICAN MERCURY 12 (October 1927): 188-94.

On the merger of vaudeville circuits, competition with the movies, fed and nurtured by vaudeville, and the necessity of "big-time" to meet the "moviemen" on their own grounds.

1098   Eaton, Walter Prichard. "The Wizards of Vaudeville." McCLURE 55 (September 1923): 43-49. Illus. (11 photos).

How B.F. Keith and E.F. Albee, starting with a dime museum, became owners of their magnificent chain of theatres.

1099   "Editor's Easy Chair." HARPER'S MONTHLY MAGAZINE 106 (April 1903): 811-15.

A fictional conversation between two editors on the virtues of vaudeville versus legitimate theatre.

1100   Elliott, Eugene Clinton. A HISTORY OF VARIETY--VAUDEVILLE IN SEATTLE. Seattle: University of Washington Press, 1944. 83 p., Illus., index. Paper.

Survey from 1852 to 1914.

1101   "Enter the Italian on the Vaudeville Stage." SURVEY 24 (7 May 1910): 198-99.

Rise of Italian and Scotch characters in vaudeville; distortion of Italian girls (much like the Negro beauty of ragtime melody and the tough girl of Irish comics).

1102   Foster, William Trufant. VAUDEVILLE AND MOTION PICTURE SHOWS. A STUDY OF THEATRE IN PORTLAND, OREGON. Portland: Reed College, 1914. 63 p.

Results of a committee study showing the effects of vaudeville on young audiences.

1103   Foy, Eddie, and Harlow, Alvin F. "Clowning Through Life." COL-LIER'S 79 (5 February 1927): 25, 28, 37; 79 (12 February): 17-18, 52-53; 79 (19 February): 28, 30, 36; 79 (26 February): 19, 36, 38-39.

Life of Eddie Foy in vaudeville and musical theatre, along with the Seven Little Foys. Memoirs of the Iroquois Theatre fire and his heroism in trying to check the panic. Expanded in the next entry.

1104 _____. CLOWNING THROUGH LIFE. New York: E.P. Dutton and Co., 1928. 331 p. Illus.

Expanded version of preceding source.

1105 Freedland, Michael. JOLSON. New York: Stein and Day, 1972. 256 p. Illus., index.

The most definitive, albeit undocumented, recent biography of Al Jolson and his career in vaudeville and revue (although not as thorough as on his later career in films).

1106 "From Honky-Tonk to Palace." LIFE 35 (7 December 1953): 38.

Editorial on Joe Laurie's book VAUDEVILLE (see item 1158).

1107 Gehman, Richard B. "Daddy of the Small Time." COLLIER'S 126 (23 September 1950): 30, 72.

Career of Gus Sun who, during his heyday, owned ten booking offices that fed acts into 275 theatres. He was also a juggler, medicine show doctor, circus proprietor, Tom show impresario, minstrel man, and theatre owner.

1108 Gilbert, Douglas. AMERICAN VAUDEVILLE: ITS LIFE AND TIMES. New York: Whittlesey House, 1940. Reprint. New York: Dover Publications, 1968. x, 428 p. Illus., index, appendix.

A standard and still useful history of vaudeville and its predecessors. Some errors corrected by later histories, especially on early variety and Pastor's contributions to vaudeville. Appendix lists fifty years of standard acts from 1880.

1109 Goewey, Edwin A. "Tony Pastor, the Starmaker." DANCE MAGAZINE 12 (August 1929): 12-13, 57, 58.

Life of the pioneer variety impresario.

1110 Golden, George Fuller. MY LADY VAUDEVILLE AND HER WHITE RATS. New York: Broadway Publishing Co., 1909. ii, 199 p. (plus 35 p. of photos).

Golden's efforts to create a union for vaudeville performers fashioned after the English model. Photographs of the officers, trustees, board of directors, secretary of directors, and general counsel of the White Rats of America.

1111   "The Golden Age of Vaudeville." CURRENT LITERATURE 42 (June 1907): 669.

    Notion that this was the golden age of vaudeville, when vaudeville had in many instances assumed the functions of legitimate drama. Quotes Ludwig Lewisohn in the Charleston NEWS AND COURIER on its value as a source of pleasure.

1112   Goodwin, Nat C. NAT GOODWIN'S BOOK. Boston: Richard G. Badger, 1914. xv, 366 p. Illus., index.

    Theatrical memoirs; good on variety and the late nineteenth-century American theatre.

1113   [Gotlieb, George A.]. "Psychology of the American Vaudeville Show. From the Manager's Point of View." CURRENT LITERATURE 60 (April 1916): 257-58.

    Analysis of the structure of the vaudeville show by the booker for the Palace Theatre in New York. Based, in part, on Page's WRITING FOR VAUDEVILLE (see item 1181).

1114   Grau, Robert. FORTY YEARS OF OBSERVATION OF MUSIC AND THE DRAMA. New York: Broadway Publishing Co., 1909. 370 p. Illus.

    Memoirs with particular attention to vaudeville. See also item 200, and sources by Grau, below.

1115   _____. "The Origin of Amateur Night." INDEPENDENT 69 (20 October 1910): 851-52.

    Brief history of this phenomenon (primarily at the Bowery Theatre) and a look at the performers. Contrast with current vogue.

1116   _____. "A Napoleon of the Vaudeville World." THEATRE 12 (October 1910): 117, x.

    On William Morris and the Morris vaudeville circuit.

1117   _____. THE BUSINESS MAN IN THE AMUSEMENT WORLD. New York: Broadway Publishing Co., 1910. 362 p. Illus., index, bibliog.

    Good study of business in theatre during the late nineteenth century, especially vaudeville and the operations of the syndicate.

1118   _____. "The Amazing Prosperity of the Vaudeville Entertainer." OVERLAND 57 (June 1911): 608-9.

Managers and performers who have become millionaires over
the preceding decade and their incomes are cataloged, including B.F. Keith, F.F. Proctor, S.Z. Poli, Martin Beck, Marcus
Loew, Felix Isman, Harry Lauder, Eva Tanquay, Alice Lloyd,
Nat Goodwin, and others.

1119 _____. "B.F. Keith." AMERICAN MAGAZINE 77 (May 1914): 86-
88.

Keith's contributions to vaudeville, especially creating what
is "refined and artistic."

1120 _____. "The Growth of Vaudeville." OVERLAND 64 (October 1914):
392-96. Illus.

Changes in vaudeville from 1892 when Grau first arrived in
New York from London. Deals primarily with rise in salaries
and possible effect on admission changes.

1121 Green, Abel. "Chas. Evans Hughes 'Saves' Albee." VARIETY (4 January 1967): 196.

1122 Green, Abel, and Laurie, Joe, Jr. SHOW BIZ FROM VAUDE TO
VIDEO. Garden City, N.Y.: Permabooks, 1953. xxiii, 613 p.
Index.

An intentionally breezy and gay history of show business from
1905 into the 1950s, written in homage to Sime Silverman,
the founder-editor-publisher of VARIETY. Especially useful
in its treatment of vaudeville.

1123 Green, Gordon C. "Seattle, Former Vaudeville Capital of the World."
WESTERN SPEECH JOURNAL 30 (Winter 1966): 26-36.

Vaudeville in Seattle in the early 1900s.

1124 Green, Helen. "The Vaudevillians." COLLIER'S 44 (23 October 1909):
20, 31-32, 34.

Largely fictional story of the difficulties of getting into vaudeville.

1123 Grinde, Nick. "Where's Vaudeville At?" SATURDAY EVENING POST
202 (11 January 1930): 44, 46, 158, 161. Illus.

Assessment of vaudeville and its possible contributions to the
movies.

1126 Hall, Ben M. THE BEST REMAINING SEATS, THE STORY OF THE

GOLDEN AGE OF THE MOVIE PALACE. New York: Clarkson N. Potter, 1961. 266 p. Illus., index.

> This superbly illustrated volume centers on the movie palaces of the 1920s, principally the Roxy Theatre in New York. In addition, however, there is good coverage of variety acts and live performance as added attractions which might be considered the tag-end of widespread vaudeville.

1127 Hapgood, Norman. "The Life of a Vaudeville Artiste." Illustrated by Archie Gunn. COSMOPOLITAN 30 (February 1901): 393-400.

> Shattering of the lines between the legitimate stage and vaudeville are explored, with a focus on the female performer.

1128 Hartley, Marsden. "Vaudeville." DIAL 68 (March 1920): 335-42.

> Suggested improvements in decor and billing; specific analysis of Ella Shields, James Watts, the Brothers Rath, and the Four Danubes.

1129 Havoc, June. EARLY HAVOC. New York: Simon and Schuster, 1959. 313 p. Illus.

> Autobiography of June Havoc and her experiences as a vaudevillian (Baby June and Dainty June) with her sister Gypsy Rose Lee and her subsequent career in marathon dancing (see her 1969 play MARATHON 33, Dramatist Play Service).

1130 _____. "Old Vaudevillians, Where Are You Now?" HORIZON 1 (July 1959): 112-20. Illus.

> Havoc recalls acts and foldways of vaudevillians from her earliest memories as "Dainty Baby June the Darling of Vaudeville."

1131 Henderson, Jerry. "Nashville in the Decline of Southern Legitimate Theatre during the Beginnings of the Twentieth Century." SOUTHERN SPEECH JOURNAL 29 (Fall 1963): 26-33.

> The rise of vaudeville between 1900 and 1920 in Nashville.

1132 Hill, Clare Maynard. "Sartorial Splendors in Vaudeville." BILLBOARD (29 November 1913): 34, 138.

> On fashion in vaudeville.

1133 Hoffman, Arthur S. "Who Writes the Jokes?" BOOKMAN 26 (October 1907): 171-81.

> Primarily a catalog of joke writers for publications, however Hoffman touches on writers for vaudeville as well.

1134   Hubbard, Elbert. IN THE SPOTLIGHT: PERSONAL EXPERIENCES OF
ELBERT HUBBARD ON THE AMERICAN STAGE. East Aurora, N.Y.:
Roycrofters, 1917. 134 p. Illus.

> Somewhat disjointed but nonetheless valuable memoirs of a
> vaudevillian working primarily on the Orpheum Circuit.
> Additional chapters by Alice Hubbard, Major Pond (Hubbard's
> manager), and O.J. Laylander.

1135   Hunter, Ruth. COME BACK ON TUESDAY. New York: Charles
Scribner's Sons, 1945. 265 p.

> Actress's chatty memoirs covering the last days of vaudeville.

1136   Hutchens, John K. "Fred Allen, Comedian's Comedian." THEATRE
ARTS MONTHLY 26 (May 1942): 307–14.

> Tribute to Allen's rare talent as a vaudeville entertainer and
> especially a radio comic.

1137   "If Troupers Make Good They'll Go Back to the Sticks." NEWSWEEK
5 (29 June 1935): 23.

> Brief article on Billy Rose's "small time" cavalcade, a group
> of thirty-six "cornbelt troubadors" brought to New York to
> perform their various vaudeville acts.

1138   Irwin, Wallace. "Country Clubs of Broadway." COLLIER'S 50 (26
October 1912): 10–12, 30.

> Vaudeville on the road.

1139   Isman, Felix. WEBER AND FIELDS: THEIR TRIBULATIONS, TRIUMPHS,
AND THEIR ASSOCIATES. New York: Boni and Liveright, 1924.
xii, [15] 345 p. Illus.

> The careers of the late nineteenth-century comic team in
> variety and vaudeville and their contemporaries. Music and
> words to eight of their most popular numbers are included.

1140   Jessel, George. SO HELP ME: THE AUTOBIOGRAPHY OF GEORGE
JESSEL. Foreword by William Saroyan. New York: Random House,
1943. xvii, 240 p. Illus., index.

> Life of Jessel and his career in vaudeville and musicals;
> coverage of his partner Gus Edwards is fairly extensive. Not
> particularly well written but lively and paints a graphic
> picture of early twentieth-century show business.

1141   _____. THIS WAY, MISS. New York: Henry Holt and Co., 1955.
xv, 229 p. Illus.

Covers his transition into films; sequel to above.

1142   Jessel, George, with Austin, John. THE WORLD I LIVED IN. Chicago: Henry Regnery Co., 1975. 213 p. Illus., index.

Candid autobiography of the performer's lengthy career in and out of show business.

1143   Johnston, Alva. "Those Mad Marx Brothers." READER'S DIGEST 29 (October 1936): 49-52.

Condensed from WOMAN'S HOME COMPANION (September 1936). The Marx Brothers' experiences in vaudeville, culminating in the 1922 production of I'LL SAY SHE IS, followed by THE COCOANUTS and ANIMAL CRACKERS.

1144   _____. "Profiles, Vaudeville to Television." NEW YORKER 22 (28 September 1946): 32-43; (5 October): 34-47; (12 October): 36-46.

Career of John F. Royal, former manager of the Cleveland Hippodrome under Albee, became vice-president of NBC. Good insight into vaudeville and the performers.

1145   Kaser, Arthur LeRoy. VAUDEVILLE TURNS. Boston: Walter H. Baker Co., 1923. 81 p. Paper.

Kaser wrote many routines for vaudeville and minstrel shows; this and the following item are included as representative. This volume contains monologues and one-act sketches for various ethnic types (Jewis, Irish, black). See next entry, item 1163, and item 1194.

1146   _____. SNAPPY VAUDEVILLE JOKES. Dayton: Paine Publishing Co., 1928. 133 p. Paper.

Short jokes on many topics and two "talking acts" demonstrating their use in a "unified act." See above entry, item 1163, and item 1194.

1147   Keaton, Buster, with Samuels, Charles. MY WONDERFUL WORLD OF SLAPSTICK. Garden City, N.Y.: Doubleday and Co., 1960. 282 p.

Life of Keaton, a major portion of which is devoted to his childhood as part of "The Three Keatons," whose proudest boast was having the rowdiest, roughest act in vaudeville.

1148   Keegan, Marcia. WE CAN STILL HEAR THEM CLAPPING. New York: Avon Books, 1975. 158 p. Illus. Paper.

A photographic essay, with text, recording the impressions and

reminiscences of former vaudevillians still living in the Times
Square area. Impression is rather sad and a bit pathetic.

1149 Kennedy, John B. "I'm a Spendthrift at Heart." COLLIER'S 79 (12
February 1927): 14, 51.

An interview with Harry Lauder during his vaudeville days
and his explanation of why Scotsmen are called tightwads.

1150 _____. "We've Forgotten How to Fight." COLLIER'S 83 (11 May
1929): 39-40, 42.

Lives and careers of Pat Rooney and his wife Marion during
their twenty-six years and twenty-five thousand public performances together. Three generations of the Rooney dynasty
are mentioned.

1151 King, Donald C. "Keith-Albee et al . . . MARQUEE 7 (3d quarter,
1975): 3-14. Illus.

A well-illustrated survey of the Keith-Albee partnership and
their involvement in various phases of show business, including
circus, vaudeville, and cinema. Focus on various theatres
under their control scattered throughout the country.

1152 "A King of the Vaudeville Stage." CURRENT LITERATURE 46 (January
1909): 84-86. Illus.

On Harry Lauder and his appeal as a vaudeville artist.

1153 Kingsley, W.J. "Reconstruction of Vaudeville." NATIONAL MAGA-
ZINE 40 (May 1919): 173-75.

1153a Lader, Lawrence. "The Palace Theater: Broadway's Shrine." CORO-
NET 32 (July 1952): 51-54.

On the New York Palace Theatre which opened as a vaudeville house in 1913.

1154 Laurie, Joe, Jr. "The Early Days of Vaudeville." AMERICAN MER-
CURY 62 (February 1946): 232-36.

Early version of a portion of his full-length history (see item
1158). Covers early nineteenth century to the rise of B.F.
Keith late in the century.

1155 _____. "Vaudeville." THEATRE ARTS 32 (August-September 1948):
54-55.

Vaudeville in 1923 as it moved away from big-time (two-a-day) toward a combination policy giving support to Hollywood.

1156 _____. "Vaudeville's Ideal Bill." NEW YORK TIMES MAGAZINE (15 May 1949): 24-25. Illus.

Photographic representation of an ideal vaudeville playbill; through text and photograph captions Laurie insists that vaudeville is still alive at the Palace Theatre and in nightclubs, radio, carnivals, and circuses. See item 1157.

1157 _____. "Is Vaudeville Dead? It's Never Been." NEW YORK TIMES MAGAZINE (14 October 1951): 25, 67, 70, 71. Illus.

Belief that vaudeville was still thriving in the early 1950s through Palace stars such as Judy Garland, and subtly living through more current forms of entertainment. See item 1156.

1158 _____ [Joseph]. VAUDEVILLE: FROM THE HONKY-TONKS TO THE PALACE. New York: Holt, 1953. Reprint. Port Washington, N.Y.: Kennikat, 1972. viii, 561 p. Index.

History, anecdotes, and reminiscences of vaudeville by a former vaudevillian containing numerous examples of routines. Still extremely valuable.

1159 Leamy, Hugh. "You Ought to Go on the Stage: An Interview with Edward F. Albee." COLLIER'S 77 (1 May 1926): 10, 36. Illus.

On finding and recognizing talent for vaudeville.

1160 Leavitt, M[ichael]. B[ennett]. FIFTY YEARS IN THEATRICAL MANAGEMENT, 1859-1909. New York: Broadway Publishing Co., 1912. xii, 735 p. Illus., index.

Extensive coverage of Leavitt's career; especially good on variety, minstrelsy, and theatre outside of New York. Five hundred illustrations.

1161 Levy, Bert. FOR THE GOOD OF THE RACE AND OTHER STORIES. New York: Ad Press, 1921. vii-xxiv, 175 p.

Somewhat fictionalized account of an artist's act on the vaudeville circuit. Levy began as a scene painter and became a performing cartoonist.

1162 Lucia, Ellis. KLONDIKE KATE: THE LIFE AND LEGEND OF KITTY ROCKWELL. New York: Hastings House Publishers, 1962. xi, 305 p. Illus., index, bibliog.

Entertaining story of a dancehall girl and a vaudeville star in the Yukon Territory at the turn of the century. Kitty Rockwell was partner and lover of Alexander Pantages before he became a vaudeville magnate.

1163 Lyons, Jimmy. ENCYCLOPEDIA OF STAGE MATERIAL. Boston: Walter H. Baker Co., 1925. 157 p. Illus.

Anthology of vaudeville material written by a vaudeville monologist. Includes jokes, skits, recitations, song lyrics, monologues, and minstrel routines. Typical of the joke book publications of the time. See items 1145-46 and 1194.

1164 McGregor, Donald. "The Supreme Court of the Two a Day." COL-LIER'S 75 (20 June 1925): 38.

On the clearinghouse for disputes between vaudeville managers and performers (Joint Complaint Bureau of the Vaudeville Managers' Protective Association and the National Vaudeville Artists, Inc.).

1165 McLean, Albert F., Jr. "Genesis of Vaudeville: Two Letters from B.F. Keith." THEATRE SURVEY 1 (1960): 82-95.

Keith's professional career in his own words; edited and introduced by McLean. Focus on his early life and contributions to the early development of vaudeville.

1166 _____. AMERICAN VAUDEVILLE AS RITUAL. Lexington: University of Kentucky Press, 1965. xvii, 250 p. Index.

Excellent study of vaudeville "as a manifestation of psychic and social forces at work in American history" and its social-historical significance. Note on sources and fully documented.

1167 _____. "U.S. Vaudeville and the Urban Comics." THEATRE QUAR-TERLY 1 (October-December 1971): 50-57.

Examination of the characters and techniques of the most famous of the comics from the 1850s to the 1930s and analysis of the nature and style of vaudeville humor in terms of a relief mechanism for the frustrations of urban industrial living with its poverty, overcrowding, and the clash of various immigrant groups and the competition for success during changing times.

1168 McNally, William. MACK'S VAUDEVILLE GUIDE. New York: Wm. McNally, 1920. 47 p. Paper.

General information on vaudeville for the professional participant.

1169   McNamara, Brooks. "'Scavengers of the Amusement World': Popular Entertainment and the Birth of the Movies." For full entry and annotation, see item 50.

1170   Marston, William, and Feller, John H. F.F. PROCTOR, VAUDEVILLE PIONEER. New York: Richard R. Smith, 1943. 191 p. Illus.

Biography of the "Dean of American Vaudeville" as told from the point of view of his wife. Covers his rise from his circus career as F.F. Le Valentine, equilibrist of the 1870s, to one of the most successful vaudeville managers in America. Discusses his numerous pioneer accomplishments, e.g., the creation of the "continuous performance." Includes a roster of his theatres and accomplishments, personal comments of contemporaries, and newspaper editorials (pp. 158-91).

1171   Marx, Groucho. GROUCHO AND ME. New York: Bernard Geis Associates, 1959. viii, 344 p. Illus. (16 p. of plates).

Tongue-in-cheek autobiography through vaudeville, musical comedy, and films up to television and YOU BET YOUR LIFE. Wit more prevalent than facts.

1172   _____. THE GROUCHOPHILE. AN ILLUSTRATED LIFE. Introduction by Hector Arce. Indianapolis and New York: Bobbs-Merrill, 1976. xvi, 384 p. Illus., index.

Of the various books by Groucho Marx, this particular one has a good chapter on the Marx Brothers in vaudeville and excellent photographs.

1173   Matlaw, Myron. "Pastor and his flock." THEATRE ARTS 42 (August 1958): 20-21. Illus.

Illustrated tribute to Tony Pastor, the "Father of Vaudeville."

1174   _____. "Tony the Trouper: Pastor's Early Years." THEATRE ANNUAL 24 (1968): 70-90.

Pastor's early life and professional career beginning 1846 to 1865, the start of his tenure as an independent manager.

1175   Meersman, Roger, and Boyer, Robert. "The National Theatre in Washington: Buildings and Audiences, 1835-1972." In RECORDS OF THE COLUMBIA HISTORICAL SOCIETY OF WASHINGTON, D.C., 1971-1972, edited by Francis Coleman Rosenberger, pp. 190-242. Washington, D.C.: published by the society, 1973. Illus.

Contains a great deal about early variety in Washington's theatres.

1176   Merrill, Katherine. "The Elective System and the Vaudeville." NEW
        ENGLAND MAGAZINE 36 (June 1907): 498-99.

>   Point of view that vaudeville appeals to the restless seeking
>   for variety, thus unwilling to concentrate attention or to
>   think connectedly, but rather they hunt for what is easy, the
>   insatiable hunger for amusement. Compares it to the "dissi-
>   pation of energy" brought about by the elective system in
>   education.

1177   Morris, Lloyd. INCREDIBLE NEW YORK. New York: Random House,
        1957. xiii, 370 p. Illus., index.

>   A discussion of the atmosphere, reputation, and dangers of
>   various concert saloons in New York (see pp. 48-52), and
>   Tony Pastor's career in variety (pp. 72-73).

1178   Moses, Montrose. "Tony Pastor--Father of Vaudeville." THEATRE
        GUILD MAGAZINE 8 (April 1931): 32-35. Illus.

>   Retrospective assessment of Pastor's contribution to vaudeville.
>   Sketchy history of his career.

1179   Musson, Bennett. "Week of One Night Stands." Illustrations by Joseph
        Cummings Chase. AMERICAN MAGAZINE 70 (June 1910): 203-13.

>   Comical look at the strict regimen of a traveling performer.

1180   Nathan, George Jean. "A Matter of Life and Death." NEWSWEEK
        13 (17 April 1939): 27.

>   On the presence of vaudeville in revues, musical shows, movie
>   houses, and so forth, despite repeated comments that it's dead.

1181   Page, Brett. WRITING FOR VAUDEVILLE. Springfield, Mass.: Home
        Correspondence School, 1915. xvi [17], 639 p. Illus., index.

>   Insiders view of vaudeville with nine complete examples of
>   various vaudeville forms by Richard Harding Davis, Aaron
>   Hoffman, Edgar Allan Woolf, Taylor Granville, Louis Weslyn,
>   Arthur Denvir, and James Madison. Excellent and important
>   guide to all aspects of vaudeville, not just writing. Includes
>   glossary of terms, analysis of a vaudeville act, physical di-
>   mensions and restrictions of the stage, how to book a vaude-
>   ville act, and much more. Diagrams of Keith's Palace and
>   vaudeville settings.

1182   Patterson, Ada. "A Dual Interview with Weber and Fields." THEATRE
        MAGAZINE 15 (April 1912): 113-16, x.

>   The comic team discuss their early career.

1183   Prill, Arthur. "The 'Small Time' King." THEATRE MAGAZINE 19
        (March 1914): 139-40, 145.

    Brief character sketch of Marcus Loew, vaudeville manager.

1184   Reed, Edward. "Vaudeville Again." THEATRE ARTS MONTHLY 17
        (October 1933): 803-6.

    Retrospective look at vaudeville and a prediction of a vaude-
    ville revival.

1185   Renton, Edward. THE VAUDEVILLE THEATRE--BUILDING--OPERATION
        --MANAGEMENT. New York: Gotham Press, 1918. 307 p.

    How to build, open, and manage a vaudeville theatre. A
    compendium of specific suggestions covering all physical and
    managerial aspects, e.g., plumbing, carpets, checkrooms; staff
    positions, advertising and publicity; and even fires and panics.

1186   Revell, Nellie. "Stars in Vaudeville." THEATRE MAGAZINE 19
        (April 1914): 199-200, 206, 208.

    Review of season but gives good sense of the types of per-
    formers and acts accepted as well.

1187   _____. The Passing of the Freak Act." THEATRE MAGAZINE 19
        (June 1914): 293-94, 316, 317.

    Notoriety is no longer a criterion for booking vaudeville and
    legitimate stage performers are now being introduced (examples
    of latter given).

1188   _____. "Good Sketches Rare as Radium in Vaudeville." THEATRE
        MAGAZINE 24 (November 1916): 278, 322.

    Lack of good vaudeville sketches with current examples.

1189   _____. "Yellow Peril Threatens Vaudeville." THEATRE MAGAZINE
        25 (May 1917): 290, 316.

    Possible results of a combination of playwright, sketch writers,
    and newspaper tyros on vaudeville.

1190   _____. "When Vaudeville Goes to War." THEATRE MAGAZINE 25
        (June 1917): 356.

    War sketches in vaudeville.

1191   _____. "Speed Mania Afflicts Vaudeville." THEATRE MAGAZINE 26
        (October 1917): 216.

Vaudeville's two-a-day as the training ground for producers, actors, writers, and composers. Also discusses the decline of the vaudeville playlet.

1192 _____. "Vaudeville Demands Cheerful Patriotism." THEATRE MAGA-ZINE 26 (December 1917): 364.

"The two-a-day fairly bristles with patriotism. But it insists on being cheerful about it." Examples of sketches of analyzed.

1193 Robinson, David. BUSTER KEATON. Bloomington and London: Indiana University Press, 1969. 198 p. Illus.

Succinct but useful chapter on Keaton's early career in vaudeville.

1194 Rossiter, Will, comp. THE VAUDEVILLE PROMPTER. Chicago: Will Rossiter Publisher, 1903. 62 p. Paper.

One of four volumes in a series; each a collection of vaudeville materials--gags and jokes, monologues, recitations, skits, parodies, one-acts, and minstrel routines. Also brief essay on various aspects of the business (makeup, how to specialize, and the dilemma of three shows a day) written by various contributors. Rossiter was a prolific writer of skits, songs, monologues, and so forth. See items 1145-46 and 1163.

1195 Royle, Edwin Milton. "The Vaudeville Theatre." SCRIBNER'S 26 (October 1899): 485-95. Illus.

Describes respectable vaudeville houses and their strict censorship rules. Also deals with the format of the program and other practices of managers, agents, and the circuit, and so forth. A useful summary.

1196 Rubin, Benny. COME BACKSTAGE WITH ME. Bowling Green, Ohio: Bowling Green University Popular Press, 1972. 218 p. Illus.

Memoirs of the vaudevillian; good sense of the life of a performer on the circuits.

1197 Samuels, Charles, and Samuels, Louise. ONCE UPON A STAGE: THE MERRY WORLD OF VAUDEVILLE. New York: Dodd, Mead and Co., 1974. viii, 278 p. Illus., index.

An informal and undocumented history of vaudeville.

1198 Savo, Jimmy. I BOW TO THE STONES. Introduction by George Freedley. Drawings by Victor J. Dowling. New York: Howard Frisch, 1963. 144 p. Illus.

Autobiography of the early life and career of a vaudeville and revue comic. Insights into amateur nights in New York, Savo's beginnings as a juggler and semi-magician in vaudeville (1912). Later Savo worked both burlesque and vaudeville, as well as appearing in revues such as the VOGUES OF 1924, MURRAY ANDERSON'S ALMANAC, EARL CARROLL'S VANITIES OF 1930, and also musical comedy. This little book, however, focuses on his early vaudeville career.

1199　Shiffman, Jack. UPTOWN, THE STORY OF HARLEM'S APOLLO THEATRE. For full entry and annotation, see item 254.

1200　Senelick, Laurence. "Variety into Vaudeville, The Process Observed in Two Manuscript Gagbooks." THEATRE SURVEY 19 (May 1978): 1-15.

Analysis and contrast of two manuscript gagbooks, one from the late 1870s (illustrating the "path of mediocrity") and the second from the early 1880s (demonstrating originality and innovation).

1201　Shayne, Eddie. DOWN FRONT ON THE AISLE. Denver: Parkway Publishing Co., 1929. 60 p. Illus. (sketches).

Described aptly by the author as "an oddly constructed melange," this slim volume briefly looks at vaudeville, its predecessors ("variety" and Western concert halls), and the differences in the forms. Told in the form of an interview with an old vaudevillian.

1202　Sherlock, Charles R. "Where Vaudeville Holds the Boards." COSMOPOLITAN 32 (February 1902): 411-20. Illus.

Evolution of the roof-garden theatre during summer months for variety and celebrities who rose to fame through vaudeville as their testing ground. Also deals with ethnic groups as reflected on stage.

1203　Smith, Bill. THE VAUDEVILLIANS. New York: Macmillan Co., 1976. vii, 278 p. Illus., index, glossary.

Thirty-one former headliners recall the era when vaudeville reached its peak with the opening of the New York Palace in 1913. An interesting, albeit sad and wistful, look at daily life on the vaudeville circuit.

1204　Snyder, Frederick Edward. "American Vaudeville Theatre in a Package: The Origins of Mass Entertainment." Ph.D. dissertation, Yale University, 1970. 166 p.

Vaudeville, the author concludes, established the conditions for the subsequent development of mass entertainment (continuous performances, universal family appeal, standardized length of routines, and uniform system of production). See next entry.

1205 _____. "Theatre in a Package." THEATRE SURVEY 12 (May 1971): 34-45.

Adapted from his dissertation (above). "The Essence of vaudeville lay in the discipline of its informing principle, its formula of standardized production, in the neat size and shape of its acts, shaved and blocked by the booker's cookie-cutter."

1206 Sobel, Bernard. A PICTORIAL HISTORY OF VAUDEVILLE. Foreword by George Jessel. New York: Citadel Press, 1961. 224 p. Illus.

Directed at a popular audience but still an accurate and informative account of vaudeville history, without documentation. Sobel divides his book into three sections: 1) "The Vaudeville Story"--an illustrated history, 2) "A Gallery of Vaudevillians" --photographs of major performers, and 3) "Visitors on the Circuits"--legitimate stars in vaudeville.

1207 "Social Welfare as Vaudeville." SURVEY 23 (26 February 1910): 794-95.

Enterprise in Chicago of inserting a talk on some phase of betterment as one of the regular "turns" at a variety theatre. Example: a South Chicago vaudeville house is singled out for illustration of the types of talks given.

1208 Spitzer, Marian. "Morals in the Two-A-Day." AMERICAN MERCURY 3 (September 1924): 35-39.

Analysis of morality in vaudeville, including an explanation of control methods, examples of deletions, and the effect on the Columbia wheel of burlesque.

1209 _____. THE PALACE. New York: Atheneum, 1969. xviii, 267 p. Illus., index.

The author, who knew the Palace from its opening in 1913 and later as a member of its staff, has written the most complete history of the Palace. Although not included here, largely because of duplication of material, it should be noted that in 1924-25 Spitzer wrote a series of useful essays on various aspects of vaudeville in SATURDAY EVENING POST (see especially issues for 12 July 1924, 24 May 1924, 7 March 1925, and 22 August 1925).

1210   "Springtime in the 40s." NEWSWEEK 33 (30 May 1949): 76-77.
       Illus.

       Brief retrospective history of vaudeville on the occasion of a
       revival of vaudeville, of sorts, at the Palace.

1211   Steegmuller, Frances. "Onward and Upward with the Arts: An Angel,
       A Flower, A Bird." NEW YORKER 45 (27 September 1969): 130-40,
       143.

       Interview with female impersonator, "Barbette" (Vander Clyde),
       who in the 1920s and '30s did a trapeze act disguised as a
       girl. This essay deals with Barbette's association with Jean
       Cocteau and his appearance in Cocteau's film THE BLOOD
       OF A POET.

1212   "Tony Pastor, Father of Vaudeville." HARPER'S WEEKLY 52 (5 Septem-
       ber 1908): 10. Illus.

       Eulogy and brief biographical sketch.

1213   Traber, J. Milton. "Pen Sketch of 'Tony' Pastor, the Father of Modern
       Variety." BILLBOARD 23 (18 February 1911): 5, 42.

       Brief biographical sketch.

1214   Tucker, Sophie, with Giles, Dorothy. SOME OF THESE DAYS: THE
       AUTOBIOGRAPHY OF SOPHIE TUCKER. Garden City, N.Y.: Double-
       day, Doran and Co., 1945. 309 p. Illus.

       Life of a strong woman, as a blackface comic ("coon shouter"),
       on the burlesque wheel, in revue, vaudeville, and in Holly-
       wood.

1215   Uraneff, Vadim. "Commedia dell' arte and American Vaudeville."
       THEATRE ARTS MONTHLY 7 (October 1923): 321-28.

       Parallels drawn between sixteenth- and seventeenth-century
       Italian theatre and American vaudeville; also a catalog of the
       fundamentals of the genuine vaudeville spirit.

1216   "The Variety Stage: Early Creators of a Remunerative Vogue." HAR-
       PER'S WEEKLY 46 (29 March, 1902): 414.

       Early performers in variety, including Kate Castleton and John
       Kelly, Tony Pastor and Jac Aberle.

1217   "The Variety Stage: Some Artists of This and Other Generations."
       HARPER'S WEEKLY 46 (12 April 1902): 466.

       Discusses Sam Ricky as a strong influence on variety and its outgrowths. Includes mention of several managers and actors, including Johnny Wild, Billy Gray, Tony Hart, Edward Harrigan, Weber and Fields.

1218 "The Variety Stage: Something of Its Early History in New York." HARPER'S WEEKLY 46 (22 March 1902): 380. Illus.

Attributes the first variety show, as such, to William Valentine. Tony Pastor is seen as the "dean of the variety profession." Includes a biography of Pastor.

1219 Willows, Maurice. "The Nickel Theatre." ANNALS OF THE AMERI-CAN ACADEMY OF POLITICAL AND SOCIAL SCIENCE 38 (July 1911): 95-99.

Biased report on the effect of cheap vaudeville and theatre on children as patrons and employees. Part of a symposium on child labor in street trades and public places.

1220 Willson, Clair Eugene. "From Variety Theatre to Coffee Shop." ARIZONA HISTORICAL REVIEW 6 (April 1935): 3-13.

Historical sketch of the Bird Cage Theatre, Tombstone, established in 1881; converted later into a coffee shop.

1221 Woolf, S.J. "Gus Edwards' Academy." NEW YORK TIMES MAGA-ZINE (23 March 1941): 12, 19. Illus.

Career of Gus Edwards, a vaudeville performer in the 1890s, later a songwriter, and early in the century a crea'or and director of vaudeville acts, and erstwhile talent scout.

1222 Zellers, Parker R. "The Cradle of Variety: The Concert Saloon." EDUCATIONAL THEATRE JOURNAL 20 (December 1968): 578-85.

History and description of early American concert saloons; the forerunner of variety. The character of patrons, the atmosphere, reputation, and waiter-girls are discussed, as well as the type and character of the shows and legal impositions. Expanded in the following entry.

1223 _____. TONY PASTOR: DEAN OF THE VAUDEVILLE STAGE. Ypsilanti: Eastern Michigan University Press, 1971. xix, 155 p. Illus., index, bibliog.

The only comprehensive study of the performer-manager; good look at New York entertainment in the 1860s and 70s and the predecessors of vaudeville. Pastor is credited with the shaping, popularizing, and refining of variety.

D. BURLESQUE AND STRIPTEASE

1224   Aldridge, A. Owen. "American Burlesque at Home and Abroad: To-
        gether with the Etymology of Go-Go Girl." JOURNAL OF POPULAR
        CULTURE 5 (Winter 1971): 565-75.

>   Origin of the striptease and the display of nudity elsewhere
>   today (Paris, London, Hamburg, Japan, and Tel-Aviv).

1225   Alexander, H.L. STRIPTEASE, THE VANISHED ART OF BURLESQUE.
        New York: Knight Publishers, 1938. xii, 124 p. (plus 34 p. of
        "candid" camera photographs).

>   Written soon after New York City outlawed the striptease,
>   with an account of those proceedings. Succinct text on early
>   history of the striptease, the Irving Place Theatre, backstage
>   with a "Minsky Grinder," "Technique and the Teasers," some
>   assessment of top strippers (Georgia Sothern, Ada Leonard,
>   Marie Cord, Betty Rowland, Ann Corio, Nadja, Carrie
>   Finnell), private lives of strippers, the comics, the producers
>   ("Money Guys"), and the like. Told in a "You Are There"
>   style.

1226   Allen, Ralph G. "Our Native Theatre." In THE AMERICAN THEATRE:
        A SUM OF ITS PARTS, edited by Henry B. Williams, pp. 273-314.
        New York: Samuel French, 1971.

>   One of the better essays on the origin and nature of burlesque;
>   a study of "Honky-Tonks, Minstrel Shows, Burlesque" up to
>   the 1930s. Good examples of burlesque bits included. As of
>   this writing, Prof. Allen is working on a full-length study of
>   burlesque.

1227   Angier, Roswell. A KIND OF LIFE: CONVERSATIONS IN THE
        COMBAT ZONE. Danbury, N.H.: Addison House, distributed by
        Light Impressions, Rochester, N.Y., 1976. 130 p. Illus.

>   A straightforward and candid look at strippers in Boston's
>   "Combat Zone."

1228   Barber, Rowland. THE NIGHT THEY RAIDED MINSKY'S. New York:
        Simon andSchuster, 1960. 351 p.

>   Fanciful account of the burlesque scene on the Lower East
>   Side of Manhattan during the 1920s and the shot in the arm
>   provided by the introduction of the striptease.

1229   Batistella, Annabel ("Fanne Fox"), with Dunleavy, Yvonne. FANNE
        FOX. New York: Pinnacle Books, 1976. 180 p. Illus. Paper.

One-dimensional autobiography capitalizing on the author's publicity stemming from the "Tidal Basin" escapade and her affair with Wilbur Mills. Includes descriptions of the kinkier striptease acts.

1230   Bigelow, Joseph. "Where is Burly Headed?" VARIETY (3 May 1936): 15.

On the changing nature of burlesque.

1231   Corio, Ann, with DiMona, Joe. THIS WAS BURLESQUE. New York: Grosset and Dunlap, 1968. 204 p. Illus.

Commentary with many illustrations and photographs on the great stars of the 1930s by one of the queens of burlesque. Suggests several possible origins for the striptease and places the phenomenon in historical perspective and in the context of burlesque form.

1232   Cummings, E.E. "Burlesque, I Love It!" In E.E. CUMMINGS: A MISCELLANY REVISED, edited by George J. Firmage, pp. 292-95. New York: October House, 1965.

Reprinted from STAGE (March 1936): On the old Howard Theatre, the National Winter Garden, the Irving Place Theatre, and the differences between them (from the filth and ugliness of the girls at the Howard to the striptease at the Irving Place). Fascinating.

1233   Green, William. "A Survey of the Development of Burlesque in America." M.A. thesis, Columbia University, 1950. 104 p.

A sensible and succinct study.

1234   _____. "Strippers and Coochers--the Quintessence of American Burlesque." In WESTERN POPULAR THEATRE, edited by David Mayer and Kenneth Richards, pp. 157-68. London: Methuen and Co., 1977.

Brief summary of the development of the "leg show" in the United States, divided into three periods: 1750-1868, the age of traditional burlesque; 1868-1922, the era during which the modern burlesque show evolved; and 1922-present, the period of nudity, smut, and decline.

1235   _____. "The Audiences of the American Burlesque Show of the Minsky Era (ca. 1920-40)." In DAS THEATER UND SEIN PUBLIKUM, pp. 225-37. Vienna: Verlag der Osterreichischen Akademie der Wissenschaften, 1977.

Good summary of the Minsky burlesque tradition in New York;

includes brief history, characterization of audiences, and description of the type of entertainment presented by the Minsky brothers.

1236 Holbrook, Stewart H. "Boston's Temple of Burlesque." AMERICAN MERCURY 58 (April 1944): 411-16.

Brief history of the old Howard burlesque house from its period of legitimate drama (1845) to burlesque beginning in the 1890s.

1237 _____. LITTLE ANNIE OAKLEY AND OTHER RUGGED PEOPLE. For full entry and annotation, see item 668.

1238 Jones, Libby. STRIPTEASE. New York: Parallax Publishing Co. Distributed by Simon and Schuster, 1967. 80 p. Illus. (drawings).

A "how-to-strip" book for the amateur stripper that guides the would-be stripteaser through bumps, grinds, stomps, and other necessary skills. A 1960s tone and attitude prevails; brief history of the art, hints on makeup and wardrobe.

1239 Joseph, Richard. "Blaze Starr." ESQUIRE 67 (July 1964): 58-62.

Describes the meteoric rise of the striptease queen to the top of the heap in Baltimore, the new capital of the strip show. (Note: the Troc, Baltimore's best-known striphouse recently closed.)

1240 Lee, Gypsy Rose. THE G-STRING MURDERS. Cleveland and New York: World Publishing, 1941. 305 p.

Old-fashioned but engrossing detective story about a string of grisly unsolved murders of strippers by a typical psychopath. Offers good backstage atmosphere of a 1930s New York striptease theatre.

1241 _____. GYPSY: A MEMOIR. New York: Harper and Bros., 1957. 337 p. Illus.

Coherent and heartwarming show business autobiography that takes the reader from vaudeville to burlesque in the persons of a stage mother and her two daughters, Gypsy Rose Lee and June Havoc (see index under Havoc). Reveals little about the stripper but offers good backstage atmosphere and penetrates the life of an itinerate performer in burlesque.

1242 Lipnitski, Bernard. "God Save the Queen." ESQUIRE 72 (August 1969): 104-7. Illus.

Photographic essay; commentary by four strippers who assail the declining morality of the hippie generation.

1243 Logan, Herschel C. BUCKSKIN AND SATIN: THE TRUE DRAMA OF TEXAS JACK AND MLLE MORLACCHI, PREMIERE DANSEUSE, ORIGINATOR OF THE CAN CAN IN AMERICA. Harrisburg, Pa.: Stackpole Co., 1954. 218 p. Illus., bibliog.

The cancan is frequently cited as the European forebearer of the striptease; this is an account of its introduction to the United States.

1244 Logan, Olive. BEFORE THE FOOTLIGHTS AND BEHIND THE SCENES. Philadelphia: Parmelee and Co., 1870. xv [17], 612 p. Illus.

Virtually the same as source below by an actress turned lecturer. Interesting section titled "Morality and Immorality in Amusements." See items 1965 and 1966.

1245 _____. THE MIMIC WORLD, AND PUBLIC EXHIBITIONS. Philadelphia: New-Word Publishing Co., 1878. 590 p. Illus.

Logan's assessment of the history and morality of the theatre in the form of a typical nineteenth-century autobiography. Still, an unusual approach in many ways. See above.

1246 McCaghy, Charles H., and Skipper, James K., Jr. "Lesbian Behavior as an Adaptation to the Occupation of Stripping." SOCIAL PROBLEMS 17 (Fall 1969): 262-70.

Study of strippers which shows that strippers experience three major conditions: 1) "isolation from affective social relationships," 2) "unsatisfactory relationships with males," and 3) "an opportunity structure allowing a wide range of sexual behavior."

1247 Meiselas, Susan. CARNIVAL STRIPPERS. New York: F., S., and G. Publishing Co. [Farrar, Straus, and Giroux], 1976. 148 p. Illus. Paper.

Forthright and honest pictorial essay on the stripper based on observations at carnival girlie shows in New England in the summer of 1973-75.

1248 Mills, Steve. "'An Artist's Studio'; A Comic Scene from Burlesque." EDUCATIONAL THEATRE JOURNAL 27 (October 1975): 342-44.

A comic bit from burlesque as described by this outstanding burlesque comic and performed first at the Apollo Theatre in New York when he was with the Minsky's. See also item 1254.

1249 "Minsky's Hideaway." NEWSWEEK 44 (8 November 1954): 95-97.

>The rise of Lili St. Cyr and the growing number of "exotic dancers," two thousand strong, in the 1950s.

1250 Newquist, Roy. SHOWCASE. Introduction by Brooks Atkinson. New York: William Morrow and Co., 1966. 412 p. Illus.

>Called by the author an "exercise in self-indulgence," this volume is a collection of essays on his favorite entertainers from John Gielgud to Jack Lemmon and Danny Kaye. The most useful interview is one with Ann Corio on burlesque.

1251 O'Connor, Lois. THE BARE FACTS: CANDID CONFESSIONS OF A STRIPPER. New York: MacFadden Books, 1964. 126 p. Paper.

>Very mediocre autobiography of the archetypical naive young girl who enters the lower echelons of the striptease business and remains there; dull but revealing in its simplemindedness. An interesting contrast to the success stories of the queens of burlesque.

1252 Pringle, Henry F. "The Minsky Kids." COLLIER'S 99 (6 March 1937): 10, 15, 60.

>On clientele sought for Minsky shows, i.e., the higher classes.

1253 Salutin, Marilyn. "Stripper Morality." TRANSACTION 8 (June 1971): 12-22.

>Sociological study of the stripper based on interviews and observation of strippers in Toronto at the Victory burlesque house. Good investigation into the motivations and corporeal ideologies of strippers and the complicated nature of their destigmatizing process and the complexities of those who have to work out a suitable identity.

1254 Sandberg, Trish. "An Interview with Steve Mills." EDUCATIONAL THEATRE JOURNAL 27 (October 1975): 331-41.

>Mills, born in 1895, spent sixty-five years in show business and has been closely associated with burlesque. He was known to contemporary audiences as the top banana in Ann Corio's THIS WAS BURLESQUE. See item 1248.

1255 Seldes, Gilbert. "Fat Ladies." NEW REPUBLIC 70 (30 March 1932): 182-83.

>On an offshoot of the downtown Minsky troupe uptown and Seldes's lament for the death of "unrefined" burlesque. Good

dissection of changes, content, and form of burlesque.

1256 _____. "Their Hearts Belong to Daddy." SOCIAL PROBLEMS 17 (Spring 1970): 33-50.

Sociological survey of Case Western Reserve sociologists exploring the psychological characteristics of strippers based on interviews with thirty-five of them.

1257 Skipper, James K., Jr., and McCaghy, Charles H. "Stripteasers: The Anatomy and Career Contingencies of a Deviant Occupation." SOICAL PROBLEMS 17 (Winter 1970): 391-405.

Includes a description of the occupation, data concerning physical, psychological, and social characteristics of strippers on a theatre circuit; also data on the situational factors surrounding their decision to enter the occupation.

1258 Sobel, Bernard. BURLEYQUE: AN UNDERGROUND HISTORY OF BURLESQUE DAYS. New York: Farrar and Rinehart, 1931. Reprint. New York: Burt Franklin, 1975. xiv, 284 p. Illus.

The first history of burlesque in the modern sense of the term. Although lacking documentation, Sobel is still a useful and recommended source. Chapters included on the origin (traces beginning to Aristophanes and parody), Lydia Thompson and the British Blondes, the first American burlesque show; Rentz-Stanley Company, Weber and Fields, Sam T. Jack, Annie Ashley, John E. Henshaw, May Howard, Honky Tonks, the Columbia Circuit, Lawrence Weber, J. Herbert Mack, Rose Sydell, Al Reeves, Al Jolson, W.C. Fields, the nineties, civic prohibitions, "The Golden Age of Burlesque," Fanny Brice, Jean Bedini and Eddie Cantor, Joe Cook, "The Bits," Fred Stone and Dave Montgomery, Henry P. Dixon, Leon Errol, Alexander Carr, Joseph Van Raalte, I. Herk, Gus Edwards, and other aspects of burlesque operation, methods, and history.

1259 _____. "Take 'Em Off!" SATURDAY REVIEW OF LITERATURE 28 (18 August 1945): 22-24.

Summary history of the American burlesque show.

1260 _____. A PICTORIAL HISTORY OF BURLESQUE. New York: Putnam, 1956. 194 p. Illus., index.

Informative text, although a sketchy history, along with excellent photographs. Other forms of popular entertainment are mentioned in Sobel's discussion of the origin of burlesque, e.g., vaudeville, minstrelsy, and honky-tonk, plus individual performers are discussed, e.g., Lydia Thompson, Lotta Crabtree, May Howard, Leon Errol, Smith and Dale, Ted Lewis, Bert Lahr, Joey Faye, Joe Welch, Weber and Fields, Adah Isaacs Menken, Millie de Leon, Gaby Deslys, Eva Tanquay, Lili St. Cyr, Gypsy Rose Lee, the Minskys, and many other personalities.

1261   Sothern, Georgia. GEORGIA. MY LIFE IN BURLESQUE. New York: Signet Books, 1972. 351 p. Illus. Paper.

The best of the stripper autobiographies; witty, highly entertaining. Sothern describes her offstage antics but also includes step-by-step instructions for a successful act and how to roll with the punches in a job that demands constant revitalization.

1262   Starr, Blaze, and Perry, Hue. BLAZE STARR: MY LIFE. New York: Warner Paperback Library, 1975. 206 p. Illus. (16 p. of photos.). Paper.

Entertaining rags-to-riches story of a poor country girl who comes to the city and becomes the undisputed queen of the striptease in the 1960s. Little concerning the actual art of the striptease.

1263   "Strippers' Retreat." NEWSWEEK 43 (11 January 1954): 72-73.

The demise of old burlesque theaters in Chicago (Minsky's Rialto) and Boston (the Howard) due to financial and legal troubles.

1264   "Le Striptease." NEWSWEEK 51 (October 1961): 98-99.

Describes the introduction and subsequent blossoming of the American art form in Paris thanks to Alain Bernardin, proprietor of Le Crazy Horse Saloon.

1265   Wilson, Edmund. THE SHORES OF LIGHT. New York: Farrar, Straus, and Young, 1952.

See "Burlesque Shows: I. The National Winter Garden" (p. 275) and "Burlesque Shows: II. Peaches--A Humdinger" (pp. 280-81). Stimulating comment by this important literary critic.

1266   Wortley, Richard. PICTORIAL HISTORY OF STRIPTEASE: 100 YEARS OF UNDRESSING TO MUSIC. Seacaucus, N.J.: Chartwell Books. Distributed by Book Sales, 1976. 160 p. Illus., index.

Rather feeble effort at a history of striptease, although its slick layout and illustrations, many in color, make an attractive book. Also includes chapters on night club dancers of Paris, New York, and London, striptease in the cinema, and a final chapter on how to strip (for the amateur).

1267 Zeidman, Irving. THE AMERICAN BURLESQUE SHOW. New York: Hawthorn Books, 1967. 271 p. Illus., index, bibliog.

The most comprehensive current history to date; the author, however, is terribly biased in an almost puritanical way and fails to document his investigation except by passing references in the text. Dates the beginning of American burlesque from THE BLACK CROOK (1866).

E. LYCEUM AND CHAUTAUQUA

The material listed in this section is related as well to chapter 14: "American Small-Town and Provincial Operations."

1268 Albert, Allen D. "Tents of the Conservative." SCRIBNER'S MAGA-ZINE 72 (July 1922): 54-59.

Discussion of chautauqua in terms of its overwhelmingly conservative influence on America and the counterweight it served to the growing radicalism of the time. See item 1285.

1269 Bestor, Arthur Eugene, Jr. CHAUTAUQUA PUBLICATIONS: AN HISTORICAL AND BIBLIOGRAPHICAL GUIDE. Chautauqua, N.Y.: Chautauqua Press, 1934. 67 p. Appendix.

Bibliography in three parts: 1) "Chautauqua Books for Home Reading and Study," 2) "Pamphlets and Serial Publications of Chautauqua," and 3) "Books and Important Pamphlets About Chautauqua."

1270 Bliven, Bruce. "Mother, Home, and Heaven." NEW REPUBLIC 37 (9 January 1924): 172-75.

Survey of chautauqua with a fictionalized reconstruction of a typical chautauqua outing. Title refers to the "inspirational" lecture known in the profession as "the mother, home and heaven stuff." Chautauqua, according to the author, depended on this, plus music and drama (the latter the most popular feature of the program).

1271 Britt, Albert. TURN OF THE CENTURY. Barre, Mass.: Barre Publishers, 1966. x, 138 p.

Memoirs of experiences in New York State at the turn of the

century, including a brief section on chautauqua, its movement, and decline.

1272   Case, Victoria, and Ormond, Robert. WE CALLED IT CULTURE: THE
STORY OF CHAUTAUQUA. Garden City, N.Y.: Doubleday and Co.,
1948. x. 272 p. Bibliog., appendix.

On the origins of chautauqua, its popularity, development
and growth, and its eventual disappearance. Includes a good
deal on the major figures, talent and types of entertainment
found in chautauqua performances. Comprehensive, informative, and well written.

1273   Castle, Marian Johnson. "Chautauqua, the Intellectual Circus."
FORUM 87 (June 1932): 369-74. Illus.

Johnson first did booking, then advance work on the road with
the chautauqua circuit. Later Johnson became a superintendent
of the actual six-day chautauqua. This essay describes and
discusses the management aspect of chautauqua. It is an informative, interesting, and somewhat irreverent look at chautauqua.

1274   Conlin, James W. "The Merom Bluff Chautauqua." INDIANA MAGA-
ZINE OF HISTORY 36 (March 1940): 23-28.

Two pioneers of chautauqua, Bishop John H. Vincent and
Lewis Miller, and the Chautauqua Association in Merom, Indiana (founded in 1905) are recounted.

1275   Detzer, Karl W. "Broadway, R.F.D.: The Rejuvenated Chautauqua is
Bigger and Better Than Ever." CENTURY MAGAZINE 116 (July 1928):
311-17.

On the updated, thriving chautauqua, then in its "middle age."
Still offering the "triumvirate--entertainment, education and
inspiration." The author provides the background of chautauqua and discusses the changes it underwent in order to still be
surviving at the time this article was written.

1276   Ellerbe, Alma, and Ellerbe, Paul. "The Most American Thing in America." WORLD'S WORK 68 (August 1924): 440-46.

Life on the chautauqua tent circuit. Chautauqua seen as a
phase of America's development, embodying the virtues "of the
race at its best," e.g., spontaneity, eagerness to be instructed,
sincerity, and honest enthusiasm.

1277   Gould, Joseph E. THE CHAUTAUQUA MOVMENT: AN EPISODE IN
THE CONTINUING AMERICAN REVOLUTION. New York: State Uni-

versity of New York, 1961. xiv, 108 p. Illus., notes.

> Covers the chautauqua movement from its conception in 1874 to the closing of the last chautauqua circuit in 1932 (though the Chautauqua Institution was still alive at the time this book was written--and is today). Discusses its rapid growth, its ever-increasing popularity, and the major figures responsible for its success. Main focus is on the movement's contribution to American education, rather than on its entertainment aspect.

1278 Harrison, Harry P., as told to Detzer, Karl. CULTURE UNDER CANVAS: THE STORY OF TENT CHAUTAUQUA. New York: Hastings House, 1958. xxvii, 287 p. Illus., index.

> Traveling tent shows recounted by the manager of the Redpath Chautauqua, covering the period 1904 to 1932.

1279 Hedges, R. Alan. "Actors Under Canvas: A Study of the Theatre of the Circuit Chautauqua, 1910-1933." Ph.D. dissertation, Ohio State University, 1976. 344 p.

> Good survey of the traveling chautauqua.

1280 High, Fred. "The Circus and the Chautauqua." BILLBOARD (22 December 1917): 14-15.

1281 _____. "Chautauqua's Growth." BILLBOARD (20 March 1920): 16-17, 204.

1282 Horner, Charles F. THE LIFE OF JAMES REDPATH AND THE DEVELOPMENT OF THE MODERN LYCEUM. New York and Newark, N.J.: Barse and Hopkins, 1926. 301 p. Illus.

> Redpath (1833-91) and the history of the lyceum movement. Rather superficial treatment of lyceum entertainment.

1283 _____. STRIKE THE TENTS, THE STORY OF THE CHAUTAUQUA. Philadelphia: Dorrance and Co., 1954. 204 p.

> Chautauqua pioneer, credited with the formula for the operation and design used by the chautauqua for nearly twenty years, tells the story of the lyceum and subsequent chautauqua circuits. Superficial firsthand account and largely superseded by subsequent histories but still gives good sense of entertainment used on the circuits and especially valuable for an explanation of the organization of the circuits (at their peak in 1922).

1284 Howard, Randall R. "Chautauqua Invades the West." SUNSET 40 (May 1918): 49-50.

Brief account of chautauqua's western expansion.

1285 "An Inveterate Chautauqua Fan." SCRIBNER'S MAGAZINE 74 (July 1923): 119-20.

Article in defense of chautauqua and its conservatism by "a dweller (by marriage) in the tents of conservatism." See item 1268.

1286 Lorch, Fred W. THE TROUBLE BEGINS AT EIGHT. MARK TWAIN'S LECTURE TOURS. Ames: Iowa State University Press, 1968. xvi, 375 p. Illus., index, bibliog., notes.

A fascinating study with informative chapters on the lyceum circuit and Twain's dealings with James Redpath.

1287 MacLaren, Gay. MORALLY WE ROLL ALONG. Boston: Little, Brown and Co., 1938. xii, 308 p. Illus., index.

On the chautauqua movement and the author's encounter with it, told with a mix of fact and fiction. Chapter 7, "Talent," discusses the leading chautauqua performers and the four groups they fell into: "the lecturers, the reader, the musical companies, and the educational features."

1288 Mead, David. "1914: The Chautauqua and American Innocence." JOURNAL OF POPULAR CULTURE 1 (Spring 1968): 339-56.

The chautauqua movement prior to the industrial and social complexities which would end the age of innocence in the Crash of 1929. Useful notes.

1289 Miller, Melvin H. "The Chautauqua in Lansing." MICHIGAN HISTORY 40 (September 1956): 257-74.

Historical survey from 1907 to 1917.

1290 Morrison, Theodore. CHAUTAUQUA. Chicago: University of Chicago Press, 1974. viii, 351 p. Illus., index, bibliog.

History of chautauqua, its development, and its role in American society. Two chapters specifically on the entertainment and artistic aspects of chautauqua. Good view of chautauqua from a more contemporary perspective; excellent photographic section.

1291 Orchard, Hugh Anderson. FIFTY YEARS OF CHAUTAUQUA; ITS BEGINNINGS, ITS DEVELOPMENT, ITS MESSAGE AND ITS LIFE. Iowa: Torch Press, 1923. 313 p. Illus.

Early history of chautauqua and two of its first pioneers, Keith Vawter and M. Roy Ellison.

1292 Price, Lucien. "Orpheus in Zion: An Idyl of Chautauqua." YALE REVIEW 19 (December 1929): 303-24.

Verbose description of the author's youth spent with the chautauqua as both an observer and later, an employee.

1293 Pringle, Henry F. "Chautauqua in the Jazz Age." AMERICAN MERCURY 16 (January 1929): 85-93.

1294 Richmond, Rebecca. CHAUTAUQUA, AN AMERICAN PLACE. New York: Duell, Sloane and Pearce, 1943. ix, 180 p. Illus., notes.

Brief history of chautauqua from its beginning to 1943 and a discussion of the movement's significance. Focus is on the original chautauqua, rather than on the circuit, with little specifically on entertainment.

1295 Row, Arthur William. "Acting in Tents in Chautauqua." POET-LORE 36 (Spring 1925): 222-31.

What it was like for an actor to tour with a chautauqua company in the 1920s.

1296 Scott, Marian. CHAUTAUQUA CARAVAN. New York: D. Appleton-Century, 1939. viii, 310 p. Illus.

Scott, a singer who toured with the chautauqua from 1916 to 1927, relates her experiences of those eleven years on the circuit. Although the book is rather trivial reminiscences, it does provide interesting information on the places she performed, with whom she performed, and life on the road in general and with the chautauqua movement in particular.

1297 Slout, L. Verne. "The Chautauqua Drama." LYCEUM MAGAZINE (April 1923): 19-20.

Brief account of the type of drama presented on the circuit.

1298 Smoot, James S. "Platform Theater. Theatrical Elements of the Lyceum--Chautauqua." Ph.D. dissertation, University of Michigan, 1954. 323 p.

Scholarly study examines the theatre/drama aspects of lyceum and chautauqua.

1299 Talley, Truman H. "The Chautauqua, an American Achievement."

WORLD'S WORK 42 (June 1921): 172-84. Illus.

Survey of chautauqua's accomplishments and history (as compared to the lyceum). Useful account of its operation.

1300 Thornton, Harrison J. "Chautauqua and the Midwest." WISCONSIN MAGAZINE OF HISTORY 33 (December 1949): 152-63.

On the movement in general and, more specifically, on its infiltration into and effect on Midwest life. More on the educational and intellectual elements of chautauqua than on the entertainment offered.

1301 Tozier, Roy Becker. "A Short Life-History of the Chautauqua." Ph.D. dissertation, University of Iowa, 1932.

1302 Warde, Frederick. FIFTY YEARS OF MAKE BELIEVE. Los Angeles: Times-Mirror, 1923. vi, 310 p. Illus.

Memoirs of the latter nineteenth century on the English and American stage, with an interesting chapter on chautauqua and lyceum circuits.

1303 Wells, L. Jeanette. A HISTORY OF THE MUSIC FESTIVAL AT THE CHAUTAUQUA INSTITUTION, 1874-1957. Washington, D.C.: Catholic University of America Press, 1958. ix, 310 p. Bibliog.

Study based on her Catholic University thesis.

1304 Wilson, Edna Erle. "Canvas and Culture: When Chautauqua Comes to Town." OUTLOOK 131 (9 August 1922): 598-600. Illus.

Somewhat romanticized view of the impact of chautauqua on small-town audiences; stresses America's need for chautauqua. Focus also on program content.

1305 Winks, Evert M. as told to Winks, Robin W. "Recollections of a Dead Art: The Traveling Chautauqua." INDIANA MAGAZINE OF HISTORY 54 (March 1958): 41-48.

Reminiscences of the traveling chautauqua in the Midwest (1916-22).

1306 Zilboorg, Gregory. "Chautauqua and the Drama. Impressions of a Travelling Stranger." DRAMA 12 (October-November 1921): 16-18, 40. Illus.

Criticizes theatre centered in large cities, particularly New York, and praises chautauqua and the way it thrives in front of small-town audiences. Discusses the yet unrealized potential of chautauqua as an indigenously American theatrical form. The author sees chautauqua as the saving grace of the American theatre.

Chapter 7

OPTICAL AND MECHANICAL ENTERTAINMENTS, STAGE MAGIC, PUPPETRY, AND TOY THEATRES

A. STAGE MAGIC

Magic books abound, especially books on "how to" do magical effects. There have been numerous volumes of bibliography on magic as well. The following list, therefore, represents only a small number of books on magic and is limited in most instances to books on the history of magic, the autobiography-biography of important magicians, or significant memoirs. Major bibliographic sources covering the entire field of magic have been listed first. The user of this guide should consult section C below and appendix A (periodicals-serials) for additional important sources. The emphasis of the sources listed below is on American and English magicians and stage magic.

1. Bibliographies

1307   Alfredson, James B., and Daily George L., Jr. A SHORT TITLE CHECK LIST OF CONJURING PERIODICALS IN ENGLISH. Lansing, Mich.: Privately printed, 1976. ii, 60 p.

> Limited to two hundred copies, a useful checklist on periodicals.

1308   Clarke, Sidney W., and Blind, Adolphe. THE BIBLIOGRAPHY OF CONJURING AND KINDRED DECEPTIONS. London: George Johnson, 1920. 84 p.

> Details on over two thousand works on conjuring and allied arts. Complete checklist of periodicals published up to 1920. Not annotated.

1309   Evans, Henry Ridgely. SOME RARE OLD BOOKS ON CONJURING AND MAGIC OF THE 16TH, THE 17TH, AND THE 18TH CENTURY. Kenton, Ohio: IBM, 1943. 21 p. Illus.

> Standard reference source on the most notable rarities of early magical literature.

1310   Findlay, James B. COLLECTORS ANNUALS. 9 vols. Isle of Wight, Engl.: Shanklin, 1949-75.

Nine annuals in all, although seven and eight do not cover the field specifically. The last annual (xii, 280 p.), with twenty-three plates and facsimiles, is a comprehensive catalog of the holdings of Findlay's collection with some six thousand titles listed. Completed in 1973, the year of the compiler's death, this is probably the largest and most comprehensive bibliography on general magic to date. The early annuals are approximately twenty-six pages each.

1311   Gill, Robert. MAGIC AS A PERFORMING ART: A BIBLIOGRAPHY OF CONJURING. London and New York: Bowker, 1976. xxii, 252 p. Index.

Annotated bibliography of over one thousand books and pamphlets on conjuring published during the past forty years (plus reprints of earlier sources). Excellent supplement to items 1310, 1312, 1313, 1315, and 1316. This is the only full-length bibliography on performing magic to evaluate the literature with descriptions of contents and assessments of value. Subject, name, and title indexes.

1312   Hall, Trevor H. A BIBLIOGRAPHY OF BOOKS ON CONJURING IN ENGLISH FROM 1580 TO 1850. Lepton, Engl.: Palmyra Press; Minneapolis: Carl Waring Jones, 1957. 96 p. Illus., index.

Most scholarly of early bibliographers on magic; 323 entries. Editions limited: two hundred fifty British and five hundred American.

1313   _____. OLD CONJURING BOOKS: A BIBLIOGRAPHICAL AND HISTORICAL STUDY. London: Duckworth, 1972; New York: St. Martin's Press, 1973. xvi, 228 [9] p. Illus., index.

Supplement to Hall above; bibliography on pages 195-211. Examination in depth of eight historical books on conjuring and "magick" from 1581 to 1801; brief analysis of most of the other major historical works on the subject. Edition limited to one thousand copies (English edition).

1314   Potter, Jack. THE MASTER INDEX TO MAGIC IN PRINT. 14 vols. Calgary, Alberta, Canada: Micky Hades, 1967-75. Looseleaf.

Includes nine supplementary lists which include items missing from the main lists. Index of approximately 2,700 monographs, in addition to the complete files of over seventy magical periodicals. Last volume contains a checklist of every work cited in the index and is an impressive bibliography of practical conjuring/magic from the earliest times to 1964.

1315　Price, Harry. SHORT TITLE CATALOGUE . . . FROM CIRCA 1450 A.D. TO 1939 A.D. London: National Laboratory of Psychical Research, 1929. 422 p. Illus.

　　　See next entry.

1316　_____. SUPPLEMENT TO SHORT TITLE CATALOGUE . . . FROM 1472 A.D. TO THE PRESENT DAY. London: University of London Council for Psychical Research, 1935. 112 p. Illus.

　　　The two catalogs above are concerned principally with spiritualism and psychic phenomena and are keyed to the Harry Price Collection at the University of London Library. Not always accurate but still an important checklist of rare and primary sources.

1317　Toole-Stott, Raymond. A BIBLIOGRAPHY OF ENGLISH CONJURING, 1581-1876. Derby, Engl.: Harpur and Sons, 1976. 288 p. Illus.

　　　Latest bibliography by the outstanding circus bibliographer (his four-volume bibliography on the circus should be consulted as well. See item 81). Limited to one thousand copies with sixteen pages of plates. Contains collations of nearly one thousand books and pamphlets on conjuring, keyed to their locations.

2. General Histories, Reference, and Autobiography and Biography

1318　Bertram, Charles. ISN'T IT WONDERFUL. London: Swan Sonnenschein and Co., 1896. 300 p. Illus.

　　　A dated history of early magic includes author's own reminiscences.

1319　_____. A MAGICIAN IN MANY LANDS. London: George Routledge and Sons; New York: E.P. Dutton and Co., 1911. xx, 315 p. Illus.

　　　Life of the late nineteenth century magician and his world tours. A number of references to the magician Harry Kellar are included.

1320　Burlingham, H.J. LEAVES FROM CONJURERS' SCRAP BOOKS. Chicago: Donohue, Henneberry and Co., 1891. 274 p. Illus., index.

　　　Survey of prominent nineteenth-century magicians.

1321　_____. HERMANN THE MAGICIAN. Chicago: Laird and Lee, 1897. 298 p. Illus.

　　　Biographies of Carl and Alexander Herrmann and a discussion of their best tricks.

1322 ____. MAGICIAN'S HANDBOOK. Chicago: Wilcox and Follet, 1942. 298 p. Illus.

Good biographical sketches of Carl and Alexander Herrmann and descriptions of their acts. An earlier edition appeared in 1897.

1323 Cannell, John Clucas. THE SECRETS OF HOUDINI. London: Hutchinson, 1931. Reprints. Ann Arbor, Mich.: Gryphon Books, 1971; New York: Dover Publications, 1973; Detroit: Gale Research Co., 1974. 279 p. Illus.

Basically a how-to book, but includes a biographical sketch.

1324 Christopher, Milbourne. "Magic in Early Baltimore." MARYLAND HISTORICAL MAGAZINE 38 (December 1943): 323-30.

Essay on the first magician to perform in Baltimore (1787), Signior Falconi.

1325 ____. PANORAMA OF PRESTIDIGITATION: MAGIC THROUGH THE AGES IN PICTURES. New York: By the author, 1955. 42 p. Illus. Paper.

Largely superseded by other works by Christopher; pictorial history of magic from the early seventeenth century to 1955.

1326 ____. PANORAMA OF MAGIC. New York: Dover Publications, 1962. viii, 216 p. Illus., index. Paper.

Not as detailed as his subsequent THE ILLUSTRATED HISTORY OF MAGIC (item 1328) but still a good history of magic and well illustrated.

1327 ____. HOUDINI: THE UNTOLD STORY. New York: Thomas Y. Crowell Co., 1969. 281 p. Illus., index.

The most comprehensive and complete biography of Houdini by this leading authority and practicing magician; covers all phases of Houdini's career, including escape artistry and psychic investigations.

1328 ____. THE ILLUSTRATED HISTORY OF MAGIC. New York: Thomas Y. Crowell Co., 1973. 452 p. Illus., index, bibliog.

One of the most important magic books of modern times and an excellent history of magic from its earliest manifestations in Egypt, Greece, and Rome to contemporary magicians. Well illustrated with prints, photographs, posters, and engravings. Bibliography worth investigating.

1329 _____. HOUDINI--A PICTORIAL LIFE. New York: Thomas Y. Crowell Co., 1976. 218 p. Index, bibliog.

More than two hundred fifty illustrations; a good pictorial biography with material not used in HOUDINI: THE UNTOLD STORY (item 1327). Recommended bibliography of works by or about Houdini.

1330 Claflin, Edward, and Sheridan, Jeff. STREET MAGIC. AN ILLUS-TRATED HISTORY OF WANDERING MAGICIANS AND THEIR CONJUR-ING ARTS. Garden City, N.Y.: Doubleday and Co., 1977. xiii, 156 p. Illus., index, bibliog. Paper.

Despite some poorly reproduced illustrations and inexpensive binding and paper, this is a worthy and recommended intro-duction to what the authors term "street magic," which is "a kind of popular entertainment in the guise of magic or illusion, performed outside the boundaries of conventional theater." In actuality, the scope is less confining, touching on the en-tire history of the street entertainer from the primitive shaman, medieval jongleur, and Hindu fakir, to Houdini, psychic phenomena, and the contemporary New York street magician.

1331 Clark, Hyla M. THE WORLD'S GREATEST MAGIC. Photographs by Paul Levin. New York: Tree Communications Edition (Crown Publish-ers), 1976. 207 p. Illus., index, bibliog.

Devoted almost entirely to magic stars of the present and to the modern performance of magic as a dramatic art. Brief introductions to magic's history. Essays and photographs on thirty-four major magicians, including Houdini, Dunninger, Dai Vernon, Cardini, Blackstone, and Doug Henning. Thirty pages devoted to "The World's Greatest Magic Secrets" as revealed by The Amazing Randi. Selected updated bibliography.

1332 Clarke, Sidney W. THE ANNALS OF CONJURING: FROM THE EARLIEST TIMES TO THE PRESENT DAY. London: George Johnson, 1929. 310 p. Illus.

Originally published as a serial in the MAGIC WAND (1924-27); a scholarly and comprehensive review of the history of magic through the early 1900s. Considered by many a stan-dard reference source on the history of magic and magicians, especially strong on performers of the Maskelyne era (including details on those who appeared at his famous halls of magic).

1333 Cook, Olive. "Victorian Magicians." In THE SATURDAY BOOK 27, edited by John Hadfield, pp. 175-83. Boston and Toronto: Little, Brown and Co., 1967. Illus.

On the use of magic lantern by Victorian magicians; illustrated with posters of the phantasmagoria, diaroscuro, and the like.

1334   Devant, David [David Wighton]. WOES OF A WIZARD. London: S.H. Bousfield and Co., 1903. 183 p.

        Admixture of autobiography, anecdotes, and magical history told in an engaging manner.

1335   _____. MY MAGIC LIFE. London: Hutchinson and Co., 1931. Reprint. Bideford, Engl.: Supreme Magic Co., 1971. 287 p. Illus., index.

        Autobiography of this magician with an introduction by J.B. Priestley and material on other contemporary magicians known by Devant.

1336   Dircks, Henry. THE GHOST! For full entry and annotation, see item 1449.

1337   Doerflinger, William. THE MAGIC CATALOGUE: A COMPREHENSIVE GUIDE TO THE WONDERFUL WORLD OF MAGIC. New York: E.P. Dutton, 1977. x, 242 p. Illus., index, select bibliog. Paper.

        Without a doubt, the most comprehensive single guide to the subject of magic available. Includes a brief illustrated history followed by sections on types of magic effects, magic dealers, magicians' societies and conventions, antique magic apparatus, catalogs and memorabilia, information on museums, books, and magazines, and courses in conjuring. Very useful.

1338   Evans, Henry Ridgely. MAGIC & ITS PROFESSORS. New York: George Routledge and Sone, 1902. v, 220 p. Illus.

        Lives and careers of the best known of the nineteenth-century magicians and their feats. Appendix: "A Visit to the Grave of Robert-Houdin."

1339   _____. THE OLD AND THE NEW MAGIC. Introduction by Dr. Paul Carus. Chicago: Open Court Publishing Co., 1906. Rev. ed. London: Kegan Paul, 1909. xxxii, 517 p. Illus.

        A classic work on the origins of the art of magic, including details of famous effects, principles, and personalities told in a rather casual and informal presentation.

1340   _____. ADVENTURES IN MAGIC. New York: Leo Rullman, 1927. 87 p. Illus. Paper.

        Detailed account of the exploits of Theodore Bamberg (Okito) and other contemporary magicians.

1341   . HISTORY OF CONJURING AND MAGIC: FROM THE
EARLIEST TIMES TO THE END OF THE EIGHTEENTH CENTURY. Rev.
ed. Kenton, Ohio: William W. Durbin, 1930. 82 p. Illus.

Overview of the development of magic.

1342   . CAGLIOSTRO: A SORCERER OF THE EIGHTEENTH CENTURY.
New York: Masonic Bibliophiles, 1931. 43 p. Illus.

Scholarly study of one of history's greatest confidence-tricksters.

1343   Findlay, J.B. ANDERSON AND HIS THEATRE. Isle of Wight, Engl.:
Shanklin, 1967. 26 p. Illus. Paper.

Prof. Anderson and his shortlived theatre in Scotland (1845).

1344   Fischer, Ottokar. ILLUSTRATED MAGIC: [WITH] AN UNPUBLISHED
CHAPTER BY THE LATE HARRY KELLAR. Translated and edited by
Fulton Oursler and J.B. Mussey. New York: Macmillan Co., 1931
and 1955. 206 p. Illus.

Translation of DAS WUNDERBUCH DER ZAUBERKUNST (Stutt-
gart, 1929). Sensitive portraits of magicians of his own time.

1345   Frost, Thomas. THE LIVES OF THE CONJURERS. 2d ed. 1881. Reprint. Detroit: Singing Tree Press, 1970. 360 p. Index.

First edition appeared in 1876; the first full-length history of
conjuring, written by a journalist and not a practicing magician. Remains a classic reference and indispensible to the
serious study of the subject.

1346   Furst, Arnold. FAMOUS MAGICIANS OF THE WORLD. Los Angeles:
Genii, 1957. 48 p. Illus. (some in color).

Details of contemporary magicians' acts which appeared originally in the magazine GENII (see item 2362).

1347   Ganson, Lewis. THE DAI VERNON BOOK OF MAGIC. London:
Harry Stanley's Unique Magic Studio, 1957. Reprint. Bideford, Engl.:
Supreme Magic Co., 1971. 240 p. Illus.

One of eight books on Vernon by the author, and the best.
An authoritative tribute to "The Professor" and his work.

1348   Gibson, Walter Brown. THE MASTER MAGICIANS--THEIR LIVES AND
MOST FAMOUS TRICKS. Garden City, N.Y.: Doubleday and Co.,
1966. xvii, 221 p. Illus., index.

Chapters on Robert-Houdin, Professor Anderson, Hermann the
Kellar, Chung Ling Soo, Thurston, Houdini and Hardeen, and
the Great Raymond.

1349 _____ . THE ORIGINAL HOUDINI SCRAPBOOK. New York: Corwin Sterling Publishing Co., 1976. 224 p. Illus., index.

> Reproductions of posters, newspaper articles, letters, books, photographs, and other memorabilia are used to trace the career of Houdini. Poor index and sepia illustrations.

1350 Gibson, Walter Brown, and Young, Morris N. HOUDINI ON MAGIC. New York: Dover Publications, 1953. xv, 280 p. Illus. Paper.

> Excellent study of Houdini's escapes and illustrations in addition to illuminating biographical detail. Well illustrated with photographs, posters, line drawings, and theatrical publicity.

1351 _____ . HOUDINI'S FABULOUS MAGIC. New York: Bell Publishing Co., 1961. viii, 214 p. Illus., Bibliog.

> A prolific author on magic, Gibson's books on Houdini, as well as other magicians run into the dozens. This work (written with Young) contains material from the above work (and others) but is here presented in a more literary form.

1352 Gresham, William L. HOUDINI: THE MAN WHO WALKED THROUGH WALLS. New York: Henry Holt and Co., 1949. xii, 306 p. Illus., bibliog.

> A generally lively and thorough biography of Houdini; one of the better of the many lives of the master magician.

1353 Hanson, Herman, and Zweers, John U. THE MAGIC MAN. Cincinnati: Haines House of Cards, 1974. 104 p. Illus.

> Career of Herman Hanson, early twentieth-century American magician who died in 1973.

1354 Hay, Henry. CYCLOPEDIA OF MAGIC. London, and New York: David McKay, 1949. 498 p. Illus.

> Alphabetical arrangement of material on conjuring terms, tricks, and sleight of hand, as well as essays on aspects of magical stagecraft (lighting, music, dress, makeup) and historical notes on great magicians (contributors include Blackstone, Houdini, Thurston, Hugard, and Okito).

1355 Henning, Doug, with Reynolds, Charles. HOUDINI, HIS LEGEND AND HIS MAGIC. New York: Times Books (division of Quandrangle-New York Times Book Co.), 1977. 190 [2] p. Illus. (18 color pls.).

> Not notable for its text, although it serves as a summary of Houdini's life and magic. It is most useful for its numerous

illustrations, including eighteen color plates, a number never before published.

1356   Hilliard, John Northern. GREATER MAGIC. London: Carl Waring Jones, 1938. xxvii, 993 p. Illus.

Considered by many the greatest single work on performing magic, especially card magic, in English, and included with this list for that reason.

1357   Hoffman, Professor [Angelo John Lewis]. MODERN MAGIC: A PRAC-TICAL TREATISE ON THE ART OF CONJURING. London: Routledge, 1876. 528 p. Illus.

An influential work that has gone through many editions (seventeenth edition, 1939) and is considered by many as the conjuror's Bible because it helped to establish many principles and effects still practiced. Although a how-to book, included for its historical importance.

1358   Houdini, Harry. THE UNMASKING OF ROBERT-HOUDIN. New York: Publishers Printing Co., 1908. 319 p. Illus.

Controversial attack on Houdini's former idol. See item 1379.

1359   Jenness, George A. MASKELYNE AND COOKE: EGYPTIAN HALL, 1873-1904. London: By the author, 1967. 93 p. Illus., index, bibliog.

Edition limited to five hundred copies; introduction by Noel Maskelyne. The history of the famed Egyptian Hall up to the transfer of the troupe to St. George's Hall. Twenty-six pages of rare photographs. Good bibliography.

1360   Jennings, John J. THEATRICAL AND CIRCUS LIFE; OR, SECRETS OF THE STAGE, GREENROOM AND SAWDUST ARENA. For full entry and annotation, see item 220a.

1361   Kaye, Marvin. THE STEIN & DAY HANDBOOK OF MAGIC. Edited by John Salisse. New York: Stein and Day, 1973. 317 p. Illus., bibliog., glossary.

Good introduction to the magicians' art; same as the 1974 English edition entitled THE COMPLETE MAGICIAN (London: Macmillan Co.).

1362   Kellock, Harold. HOUDINI: HIS LIFE STORY. London: Heinemann, 1928. 384 p. Illus.

Biography compiled from documents and recollections of
Beatrice Houdini.

1363   Lamb, Geoffrey Frederick. PEGASUS BOOK OF MAGIC AND MAGI-
CIANS. London: Dobson, 1968. 190 p.

Superficial survey of magic and its most famous practitioners
from the earliest times to the mentalism of the Piddingtons.

1364   _____. VICTORIAN MAGIC. London, Henley, and Boston: Routledge
and Kegan Paul, 1976. xii, 136 p. Illus., index, bibliog.

Specific chapters on famous Victorian magicians and magic
theatre, including Professor Anderson, "Wizard of the North,"
Professor Pepper, "Colonel" Stodare, J.N. Maskelyne and the
Egyptian Hall, the Davenport Brothers, and Charles Bertram.
Although an entertaining volume, Lamb's coverage is superficial
and lacks documentation.

1365   McArdle, John. McARDLE'S INTERNATIONAL DICTIONARY OF MAGI-
TAIN. Newtown, Conn.: Published by author, 1963. 142 p.

Edition limited to fifty copies; seventy-three biographies of
magicians from the sixteenth century to the twentieth. Among
the entries are a history of automata, chautauqua, vaudeville,
effects, and terminology associated with magic.

1366   Maskelyne, Jasper. WHITE MAGIC: THE STORY OF THE MASKELYNES.
London: Stanley Paul, 1936. 287 p. Illus., index.

Historical account of three generations of the famous Maskelyne
family, their performances at the Egyptian Hall and St. George's
Hall in London, and the world-famous magicians who worked
for them.

1367   Maskelyne, Nevil, and Devant, David [David Wighton]. OUR MAGIC.
2d ed. Berkeley Heights, N.J.: Fleming Book Co., 1946. Reissue.
Bideford, Engl.: Supreme, 1971. xvi, 318 p. Illus., index.

A classic work and the first to treat magic as a valid dramatic
art. Divided into three parts: "Art in Magic," "Theory of
Magic," and "Practice of Magic."

1368   Meyer, Bernard C. HOUDINI: A MAN IN CHAINS. A PSYCHO-
ANALYTIC PORTRAIT. New York: E.P. Dutton and Co., 1976. xix,
197 p. Illus., index, notes.

Less of a biography than a psychiatric explanation for Houdini's
actions and behavior. A somewhat far-fetched portrait of the
magician as a tortured and neurotic man whose tricks and es-
capes were the product of a bizarre mind.

1369   Mulholland, John.   QUICKER THAN THE EYE--THE MAGIC & THE
        MAGICIANS OF THE WORLD.   Illustrated by Cyrus Leroy Baldridge.
        Bobbs-Merrill Co., 1932.   259 p.

        A survey account.

1370   _____.   JOHN MULHOLLAND'S STORY OF MAGIC.   New York:
        Loring and mussey, 1935.   79 p.   Illus.

        General history of magic with specific treatment of such
        magicians as Jack Gwynne, Edward Victor, and Nate Leipzig.
        Generally superseded by more recent histories.

1371   _____.   THE EARLY MAGIC SHOWS.   New York: By the author,
        1945.   18 p.   Illus.   Paper.

        Brief summary of the early origins of modern magic (mounte-
        banks, traveling performers, fairground tricksters, and the like)
        by the collector and magic expert.

1372   Olf, Julian M.   "The Actor and the Magician."   DRAMA REVIEW
        18 (March 1974):   53-58.

        Useful summary of the similarities between the art of the
        actor and the magician.

1373   Pecor, Charles.   THE MAGICIAN ON THE AMERICAN STAGE, 1752-
        1874.   Washington, D.C.:   Emerson and West, 1977.   313 p. (plus
        90 p. of footnotes).   Illus., bibliog.

        Adaptation of the author's dissertation; excellent source on all
        types of performers and performances of all kinds in colonial
        America.   Scope: from the arrival of the Hallam theatre com-
        pany in 1752 to the death of John Henry Anderson, the first
        star magician to visit America (also the year of Houdini's
        birth and the year Alexander Herrmann arrived in America).
        Divided into four sections: "The Early Struggles, 1752-1799,"
        "Growth and Expansion, 1800-1824," "A Time of Transition,
        1825-1849," and "The Dawning of the Golden Age, 1850-
        1874."   Contains ninety pages of footnotes.

1374   Randi, The Amazing, and Sugar, Bert Randolph.   PRESENTING HOU-
        DINI: HIS LIFE AND ART.   New York: Grosset and Dunlap, 1976.
        191 p.   Illus., index.   Paper.

        Good collection of illustrations; one of many books published
        on the fiftieth anniversary of the magician's death.   Otherwise,
        an undistinguished biography.

1375   Reynolds, Charles, and Reynolds, Regina.   100 YEARS OF MAGIC

POSTERS. New York: Grosset and Dunlap, 1976. 117 p. Illus. Paper.

Large (11 inch by 16 inch), full-color posters of the world's greatest magicians and their famous illusions reproduced. Biography of each magician and an explanation of how and why the posters were accomplished in the introduction.

1376 Robert-Houdin, Jean Eugene. MEMOIRS OF ROBERT-HOUDIN. Translated by R. Shelton MacKenzie. London: T. Werner Laurie, 1942. 376 p., London: Carl Waring Jones, 1944. xii, 458 p. Illus., New York: Dover Publications, 1964. 336 p. Illus., index.

First translation of this classic work appeared in 1859; later editions include a chapter on the life and performances of a typical French mountebank. The Dover edition contains an introduction by Milbourne Christopher, is translated by Lascelles Wraxall, and is a reprint of the two-volume 1859 English edition. The title of this edition is KING OF CONJURORS: MEMOIRS OF ROBERT-HOUDIN.

1377 Ronnie, Art. "Houdini's High-Flying Hoax." AMERICAN HERITAGE 23 (April 1972): 106-109. Illus.

Houdini's experiences in 1919 while filming THE GRIM GAME and his supposed daring-do in transferring from one plane to another--actually accomplished by an ex-Air Service flier, Robert E. Kennedy.

1378 Rydell, Wendy, and Gilbert, George. THE GREAT BOOK OF MAGIC. New York: Harry N. Abrams, 1976. 271 p. Illus. (many in color), index, bibliog.

Half of this book deals with the history of magic and famous magicians (Robert-Houdin, Herrmann brothers, John Nevil Maskelyne, Harry Kellar, Howard Thurston, Houdini, Blackstone, and others).

1379 Sardina, Maurice. WHERE HOUDINI WAS WRONG. Edited and translated by Victor Farelli. London: Magic Wand, 1950. 120 p. Illus.

A response to Houdini's THE UNMASKING OF ROBERT-HOUDIN (see item 1358) and a defense of the French magician's integrity.

1380 Severn, Bill. MAGIC AND MAGICIANS. New York: David McKay Co., 1958. 178 p. Illus., index.

Discusses Robert-Houdin, Herrmann, Kellar, Houdini, and Thurston, as well as a number of more contemporary magicians.

1381 Tarbell, Harlan. THE TARBELL COURSE IN MAGIC. 7 vols. New

York: Louis Tannen, 1941–72. Illus., index in Vol. 7 (pp. 377–490).

> The exception to the rule of this bibliography; a voluminous
> how-to work covering virtually every aspect of the art and
> practice of magic.

1382   Volkmann, Kurt. THE OLDEST DECEPTION. Translated by J. Barrows
Mussey. Foreword by Harold Joachin. Minneapolis: Carl Waring
Jones, 1956. 48 p. Illus.

> Interesting study of the cups and balls trick in the fifteenth
> and sixteenth centuries; much informative and scholarly com-
> ment for the student and historian.

1383   Williams, Beryl, and Epstein, Samuel. THE GREAT HOUDINI: MAGI-
CIAN EXTRAORDINARY. New York: Julian Messner, 1954. viii,
183 p. Illus., bibliog.

> Not a particularly distinguished biography but gives a fair
> sense of Houdini's personality.

B. PUPPETRY AND TOY THEATRES (JUVENILE DRAMA)

The majority of sources on puppetry are devoted to the making of puppets and
the creation of puppet shows. This list excludes all sources devoted exclusively
to production, although a referral to items 1389 and 1400 will lead one to
major sources on puppet production. The emphasis in this select list is on the
history of puppetry and the toy theatre, the latter a topic that has received
scant coverage, especially the American form. The listing also excludes a
large number of sources on puppetry outside of the United States and England;
these too can be found in items 1389 and 1400.

1384   Baird, Bil. THE ART OF THE PUPPET. New York: Bonanza Books,
1973. 251 p. Illus., index, select bibliog.

> Magnificent colored photographs adorn this undocumented world
> history of puppetry from its remotest beginnings to the present.
> Only one major chapter is devoted to putting on a puppet show.
> International bibliography.

1385   Baring, Maurice. PUNCH AND JUDY & OTHER ESSAYS. London:
Heinemann, 1924. x, 370 p.

> Most of these essays are on playwrights. The title essay, how-
> ever, is an interesting comparison between Punch and Judy
> shows and early film (pp. 3–24).

1386   Batchelder, Marjorie. THE PUPPET THEATRE HANDBOOK. New York:
Harper and Bros., 1947. 300 p. Illus. (68 black-and-white pls.),
bibliog.

Comprehensive study of puppetry, including brief history of
world puppetry, puppet and marionette construction, and stage
construction. Dated list of suppliers.

1387   Bohmer, Gunter. PUPPETS THROUGH THE AGES: AN ILLUSTRATED
HISTORY. Translated by Gerald Morice. London: MacDonald and
Co., 1971; Boston: Plays, Inc., 1971. 156 p. Illus. (some in color).

History drawn from the puppet collection of the city of
Munich, Germany.

1388   Collier, John Payne. PUNCH AND JUDY, WITH ILLUSTRATIONS
DESIGNED AND ENGRAVED BY GEORGE CRUIKSHANK. ACCOM-
PANIED BY THE DIALOGUE OF THE PUPPET-SHOW, AN ACCOUNT
OF ITS ORIGIN, AND OF PUPPET-PLAYS IN ENGLAND. London:
S. Prowett, 1828. [10] 248 p. Illus. (24 pls.).

Important early history of Punch and Judy; especially valuable
for Cruikshank's engravings. Numerous editions and reissues.

1389   Crothers, J. Frances. THE PUPPETEER'S LIBRARY GUIDE: THE
BIBLIOGRAPHIC INDEX TO THE LITERATURE OF THE WORLD PUPPET
THEATRE. Metuchen, N.J.: Scarecrow Press, 1971. 474 p. Index,
list of puplishers.

The first volume in on puppet history; six volumes are projected.

1390   Currell, David. THE COMPLETE BOOK OF PUPPETS. Boston: Plays
Inc., 1975. 204 p. Illus.

History, construction, special professional tricks, and manipu-
lation of marionettes.

1391   Hill, Lyn Stiefel. "There Was an American Toy Theatre." THEATRE
SURVEY 26 (November 1975): 166-84. Illus.

An examination of this popular pastime in America in the late
nineteenth century and early twentieth century. The author
explores the American publication of toy theatre plays. In
part, a rebuttal to Speaight (see item 1413).

1392   Joseph, Helen Haiman. A BOOK OF MARIONETTES. London: Allen
and Unwin, 1931. 248 p. Illus. (47 pls.).

History of marionettes in Italy, Germany, England, America,
and elsewhere.

1393   McNamara, Brooks. "An Interview with Percy Press and a Portfolio of
Buskers." EDUCATIONAL THEATRE JOURNAL 27 (October 1975): 313-
22. Illus.

An interview with a performer called "the greatest modern
Punch and Judy showman." An excellent example of a dying
breed of English busker. Concludes with a series of nineteenth-
and early twentieth-century engravings of street entertainers.

1394   McPharlin, Paul. THE PUPPET THEATRE IN AMERICA. Rev. ed.
Boston: Plays, 1969. xi, 734 p. Illus., index.

The definitive history, 1524-1948 (with a supplement to the
1949 edition updating to the present by Marjorie Batchelder
McPharlin) of puppets in America.

1395   Matthews, Brander. "A Moral from a Toy Theatre." SCRIBNER'S
MAGAZINE 58 (October 1915): 405-12. Illus.

Robert Louis Stevenson took to playwriting inspired by Skelts's
Juvenile Drama and popular melodrama, according to this
source. This essay is a criticism of Stevenson's playwriting
stating that his models were poorly chosen and the genre he
wrote in, i.e., melodrama, was inferior. Article also discusses English toy theatres and melodrama to a considerable
extent.

1396   Morice, Gerald. "Long Live the Juvenile Drama." NOTES AND
QUERIES 186 (25 March 1944): 157-58.

Data on "Pollock's" toy theatre shop in Hoxton and the decline of this business. See item 1397.

1397   _____. "Victorian Toy Theatres, Parlour Pastimes and Pursuits, and
Street Games." NOTES AND QUERIES 187 (7 October 1944): 157-
59.

Notes on aspects to toy theatres; manufacturers' advertisements
the principal source of this essay (H.G. Clark productions).

1398   _____. "Further Long Life to the Juvenile Drama." NOTES AND
QUERIES 187 (2 December 1944): 253-55.

Continuation of item 1396.

1399   Morice, Gerald, and Speaight, George. "New Light on the Juvenile
Drama." THEATRE NOTEBOOK 26 (Spring 1972): 115-21.

Essay based on 1850 interview between Henry Mayhew and
William West, the publisher of juvenile drama and theatres.

1400   Philpott, A.R. DICTIONARY OF PUPPETRY. London: MacDonald
and Co., 1969; Boston: Plays, Inc., 1969. 291 p. Illus., bibliog.

Entries on virtually every topic having to do with puppets, including several pages relating to Punch and his origins and names of famous Punchmen.

1401 Seaton-Reid, D. "An Early West Sheet?" THEATRE NOTEBOOK 4 (January–March 1950): 36–37. Illus.

The author discusses a sheet of characters from the juvenile drama version of John Millingen's THE BEEHIVE (Lyceum, 19 January 1911):

1402 _____. "Early West Plates." THEATRE NOTEBOOK 5 (January–March 1951): 43–43.

On rare 1811 plates of juvenile drama.

1403 _____. "A Portrait of William West." THEATRE NOTEBOOK 6 (January–March 1952): 43–44.

Brief biography of the early nineteenth-century publisher of juvenile drama.

1404 Simmen, Rene. THE WORLD OF PUPPETS. New York: Thomas Y. Crowell Co., 1975. 135 p. Illus., select. bibliog., notes.

Superficial world history but good photographs of all types of puppets, especially European examples. Brief section on the English "Punch." First published in Zurich in 1972.

1405 Speaight, George. "Pope in the Toy Theatre." THEATRE NOTEBOOK 7 (April–June 1953): 62–63.

Demonstrates the use of Pope's ILIAD in a juvenile version of George Almar's THE CEDAR CHEST.

1406 _____. THE HISTORY OF THE ENGLISH PUPPET THEATRE. London: G. Harrap, 1955; New York: John De Graff, n.d. 350 p. Illus., index, notes.

The definitive history; the Punch and Judy aspect is improved and expanded in his later book (see item 1411). Well-documented and lively narration. Appendixes: "Puppet Show-men in England, 1600–1914" and "Plays Performed by Puppets in England."

1407 _____. "The M.W. Stone Collection." THEATRE NOTEBOOK 11 (January–March 1957): 62–63.

Survey of the Juvenile Drama Collection in the Enthoven Collection at the Victoria and Albert Museum (now part of the British Theatre Museum).

1408 _____. "Juvenile Drama and Puppetry Research." THEATRE NOTE-
BOOK 21 (Autumn 1966): 24-26.

> Recent research and discoveries in juvenile drama and pup-
> petry are outlined.

1409 _____. THE HISTORY OF THE ENGLISH TOY THEATRE. Boston:
Plays, Inc., 1946. Rev. ed., 1969. 182 p. Illus., index, bibliog.,
appendixes.

> First published as JUVENILE DRAMA: THE HISTORY OF THE
> ENGLISH TOY THEATRE (London: MacDonald and Co.). The
> standard source on the topic; discusses the adaptation of Eng-
> lish popular theatre forms, in particular harlequinades and
> pantomime, into toy theatre. Appendixes list publishers of
> toy theatre plays, lists of collections, and a short bibliography.

1410 _____. "The Brigand in the Toy Theatre." In THE SATURDAY BOOK
29, edited by John Hadfield, pp. 206-15. New York: Clarkson N.
Potter, 1969. Illus. (some in color).

> History and description of the juvenile drama version of James
> Robinson Planche's THE BRIGAND and the toy theatre.

1411 _____. PUNCH AND JUDY: A HISTORY. Rev. ed. Boston: Plays,
Inc., 1970; London: Studio Vista, 1970. 160 p. Illus., index,
bibliog.

> Portions of this book are based on material previously included
> in his THE HISTORY OF THE ENGLISH PUPPET THEATRE (see
> item 1406). Includes eight pages of full color, and more
> than fifty black-and-white illustrations. The best single source
> on the subject and most of the major primary and early sources
> are listed in his bibliography.

1412 _____. "The Toy Theatre." HARVARD LIBRARY BULLETIN 19 (July
1971): 307-13. Illus.

> Good summary history of toy theatre (juvenile drama) with spe-
> cific reference to the Harvard Theatre Collection holdings.

1413 _____. "Was There Ever an American Toy Theatre?" NINETEENTH
CENTURY THEATRE RESEARCH 1 (Autumn 1973): 89-93.

> Belief that there was no true indigenous toy theatre in the
> United States, although a toy theatre did begin to emerge
> about 1870 with a repertory basically English in origin. See
> Hill, item 1391.

1414 Spencer, H.D. "A West Artist." THEATRE NOTEBOOK 4 (January-
March 1950): 37-38.

Deals with a C. Tompkins whose signature appears on some
West portraits, ca. 1817-19.

1415 _____. "The Juvenile Drama Artists: William Heath's Early Sheets."
THEATRE NOTEBOOK 5 (January-March 1951): 43-44.

Evidence presented on William Heath's early contributions to
juvenile drama.

1416 Stead, Philip John. MR. PUNCH. London: Evans Brothers, 1950.
165 p. Illus., index, note on sources.

Undistinguished but serviceable history of Punch; superseded by
Speaight's definitive work (see item 1406).

1417 Stone, M.W. "Juvenile Drama and J.H. Jameson." THEATRE NOTE-
BOOK 1 (October 1945): 5-6.

Early publisher of juvenile drama with a list of plays he published.

1418 _____. "William Blake and the Juvenile Drama." THEATRE NOTE-
BOOK 1 (July 1946): 41.

Disproves notion that Blake worked as illustrator-designer for
William West, the juvenile drama publisher.

1419 _____. Juvenile Drama Publishers--The Dyers." THEATRE NOTE-
BOOK 1 (January 1947): 80.

On early nineteenth-century juvenile drama publications, includes list of Dyer Company plays.

1420 _____. "Shakespeare and the Juvenile Drama." THEATRE NOTEBOOK
8 (April-June 1954): 65-66.

Early nineteenth-century juvenile drama adapted from Shakespeare with a list of adaptations.

1421 Taylor, Vic. REMINISCENCES OF A SHOWMAN. Introduction by
David Robinson. London: Allen Lane, 1971. ix [x], 115 [6] p.
Illus.

Memoirs of a twentieth-century Punch and Judy showman and
magician in England.

1422 Walton, Thomas. "Notes for a History of Juvenile Drama." THEATRE
NOTEBOOK 3 (July-September 1949): 64-66.

Random and rather disjointed notes from Thomas Dibdin's
REMINISCENCES.

1423   Williams, Charles D.   "A Note on H.G. Clarke Productions."   NOTES
       AND QUERIES 186 (1 January 1944): 19-20.

       Brief history of Clarke, publisher of "penny plain, twopence
       coloured."

1424   _____.   "A Note on Toy Theatre Lighting."   NOTES AND QUERIES
       187 (4 November 1944): 212.

       Possible form of lighting used for toy theatres; extremely
       brief.

1425   _____.   "A Note on Wells Gardner Darton & Co., Ltd."   NOTES
       AND QUERIES 187 (18 November 1944): 232-33.

       On the toy theatre publishing firm.

1426   Wilson, A[lbert]. E[dward].   PENNY PLAIN TWOPENCE COLOURED:
       A HISTORY OF THE JUVENILE DRAMA.   Foreword by Charles B.
       Cochran.   London: Harrap, 1932.   Reprint.   New York, and London:
       Benjamin Blom, 1969.   118 p.   Illus., bibliog.

       Earliest study of juvenile drama with numerous illustrations.
       Two appendixes: list of publishers and list of plays published
       by William West between 1811 and 1831.   Superseded by
       Speaight, 1409.

C. STAGE ILLUSIONS, PANORAMA AND DIORAMA, AND
EARLY OPTICAL AND MECHANICAL ENTERTAINMENTS

See also sources in section A, above.   Altick's SHOWS OF LONDON should
be consulted for important chapters on various forms of optical and mechanical
exhibitions and for additional sources on English forms, especially.   See item
279.

1427   Allen, Ralph G.   "The Eidophusikon."   THEATRE DESIGN & TECHNOL-
       OGY 7 (December 1966): 12-16.   Illus.

       De Loutherbourg's scenic spectacle first exhibited in 1781; a
       summary of contemporary information.

1428   Andrews, Herbert C.   "The Leicester Square and Strand Panoramas:
       Their Proprietors and Artists."   NOTES AND QUERIES 159 (26 July
       1930): 57-61; 159 (2 August 1930): 75-78.

       Good summary of the history of these two exhibition halls for
       panoramas and their various proprietors.

1429   Apperson, G.L.   "The Early History of Panoramas."   ANTIQUARY 40
       (1904): 299-304.

Useful for background information and early history of English examples.

1430 Arnold, Richard L. "Animated Scenery." EDUCATIONAL THEATRE JOURNAL 16 (October 1964): 249-52.

Deals with those effects which gave "animation or a sense of motion to otherwise static settings." Describes how these effects were achieved.

1431 Arrington, Joseph Earl. "Leon D. Pomarede's Original Panorama of the Mississippi Rover." MISSOURI HISTORICAL SOCIETY BULLETIN 9 (April 1953): 261-73.

Study of Pomarede's career as a panoramist and his 1849 Mississippi panorama. Detailed description and study of its various exhibitions between St. Louis and Newark, New Jersey.

1432 _____. "The Story of Stockwell's Panorama." MINNESOTA HISTORY 33 (Autumn 1953): 284-90. Illus.

Samuel B. Stockwell, born 1813 in Boston; his career as a scene artist and his Mississippi panorama first displayed in Boston in 1839.

1433 _____. "Lewis and Bartholomew's Mechanical Panorama of the Battle of Bunker Hill." OLD-TIME NEW ENGLAND 52 (Fall 1961): 50-58, 81-89. Illus.

Description of a panorama painted by Minard Lewis and Truman C. Bartholomew in 1838 and exhibited for almost twenty years.

1434 Bapst, Germaine. ESSAI SUR L'HISTOIRE DES PANORAMAS ET DES DIORAMAS. Paris: Imprimerie Nationale, 1891. 30 p. Illus.

Panorama as an international phenomenon. In French.

1435 Blegen, Theodore C. "The 'Fashionable Tour' on the Upper Mississippi." MINNESOTA HISTORY 20 (December 1939): 377-96.

Focus on the panorama's influence on travel, its attempt at realism, and its great popularity, especially Banvard's. Other panoramic painters mentioned include Leon Pomarede, H. Lewis, J.R. Smith, and S.B. Stockwell.

1436 Boe, Roy A. "The Panoramas of the Mississippi." MISSISSIPPI QUARTERLY 16 (Fall 1963): 203-19. Illus.

Panoramas of the 1830s and '40s, principally those of John Banvard, are discussed. Also mentioned are John Rowson

Smith, Harry Lewis, Sam Stockwell, Leon Pomarede, and Samuel Hudson. A useful summary.

1437   Born, Wolfgang. "Early Peep-Shows and the Renaissance Stage." CON-COISSEUR 107 (February 1941): 67-7; (April 1941): 161-64, 180. Illus.

Survey of early peep shows and Renaissance staging.

1438   _____. "The Panoramic Landscape as an American Art Form." ART IN AMERICA 36 (1948): 3-19. Illus.

The origin of the panorama and its influence on the development of "panoramic painting" in the Hudson River School is discussed with the use of pictorial examples. Relationship between well-known artists and panoramists is established.

1439   Carothers, Robert L., and Marsh, John L. "The Whale and the Panorama." NINETEENTH-CENTURY FICTION 26 (December 1971): 319-28.

The Benjamin Russell-Caleb Purrington Panorama, "A Whaling Voyage Round the World" (1849), as a possible inspiration for Melville's writing of MOBY DICK. Includes a description of the panorama and its history.

1440   Carroll, Charles Michael. THE GREAT CHESS AUTOMATION. New York: Dover Publications, 1975. xi, 116 p. Illus., index, bibliog.

History of one of the most famous of the automata; excellent bibliography.

1441   Ceram, C.W. [Kurt W. Marek]. ARCHAEOLOGY OF THE CINEMA. Translated by Richard Winston. Illustrations edited by Olive Cook. New York: Harcourt, Brace, and World, [1965]. 264 p. Illus., index, bibliog.

History of the genesis of the cinema to 1897. Although not an in-depth study, this book is a valuable introduction to early Optical entertainments (magic lanterns, the diorama, panorama, and so forth. An essential extension to the text are the 293 illustrations on forerunners of the cinema. Recommended.

1442   Chapuis, Alfred, and Droz, Edmund. AUTOMATA. Translated by Alec Reid. New York: Central Book Co., 1958. 411 p. Illus., notes and additions.

Original title: LES AUTOMATES DAN LES OUEVRES D' IMAGINATION (Switzerland, 1947). Standard study of mechanical devices for entertainment from antiquity to the 1940s. Most useful and pertinent chapters are: 12, "Sooth-

Sayers, Magicians and Conjurers," 13, "Mechanical Music and Automaton Musicians," 14, "Automaton Writers and Draughtsmen," 15, "Walking and Talking Automata," 17, "Animated Display," 18, "Trick Machinery, Fake Automata Plays and Semi-Automata."

1443   Cook, Olive. MOVEMENT IN TWO DIMENSIONS. A STUDY OF THE ANIMATED AND PROJECTED PICTURES WHICH PRECEDED THE INVENTION OF CINEMATOGRAPHY. London: Hutchinson and Co., 1963. 142 [3] p. Illus., index, bibliog.

Topics covered include "mirrors and magic," peep shows and panoramas, Far Eastern shadows, Chinese shades (shadow shows), and the magic lantern.

1444   Cooke, Conrad William. AUTOMATA OLD AND NEW. London: Cheswick Press, 1893. 98 p. Illus.

Brief but classic work.

1445   Daguerre, Louis J.M. AN HISTORICAL AND DESCRIPTIVE ACCOUNT OF THE VARIOUS PROCESSES OF THE DAGUERREOTYPE AND THE DIORAMA. London, 1839. Reprint. New York: Kraus Reprint, 1969. 86 p. plus 4 p. essay.

Most applicable chapter is the last, a descriptive of the process of painting and effects of light applied by Daguerre to the pictures of the diorama. Includes four-page essay by William A. Aikin, "Theory of the Daguerreotype Process."

1446   Dahl, Curtis. "Panoramas of Antiquity." ARCHAEOLOGY 12 (Winter 1959): 258-63. Illus.

Explanation of types of panoramas popular 1800-1870, a list of archeological subjects exhibited in London, and a discussion of American examples. A useful survey.

1447   _____. "Artemus Ward; Comic Panoramist." NEW ENGLAND QUARTERLY 32 (December 1959): 476-85.

Ward's 1863 parody; an accurate and amusing caricature of the 1840s panoramas. Documented with numerous sources suggested.

1448   _____. "Mark Twain and the Moving Panoramas." AMERICAN QUARTERLY 13 (Spring 1961): 20-32.

Twain's satirization of the moving panorama and its grandiloquent lecture. Documented.

1449   Dircks, Henry. THE GHOST! AS PRODUCED IN THE SPECTRE DRAMA

. . . BY THE APPARATUS CALLED THE DIRCKSIAN PHANTASMAGORIA. London: Spon, 1863. 102 p. Illus.

Description of "Pepper's Ghost," the optical illusion invented by Dircks. See also Speaight (item 1480) and sources in section A.

1450   Dondore, Dorothy. "Banvard's Panorama and The Flowering of New England." NEW ENGLAND QUARTERLY 11 (December 1938): 817-26.

Banvard's Mississippi panorama and its stimulation of New England writers, e.g., J.G. Whittier, Longfellow, and Van Wyck Brooks.

1451   Fay, Arthur. BIOSCOPE SHOWS AND THEIR ENGINES. Lingfield, Surrey, Engl.: Oakwood Press, 1966. 36 p. Illus. Paper.

Published to commemorate the seventieth birthday of cinematography (i.e., in Great Britain). Brief history of optical illusion and more detail on early traveling cinema shows with allusions to Pepper's Ghost, marionette shows, waxwork exhibitions, menageries, and so forth. Especially good on transportation up to about 1916.

1452   Gage, John. "Loutherbourg: Mystagogue of the Sublime." HISTORY TODAY 13 (May 1963): 332-39. Illus.

De Loutherbourg's career summarized with a focus on his "Eidophusikon" and its influence.

1453   Gernsheim, Helmut, and Alison, L.J.M. DAGUERRE: THE HISTORY OF THE DIORAMA AND THE DAGUERROTYPE. New York: Dover Publications, 1968. xxii, 226 p. Illus., index, bibliog., notes, appendixes. Paper.

Contains succinct account of the photographic pioneer's (1787-1851) contributions to the art of the panorama (1807-16), scene design, and later his development of the diorama (1820s). Rival dioramas are discussed also, as is the history of the panorama. Appendix lists subjects shown at Paris and London Dioramas (beginning in the 1820s). Extensively illustrated.

1454   Gordon, Lesley. PEEPSHOW INTO PARADISE: A HISTORY OF CHILDREN'S TOYS. London: Harrap; New York: J. DeGraff, 1953. 264 p. Illus. (6 pls.), bibliog.

Six plates in color with line drawings by the author. Material on automata.

1455   Heather, J[ohn]. F[ry]. OPTICAL INSTRUMENTS. London: Lockwood, 1888. viii, 141 p.

Chapter 7 (pp. 100-108), "Instruments for Exhibiting Magni-
fied Pictures of Objects to an Assemblage of Spectators' most
useful (on magic lanterns and the solar microscope).

1456 Hedgbeth, Llewellyn Hubbard. "Extant American Panoramas: Moving
Entertainments of the Nineteenth Century." Ph.D. dissertation, New
York University, 1977. 533 p.

The author discusses the general history of panoramas and
gives the history and descriptions of various extant American
moving panoramas, e.g., C.C.A. Christensen's "Mormon
Panorama," the Russel-Parrington "Whaling Voyage Round the
World," the Dickeson-Egan "Monumental Grandeur of the
Mississippi Valley," John Steven's "Sioux War Panorama,"
Gordon's "Battle Scenes of the Rebellion," Ruger's "Andrews'
Railroad Raid, 1862," the Mastin Collection, and Thomas
Nast's "Grand Caricaturama."

1457 Heilbron, Bertha L. "Henry Lewis' 'Das Illustrirte Mississippithal'; A
Contemporary Advertisement." BIBLIOGRAPHIC SOCIETY OF AMERICA
PAPERS 43 (3d quarterly 1949): 344-45.

Letter written by Heilbron including an advertisement of H.
Lewis's book on panorama citing its form and value.

1458 _____. "Documentary Panorama." MINNESOTA HISTORY 30 (March
1949): 14-23.

Story of the Minnesota Panorama painted by John Stevens.
The panorama is explained as a documentary of the history of
Minnesota; Stevens's other panoramas are mentioned in detail
and highly praised.

1459 Hillier, Mary. AUTOMATA AND MECHANICAL TOYS--AN ILLUS-
TRATED HISTORY. London: Jupiter Books, 1976. 200 p. Illus.,
index, bibliog.

Emphasis on the eighteenth century onwards; excellent illustrations, some in color. Chapter on "Wizards and Showmen"
more pertinent than other chapters. Includes a chronological
bibliography and index of mechanical toy and automata makers
in an appendix.

1460 Hopkins, Albert A., ed. and comp. MAGIC: STAGE ILLUSIONS AND
SCIENTIFIC DIVERSIONS INCLUDING TRICK PHOTOGRAPHY. Intro-
duction by Henry Ridgely Evans. New York, 1897. Reprints. New
York: Benjamin Blom, 1967; New York: Arno Press, 1977. xii, 556 p.
Illus., index, bibliog.

Compendium of stage tricks, optical illusions, machines, and so forth with a broad survey of the history of legerdemain, ventriloquism, and shadowgraphy. Though dated, this is a marvelous source for nineteenth-century art of illusion. Although meant as a revelation of tricks, Hopkins is useful today as a historical document. Over four hundred illustrations.

1461 Lausanne, Edita. THE GOLDEN AGE OF TOYS. London: Patrick Stephens, 1967. Illus.

Chapter 12 (pp. 219 f.): Good summary survey of optical toys of the nineteenth century, including Auguste Lapierre's magic lanterns and subsequent versions. Deals also with more complex optical devices.

1462 McDermott, John Francis. "Banvard's Mississippi Panorama Pamphlets." BIBLIOGRAPHIC SOCIETY OF AMERICA PAPERS 43 (1st quarter 1949): 48-62. Illus.

Descriptions of the form, contents, and editions of John Banvard's pamphlets, illustrated with three posters of advertisements.

1463 _____. "Henry Lewis' 'Das Illustrirte Mississippithal'." BIBLIOGRAPH-IC SOCIETY OF AMERICA PAPERS 45 (2d quarter 1951): 152-55.

Letter from McDermott in which he discusses the bilingual irregularity of the pictorial captions in the German edition of Lewis's books and describes the content and its importance as an art form. See item 1457.

1464 _____. THE LOST PANORAMAS OF THE MISSISSIPPI. Chicago: University of Chicago Press, 1958. xvii, 211 p. Illus., index, bibliog.

The definitive study of the origins and early history of the American panorama of the 1840s. A major portion of the book deals with such panoramists as John Banvard, Henry Lewis, John Rowson Smith, Sam Stockwell, and Leon Pomarede; concludes with statements on the physical structure of the panorama. Excellent bibliography.

1465 McLanathan, Richard. THE AMERICAN TRADITION IN THE ARTS. New York: Harcourt, Brace and World, 1968. xv, 492 p. Illus., index, bibliog.

Author includes a survey of panoramas in the United States (pp. 229-30 and 302-10).

1466 Marion, F. THE WONDERS OF OPTICS. Translated by Charles W. Quin. London: Sampson Low, Son, and Marston, 1868; New York:

Charles Scribner's Sons, 1870. xiv[15], 276 p. Illus.

Chapter 1, part 3 (pp. 160-67): a simple explanation and illustration of the Magic Lantern.

1467 Marsh, John L. "The Moving Panorama." PLAYERS, THE MAGAZINE OF AMERICAN THEATRE 45 (August-September 1970): 272-75. Illus.

Brief history of the panorama, A WHALING VOYAGE ROUND THE WORLD, which began at Fairhaven and New Bedford, Massachusetts, in 1848.

1468 _____. "Captain E.C. Williams and the Panoramic School of Acting." EDUCATIONAL THEATRE JOURNAL 23 (October 1971): 289-97.

A purveyor of panoramas on the American stage is traced. The SOUTH SEA WHALING VOYAGE began in 1868 and lasted almost a decade; Williams was its owner and delineator.

1469 "Moving (Dioramic) Experiences." ALL THE YEAR ROUND 17 (1867): 304-307.

Witty account of moving dioramic exhibitions in England; includes information on methods of operation and audience responses.

1470 "On Cosmoramas, Dioramas, and Panoramas." PENNY MAGAZINE 11 (1842): 363-64.

Brief survey of each form.

1471 Ord-Hume, Arthur W.J.G. CLOCKWORK MUSIC. New York: Crown Publishers, 1973. 334 p. Illus.

A not always reliable illustrated history of mechanical instruments from the music box to the pianola, from automaton lady virginal players to orchestrion.

1472 Parry, Lee. "Landscape Theatre in America." ART IN AMERICA 59 (November-December 1971): 52-61. Illus. (some in color).

Documented study of the influence of panoramic exhibitions of the early nineteenth century on landscape painters. Discusses work of John Banvard and John Vanderlyn, and provides English and French examples, as well as American ones.

1473 Phillabaum, Corliss E. "Panoramic Scenery at Sadler's Wells." OHIO STATE UNIVERSITY THEATRE COLLECTION BULLETIN 6 (1959): 20-25. Illus.

Use of panoramas in Samuel Phelps's productions of: THE

TEMPEST (1840), TIMON OF ATHENS (1851 or 1856), and
PERICLES (1854).

1474   Preston, Lillian E. "Philippe Jacques de Loutherbourg: Eighteenth
Century Romantic Artist and Scene Designer." Ph.D. dissertation, University of Florida, 1957. 315 p.

Survey of his career and an assessment of his theatrical contributions, including scenic innovations.

1475   Quigley, Martin. MAGIC SHADOWS: THE STORY OF THE ORIGINAL
MOTION PICTURE. Washington, D.C.: Georgetown University, 1948.
Reprint. New York: Quigley Publishing, 1960. 190 p. Illus.,
index, bibliog.

Useful prehistory of the motion picture from the earliest
"magic shadow shows" to the New York premiere of screen
projection at Koster and Bial's Music Hall in New York (23
April 1896). As a summary of the evolution of optical entertainment, this is a valuable study.

1476   Rathbone, Perry T., ed. MISSISSIPPI PANORAMA: THE LIFE AND
LANDSCAPE OF THE FATHER OF WATERS AND ITS GREAT TRIBUTARY,
THE MISSOURI. St. Louis: City Art Museum, 1949. 351 p. Illus.

Written as a guide to an exhibit at the City Art Museum;
chapters by Rathbone, Charles van Ravenswaay, and H.
Steward Leonard. The focus of the exhibit was the "Panorama
of the Monumental Grandeur of the Mississippi Valley" (1850),
a fifteen thousand foot canvas which toured the country in
1852. Dr. Montroville W. Dickeson and I.J. Egan were
responsible for this panorama. Features 188 illustrations.

1477   Rosenfeld, Sybil. "The Eidophusikon Illustrated." THEATRE NOTE-
BOOK 18 (Winter 1963-64): 52-54. Illus.

Plate and text illuminate De Loutherbourg's miniature scenic
entertainment of the 1780s.

1478   _____. A SHORT HISTORY OF SCENE DESIGN IN GREAT BRITAIN.
Totowa, N.J.: Rowman and Littlefield, 1973. xviii, 214 p. Illus.,
index, bibliog.

Covers all aspects of design historically and includes useful
sections on the origin and influences of the panorama and
the diorama.

1479   Southern, H. "The Centenary of Panorama." THEATRE NOTEBOOK 5
(April-June 1951): 67-69.

Summary of the history of Hamilton and Poole's panoramas in England.

1480 Speaight, George. "Professor Pepper's Ghost." REVUE D'HISTOIRE DU THEATRE 15 (January–March 1963): 48–56. Illus.

Magic Lantern and the invention by Dircks (mid-nineteenth century) of his optical illusion and its ultimate perfection and exploitation by J.H. Pepper of the Royal Polytechnic Institution. Good drawings illustrate its evolution and methodology.

1481 Telbin, William [the younger]. "The Painting of Panoramas." MAGAZINE OF ART 24 (1900): 558–58. Illus.

The scene designer and painter discusses nineteenth-century English panoramas.

1482 van Ravenswaay, Charles. "Our Cover." MISSOURI HISTORICAL SOCIETY JOURNAL 4 (July 1948): 196.

Short biography of Henry Lewis focuses on the where and when of his panorama.

1483 Von Hagen, Victor Wolfgang. FREDERICK CATHERWOOD, ARCHITECT. New York: Oxford University Press, 1950. xix, 177 p. Illus., index, bibliog.

Focus on Catherwood as an artist-archeologist but covers early career when Catherwood worked as a panoramist for R. Burford of London's Leicester Square after his documentary research painting of ancient temples proved unprofitable. His European, Easter, and American panoramas are discussed fully, both at their commercial entertainment and artistic documentational levels.

1484 Wickman, Richard Carl. "An Evaluation of the Employment of Panoramic Scenery in the Nineteenth-Century Theatre." Ph.D. dissertation, Ohio State University, 1961. 376 p.

The panorama and diorama as a form of exhibition and also their use as theatrical scenery.

Chapter 8

EARLY MUSICAL THEATRE AND REVUES

In addition to specific sources on the early history of musical theatre and the later revue phenomenon, this chapter includes major survey histories covering the history of the musical stage to the present. See the preface for an explanation of exclusions. The focus in this chapter is on the nineteenth century, although a few select sources on the eighteenth century are included. Sources on both English and American forms are included, with a stress on the latter. Only select musical biographies and autobiographies are included and only if they shed light on the development of musical form. See also sources in chapters 3 and 6 (A and B).

1485 Anderson, John Murray, and Anderson, Hugh Abercrombie. OUT WITH-
      OUT MY RUBBERS: THE MEMOIRS OF JOHN MURRAY ANDERSON.
      New York: Library Publishers, 1954. x, 253 p. Illus., index.

      Autobiography of John M. Anderson (1886-1954), producer of
      revues in New York, in particular the Greenwich Village
      Follies, plus a brief history of the revue form and the best
      known producers--Flo Ziegfeld, Hassard Short, George White,
      and Earl Carroll.

1486 Aronson, Rudolph. THEATRICAL AND MUSICAL MEMOIRS. New York:
      McBride, Nast and Co., 1913. 283 p. Illus., index.

      Good on the New York Casino in the 1880s and '90s.

1487 Bantock, Granville, and Aflalo, F.G. ROUND THE WORLD WITH
      "A GAIETY GIRL." London: John Macqueen, 1896. 172 p. Illus.

      Account of international tour (Europe, United States, and Aus-
      tralia) by members of George Edwardes's company, performing
      the musical comedy "A Gaiety Girl."

1488 Baral, Robert. REVUE: THE GREAT BROADWAY PERIOD. New York:
      Fleet Press, 1962. 296 p. Illus., index.

      A comprehensive study of New York revues, including history,

anecdotes, descriptions of individual revues, and biographies
of performers and producers. Also touches on English and
French forms. Appendix: Listing of revues on Broadway beginning with Weber and Ziegfeld productions (includes cast
lists).

1489   Barker, Barbara M. "The Case of Augusta Sohlke vs. John DePol."
EDUCATIONAL THEATRE JOURNAL 30 (May 1978): 232-39. Illus.

Dancer in THE DEVIL'S AUCTION (one of the many spectacles
produced to compete with THE BLACK CROOK) in 1867 and
her contractual difficulties with her producer John DePol at
Banvard's Museum and Opera House.

1490   Berry, W.H. (Bill). FORTY YEARS IN THE LIMELIGHT. Foreword by
Seymour Hicks. London: Hutchinson and Co., 1939. 256 p. Illus.,
index.

Autobiography of English musical comedy star, whose career
began in 1890. Table of performances by Berry, 1905-35, including twenty consecutive years at Daly's and the Adelphi.
Frequent references to George Edwardes.

1491   Blesh, Rudi, and Janis, Harriet. THEY ALL PLAYED RAGTIME. New
York: Alfred A. Knopf, 1950. xviii, 338 p. Illus., index (xviii p.),
appendixes.

Ragtime music and musicians examined; good background material and lists of useful information on music, publishers, phonograph records, and piano rolls.

1492   Bloom, Ursula. CURTAIN CALL FOR THE GUV'NOR. A BIOGRAPHY
OF GEORGE EDWARDES. London: Hutchinson and Co., 1954. 238 p.
Illus.

Undistinguished biography of the Gaiety Theatre impresario.

1493   Bolitho, Hector. MARIE TEMPEST. London: Cobden-Sanderson, 1936;
Philadelphia: J.B. Lippincott Co., 1937. 320 p. Illus., index.

Biography of the English singer-actress and her career in England and America. Includes a record of her appearances,
1885-1935. Tempest died in 1942 at the age of seventy-eight.

1494   Bond, Jessie. THE LIFE AND REMINISCENCES OF JESSIE BOND,
THE OLD SAVOYARD. AS TOLD BY HERSELF TO ETHEL MacGEORGE.
London: John Lane 1930. xvi, 244 p.

Bond (1833-42) memoirs; long-time Savoy performer. Good
plates showing the actress-singer in Gilbert and Sullivan roles.

1495 Burke, Billie, with Shipp, Cameron. WITH A FEATHER ON MY NOSE. New York: Appleton-Century, 1949. ix, 272 p. Illus.

> First of two memoirs by the actress and Flo Ziegfeld's second wife. See next entry.

1496 _____. WITH POWDER ON MY NOSE. New York: Coward-McCann, 1959. 249 p. Illus.

> Second of two memoirs, (see above).

1497 Burton, Jack. BLUE BOOK OF BROADWAY MUSICALS. Rev. ed. Watkins Glen, N.Y.: Century House, 1974. 328 p. Illus., index.

> Reference work on the American musical; pre-1900 essay plus six other time-span essays and data on individual major musicals.

1498 Byram, John. "Famous American Theatres." THEATRE ARTS 41 (December 1957): 74-75, 92. Illus.

> Brief history of the Hippodrome in New York (1905). See item 1507.

1499 Cantor, Eddie, with Ardmore, Jane Kesner. TAKE MY LIFE. Garden City, N.Y.: Doubleday and Co., 1957. 288 p. Illus.

> Cantor's autobiography; chapters on Fanny Brice, George Jessel, Al Jolson, Will Rogers, Flo Ziegfeld, W.C. Fields, and references to Earl Carroll and Oliver Morosco.

1500 Cantor, Eddie, as told to Freedman, David. MY LIFE IS IN YOUR HANDS. Foreword by Will Rogers. New York: Blue Ribbon Books, 1932. xiv, 309 p. Illus.

> Comments on Ziegfeld's Follies. See also item 1075.

1501 Cantor, Eddie, and Freedman, David. "Ziegfeld and His Follies." COLLIER'S 93 (13 January 1934): 7-9 ; 93 (20 January): 22, 26, 47-48; 93 (27 January): 24-25, 45-56; 93 (3 February): 18-19, 32; 93 (17 February): 22, 38, 40. Illus.

> Series of articles on Ziegfeld: 1) elegy for Ziegfeld and introduction to the "Follies" and its early history, 2) from the Anna Held days through 1917, 3) portraits of Ziegfeld stars, including Billie Burke, Lillian Lorraine, Gene Buck, and Fannie Brice, 4) focus on Cantor in the "Follies" and descriptions of various acts, and 5) last years of Ziegfeld's career, dispersion of the stars to Hollywood, the crash of 1929, and Ziegfeld's decline. See next entry.

1502   _____ . ZIEGFELD THE GREAT GLORIFIER. New York: Alfred King, 1934. 166 p. Illus.

> Basically a reprint in book form of the articles listed in item 1500. Good insight into the personality and tactics of Florenz Ziegfeld, Jr.

1503   Carter, Randolph. THE WORLD OF FLO ZIEGFELD. New York and Washington, D.C.: Praeger, 1974 [7], 146 p. Illus. (16 color pls.), index, bibliog., appendix.

> Pictorial history of the "Follies," 1907-31, plus background material on Ziegfeld's early experiences and significant participants in the "Follies." List of productions and principals in appendix.

1504   Castle, Irene, as told to Bob and Wanda Duncan. CASTLES IN THE AIR. Garden City, N.Y.: Doubleday and Co., 1958. 264 p. Illus.

> Autobiography of the dancer in revues and films (along with her partner, husband Vernon Castle).

1505   Charters, Ann. NOBODY: THE STORY OF BERT WILLIAMS. New York: Macmillan Co., 1970. 157 p. Illus., index, discography.

> Undistinguished biography of the black performer who was a star in vaudeville and revue from 1892 to 1922. Best remembered for his appearances in the Ziegfeld Follies and the introduction of such songs as "I'm a Jonah Man" and "Nobody," the words and music for which are included in this volume, along with eight other examples from Williams's repertoire.

1506   Churchill, Allen. THE THEATRICAL TWENTIES. New York: McGraw-Hill, 1975. 326 p. Illus., index, bibliog.

> Good on the revue form. See also item 183.

1507   Clarke, Norman. THE MIGHTY HIPPODROME. New York and South Brunswick, N.J.: A.S. Barnes and Co., 1968. 144 p. Illus., index, bibliog.

> Only book-length history of the Hippodrome Theatre in New York (1905-39), home of lavish musicals and circus attractions.

1508   Cohan, George M. TWENTY YEARS ON BROADWAY; AND THE YEARS IT TOOK TO GET THERE. New York: Harper and Bros., 1924. 264 p. Illus.

> Autobiography of the dynamic showman but containing little significant information. See also items 1597 and 1614.

1509   Collier, Constance. HARLEQUINADE: THE STORY OF MY LIFE.
London: John Lane the Bodley Head, 1929. xii, 294 p. Illus.,
index.

>   Collier (1878-1955), a major star in the United States and
>   England after 1908, began acting as a child and was a Gaiety
>   Girl under George Edwardes at the Gaiety and Daly's. Al-
>   though most of her autobiography is devoted to her later ca-
>   reer as a serious actress, the chapters on her Gaiety experi-
>   ences are most pertinent to this chapter.

1510   Conrad, Earl. BILLY ROSE; MANHATTAN PRIMITIVE. Cleveland:
World Publishing, 1968. xvi, 272 p. Illus.

>   Biography of the Broadway producer.

1511   "Costumes: Baubles, Bangles, and Bright Shiny Beads." THEATRE
CRAFTS 10 (March-April 1976): 10-13, 42, 44. Illus.

>   Essay on the costume designers, construction, and storage of
>   costumes for Las Vegas revues.

1512   Coward, Noel. PRESENT INDICATIVE. Garden City, N.Y.: Doubleday, Doran, and Co., 1937. viii, 371 p. Illus., index.

>   Autobiography of Coward from birth to age thirty-one.

1513   _____. FUTURE INDEFINITE. Garden City, N.Y.: Doubleday and
Co., 1954. 352 p. Illus., index.

>   Continuation of Coward's autobiography; from 1939 through
>   1945.

1514   Crowley, Alice Lewinsohn. THE NEIGHBORHOOD PLAYHOUSE.
New York: Theatre Arts Books, 1959. Illus., index, appendix.

>   Chapter: "The Grand Street Follies" (pp. 116-20) contains a
>   detailed account of the nature, origin, and development of
>   the Follies.

1515   Croy, Homer. OUR WILL ROGERS. New York: Duell, Sloan, and
Pearce; Boston: Little, Brown, and Co., 1953. xii, 377 p. Index.

>   Biography of Rogers based largely on firsthand observation and
>   interviews, including his stint in revues.

1516   Cummings, E.E. "Vive la Folie!" In E.E. CUMMINGS: A MISCEL-
LANY REVISED, edited by George J. Firmage, pp. 159-63. New
York: October House, 1965.

>   Reprinted from VANITY FAIR (September 1926). Cummings

analyzes the "revue" in general and the Parisian revue in particular. Applauds French version and debunks the Earl Carroll-Flo Ziegfeld variety.

1517 Dale, Alan. "Stage Beauty and Brains." COSMOPOLITAN 50 (March 1911): 517-22. Illus.

Dale praises the virtues of American actresses of the time over English and European actresses, especially in terms of versatility (musical comedy to legitimate theatre).

1518 Day, Donald, ed. THE AUTOBIOGRAPHY OF WILL ROGERS. Boston: Houghton Mifflin Co., 1949. ix, 410 p. Index.

Rogers's rise in show business from Wild West shows to the Ziegfeld Follies in 1919 and beyond. Told in Rogers's inimitably witty style.

1519 _____. WILL ROGERS: A BIOGRAPHY. New York: David McKay Co., 1962. xiii, 370 p. Illus., index.

More extensive coverage of his early show business career than the previous source, especially in vaudeville and with Ziegfeld. Also superior to Croy item 1515.

1520 Day, Susan Stockbridge. "Productions at Niblo's Garden Theatre, 1862-1868, During the Management of William Wheatley." Ph.D. dissertation, University of Oregon, 1972. 362 p.

Includes descriptions of the spectacles with music: THE BLACK CROOK and THE WHITE FAUN.

1521 Deghy, Guy. PARADISE IN THE STRAND. THE STORY OF ROMANO'S. London: Richards Press, 1958. 256 p. Illus., index, bibliog.

The history of the famous London restaurant (heyday, 1877-90); chapters on the Gaiety Theatre and George Edwardes.

1522 de Mille, Agnes. SPEAK TO ME, DANCE WITH ME. Boston: Little, Brown and Co., 1973. x, 404 p. Illus., index.

Excellent autobiography of the choreographer of OKLAHOMA! who began her career during the depression years of 1932-35.

1523 Dircks, P.T. "James Robinson Planche and the English Burletta Tradition." THEATRE SURVEY 17 (May 1976): 68-81.

A useful study of this early form of musical theatre in nineteenth-century England.

1524 Duff-Gordon, Lady Lucile. DISCRETIONS AND INDISCRETIONS.

London: Jarrolds; New York: Frederick A. Stokes Co., 1932. 333 p. Illus.

Memoirs of the costume designer for the Ziegfeld Follies at its height (the teens); limited factual information.

1525　Duke, Vernon. PASSPORT TO PARIS. Boston and Toronto: Little, Brown and Co., 1955. 502 p. Illus., index.

Autobiography of the composer Duke (also known as Vladimir Dukelsky, a "serious" composer); most useful on his memories of the late Ziegfeld Follies, the Shuberts, and musicals of the 1930s and '40s.

1526　Engel, Lehman. THE AMERICAN MUSICAL THEATRE. A CBS LEGACY COLLECTION BOOK. New York: Macmillan Co., 1967. xiii, 236 p. Illus., index, bibliog.

Good historical survey with focus on technical aspects; valuable for three appendixes: discography, published librettos, and published vocal scores.

1527　_____. WORDS WITH MUSIC. New York: Macmillan Co., 1972. 358 p. Index, bibliog.

Analysis of the musical theatre form with some allusions to the early period.

1528　_____. THE WORDS ARE MUSIC: THE GREAT THEATER LYRICISTS AND THEIR LYRICS. New York: Crown Publishers, 1975. xii, 276 p. Illus., index.

Includes chapters on early lyricists (1900-1920 era), the American musical theatre from 1925 to 1972, Kurt Weill collaborators, lyrics from musicals shows, 1920-74, and a section on as yet unproduced lyricists.

1529　Ewen, David. "Down Falls the Hippodrome." THEATRE GUILD MAGAZINE 7 (April 1930): 39-41. Illus.

Spectacle at the Hippodrome (1905-15) assessed and a cursory history to the 1920s presented.

1530　_____. THE STORY OF GEORGE GERSHWIN. New York: Henry Holt and Co., 1943. vii, 211 p. Illus., brief bibliog.

Somewhat sentimental biography of Gershwin, mostly undocumented, but useful for a listing of musical comedies, revues, and films for which Gershwin wrote music and a chart showing world events and musical events that correspond to different periods in the composer's life.

1531 _____. THE LIFE AND DEATH OF TIN PAN ALLEY. New York:
Funk and Wagnalls, 1964. xv, 380 p. Index, bibliog.

> Covers the period 1880–1930, "the Golden Age of American
> popular music," and discusses popular songs of that period in
> America, including composers, publishers, and performers of
> these songs and the way they reflected American life at the
> time. Appendixes: "The Golden 100: Tin Pan Alley Stan-
> dards, 1880–1920" and "The Elect of Tin Pan Alley: Lyricists
> and Composers, 1880–1930."

1532 _____. THE STORY OF AMERICA'S MUSICAL THEATRE. Rev. ed.
New York and Philadelphia: Chilton Book Co., 1968. v, 278 p.
Index.

> Ewen dates the beginning of musical theatre in America from
> FLORA (1735). Although sketchy and undocumented, generally
> reliable historical outline of the American musical, with over
> half devoted to the early period prior to OKLAHOMA! This
> revised edition concludes with MAN OF LA MANCHA.

1533 _____. NEW COMPLETE BOOK OF THE AMERICAN MUSICAL
THEATRE. New York: Holt, Rinehart and Winston, 1970. 800 p.

> A chronological history focused on the composers; good refer-
> ence work for brief histories of specific productions. An
> earlier edition (COMPLETE BOOK OF THE AMERICAN MUSI-
> CAL THEATER, Holt) appeared in 1958.

1534 _____. GREAT MEN OF AMERICAN POPULAR SONG. Englewood
Cliffs, N.J.: Prentice-Hall, 1970.

> Biographies, personal portraits, and critical evaluations of
> thirty American composers––includes Dan Emmett, Stephen
> Foster, James A. Bland, Gus Edwards, Victor Herbert,
> George M. Cohan, Irving Berlin, Jerome Kern, the Gershwins,
> and other composers of music for various forms of popular en-
> tertainment.

1535 Farnsworth, Marjorie. THE ZIEGFELD FOLLIES. London: Peter Davies;
New York: Bonanza Books, 1956. 194 p. Illus., index.

> The history of the Follies, including Florenz Ziegfeld's profes-
> sional background and development, and that of numerous
> performers. Occasionally unreliable on factual data but illus-
> trations are excellent. Appendix: Ziegfeld Follies productions,
> 1907–31.

1536 Flood, Priscilla. "The Follies, Scandals, and Delights of Erte." HORI-
ZON 17 (Summer 1975): 20–31. Illus.

The style of and renewed interest in Erte, the revue designer
(George White's SCANDALS, Folies-Bergere). Includes an
impressive colored portfolio of his theatre designs.

1536a Forbes-Winslow, D. DALY'S, THE BIOGRAPHY OF A THEATRE.
London: W.A. Allen and Co., 1944. 220 p. Illus., index.

Story of the theatre built by George Edwardes and named after
Augustin Daly in London in 1893; home of popular comedies
and musicals, in the vein of Edwardes's "Gaiety" productions.

1537 Fordin, Hugh. GETTING TO KNOW HIM; A BIOGRAPHY OF OSCAR
HAMMERSTEIN II. Introduction by Stephen Sondheim. New York:
Random House, 1977. xiv, 383 p. Illus., index, selected bibliog.

This most recent biography of Hammerstein is rather tedious
and lacking in objectivity but gives an adequate coverage of
the lyricist's early career and the careers of his uncle and
grandfather as pioneers in the American theatre, specifically
in variety and musical theatre.

1538 Foy, Peter. "Special Effects Casebook: Problem Solving in Las
Vegas." THEATRE CRAFTS 10 (March-April 1976): 24-25.

Special effects and transformations in large production numbers;
scenic design aspects of Las Vegas-type revues.

1539 Freedland, Michael. JOLSON. New York: Stein and Day, 1972.
256 p. Illus., index.

Touches on his career in revues. See also item 1105.

1540 Freeman, Graydon La Verne. THE MELODIES LINGER ON: FIFTY
YEARS OF POPULAR SONG. New York: Century House, 1951. 212
p. Illus.

Survey of popular songs in the United States from 1900 to 1950.
Chronology of popular hit songs on pages 193-212.

1541 Friedman, Robert. "The Contributions of Harry Bache Smith (1860-1936)
to the American Musical Theatre." Ph.D. dissertation, New York University, 1976. 351 p.

Life and contributions of one of the most prolific of American
librettists and lyricists of his time.

1542 Gershwin, George, and Gershwin, Ira. GEORGE AND IRA GERSHWIN
SONGBOOK. Foreword by Ira Gershwin. New York: Simon and
Schuster, 1960. xiv, 178 p. Index.

Appendix: list of songs by George Gershwin with lyrics by
Ira and others (1916-45).

1543   Gershwin, Ira. LYRICS ON SEVERAL OCCASIONS. New York:
        Viking Press, 1974. xv [i], 362 p. Index (i-ix).

      Gershwin's lyrics plus commentary.

1544   Goldberg, Isaac. TIN PAN ALLEY: A CHRONICLE OF THE AMERI-
        CAN POPULAR MUSIC RACKET. Introduction by George Gershwin.
        New York: John Day Co., 1930. xi, 341 p. Illus., index.

      Good discussion of Harrigan and Hart and the minstrel show,
      as well as general information on the music world.

1545   Graves, George. GAIETIES AND GRAVITIES. Foreword by Charles B.
        Cochran. London: Hutchinson and Co., 1931. xiii, [14] 287 p.
        Illus., index.

      Autobiography of the English comic, considered by some the suc-
      cessor of Arthur Roberts (see item 1623). Graves appeared in
      Gaiety musicals under George Edwardes, in pantomimes, in vari-
      ety, and in a number of important early British musical shows.

1546   Green, Stanley. THE WORLD OF MUSICAL COMEDY. New York:
        Grosset and Dunlap, 1962. xvi, 397 p. Illus., index, discography.
        2d ed. South Brunswick, N.J.: A.S. Barnes, 1968. xvi, 541 p.
        Illus., index, discography.

      A chapter is included on every major composer who wrote for
      American musical comedy; discusses composer's music, the
      show as a whole, and the performances. Slightly revised
      version (1968) shows little change in the treatment of the
      early examples.

1547   _____ . RING BELLS! SING SONGS! BROADWAY MUSICALS OF
        THE 1930S. New York: Galahad Books, 1971. 358 p. Illus., index,
        bibliog., discography.

      Illustrated history of musical theatre from STRIKE UP THE
      BAND to DUBARRY WAS A LADY. Casts and credits for
      175 musicals included.

1548   _____ . ENCYLOPAEDIA OF THE MUSICAL THEATRE. New York:
        Dodd, Mead and Co., 1976. vi, 488 p. Bibliog., discography.

      Reference guide to over two thousand performers, writers,
      directors, productions, and songs of the musical stage, both
      in New York and London.

1549   Gressler, Thomas H. "A Review of the Term Revue." PLAYERS, THE
        MAGAZINE OF AMERICAN THEATRE 48 (June-July 1973): 224-29.

      An attempt to come to grips with the origin of the term and
      the various theatrical usages, from Ziegfeld to quasirevues.
      A useful essay on this confusing concept.

1550   Grossmith, George. A SOCIETY CLOWN: REMINISCENCES BY
       GEORGE GROSSMITH. Bristol: J.W. Arrowsmith; London: Simpkin,
       Marshall and Co., 1888. 192 p.

       Autobiography of the English actor–singer (1847–1912). See
       next entry.

1551   _____. PIANO AND I: FURTHER REMINISCENCES BY GROSSMITH.
       Bristol: J.W. Arrowsmith; London: Simpkin, Marshall, Hamilton, Kent
       and Co., 1910. 199 p. Illus.

       See previous entry.

1552   Grossmith, George, and Grossmith, Weedon. THE DIARY OF A NO-
       BODY. Bristol: J.W. Arrowsmith, [1892]. 300 p. Illus.

       There have been seven editions of this work, which includes
       material on musical theatre in London, between 1892 and
       1955. The elder George Grossmith and Weedon were brothers.

1553   Grossmith, George, Jr. G.G. London: Hutchinson and Co., 1933.
       288 p. Illus., index.

       Grossmith's autobiography covering the time from the beginning
       of his acting career in 1893 at London's Gaiety Theatre through
       1932. Includes many reminiscences of his work in theatres,
       revues, cabarets, films, and broadcasting both at home in
       London and abroad. A good deal of information on other per-
       sonalities of that period.

1554   Hackett, Frances. "The Follies." NEW REPUBLIC 11 (7 July 1917):
       278.

       A denunciation of "ostentatious and boring" Follies (Ziegfeld's
       and the "Tired Business man" audience which patronized it).

1555   Hall, Roger Allan. "Nate Salsbury and His Troubadors: Popular Ameri-
       can Farce and Musical Comedy, 1875–1887." Ph.D. dissertation, Ohio
       State University, 1974. 186 p.

       A useful documented study of early American musical theatre.
       See next entry.

1556   _____. "The Brook: America's Germinal Musical?" EDUCATIONAL
       THEATRE JOURNAL 27 (October 1975): 323–29.

       THE BROOK cannot be considered the "germinal cell" of Ameri-
       can musical comedy since, among other reasons, the majority
       of its music was borrowed from popular music of the time. The
       essay shows how THE BROOK was significant in that, for
       example, it pulled together as a more cohesive whole with
       some sort of plot the different elements of American popular

theatre, such as those found in minstrel shows and variety.

1557 Hammerstein, Oscar II. LYRICS. New York: Simon and Schuster, 1949. xv, 215 p.

Lyrics by Hammerstein plus explanatory introduction.

1558 Haskins, Jim. THE COTTON CLUB: A PICTORIAL AND SOCIAL HISTORY OF THE MOST FAMOUS SYMBOL OF THE JAZZ ERA. New York: Random House, 1977. 170 p. Illus., select bibliog. Paper.

Survey of the Cotton Club's history, its heyday in the 1930s, and its demise in 1940 [it has recently reopened]. Vivid portraits of the black celebrities associated with the club, many of whom were prominent on other musical platforms as well.

1559 Heaps, Willard A., and Heaps, Porter W. THE SINGING SIXTIES. Norman: University of Oklahoma Press, 1960. xiv, 423 p. Illus., index.

Popular songs of the 1860s and how they reflected the spirit of the split nation during the Civil War. The authors note the rapid increase in music publication and the nationwide love of popular songs. Good for background material; little specifically on musical theatre.

1560 Held, Anna. MEMOIRES, UNE ETOILE FRANCAISE AU CIEL DE L'AMERIQUE. Preface by Jacques-Charles. Paris: La Nef de Paris, 1954. 210 p.

Memoirs, in French, of Flo Ziegfeld's first wife and star of the Follies.

1561 Hicks, Seymour. SEYMOUR HICKS: TWENTY-FOUR YEARS OF AN ACTOR'S LIFE. London: Alston Rivers, 1910. 321 p. Index.

Autobiography of the actor-singer with a useful chapter on the Gaiety and George Edwardes.

1562 Higham, Charles. ZIEGFELD. Chicago: Henry Regnery Co., 1972. 245 p. Illus., index.

Biography of Florenz Ziegfeld with a good deal of information on some of his more prominent stars, Fanny Brice, Anna Held, and Billie Burke. Excessive inconsequential trivia; but little documentation.

1563 Hollingshead, John. MY LIFETIME. 2 vols. London: Sampson, Low, Marston and Co., 1895.

Autobiography of the manager (1827-1904) of The Gaiety for almost twenty years. See next two entries.

1564 _____. GAIETY CHRONICLES. London: Constable, 1898. xvi, 493 p.

Memoirs of the Gaiety by its first manager. See item 1563 and 1565.

1565 _____. "GOOD OLD GAIETY": AN HISTORIETTE AND A REMEM-BRANCE. London: Gaiety Theatre Co., 1903. 79 p. Illus.

Informal memoirs of the Gaiety. See above.

1566 Hughes, Gervase. COMPOSERS OF OPERETTA. ca. 1962. Reprint. Westport, Conn.: Greenwood Press, 1974. xi, 283 p. Illus., bibliog.

A generally reliable introduction to the operettic stage and its composers.

1567 Hyman, Alan. THE GAIETY YEARS. London: Cassell, 1975. xi, 230 p. Illus., index, bibliog.

Disappointing biography of George Edwardes covering the time of his life when he was manager of the Gaiety Theatre in London. Also a history of the Gaiety and its personalities during its most active years (1868-1915). Some documentation.

1568 Jablonski, Edward. HAROLD ARLEN: HAPPY WITH THE BLUES. Garden City, N.Y.: Doubleday and Co., 1961. 286 p. Illus., index.

Biography of Harold Arlen the composer includes a list of his works and a selected discography.

1569 Jablonski, Edward, and Stewart, Lawrence D. THE GERSHWIN YEARS. Garden City, N.Y.: Doubleday and Co., 1958. 313 p. Illus., index.

Covers the lives and careers of the two composer brothers with information on their acquaintances and associates and the times in which they wrote. Well illustrated.

1570 Jackson, Allan S. "Edward Everett Rice and Musical Burlesque." PLAYERS, THE MAGAZINE OF AMERICAN THEATRE 51 (Summer 1976): 154-66. Illus.

Twenty-five year career of the producer (1847-1924) and his musical burlesques. Discusses the ingredients of the American hybrid form.

1571 Jackson, Arthur. THE BEST MUSICALS FROM SHOW BOAT TO A
      CHORUS LINE: BROADWAY, OFF-BROADWAY, LONDON. Foreword
      by Clive Barnes. New York: Crown Publishers, 1977. 208 p. Illus.,
      index, bibliog., discography, filmography.

      A compendium of information musical theatre, in scope and
      design a cross between a handsome and entertaining coffee
      table book and a reference work, with a somewhat superficial
      and uncritical historical survey of the musical beginning with
      THE BLACK CROOK (1866). Includes 174 illustrations (six-
      teen pages in color), a who's who of show and film music, a
      musical calendar (1866-1977), a list of songs and their sources,
      a list of long runs on and off Broadway, and a section mis-
      leadingly called "Plot Summaries" (actually nothing more than
      a listing of shows with pertinent data and brief descriptions).

1572 Jolson, A[l]. "If I Don't Get Laughs and Don't Get Applause--The
      Mirror Will Show Me Who Is To Blame." AMERICAN MAGAZINE 87
      (April 1919): 18-19, 154-58.

      Useful analysis of audience orientation of the popular enter-
      tainer.

1573 Johnson, James Weldon. BLACK MANHATTAN. New York: Alfred
      A. Knopf, 1940. xvii, 284 p. Illus., index (pp. xxi-xxxiv).

      Firsthand account of the development of Negro musicals.

1574 Jupp, James. THE GAIETY STAGE DOOR: THIRTY YEARS' REMINIS-
      CENCES OF THE THEATRE. Boston: Small, Maynard and Co., n.d.;
      London: Jonathan Cape, 1923. 352 p. Illus.

      Stage doorman at the Gaiety for more than thirty years remi-
      nisces about its heyday in the 1890s.

1575 Kahn, E.J., Jr. THE MERRY PARTNERS: THE AGE AND STAGE OF
      HARRIGAN AND HART. New York: Random House, 1955. 302 p.
      Illus.

      History of the musical-comedy team that flourished from 1871
      through 1885. Suffers from lack of index and documentation.

1576 Katkov, Norman. THE FABULOUS FANNY: THE STORY OF FANNY
      BRICE. New York: Alfred A. Knopf, 1953. 337 p.

      Chatty (and gushy) biography of Brice, but little on her
      performing career per se.

1577 Kimball, Robert, ed. COLE. New York: Holt, Rinehart and Winston,
      1971. xix, 283 p. Illus.

Chronological collection of illustrations, correspondence, and anecdotes, plus examples of Porter's lyrics. Useful biographical essay by Brendan Gill.

1578   Kimball, Robert, and Balcom, William. REMINISCING WITH SISSLE AND BLAKE. New York: Viking Press, 1973. 254 p. Illus.

Largely pictorial memoir of the musical team of Noble Sissle and Eubie Blake, who first teamed in 1915 as vaudeville headliners and worked together for fifty-seven years. Authors of the landmark musical SHUFFLE ALONG in 1921 which restored authentic black artistry to the American theatre. Appendixes include: chronological list of songs and productions, an alphabetical list of selected Sissle-Blake songs, discography, list of Sissle-Blake films, and other data on the team and their individual accomplishments.

1579   Kimball, Robert, and Simon, Alfred. THE GERSHWINS. Foreword by Richard Rodgers. Introduction by John S. Wilson. New York: Atheneum, 1973. xlii[i], 292 p. Illus. (some in color), bibliog.

Largely pictorial essay; most valuable for Wilson's introduction and a chronological list of shows (1919-29), list of songs, discography, and piano rollography.

1580   Knapp, Margaret M. "Theatrical Parody in the Twentieth-Century American Theatre: The Grand Street Follies." EDUCATIONAL THEATRE JOURNAL 27 (October 1975): 356-68.

Discusses the tone, subject matter, performers in and history of the "Grand Street Follies."

1581   Kreuger, Miles. SHOW BOAT: THE STORY OF A CLASSIC AMERICAN MUSICAL. New York: Oxford University Press, 1977. x, 247 p. Illus., index, seven appendixes.

First full history of this historically important musical. See also item 2330.

1582   Krutch, Joseph Wood. "Of Revues." NATION 120 (13 January 1926): 40-41.

Krutch supports revues as unpretentious displays of charm; includes a comparison of the "Greenwich Street Follies" and "Vanities."

1583   _____. "Bigger and Better." NATION 122 (June 1926): 616.

Popularity of the revue is due largely to its passive nature, according to Krutch. Includes a brief review of "The Great Temptations."

1584 _____. "Prodigal Enough." NATION 135 (19 October 1932): 365-76.

    Deals with the elements of the revue and suggests that its mechanical perfection has become boring.

1585 Laufe, Abe. BROADWAY'S GREATEST MUSICALS. Rev. ed. New York: Funk and Wagnalls, 1977. x, 519 p. Indexes (titles and names), bibliog., appendix ("The Long-Running Musicals").

    Laufe discusses Broadway's greatest hits from 1884 to the late '60s (the new edition briefly brings it up to the '70s) and why and how they were so successful. The latest revised edition offers few significant changes over the 1969 edition.

1586 Lawrence. Gertrude. A STAR DANCED. Garden City, N.Y.: Doubleday, Doran and Co., 1945. 238 p.

    The singer-actress's career in London revues staged by Andre Charlot in the 1920s and '30s.

1587 Lerche, Frank Martin. "The Growth and Development of Scenic Design for the Professional Musical Comedy Stage in New York from 1866 to 1920." Ph.D. dissertation, New York University, 1969. 490 p.

    From the examination of one hundred productions, the author divides major changes in terms of painted illusionism (1866-99), built-up illusionism (1900-1909), and the New Stagecraft (1909-20). In the latter category, the work of Joseph Urban, Ziegfeld's designer, is stressed.

1588 Levant, Oscar. THE MEMOIRS OF AN AMNESIAC. New York: G.P. Putnam's Sons, 1965. 320 p. Illus.

    Irreverent memoirs of the pianist-entertainer; observations on revues and musical productions of the 1920s are useful, though inexact, especially his recollections of the hit BURLESQUE.

1589 Lewine, Richard, and Simon, Alfred. ENCYCLOPEDIA OF THEATRE MUSIC. New York: Random House, 1961. vii, 248 p. Index (shows).

    A comprehensive listing of more than four thousand songs from Broadway and Hollywood, 1900-1950. Useful reference.

1590 _____. SONGS OF THE AMERICAN THEATER: A COMPREHENSIVE LISTING OF MORE THAN 12,000 SONGS, INCLUDING SELECTED TITLES FROM FILM AND TELEVISION PRODUCTIONS. Introduction by Stephen Sondheim. New York: Dodd, Mead and Co., 1973. 820 p. Index.

Revision of above, adds a more complete chronology of productions and an index of composers and lyricists.

1591 Liebman, Max. "A Broadway Revue Every Week." THEATRE ARTS 37 (May 1953): 75-77.

The adjustment from working live revues to televised "revue" such as "Your Show of Shows."

1592 "Lighting: Glitter and Glamorize." THEATRE CRAFTS 10 (March-April 1976): 14-17, 46, 48. Illus.

The instruments, techniques, and demands of lighting in Las Vegas revues.

1593 Lillie, Beatrice, with Braugh, James. EVERY OTHER INCH A LADY. Aided and abetted by John Philip; Garden City, N.Y.: Doubleday and Co., 1972. 360 p. Illus.

Autobiography of the Canadian-born performer, best known for her appearances in cabaret and revue. Includes much on her experiences in Charlot's Revue in 1925.

1594 Litton, Glenn. "The American Musical Theatre in the 1950s." THEATRE ANNUAL 32 (1976): 7-111.

A monograph devoted to the history of musicals in the 1950s; projected to appear in a new edition of MUSICAL COMEDY IN AMERICA by Cecil Smith (see item 1634) to be published by Theatre Arts Books. Contains little of value on early musicals.

1595 Locke, Alain. THE NEGRO AND HIS MUSIC & NEGRO ART: PAST AND PRESENT. For full entry and annotation, see item 1016.

1596 Lubbock, Mark. THE COMPLETE BOOK OF LIGHT OPERA. With an American section by David Ewen. New York: Scholarly Press, 1962. xviii, 953 p. Illus., index.

The American section is on pages 753-935; the volume includes plot synopses of major light operas.

1597 McCabe, John. GEORGE M. COHAN: THE MAN WHO OWNED BROADWAY. Garden City, N.Y.: Doubleday and Co., 1973. xii, 296 p. Illus., index.

Well-illustrated biography; appendix A: listing of George M. Cohan productions in New York (1901-40) and appendix B: plays written by Cohan (1895-1941).

1598 MacKay, Patricia. "Las Vegas Spectacular." THEATRE CRAFTS 10 (March-April 1976): 28-31, 34, 36-44, Illus.

Brief history and nature of the Las Vegas revue, including descriptions of typical revue numbers.

1599 Macqueen-Pope, W. GAIETY, THEATRE OF ENCHANTMENT. London: W.H. Allen, 1949. 498 p. Illus., index.

Standard history of the Gaiety, home of variety under John Hollingshead and English musical comedy under George Edwardes. Not a scholarly, documented account.

1600 _____. NIGHTS OF GLADNESS. London: Hutchinson and Co., 1956. 268 p. Illus., index (names).

Undocumented and flowery history of the English musical stage in its various forms, exclusive of the music hall and revue.

1601 _____. THE FOOTLIGHTS FLICKERED. London: Herbert Jenkins, 1959. 256 p. Illus., indexes (names, titles, theatres).

History of English musicals and revues of the 1920s.

1602 Mander, Raymond, and Mitchenson, Joe. MUSICAL COMEDY: A STORY IN PICTURES. Foreword by Noel Coward. London: Peter Davis, 1969; New York: Taplinger Publishing Co., 1970. 64 p. Illus., indexes.

Summary of the development of musical comedy, primarily in England, from 1892 to the 1968 productions of MAN OF LA MANCHA and HAIR. As is usual with Mander and Mitchenson volumes, the over 240 photographs make the work invaluable.

1603 _____. REVUE: A STORY IN PICTURES. Foreword by Noel Coward. London: Davies, 1971; New York: Taplinger Publishing Co., 1971. viii, 168 p. (112 p. of pls.). Illus., index.

Entertaining study of the revue, its formal beginnings more than one hundred fifty years ago with the focus on England.

1604 Marks, Edward Bennett. THEY ALL SANG: FROM TONY PASTOR TO RUDY VALLEE. For full entry and annotation, see item 233.

1605 _____. THEY ALL HAD GLAMOUR: FROM THE SWEDISH NIGHTIN-GALE TO THE NAKED LADY. For full entry and annotation, see item 234.

1606 Mates, Julian. THE AMERICAN MUSICAL STAGE BEFORE 1800. New

Brunswick, N.J.: Rutgers University Press, 1962. ix, 331 p. Illus.,
index.

The standard history of musical drama to 1800, carefully documented with a fifteen-page bibliography.

1607 _____. "THE BLACK CROOK Myth." THEATRE SURVEY 7 (May 1966):
31–43.

The significance of the BLACK CROOK (1866) in the history
of American musical theatre.

1608 _____. "American Musical Theatre: Beginnings to 1900." In THE
AMERICAN THEATRE: A SUM OF ITS PARTS, edited by Henry B.
Williams, pp. 225–45. New York: Samuel French, 1971.

Excellent summary with a useful bibliography.

1609 Mattfeld, Julius. VARIETY MUSIC CAVALCADE: MUSICAL-HISTORICAL
REVIEW, 1620-1969. 3d ed. New York: Prentice-Hall, 1971. xx,
766 p. Index.

Chronological checklist of popular music in the United States
from the Pilgrims to 1969. Useful introductory essays to each
year with numerous references to theatre music.

1610 Meyer, Hazel. THE GOLD IN TIN PAN ALLEY. New York: J.B.
Lippincott Co., 1958. 258 p. Index.

Detailed and informative history of the music publishing business in New York's famed Tin Pan Alley. Deals with all the
big publishers, policies, popular song personalities, and the
like.

1611 Miller, Ruby. CHAMPAGNE FROM MY SLIPPER. London: Herbert
Jenkins, 1962. 192 p. Illus.

Autobiography of the actress who began her career as a
"Gaiety Girl" in 1903 and became a star of the stage and
screen.

1612 Morath, Max. "The Ninety-Three Years of Eubie Blake." AMERICAN
HERITAGE 27 (October 1976): 56–65. Illus.

Interview with Blake; touches on his experiences with medicine
shows, minstrels, vaudeville, and musical comedy.

1613 Mordden, Ethan. BETTER FOOT FORWARD: THE HISTORY OF AMERI-
CAN MUSICAL THEATRE. New York: Grossman Publishers (a division
of the Viking Press), 1976. xii, 369 p.

A pretentious and precious history that adds little but aggrava-
tion to earlier histories.

1614   Morehouse, Ward. GEORGE M. COHAN: PRINCE OF THE AMERI-
CAN THEATRE. Philadelphia: J.B. Lippincott, 1943. 240 p. Illus.

Popularized biography of the showman to his death in 1942;
chronology of his life in an appendix.

1615   _____. "The Ziegfeld Follies--A Formula with Class." THEATRE
ARTS 40 (May 1956): 66–69, 87. Illus.

The Ziegfeld Follies changed the pattern and set the structure
for the evolving American revue. Personal acquaintance and
critic analyzes the formula used by Ziegfeld; beautiful girls,
dazzling backgrounds, and first-rate comedians.

1616   Morell, Parker. LILLIAN RUSSELL. THE ERA OF PLUSH. New York:
Random House, 1940. 319 p. Illus., index.

Undocumented biography of the actress-singer (1861-1922).

1617   Murray, Ken. THE BODY MERCHANT: THE STORY OF EARL
CARROLL. Pasadena: Ward Ritchie Press, 1976. xiii, 243 p. Illus.,
index.

Ostensibly the life of the revue producer Earl Carroll, focusing on his sexual exploits; only indirectly does Murray deal
with his "Vanities," which lasted from 1923-32.

1618   Nathan, George Jean. THE ENTERTAINMENT OF A NATION: OR,
THREE SHEETS IN THE WIND. New York: Alfred A. Knopf, 1942.
Reprint. Rutherford, N.J.: Fairleigh Dickinson University Press, 1971.

See pp. 107-17, "The Musical Shows." A discussion of the
"girlie" nature of musical shows and revues, and the decline
in the 1940s of the quality of these productions.

1619   Naylor, Stanley. GAIETY AND GEORGE GROSSMITH: RANDOM
REFLECTIONS ON THE SERIOUS BUSINESS OF ENJOYMENT. London:
Stanley Paul and Co., 1913. 263 p. Illus.

Somewhat scant biography of Grossmith and limited insights
into the Gaiety Theatre and the "Gaiety Girls" and musical
burlesques.

1620   O'Brien, P.J. WILL ROGERS: AMBASSADOR OF GOOD WILL,
PRINCE OF WIT AND WISDOM. Philadelphia: John C. Winston Co.,
1935. 288 p. Illus.

Early biography of Rogers; brief coverage of his stage career but with photographs not in other biographies.

1621 Phillips, Julien. STARS OF THE ZIEGFELD FOLLIES. Minneapolis: Lerner Publications Co., 1972. 79 p. Illus.

Children's introduction to the Follies and eight major stars' brief biographies (Sandow, Anna Held, Bert Williams, Fanny Brice, W.C. Fields, Marilyn Miller, Will Rogers, and Eddie Cantor).

1622 Richards, Sandra L. "Bert Williams: The Man and the Mask." MIME, MASK & MARIONETTE 1 (Spring 1978): 7-24. Illus.

Study of "the private personality and the public persona," with a focus on Williams's work with George Walker and later with the Ziegfeld Follies.

1623 Roberts, Arthur. FIFTY YEARS OF SPOOF. London: John Lane, 1927. x, 255 p. Illus., index.

Autobiography of music hall and musical comedy star in England. See also item 1818.

1624 Rodgers, Richard. MUSICAL STAGES: AN AUTOBIOGRAPHY. New York: Random House, 1975. 341 p. Illus., index.

A superb autobiography of the dean of the American musical theatre who, for more than five decades, has been composing songs for revues and musicals and who achieved his first success with Lorenz Hart in 1925 (first edition of THE GARRICK GAIETIES). Good personal insights into the early years of America's musical theatre heyday.

1625 Rowland, Mabel, ed. BERT WILLIAMS: SON OF LAUGHTER. New York: English Crafters, 1923. Reprint. New York: Negro Universities Press, 1969. vii, 281 p. Illus.

Collection of tributes to the vaudeville-revue star.

1626 Schwartz, Charles. COLE PORTER, A BIOGRAPHY. New York: Dial Press, 1977. xvi, 365 p. Illus., index, bibliog., appendixes.

The most recent biography of Porter with an excellent bibliography of previously published sources. Appendixes include works by Porter, a list of musical works, and a selected discography.

1627 "Setting: See Moscow Burn; Witness the Great Flood." THEATRE CRAFTS 10 (March-April 1976): 18-23, 44-46. Illus.

Spectacular effects in Las Vegas revues, scenic transformations and traditions.

1628   Sheean, Vincent. THE AMAZING OSCAR HAMMERSTEIN I: THE LIFE AND EXPLOITS OF AN IMPRESARIO. New York: Simon and Schuster, 1956. xx, 363 p. Illus., index.

Life of the theatrical impresario (ca. 1847-1919) and his times. Good on early musical entertainments in New York.

1629   Sherman, Jan. "A Denishawn Dancer with the Ziegfeld Follies." DANCE MAGAZINE 48 (June 1975): 32-37. Illus.

Essay on the Ziegfeld tab shows, the signing of Denishawn "interpretive" dancers, and their backstage life.

1630   Short, Ernest. FIFTY YEARS OF VAUDEVILLE. London: Eyre and Spottiswoode, 1946. ix, 271 p. Illus., index.

History of vaudeville, English style, up to the 1940s. Only indirectly related to music hall. Topics cover musical comedy, revue, comic and romantic opera, and other related concerns. Specific references to such pioneers as George Edwardes, Mme. Vestris, Nellie Farren, Albert Chevalier, Herbert Farjeon, Gracie Fields, Bea Lillie, Lupino Lane, and others. A romanticized account with an unfortunate proclivity toward inaccuracies and misquotations.

1631   Sieben, Pearl. IMMORTAL JOLSON: HIS LIFE AND TIMES. New York: Frederick Fell, 1962. 231 p.

Undocumented, chatty biography of Al Jolson.

1632   Sillman, Leonard. "Who Said the Revue is Dead?" THEATRE ARTS 46 (March 1961): 16-19, 76. Illus.

The producer of the "New Faces" series claims that reports that revue is dead are not only premature but pure poppycock, "but the formula for keeping it alive is extremely tricky."

1633   Slout, William L. "The Black Crook: First of the Super Nudies." PLAYERS, THE MAGAZINE OF AMERICAN THEATRE 50 (Fall-Winter 1975): 16-19. Illus.

Evolution and history of the musical burlesque production at Niblo's Garden, 1866.

1634   Smith, Cecil. MUSICAL COMEDY IN AMERICA. New York: Theatre Arts, 1950. x, 374 p. Illus., index.

One of the better, more comprehensive histories of the Ameri-

can musical with 199 pages dealing with musical theatre up
to 1916, beginning with minstrel shows in the 1840s.

1635 _____. WORLDS OF MUSIC. Philadelphia: J.B. Lippincott, 1952.
Reprint. Westport, Conn.: Greenwood Press, 1973. 328 p. Index.

Survey of various types of music in the United States; little
specifically on musicals.

1636 Sobel, Bernard. "Musical Comedy, Quo Vadis?" THEATRE ARTS
MONTHLY 12 (August 1928): 566-68, 573-75.

Evaluation of the state of musical comedy in the late 1920s
by the critic-agent.

1637 _____. "This was Ziegfeld." AMERICAN MERCURY 60 (January
1945): 96-102.

Anecdotal account of Ziegfeld's backstage activities, a brief
biography of Ziegfeld in his business matters, and a discussion
of his rapport with performers and business associates.

1638 _____. BROADWAY HEARTBEAT: MEMOIRS OF A PRESS AGENT.
For complete entry and annotation, see item 256.

1639 Sonneck, Oscar G. EARLY OPERA IN AMERICA. New York: G.
Schirmer, 1915. Reprint. New York: Benjamin Blom, 1974. viii,
230 p. Illus.

History of early opera in America to 1800.

1640 Spaeth, Sigmund. A HISTORY OF POPULAR MUSIC IN AMERICA.
For full entry and annotation, see item 258.

1641 Spencer, Charles. ERTE. London: Studio Vista; New York: Charles N.
Potter, 1970. ix, 198 p. Illus., index, bibliog., notes on illustrations.

Brief text deals with Erte's costume and set designs for operas,
ballets, revue, theatrical production, and films in America
and abroad from 1913 to 1970. Seventy-five percent of the
book is comprised of superb illustrations with some in color.

1642 Stagg, Jerry. THE BROTHERS SHUBERT. A HALF-CENTURY OF SHOW
BUSINESS AND THE FABULOUS EMPIRE OF THE BROTHERS SHUBERT.
New York: Random House, 1968. xii, 431 p. Illus., index.

History of the rise and fall of the Shubert empire from 1900
to 1950, including biographical material on the three brothers
and a listing of Shubert-produced musicals, revues, and plays
in New York from 1901 through 1954.

1643   Stambler, Irwin. ENCYCLOPEDIA OF POPULAR MUSIC. New York: St. Martin's Press, 1965. xiii, 359 p. Illus., bibliog., discography.

Limited use for early musicals, although select musicals and composers are included.

1644   Strang, Lewis Clinton. CELEBRATED COMEDIANS OF LIGHT OPERA AND MUSICAL COMEDY IN AMERICA. Boston: L.C. Page and Co., 1901. Reprint. New York: Benjamin Blom, 1972. 293 p. Illus., index.

Brief sketches of twenty-three musical comedy stars on the American stage at the turn of the century.

1645   Terriss, Ellaline. JUST A LITTLE BIT OF STRING. Foreword by Beverley Nichols. London: Hutchinson and Co., 1955. 296 p. Illus., index.

Terriss (1871-1971), daughter of the actor William Terriss, (see item 1561), was a "Gaiety Girl" under George Edwardes and became a famous Edwardian musical comedy star.

1646   Vincent, W.T. RECOLLECTION OF FRED LESLIE. 2 vols. London: Kegan Paul, Trench, Trubner and Co., 1894. Illus.

Life of Frederick Hobson (Fred Leslie), who died in 1892 at the young age of thirty-seven. Biography includes information on the singer-actor's career at the Gaiety Theatre.

1647   Washington, Booker T. "Bert Williams." AMERICAN MAGAZINE 70 (May-October, 1910): 600-604. Illus.

Brief article on the life and career of the black comedian-singer.

1648   Whitton, Joseph. "THE NAKED TRUTH!" AN INSIDE HISTORY OF THE BLACK CROOK. Philadelphia: H.W. Shaw, 1897. 32 p. Paper.

History of THE BLACK CROOK (1866) by the business manager of Niblo's Garden.

1649   Wilder, Alec. AMERICAN POPULAR SONG, THE GREAT INNOVA-TORS 1900-1950. Edited with introduction by James T. Machee. New York: Oxford University Press, 1972. xxxix, 536 p. Indexes (composers, song titles).

Study of the development of the popular song; separate chapters on Jerome Kern, Irving Berlin, George Gershwin, Richard Rodgers, Cole Porter, and Harold Arlen.

1650   Williams, Bert. "The Comic Side of Trouble." AMERICAN MAGAZINE

85 (January 1918): 33-35, 58-61.

Astute observations on comedy and racial discrimination.

1651　Wilson, Francis. FRANCIS WILSON'S LIFE OF HIMSELF. For full entry and annotation, see item 271.

1652　Winslow, D. Forbes. DALY'S, THE BIOGRAPHY OF A THEATRE. London: W.A. Allen and Co., 1944. 220 p. Illus., index.

Story of the theatre built by George Edwardes and named after Augustin Daly in London in 1893; home of popular comedies and musicals, in the vein of Edwardes's "Gaiety" productions.

1653　Wodehouse, P.G., and Bolton, Guy. BRING ON THE GIRLS: THE IMPROBABLE STORY OF OUR LIFE IN MUSICAL COMEDY. New York: Simon and Schuster, 1953. 278 p. (plus portfolio of photos). Index.

The period 1914 to the 1950s; story of a famous collaboration in early musical comedy writing.

1654　Ziegfeld, Florenz, Jr. "Picking Out Pretty Girls for the Stage." AMERICAN MAGAZINE 88 (December 1919): 120-22, 125-26, 129. Illus.

The different types of Follies women delineated; a discussion of various performers, the life of a showgirl, her makeup, salary, rehearsal demands, and audition practices at the "Follies."

1655　Ziegfeld, Patricia. THE ZIEGFELDS' GIRL. Boston: Little, Brown and Co., 1964. 210. Illus.

Autobiography of Patricia Ziegfeld, daughter of Flo Ziegfeld and Billie Burke. Excessive in useless trivia; short on insightful information.

Chapter 9

MAJOR SOURCES ON PRINCIPAL ENGLISH FORMS

A. PANTOMIME

The following sources have been selected from major and recent publications and unpublished dissertations. Since very little of value has been written on American pantomime, the majority of these select sources deal with English pantomime, with the exception of items 1677, 1678, and 1714.

In addition to the sources listed below, the bibliography by Mayer (item 1700) should be consulted for a more complete compilation. Also, there are numerous items that relate to pantomime in the next section (B) on music hall and in chapters 3 (B), 4, and 11.

1656   Allen, Ralph G. "The Stage Spectacle of Philip James De Loutherbourg." D.F.A. dissertation, Yale University, 1960. 368 p.

        Allen reconstructs thirty-one productions; he has authored numerous essays based on this dissertation. In addition to the essays listed in items 1657, 1658, and 1659, see Allen in the index.

1657   _____. "THE WONDERS OF DERBYSHIRE: A Spectacular Eighteenth-Century Travelogue." THEATRE SURVEY 2 (1961): 54-66.

        De Loutherbourg's scenery for this 1779 harlequinade at Drury Lane.

1658   _____. "De Loutherbourg and Captain Cook." THEATRE RESEARCH/RECHERCHES THEATRALES 4 (1962): 195-211.

        De Loutherbourg's scenery for the pantomime: OMAI, produced at Covent Garden in 1785.

1659   _____. "A CHRISTMAS TALE, or, Harlequin Painter." TENNESSEE STUDIES IN LITERATURE 19 (1974): 149-61.

Scenery and lighting effects by De Loutherbourg for the Drury Lane pantomime in 1773.

1660   [Arthur, Thomas]. THE LIFE AND ADVENTURES OF BILLY PURVIS, THE EXTRAORDINARY, WITTY, AND COMICAL SHOWMAN, CONTAINING MANY HUMOROUS INCIDENTS AND ANECDOTES, NOT HITHERTO PUBLISHED. Newcastle-on-Tyne, Engl.: Daniel Bowman, 1875. 144 p.

Excellent early biography of the North Country showman and pantomime clown. See Mayer, item 1697.

1661   Avery, Emmett L. "Dancing and Pantomime on the English Stage." STUDIES IN PHILOLOGY 21 (1934): 403-31.

Seminal essay on the early forms of pantomime. See next entry.

1662   Avery, Emmett L., et al. THE LONDON STAGE, 1660-1800. 5 parts in 11 vols. Carbondale: Southern Illinois University Press, 1960-68. Illus., index, bibliog.

Pantomime is discussed in all the prefaces but the first; most valuable are the preface to part 2, 1700-1729, edited by Emmett L. Avery, part 4, 1747-77, edited by George Winchester Stone, Jr., and part 5, 1776-1800, edited by Charles Beecher Hogan. Mayer has pointed out that Stone's essay is an especially excellent account of pantomime at this state of evolution, especially his description of John Rich's 1753 revival of: HARLEQUIN SORCERER.

1663   Beaumont, Cyril W. THE HISTORY OF HARLEQUIN. London, 1926. Reprint. New York: Benjamin Blom, 1967. 156 p. Illus.

Contains two rather brief chapters on English Harlequins.

1664   Blanchard, Edward Laman. THE LIFE AND REMINISCENCES OF E.L. BLANCHARD. Edited by Clement Scott and Cecil Howard. 2 vols. London: Hutchinson and Co., 1891. Illus.

Autobiography of the most prolific writer of pantomime libretti in the last half of the nineteenth century. Based in part on Blanchard's diary. Biographical sketch by D. Meadows.

1665   Brandreth, Gyles. DISCOVERING PANTOMIMES. Discovering series. Aylesbury, Engl.: Shire Publications, 1973. 55 p. Illus., index, bibliog. Paper.

Brief but useful introduction to pantomime.

1666 _____. I SCREAM FOR ICE CREAM. PEARLS FROM THE PANTO-MIME. London: Eyre Metheun, 1974. 150 p. Illus., index. Paper or hardback.

Collection of songs and humor, jokes and routines, scenes and speeches from English pantomime, including sections on specific pantomime characters and a brief history of the form. Most useful on pantomime since the nineteenth century. Written by the director of the British Pantomime Association (see item 2450).

1667 Broadbent, R.J. A HISTORY OF PANTOMIME. London: Simpkin, Marshall, Hamilton, Kent, 1901. Reprint. New York: Benjamin Blom, 1964; New York: Citadel Press, 1965. 226 p.

An early attempt to treat pantomime seriously; valuable for scholar and general reader if used collaterally with other sources. Lacks illustrations and documentation; little included on the nineteenth century. One brief chapter on Joseph Grimaldi.

1668 Burgess, C.F. "Some Unpublished Items of John Rich and Something of a Puzzle." RESTORATION AND 18TH CENTURY THEATRE RESEARCH 7 (November 1968): 37-47.

The author deals with Rich's eccentricities and alleged illiteracy.

1669 Clinton-Baddeley, V.C. SOME PANTOMIME PEDIGREES. London: Society for Theatre Research, 1963. 38 p. Paper.

Description of Joseph Grimaldi's most famous pantomimes and a brief glance at the history of these roles.

1670 Coggin, Frederick Marsh. "The Pantomimes of Augustus Harris: Drury Lane 1879-1895." Ph.D. dissertation, Ohio State University, 1973. 205 p.

1671 Cole, Richard J. PANTOMIME BUDGETS, AND BY SPECIAL COMMAND A TETE-A-TETE BETWEEN SIR JOHN BARLEYCORN AND THE OLD LADY OF THREADNEEDLE STREET. London: J. Cross and Sons, 1853. iii, 4-70 p.

Deals with economics of pantomime production.

1672 Cook, Dutton. "Pantomimic Families." THEATRE: A MONTHLY REVIEW OF THE DRAMA, MUSIC, AND THE FINE ARTS N.S. 1 (January-June 1883): 3-9.

Grimaldi's influence on other performers; includes lineages of performers.

1673   "Crowquill, Alfred" [Alfred Henry Forrester]. PANTOMIME AS IT IS,
        WAS, AND WILL BE. London: J. Harwood, 1894.

>   See item 1666 for a more accessible source (reprint) of the
        cartoon portion of "Crowquill" commenting on the form and
        content of early Victorian pantomime.

1674   Decastro, Jacob. THE MEMOIRS OF THE LIFE OF J. DECASTRO,
        COMEDIAN. Edited by R. Humphreys. London: Sherwood, Jones
        and Co., 1824. xx, 279 p. Illus., index.

>   Equestrian pantomimes and pantomimists discussed in anecdotal
        biography. Also deals with early English circus (see also item
        408) and Sadler's Wells.

1675   Dickens, Charles. MEMOIRS OF JOSEPH GRIMALDI. Edited by
        Richard Findlater. New York: Stein and Day; London: MacGibbon
        and Kee, 1968. 311 p. Illus., index, appendixes.

>   Joseph Grimaldi (1778-1837) was perhaps England's greatest
        clown and pantomime artist. Dickens's original edited version
        appeared first in 1838. Findlater has edited Dickens's origi-
        nal version in the light of more recent research, including his
        own biography (see item 1680). The footnotes, for example,
        are his.

1676   Disher, Maurice Willson. CLOWNS AND PANTOMIMES. London:
        Constable and Co., 1925. Reprint. New York and London: Benjamin
        Blom, 1968. xx, 344 p. Illus., index.

>   Although heavily indebted to earlier sources, not acknowledged
        by the author, this is a useful and fairly reliable source on
        pantomime from its origin to its twentieth-century forms. Also
        good for other types of clowns from the commedia dell' arte
        to the circus clown.

1677   Draper, Walter Headen. "George L. Fox, Comedian, In Pantomime
        and Travesty." Ph.D. dissertation, University of Illinois, 1958. 183 p.

>   Somewhat disappointing study of this famous American panto-
        mime artist (1825-75). See next entry.

1678   _____. "George L. Fox's Burlesque." QUARTERLY JOURNAL OF
        SPEECH 50 (December 1964): 378-84.

>   A study of the burlesque performances of America's most famous
        nineteenth-century pantomimist. Deals in detail with his bur-
        lesque of HAMLET (1870). Based, in part, on preceding source.

1679   [Farmer, Peter]. "Pantomime." THEATRE ARTS 46 (January 1962):
        56-63. Illus.

A portfolio of characters from the Christmas pantomime drawn by Peter Farmer; represented are Joseph Grimaldi, an Old King Cole figure from 1900, an Ugly Sister in CINDERELLA (1880 version), a traditional Principal Boy (1890 pantomime), Simple Simon (1890), and "Annabelle" the Ugly Sister.

1680 Findlater, Richard. GRIMALDI, KING OF CLOWNS. London: Macgibbon and Kee, 1955. 240 p. Illus., index, bibliog. 2d ed. New York and London: Cambridge University Press, 1979. 260 p. Illus., notes, index, appendix.

The only full-length documented biography of the English pantomime clown of the late eighteenth and early nineteenth centuries. Contains Grimaldi family tree in an appendix, plus information on James Barnes (Pantaloon) and Thomas Ellar (Harlequin), notes on Grimaldi's autobiography and Dickens' edition of the same, and samples of Grimaldi's most famous songs. See Dickens, item 1675.

1681 Fiske, Roger. ENGLISH THEATRE MUSIC IN THE EIGHTEENTH CENTURY. For full entry and annotation, see item 314.

1682 Fleetwood, Frances, in collaboration with Conquest, Betty. CONQUEST: THE STORY OF A THEATRE FAMILY. Preface by A.E. Wilson. London: W.H. Allen, 1953. xiv, 282 p. Illus., index, bibliog.

Story of the Conquest family (Benjamin Oliver Conquest, 1805-72, et al.) in pantomime and popular theatre fare. Appendixes include a complete list of plays produced by the Conquests at the Grecian Theatre (1851-82) and later the Surrey Theatre (1881-1904), pantomimes between 1831 and 1903, and the Conquest family tree.

1683 Fletcher, Ifan K. "Harlequinades." THEATRE NOTEBOOK 1 (July 1946): 46-48.

Note on the characteristics of the eighteenth-century harlequinade and a list of harlequinades published by Sayer and other publishers.

1684 Forsyth, Gerald. "Notes on Pantomime, with a List of Drury Lane Pantomimes, 1879-1914." THEATRE NOTEBOOK 2 (January-March 1948): 22-30.

Inexact list of pantomimes taken from playbills compiled by a patron of Drury Lane beginning in 1885.

1685 Green, William. "King Panto and King Cotton: The American Civil War . . . as Reflected in Christmas Pantomime." THEATRE QUARTERLY

6 (Winter 1976-77): 7-12. Illus.

The relationship of the traditional Christmas pantomime in Manchester ("Cottonopolis") during the mid-nineteenth century and events of the Civil War are explored.

1686   Halliday, Andrew. COMICAL FELLOWS; OR, THE HISTORY AND MYSTERY OF THE PANTOMIME, WITH SOME CURIOSITIES AND DROLL ANECDOTES CONCERNING CLOWN AND PANTALOON, HARLEQUIN AND COLUMBINE. London: J.H. Thompson, 1863. 96 p.

The relationship of the traditional Christmas pantomime in Good for mid-nineteenth-century pantomime; a scarce source.

1687   Hunt, Douglas, and Hunt, Kari. PANTOMIME. THE SILENT THEATRE. New York: Atheneum, 1964. xii, 114 p. Illus., bibliog.

A superficial history of pantomime from primitive times to the present; chapters on Medieval entertainment, the commedia dell' arte, English pantomime, clowns, magicians, and movie pantomime. Most of this source does not deal with pantomime in the English sense.

1688   Lebel, J[ean].-P[atrick]. BUSTER KEATON. Translated by P.D. Stovins. International Film Guide Series. New York: A.S. Barnes, 1967. 179 p. Illus.

Not an extremely important source other than for its description of physical tricks common before Keaton, namely those used by Joseph Grimaldi. Interesting connections between the two suggested.

1689   Lewes, John Lee, ed. THE MEMOIRS OF CHARLES LEE LEWES. 4 vols. London: Richard Phillips, 1805.

Life of the actor known for his Harlequin in the late eighteenth century.

1690   Lupino, Stanley. FROM THE STOCKS TO THE STARS. AN UNCONVENTIONAL AUTOBIOGRAPHY. London: Hutchinson and Co., 1934. 288 p. Illus.

Lupino (1893-1942) first appeared on the stage as a child; he then moved to variety with an acrobatic group; later he appeared in pantomime for many years at Drury Lane, and was seen also in revues and musical comedies.

1691   Mander, Raymond, and Mitchenson, Joe. PANTOMIME: A STORY IN PICTURES. Foreword by Danny La Rue. London: Peter Davies; New York: Taplinger Publishing Co., 1973. [viii], 56 p. Illus.

An excellent collection of illustrations, although the brief
text which precedes them is not always reliable. Nonetheless, an excellent introduction to pantomime for the uniniti-
ated. Section of 249 illustrations.

1692   Maurice, Arthur B. "Two Classic Clowns: Joseph Grimaldi and
George L. Fox." MENTOR 12 (December 1924): 18-19. Illus.

Very brief comparison of the English and American pantomime
clowns.

1693   Mawer, Irene. THE ART OF MIME. ITS HISTORY AND TECHNIQUE
IN EDUCATION AND THE THEATRE. London: Methuen and Co.,
1955. xii, 249 p. Illus.

Some coverage of English pantomime but frequently inaccurate;
typical, however, of the practical guides to mime and pantomime (in the modern sense) in its dealing with the topic historically.

1694   Mayer, David [III]. "The Pantomime Olio and Other Pantomime Variants." THEATRE NOTEBOOK 19 (Autumn 1964): 23-29.

Description of Grimaldi's business in several well-known pantomimes.

1695   _____ . "Dandyism in Regency Pantomime." THEATRE NOTEBOOK 19
(Spring 1965): 93-101.

Description of Grimaldi's and others roles in satirizing dandyism in early pantomime.

1696   _____ . HARLEQUIN IN HIS ELEMENT. Cambridge, Mass.: Harvard
University Press, 1969. xvii, 400 p. Illus., indexes, note on sources.

Exhaustive study of the important period in the history of English pantomime, fully illustrated and documented. Mayer is
acknowledged to be the current authority on the subject and
his work has superseded much that was done before him. He
is the first scholar to explore meaningfully the English Regency
pantomime. Appendixes on pantomime trickwork and music
complete the study.

1697   _____ . "Billy Purvis: Travelling Showman." THEATRE QUARTERLY 1
(October-December 1971): 27-34.

The career of Billy Purvis, a traveling showman (from 1810 to
1849) on the circuit of northern racetracks in England. He
appeared as Fantoccini (marionettes) exhibitor, conjuror,
clown, and manager of a troupe. Good glimpse at a booth
theatre operation. See also item 1660.

1698   ____. "The Pantomime of the Poor." PANTO! no. 2 (Christmas 1973): 2-11.

> The experiences of a Penny-Gaff clown in the mid-nineteenth century as extracted from Henry Mayhew's LONDON LABOUR AND THE LONDON POOR (see items 334 and 1701).

1699   ____. "The Sexuality of Pantomime." THEATRE QUARTERLY 4 (February-April 1974): 55-64.

> An analysis of the sexual ambiguities of the nineteenth-century Principal Boy.

1700   ____, comp. ANNOTATED BIBLIOGRAPHY OF PANTOMIME AND GUIDE TO STUDY SOURCES. London: Commission for a British Theatre Institute, 1975. 12 p. Paper.

> Major sources on pantomime, many excluded in this brief listing, by the major authority on the subject. Listed under books about pantomime or with sections relating to pantomime, memoirs and biographies, articles, bibliographies and catalogs of manuscript collections, collections of pantomime libretti, sources of illustrations, and other sources of information. I have used his bibliography extensively as a guide in the selection of sources for this list. Available from the Commission for a British Theatre Institute, 9 Fitzroy Square, London W1P 6AE.

1701 Mayhew, Henry. LONDON LABOUR AND THE LONDON POOR. Vol. 3: LONDON STREET FOLK. London: Charles Griffin and Co., 1864. Illus. Reprint. 4 vols. New York: A.M. Kelly, 1967. Reprint. 4 vols. New York: Dover Publications, 1968.

> Mayhew's essays "The Penny-Gaff Clown," "The Canvas Clown," and the "Ballet Performers" are authoritative accounts of popular pantomimes performed before the working-class audiences in the mid-nineteenth century. Direct transcriptions of pantomimists' accounts are included. See items 338 and 1698.

1702 Miesle, Frank Leland. "The Staging of Pantomime Entertainments on the London Stage, 1715-1808." Ph.D. dissertation, Ohio State University, 1955. 376 p.

> All aspects of production discussed: programming literary aspects, performers and their styles, scenes, scene changing, mechanical tricks, and grand finales.

1703 Miles, Henry Downes. THE LIFE OF JOSEPH GRIMALDI; WITH ANECDOTES OF HIS CONTEMPORARIES. London: Christopher Harris, 1838. 194 p.

Published as a rival to Dickens's edition (see item 1675).

1704   Morrow, John Charles. "The Staging of Pantomime at Sadler's Wells
        Theatre, 1828-1860." Ph.D. dissertation, Ohio State University, 1963.
        393 p.

> The scenery, special effects, and acting of pantomime; focus
> on the production and the theatrical appeal of extravaganza
> pantomime.

1705   Oulton, W.C. A HISTORY OF THE THEATRES OF LONDON. For
        full entry and annotation, see item 336.

1706   Reed, Edward. "Grimaldi: Michaelangelo of Buffonery." THEATRE
        ARTS MONTHLY 21 (June 1937): 483-87.

> Brief biographical sketch of Joseph Grimaldi.

1707   Robson, Joseph P[hilip]. THE LIFE AND ADVENTURE OF FAR-FAMED
        BILLY PURVIS. Newcastle-on-Tyne, Engl. J. Clarke, 1849. 240 p.

> Early biography of the North country clown-pantomimist. See
> items 1660 and 1697.

1708   Sawyer, Paul. "The Popularity of Various Types of Entertainment at
        Lincoln's Inn Fields and Covent Garden Theatres, 1720-1733." THEATRE
        NOTEBOOK 24 (Summer 1970): 154-63.

> Survey, with charts, demonstrating the popularity of panto-
> mime, drama, ballad opera, opera, and dancing at these two
> London playhouses. Especially useful in showing the enormous
> popularity of John Rich's pantomimes.

1709   _____. "Was John Rich Illiterate?" THEATRE NOTEBOOK 27
        (Autumn 1972): 36-39.

> Defense of the literacy of John Rich the manager and panto-
> mime artist.

1710   _____. "John Rich's Contribution to the Eighteenth Century Stage."
        In THE EIGHTEENTH CENTURY STAGE, edited by Kenneth Richards and
        Peter Thomson, pp. 85-104. London: Methuen and Co., 1972.

> Summary of the contributions of the manager-pantomist. Pre-
> liminary work on a full-length biography.

1711   Saxe-Wyndham, Henry. THE ANNAL OF COVENT GARDEN THEATRE
        FROM 1732 TO 1897. 2 vols. London: Chatto and Windus, 1906.

> A general history but most useful for its occasional references
> to pantomime and pantomimists.

1712   Saxon, A.H. ENTER FOOT AND HORSE: A HISTORY OF HIPPODRAMA IN ENGLAND AND FRANCE. For full entry and annotation, see item 2127.

1713   Scott, Virginia P. "The Infancy of English Pantomime: 1716-1723." EDUCATIONAL THEATRE JOURNAL 24 (May 1972): 125-34.

       Certainly one of the best of the academic studies and the most insightful to date on the early years of English pantomime. Reprinted in PANTO! (no. 3, 1975).

1714   Senelick, Laurence. "George L. Fox and American Pantomime." NINETEENTH CENTURY THEATRE RESEARCH. 7 (Spring 1979): 1-25. Illus.

       This is the most perceptive essay yet written on the American pantomime artist. For this guide the essay was read in manuscript.

1715   Sims, George R. MY LIFE: 60 YEARS OF BOHEMIAN LONDON. London: Eveleigh Nash Co., 1917. vii, 351 p. Illus.

       Author and playwright (1847-1922) of pantomimes, burlesques, and other popular forms.

1716   Speaight, George. "Pantomime." In THE SATURDAY BOOK 34, edited by John Hadfield, pp. 10-23. New York: Clarkson N. Potter, 1975. Illus.

       Good cursory survey of English pantomime, its origin and changes. Excellent illustrations, several in color.

1717   Tulin, Miriam S. "Mr. Grimaldi in the English Pantomime." Ph.D. dissertation, Yale University, 1943.

1717a   Van Lennep, William. "Dykwynkyn of Old Drury." THEATRE ANNUAL (1946): 62-72. Illus.

       Study of Richard Wynne Keene's designs for the 1852 pantomime at Drury Lane. Seven pages of plates.

1718   Wagner, Leopold. THE PANTOMIMES AND ALL ABOUT THEM, THEIR ORIGIN, HISTORY, ETC. London: J. Heywood, 1881. 60 p.

       A brief but valuable book on late-Victorian pantomime.

1719   [Ward, Edward]. THE DANCING DEVILS; OR, THE ROARING DRAGON. A DUMB FARCE. AS IT WAS LATELY ACTED AT BOTH

HOUSES, BUT PARTICULARLY AT ONE, WITH UNACCOUNTABLE SUC-
CESS. London: A. Bettesworth, 1724. 70 p.

An early attack on pantomimes and other minor forms of amusement.

1720   Wells, Mitchell P. "Pantomime and Spectacle on the London Stage,
1714-1761." Ph.D. dissertation, university of North Carolina, 1935.

1721   Wells, Staring, ed. A COMPARISON BETWEEN TWO STAGES. London, 1702. Edited edition. Princeton, N.J.: Princeton University
Press, 1942. xxi, 206 p. Index, bibliog., notes.

This anonymous treatise includes descriptions of a "night
scene," an immediate ancestor of the harlequinade. There
are also references to the Allard brothers, Louis Nivellon,
and Richard Baxter, direct from the Paris fairs. The night
scene mingled characters from the Italian commedia dell'arte
with characters representing English shopkeepers and artisans.

1722   Wilson, A[lbert]. E[dward]. CHRISTMAS PANTOMIME: THE STORY
OF AN ENGLISH INSTITUTION. London: Allen and Unwin, 1934.
262 p. Illus., index, bibliog.

Covers the entire history of English pantomime but is most useful for the Victorian and Edwardian eras. Adequate chapters
on Augustus Harris, Drury Lane, and Dan Leno.

1723   _____. KING PANTO: THE STORY OF PANTOMIME. New York:
E.P. Dutton, 1935. 262 p. Illus., index, bibliog.

This critic's generally reliable history of English pantomime
from its origin up to the 1930s.

1724   _____. PANTOMIME PAGEANT. A PROCESSION OF HARLEQUINS,
CLOWNS, COMEDIANS, PRINCIPAL BOYS, PANTOMIME-WRITERS,
PRODUCERS AND PLAYGOERS. London: Stanley Paul, 1946. 136 p.
Illus., index.

Good for pantomime in the first half of the twentieth century.

1725   _____. THE STORY OF PANTOMIME. London: Home and Van Thal,
1949. Reprint. Introduction by Roy Hudd. Wakefield, Engl.: E.P.
Publishing Co., 1974. 142 p. Illus.

Revision of KING PANTO (see item 1723) brought up to date
for younger readers. Study suffers from Wilson's chatty jour-
nalistic style lacking in careful research and thus providing
some misleading facts.

1726   Winter, Marian Hannah. THE PRE-ROMANTIC BALLET. London: Sir Isaac Pitman and Sons, 1974; Brooklyn: Dance Horizons, 1975. xxii, 306 p. Illus., index, bibliog.

Scholarly and documented study of the contributions made to pantomime by John Weaver, John Rice, Noverre, and the acrobat-dancers of the Parisian fairs.

B. MUSIC HALL: PRINCIPAL AND RECENT SOURCES

A valuable guide to sources on the music hall is currently in preparation by David Cheshire, Ulrich Schneider, and Laurence Senelick. The tentative title is A BIBLIOGRAPHIC GUIDE TO BRITISH MUSIC HALLS 1840-1930 and is scheduled to be published by the Shoe String Press (Hamden, Conn.), in 1979 or 1980. This should prove to be an exhaustive listing of sources on the halls. See index for additional sources listed elsewhere in this guide.

1727   Anderson, J[ean]., ed. LATE JOYS AT THE PLAYERS' THEATRE. London: T.V. Boardman and Co., 1943. 119 p. Illus.

Portrait of the Players' Theatre from its original site as Evans' Supper Rooms in Covent Garden to its removal to Albermarle Street, Piccadilly. See Sheridan, item 1831.

1728   Archer, William. "The County Council and the Music Hall." CONTEMPORARY REVIEW 67 (March 1895): 317-27.

Discussion of early derivations from the in-between pieces of the serious London stage; traces the transition from amateurism to professionalism. Archer supports County Council control of the "halls" as opposed to the jurisdiction of the Lord Chamberlain.

1729   Bamberger, Louis. BOW BELL MEMORIES. London: Sampson Low, Marston, [ca. 1930]. x, 246 p. Illus. (16 pls.).

Recollections of London's music halls and theatre.

1729a   Bason, Fred. "Music Hall Memories." In THE SATURDAY BOOK 30, edited by John Hadfield, pp. 121-24. New York: Clarkson N. Potter, 1970.

Reminiscences of a music hall fan.

1730   Beerbohm, Max. "The Laughter of the Public." LIVING AGE 233 (5 April 1902): 52-57.

On the source of humor in the "old-fashioned music-hall" with their "unpretentious raciness, their quaint monotony, the reality of the enjoyment on all those stolidly ept faces in the audience." For other relevant sources by Beerbohm, see items 285-87.

1731 Boardman, W[illiam]. H. ("Billy"). VAUDEVILLE DAYS. Edited by David Whitelaw. London: Jarrolds, 1935. 288 p. Illus.

Reminiscences by the variety manager of such artists as Sarah Bernhardt, Yvette Guilbert, Pavlova, and other legitimate stars of the stage.

1732 Booth, Charles. LIFE AND LABOUR OF THE PEOPLE IN LONDON. 17 vols. London: Macmillan and Co., 1889-1902.

Booth, a successful Liverpool businessman, set out in 1875 to disprove reports reports of widespread poverty and finished by supporting this thesis. His study includes an important account of music hall performers' income and the relationship between established music halls and working men's clubs; also describes methods by which artists sought employment. (For excerpts from Booth, see THEATRE QUARTERLY 1 (October-December 1971): 46.)

1733 Bradley, John L[ewis]. ROGUE'S PROGRESS. THE AUTOBIOGRAPHY OF "LORD CHIEF BARON" NICHOLSON. Cambridge, Mass.: Houghton Mifflin Co., 1965. xiii, 330 p.

Firsthand observation and participation in the obscene through hilarious mock trials in the "night cellars," a predecessor of the music hall and a feature of London night life for twenty years beginning during the Regency period. Also, information on Joseph Grimaldi and pantomime.

1734 Bratton, J[acquelin]. S. THE VICTORIAN POPULAR BALLAD. London: Macmillan Co.; Totowa, N.J.: Rowman, Littlefield, 1975. 275 p. Index, bibliog.

Valuable on nineteenth-century British popular theatre, especially the music hall, the songs of which the author examines for social, political, moral, sexual, and economic attitudes. Also good generalizations about nineteenth-century popular entertainment in general.

1735 _____. WILTON'S MUSIC HALL. London: Consortium for Drama and Media in Higher Education, 1975. 43 p., bibliog., slide set. Paper.

This is a guide to a set of thirty-nine slides depicting an uniquely preserved London music hall, the oldest music hall building still standing. It was built in 1859 and closed its doors in 1880. The guide and slides are available from the Consortium, % BUFC, Royalty House, 72 Dean Street, London W1V 5HB. An excellent visual source on the music hall and the performers that appeared there.

1736   Bristow, Eugene K. "'Tapping the Pockets' in 1860: An Economic Portrait of Sam Cowell's American Tour." THEATRE ANNUAL 22 (1965-66): 48-64.

Largely based on Mrs. Cowell's financial notations in her diary (see item 1755).

1736a   Brandreth, Gyles. THE FUNNIEST MAN ON EARTH: THE STORY OF DAN LENO. London and North Pomfret, Vt.: Hamish Hamilton, 1977. x, 105 p. Illus., index, bibliog., appendix.

The most reliable biography to date of Leno, although lacking in documentation. More useful than items 1792 or 1851.

1737   Brown, Ivor. "The English Drolls." THEATRE ARTS MONTHLY 22 (September 1939): 649-55.

Revival of English music hall and its importance as a source of talent for films and the stage.

1738   Burnand, Sir Francis C. RECORDS AND REMINISCENCES, PERSONAL AND GENERAL. 2 vols. London: Methuen and Co., 1904. Illus.

Good general source on English popular entertainment and theatre, but especially useful insights into early music hall and such a performer as W.G. Ross and his greatest success "Sam Hall."

1739   Busby, Roy. BRITISH MUSIC HALL: AN ILLUSTRATED WHO'S WHO FROM 1850 TO THE PRESENT DAY. London and Salem, N.H.: Paul Elek, 1976. 191 p. Illus., glossary.

Despite many exclusions and numerous errors, this is the only such reference work on music hall available. Five hundred biographical entries; approximately two hundred fifty illustrations plus a brief historical survey.

1740   Byng, Douglas. AS YOU WERE, REMINISCENCES. London: Duckworth, 1970. 176 p. Illus., index.

An artist in the latterday of music hall, cabaret, and other entertainment media, famous for his outrageous comedy songs.

1741   Calthrop, D[ion]. C[layton]. MUSIC-HALL NIGHTS. London: John Lane, 1925. vi, 147 p. Illus.

Inevitably listed among major sources on music hall; actually
a rather poor source, although some useful summaries of late-
Victorian music hall events are included.

1742 Cheshire, David F. "A Chronology of Music Hall." THEATRE QUAR-
TERLY 1 (October–December 1971): 41–45.

Highlights from 1819, birth of Charles Morton, to 1923, the
first BBC broadcast of a full-scale variety show.

1743 _____. MUSIC HALL IN BRITAIN. Newton Abbot, Devon, Engl.:
David and Charles; Rutherford, N.J.: Fairleigh Dickenson University
Press, 1974. 112 p. Illus., bibliog.

Cheshire stresses the variety element of the music halls and
their commercial nature; he divides the history of the halls
into four periods: up to 1843, 1843–90, 1890–1912, and
1912–23. Outstanding telling of the halls' history in documents and pictures.

1744 Chevalier, Albert. BEFORE I FORGET: THE AUTOBIOGRAPHY OF
CHEVALIER D'INDUSTRIE. London: T. Fisher Unwin, 1901. xvi,
258 p. Illus.

Further reminiscences; see below.

1745 Chevalier, Albert, and Daly, Brian. A RECORD BY HIMSELF. London:
John Macqueen, 1895. xii, 295 p. Illus.

Chevalier (1862–1923) was one of the more popular coster
comedians.

1746 Chevalier, Florenz. ALBERT CHEVALIER COMES BACK. London:
Rider and Co., [1927]. 200 p. Illus.

Bizarre biography of the music hall performer based on spiritu-
alistic experiences.

1747 Chirgwin, G.H. CHIRGWIN'S CHIRRUP. BEING THE LIFE AND
REMINISCENCES OF GEORGE CHIRGWIN, THE "WHITE EYED MUSI-
CAL KAFFIR." London: J and J Bennett, 1912. 134 p. Illus.

Autobiography of Chirgwin (1854–1922), an eccentric music
hall comedian.

1748 Coburn, Charles. "THE MAN WHO BROKE THE BANK." MEMORIES
OF THE STAGE AND MUSIC HALL. London: Hutchinson and Co.,
[1928]. 286 p. Illus.

Coburn (1852–1945) was revered as "The Father of the Profession."

1749   Cotes, Peter. GEORGE ROBEY: THE DARLING OF THE HALLS.
        Foreword by Neville Cardus. London: Cassell, 1972. xx, 204 p.
        Illus., index, brief bibliog.

> Reasonably good modern biography of Robey (1869-1954), al-
> though undocumented. Robey was both a music hall comedian
> and a famous pantomime dame. Three appendixes: selections
> from his writings; highlights of his career (1888-1954), produc-
> tions in which he appeared (excluding music hall and panto-
> mime) from 1916 to 1952, and songs sung by Robey and books
> by him (fourteen in all). His most useful books are listed in
> items 1820 and 1821.

1750   Cowen, John. "Music Halls and Morals." CONTEMPORARY REVIEW
        110 (November 1916): 611-20.

> Cowen endorses the laws against the "Promenades" on the
> grounds of the visible destruction of lives by "sexual disease"
> and singles out Harry Lauder as a rare example of decency
> in the halls.

1751   Croxton, Arthur, CROWDED NIGHTS AND DAYS. London: Sampson
        Low, Marston and Co., [1930]. xviii, 398 p. Illus., index.

> Autobiography; most useful for his observations on the variety
> and music hall stages.

1752   Davison, Peter, comp. and ed. SONGS OF THE BRITISH MUSIC HALL.
        New York: Oak Publications (a division of Embassy Music Corp.),
        1971. 244 p. Illus., index, bibliog. Paper.

> Excellent checklist of major sources (published), a selective
> discography, and a superb introduction and conclusion, bal-
> anced with perceptive criticism of the songs included in the
> volume, from "Sam Hall" to "Heaven Will Protect an Honest
> Girl." Though the author disclaims this collection as a his-
> tory or an exact sample of songs sung in the halls, it remains
> an excellent collection, with commentary, of the songs of the
> music hall from W.G. Ross to Gracie Fields by a discerning
> and informed critic-musician. Fifty songs are included with
> words, music, and variants.

1753   De Frece, Lady [Vesta Tilley]. RECOLLECTIONS OF VESTA TILLEY.
        Foreword by Oswald Stoll. Appreciation by Sir Alfred Butt. London:
        Hutchinson and Co., 1934. 295 p. Illus., index.

> Autobiography of Tilley (1864-1952), probably the finest of
> the music hall's male impersonators.

1754   Disher, M[aurice]. Willson. "The Music-Hall." QUARTERLY REVIEW

252 (April 1929): 259-71.

Cursory history of the "halls" from the "Song and Supper" rooms to the latterday variety. Reasonably useful survey.

1755   ____, ed. THE COWELLS IN AMERICA: BEING THE DIARY OF MRS. SAM COWELL, 1860-61. London: Oxford University Press, 1934. lxv, 426 p. Illus., index

Cowell (1820-64), an early English star of the music hall, toured the United States in 1860-61. His wife's (Emilie Ebsworth) diary, edited by Disher, is preceded by a detailed introduction to the Cowells. See item 1736.

1756   ____. WINKLES AND CHAMPAGNE: COMEDIES AND TRAGEDIES OF THE MUSIC HALL. London: B.T. Batsford, 1938. xii, 147 p. Illus., index.

Not totally devoted to music hall but extremely good for illustrations (114) and commentary. Published in the United States (New York: Charles Scribner's Sons, 1938) as MUSIC HALL PARADE.

1757   Dunville, T.E. THE AUTOBIOGRAPHY OF AN ECCENTRIC COMEDIAN. London: Everett and Co., [1912]. x, 102 p.

Dunville (1870-1924) was an "eccentric" comedian and known for his outlandish costume and clownish makeup and the nonsensical songs he sang.

1758   Eliot, T.S. SELECTED ESSAYS: 1917-32. New York: Harcourt, Brace and Co., 1932.

In his 1923 eulogy, "Marie Lloyd" (369 f.) Eliot bemoans the passing of the music hall in the era of cinema and gramophone and other passive entertainment.

1759   Elkin, Robert. QUEEN'S HALL 1893-1941. Foreword by Dr. Malcolm Sargent. London: Rider and Co., [1944]. 160 p. Illus.

History of Queen's Hall Music Hall.

1760   ____. THE OLD CONCERT ROOMS OF LONDON. London: Edward Arnold, 1955. 167 p. Illus.

On one of the music hall's predecessors.

1761   Farson, Daniel. MARIE LLOYD AND THE MUSIC HALL. London: Tom Stacey, 1972. 176 p. Illus., index.

An unsatisfying biography of the great music hall star (1870-

1922). Her tragic life is portrayed as perpetuated on the premise that "The English public will open its arms to vice, provided it is presented as a frolic." Traces the origins of music hall and shows how they came together in the form of a "people's entertainment."

1762 Felstead, S. Theodore. STARS WHO MADE THE HALLS. London: T. Werner Laurie, 1946. x, 192 p. Illus., index.

Firsthand impressions of music hall stars and a history of the halls. A useful source.

1763 Fergusson, Sir Louis. OLD-TIME MUSIC HALL COMEDIANS. Leicester, Engl.: C.H. Gee and Co., 1949. 63 p.

Brief survey of best known comedians.

1764 Finck, Herman. MY MELODIES MEMOIRS. London: Hutchinson and Co., 1937. 304 p. Illus.

Music hall memoirs by the orchestra conductor of the Palace Theatre (London).

1765 Fisher, John. FUNNY WAY TO BE A HERO: BEING A PENETRATING HISTORY OF HALF A CENTURY OF BRITISH MUSIC HALL COMEDY. London: Frederick Muller, 1973. 336 p. Illus., index, bibliog.

Deals with music hall, as well as cabarets, theatres, and variety. Focus on the comedians in these forms.

1766 Fitzgerald, Percy. MUSIC HALL LAND, AN ACCOUNT OF THE NA-TIVES, MALE AND FEMALE, PASTIMES, SONGS, ANTICS, AND GENERAL ODDITIES OF THAT STRANGE COUNTRY. Illustrated by Alfred Bryan. London: Ward and Downey, 1890. vi, 90 p.

An unusual source on the halls but of limited use.

1767 Foster, George. THE SPICE OF LIFE. London: Hurst and Blackett, 1939. 288 p. Illus.

Sixty-five years in the "Glamour World" as told by an agent. Personal account of music halls with anecdotes on the principal stars.

1768 Gamble, George. THE 'HALLS'. Illustrated by G.F. Scotson-Clark. London: T. Fisher Unwin, [1899]. 48 p. Illus.

Most useful for its twenty-four plates and early commentary, though limited as a factual source.

1769 Gammond, Peter. YOUR OWN, YOUR VERY OWN. London: Ian Allen, 1971. 96 p. Illus., bibliog., discography. Paper.

Scrapbook format with interesting pictorial material but very inaccurate historical test. List of one hundred music hall songs.

1770 _____, ed. BEST MUSIC HALL AND VARIETY SONGS. London: Wolfe (Wolfe Old Time Stars' Book), 1972. 512 p.

Disappointing collection with only one major music hall performer (Albert Chevalier) represented. Most selections were songs from revuews, pantomimes, and musical comedies or radio comedy. Uneven introduction by the compiler.

1771 Garrett, John M. SIXTY YEARS OF BRITISH MUSIC HALL. London: Chappell and Co., 1976. [252] p. Illus.

Thirty-five music hall songs reproduced with words and music (as originally published). Forty five illustrations of the original color covers are reproduced. There are introductory chapters that briefly trace the history of music hall and the production of music for the performers. Data on each song and artist is also included.

1772 Geary, William Neville Montgomerie. THE LAW OF THEATRES AND MUSIC-HALLS. London: Stevens and Sons, 1885. xiii, 230 p.

Includes contracts and precedents of contracts with a historical introduction by James Williams.

1773 Glasstone, Victor. VICTORIAN & EDWARDIAN THEATRES. For full entry and annotation, see item 317.

1774 Greenwall, Harry James. THE STRANGE LIFE OF WILLY CLARKSON. AN EXPERIMENT IN BIOGRAPHY. London: John Long, 1936. 288 p. Illus.

Biography of a theatrical wigmaker, with much information on the halls. Fifteen pages of plates.

1775 Haddon, Archibald. THE STORY OF THE MUSIC HALLS. London: Fleetway Press, 1935. 204 p. Illus. (66 pls.).

Superficial account of the halls.

1776 Hibbert, H.G. FIFTY YEARS OF A LONDONER'S LIFE. Preface by T.P. O'Conner. London: Grant Richard; New York: Dodd, Mead and Co., 1916. xv, 303 p. Illus.

One of two autobiographies with firsthand observations on the halls. See next entry.

1777 _____. A PLAYGOER'S MEMORIES. Preface by William Archer. London: Grant Richards, 1920. 303 p.

Additional memoirs. See above.

1778 Hilliam, B[entley]. C[ollingwood]. FLOTSAM'S FOLLIES. THE AUTO-BIOGRAPHY OF B.C. HILLIAM, "FLOTSAM." Foreword by Sir Louis Sterling. London: Arthur Barron, 1948. xv, 178 p. Illus.

Music hall reminiscences.

1779 Holloway, Stanley, as told to Richards, Dick. WIV A LITTLE BIT O' LUCK. THE LIFE STORY OF STANLEY HOLLOWAY. London: Leslie Frewin; New York: Stein and Day, 1967. 223 p. Illus.

Late music hall performer's autobiography.

1780 Honri, Peter. WORKING THE HALLS. Farnborough, Hampshire, Engl.: Saxon House, 1973. xv, 215 p. Illus., index, bibliog.

Story of four generations of music hall performers, beginning in the 1870s. Interesting illustrations, several in color.

1781 Howard, Diana. LONDON THEATRES AND MUSIC HALLS 1850-1950. London: Library Association, 1970. Distributed in the United States by Gale Research Co., Detroit. xiv, 292 p. Illus., bibliog.

Details of architecture, management, and so forth of over nine hundred music halls, theatres, and public houses with entertainment licenses in London. Each entry lists the building details of each structure on the site, managers, and a bibliography of references to official records, contemporary accounts in periodicals, and historical accounts in books. Other data, including list of collections and an excellent bibliography, are included in appendixes. Recommended.

1782 Hudd, Roy. MUSIC HALL. London: Eyre Methuen, 1976. Unpaged. Illus. Paper.

Celebration in words and pictures by the British comedian but not of much factual value. Features 126 illustrations.

1783 Irving, Gordon. GREAT SCOT, THE LIFE STORY OF SIR HARRY LAUDER, LEGENDARY LAIRD OF THE MUSIC HALL. London: Leslie Frewin, 1968. 184 p. Illus., index.

Popularized biography; appendix: list of Lauder's songs. Lauder was also popular in American variety and vaudeville, and later, films.

1784 Jacob, Naomi. OUR MARIE. London: Hutchinson and Co., [1936]. 287 p. Illus., index.

Sympathetic, anecdotal account of Marie Lloyd's life, stressing her finer qualities. Lloyd's real name was Matilda Wood (1870-1922). Illustrated frontispiece.

1785 Kavanagh, Ted. TOMMY HANDLEY. London: Hodder and Stoughton, 1949. 256 p. Illus.

Biography of comedian most popular in radio. Thirty-three pages of illustrative plates.

1786 Knowles, R[ichard]. G[eorge]. A MODERN COLUMBUS. London: T. Werner Laurie, 1918. xii, 301 p. Illus.

Life of the Canadian-born comedian (1858-1919) known as the "Very Peculiar American Comedian."

1787 Langdon, Claude. EARL'S COURT. Foreword by the Marquess of Milford Haven. London: Stanley Paul and Co., 1953. 223 p. Illus.

Autobiography with material on the music hall.

1788 Lauder, Harry. AT HOME AND ON TOUR BY MA' SEL'. London: Greening and Co., 1907. 126 p. Illus.

Early autobiography of the Scottish singer-comedian. See items 1789, 1790, and 1791.

1789 _____. A MINSTREL IN FRANCE. New York: Hearst's International Library Co., 1918. [6], 338 p. Illus.

Autobiography covering the years 1914-18. See items 1788, 1790, and 1791.

1790 _____. BETWEEN YOU AND ME. New York: James A. McCann Co., 1919. 324 p.

Another rambling autobiography. See items 1788, 1789, and 1791.

1791 _____. ROAMIN' IN THE GLOAMIN'. Philadelphia and London: J.B. Lippincott, 1928. 300 p. Illus.

The most complete of his several autobiographies; covers his career in Great Britain and the United States.

1792 Leno, Dan. HYS BOOKE: A VOLUME OF FRIVOLITIES. 1901. Abridged reprint, edited by Roy Hudd. London: Hugh Evelyn, 1968. 59 p. Illus.

Entertaining little autobiography of the music hall comic who

died in 1904 at the age of forty-three. A brief introduction
and even briefer biographical notes are supplied by Hudd.
See items 1736a and 1851.

1793 Le Roy, George. MUSIC HALL STARS OF THE NINETIES. London:
British Technical and General Press, 1952. 70 p. Illus.

Principally concerned with the singers of the music hall.

1794 MacInnes, Colin. SWEET SATURDAY NIGHT. London: MacGibbon
and Kee, 1967; London: Panther Books, 1969. 160 p.

A semisociological study of the music hall with strange preju-
dices and numerous inaccuracies, dominated by nostalgic,
discursive comments.

1795 Macqueen-Pope, W[alter]. MARIE LLOYD, QUEEN OF THE MUSIC-
HALLS. London: Oldbourne, n.d. 186 p.

One of the three full-length studies of Marie Lloyd and the
least reliable; often inaccurate and gossipy. Contains portrait
of Lloyd

1796 _____. THE MELODIES LINGER ON. THE STORY OF MUSIC HALL.
London: W.H. Allen, [1950]. 459 p. Illus.

Lengthy history written in the author's typically flowery and
emotional style; not very accurate or specific.

1797 Mander, Raymond, and Mitchenson, Joe. BRITISH MUSIC HALL. Rev.
ed. London: Gentry Books, 1974. 243 p. Illus., index.

Revised version of 1965 edition (London: London House and
Maxwell); no formal bibliography but sources are indicated in
an acknowledgement. Basically an illustrated history from the
eighteenth century to the early 1960s, with useful summary
introductions and information in extended captions for the 301
plates. Serves as a good introduction to music hall. Provides list of performers for the Royal Command Performance,
Palace Theatre, 1 July 1912, London Coliseum, 28 July 1919,
and Royal Variety Performances 1921–73. Select discography.

1798 Mellor, G[eoffrey]. J[ames]. POMS POMS AND RUFFLES. Clapham,
Lancaster, Engl.: Dalesman, 1966 72 p. Illus. Paper.

The story of Northern seaside entertainment; interesting look
at music hall outside of London.

1799 _____. THE NORTHERN MUSIC HALL: A CENTURY OF POPULAR
ENTERTAINMENT. Introduction by Ken Dodd. Foreword by George

Wood. Newcastle-on-Tyne, Engl.: Graham, 1970. 224 p. Illus.,
index.

Amateur compilation with a good deal of unrecorded information; still, a decent account of music hall in general outside
of London in particular.

1800 Mozart, George [David John Gillings]. LIMELIGHT. London: Hurst
and Blackett, 1938. 284 p. Illus.

Autobiography of Mozart (1864-1947) known for his character
comedic one-man sketches.

1801 Morton, W[illiam]. H., and Newton, H[enry]. Chance [Heath Cranton].
SIXTY YEARS' STAGE SERVICE, BEING A RECORD OF THE LIFE OF
CHARLES MORTON, "THE FATHER OF THE HALLS." London: Gale
and Polden, 1905. viii, 208 p. Illus.

Life of Morton (1819-1904); information on his contribution to
music hall and his halls (the Canterbury and the Oxford) and
valuable incidental information.

1802 Munro, John M. "Queer Fish at the Aquarium: The Failure of a
Victorian Compromise." DRAMA AND THEATRE 9 (1970-71): 75-80.

Expanded in his book, below.

1803 _____. THE ROYAL AQUARIUM: FAILURE OF A VICTORIAN COM-
PROMISE. Beirut, Lebanon: American University of Beirut Press, 1971.
xii, 71 p. Illus., bibliog.

Account of the ill-fated institution which was demolished in
1903 after developing into a cross between a music hall and
a fairground (originally conceived as an institution which
would combine the virtues of an exhibition with those of a
pleasure garden).

1804 Nevill, Ralph [Henry], and Jerningham, Charles Edward. PICCADILLY
TO PALL MALL: MANNERS, MORALS, AND MAN. London: Duckworth and Co., 1908. 310 p. Illus., index.

Pages 111-27 deals with the latter-day music hall and the
Gaiety Theatre.

1805 Newton, H. Chance [Heath Cranton]. IDOLS OF THE "HALLS."
London: Heath Cranton, 1928. 256 p. Illus., index.

Intimate memoirs by "Carados," critic and gossipmonger for
the REFEREE, but inaccurate on facts. Still, interesting first-
hand observations when used discriminately.

1806 O'Rourke, Eva, comp. LAMBETH AND MUSIC HALL: A TREASURY
OF MUSIC HALL MEMORABILIA. London: London Borough of Lambeth
Directorate of Amenity Services, 1977.

A portfolio containing biographical notes with photographs,
original reviews and quotations on Dan Leno, George Robey,
Fred Karno, and Bransby Williams. Facsimile reproductions
of early music hall programs of the Canterbury Theatre and
the Empress Theatre Brixton; historical notes and engravings of
"The Canterbury" and "The Old Vic"; reproduction of the
famous painting "Popularity" with 226 portraits of music hall
artists, together with a key, information on the early days of
Gertrude Lawrence, and a booklist and introductory notes.

1807 [Page, Will A.]. "How Harry Lauder Composed His Famous Songs."
THEATRE MAGAZINE 8 (December 1908): 322, 324.

Lauder explains the compositions of "I Have a Lassie," "The
Weddin Bells," and other songs associated with him.

1808 Palmer, John. THE FUTURE OF THE THEATRE. London: G. Bell and
Sons, 1913. xi, 196 p.

Contrast between the attraction of the music hall and the
legitimate theatre.

1809 Pearsall, Ronald. VICTORIAN SHEET MUSIC COVERS. Detroit:
Gale Research Co., 1972. 112 p. Illus., index.

Contains a good deal on Victorian music hall songs and
specific performers. See next source.

1810 _____. VICTORIAN POPULAR MUSIC. Newton Abbot, Devon, Engl.:
David and Charles, 1973. 240 p. Illus., index, bibliog.

Includes all forms of music--brass bands, choirs, mechanical
music in the home, concerts featuring Monster Quadrilles and
Beethoven symphonies accompanied by four brass bands, music
hall, ballet, opera, outdoor music, and dancing.

1811 Peers, Donald. PATHWAY. London: Werner Laurie, 1951. 224 p.
Illus.

Autobiography of the English singer and broadcaster who, started
his career in the music halls.

1812 Prentis, Terence, ed. MUSIC-HALL MEMORIES. Foreword by Harry
Lauder. Illustrations by Elizabeth Pyke. London: Selwyn and Blount,
1972. x, [11] 94 p. Illus.

General source on music hall songs.

1813 Pulling, Christopher. THEY WERE SINGING AND WHAT THEY SANG
ABOUT. London: George C. Harrap and Co., 1952. 276 p. Illus.,
indexes, select bibliog.

> Perceptive study of the music of the halls and its relation to
> the social background; lacks specific dates but is most con-
> cerned with Victorian music hall examples. Index of singers
> and actors, songs with their singers, and a general index.
> Compared to many music hall sources, this is fairly reliable
> and recommended. Line decorations by Muriel Box.

1814 Randall, Harry. HARRY RANDALL, OLD TIME COMEDIAN. Foreword
by Charles B. Cochran. London: Sampson Low, Marston and Co.,
[1930]. xiii, 242 p. Illus.

> Memoirs of Randall (1860-1932), including his appearances in
> pantomime and those of his contemporaries.

1815 Reeve, Ada. TAKE IT FOR A FACT: A RECORD OF MY SEVENTY-
FIVE YEARS ON THE STAGE. Foreword by Sir Compton Mackenzie.
London: Heinemann, 1954. 263 p. Illus., index.

> Memoirs of Reeve (1874-1966), stage name of Adelaide Mary
> Isaac. Illustrations from the Mander and Mitchenson collection.

1816 Relph, Harry [Little Tich]. A BOOK OF TRAVELS (AND WANDERINGS).
London: Greening and Co., 1911. 135 p. Illus.

> Career of Little Tich (1867-1928), famous music hall comedian.

1817 Ritchie, James [Ewing]. DAYS AND NIGHTS IN LONDON; OR,
STUDIES IN BLACK AND GRAY. London: Tinsley Bros., 1880. viii,
295 p.

> Music hall reminiscences; see also his NIGHT SIDE OF LON-
> DON (item 340).

1818 Roberts, Arthur. THE ADVENTURES OF ARTHUR ROBERTS BY RAIL,
ROAD AND RIVER. TOLD BY HIMSELF AND CHRONICLED BY R.
MORTON. Bristol: J.W. Arrowsmith, 1895. 198 p.

> Early reminiscences of the actor-music hall performer (1852-
> 1933).

1819 _____. FIFTY YEARS OF SPOOF. For full entry and annotation, see
item 1623.

1820 Robey, George. MY LIFE UP TO NOW, A NAUGHTIBIOGRAPHY.
London: Greening and Co., 1908. xv, 128 p. Illus.

Autobiography of Robey (1869-1954), "The Prime Minister of Mirth". See also next entry and item 1749.

1821 _____. LOOKING BACK ON LIFE. Introduction by J.M. Barrie. London: Constable and Co., 1933. xviii, 318 p. Illus., index.

The last of Robey's fourteen books. Robey was also important in English pantomime. See also the preceding entry and item 1749.

1822 Rose, Clarkson. WITH A TWINKLE IN MY EYES. Foreword by Sir Barry Jackson. Preface by Collie Knox. Introduction by George F. Reynolds. London: Museum Press, 1951. 272 p. Illus.

Memoirs of Rose (1890-1968), variety comedian and excellent dame in pantomime. More reminiscences are contained in the following two items.

1823 _____. BESIDE THE SEASIDE. London: Museum Press, 1960. 148 p. Illus.

1824 _____. RED PLUSH AND GREASEPAINT, A MEMORY OF THE MUSIC-HALL AND LIFE AND TIMES FROM THE '90'S TO THE '60'S. London: Museum Press, 1964. 152 p. Illus.

1825 Scott, Christopher, and Scott, Amoret. "The Music of the Halls." In THE SATURDAY BOOK 20, edited by John Hadfield, pp. 122-35. London: Hutchinson and Co., 1960. Illus.

Brief history of printed music from the music halls, illustrated with music covers.

1826 Scott, Harold, ed. and comp. AN ENGLISH SONG BOOK. Introduction by Harold Scott. London: Chapman and Hall, 1925; New York: Robert M. McBride and Co., 1926. xviii, 149 p. Illus.

Eighteenth- and nineteenth-century popular songs (melodies only).

1827 _____. THE EARLY DOORS--ORIGINS OF THE MUSIC HALL. London: Nicholson and Watson, 1946. 259 p. Illus., indexes, (song and general), bibliog., appendixes.

First carefully researched music hall history, especially strong on the early phase and the origins of the halls. The closest work to a classic written to date, in this compiler's opinion. Examples of songs in six appendixes.

1828 Senelick, Laurence. "A Brief Life and Times of the Victorian Music-

Hall." HARVARD LIBRARY BULLETIN 19 (October 1971): 375-98.
Illus.

Although Senelick's expertise in this field has grown since
this essay was written, he has produced here a superb summary
of the music hall's life and times during the Victorian period.
Recommended.

1829 _____. "All Trivial Fond Records: On the Uses of Early Recordings
of British Music Hall Performers." THEATRE SURVEY 26 (November
1975): 135-49.

Excellent survey of early music hall recordings.

1830 _____. "Politics as Entertainment: Victorian Music Hall Songs."
VICTORIAN STUDIES 19 (December 1975): 149-80.

Stresses the vapidness of political satire in the songs of the
halls and discusses the competition between music hall songs
which were associated with a single performer who used the
same songs for years and the broadside ballads which were
distributed widely and of which there were new ones every
week.

1831 Sheridan, Paul. LATE AND EARLY JOYS AT THE PLAYERS' THEATRE.
Foreword by Sybil Thorndike. London: T.V. Boardman, 1952. 97 p.
Illus.

Sequel to LATE JOYS AT THE PLAYERS' THEATRE, 1943 (see
item 1727).

1832 Short, Ernest, and Compton-Rickett, Arthur. RING UP THE CURTAIN,
BEING A PAGEANT OF ENGLISH ENTERTAINMENT COVERING HALF
A CENTURY. London: Herbert Jenkins, 1938. 319 p. Illus., index.

Chapter 7: "The Palaces of Variety Round About Leicester
Square" provides the history, development, and downfall of
England's palaces of variety, including the Alhambra, Empire
Palace of Variety, the Palace, the Hippodrome, the Palladium,
and a discussion of the stars, managers, and important people
connected with these variety-music hall houses. See also
item 345.

1833 Soldene, Emily. MY THEATRICAL AND MUSICAL RECOLLECTIONS.
London: Downey and Co., 1898. xx, 315 p. Illus.

Amusing account of a respectable young lady's first impressions
of the Canterbury Hall of Charles Morton. She was hired by
Morton in 1865. Soldene (1840-1912) was a music hall performer who first appeared as Miss Fitzhenry at The Canterbury.

1834   Soutar, Robert, ed. A JUBILEE OF DRAMATIC LIFE AND INCIDENT OF JOSEPH A. CAVE. London: T. Vernon, [1894]. 218 p.

       Life of the music hall manager (1823-1912).

1835   Speaight, George, comp. BAWDY SONGS OF THE EARLY MUSIC HALL. Newton Abbot, London and Vancouver: David and Charles, 1975. 96 p. Illus., notes.

       Songs of the "Song and Supper Rooms" in the early nineteenth century. Ten-page introduction to this phenomenon and its songs is useful.

1836   Stuart, C[harles]. D[ouglas]., and Park, A.J. THE VARIETY STAGE, A HISTORY OF THE MUSIC HALLS FROM THE EARLIEST PERIOD TO THE PRESENT TIME. London: T. Fisher Unwin, [1895]. [vii]-xii, 255 p.

       The first treatise on music hall written while the form was still thriving; although undocumented and illustrated, this is a fascinating account, invaluable for contemporary information on the halls and the incidental characters.

1837   Stump, Walter Ray. "British Parliamentary Hearings on the Theatre Between 1843 and 1909: The Struggle for a Free Stage in London Revisited." Ph.D. dissertation, Indiana University, 1973. 372 p.

       Saloon taverns, music halls, and the licensing of legitimate theatre and the halls. See sources on censorship and the law under popular theatre (chapter 11).

1838   Symons, Arthur. CITIES AND SEA COASTS AND ISLAND. London: W. Collins Sons and Co.; New York: Brentanos, 1919. vii, 352 p.

       Comments by the critic on music hall.

1839   Taylor, Vic. REMINISCENCES OF A SHOWMAN. Introduction by David Robinson. London: Allen Lane, 1971. x, 116 p. Illus.

       A late performer in variety (b. 1900) reminisces.

1840   Thackeray, William Makepeace. THE NEWCOMES: MEMOIRS OF A MOST RESPECTABLE FAMILY. 2 vols. London: Brodbury and Evans, 1855.

       Chapter 1 of Thackeray's novel contains a vivid and fairly reliable description of the Cider Cellar. Thackeray's fiction is frequently a good source on English popular entertainments.

1841   Titterton, William Richard. FROM THEATRE TO MUSIC HALL. London: Stephen Swift and Co., 1912. 242 p.

A relatively unimportant source on the music hall.

1842   Unthan, Carl Hermann. THE ARMLESS FIDDLER. A PEDISCRIPT.
        BEING THE LIFE STORY OF A VAUDEVILLE MAN. Preface by J.
        Malcolm Forbes. London: G. Allen and Unwin, 1935. 287 p. Illus.

        The autobiography of one of the more unusual English variety
        and music hall performers.

1843   Watters, Eugene, and Murtagh, Mathews. INFINITE VARIETY. DAN
        LOWREY'S MUSIC HALL, 1879-97. Dublin: Gill and MacMillan,
        1975. 176 p. Illus., indexes.

        The Olympia, Dublin's only surviving music hall, built by
        Lowrey and visited by most of the great stars during his
        seventeen years of management is chronicled.

1844   Wewiora, G.E. "Manchester Music-Hall Audiences in the 1880s."
        MANCHESTER REVIEW 12 (1972): 124-28.

        Useful analysis of provincial music hall audiences.

1845   Williams, Bransby. AN ACTOR'S STORY. London: Chapman and
        Hall, 1909. xiii, 270 p. Illus.

        Williams (1870-1961) was known as "The Hamlet of the Halls."
        This is the first of several autobiographies. See two items
        below.

1846   _____. THE OLD TIME ACTOR AND PENNY SHOWMAN. New
        York and London: Samuel French, [1913]. 6 p. Paper.

1847   _____. BY HIMSELF. London: Hutchinson and Co., 1954. 240 p.
        Illus.

1848   Wilson, A[lbert]. E[dward]. PRIME MINISTER OF MIRTH. London:
        Odhams Press, 1956. 256 p. Illus., index.

        Life of George Robey, the famous music hall entertainer known
        as "The Prime Minster of Mirth."

1849   Wood, Georgie. I HAD TO BE "WEE." London: Hutchinson and Co.,
        [1948]. 196 p. Illus.

        Autobiography of the dimunitive music hall performer (b. 1895).

1850   _____. ROYALTY, RELIGION AND RATS! AN AUTOBIOGRAPHICAL
        SCRAPBOOK MISCELLANY. London: privately printed, 1963. [4],
        256 p. Illus.

Edition limited to two thousand copies. A potpourri of events and people in Wood's life, told in a disjointed narrative. Fairly useful on The Rats (Grand Order of Water Rats).

1851 Wood, J[ay]. Hickory. DAN LENO. London: Methuen and Co., 1905. xiv, 285 p. Illus.

Biography of the best music hall comedian of his day written by the well-known pantomime author. Leno was also active in pantomime.

Part III

POPULAR THEATRE: ENGLISH AND AMERICAN

Chapter 10

POPULAR THEATRE: GENERAL SOURCES, UNITED STATES

The sources listed below should not be construed as representative or approximating completeness. The sources have been chosen for this section because of their major relevance to popular theatre, their currentness, or emphasis on specific aspects of popular theatre not covered elsewhere in this guide. Virtually all sources on American theatre and drama could be included in this section. The user of this guide is thus urged to refer to item 93 for additional sources. Most well-known general histories have been excluded. See also sources in chapter 3, section A.

1852   Abbott, George. MISTER ABBOTT. New York: Random House, 1965. 279 p.

> Autobiography of the actor, director, producer; contains a chronological list of his theatre activities, 1913-62.

1853   Anderson, John. THE AMERICAN THEATRE. For full entry and annotation, see item 156.

1854   Appelbaum, Stanley, ed. THE NEW YORK STAGE: FAMOUS PRODUCTIONS IN PHOTOGRAPHS. New York: Dover Publications, 1975. vi, 154 p. Index. Paper.

> Contains 148 photographs (1883-1939) from the Theatre and Music Collection of the Museum of the City of New York. Many of the productions represented fall into the category of popular theatre fare.

1855   _____. SCENES FROM THE NINETEENTH-CENTURY STAGE. New York: Dover Publications, 1977. xv, 152 p. Indexes. Paper.

> Fascinating collection of 268 woodcuts giving a representative overview of productions from primarily the 1860s to 1974. The majority of these examples were popular fare and the editor has included a useful description of the theatrical genres and some points of stagecraft of the period.

1856   Atkinson, Brooks. BROADWAY. For full entry and annotation, see
item 158.

1857   Barnabee, Henry Clay. MY WANDERINGS. REMINISCENCES OF
HENRY CLAY BARNABEE. BEING AN ATTEMPT TO ACCOUNT FOR
HIS LIFE, WITH SOME EXCUSES FOR HIS PROFESSIONAL CAREER.
Edited by George Leon Varney. Boston: Chapple Publishing Co.,
1913. 461 p. Illus.

Especially good for the Boston Museum and the Boston Theatre.

1858   Barnes, Djuna. "When Stock Was Work." THEATRE GUILD MAGA-
ZINE 7 (February 1930): 33-34.

Description of stock acting and conditions at the turn of the
century as related by Sam Forrest, a veteran of stock.

1859   Belasco, David. THE THEATRE THROUGH ITS STAGE DOOR. New
York: Harper and Bros., 1919. 246 p. Illus.

The autobiography of the producer-director-playwright, replete
with his biased and often uncorroborated claims; still useful
on popular theatre during the late nineteenth century. See
item 1962.

1860   Bennett, Joan. THE BENNETT PLAYBILL. For full entry and annotation, see item 160.

1861   Bernheim, Alfred. THE BUSINESS OF THE THEATRE. New York:
Actors' Equity Association, 1932. Reprint. New York: Benjamin Blom,
1964. xii, 218 p.

Contains an excellent economic history of the legitimate
theatre from the colonial period to 1929. Useful background
for popular theatre.

1862   Blumenthal, George. MY SIXTY YEARS IN SHOW BUSINESS. For
full entry and annotation, see item 162.

1863   Bond, Frederick W. THE NEGRO AND THE DRAMA. For full entry
and annotation, see item 163.

1864   Brazier, Marion Howard. STAGE AND SCREEN. Boston: M.H.
Brazier, 1920. 130 p.

Plays and players from stock days (1870s) to the rise of early
cinema.

1865   Breitenbach, Edgar. "Historical Development of the American Theatrical

Poster in the Nineteenth Century." OHIO STATE UNIVERSITY THEATRE COLLECTION BULLETIN no. 10 (1963): 3-6.

> Interesting but brief study of the evolution of the theatrical poster in America. See also Winter, item 95, and Halliday, item 1894.

1866 Brown, David J. "Footlight Favorites Forty Years Ago." For full entry and annotation, see item 167.

1867 Brown, Henry Collins, ed. VALENTINE'S MANUAL, 1927. For full entry and annotation, see item 168.

1868 _____. IN THE GOLDEN NINETIES. For full entry and annotation, see item 169.

1869 Brown, John Mason. TWO ON THE AISLE. For full entry and annotation, see item 170.

1870 Brown, T. Allston. HISTORY OF THE NEW YORK STAGE. For full entry and annotation, see item 171.

1871 Churchill, Allen. THE GREAT WHITE WAY. For full entry and annotation, see item 182.

1872 _____. THE THEATRICAL TWENTIES. For full entry and annotation, see item 183.

1873 Clapp, William W., Jr. A RECORD OF THE BOSTON STAGE. For full entry and annotation, see item 184.

1874 Cook, Doris E. SHERLOCK HOLMES AND MUCH MORE; OR SOME OF THE FACTS ABOUT WILLIAM GILLETTE. Hartford: Connecticut Historical Society, 1970. viii, 112 p. Notes. Paper.

> The only full-length, documented study of the actor-playwright (1855-1937) who was such a popular figure on the popular stage.

1875 Crawford, Mary Caroline. THE ROMANCE OF THE AMERICAN THEATRE. New York: Halcyon House, 1940. xiv, 508 p. Illus., index.

> Mose useful on popular theatre of the nineteenth century.

1876 Daly, Joseph Francis. LIFE OF AUGUSTIN DALY. New York:

Macmillan Co., 1917. xi, 672 p. Illus., index.

Life of the author-manager-regisseur by his brother, no doubt responsible, at least in part, for many of Daly's plays.

1877 Dempsey, David, and Baldwin, Raymond P. THE TRIUMPHS AND TRIALS OF LOTTA CRABTREE. New York: William Morrow, 1968. viii, 341 p. Illus., index, bibliog.

Reasonably reliable biography of the popular theatre performer. Includes a chronology of important events in her life and a list of plays in which she appeared.

1878 [Dithmar, Edward A.]. MEMORIES OF DALY'S THEATRE. New York: privately printed, 1897 143 p. Paper.

Romanticized and puffed record of Augustin Daly's management but useful information nonetheless, especially summaries of Daly's seasons (1869-95).

1879 Drew, John. MY YEARS ON THE STAGE. Foreword by Booth Tarkington. New York: E.P. Dutton and Co., 1922. xii, 242 p. Index.

Largely anecdotal autobiography by the great nineteenth-century comic actor who worked largely under Augustin Daly and Charles Frohman.

1880 Durang, John. THE MEMOIR OF JOHN DURANG (AMERICAN ACTOR, 1785-1816). Fur full entry and annotation, see item 189.

1881 Eaton, Walter Prichard. THE AMERICAN STAGE OF TODAY. Boston: Small, Maynard and Co., 1908. x, 338 p.

American theatre at the turn of the century.

1882 Edwards, Samuel. QUEEN OF THE PLAZA. A BIOGRAPHY OF ADAH ISAACS MENKEN. London: Alvin Redman, 1965. New York: Funk and Wagnalls Co., 1964. 307 p. Index, bibliog.

Undistinguished biography; suffers from lack of illustrations of the famous equestrian actress (MAZEPPA). See next entry and Lewis, item 1915.

1883 Falk, Bernard. NAKED LADY; OR STORM OVER ADAH; A BIOGRAPHY OF ADAH ISAACS MENKEN. London: Hutchinson and Co., 1934. 306 p. Illus., index.

Well-illustrated, readable biography; fairly accurate and probably the best of the numerous Menken biographies but still not well documented. See items 1882, 1914, and 1915.

1884 Felheim, Marvin. THEATER OF AUGUSTIN DALY: AN ACCOUNT OF THE LATE NINETEENTH CENTURY AMERICAN STAGE. Cambridge, Mass.: Harvard University Press, 1956. 329 p. Illus., index.

A full account of the career of the manager-playwright (1839-99), a major figure of the popular theatre in New York. See item 1876.

1885 Foley, Doris. THE DIVINE ECCENTRIC: LOLA MONTEZ AND THE NEWSPAPERS. Los Angeles: Westernlore Press, 1969. xii, 228 p. Illus., bibliog.

Good source on her Pacific Coast career; a useful list of sources.

1886 Frohman, Daniel. DANIEL FROHMAN PRESENTS. New York: Claude Kendall and Willoughby Sharp, 1935. xv, 397 p. Illus., index.

Frohman's second volume of reminiscences; this one contains comments on numerous figures of the popular theatre, e.g., William Gillette, Mae West, Billie Burke, Will Rogers, George M. Cohan, Charlie Chaplin, and Cecilia Loftus, among others.

1887 Fyles, Franklin. THE THEATRE AND ITS PEOPLE. New York: Double-day, Page and Co., 1900. viii, 259 p. Illus.

The theatre as a business and as a profession in America at the turn of the century. Very chatty and full of trivia.

1888 Gallagher, Kent G. THE FOREIGNER IN EARLY AMERICAN DRAMA: A STUDY IN ATTITUDES. The Hague: Mouton and Co., 1966. Index, bibliog., appendix (list of plays).

Chapter 4 covers all the "comic foreigners' found in early plays: Irish, English, French, and the like.

1889 _____. ["Nineteenth-Century American Theatre"]. EMERSON SO-CIETY QUARTERLY 20 (3d quarter 1974): 143-47.

Introduction to a special issue devoted to nineteenth-century American theatre.

1890 Gerson, Noel B[ertram]. [Paul Lewis]. LILLIE LANGTRY: A BIOG-RAPHY. London: Hale, 1972; BECAUSE I LOVED HIM. THE LIFE AND LOVES OF LILLIE LANGTRY. New York: William Morrow, 1971. 255 p. Illus., index, bibliog.

Biography of the actress-performer with an emphasis on her personal life.

1891   Gilbert, Mrs. Anne Jane Hartley. STAGE REMINISCENCES OF MRS.
       GILBERT. Edited by C.M. Martin. New York: Charles Scribner's
       Sons, 1901. xii, 248 p. Illus.

       Autobiography of Mrs. Gilbert, who, under Augustin Daly,
       became one of the "Big Four" along with Ada Rehan, John
       Drew, and James Lewis.

1892   Goodwin, Nat C. NAT GOODWIN'S BOOK. For full entry and
       annotation, see item 1112.

1893   Hagler, Nevis Ezelk, Jr. "William A. Brady: Theatre Entrepreneur."
       Ph.D. dissertation, University of Florida, 1975. 179 p.

       Survey of Brady's career and contributions to theatre in New
       York.

1894   Halliday, E.M. "Curses, Foiled Again!" AMERICAN HERITAGE 15
       (December 1963): 12-23. Illus.

       The principle purpose of this piece is to illustrate and anno-
       tate the poster art used to advertise turn of the century popu-
       lar theatre, in particular melodrama. See also items 95 and
       1865.

1895   Harlow, Alvin F. OLD BOWERY DAYS. New York: D. Appleton,
       1931. xi [i], 564 [5] p. Illus., index, bibliog.

       "The chronicles of a Famous Street" including the history of
       the Bowery Theatre (pp. 234-56), the Park, the Chatham
       Garden Theatre, Chanfrau's National, and other places of
       entertainment in the Bowery district up to the early 1900s.

1896   Harrison, Gabriel. A HISTORY OF THE PROGRESS OF THE DRAMA,
       MUSIC AND FINE ARTS IN THE CITY OF BROOKLYN. Brooklyn:
       N.p., 1884. 64 p. Illus.

       Reprinted from THE ILLUSTRATED HISTORY OF KINGS
       COUNTY edited by Dr. H.R. Stetis, published by W.W.
       Munsell and Co. Twenty-one pages are devoted exclusively
       to forms of theatre.

1897   Hart, William S. MY LIFE EAST AND WEST. Boston and New York:
       Houghton Mifflin Co., 1929. viii, 363 p. Illus., index.

       Autobiography of the cowboy-actor, his career as a legitimate
       actor, appearances in popular dramas on the West, and his
       rise to fame in films.

1898   Henderson, Mary C. THE CITY AND THE THEATRE. Clifton, N.J.:

James T. White, 1973. xiv, 323 p. Illus., index, bibliog., notes.

Development of the physical stage in New York, includes eighty-two "biographies" of legitimate houses in the Times Square district from the late nineteenth century, plus a general survey of theatres from 1700. Good background on the city as well. See also item 209.

1899   Holdredge, Helen. THE WOMAN IN BLACK--THE LIFE OF LOLA MONTEZ. New York: G.P. Putnam's Sons, 1955. x, 309 p. Illus., index, bibliog.

The best of the Montez biographies in dealing with her American career.

1900   Hutton, Laurence. CURIOSITIES OF THE AMERICAN STAGE. New York: Harper and Bros., 1891. xv, 347 p. Illus., index.

An entertaining volume that touches on various aspects of popular entertainment and theatre, e.g., native type characters, literary burlesque, and so forth.

1901   Ireland, Joseph N. RECORDS OF THE NEW YORK STAGE FROM 1750 TO 1860. 2 vols. New York: Morrell, 1866.

Survey history largely superseded by Odell (see item 248).

1902   James, Reese D. CRADLE OF CULTURE, 1800-1810: THE PHILADELPHIA STAGE. For full entry and annotation, see item 217.

1903   [Jefferson, Joseph III]. THE AUTOBIOGRAPHY OF JOSEPH JEFFERSON. New York: Century Co., 1890. xv, 309 p. Illus., index.

The autobiography of Jefferson (1829-1905), one of America's most beloved figures on the stage, remains an important source on popular theatre in nineteenth-century America. Excellent portrait of barnstorming and its pitfalls. There have been numerous editions of his autobiography, including contemporary reprints edited by Alan S. Downer (1964) and by Eleanor Farjeon (1949).

1904   [Jeffrey, John B., ed.]. JNO. B. JEFFREY'S GUIDE. For full entry and annotation, see item 219.

1905   Jenkins, Stephen. THE GREATEST STREET IN THE WORLD--BROADWAY. For full entry and annotation, see item 220.

1906   Johnson, Raoul Fenton. "United States and British Patents for Scenic and Lighting Devices for the Theatre from 1861 to 1915." Ph.D. dissertation, University of Illinois, Urbana-Champaign, 1966. 278 p.

Covers the period of popular theatre's heyday, includes patents for lighting devices, illusionistic effects, and scenery-changing apparatus.

1907 JULIUS CAHN'S OFFICIAL THEATRICAL GUIDE. For full entry and annotation, see item 223.

1908 Keese, William L. WILLIAM E. BURTON, ACTOR, AUTHOR, AND MANAGER. New York: G.P. Putnam's Sons, 1885. xi, 230 p. Illus., index.

The first book-length study of the popular comic actor-manager (1804-60).

1909 [Knowlton, Dora]. DIARY OF A DALY DEBUTANTE; BEING PASSAGES FROM THE JOURNAL OF A MEMBER OF AUGUSTIN DALY'S FAMOUS COMPANY OF PLAYERS. New York: Duffield, 1910. [3], 249 p. Illus.

Daly's theatre in the 1880s.

1910 Krows, Arthur E. PLAY PRODUCTION IN AMERICA. New York: Henry Holt and Co., 1919. x, 414 p. Illus., index, bibliog.

Practical aspects of all forms of theatre production during the early twentieth century.

1911 Langtry, Lillie [Lady de Bathe]. THE DAYS I KNEW. Foreword by Richard Le Gallienne. 2d ed. London: Hutchinson and Co., n.d.; New York: George H. Doran Co., 1925. 319 p. Illus.

Very personal memoir of the popular actress-entertainer (1853-1929).

1912 Laufe, Abe. THE WICKED STAGE: A HISTORY OF THEATER CENSOR-SHIP AND HARASSMENT IN THE UNITED STATES. New York: Frederick Ungar Publishing Co., 1978. xvi, 191 p. Illus., index, bibliog.

A cursory history from the beginnings of the American theatre to the 1970s, with brief mentions of burlesque, revue, extravaganzas (THE BLACK CROOK), MAZEPPA and Adah Isaacs Menken, popular theatre fare, and other related topics.

1913 Leman, Walter M. MEMORIES OF AN OLD ACTOR. San Francisco: A. Roman Co., 1886. xv, 406 p.

Memoirs of the mid-nineteenth-century American theatre, including mention of most major performers, as well as theatre

in New York, Philadelphia, St. Louis, Baltimore, Virginia
City (Nevada), Salt Lake City, and California.

1914   Lesser, Allen. ENCHANTING REBEL: THE SECRET OF ADAH ISAACS
MENKEN. New York: Beechhurst Press, 1947. 284 p. Illus., index,
bibliog.

The most sentimental of the Menken studies. See items 1882,
1883, and 1915.

1915   Lewis, Paul [Noel B. Gerson]. QUEEN OF THE PLAZA. New York:
Funk and Wagnalls, 1964. 307 p. Index, bibliog.

Biography of Menken based largely on her diary and autobiographical prose fragments at Harvard. Rather careless and inaccurate study. See items 1882, 1883, and 1914.

1916   Lippincott, Horace Mather. "Amusements in the Nineties." THE
GENERAL MAGAZINE AND HISTORICAL CHRONICLE 52 (Summer
1950): 239-51.

Survey of entertainment in Pahiladelphia, 1893-97.

1917   Logan, Olive. BEFORE THE FOOTLIGHTS AND BEHIND THE SCENES;
also, THE MIMIC WORLD, AND PUBLIC EXHIBITIONS. For full entry
and annotation, see items 1965 and 1966.

1918   Loring, Janet. "Belasco: Preface to a Re-Evaluation." WESTERN
SPEECH JOURNAL 23 (Fall 1959): 207-11.

Belasco's comments on realism should be clarified by a detailed
reexamination, according to this author.

1919   Ludlow, Noah M. DRAMATIC LIFE AS I FOUND IT. St. Louis: G.I.
Jones, 1880. Reissue. New York: Benjamin Blom, 1966. xlvii,
779 p. Index.

Blom edition contains a good introduction by Francis Hodge.
This is an important source on early barnstorming along the
Ohio and Mississippi. Ludlow, like his partner Solomon
Smith, is often misleading and thus his facts should be veri-
fied. Ludlow's book is generally more valuable than Smith's
works, excluded in this guide.

1920   McCullough, Jack W. "Edward Kilanyi and American Tableaux Vivants."
THEATRE SURVEY 16 (May 1975): 25-41.

An area of popular theatre rarely discussed, "living pictures"
or "living statues" on the late nineteenth-century American
stage. The same could be said for this phenomenon on the
English stage.

1921   McGee, Thomas R., Jr.   "Belasco's Realism." WESTERN SPEECH
       JOURNAL 21 (Fall 1957): 218-21.

       Belasco's realism reflected in settings, lighting, and costuming.

1922   McGlinchee, Claire. THE FIRST DECADE OF THE BOSTON MUSEUM.
       Boston: Bruce Humphries, 1940. 370 p. Illus., index, bibliog.

       History of one of America's most popular stock companies
       (1841-51). All entertainments for the decade under examina-
       tion are listed in an appendix. See next entry.

1923   Mammen, Edward W. THE OLD STOCK COMPANY SCHOOL OF
       ACTING. Boston: Trustees of the Public Library, 1945. 89 p. Illus.
       Paper.

       Standard work on the stock companies of the nineteenth cen-
       tury, using the Boston Museum as the prototype. See previous
       entry.

1924   Marks, Edward Bennett. THEY ALL HAD GLAMOUR: FROM THE
       SWEDISH NIGHTINGALE TO THE NAKED LADY. For full entry and
       annotation, see item 234.

1925   Moody, Richard. AMERICA TAKES THE STAGE. Bloomington: Indiana
       University Press, 1955. viii, 322 p. Illus., index, bibliog.

       "Romanticism in American drama and theatre, 1750-1900."
       Deals prominently with the Yankee, Negro minstrelsy, and
       romanticism in scene design. A selected play list for the
       period is included.

1926   _____, ed. DRAMAS FROM THE AMERICAN THEATRE, 1762-1909.
       With introductory essays. Cleveland and New York: World Publishing
       Co., 1966. xiii, 873 p. Illus., bibliog.

       In addition to a fine bibliography and excellent introductions
       to representative American plays, many of the popular variety,
       Moody includes minstrel show routines and the first printing of
       Harrigan's THE MULLIGAN GUARD BALL (1879).

1927   Morehouse, Ward. MATINEE TOMORROW. For full entry and annota-
       tion, see item 240.

1928   Morsberger, Robert E., and Mossberger, Katherine M.   "'Christ and a
       Horse-Race': BEN-HUR on Stage." JOURNAL OF POPULAR CULTURE
       8 (Winter 1974): 489-502.

       The transference of Lew Wallace's novel to the stage and its
       stage history, 1899-1920.

1929   Moses, Montrose J.   "David Belasco: The Astonishing Versatility of a
        Veteran Producer."   THEATRE GUILD MAGAZINE 7 (November 1929):
        27-30, 51.   Illus.

>   Good summary of Belasco's accomplishments and personal in-
        sights into the man.

1930   _____.   "William Gillette Says Farewell."   THEATRE GUILD MAGA-
        ZINE 7 (January 1930):   30-35, 56.   Illus.

>   Estimate of Gillette's talent as actor, director, and play-
        wright over a fifty-year period.

1931   Nathan, George Jean.   THE POPULAR THEATRE.   For full entry and
        annotation, see item 242.

1932   _____.   THE THEATRE, THE DRAMA, THE GIRLS.   For full entry and
        annotation, see item 243.

1933   _____.   THE WORLD IN FALSEFACE.   For full entry and annotation,
        see item 244.

1934   _____.   ENCYCLOPAEDIA OF THE THEATRE.   For full entry and
        annotation, see item 245.

1935   _____.   THE WORLD OF GEORGE JEAN NATHAN.   Edited by
        Charles Angoff.   For full entry and annotation, see item 246.

1936   Northall, William Knight.   BEFORE AND BEHIND THE CURTAIN.   For
        full entry and annotation, see item 247.

1937   Odell, George C.D.   ANNALS OF THE NEW YORK STAGE.   For full
        entry and annotation, see item 248.

1938   _____.   "Some Theatrical Stock Companies of New York."   THEATRE
        ANNUAL 9 (1951):   7-26.

>   Coverage includes companies of William Mitchell, William E.
        Burton, James and Lester Wallack, Augustin Daly, and
        Albert M. Palmer.

1939   Owens, Mrs. John E.   MEMORIES OF THE PROFESSIONAL AND
        SOCIAL LIFE OF JOHN E. OWENS, BY HIS WIFE.   Baltimore: John
        Murphy and Co., 1892.   vii, 292 p.   Illus.

>   Owens (1823-86) was known principally for his Yankee charac-
        ters and eccentric comic roles.

1940   Parrott, Frederick J. "The Mid-Nineteenth Century American Theatre 1840-1860. A Survey of Theatre Production, Comment, and Opinion." Ph.D. dissertation, Cornell University, 1948.

1941   Parsons, Bill. "The Debut of Adah Isaacs Menken." QUARTERLY JOURNAL OF SPEECH 46 (February 1960): 8-13.

      Debut at the James S. Charles Theatre in Shreveport, Louisiana, in March 1857.

1942   Pitou, Augustus. MASTERS OF THE SHOW. New York: Neale Publishing Co., 1914. 186 p. Illus.

      Memoirs of actor-manager for over fifty years; good on transition from stock to the combination company. Mentions most major figures at the turn of the century.

1943   Poggi, Jack. THEATER IN AMERICA: THE IMPACT OF ECONOMIC FORCES, 1870-1967. Ithaca, N.Y.: Cornell University Press, 1968. xx, 328 p. Illus., index, bibliog.

      Theatre economics and their impact; stock system to combination system, the decline of the road, and some mention of vaudeville.

1944   Powers, James T. TWINKLE LITTLE STAR: SPARKLING MEMORIES OF SEVENTY YEARS. New York: G.P. Putnam's Sons, 1939. xiv [17], 379 p. Illus., index.

      Informative autobiography of the American comedian; good firsthand account of all aspects of popular theatre during the latter part of the nineteenth century. More than one hundred illustrations. A recommended primary source.

1945   Quinn, Arthur Hobson. A HISTORY OF THE AMERICAN DRAMA FROM THE BEGINNING TO THE CIVIL WAR. 2d ed. New York: Appleton-Century-Crofts, 1943. xvi, 530 p. Index, bibliog.

      See below.

1946   _____. A HISTORY OF THE AMERICAN DRAMA FROM THE CIVIL WAR TO THE PRESENT DAY [1936]. Rev. ed. New York: Appleton-Century-Crofts, 1936. xxv, 432 p. Illus., index, bibliog.

      Standard works (see above) on American drama, including native types and popular theatre. Extensive bibliographies and lists of plays. A series of volumes by Walter J. Meserve on American drama to be published by Indiana University Press should, in time, supersede Quinn's studies. The first volume (1978) of this series, up to 1828, contains little, however, relevant to this guide.

1947   Reardon, William R.   "The American Drama and Theatre in the Nine-
        teenth Century: A Retreat from Meaning."   EMERSON SOCIETY
        QUARTERLY 20 (3d quarter 1974): 170–86.

>   An attempt to account for the "comparative lack of achieve-
        ment" in American nineteenth-century theatre and drama.

1948   Reardon, William R., and Bristow, Eugene K.   "The American Theatre,
        1864–1870: An Economic Portrait."   SPEECH MONOGRAPHS 33
        (August 1966): 438–43.

>   Excellent analysis of a decade of change from stock company
        operation to traveling theatre. Eight tables illustrate the
        economic profile.

1949   Reed, Ronald Michael.   "The Nature of the Scenic Practices in
        Augustin Daly's New York Production, 1869–1899."   Ph.D. dissertation,
        University of Oregon, 1968. 360 p.

1950   Rinear, David L.   "Burlesque Comes to New York: William Mitchell's
        First Season at the Olympic."   NINETEENTH CENTURY THEATRE
        RESEARCH 2 (Spring 1974): 23–34.

>   An account of Mitchell's maiden season as manager of the
        Olympic, 1839–40.

1951   Ruggles, Eleanor. PRINCE OF PLAYERS: EDWIN BOOTH.   New York:
        W.W. Norton and Co., 1953. xii, 491 p. Illus., index, note on
        sources.

>   Although dated and a popularized biography, this remains the
        most readable of the biographies of the actor. In terms of
        popular theatre, useful for Booth's early performances in Cali-
        fornia and various tours on the road.

1952   Ryan, Kate. OLD BOSTON MUSEUM DAYS.   Boston: Little, Brown
        and Co., 1915. xii, 264 p. Illus.

>   Reminiscences of the Boston Museum from 1841 through 1893
        by a member of the company.

1953   Schaal, David.   "The Rehearsal Situation at Daly's Theatre."   EDUCA-
        TIONAL THEATRE JOURNAL 14 (March 1962): 1–14.

>   An examination of Augustin Daly's directorial practices between
        1869 and 1899.

1954   Schmidt, Emile.   "The Bowery! The Bowery!"   PLAYERS, MAGAZINE
        OF AMERICAN THEATRE 45 (June–July 1970): 223–27. Illus.

Nineteenth-century theatres in the Bowery district of New York and a survey history of the Bowery Theatre, home of melodrama, from 1826 until its sixth and final fire in 1929.

1955 Scrimgeour, Gary. "Drama and Theatre in the Early Nineteenth Century. " Ph.D. dissertation, Princeton University, 1968. 555 p.

Good survey of popular theatre during the great period of change, 1790-1830.

1956 Shafer, Yvonne. "A Sherlock Holmes of the Past: William Gillette's Later Years." PLAYERS, MAGAZINE OF AMERICAN THEATRE 46 (June-July 1971): 229-34. Illus.

Survey of the actor's later career to 1937 with a summary of his early years.

1957 Shank, Theodore J. "Theatre for the Majority: Its Influence on a Nineteenth-Century American Theatre." EDUCATIONAL THEATRE JOURNAL 11 (October 1959): 188-99.

Taken in part from his 1956 Stanford dissertation ("The Bowery Theatre, 1826-1836"). Investigates how and why, under Thomas S. Hamblin (from 1830), the Bowery Theatre ceased to cater to aristocracy and became the home for melodrama, in turn, shaping some of the production methods of melodrama which have continued to the present. Essay concludes with the burning of the second Bowery in 1836.

1958 Shaw, Mary. "The Boston Museum and Daly's Theatre." SATURDAY EVENING POST 182 (20 May 1911): 14, 15, 34.

Comparison of the two nineteenth-century stock companies and theatres.

1959 Sheaffer, Louis. O'NEILL, SON AND PLAYWRIGHT. Boston: Little, Brown and Co., 1968. xx, 543 p. Illus., index, bibliog.

Volume 1 of a two-volume biography of Eugene O'Neill; useful information on James O'Neill and his association with the melodrama, COUNT OF MONTE CRISTO.

1960 Sichel, Pierre. THE JERSEY LILY: THE STORY OF THE FABULOUS MRS. LANGTRY. Englewood Cliffs, N.J.: Prentice-Hall, 1958. 456 p. Illus., index.

Poorly documented biography of the actress (1853-1929) and her American tours.

1961 Stagg, Jerry. THE BROTHERS SHUBERT. For full entry and annotation, see item 1647.

1962   Timberlake, Craig. THE BISHOP OF BROADWAY: DAVID BELASCO, HIS LIFE AND WORK. New York: Library Publishers, 1954. 491 p. Illus., index, bibliog.

> Useful biography of Belasco, especially in terms of staging and effects. Includes a chronological list of his New York productions (1880-1930). William Winter also wrote a biography of Belasco (see item 1968), which is extremely biased. See also item 1859.

1963   Tompkins, Eugene, and Kilby, Quincy. THE HISTORY OF THE BOSTON THEATRE, 1854-1901. Boston: Houghton Mifflin Co., 1908. xvi, 551 p. Illus., index.

> Personalized history of the Boston Theatre by its manager and treasurer.

1964   Turner, Darwin T. "Jazz-Vaudeville Drama in the Twenties." EDUCATIONAL THEATRE JOURNAL 11 (May 1959): 110-16.

> Attempt by left-wing dramatists to use the vigor and originality of jazz and vaudeville to provide a rhythm and tempo for their criticisms of American society.

1965   Wills, J. Robert. "The Riddle of Olive Logan: A Biographical Profile." Ph.D. dissertation, Case Western Reserve, 1971. 349 p. See items 1244-45, and 1966.

1966   _____. "Olive Logan Vs. the Nude Woman." PLAYERS, MAGAZINE OF AMERICAN THEATRE 47 (October-November 1971): 37-43.

> Logan's campaign against "naked drama" in 1869.

1967   Winter, William. ADA REHAN. New York: Privately printed for Augustin Daly, 1898. 211 p. Illus.

> Sketchy biography of Augustin Daly's leading lady (1860-1916). Includes a useful chronology of her life.

1968   _____. THE LIFE OF DAVID BELASCO. 2 vols. New York: Moffat, Yard and Co., 1919. Illus., index.

> Detailed but imperfect biography of the director-playwright published after the author's death. Sixty-six page chronology at the conclusion of volume 2.

Chapter 11

POPULAR THEATRE:

GENERAL SELECT SOURCES, GREAT BRITAIN

This chapter contains a highly selective group of sources. A more extensive list of sources on nineteenth-century English theatre can be found in item 18. Like the preceding chapter, most major sources on English theatre and drama could be included in this section. Since the focus here is on balance rather than completeness, most of these have been excluded. Additional sources relating to popular theatre can be found in chapter 3, section B.

1969 Appleton, William W. MADAME VESTRIS AND THE LONDON STAGE. New York and London: Columbia University Press, 1974. 231 p. Illus., index, notes.

> The most complete and best-documented study of the stage career of Madame Vestris (1797-1856); deals well with the popular forms associate with her, in particular extravaganza. Extensive coverage of James Robinson Planche's contributions.

1970 Archer, William. THE OLD DRAMA AND THE NEW. London: Heinemann; Boston: Small, Maynard and Co., 1923. viii, 396 p. Index.

> The influential "modern" critic presents his biased opinions on popular drama in England during the eighteenth and nineteenth centuries.

1971 Armstrong, William A. "The Art of the Minor Theatres in 1860." THEATRE NOTEBOOK 10 (April-June 1956): 89-94.

> On minor theatres and scene painting; based on T.W. Erle's LETTERS FROM A THEATRICAL SCENE-PAINTER (London, 1880).

1972 _____. "Madame Vestris: A Centenary Appreciation." THEATRE NOTEBOOK 11 (October-December 1957): 11-18. Illus.

> Succinct assessment of her contributions.

1973 Arundell, Dennis. THE STORY OF SADLER'S WELLS, 1683-1977. For full entry and annotation, see item 280.

1974 Baker, H. Barton. HISTORY OF THE LONDON STAGE AND ITS FAMOUS PLAYERS (1576-1903). For full entry and annotation, see item 281.

1975 Baker, Michael. THE RISE OF THE VICTORIAN ACTOR. London: Croom Helm; Totowa, N.J.: Rowman and Littlefield, 1978. 249 p. Index, bibliog., notes, appendixes.

Useful social history of Victorian actors which seeks to show how wider social attitudes and developments affected the changing status of acting as a profession. In addition to popular theatre of the period 1830-80, there are numerous references to pantomime and music hall. Very useful bibliography for the Victorian period.

1976 Barker, Clive. "The Chartists, Theatre, Reform and Research." THEATRE QUARTERLY 1 (October-December 1971): 3-10.

Study of a working-class theatre in London and the rise of the minor theatres. Focus in on the Britannia Theatre, Hoxton, and how the theatre got caught up in the general agitation for reform in the 1830s.

1977 Bishop, Conrad Joy. "Melodramatic Acting: Concept and Technique in the Performance of Early Nineteenth Century English Melodrama." Ph.D. dissertation, Stanford University, 1967. 269 p.

1978 Booth, Michael R. "The Acting of Melodrama." UNIVERSITY OF TORONTO QUARTERLY 34 (1964): 31-48.

Persuasive defense of melodramatic acting by the notable English authority of melodrama.

1979 _____. "Going on Stage." In THE MIND AND ART OF VICTORIAN ENGLAND, edited by Josef L. Altholz, pp. 107-123. Minneapolis: University of Minnesota Press, 1976. Illus., bibliog., notes, index.

The life and problems of struggling Victorian actors and methods employed in entering the acting profession.

1980 _____. "East End and West End: Class and Audience in Victorian London." THEATRE RESEARCH INTERNATIONAL 2 (February 1977): 98-103.

". . . the middle-class West End playgoer was part of a numerical minority, the vast sub-stratum of working-class theatre. . . dominated it by sheer bulk and represented a mass popular entertainment market of considerable proportions." A survey and a challenge for more research.

1981   Chancellor, Edwin Beresford.   THE PLEASURE HAUNTS OF LONDON DURING FOUR CENTURIES.   For full entry and annotation, see item 299.

1982   Clinton-Baddeley, V.C.   ALL RIGHT ON THE NIGHT.   For full entry and annotation, see item 303.

1983   Colby, Elbridge.   "A Supplement on Strollers."   PUBLICATION OF THE MODERN LANGUAGE ASSOCIATION 39 (September 1924): 642-54.

    Provincial strolling players in England during the eighteenth century.   See item 2049.

1984   Conolly, L.W.   THE CENSORSHIP OF ENGLISH DRAMA 1737-1824.   San Marino, Calif.: Huntington Library, 1976.   x, 233 p.   Illus.

    Excellent study of the Stage Licensing Act of 1737 and its various implications, including those on popular forms (although not stressed in this study).

1985   Cook, Dutton.   A BOOK OF THE PLAY.   For full entry and annotation, see item 304.

1986   Daam, Paul Alexander.   "The Royal Circus 1782-1809: An Analysis of Equestrian Entertainments."   For full entry and annotation, see item 404.

1987   Davies, Thomas.   MEMOIRS OF THE LIFE OF DAVID GARRICK.   2 vols.   London: Longman, Hurst, Rees, and Orms, 1808.

    Although one of the early lives of Garrick, these volumes nonetheless contain good accounts of Garrick's participation in pantomime, farce, and other related forms.

1988   Dent, Edward J.   A THEATRE FOR EVERYBODY: THE STORY OF THE OLD VIC AND SADLER'S WELLS.   London and New York: T.V. Boardman, 1946.   167 p.   Illus.

    History of the Old Vic, formerly the Royal Coburg, with an emphasis on the period under Emma Cons from 1880 and Lilian Baylis from 1912.   Under Cons, the "Royal Victoria Hall and Coffee Tavern" was intended to be an inexpensive and decent place for family entertainment.

1989   Dibdin, Charles.   THE PROFESSIONAL LIFE OF MR. DIBDIN.   2 vols.   London: By the author, 1809.

    Autobiography of the writer of pantomimes and ballad operas

who was also a performer, known for his one-man entertainments. Text includes some of the songs from his scripts.

1990   Dickens, Charles. THE DICKENS THEATRICAL READER. For full entry
and annotation, see item 307.

1991   Disher, M. Willson. GREATEST SHOW ON EARTH. For full entry
and annotation, see item 410.

1992   East, John M. 'NEATH THE MASK. THE STORY OF THE EAST
FAMILY. London: George Allen and Unwin, 1967. 356 p. Illus.,
indexes.

Careers of John and Charles East as illustrative of life in the
melodramatic theatre of the 1880s. Good portrait of the
blood and thunder drama preferred by London suburban and
provincial playgoers. Also useful on early films in England.

1993   _____. "Karno's Folly, or How to Lose a Show-Business Fortune."
THEATRE QUARTERLY 1 (July–September 1971): 60–62.

Brief biographical sketch of Fred Karno (d. 1941), an English
performer-impresario of comedy companies, and discoverer of
Stan Laurel, Charlie Chaplin, and others.

1994   _____. "Andrew Ducrow: The World's Greatest Equestrian Performer."
THEATRE QUARTERLY 1 (October–December 1971): 37–39.

Brief life and career of th equestrian performer, including a
good deal of information on his performances at Astley's Amphitheatre. For the most complete sources on Ducrow, see listings for Saxon in the index.

1995   Fagg, Edwin. THE OLD "OLD VIC": A GLIMPSE OF THE OLD
THEATRE, FROM ITS ORIGIN AS "THE ROYAL COBURG," FIRST MAN-
AGED BY WILLIAM BARRYMORE, TO ITS REVIVAL UNDER LILIAN
BAYLIS. [London]: Vic Well's Association, 1936. 124 p.

Sketchy account of its various periods, including its time as a
popular theatre house.

1996   Favorini, Attilio. "The Old School of Acting and the English Provinces."
QUARTERLY JOURNAL OF SPEECH 58 (April 1972): 199–208.

Impact of provincial theatre and the profession of the strolling
player as a "dramatic school" for training actors during the
seventeenth and eighteenth centuries and the break in this
tradition in the nineteenth century.

1997   Findlater, Richard. BANNED! A REVIEW OF THEATRICAL CENSOR-
SHIP IN BRITAIN. London: MacGibbon and Kee, 1967; London:
Panther Books, 1968. 284 p. Index, bibliog. Paper.

General history of the subject with little specifically on
popular entertainment forms or the implications of censorship
and legal restrictions on these forms. Still provides basic
background of the struggle between the minor theatres and
the patent houses.

1998   Fitzgerald, Percy. THE WORLD BEHIND THE SCENES. London: Chatto
and Windus, 1881. 320 p.

Useful section concerned with theatrical machinery, effects,
and the like; not limited to minor forms but much that is applicable.

1999   Forbes-Winslow, D. DALY'S, THE BIOGRAPHY OF A THEATRE. London: W.A. Allen and Co., 1944. 220 p. Illus., index.

History of the London theatre named after Augustin Daly, with
two chapters devoted to coverage of Daly's actual brief connection with the theatre and fuller coverage of subsequent
popular fare, especially musical offerings, at Daly's.

2000   Glasstone, Victor. VICTORIAN & EDWARDIAN THEATRES. For
full entry and annotation, see item 316.

2001   Grant, James. "Eye-Witness at the Penny Gaffs." THEATRE QUAR-
TERLY 4 (October-December 1971): 15-18.

Penny "gaffs" were the theatres of the young lower working
class in nineteenth-century England. Strictly seen as a source
of entertainment. Written to suppress their activity, Grant's
1838 work, SKETCHES IN LONDON, gives considerable detail of the organization and finance of these theatres. The
complete essay, PENNY THEATRES, was published as a pamphlet by the Society for Theatre Research (London) in 1952
(35 p.).

2002   Hamilton, Cicely, and Baylis, Lilian. THE OLD VIC. London: Cape,
1926. 285 p. Illus.

An informal account of the theatre, originally the Royal
Coburg (beginning in 1816), which became a local theatre
and home of melodrama and later a house known for its tough
audience and rough shows until Emma Cons and later her
niece Lilian Baylis brought it respectability. It also served
as a music hall.

2003   Hanson, Frank Burton. "London Theatre Audiences of the Nineteenth Century." Ph.D. dissertation, Yale University, 1953. 464 p.

2004   Hatton, Joseph. REMINISCENCES OF J.L. TOOLE. 2 vols. London: Hurst and Blackett, 1889. Illus., index.

     Life of the English actor and theatre manager (1830-1906) who appeared in burlesques under Hollingshead at the Gaiety and after 1879 at his own theatre in plays by H.J. Byron.

2005   Hicks, Seymour. BETWEEN OURSELVES. London: Cassell and Co., 1930. 252 p. Illus., index.

     The actor-singer's memories of actors, playwrights, and other celebrities and institutions from the Edwardian period (e.g., J.L. Toole, Gabys Deslys, George Edwardes, W.S. Gilbert, Lily Langtry, Dan Leno, the music hall, William Terriss, and so forth).

2006   Hughes, Leo. THE DRAMA'S PATRONS: A STUDY OF THE EIGH-TEENTH CENTURY LONDON AUDIENCE. Austin: University of Texas Press, 1971. viii, 209 p. Index, bibliog.

     Changes in the audience's taste from Dryden's day to Sheridan's, including a fairly complete section on pantomime.

2007   Jackson, Allan S[tuart]., and Morrow, John C[harles]. "Aqua Scenes at Sadler's Wells Theatre, 1804-1824." OHIO STATE UNIVERSITY COLLECTION BULLETIN 9 (1962): 22-47. Illus.

     The water tank built below the Wells stage and the scenery and special effects for "Aquadramas" are discussed and de-scribed. Includes a list of aquadrama producers, 1804-24.

2008   Kernodle, George R. "Stage Spectacle and Victorian Society." QUAR-TERLY JOURNAL OF SPEECH 40 (February 1954): 31-36.

     Stage effects as "well devised expressions of certain recurrent themes of the isolated individual and his conflict with the social sanctions of the time."

2009   MacQueen-Pope, W. CARRIAGES AT ELEVEN: THE STORY OF THE EDWARDIAN THEATRE. For full entry and annotation, see item 327.

2010   _____. GHOSTS AND GREASEPAINT. For full entry and annotation, see item 328.

2011   _____. PILLARS OF DRURY LANE. London: Hutchinson and Co., 1955. 256 p. Illus.

Like all of his books, this one, too, is frequently unreliable but nonetheless a useful summary of late nineteenth- and twentieth-century theatre and pantomime at Drury Lane. More useful than his earlier book, THEATRE ROYAL DRURY LANE: THE BIOGRAPHY OF THE GREATEST THEATRE IN THE WORLD (London: W.H. Allen, 1945).

2012 Mander, Raymond, and Mitchenson, Joe. THE LOST THEATRES OF LONDON. For full entry and annotation, see item 330.

2013 Mayer, David. "Nineteenth Century Theatre Music." THEATRE NOTE-BOOK 3, no. 3 (1976): 115-22. Illus.

Survey of the range of material available on the subject of nineteenth-century theatre music, in particular the English melodrama. Illustrated with the musical score for the final moments of THE MILLER AND HIS MEN (II,v).

2014 Morley, Henry. JOURNAL OF A LONDON PLAYGOER, FROM 1851 TO 1866. For full entry and annotation, see item 335.

2015 Morley, Malcolm. "More on the Minor Theatre." THEATRE NOTE-BOOK 19 (Autumn 1964): 29.

Discovery of a nineteenth-century minor theatre in Catherine Street (Theatre of Astronomy). Contains map.

2017 Nicholson, Watson. THE STRUGGLE FOR THE FREE STAGE IN LON-DON. Boston and New York: Houghton Mifflin and Co., 1906. xii, 475 p. Index, bibliog.

Good account of the breaking of the patent monopoly held by Drury Lane and Covent Garden and the introduction of the 1843 Theatres Regulation Act, which in turn led to the licensing of other theatres. Excellent on minor theatres.

2018 Nicoll, Allardyce. A HISTORY OF ENGLISH DRAMA, 1660-1900. 6 vols. Cambridge: Cambridge University Press, 1952-60.

The most useful volume for popular theatre is volume five (1850-1900), LATE NINETEENTH CENTURY DRAMA, 1959. vi, 901 p. This includes a two-hundred page history followed by seven hundred pages of lists of theatres and plays, the most useful part of the volume. In 1973 a seventh volume (1900-1930) was published.

2019 Palmer, John. THE CENSOR AND THE THEATRES. London: T. Fisher Unwin, 1912. 307 p.

Account of the 1909 Joint Select Committee of the House of

Lords and the House of Commons on Stage Plays (censorship) by a staunch opponent of censorship.

2020 Paterson, Peter [James Glass Bertram]. GLIMPSES OF REAL LIFE AS SEEN IN THE THEATRICAL WORLD AND IN BOHEMIA: BEING THE CONFESSIONS OF PETER PATERSON, A STROLLING COMEDIAN. Edinburgh: William P. Nimmo, 1864. xii, 352 p.

Useful as a firsthand account of a strolling player and for information on English nineteenth-century booth theatricals.

2021 Pearce, Charles E. MADAME VESTRIS AND HER TIMES. London: Stanley Paul, 1923. Reprint. New York and London: Benjamin Blom, 1969. 314 p. Illus.

Life of the actress-manager (1797-1856), includes a list of Vestris's appearances at the Olympic, 1831-39. Less useful and reliable than items 1969 and 2055.

2022 Price, Cecil. THEATRE IN THE AGE OF GARRICK. Totowa, N.J.: Rowman and Littlefield, 1973. 212 p. Illus., index, bibliog.

Probably more useful than most of the biographies of Garrick in dealing succinctly and cogently with the spectacle presented under Garrick's management. See especially pages 61-83.

2023 Reynolds, Ernest. EARLY VICTORIAN DRAMA (1830-1870). Cambridge, New York: Benjamin Blom, 1956. vii, 163 p. Index, bibliog.

Brief but serious study of both drama and theatre for this period.

2024 Richards, Kenneth, and Thomson, Peter, eds. NINETEENTH CENTURY BRITISH THEATRE. London: Methuen and Co., 1971. ix, 195 p. Illus., notes.

The proceedings of a symposium sponsored by the Manchester, England, Department of Drama in 1970. Essays on the theatre, drama, and Shakespearean production in the nineteenth century. Essays by Clive Barker, Donald Roy, M. Glen Wilson, Paul Wadleigh, Thomson, William Ruddick, Michael R. Booth, John Hopkin, Joseph W. Donohue, Arthur Colby Sprague, Jan McDonald, W. Moelwyn Merchant, and Kenneth Richards.

2025 Rohrig, Gladys M. "An Analysis of Certain Acting Editions and Prompt-books of Plays by Dion Boucicault." Ph.D. dissertation, Ohio State University, 1956. 208 p.

Applicable to both the English and American stages (1841-74).

2026 Rosenfeld, Sybil. STROLLING PLAYERS & DRAMA IN THE PROVINCES 1660-1765. Cambridge: Cambridge University Press, 1939. viii, 333 p. Illus., indexes (plays, persons, places, subjects).

The definitive study on the subject.

2027 _____ . THE THEATRE OF THE LONDON FAIRS IN THE EIGHTEENTH CENTURY. Cambridge: Cambridge University Press, 1960. xii, 194 p. Illus., indexes (persons and subjects, entertainments).

The most complete study of the performances at Bartholomew Fair, Southwark Fair, May Fair, and several lesser fairs.

2028 _____ . "A Sadler's Wells Scene Book." THEATRE NOTEBOOK 15 (Winter 1960-61): 57-62. Illus.

Designers under Charles Dibdin (Robert C. Andrews, Luke Clint, and John Henderson Grieve).

2029 _____ . "Early Lyceum Theatres." THEATRE NOTEBOOK 18 (Summer 1964): 129-34. Illus.

Brief notes on theatres bearing the lyceum name during the period 1765-1816.

2030 _____ . "Muster Richardson--'The Great Showman.'" In WESTERN POPULAR THEATRE, edited by David Mayer and Kenneth Richards, pp. 105-22. London: Methuen and Co., 1977. Illus.

Study of John Richardson and his famous booth theatre during the eighteenth and early nineteenth centuries. Useful notes.

2031 Rowell, George. THE VICTORIAN THEATRE. London: Oxford University Press, 1956. xiii, 209 p. Illus., index, bibliog. 2d ed. London and New York: Cambridge University Press, 1979. xiii, 239 p. Illus., index, bibliog.

Outstanding survey up to 1914 in which the author stresses the inseparability of the Victorian theatre and Victorian drama. Although music hall and pantomime receive only passing mention, Rowell is good on melodrama and musical comedy. Comprehensive bibliography; playlist, 1792-1914.

2032 _____ . VICTORIAN DRAMATIC CRITICISM. For full entry and annotation, see item 341.

2033 Ryan, Thomas Richard, Jr. "The Surrey Theatre Under the Management of Thomas Dibdin: 1816-1822." Ph.D. dissertation, University of Wisconsin, 1974. 228 p.

2034   Saxon, A.H. "Shakespeare and Circuses." THEATRE SURVEY 7 (November 1966): 59-79. Illus.

      Heavily documented account of eighteenth- and nineteenth-century equestrian productions of Shakespeare. See also items 499, 2035-37, and 2127.

2035   _____. "The Tyranny of Charity: Andrew Ducrow in the Provinces." NINETEENTH CENTURY THEATRE RESEARCH 1 (Autumn 1973): 95-105.

      Ducrow (1793-1842), the English equestrian, rope-dancer, mime, and manager of Astley's Amphitheatre in London, and his provincial tours in the second quarter of the nineteenth century. Focus is on his charitable endeavors. See items 2034, 3036, and 2037. For Saxon's definitive works on Astley's and Ducrow, see items 499 and 2127.

2036   _____. "Andrew Ducrow, England's Mime on a Moving Stage. The Years in France." THEATRE RESEARCH 13 (1973): 15-21.

      Ducrow's career prior to his management of Astley's. See Saxon sources above (items 2034-36) and items 499 and 2127.

2037   _____. "Capon, The Royal Circus and The Destruction of the Bastille." THEATRE NOTEBOOK 28, no. 3 (1974): 133-35. Illus.

      Identification of an engraving as that of a production at the Royal Circus in the summer of 1789 designed by William Capon.

2038   Scott, Clement. THE DRAMA OF YESTERDAY AND TODAY. For full entry and annotation, see item 342.

2039   Sharp, R. Farquharson. "Travesties of Shakespeare's Plays." THE LIBRARY, 4th Series, 1 (1920): 1-20.

      Discussion of nineteenth-century parodies of Shakespeare.

2040   Sherson, Erroll. LONDON'S LOST THEATRES OF THE NINETEENTH CENTURY. For full entry and annotation, see item 343.

2041   Southern, Richard. "Trick-Work in the English Nineteenth Century Theatre." LIFE AND LETTERS TO-DAY 21 (1939): 94-101.

      Stage traps and other stage tricks used in popular forms.

2042   _____. "Visions of Leaps." LIFE AND LETTERS TO-DAY 30 (September 1941): 219-27.

      An account of a Hanlon-Lees acrobatic act and description of the intricate system of traps they used. See item 347.

2043 _____. CHANGEABLE SCENERY, ITS ORIGIN AND DEVELOPMENT IN THE BRITISH THEATRE. For full entry and annotation, see item 346.

2044 _____. THE VICTORIAN THEATRE. For full entry and annotation, see item 347.

2045 Speaight, George, ed. PROFESSIONAL & LITERARY MEMOIRS OF CHARLES DIBDIN THE YOUNGER. DRAMATIST AND UPWARD OF THIRTY YEARS MANAGER OF MINOR THEATRES. London: Society for Theatre Research, 1956. x, 175 p. Illus., indexes, appendixes.

> Well-edited, previously unpublished memoirs, completed in 1830. Speaight provides in his introduction a brief history of Sadler's Wells, Astley's the Royal Circus, and the Royalty, the minor theatres with which Dibdin was associated.

2046 _____. "Ilustration of Minor Theatres." THEATRE NOTEBOOK 12 (Spring 1958): 94-96.

> Drawings by an unknown artist of minor theatre in the early 1830s are listed and discussed.

2047 Sprague, Rosemary. "The Victorian Scene on the London Stage 1843-1883." Ph.D. dissertation, Western Reserve University, 1950.

2048 Stephens, John Russell. "Dramatic Censorship During the Reign of Victoria." Ph.D. dissertation, University of Wales, 1972.

2049 Thaler, Alwin. "Strolling Players and Provincial Drama After Shakespeare." PUBLICATION OF THE MODERN LANGUAGE ASSOCIATION 37 (March 1922): 243-80.

> Seventeenth- and eighteenth-century strolling players in England. See item 1983.

2050 Thomas, Russell B. "Spectacle in the Theatres of London from 1767 to 1802." Ph.D. dissertation, University of Chicago, 1942. 255 p.

2051 Troubridge, St. Vincent. "Minor Victorian Playhouses." NOTES & QUERIES 179 (14 September 1940): 195.

> Note on the Garrick, Leman Street, and Whitechapel theatres in 1873.

2052 Tuttle, George Palliser. "The History of the Royal Circus . . . . " For full entry and annotation, see item 526.

2053 Waitzkin, Leo. THE WITCH OF WYCH STREET. A STUDY OF THE
      THEATRICAL REFORMS OF MADAME VESTRIS. Cambridge, Mass.:
      Harvard University Press, 1933. 67 p.

> Early and inadequate appraisal of her contributions to the Eng-
> lish theatre.

2054 Walsh, Townsend. THE CAREER OF DION BOUCICAULT. New York:
      Dunlap Society Publications, 1915. xviii, 225 p. Illus.

> The life and career of the actor-author who died in 1890.
> Bibliography of his works (pp. 220-24) in chronological order.
> Useful for the American theatre as well.

2055 Williams, Clifford John. MADAME VESTRIS, A THEATRICAL BIOG-
      RAPHY. London: Sidgwick and Jackson, 1973. xiv, 240 p. Illus.,
      index, bibliog.

> Biography of Lucia Elizabeth Vestris (1797-1856) as performer-
> manageress. Attempt to discover the magic of her attraction.
> Three relatively insignificant appendixes. Not as comprehen-
> sive as item 1969.

2056 Wilson, A[lbert]. E[dward]. THE LYCEUM. London: Dennis Yates,
      1952. 208 p. Illus., index.

> Undocumented history of the theatre that housed the burnt-out
> Drury Lane company and later offered lavish Melville Brothers'
> pantomimes. Illustrated from the Raymond Mander and Joe
> Mitchenson Theatre Collection.

2057 _____. EAST END ENTERTAINMENT. For full entry and annotation,
      see item 354.

2058 Wisely, Edward Burdock. "Charles Dibdin and the Table Entertainment."
      Ph.D. dissertation, Columbia University, 1951. 358 p.

> Twenty seasons of a one-man show at his San Souci Theatres.

Chapter 12

MAJOR DRAMATIC GENRES AND FORMS:
ENGLISH AND AMERICAN

Sources listed in chapters 10 and 11 also contain material relevant to popular theatre literary forms, genres, and specialized staging techniques and practices, such as aquatic or equestrian drama.

2059   Adams, William Davenport. A BOOK OF BURLESQUE SKETCHES OF ENGLISH STAGE TRAVESTIE AND PARODY. London: Henry and Co., 1891. vi [1], 220 p. Illus.

Introduction to English stage burlesque with examples of various categories. An opening chapter surveys English burlesque's palmy days, followed by a chapter on the beginnings of burlesque (literary), and a final chapter ("The New Burlesque") which focuses on post-1885 burlesque.

2060   Apter, Andrew W. "Popular American Drama as an Expression of American Society, 1900-1910." Ph.D. dissertation, Indiana University, 1976. 269 p.

Studies a number of authors of popular fare, e.g., David Belasco, Clyde Fitch, Augustus Thomas, Edwin Locke, Charles Klein, and others.

2061   Baker, Seymour O. "The English Farce from 1800-1880." Ph.D. dissertation, Harvard University, 1948.

2062   Bergainnier, Earl F. "Melodrama as Formula." JOURNAL OF POPULAR CULTURE 8 (Winter 1975): 726-33.

The author suggests a new way to examine popular art, in particular the melodrama.

2063   Blayney, Glenn H. "City-Life in American Drama, 1825-1860." In STUDIES IN HONOR OF JOHN WILCOX, edited by A. Doyle Wallace and Woodburn Ross, pp. 99-128. Detroit: Wayne State University Press, 1958.

Incisive, documented essay on the topic; deals with the city setting as a leading force in dramatic development. Thirty-six plays discussed.

2064   Booth, Michael R. HISS THE VILLAIN: SIX ENGLISH AND AMERI-CAN MELODRAMAS. London: Eyre and Spottiswoode, 1964; New York: Benjamin Blom, 1964. 390 p. Illus., note on authors and sources.

Good representative collection and commentary on representative melodramas.

2065   _____. "The Drunkard's Progress: Nineteenth Century Temperance Drama." DALHOUSIE REVIEW 44 (1964-65): 205-12.

Excellent essay demonstrating the extreme form of temperance propaganda in nineteenth-century melodrama.

2066   _____. ENGLISH MELODRAMA. London: Herbert Jenkins, 1965. 223 p. Illus., index, bibliog.

Excellent study of the genre; especially good in distinguishing the various kinds of melodramas and deals well with the subject of acting styles. Useful bibliography.

2067   _____, ed. ENGLISH PLAYS OF THE NINETEENTH CENTURY. Vols. 1 and 2. Oxford: Clarendon Press, 1969.

Excellent collections of English melodramas and commentary. Volume 1: xi, 315 p. Illus., appendix. (covers the period 1800-1850), volume 2: vii, 427 p. Illus. (covers the period 1850-1900).

2068   _____. "Early Victorian Farce: Dionysus Domesticated." In NINE-TEENTH CENTURY BRITISH THEATRE, edited by Kenneth Richards and Peter Thomson, pp. 95-110. London: Methuen and Co., 1971.

Analysis of the audience and the form with examples of Victorian farce analyzed.

2069   _____, ed. ENGLISH PLAYS OF THE NINETEENTH CENTURY. Vol. 5: PANTOMIMES, EXTRAVAGANZAS, AND BURLESQUES. London: Clarendon Press, 1976. 534 p. Illus., index, notes.

An invaluable source; much more than a collection of plays. Contains good examples of pantomimes, burlesques, and extravaganzas performed between 1800 and 1900, preceded by a useful and lengthy introduction. Each text has an informative preface and an appendix entitled "Pantomime Rehearsal, Production, and Performance" concludes the volume.

2070 _____. "East End Melodrama." THEATRE SURVEY 17 (May 1976):
57-67.

> Survey of the working-class theatres of East London during
> Victorian times and an analysis of the popular theatrical fare
> (melodrama) presented there.

2071 Clinton-Baddeley, V.C. THE BURLESQUE TRADITION IN THE EN-
GLISH THEATRE AFTER 1660. London: Methuen and Co., 1952. xvi,
152 p. Illus., index, bibliog.

> The standard study of dramatic burlesque in the English
> theatre from Davenant and Buckingham to pantomime and
> ballet. Figures examined include Thomas Duffet, John Gay,
> Henry Fielding, Henry Carey, R.B. Sheridan, John Hookham
> Frere and George Canning, Thomas Dibdin, Charles Dickens,
> J.R. Planche, W.S. Gilbert, Bernard Shaw, Stephen Leacock,
> and Max Beerbohm.

2072 Croghan, Leland A. "New York Burlesque: 1840-1870." Ph.D. dissertation, New York University, 1968. 402 p.

> Following a definition of literary burlesque, this analyzes the
> work of George L. Fox, William Mitchell, John Brougham,
> William Burton, George Holland, Joseph Jefferson III, Dion
> Boucicault, Mrs. John Wood, and Tony Pastor.

2073 Cross, Gilbert B. NEXT WEEK--EAST LYNNE: DOMESTIC DRAMA
IN PERFORMANCE 1820-1874. Lewisburg, Pa.: Bucknell University
Press; London: Associated University Presses, 1977. 281 p. Illus.,
index, bibliog.

> Based on the author's 1971 dissertation (University of Michigan).
> Study of domestic drama, primarily in England, from 1820
> (first performance of William Moncrieff's THE LEAR OF PRI-
> VATE LIFE) to 1874 (production of T.A. Palmer's version of
> EAST LYNNE). Examines plot, character, setting, and
> spectacle, viewing the plays in performance. Stresses impor-
> tance of costume, makeup, gesture, and audience participa-
> tion, and relates the subject matter of the plays to contempo-
> rary society, especially as it reflected England's change from
> a semifeudal to an increasingly democratic society.

2074 Cutler, Jean Valjean. "Realism in Augustin Daly's Productions of
Contemporary Play." Ph.D. dissertation, University of Illinois, 1963.
181 p.

2074a Daum, Paul Alexander. "The Royal Circus 1782-1809: An Analysis of
Equestrian Entertainment." For full entry and annotation, see item 404.

2075   Davis, Owen. "Why I Quit Writing Melodrama." AMERICAN MAGA-
ZINE 78 (September 1914): 28-31, 77, 78-79, 80. Illus.

> Davis discusses how and why he chose his profession as writer
> of melodramas. He analyzes his success and provides the
> formula for constructing a successful melodrama. At the con-
> clusion he confides that as a writer of melodrama his reputation
> as a serious writer was being ruined.

2076   _____. I'D LIKE TO DO IT AGAIN. New York: Farrar and Rinehart, 1931. viii, 233 p. Illus.

> Autobiography of the author of melodramas.

2077   Degen, John Alden III. "A History of Burlesque-Extravaganza in
Nineteenth-Century England." Ph.D. dissertation, Indiana University,
1977. 420 p.

> Companies and actors who performed it; authors who wrote it,
> from Planche in the 1830s to the 1890s.

2078   _____. "Victorian Drama." INDIANA UNIVERSITY BOOKMAN 12
(December 1977): 5-25.

> Ostensibly a description of the scope of the Indiana University
> Lilly Library's holdings (in the Stock Collection) in nineteenth-
> century theatre and drama, but additionally useful for the
> author's brief discussion of various genres of popular theatre
> and suggestions of possible research approaches to this material.

2079   Dircks, P.T. "James Robinson Planche and the English Burletta Tradition." THEATRE SURVEY 17 (May 1976): 68-81.

> Consideration of "Planche's classical burlettas in terms of the
> ongoing tradition of the burletta form on the English stage."

2080   Disher, Maurice Willson. "The Equestrian Drama." NINETEENTH
CENTURY 102 (1927): 830-39, 103 (1928): 124-32.

> Disher proclaims this article the "obituary" of equestrian
> drama after a century of existence. He gives a brief history
> of and commentary on equestrian drama citing many examples
> and discussing the leading figures in the genre.

2081   _____. BLOOD AND THUNDER: MID-VICTORIAN MELODRAMA
AND ITS ORIGIN. London: Frederick Muller, 1949. 280 p. Illus.,
index; list of plays.

> One of the first studies of mid-Victorian melodrama; still a
> reasonable, good basic approach to the subject. English,
> French, and American examples are included. Disher presents
> his subject with a good sense of the theatrical context.

2082 _____. MELODRAMA: PLOTS THAT THRILLED. London: Rockliff
Publishing, 1954. xiv, 210 p. Illus., indexes. (persons and places,
plays, films, theatres).

> Disher attempts to trace the theme of virtue in conflict with
> vice in melodrama from 1850 to circa 1950. Chapters include
> virtually every possible category of melodrama, from "Mag-
> dalens" to "Melodrama Mocked" and includes numerous
> examples for each category examined. Excellent illustrations.

2083 Dolkey, Matthew. "Follies in Fashion: The Afterpiece in the American
Theatre." Ph.D. dissertation, New York University, 1974. 149 p.

2084 Donohue, Joseph. "Burletta and the Early Nineteenth-Century English
Theatre." NINETEENTH CENTURY THEATRE RESEARCH 1 (Spring 1973):
29-51.

> Excellent reexamination of the origin of burletta and its exact
> meaning. "Fresh scrutiny of the subject will show that the
> exact historical dimensions of burletta have an importance far
> greater than its apparently minor generic nature might suggest."

2085 Donohue, Joseph, and Ellis, James, eds. "The British Theatre 1800-
1900: Essays on the Nineteenth-Century Stage." THEATRE SURVEY 17
(May 1976): 123 p. Illus.

> Papers from the Conference on the Nineteenth-Century British
> Theatre held at the University of Massachusetts, Amherst,
> 10-12 May 1974.

2086 Dye, William S[eddinger]., Jr. A STUDY OF MELODRAMA IN ENG-
LAND FROM 1800 TO 1840. State College, Pa.: Nittany Printing
and Publishing Co., 1919. 54 p. Bibliog. Paper.

> Based on his 1915 Ph.D. thesis. Includes a partial list of
> melodramas written between 1800 and 1840.

2087 Eaton, Julia. "Classic and Popular Elements in English Comedy of the
Eighteenth and Nineteenth Centuries." Ph.D. dissertation, Cornell
University, 1943.

2088 Eaton, Walter Prichard. "The Return of Farce." AMERICAN MAGA-
ZINE 71 (December 1910): 264-73. Illus.

> Eaton gives his definition of farce and discusses the great
> renewed success that genre was having in America at that
> time, just when critics had pronounced it dead. Cites
> several examples and discusses the more popular farces of
> the time.

2089 _____. "Why Do You Fear Me, Nellie?" HARPER'S 183 (July 1941):
164-70.

On turn of the century melodramas.

2090 Estill, Robin. "The Factory Lad: Melodrama as Propaganda." THEATRE
QUARTERLY 1 (October-December 1971): 22-26.

Analysis of the melodrama script, THE FACTORY LAD (1832)
by John Walker, as propaganda; also considers other politi-
cally motivated entertainments in the period.

2091 Girard, Chet Anthony. "The Equestrian Drama of the Nineteenth Century." Ph.D. dissertation, Louisiana State University, 1939.

2092 Glenn, Frank Warren. "An Historical and Critical Evaluation of the
Plays of George M. Cohan, 1901-1920." Ph.D. dissertation, Bowling
Green State University, 1976. 450 p.

Cohan examined as a popular playwright.

2093 Glenn, Stanley L. "Ludicrous Characterizations in American Comedy
from the Beginning Until the Civil War." Ph.D. dissertation, Stanford
University, 1955. 519 p.

Divided into three sections, this study attempts to show how
the development of American thought and characters was
reflected in the development of indigenous American comedy.

2094 Goff, Lewin. "The Owen Davis-Al Woods Melodrama Factory." EDU-
CATIONAL THEATRE JOURNAL 11 (October 1959): 200-207.

An analysis of the popular priced melodrama at the turn of the
century, typified by the works of Davis and Woods. Based
in part on Goff's 1948 Western Reserve University Ph.D.
thesis ("The Popular Melodrama in America, 1890-1910, With
Its Origins and Development to 1890").

2095 Goodlad, J.S. A SOCIOLOGY OF POPULAR DRAMA. Totowa, N.J.:
Rowman and Littlefield, 1972. x, 230 p. Indexes, appendixes.

A close analysis of the role and function of drama in society;
concludes that popular drama "is concerned with the survival
of the social system."

2096 Grimsted, David. MELODRAMA UNVEILED: AMERICAN THEATRE
AND CULTURE, 1800-1850. Chicago: University of Chicago Press,
1968. xii, 285 p. Index, bibliog.

A scholarly work, well documented, that includes chapters on

critics, audiences, stages, and plays. A perceptive analysis
of the cultural milieu in which melodrama thrived. Recommended.

2097 Hamilton, Clayton. "Melodrama and Farces." FORUM 41 (January
1909): 23-32.

Explains the inherent differences between tragedy and melodrama, comedy and farce, giving his definition of each of
the four genres. He then discusses examples in terms of his
definitions.

2098 _____. "Melodrama, Old and New." BOOKMAN 33 (May 1911):
309-14.

Discusses pure melodrama, choosing to ignore its derogatory
connotations. Good analysis of the genre and its effects on
audiences.

2099 Hughes, Leo. A CENTURY OF ENGLISH FARCE. London: Oxford
University Press, 1956. 307 p. Index, bibliog.

Reasonably good chapter on "Rival Entertainments" (pantomime,
burlesque, satire, sentiment). Also a summary chapter on
fairs and strollers. Drawn heavily from other sources. Period
covered is 1660 to the mid-eighteenth century.

2100 Jerome, Jerome K. STAGE-LAND: CURIOUS HABITS AND CUSTOMS
OF ITS INHABITANTS. Illustrated by J. Bernard Partridge. London:
Chatto and Windus, 1890. 80 p. Illus.

Amusing, illustrated account of character types in contemporary
late nineteenth-century melodrama.

2101 Jump, John D. THE CRITICAL IDIOM: BURLESQUE. New York:
Methuen and Co., 1972. x, 77 p. Index, bibliog.

Brief but useful outline chapter on dramatic burlesque of the
English tradition (pp. 52-74) from the Pyramus-Thisbe burlesque
in MIDSUMMER'S NIGHT DREAM to Shaw's THE ADMIRABLE
BASHVILLE.

2102 Kahan, Stanley. "Pre-Victorian Melodrama." Ph.D. dissertation,
University of Wisconsin, 1959. 538 p.

Techniques and themes in melodrama from 1790 to 1837.

2103 Kahn, E.J., Jr. THE MERRY PARTNERS: THE AGE AND STAGE OF
HARRIGAN AND HART. For full entry and annotation, see item
1575.

2104   Krutch, Joseph Wood. "What is Melodrama?" THE NATION 138
        (9 May 1934): 544, 546.

        Definition, history (brief), and discussion of its purpose and
        change from its origin.

2105   Kummer, George. "The Americanization of Burlesque, 1840-1860."
        THEATRE ANNUAL 27 (1971-72): 47-56.

        Influence of literary British burlesque on the productions of
        William Mitchell, William Burton, and John Brougham.
        Largely historical in approach.

2106   McConachie, Bruce Alan. "Economic Values in Popular American
        Melodramas, 1815-1860." Ph.D. dissertation, University of Wisconsin-
        Madison, 1977. 454 p.

        Relates early industrial revolution to the changing form and
        content of melodrama in America.

2107   McGlinchee, Claire. "The Marvelous in the Pantomimes, Spectacles
        and Extravaganzas in the Nineteenth Century American Theatre." RE-
        VUE D'HISTOIRE DU THEATRE 15 (January-March 1963): 63-70.

        American extravaganzas and burlesques as derivations of
        England's Christmas pantomime; author examines the evolution
        of the form on the American stage with examples.

2108   Mandeville, Gloria E. "A Century of Melodrama on the London Stage,
        1790-1890." Ph.D. dissertation, Columbia University, 1954. 370 p.

        Analysis of major figures and representative plays.

2109   Marker, Lise-Lone. DAVID BELASCO: NATURALISM IN THE AMERI-
        CAN THEATRE. Princeton, N.J.: Princeton University Press, 1975.
        xiv, 248 p. Illus., index, bibliog.

        Good reassessment of Belasco's place in theatre and dramatic
        history, with detailed production reconstructions of four typical
        productions. Good insight into his form of popular drama.

2110   Matlaw, Myron. "Persiflage on the Nineteenth-Century Stage." EDU-
        CATIONAL THEATRE JOURNAL 11 (October 1959): 212-21.

        Discusses the lack of "stature" in English drama for over half
        of the nineteenth century (period between Sheridan and
        Robertson) and the consequent flourishing at that time of
        popular entertainments including the burlesquing of serious
        drama.

2111   Meisel, Martin. "Political Extravaganza: A Phase of Nineteenth-

Century British Theatre." THEATRE SURVEY 3 (1962): 19-31.

> Discusses politics on the English stage and the main vehicle
> for topical political satire, the Burlesque-Extravaganza.

2112 Mendelson, Andrew David. "The Rise of Melodrama and the Schematization of Women in England, 1760-1840: The Relationship Between Theatrical Stereotype, Social Mythology, and Social Change During the Industrial Revolution." Ph.D. dissertation, Stanford University, 1977. 500 p.

2113 Moody, Richard. "Edward Harrigan." MODERN DRAMA 19 (December 1976): 319-25.

> The author of the "Mulligan" series of farces is examined from the
> the standpoint of the serious critics of the day and his own
> thoughts on drama and theatre. Moody is currently projecting
> a full-length study of Harrigan.

2114 Moses, Montrose J. "Harrigan, American." THEATRE GUILD MAGAZINE 7 (June 1930): 24-29, 64. Illus.

> Retrospective assessment of Edward Harrigan's contributions to
> to the American theatre in "making Americans conscious of
> the new racial and social strains in their midst."

2115 Nadeau, Albert Henry. "James Robinson Planche, Craftsman of Extravaganza." Ph.D. dissertation, University of Michigan, 1955. 264 p.

> Forty-four extravaganza scripts, memoirs, periodicals, and
> newspapers are used to examine Planche's work.

2116 Nardin, James T. "A Study in Popular American Farce, 1865-1914." Ph.D. dissertation, University of Chicago, 1950.

2117 Newton, H. Chance [Heath Cranton]. CRIME AND THE DRAMA, OR, DARK DEEDS DRAMATIZED. Introduction by Sir John Martin-Harvey. London: Stanley Paul and Co., 1927. 284 p. Illus.

> Chatty but useful account of criminal melodramas of the later
> nineteenth century in England.

2118 Orr, Lynn E. "Dion Boucicault and the Nineteenth-Century Theatre." Ph.D. dissertation, Louisiana State University, 1953.

2119 Quinn, Arthur Hobson. "In Defense of Melodrama." BOOKMAN 61 (June 1925): 413-17.

> Examines popular reaction to melodrama and then its essential
> elements. A persuasive defense of the genre.

2120 Planche, James Robinson. THE RECOLLECTIONS AND REFLECTIONS OF J.R. PLANCHE. 2 vols. London: Tinsley Bros., 1872. Illus.

Important source on the development of the extravanza as a rival of the pantomime.

2121 Rahill, Frank. "Melodrama." THEATRE ARTS 16 (April 1932): 285-94.

Essay on melodrama in which the author discusses briefly the origins of the form and the eclecticism of the form; shows how melodrama borrowed a great deal from other art forms, particularly popular ones.

2122 _____. "The Murder Mystery Melodrama." THEATRE ARTS 25 (March 1941): 233-42. Illus.

Discusses the genre of the murder-mystery melodrama, beginning in 1863, and then discusses its various formulas, citing numerous examples and briefly examing mutations of the form.

2123 _____. "When Heaven Protected the Working Girl." THEATRE ARTS 38 (October 1954): 10, 78-80, 91-92. Illus.

On the ten-twent'-thirt' popular melodrama and the producers, writers, and performers who got their theatrical start in it. Discusses the content of these plays citing several examples.

2124 _____. THE WORLD OF MELODRAMA. University Park: Pennsylvania State University Press, 1967. 334 p. Index, bibliog.

Good treatment of theatre as a social institution, as well as an important treatment of the genre during the nineteenth century. Coverage not limited to the United States (a good deal on England and France). Extensive bibliography.

2125 Reynolds, Ernest. EARLY VICTORIAN DRAMA (1830-1870). Cambridge, Engl.: W. Heffer and Sons, 1936. Reprint. New York: Benjamin Blom, 1956. vii, 163 p. Index, bibliog.

Good documented account of melodrama in its theatrical context; appendixes include the dramatization of fiction and notable authors of the period. See also item 2023.

2126 Ryan, Pat M. "John Brougham: The Gentle Satirist." BULLETIN OF THE NEW YORK PUBLIC LIBRARY 63 (December 1959): 619-40.

Critique of his writing and a checklist and census of his plays.

2127 Saxon, A.H. ENTER FOOT AND HORSE: A HISTORY OF HIPPO-DRAMA IN ENGLAND AND FRANCE. New Haven: Yale University

Press, 1968. xiv, 249 p. Illus., index, bibliog.

A first-rate scholarly study of the roots of the American circus which focuses on the unique facilities for hippodrama or equestrian drama in London and Paris (Astley's and the Cirque Olympique). Also strongly recommended as a social history of the times as seen through the plays of this genre and their productions. See index for additional sources on hippodrama by Saxon, the acknowledged authority.

2128   Sedgwick, Ruth W. "Those Dear, Dead Days of Melodrama." STAGE [New York] 12 (August 1935): 11, 38-41. Illus.

History of melodrama from the late 1700s through 1912. Discusses melodrama's more prominent managers, producers, and playwrights.

2129   Smith, Harry James. "The Melodrama." ATLANTIC MONTHLY 99 (March 1907): 320-28.

Good article analyzing the nature of melodrama, particularly those produced at the Thalia Theatre, its character and its appeal.

2130   Smith, James L. MELODRAMA. London: Methuen and Co., 1973. viii, 96 p. Index, bibliog.

Brief but useful introduction to the genre; discusses the nature of the form and defends the more skillfully wrought manifestations of the form. Three sections deal with the formulas for melodramas of triumph, defeat, and protest.

2131   Speaight, George. "Some Comic Circus Entrees." For full entry and annotation, see item 502.

2132   Taylor, Dwight. BLOOD-AND THUNDER. New York: Atheneum, 1962. x, 232 p.

An "unofficial" biography of Charles A. Taylor, American author of many melodramas, by his son, Dwight.

2133   Thompson, Alan Reynolds. "A Study of Melodrama as a Dramatic Genre." Ph.D. dissertation, Harvard University, 1926.

2134   Trussler, Simon. "A Chronology of Early Melodrama." THEATRE QUARTERLY 4 (October-December 1971): 19-21, 93.

Brief chronology (1764-1840) highlights the stages of melodrama's development in England, noting early treatments of its various staple themes, and the significant events which sometimes "seem to be more than coincidentally reflected in the plays."

2135   Tsai, Andre Tii-Kang. "The British Nautical Drama, 1824-1843." Ph.D. dissertation, Ohio State University, 1964. 264 p.

Examination of twenty-five plays of the genre, focuses on the works of Edward Fitzball and Douglas Jerrold.

2136   Tuttle, George Palliser   "The History of the Royal Circus, Equestrian and Philharmonic Academy, 1782-1816, St. George's Fields, Surry, England." Ph.D. dissertation, Tufts University, 1972. 416 p.

On equestrian drama. See also item 526.

2137   Warner, Frederick Elliott. "The Burletta in London's Minor Theatres During the Nineteenth Century, With a Handlist of Burlettas." Ph.D. dissertation, Ohio State University, 1972. 170 p.

2138   Watson, Ernest Bradlee. SHERIDAN TO ROBERTSON. A STUDY OF THE NINETEENTH-CENTURY LONDON STAGE. Cambridge, Mass.: Harvard University Press, 1926. xix, 485 p. Illus., index, bibliog., map.

Although largely superseded by subsequent works, still a useful survey of this transitional period and greatest era of popular theatre in London. Adds to Nicholson's THE STRUGGLE FOR A FREE STAGE (see item 2017) in its discussion of legal problems and minor forms. Appendix: essay on "Lesser Theatres and Places of Amusement," including outdoor theatres and exhibitions of scenic illusion. Map is included which shows the location of London theatres and similar places of amusement from 1800 to 1870. All in all, a lively defense of nineteenth-century drama.

2139   Wells, Stanley. "Shakespeare in Planche's Extravaganzas." In SHAKESPEARE SURVEY 16, pp. 103-17. Birmingham, Engl.: Cambridge University Press, 1963. Illus.

A study of James Robinson Planche's use of Shakespeare in his extravaganzas. Cites allusions in these works to lines and speeches of Shakespeare and gives numerous examples of Planche's clever parodying of lines, speeches, and entire scenes from Shakespeare's work. Also deals with the staging of these extravaganzas.

2140   Winesanker, Michael. "The Record of English Musical Drama, 1750-1800." Ph.D. dissertation, Cornell University, 1944.

Chapter 13

NATIVE AMERICAN TYPES FROM THE YANKEE TO TOBY

See also sources in chapters 12 and 14.

2141 Amacher, Richard E. "Behind the Curtain with the Noble Savage: Stage Managment of Indian Plays, 1825-1860." THEATRE SURVEY 7 (November 1966): 101-14. Illus.

Survey of Indian plays and their productions.

2142 Bank, Rosemarie Katherine. "Rhetorical, Dramatic, Theatrical, and Social Contexts of Selected American Frontier Plays, 1871 to 1906." Ph.D. dissertation, University of Iowa, 1972. 247 p.

2143 Belcher, Fannis S., Jr. "The Place of the Negro in the Evolution of the American Theatre, 1767 to 1940." Ph.D. dissertation, Yale University, 1945.

2144 Birdoff, Harry. THE WORLD'S GREATEST HIT--UNCLE TOM'S CABIN. New York: S.F. Vanni, 1947. xiv, 440 p. Illus.

A history of the dramatization of Stowe's novel from 1852 to 1936, plus an analysis of "Tommers" and derivations from the original. Appendix of cast lists and other pertinent data.

2145 Blair, Walter. NATIVE AMERICAN HUMOR. For full entry and annotation, see item 107.

2146 Brasmer, William. "The Wild West Exhibition and the Drama of Civilization." For full entry and annotation, see item 614.

2147 Clark, Larry D. "Toby Shows: A Form of American Popular Theatre." Ph.D. dissertation, University of Illinois, 1963. 163 p.

Clark describes, analyzes and gives a brief history of Toby shows.

2148 _____. "The Toby Show: A Rural American Harlequinade." CEN-TRAL STATES SPEECH JOURNAL 19 (Summer 1968): 91-95.

Popular character dominated tent theatre from about 1920 to the present.

2149 Cline, Julia. "Rise of the American Stage Negro." DRAMA 21 (January 1931): 9-10.

Cursory survey from FASHION (1845) to THE GREEN PASTURES.

2150 Coleman, William S.E. "Buffalo Bill on Stage." PLAYERS, MAGAZINE OF AMERICAN THEATRE 47 (December-January 1972): 80-91. Illus.

William F. Cody's career in melodrama, beginning in 1872 and concluding in 1883.

2151 Collier, Gaylan. "George Handel Hill: The Yankee of Them All." SOUTHERN SPEECH JOURNAL 24 (Winter 1958): 91-93.

Life of the Yankee specialist.

2152 Corbett, Elizabeth F. "A Foot Note to 'THE DRAMA.'" DRAMA 16 (May 1926): 285-86.

Corbett discusses the isolated American town of the 1870s and '80s and states that such towns had only two links with the "outside world"--the circus that toured in the summer and, in the winter, UNCLE TOM'S CABIN, which Corbett calls "our one folk play." Article focuses on the play and its time on the road.

2153 _____. "Uncle Tom Is Dead." THEATRE GUILD MAGAZINE 8 (January 1931): 16-20. Illus.

Assessment of UNCLE TOM'S CABIN's history during the first year in which no company was playing it since 1853. Illustrations from the Albert Davis Collection.

2154 Cox, Paul Ronald. "The Characterization of the American Indian in American Indian Plays 1800-1860 As a Reflection of the American Romantic Movement." Ph.D. dissertation, New York University, 1970. 282 p.

2155 Curvin, Jonathan W. "The Stage Yankee." In STUDIES IN SPEECH AND DRAMA IN HONOR OF ALEXANDER M. DRUMMOND, pp. 139-51. Ithaca, N.Y.: Cornell University Press, 1944.

Summary of Yankee plays and specialist, from THE CONTRAST (1783) to THE OLD HOMSTEAD (1886).

2156 David, J. Frank. "Tom Shows." SCRIBNER'S MAGAZINE 77 (April 1925): 350-60. Illus.

The structure and content of Tom Shows; briefly discusses the demise of the Tom Show. Good insight into the wide range of quality, content, and production methods found within the various Tom Shows.

2157 Dorn-Heft, Dolores. "Toby: The Twilight of a Tradition." THEATRE ARTS 42 (August 1958): 52-55, 80. Illus.

Toby shows in the Midwest and the Neil Schaffner Players.

2158 Dorson, Richard M. "The Yankee on the Stage--a Folk Hero of American Drama." NEW ENGLAND QUARTERLY 13 (September 1940): 467-93.

Description and analysis of stereotyped stage Yankee.

2159 _____. "Mose the Far-Famed and World Renowned." AMERICAN LITERATURE 15 (November 1943): 288-300.

Heavily documented survey and analysis of the character Mose the Bowery b'hoy. Checklist of Mose plays (1848-56).

2160 _____. "The Story of Sam Patch." AMERICAN MERCURY 64 (June 1947): 741-47.

The life of the real Sam Patch and Dan Marble's portrayal of Patch in the 1830s.

2161 Downing, Robert. "Toby." THEATRE ARTS 30 (November 1946): 651-54. Illus.

On the character of Toby; article discusses his origin, nature, appearance, and the type of theatres and productions in which he appeared.

2162 _____. "Folding of Last of Toby Troupes Ends Another Show Biz Tradition." VARIETY (16 May 1962): 61, 67.

On the retirement of Neil Schaffner.

2163 Eaton, Walter Prichard. "Dramatic Evolution and the Popular Theatre; Playhouse Roots of Our Drama." For full entry and annotation, see item 989.

2164 Eich, Louis M. "The Stage Yankee." QUARTERLY JOURNAL OF SPEECH 27 (February 1941): 16-25.

Brief survey of Yankee plays and specialists.

2165 Fruth, Mary Ann. "Scenery and Staging of UNCLE TOM'S CABIN: Allegory and Ohio River Scenes." OHIO STATE UNIVERSITY THEATRE COLLECTION BULLETIN no. 10 (1963): 31-39. Illus.

Mechanics of two scenes from the Harmount UNCLE TOM'S CABIN.

2166 Furnas, J.C. GOODBYE TO UNCLE TOM. New York: William Sloane Associates, 1956. 435 p. Illus., index, notes.

A Canadian's view of UNCLE TOM'S CABIN and an analysis of its effect on the American Negro image.

2167 Hill, George H. SCENES FROM THE LIFE OF AN ACTOR. New York, 1853. Reprint. New York: Benjamin Blom, 1972. viii, 246 p. Illus.

Autobiography of the Yankee specialist compiled from journals, letters, and memoranda.

2168 Hodge, Francis. "Biography of a Lost Play: LION OF THE WEST." THEATRE ANNUAL 12 (1954): 48-61.

History of the play and James Hackett's association with it (first produced in 1831).

2169 _____. "Yankee in England: James Henry Hackett and the Debut of American Comedy." QUARTERLY JOURNAL OF SPEECH 45 (December 1959): 381-90.

2170 _____. YANKEE THEATRE: THE IMAGE OF AMERICA ON STAGE 1825-1850. Austin: University of Texas Press, 1964. 320 p. Illus., index, bibliog.

The definitive history of the stage Yankee during its peak period; includes an appendix on Yankee stage speech.

2171 Hunt, Douglas L. "Charles H. Hoyt: Playwright-Manager." THEATRE ANNUAL 1 (1942): 42-50.

Biography and assessment of Hoyt in the theatre (1883-1900).

2172 Lund, Ralph Eugene. "Trouping with Uncle Tom." THE CENTURY 115 (January 1928): 329-37.

Chatty article on life on the road with touring companies of
UNCLE TOM'S CABIN. Essay focuses on the role of Little
Eva and those who played her, including Fay Templeton and
Mary Pickford.

2173 MacDonald, Cordelia Howard. "Memoirs of the Original Little Eva."
EDUCATIONAL THEATRE JOURNAL 8 (December 1956): 267-82.

Foreword by George P. Howard; memoirs of the first Little
Eva in the George C. Howard production (based on George L.
Aiken's dramatization) written in 1928.

2174 McDowell, John H. "Original Scenery and Documents for Productions
of UNCLE TOM'S CABIN." REVUE D'HISTOIRE DU THEATRE 15
(January-March 1963): 71-79.

Principally on the Harmount UNCLE TOM'S CABIN show beginning in 1903; study of the scenery and other pictorial
materials in the Ohio State University collection.

2175 _____ . "Scenery and Staging of UNCLE TOM'S CABIN: Selected
Scenes." THE OHIO STATE UNIVERSITY THEATRE COLLECTION
BULLETIN no. 10 (1963): 19-30. Illus.

Analysis and description of scenery used by the Harmount
Company. Photographs of scenery and posters.

2176 Meserve, Walter J. "The Dramatists and Their Plays." In THE REVELS
HISTORY OF DRAMA IN ENGLISH. Vol. 3: AMERICAN DRAMA,
edited by T.W. Craik, pp. 149-296. London: Methuen and Co.;
New York: Barnes and Noble Books, 1977.

Survey history of American drama; good introduction to native
characters in American drama.

2177 Mickel, Jere C. "The Genesis of Toby. A Folk Hero of the American
Theater." JOURNAL OF AMERICAN FOLKLORE 80 (October-December
1967): 334-40.

Excellent survey of the character Toby's evolution; corrects
previous errors. See also item 2277.

2178 Monaghan, Jay. "The Stage Career of Buffalo Bill." JOURNAL OF
THE ILLINOIS HISTORICAL SOCIETY 31 (December 1938): 411-23.
Illus.

Cody's career in melodrama prior to 1893.

2179 Moody, Richard. "Uncle Tom, The Theater and Mrs. Stowe." AMERI-
CAN HERITAGE 6 (October 1955): 29-33, 102-3. Illus.

Succinct history of the plays and an analysis of its ingredients which combined to produce an enduring drama, although an undistinguished literary effort.

2180 Moody, Richard, and Drummond, A.M. "The Hit of the Century: UNCLE TOM'S CABIN." EDUCATIONAL THEATRE JOURNAL 4 (December 1952): 315-22.

Survey of the play's history from 1852 to 1952.

2181 Morris, Joe Alex. "Corniest Show on the Road." SATURDAY EVENING POST 228 (17 September 1955): 30-31, 60-62, 66, 70. Illus. (color).

Neil Schaffner and the Schaffner Players while his Toby shows were still the most popular form of entertainment in the farm belt.

2182 Morrow, John C. "The Harmount Company: Aspects of an UNCLE TOM'S CABIN Company." OHIO STATE UNIVERSITY THEATRE COLLECTION BULLETIN no. 10 (1943): 10-18. Illus.

Harmount tours of UNCLE TOM'S CABIN beginning in 1903 and extending until 1929. Interesting analysis of operation, structure, and transportation of the company.

2183 Nolan, Paul T. "When Curtains Rise, Scouts Fall Out." SOUTHERN SPEECH JOURNAL 29 (Spring 1964): 175-86.

The master scout as stage hero and an account of John Wallace Crawford's quarrel with William F. Cody over an "accident" on stage in 1877 during a performance of THE RIGHT RED HAND.

2184 _____. "J.W. Crawford: Poet Scout of the Black Hills." SOUTH DAKOTA REVIEW 2 (Spring 1965): 40-47.

The theatrical relationship of Buffalo Bill Cody and John Wallace Crawford in 1876 after the battle at the Little Big Horn.

2185 _____. "The Western Hero on Stage." REAL WEST 11 (October 1968): 37-38, 56-57, 66, 74-75.

Good summary of real live western heroes transferred to the stage, as epitomized by Bill Cody.

2186 Northall, W[illiam]. K., ed. LIFE AND RECOLLECTIONS OF YANKEE HILL. New York: W.F. Burgess, 1850. 203 p. Paper.

A rather quaint volume with a ninety-seven-page biographical sketch of the Yankee specialists and the remainder "anecdotes and incidents."

2187 Obee, Harold B. "A Prompt Script Study of Nineteenth-Century Legitimate Stage Versions of Rip Van Winkle." Ph.D. dissertation, Ohio State University, 1961. 358 p.

Study of twenty promptbooks and nine scripts of the play "in order to evaluate current historical studies related to this play and to theatre production of the nineteenth century."

2188 Pettit, Paul B. "The Important American Dramatic Types to 1900. A Study of the Yankee, Negro, Indian and Frontiersman." Ph.D. dissertation, Cornell University, 1949.

2189 Quarnstorm, I. Blaine. "Early Twentieth-Century Staging of UNCLE TOM'S CABIN." OHIO STATE UNIVERSITY THEATRE COLLECTION BULLETIN no. 15 (1968): 32-42.

Research on the Harmount's Tom Show.

2190 Rahill, Frank. "America's Number One Hit." THEATRE ARTS 36 (October 1952): 18-24. Illus.

Good theatrical history of UNCLE TOM'S CABIN.

2191 Ranney, Omar. "Forever Toby." THEATRE ARTS 37 (August 1953): 73, 95.

Short article on Toby shows, particularly in the character of Toby, which were still being performed in tents in the rural Southwest and Midwest.

2192 "Rose Melville--The Feminine Denman Thompson." THE THEATRE 8 (January 1908): 28-29. Illus.

Story of the acting career of Melville, beginning with the acts she did with her sisters and covering her origination of the "Sis Hopkins" role in 1891, a role which she continued to play for the rest of her career. "Sis Hopkins" (Toby's female counterpart) began as an entracte specialty and later had a full-length play written about her.

2193 Rourke, Constance. AMERICAN HUMOUR: A STUDY OF THE NATIONAL CHARACTER. For full entry and annotation, see item 144.

2194 "Rural Invasion." HARPER'S MAGAZINE 209 (November 1954): 82-84.

On Neil Schaffner and the "Toby and Susie" shows.

2195 Schaffner, Neil E., with Johnson, Vance. THE FABULOUS TOBY AND ME. Englewood Cliffs, N.J.: Prentice-Hall, 1968. x, 212 p. Illus., index.

> Story of Neil Schaffner, the last of the well-known tent repertoire showmen, who, in the 1920s, created the Schaffner Players, which he and his wife, Caroline, owned and operated until their retirement in 1962. Neil ultimately became inseparable with the character Toby and his wife, Susie. See also item 2250.

2196 Schultz, Charles Albert. "The Yankee Figure in Early American Theatre Prior to 1820." Ph.D. dissertation, Bowling Green State University, 1970. 212 p.

> Survey of the development of the Yankee to 1820; six plays analyzed in detail.

2197 Sitton, Fred. "The Indian Play in American Drama, 1750-1900." Ph.D. dissertation, Northwestern University, 1962. 152 p.

2198 Snyder, Sherwood III. "The Toby Shows." Ph.D. dissertation, University of Minnesota, 1966. 403 p.

> Study of Toby Shows describing the Toby character, shows written around him, companies which performed these shows. Snyder concludes that Toby and Toby Shows are the closest thing America has seen to true folk theatre on a national scale.

2199 Stout, Wesley Winans. "Little Eva is Seventy-Five." SATURDAY EVENING POST 200 (8 October 1927): 10+. Illus.

> On the original UNCLE TOM'S CABIN dramatization.

2200 Turner, Willis L. "City Low-Life on the American Stage to 1900." Ph.D. dissertation, University of Illinois, 1956. 215 p.

> "Study of the use of city low-life themes, characters, and locales in the native drama and theatre of the nineteenth century."

2201 Waterman, Arthur E. "Joseph Jefferson as Rip Van Winkle." JOURNAL OF POPULAR CULTURE 1 (Spring 1968): 371-78.

> Jefferson's close association with the role for over forty years and its nineteenth-century association.

Chapter 14

AMERICAN SMALL-TOWN

AND PROVINCIAL OPERATIONS

See also sources in chapter 13.

2202   Adams, Allen J. "Mining Theatre History." PLAYERS, MAGAZINE OF AMERICAN THEATRE 44 (December–January 1969): 62–65. Illus.

        History of Cripple Creek Colorado Theatre, 1897–1907.

2203   Baxter, Alice. "Fifty-Five Years on the Stage and Doing One-Night Stands." BILLBOARD (11 September 1908): 17.

        Brief memoirs of touring experiences.

2204   Bell, Campton. "The Early Theaters, Cheyenne, Wyoming, 1867–1882." ANNALS OF WYOMING 25 (January 1953): 3–21.

        Includes partially complete list of theatres and variety halls between 12 October 1867, and 7 December 1902.

2205   Berkeley, Philip. "Watchman, What of the Road? A Sentimental Record of Twenty Years of Road Shows As They Passed Through a Typical Town." THEATRE ARTS MONTHLY 19 (October 1935): 780–85.

        The Kempner Theatre in Little Rock, Arkansas, from 1913 to 1928.

2206   Briggs, Harold E., and Bennett, Ernestine. "The Early Theatre on the Northern Plains." MISSISSIPPI VALLEY HISTORICAL REVIEW 37 (September 1950): 231–64.

        The period 1867–82 in Sioux City, Iowa; Yankton, South Dakota; Fargo and Bismarck, North Dakota; Miles City, Montana; and Cheyenne, Wyoming.

2207   Bunn, George W. "The Old Chatterton. A Brief History of the Famous Old Opera House." JOURNAL OF THE ILLINOIS STATE HISTORICAL

SOCIETY 36 (March 1943): 8-20. Illus.

Built in 1866 in Springfield; history to the turn of the century.

2208   Carson, William G.B. THE THEATRE ON THE FRONTIER: THE EARLY
YEARS OF THE ST. LOUIS STAGE. Chicago: University of Chicago
Press, 1932. Reprint. New York: Benjamin Blom, 1965. xi, 361 p.
Illus., index, bibliog., appendix.

History of dramatic enterprises in St. Louis from 1815 to
1839; good on early pioneers. Appendix lists record of performances of individual plays

2209   _____. "Night Life in St. Louis a Century Ago." MISSOURI HISTO-
RICAL SOCIETY BULLETIN 1 (April 1945): 3-9, 2 (October 1945):
3-10.

Lectures, concerts, and the theatre in St. Louis in the 1840s.

2210   _____. MANAGERS IN DISTRESS: THE ST. LOUIS STAGE, 1840-
1844. St. Louis: St. Louis Historical Documents Foundation, 1949.
xv, 329 p. Illus., index, bibliog.

Important study of critical period in St. Louis theatre history
involving Solomon Smith and Noah Ludlow (see item 1919).

2211   _____. "Under the Calcium Lights." MISSOURI HISTORICAL SO-
CIETY BULLETIN 12 (July 1956): 333-57.

George Barton Berrell and DeBar's Opera House in St. Louis,
1875-77.

2212   Chase, Edwin T. "Forty Years on Main Street." IOWA JOURNAL OF
HISTORY AND POLITICS 34 (July 1936): 227-61.

Atlantic, Iowa, during the latter part of the nineteenth century; a portrait of a typical town on the kerosene circuit
(one-night stands).

2213   Coburn, Charles. "Within These Walls." THEATRE ANNUAL 1 (1942):
29-36.

Deals with the actor-manager system at the Savannah Theatre
in the 1890s.

2214   Cosgrave, Luke. THEATER TONIGHT. Hollywood: House-Warven,
1952. 245 p. Illus.

Autobiography of Irish-born actor who immigrated to the United
States in 1870. Useful look at an itinerant, touring actor in
the West and Midwest between the 1880s and the 1920s. As
a character actor Cosgrave made films in the 1940s.

2215   Crane, William. "A Forgotten Theatre: The Eagle Variety House."
        THEATRE ANNUAL 10 (1952): 61-68.

> History of the theatre in New York which opened in 1875;
> later known as the Standard and Manhattan.

2216   Crane, William H. "The Modern Cart of Thespis." NORTH AMERI-
        CAN REVIEW 94 (April 1892): 472-79.

> On theatrical life on the road in 1892 and predictions for the
> road's future.

2217   Davis, Ronald L. "They Played for Gold: Theater on the Mining
        Frontier." SOUTHWEST REVIEW 51 (Spring 1966): 169-84.

> General survey of theatre throughout the West after the gold
> rush.

2218   _____. "Sopranos and Six Guns: The Frontier Opera House as a
        Cultural Symbol." AMERICAN WEST 7 (November 1970): 10-17.
        Illus.

> Study of the frontier opera house during the last third of the
> nineteenth century.

2219   De Angelis, Jefferson, and Harlow, Alvin F. VAGABOND TROUPER.
        New York: Harcourt, Brace and Co., 1931. 325 p. Illus.

> Biography of the actor Jeff De Angelis (b. 1859). Good in-
> sight into barnstorming in the nineteenth century, especially
> in the West.

2220   Degitz, Dorothy M. "History of the Tabor Opera House at Leadville."
        COLORADO MAGAZINE 13 (May 1936): 81-89.

> On the opera house built in 1878 by H.A.W. Tabor.

2221   Dixson, Harry L. "Doff Your Hat to the Tent Shows." BILLBOARD
        (20 March 1926): 9, 13, 218-20.

> Homage paid to the early twentieth-century traveling tent
> show.

2222   Dunbar, Willis Frederick. "The Opera House as a Social Institution in
        Michigan." MICHIGAN HISTORY MAGAZINE 26 (October-December
        1943): 661-72.

2223   Eaton, Walter Prichard. "On the One-Night Stand." AMERICAN
        MAGAZINE 72 (June 1911): 246-56. Illus.

> Eaton's ideas and proposals for improving the state of "one-

night stand" performance fare "on the road" in America. Strongly urges community support of the theatre so that higher quality productions could be brought in.

2224 _____. "What's the Matter With the Road?" AMERICAN MAGAZINE 74 (July 1912): 359-68. Illus.

Theatre business was not good in 1911-12 either on the road or in major cities. Eaton cites reasons for this: growth of movie industry, poor management of small town theatres, "loss of public confidence in the theatre" (particularly in the quality of the road shows), and New York producers sending poor second companies on the road.

2225 _____. "The Repertoire Theatre in America." AMERICAN MAGA-ZINE 75 (June 1913): 58-63. Illus.

Laments the state of repertory theatre in Amerca at that time and expresses some hope for its future. Suggestions made for a more flourishing theatre in cities and towns outside the few major cultural capitals in the United States.

2226 Emmett, Frank. "Trouping Under Canvas." BILLBOARD (9 December 1911): 24, 97.

Repertoire theatre presented in traveling tent theatres.

2227 "End of an Era." NEWSWEEK 60 (27 August 1962): 54.

Death of tent show repertoire and Toby shows.

2228 Ericson, Robert Edward. "Touring Entertainment in Nevada During the Peak Years of the Mining Boom, 1876-1878." Ph.D. dissertation, University of Oregon, 1970. 309 p.

A study of the great number of performance tours to Nevada during this period, its greatest economic period in the nineteenth century. The kinds of entertainment brought in exemplified the most popular forms of entertainment of that period in America.

2229 Ernst, Alice Henson. TROUPING THE OREGON COUNTRY. Portland: Oregon Historical Society, 1961. xvii, 197 p. Illus., index, bibliog.

Frontier theatre in Oregon and Washington state (from the 1840s).

2230 Eytinge, Rose. MEMORIES OF ROSE EYTINGE. New York: Frederick A. Stokes, 1905. xii, 311 p. Illus.

Theatrical memoirs; good on Western theatres, especially in California and Nevada.

2231   Ford, George D. THESE WERE ACTORS. THE STORY OF THE CHAPMANS AND THE DRAKES. New York: Library Publishers, 1955. xx, 314 p. Illus., index.

Theatre on the frontier as exemplified by the families of Samuel Drake and William Chapman, Sr.

2232   Foster, J. Walter. "A Brief History of the Princess Stock Company." ANNALS OF IOWA 41 (Summer 1972): 969-94. Illus.

History of theatre and stock company in Des Moines, Iowa, from 1909 to 1930.

2233   Gaer, Joseph, ed. THEATER OF THE GOLD RUSH DECADE IN SAN FRANCISCO. New York: Burt Franklin, 1970. 101 p. Index (authors).

First published in 1935, this study begins with a five-page introduction followed by lists of plays, minstrel shows, extravaganzas, ballets, pantomimes, and operas.

2234   Gagey, Edmond McAdoo. THE SAN FRANCISCO STAGE. New York: Columbia University Press, 1950. xv, 264 p. Illus., index, bibliog.

Survey history; focus on the nineteenth century.

2235   Gallegly, Joseph [S.]. FOOTLIGHTS ON THE BORDER. The Hague, Netherlands: Mouton, 1962. 262 p. Illus., index.

History of theatre in Galveston and Houston, Texas, 1838 to the end of the century.

2236   Gilbert, Vedder M. "The American Theatre: Missoula, 1910, a Case History." MONTANA, THE MAGAZINE OF WESTERN HISTORY 18 (October 1968): 56-68.

The bill of fare at the Harnois Theatre (opened 1909), demolished 1968) in 1910; interesting look at a small town operation.

2237   Green, Elvena Marion. "Theatre and Other Entertainments in Savannah, Georgia, From 1810 to 1865." 2 vols. Ph.D. dissertation, University of Iowa, 1971.

2238   Hall, Linda. "Lillie Langtry and the American West." JOURNAL OF POPULAR CULTURE 7 (Spring 1974): 873-81.

Langtry's effect on the West, including coverage of her Western tours.

2239　Harrison, Shirley Madeline. "The Grand Opera House (Third Varieties Theatre) of New Orleans, Louisiana, 1971 to 1906. A History and Analysis." Ph.D. dissertation, Louisiana State University, 1965. 1,421 p.

2240　Hill, West T. THE THEATRE IN EARLY KENTUCKY, 1790–1820. Lexington: University Press of Kentucky, 1971. xiii, 205 p. Illus., index, bibliog.

Includes an exhaustive record of performances announced in Kentucky towns and in Cincinnati, Ohio, between 1790 and 1820.

2241　Hingston, Edward P. THE GENIAL SHOWMAN AND PICTURES OF A SHOWMAN'S CAREER IN THE WESTERN WORLD; BEING REMINISCENCES OF THE LIFE OF ARTEMUS WARD. London: John Camden Hotten, [1870]. vii, 519 p. Illus.

Account of Hingston's experiences on the road with Artemus Ward; describes Ward's "public career," the adventures they shared, the people and scenes they encountered. Entertaining, well-illustrated portrait of a showman on the frontier.

2242　Hogan, William Ransom. "The Theatre in the Republic of Texas." SOUTHWEST REVIEW 19 (July 1934): 374–401.

Actors and vaudevillians who blazed a theatrical trail into the Texas territory in the 1830s and '40s.

2243　Hollister, Katharine Stevens. "The Theatre in Jackson, 1890–1910." JOURNAL OF MISSISSIPPI HISTORY 17 (April 1955): 127–34.

History of a "one-night stand" city; minstrels, vaudeville, and theatre.

2244　Hood, Charles Newton. "The One-Night Stand. Some Memories of a Local Manager." SCRIBNER'S MAGAZINE 71 (March 1927): 285–94. Illus.

Firsthand account by a former local manager. Contains a good deal of specific information on such operations, such as finances, type of attractions, booking procedures, and complications. Programs illustrated. See next entry.

2245　_____. "Running a One-Night Stand in 'The Sticks.'" THEATRE MAGAZINE 48 (August 1928): 15, 52.

Nostalgic look at the "one-night stand" small-town theatres
in the days when they were most popular, i.e., 1890 to
1910, by a former small-town "opry" house manager. See
above.

2246   Hoyt, Harlowe. TOWN HALL TONIGHT. New York: Bramhall House,
       1955. ix, 292 p. Illus., index.

       History of entertainment in the 1880s and '90s on the stages
       of town halls and similar places of performance in small
       towns throughout the United States. Excellent introduction
       to the understanding of what show business was like in late
       nineteenth-century American heartland.

2247   Hume, Charles V. "First of the Gold Rush Theatres." THE CALIFOR-
       NIA HISTORICAL SOCIETY QUARTERLY 46 (December 1967): 337-44.
       Illus.

       History of The Eagle Theatres in Sacramento (built 1849) and
       San Francisco (1850).

2248   _____. "The Gold Rush Actor: His Fortunes and Misfortunes in the
       Mining Camps." AMERICAN WEST 9 (May 1972): 14-19. Illus.

       The hardships and privations that faced entertainers in the
       1850s.

2249   Jensen, Andrew F. "Two Decades of Trouping in Minnesota, 1865-1885."
       MINNESOTA HISTORY 28 (June 1947): 97-119. Illus.

       Detailed investigation into traveling troups which accounted
       almost entirely for the professional productions seen in Minne-
       sota.

2250   Johnson, Vance. "Hits in the Tall Corn." COLLIER'S 124 (20 August
       1949): 16-17, 72-73. Illus.

       Tent repertoire during its late period; on the Schaffner Players,
       the Madge Kinsey Players, and the Harley Sadler Co. Also
       a good deal on the character of Toby.

2251   Kelm, William E. "The People's Theatre." PALIMPSEST 9 (March
       1928): 89-105.

       On theatrical activity in Dubuque, Iowa, in the 1850s.
       Essay gives a good indication of what Midwest theatrical ac-
       tivity consisted of in general during this period.

2252   Kemmerling, James D. "A History of the Whitley Opera House in
       Emporia, Kansas: 1881-1913." EMPORIA STATE RESEARCH STUDIES

18 (March 1970): 1-72. Illus.

History of Whitley Opera House with a list of all theatrical and nontheatrical productions during the period covered.

2253 Klussen, Robert Dean. "The Tent-Repertoire Theatre: A Rural American Institution." Ph.D. dissertation, Michigan State University, 1970. 351 p.

Tent rep examined and conditions which contributed to its growth are analyzed. The Rosier Players of Jackson, Michigan are used as an example.

2254 Kusell, Maurice L., and Merritt, M.S. MARQUEE BALLYHOO. Los Angeles: Overland-Out West Publications, 1932. 276 p. Glossary.

Fictional account of the tent repertoire show.

2255 Leavitt, M[ichael]. B[ennett]. FIFTY YEARS IN THEATRICAL MANAGEMENT, 1859-1909.

For full entry and annotation, see item 1160.

2256 Lemmon, Sarah McCulloh. "Entertainment in Raleigh in 1890." NORTH CAROLINA HISTORICAL REVIEW 40 (Summer 1963): 321-37.

Covers all forms of entertainment, including theatre and the Metropolitan Hall with the McLean-Prescott Company.

2257 Lewis, Philip C. TROUPING: HOW THE SHOW CAME TO TOWN. New York: Harper and Row, 1973. 266 p. Illus., index.

A pleasant but frequently unreliable history of touring in America around the turn of the century. Good sense of atmosphere created, however.

2258 Ludwig, Jay F. "James H. McVicker and His Theatre." QUARTERLY JOURNAL OF SPEECH 46 (February 1960): 14-25.

Study of McVicker's theatre in Chicago illustrates the reduction in status of the provincial theatre manager in America. Period covered is 1857-96.

2259 Lyman, George D. THE SAGA OF THE COMSTOCK LODE: BOON DAYS IN VIRGINIA CITY. New York and London: Charles Scribner's Sons, 1934. xii, 399 p. Illus., notes.

Most useful for background material, although there is a specific section on Adah Isaacs Menken and MAZEPPA (pp. 270-84).

2260   McDermott, Douglas. "Touring Patterns on California's Theatrical Frontier, 1849-1859." THEATRE SURVEY 15 (May 1974): 18-28. Map.

Excellent analysis of touring system.

2261   _____. "The Development of Theatre on the American Frontier, 1750-1890." THEATRE SURVEY 19 (May 1978): 63-78. Map.

Author provides a framework within which one might grasp the nature and significance of the frontier and its theatre for the overall history of theatre in America. Extensive notes.

2262   McKennon, Marian. TENT SHOW. New York: Exposition Press, 1964. 192 p.

Narrative story of a traveling tent show playing popular reper-toire. Based on fact but written in a fictional form with no documentation.

2263   MacMinn, George R. THE THEATER OF THE GOLDEN ERA IN CALI-FORNIA. Caldwell, Idaho: Caxton Printers, 1941. 529 p. Illus., index, bibliog.

Selective history of mid-nineteenth-century theatre in Califor-nia; legitimate theatre and minor forms are included in this study.

2264   McVicker, James H. THE THEATRE: ITS EARLY DAYS IN CHICAGO. Chicago: Knight and Leonard, 1884. 88 p.

McVicker (1822-96), the pioneer theatre impresario, gives his own biased history of early Chicago theatre.

2265   Mahan, Bruce E. "At the Opera House." PALIMPSEST 5 (November 1924): 408-23.

Opera houses in Iowa up to 1884-85, with a discussion of various entertainments held in them.

2266   Malin, James C. "Traveling Theatre in Kansas: The James A. Lord Chicago Dramatic Company, 1869-1871." KANSAS HISTORICAL QUARTERLY 23 (Autumn 1957): 298-322; (Winter 1957): 401-38.

Detailed account of the Lord Company, 1869-71.

2267   Maloney, Martin J. "The Frontier Theatre." PLAYERS MAGAZINE 15 (July-August 1939): 6; 16 (October 1939): 6; (November 1939): 6; (December 1939): 6.

A "Six Gun Theatre" in Dodge City, Kansas, 1878-79.

2268   Marsh, John L. "Troupers at Tidioute." PLAYERS, MAGAZINE OF AMERICAN THEATRE 47 (February–March 1972): 138–44. Illus.

         History and description of the Grandin Opera House in Tidioute, Pennsylvania, from the 1860s to the turn of the century. Incorporated, in part, in items 2269 and 2271.

2269   _____, [and Acklin, Frank B.]. "Passion, Pathos and Platitude at the Grandin Opera House." STEPPING STONES 16 (January 1972): 454–57. Illus.

         Popular theatre fare at the Grandin Opera House, 1872–1904. Partially incorporated in item 2271.

2270   _____. "Esmeralda, A Drama for the Oil Region." STEPPING STONES 16 (September 1972): 482–86. Illus.

         Production of Frances Hodgson Burnett and William Gilette's ESMERALDA at the Library Hall, Warren, Pennsylvania, in 1883.

2271   _____. THE GRANDIN OPERA HOUSE, OR THEATRE ON THE KERO-SENE CIRCUIT, 1872–1904. Northwestern Pennsylvania Historical Study, no. 4. Warren, Pa.: Warren County Historical Society, 1973. [3], 50 p. Illus., notes and sources. Paper.

         History of the Grandin Opera House in Tidioute, Pennsylvania.

2272   _____. "Frank Coltman: Trouper from Tidioute." THEATRE SURVEY 16 (November 1975): 121–34.

         Career of a minor actor (fl. 1870–1900) and serves as a "case study of the combination system at work and the hardships of an actor typed into one role."

2273   _____. "For One Night Only, or a Look at Theatre on the Kerosene Circuit." PENNSYLVANIA MAGAZINE OF HISTORY AND BIOG-RAPHY 101 (April 1977): 205–16.

         History of the opera house in St. Petersburg, Pennsylvania, during the last half of the nineteenth century and its attractions. Taken together, Marsh's essays give an excellent picture of the typical small town theatre operation during the last half of the nineteenth century.

2274   Massett, Stephen C. DRIFTING ABOUT: OR, WHAT JEEMS PIPES OF PIPESVILLE SAW--AND--DID. New York: Carleton, 1863. 371 p. Illus.

         Massett arrived in San Francisco in 1849 and recounts conditions and theatrical personalities in that town and nearby towns during his frequent visits between 1849 and 1856.

2275 Mawson, Harry P. "In Stock." THEATRE MAGAZINE 17 (July 1913): 27-30. Illus.

Discusses the logistics and details of "stock" theatre operations in the teens.

2276 Meade, Edward Hoag. DOUBLING BACK, AUTOBIOGRAPHY OF AN ACTOR, SERIO-COMICAL. Chicago: Hammond Press, 1916. 180 p. Illus.

Life of a touring trouper from the 1880s to 1912 in the Midwest and West. Interesting look at the vagaries of a small-time player on the road in second-rate fare and in stock.

2277 Mickel, Jere C. FOOTLIGHTS ON THE PRAIRIE. St. Cloud, Minn.: North Star Press, 1974. [x], 226 p. Illus., index, bibliog., glossary.

History of many of the tent show theatre groups which traveled Midwestern small towns from the mid-1850s to World War II. One of the more complete histories.

2278 Miles, Carlton. "Doubling in Brass." THEATRE ARTS 10 (October 1926): 685-88.

Tent shows; an assessment of their status in 1926.

2279 Monson, William Neil. "Frontier Theatre Town. An Historical Study of Some Paratheatrical Activities in Visalia, California, 1852 to 1889." Ph.D. dissertation, University of Oregon, 1976. 406 p.

Chronological study, including accounts of dramatic, musical, variety, and circus attractions.

2280 Naeseth, Henrietta C.K. "Drama in Early Deadwood, 1869-1879." AMERICAN LITERATURE 10 (November 1938): 289-312.

Lists 168 plays performed between 1876-79.

2281 Nobles, Milton. "Some Unwritten Stage History." THEATRE MAGAZINE 24 (July 1916): 31-32.

Popular theatre in Omaha, Nebraska, 1867-68.

2282 O'Connor, Richard. "Thespis in Deep Freeze." In his HIGH JINKS ON THE KLONDIKE, New York: Bobbs-Merrill Co., 1954. Index, bibliog. Pp. 140-57.

Chapter 8 (pp. 140-57) "Thespis in Deep Freeze" deals with late nineteenth-century theatre on the Yukon. The author points out that it was on an approximate level with traveling tent shows and Uncle Tom companies in the States.

2283 O'Neil, Nance. "One-Night Stands of America." HARPER'S WEEKLY
54 (3 December 1910): 23.

> Brief article praising the "one-night stand" performance routine.
> O'Neil claims that the audience in small towns on the road
> were more attentive and receptive than those of major cities.

2284 Popkin, Zelda F. "The Tent Show Turns to Sex." OUTLOOK AND
INDEPENDENT 156 (24 September 1930): 128-30, 157. Illus.

> On traveling "Tent Show" repertoire companies and the "senti-
> mental and moralistic" melodramas they perform in which "sex"
> is the key element. Discusses audiences, company personnel,
> and preshow set up.

2285 Ranck, Edwin Carty. "What's Wrong with the Road?" THEATRE
MAGAZINE 26 (October 1917): 218.

> "The road" in 1917 was "beginning to think." Attractions
> had to be more carefully selected according to the more re-
> fined tastes of the individual communities.

2286 Revett, Marion S. A MINSTREL TOWN. New York: Pageant Press,
1955. xvi, 335 p. Illus., bibliog.

> Entertainment in Toledo, Ohio, from the 1840s to the turn of
> the century.

2287 Robinson, Clyde. "Tennessee Goes to the Show." THEATRE ARTS 16
(April 1932): 316-22.

> On Iberson's Tent Show Attraction; reconstructs a night's per-
> formance in Bolivar, Tennessee.

2288 Rodescape, Lois. "Tom Maguire, Napoleon of the Stage." CALIFOR-
NIA HISTORICAL SOCIETY QUARTERLY 20 (December 1941): 289-314;
21 (September 1942): 239-75.

> Good essay on Maguire's pioneer efforts in San Francisco from
> the 1850s to his death in 1896.

2289 Rohrer, Mary Katherine. THE HISTORY OF SEATTLE STOCK COM-
PANIES. Seattle: University of Washington Press, 1945. xiii, 76 p.
Index, bibliog., appendixes.

> History of stock companies in Seattle from 1890 to 1934.

2290 Rourke, Constance. TROUPERS OF THE GOLD COAST, OR THE RISE
OF LOTTA CRABTREE. New York: Harcourt, Brace and Co., 1928.
xiii, 262 p. Illus., index.

Biography of the actress and coverage of early theatre in California (1850s-80s).

2291 Rulfs, Donald J. "The Professional Theatre in Wilmington, 1870-1900." NORTH CAROLINA HISTORICAL REVIEW 28 (July 1951): 316-31.

Historical survey of all forms of entertainment.

2292 _____. "The Professional Theatre in Wilmington, 1900-1930." NORTH CAROLINA HISTORICAL REVIEW 28 (October 1951): 463-85.

Continuation of the above.

2293 Ryan, Pat M. "Tombstone Theatre Tonight." SMOKE SIGNAL no. 13 (Spring 1966): 50-76. Illus.

"A chronicle of entertainment on the Southwestern mining frontier" in Tombstone, Arizona, from 1879 into the 1890s.

2294 _____. "Wild Apaches in the Effete East: A Theatrical Adventure of John P. Clum." THEATRE SURVEY 6 (November 1966): 147-56. Illus.

Clum, an Indian agent, and Apaches performed in 1876 at the Olympic Theatre, St. Louis, Missouri.

2295 Schick, Joseph S. THE EARLY THEATRE IN EASTERN IOWA: CULTURAL BEGINNINGS AND THE RISE OF THE THEATRE IN DAVENPORT AND EASTERN IOWA, 1836-63. Chicago: University of Chicago Press, 1939. ix, 384 p. Bibliog. Paper.

Documented history; appendix lists all known theatrical performances and assorted entertainments in Davenport during period.

2297 Shafer, Yvonne B. "Tabor Opera House." PLAYERS, MAGAZINE OF AMERICAN THEATRE 43 (June-July 1968): 151-53. Illus.

Description of the opera house, built in 1879 in Leadville, Colorado, and the story of H.W. Tabor and his wife, Baby Doe.

2298 Shaw, Mary. "The Actress on the Road." McCLURE'S 37 (June 1911): 263-72.

Anecdotes and memoirs by a female trouper; illustrates dangers and hardships of the profession.

2299 Sherman, Robert L. CHICAGO STAGE, ITS RECORDS AND ACHIEVEMENTS. Chicago: Privately printed, 1947. 792 p. Illus.

History from 1834 to 1871 (the Great Fire).

2300   Slout, William Lawrence. THEATRE IN A TENT: THE DEVELOPMENT
        OF A PROVINDIAL ENTERTAINMENT. Bowling Green, Ohio: Bowling
        Green University Popular Press, 1972. 153 p. Illus., index, bibliog.

        Limited survey of repertoire tent shows in the United States
        from the late nineteenth century to the ultimate development
        of "Toby" as a stock character in the twentieth century.
        Especially good account of operational practices; useful bibli-
        ography.

2301   Stallings, Roy. "The Drama in Southern Illinois (1865-1900)." JOUR-
        NAL OF THE ILLINOIS STATE HISTORICAL SOCIETY 33 (June 1940):
        190-202.

        Focus on Cairo, particularly at the Athenaeum and the New
        Opera House.

2302   Stevens, Henry Bailey. "The Farmer Goes to the Theatre." DRAMA
        MAGAZINE 21 (May 1931): 7-8. Illus.

        On the nature of rural drama in the half century prior to
        1931. Discusses taste of the audience and the desire for
        higher quality production and more substantive plays.

2803   Stewart, George R., Jr. "The Drama in a Frontier Theater." In THE
        PARRIOTT PRESENTATION VOLUME, edited by Hardin Craig, pp. [183]-
        204. Princeton, N.J.: Princeton University Press, 1935.

        Productional reconstruction in the frontier theatre of Nevada
        City in the 1850s.

2304   Taylor, Justus Hurd. JOE TAYLOR, BARNSTORMER, HIS TRAVELS,
        TROUBLES AND TRIUMPHS, DURING FIFITY YEARS IN FOOTLIGHT
        FLASHES. New York: William R. Jenkins Co., 1913. [3], 248 p.
        Illus.

        A theatrical career that took Taylor during the 1850s to such
        frontier California towns as Volcano, Omega, Washington Flat,
        Sacramento, Petaluma, San Francisco, and Eureka.

2305   "A Theatrical Press Agent's Confession and Apology." INDEPENDENT
        59 (27 July 1905): 191-95.

        The imagination of a press agent on the road.

2306   Ware, Helen. "The Road." THEATRE 26 (July 1917): 26, 52.

        Ware's nostalgic look at the part of her career spent on the
        road.

2307   Watson, Margaret. SILVER THEATRE, AMUSEMENTS OF THE MINING

FRONTIER IN EARLY NEVADA, 1850-1864. Glendale, Calif.: Arthur H. Clark Co., 1964. 387 p. Illus., index, bibliog.

Well-illustrated and documented history.

2308 White, William Allen. "A Typical Kansas Community." ATLANTIC MONTHLY 80 (August 1897): 171-77.

A typical, fictional Midwestern town is characterized; low quality of theatre and the opera house is described.

2309 Willson, Clair Eugene. MIMES AND MINERS: A HISTORICAL STUDY OF THE THEATER IN TOMBSTONE. Tucson: University of Arizona Press, 1935. 207 p. Illus., bibliog. Paper.

Historical summary, 1881-1918, including details on the Bird Cage Variety Theater and Schieffelin Hall.

2310 Wilson, W.L. "The Tented Theatre." BILLBOARD (23 March 1912): 34, 84.

On tent repertoire theatre.

2311 Woods, Alan. "Popular Theatre in Los Angeles at the Turn of the Century." PLAYERS, THE MAGAZINE OF AMERICAN THEATRE 48 (April-May 1973): 173-78. Illus.

Operations of the New Los Angeles Theatre during the years 1896-1898.

2312 _____. "Frederick B. Warde: America's Greatest Forgotten Tragedian." EDUCATIONAL THEATRE JOURNAL 29 (October 1977): 333-44. Illus.

Study of a turn-of-the-century touring tragedian in the provinces. Excellent demonstration of the use of unpublished theses and dissertations in historical research.

2313 Yates, L.B. "Hittin' The Grit." SATURDAY EVENING POST 194 (13 August 1921): 8-9, 92-94. Illus.

Rural theatre in the United States.

2314 Zilboorg, Gregory. "The Stageless Road." DRAMA 11 (August-September 1921): 395-96, 401.

On lack of regional theatre in the '20s and a plea for the decentralization of the theatre.

Chapter 15

THE AMERICAN SHOWBOAT (FLOATING THEATRES)

This is a selective list of sources on showboats. The major purpose has been to annotate representative items and to supplement the excellent bibliography in Graham (item 2212).

2315   Aylward, William J. "Steamboating Through Dixie." HARPER'S MAG-
        AZINE 131 (September 1915): 512-22. Illus.

        Description of embryonic floating theatres on the Mississippi
        and a discussion of their origins.

2316   Basso, Hamilton. "Cotton Blossom, the South from a Mississippi Show-
        boat." SEWANEE REVIEW 40 (October 1932): 385-95.

        Description of a performance aboard the "Cotton Blossom,"
        detailing the theatre, play, actors, and audience. Great
        attention is paid to atmosphere.

2317   Briggs, Harold Edward. "Floating Circuses." EGYPTIAN KEY 3 (Sep-
        tember 1951): 19-23.

        Showboats at Cairo, Illinois, 1848-58.

2318   Bryant, Billy. CHILDREN OF OL' MAN RIVER: THE LIFE AND
        TIMES OF A SHOW-BOAT TROUPER. New York: L. Furman, [1936].
        xiv, 303 p. Illus.

        Story of a late showboat family in Ohio during the early
        twentieth century. Anecdotal and lacking in factual exact-
        ness.

2319   Burman, Ben Lucian. BIG RIVER TO CROSS. New York: John Day
        Co., 1940. Illus.

        See pages 163-85 for an explanation of showboat business in
        the 1930s, with sketches of captains, entertainers, and per-
        formances.

2320 Cocroft, Thoda. "The Floating Theatre Thrives." BOOKMAN 66 (December 1927): 396-98.

> Primarily a description of Captain Menke's "Golden Rod" (with photo), it also examines the ins and outs of showboating in the early 1900s and speculates as to the effects of Edna Ferber's SHOW BOAT on box office sales.

2321 Chrichton, Kyle. "Showboat" 'Round the Bend.'" COLLIER'S 104 (15 July 1939): 19, 40-41. Illus.

> Study of Captain Reynold's "Majestic" and a review of other showboats in operation at the time. Also discusses current attitudes toward the business and particular forms of entertainment.

2322 Donovan, Frank. RIVERBOATS OF AMERICA. New York: Thomas Y. Crowell, 1966. 298 p. Illus., index, select bibliog.

> Thorough history of riverboats, including chapters on "Floating Palaces" and "Drama and Glamour Afloat." Useful summary.

2323 Ford, George D. THESE WERE ACTORS. THE STORY OF THE CHAPMANS AND THE DRAKES. For full entry and annotation, see item 2231.

2324 Gordon, Jan, and Gordon, Cora. "Two English Tourists on a Showboat." LITERARY DIGEST 99 (29 December 1928): 38-41. Photo.

> A personal account of an evening spent on Captain Hi's "River Maid" (1918-29); notes the composition of the audience, the nature of the entertainment, and background of various performers.

2325 Graham, Philip. SHOWBOATS. THE HISTORY OF AN AMERICAN INSTITUTION. Austin: University of Texas Press, 1969. x, 224 p. Illus., index, bibliog., appendix.

> The most definitive study of America's floating theatre from 1831 to 1937. Covers the vehicles, stages, entertainments, entertainers, audiences, businessmen, and progress of its various forms. An appendix lists chronologically the principal showboats. Extensive bibliography. Originally printed in 1951.

2326 _____. "Showboats in the South." GEORGIA REVIEW 12 (Summer 1958): 174-85.

> Early development (1831-60), peak period (1878-1910), and decline (1911-43) of the showboat on the Southern waterways.

2327   Hunter, John Marvin. "Mollie Bailey, Great Showwoman." FRON-
       TIER TIMES 27 (April 1950): 183-93.

       Showboat performers on the Mississippi, about 1866, and the
       Bailey Family Show in Arkansas and Texas.

2328   Judd, "Doctor." "The Water Days of the Drama." THEATRE MAGA-
       ZINE 3 (August 1903): 202-204.

       Brief essay on Butler's Floating Theatre in the 1830s and the
       Chapman family of performers.

2329   Knox, Rose B. FOOTLIGHTS AFLOAT. Illustrated by E.P. Couse.
       Garden City, N.Y.: Doubleday, Doran and Co., 1937. xiii, 300 p.

       Fictional story of a showboat based on "French's New Sensa-
       tion" showboat and Captains A.B. and Callie French. The
       most famous fictional story of a showboat is, of course, Edna
       Ferber's. See Kreuger, below.

2330   Kreuger, Miles. SHOW BOAT: THE STORY OF A CLASSIC AMERI-
       CAN MUSICAL. New York: Oxford University Press, 1977. x, 247 p.
       Illus., index, seven appendixes.

       First full-history of the Kern-Hammerstein II musical. Al-
       though as a history of the musical, the text is somewhat disap-
       pointing, the opening chapter on the Edna Ferber novel (1926)
       gives a fair summary of showboat history, the nature of the
       boats, and the type of entertainment offered. Good illustra-
       tions of historic showboats.

2331   Lanthrop, West. RIVER CIRCUS. For full entry and annotation, see
       item 457.

2332   Martin, Pete. "River Singer." SATURDAY EVENING POST 220 (16
       August 1947): 30-31, 50, 52-54, 56; 220 (23 August): 28, 104-106,
       108; 220 (30 August): 26, 70, 73-74.

       The story of the Hughes' Floating Enterprise," a minor show-
       boat which sank after two years on the Ohio. Many vivid
       details of the construction of the theatre, the recruitment of
       acts and actors, the day-to-day life of the troupe, and the
       showboat scene of the late nineteenth and early twentieth
       centuries.

2333   M'Clure, W. Frank. "A Floating Theatre." SCIENTIFIC AMERICA 90
       (9 January 1904): 24. Illus.

       Discussion of the typical itinerary, design, and entertainments
       of a "modern" showboat.

2334   Pettit, Paul Bruce. "The Showboat Theatre." QUARTERLY JOURNAL
        OF SPEECH 31 (April 1945): 167-75.

> The showboat as a symbol of the spirit of the American fron-
> tier. Brief history from 1817 to 1937.

2335   Price, Willard. THE AMAZING MISSISSIPPI. New York: John Day
        Co., 1963. 188 p. Illus., index.

> Discussion of shows, showboats, and captains found on the
> Mississippi in the early 1960s.

2336   Schick, Joseph S. "Early Showboat and Circus in the Upper Valley."
        MID-AMERICA 32 (October 1950): 211-25.

> A study of the amalgamation of showboats and circus, particu-
> larly those vessels operated by the Spaulding and Rogers Circus
> Company in the Upper Mississippi Valley, 1833-58.

2337   Simpich, Frederick. "So Much Happens Along the Ohio River."
        NATIONAL GEOGRAPHIC MAGAZING 97 (February 1950): 177-212.
        Illus. (color).

> General description of civilization in the Ohio River Valley,
> including the showboats that frequented this waterway.

2338   Snook, Sidney. "The Showboat Drifts Downstream." SOUTH ATLANTIC
        QUARTERLY 41 (July 1942): 321-26.

> Summary survey of showboats, existent and extinct, emphasiz-
> ing the entertainer and the audience, now (1942) and in the
> past.

2339   Spears, Raymond S. "The Mississippi Boat Theatres." HARPER'S WEEKLY
        53 (4 September 1909): 13.

> Cursory history of showboats and their status in 1909; includes
> "circus-boats," "Medicine-boats," and "theatre-boats."

2340   Striker, Hopper. "Cruising Theatres of Long Ago." LITERARY DIGEST
        53 (22 July 1916): 189.

> Review of the floating theatres of the mid-1800s, detailing
> their origins and most memorable entertainers and performances.

APPENDIXES

Appendix A

SELECTED PERIODICALS AND SERIALS

A note on suspended periodicals and serials: Any serious student of popular entertainment and popular theatre should investigate beyond the selected resources listed below. There are literally dozens of periodicals devoted to specific forms that deserve attention. The field of magic alone has had a score of periodicals devoted to that art, although most are of the "how-to" variety; English periodicals devoted to variety or music hall were common. The sources listed here cover the peak period of popular entertainment or represent the best current periodicals on various forms, plus general scholarly journals of note. For a more detailed list of suspended periodicals of value in these areas, consult Arnott and Robinson (item 3) which lists over forty-five hundred sources, including a useful section on periodicals, and the following:

2341   Stratman, Carl J. AMERICAN THEATRICAL PERIODICALS, 1798-1967. A BIBLIOGRAPHICAL GUIDE. Durham, N.C.: Duke University Press, 1970. xxii, 133 p. Index.

>   The definitive guide to American theatrical periodicals, including those that deal with popular entertainment. Some 685 periodicals published in 122 cities and thirty-one states, with locations of issues noted in 137 libraries in the United States, Canada, and the British Library (formerly the British Museum) are listed. An indispensible source.

2342   _____. BRITAIN'S THEATRICAL PERIODICALS, 1720-1967: A BIBLIOGRAPHY. 2d ed. New York: New York Public Library, 1972. xxiv, 160 p. Index.

>   The major guide to British theatre periodicals, not only those that deal with legitimate theatre but dance, magic, variety, and so forth. The list is arranged chronologically and gives publishing information, plus locations of copies in the United States and in British libraries. Major revisions of the 1962 edition.

PERIODICALS AND SERIALS

2343   AMERICAN MUSEUM OF MAGIC NEWSLETTER. Marshall, Mich.:

1977-- . Irregular.

Address: Box 5, Marshall, Michigan 49068.

2344 AMUSEMENT BUSINESS. Nashville, Tenn. 1961-- . Weekly.

A Billboard Publication. Address: 1717 West End Avenue, Nashville, Tennessee 37203. Especially useful is the 75th anniversary issue, volume 81, no. 52, December 1969.

2345 BANDWAGON. Columbus, Ohio: Circus Historical Society, 1951-- . Bimonthly.

Address: 2515 Dorset Road, Columbus, Ohio 43221.

2346 BILLBOARD. Cincinnati, Ohio. Vols. 1-72. 1 November 1894-31 December 1960. Weekly (monthly, 1894-May 1900). Title and frequency vary.

Excellent source for popular entertainment. AMUSEMENT BUSINESS is a spinoff of BILLBOARD.

2347 BULLETIN FOR FRIENDS OF MAGIC HISTORY. Toledo, Ohio. Quarterly.

Address: Tigner Magic Supply Co., P.O. Box 7149, Toledo, Ohio 43615.

2348 THE CALL BOY. London: British Music Hall Society, 1963-- . Quarterly.

Address: 1 King Henry St., London N16.

2349 CALLIOPE. Baltimore, Md.: Clowns of America. Frequency varies.

Address: 717 Beverly Road, Baltimore, Maryland 21222.

2350 CHAPTER ONE. New York: Greater New York Chapter of ANTA, 1 (January 1954)-12 (Winter 1965). Monthly (irregular).

2351 THE CHAUTAUQUAN. Chautauqua, N.Y.: Chautauqua Literary and Scientific Circle, 1880-1913. Monthly.

2352 THE CHAUTAUQUAN DAILY (originally THE ASSEMBLY HERALD). Chautauqua, N.Y.: Chautauquan Institution, 1876-- . Daily (during annual session).

Records activities and news of Institution during its annual session.

2353 LE CIRQUE DANS L'UNIVERS. Vincennes, France: Club du Cirque, 1950-- . Quarterly.

Source of many excellent articles on circus history. Address: 11 Rue Ch-Silvestri, 94300 Vincennes, France.

2354 THE CONJURERS' MONTHLY MAGAZINE. New York. Vols. 1-2. September 1906-August 1908. Monthly.

Published and edited by Harry Houdini (The Conjurer's Magazine Publishing Co.), who contributed essays on the history of magic drawn from his own library and collection.

2355 DANCE RESEARCH JOURNAL. New York: Committee on Research in Dance, 1969-- . Biannual.

Address: See item 2455.

2356 THE DRAMA REVIEW. New York. 1955-- . Quarterly.

The single best source for essay dealing with the influence of popular entertainment on the avant-garde. Address: 51 West 4th Street, Room 300, New York, N.Y. 10012.

2357 EDUCATIONAL THEATRE JOURNAL. Washington, D.C.: University and College Theatre Association of the American Theatre Association, 1949-- . Quarterly.

Beginning with the March 1979 issue the title will change to THE THEATRE JOURNAL. Address: 1000 Vermont Avenue, N.W., Washington, D.C. 20005.

2358 THE ENTR'ACTE ALMANACK AND THEATRICAL & MUSIC HALL ANNUAL. 34 vols. London: W.H. Combes, 1873-1906.

Also called: THE ENTR'ACTE AND LIMELIGHT ALMANACK, and, from 1886, THE ENTR'ACTE ANNUAL. Marvelous comical cartoons of theatrical and popular entertainment personalities by Alfred Bryan highlight this publication.

2359 EQUITY. New York: Actors' Equity Association, 1915-- . Monthly.

Address: 1500 Broadway, New York, N.Y. 10036.

2360 THE ERA. 103 vols. London: Era Office, 1838-1939. Weekly.

Excellent on English forms of popular entertainment.

2361 THE ERA ALMANACK. Edited by Edward Ledger, Frank Desprez, and Alfred Barnard. London: "The Era," 1868-1919. Annual.

2362 GENII. Los Angeles, Calif. 1936-- . Monthly.

> Excellent general magic magazine. Address: P.O. Box 36068, Los Angeles, California 90036.

2363 THE GREEN ROOM BOOK. New York: Vols. 1-4. 1906-9. Annual.

> A who's who on the stage and an annual biographical record of the dramatic, musical, and variety world.

2364 GUIDE TO THE PERFORMING ARTS. New York: Scarecrow Press, 1957-- . Annual.

> Address: 52 Liberty Court, Metuchen, N.J. 08840.

2365 HOUDINI'S MAGIC MAGAZINE. Englewood Cliffs, N.J.: Stories Layouts and Press, 1977-- . Bimonthly.

> Address: 191 Middlesex Avenue, Englewood Cliffs, New Jersey 07632.

2366 JOURNAL OF POPULAR CULTURE. Bowling Green, Ohio: Popular Culture Association, 1967-- . Quarterly.

> Address: University Hall, Bowling Green University, Bowling Green, Ohio 43404.

2367 THE LINKING RING. Palatine, Ill.: International Brotherhood of Magicians, 1922-- . Monthly.

> Although not consistently strong on the history of magic, it should be consulted for the better years. Address: 820 North Inverway Road, Palatine, Illinois 60067.

2368 MAGIC, UNITY, AND MIGHT (M.U.M.). Lynn, Mass.: Society of American Magicians, 1911-- . Monthly.

> The early issues (1911-25) are rich in articles on the history of magic, including a number by Houdini. In the 1950s Milbourne Christopher contributed a number of valuable articles. Address: Lock Drawer 789-G, Lynn, Massachusetts 01903.

2369 MAGIC CIRCULAR. London: International Brotherhood of Magicians in England, 1906-- . Irregular.

2370 MAGICIAN MONTHLY. London, Engl. Vols. 1-35, no. 9. December 1904-August 1939. Monthly.

2371 MAGICOL. Chicago, Ill.: Magic Collectors Association, 1950-- . Quarterly.

> Address: 5103 North Lincoln Avenue, Chicago, Illinois 60625.

2372 MAHATMA. New York. Vols. 1-9. 1895-1906 (February). Weekly, monthly (irregular).

> Advertised as "The Only Paper in the United States Devoted to the Interests of Magicians, Spiritualists, Mesmerists." From July 1898 until it ceased publication, it was called the VAUDEVILLE, DEVOTED TO THEATRICALS. "LATE MAHAT-MA."

2373 MARQUEE: THE JOURNAL OF THE THEATRE HISTORICAL SOCIETY. Alameda, Calif.: Theatre Historical Society, 1969-- . Quarterly.

> The primary interest of this journal is in motion picture theatres. Address: P.O. Box 2416, Alameda, California 94501.

2374 MIME, MASK & MARIONETTE: A QUARTERLY JOURNAL OF PER-FORMING ARTS. New York: Marcel Dekker, 1978-- .

> Focus is on the forms of expression that rely on the movement and image of the body. Address: P.O. Box 11305, Church St. Station, New York, N.Y. 10249.

2375 MIME NEWS. Spring Green, Wis.: International Mimes and Panto-mimists, 1977-- . Bimonthly newsletter.

> Address: Spring Green, Wisconsin 53588.

2376 THE MUSIC HALL AND THEATRE REVIEW. London. Vols. 1-3. 1889-1912. Weekly.

2377 A NEWSLETTER FOR THE AMERICAN MUSICAL THEATER. Anchorage, Ala. 1975-- . Three times yearly.

> Address: University of Alaska, 3221 Providence Avenue, Anchorage, Alaska 99504.

2378 NEW YORK CLIPPER. New York. Vols. 1-72, no. 23. 1853-1924 (12 July). Weekly.

> Absorbed by VARIETY, 19 July 1924. Important publication, especially for information on vaudeville between 1900-1918 and for an early serialized history of the circus by T. Allston Brown in the early 1860s.

2379   NEW YORK CLIPPER ANNUAL. 7 vols. New York: F. Queen
       Publishing Co., 1874-1901.

2380   NEW YORK MIRROR. New York. Vols. 1-95. 1879-89 (19 January).
       Title variations as follows: NEW YORK DRAMATIC MIRROR, 26 Janu-
       ary 1889-1910 February 1917; then, DRAMATIC MIRROR, 17 February
       1917-9 October 1920; then, DRAMATIC MIRROR AND THEATRE WORLD,
       16 October 1920-24 December 1921; then, NEW YORK MIRROR, 31
       December 1921-April 1922. Weekly prior to April 1922, thereafter,
       monthly.

       Extremely important periodical.

2381   NINETEENTH CENTURY THEATRE RESEARCH. Tucson, Ariz. and
       Edmonton, Alberta, Canada. 1973-- . Biannual.

       Addresses: Department of English, University of Arizona,
       Tucson, Arizona 85721; Department of English, University of
       Alberta, Edmonton, Alberta, Canada T6G 2E5.

2382   OHIO STATE UNIVERSITY THEATRE COLLECTION BULLETIN. Colum-
       bus: Ohio State University, 1953-- . Annual (irregular; title varies).

       After 1971, title changed to THEATRE STUDIES. Address:
       Department of Theatre, Ohio State University, 154 North
       Oval Drive, Columbus, Ohio 43210.

2383   OUR PLAYERS GALLERY. New York. Vol. 1, nos. 1-2. 1900.
       Title variations as follows: THE THEATRE. Vols. 1-26. December
       1900-July 1917; then, THE THEATRE MAGAZINE. Vols. 27-53.
       August 1917-April 1931. Frequency varies.

       Issued quarterly from October 1900 to January 1901, then
       monthly from May 1901 to April 1931. Important publication
       and frequent articles on vaudeville and other forms of Ameri-
       can popular entertainment.

2384   PANTO! THE JOURNAL OF THE BRITISH PANTOMIME ASSOCIATION.
       London: British Pantomime Association, 1973-- . Semiannual.

       Address: 170 Clarence Gate Gardens, London NW1 6AR,
       England.

2385   THE PASSING SHOW: NEWSLETTER OF THE SHUBERT ARCHIVES.
       New York: Shubert Foundation, 1977-- . Biannual.

       Progress reports and surveys of the Shubert collection. See
       item 2440.

2386   PERFORMING ARTS RESOURCES. New York: Drama Book Specialists,
       1975-- . Annual.

Published in cooperation with the Theatre Library Association. Address: 150 West 52d Street, New York, New York 10019.

2387 PLAYBILL. New York: American Theatre Press, September 1957-- . Weekly.

Frequent brief essays of interest. Address: 151 East 50th Street, New York, New York 10022.

2388 THE PLAYER. New York: The White Rats of America, 1 (10 December 1909)-9 (April 1917). Weekly (subtitle varies).

Publication of the vaudeville performer's union. Suspended between 21 November 1913 and 22 December 1916.

2389 PLAYERS, MAGAZINE OF THE AMERICAN THEATRE. Dekalb.: Northern Illinois University, 1924-- . Monthly (October-May).

Since 1961, PLAYERS has been publishing more relevant essays on American popular entertainment. Address: National Collegiate Players, University Theatre, Northern Illinois University, Dekalb, Illinois 60015. Note: as of this writing, PLAYERS was planning to change addresses; its future seems uncertain.

2390 THE PUPPET MASTER. JOURNAL OF THE BRITISH PUPPET AND MODEL THEATRE GUILD. Yeading, Engl.: British Puppet and Model Theatre Guild, Irregular.

Address: 18 Maple Road, Yeading, Nr. Hayes, Middlesex, Engl.

2391 PUPPETRY JOURNAL. Pasadena, Calif.: Puppeteers of America, 1949-- . Bimonthly.

Address: Box 1061, Ojai, California 92023.

2392 QUARTERLY JOURNAL OF SPEECH COMMUNICATION: Falls Church, Va.: Speech Communications Association, 1915-- .

From 1915 to 1918, title was QUARTERLY JOURNAL OF PUBLIC SPEAKING; 1919-27, QUARTERLY JOURNAL OF SPEECH EDUCATION. Address: 5205 Leesburgh Pike, Falls Church, Virginia 22041.

2393 REVUE D'HISTOIRE DU THEATRE. Paris: Societ d'Histoire du Theatre, 1948-- . Quarterly.

Address: 98 Kellerman Boulevard, Paris (13e), France. Essays in English and French.

2394 THE SATURDAY BOOK. London, Engl. 1952-- . Annual.

A yearbook (various publishers) that contains numerous essays on topics of interest. George Speaight and Olive Cook, for example have been frequent contributors. Excellent illustrations.

2395 THE SHOW WORLD. Chicago: Show World Publishing Co., 1 (1907)-8, no. 6 (August 1911). Weekly.

All forms of entertainment covered--especially good on circus.

2396 SHOW WORLD. THE BLUE BOOK OF SHOW LANDS. New York: Show World Publishing Co., 1 (1925)-7, no. 3 (February 1928). Semi-monthly.

2397 SPHINX. Chicago (later New York). Vols. 1-52, no. 1. March 1902-March 1953. Monthly, then quarterly.

Many magicians consider this the best magic magazine ever published. John Mulholland, a noted magic historian, was its editor for many years. Numerous essays appeared in this journal on the history of magic.

2398 THE SPIRIT OF THE TIMES: A CHRONICLE OF THE TURF, AGRICULTURE, FIELDSPORTS, LITERATURE AND THE STAGE. New York. Vols. 1-31. 10 December 1831-22 June 1861. Also: THE SPIRIT OF THE TIMES AND NEW YORK SPORTSMAN. 10 September 859-13 December 1902. Weeklies.

Valuable sources of information on all phases of popular theatre during the time coverage of these publications; more useful than the daily newspapers.

2399 THE STAGE YEAR BOOK (title varies). London, Engl.: Carson and Comerford, 1908-- .

Theatrical directory and yearbook of British and Australian theatre. Earlier editions useful for music hall locations.

2400 THEATRE ANNUAL. Hiram, Ohio: Hiram College, 1942-- . Annual.

As of 1976 there have been thirty-two volumes; 1948-49, 1957-59, 1965-66 were combined issues. Address: Hiram College, Hiram, Ohio 44234.

2401 THEATRE ARTS MAGAZINE. Detroit (later New York): Society of Arts and Crafts, 1 (November 1916)-48 (December 1923).

Frequency and city of publication vary. Title variations as

follows: THEATRE ARTS MONTHLY, January 1924–October 1939; then, THEATRE ARTS, November 1939–January 1974. From December 1917 to January 1964 published in New York. Issued quarterly from November 1916 to October 1923, monthly from January 1924 to January 1964. Important magazine with frequent essays on all forms of popular entertainment.

2402   THEATRE NOTEBOOK. London, Engl.: Society for Theatre Research, 1945-- . Frequency varies.

Excellent for English forms of popular entertainment, especially pantomime in its early form. Address: 77 Kinnerton Street, London, S.W. 1.

2403   THEATRE QUARTERLY. Los Angeles and London, Engl.: Theatre Quarterly, January–March 1971-- . Quarterly.

American address: Division of Drama, University of Southern California, University Park, Los Angeles, California 90007.

2404   THEATRE RESEARCH INTERNATIONAL. Location has varied: International Federation for Theatre Research, 1958-- . Annual (irregular). Title varies.

Prior to October 1975 the title was THEATRE RESEARCH/RE-CHERCHES THEATRALES. Published now by Oxford University Press, London. In English and French.

2405   THEATRE SURVEY. Pittsburgh, Pa.: American Society for Theatre Research, 1960-- . Semiannual.

Frequency has varied; currently semiannual. Address: 1117 Cathedral of Learning, University of Pittsburgh, Pittsburgh, Pennsylvania 15213.

2406   THEATRICAL VARIETY GUIDE. Los Angeles: Theatrical Variety Publications, 1966-- . Annual.

Issued on behalf of the American Guild of Variety Artists. On contemporary variety in the United States; includes names and addresses of producers, agents, managers, plus other useful information for performers. Address: 1400 Cahuenga Boulevard, Los Angeles, California 90028.

2407   VARIETY. New York: Variety, 1905-- . Weekly.

Still the basic trade magazine for all forms of show business. Address: 154 West 46th St., New York, New York 10036.

2408   WHITE TOPS MAGAZINE. Indianapolis, Ind.: Circus Fans of America, 1928-- . Bimonthly.

Address: 4931 Rosslyn, Indianapolis, Indiana 46205. Issues have frequently been irregular.

2409   WHO'S WHO IN SHOW BUSINESS. THE NATIONAL DIRECTORY OF SHOW PEOPLE. New York: Who's Who in Show Business, 1950-- . Annual.

Performing artists and entertainers are listed under various categories.

2410   THE WORLD'S FAIR. Oldham, Engl.: 1904-- . Weekly newspaper.

The trade publication of the English fair and outdoor amusement industry. Address: Union Street, Oldham, England.

Appendix B

SPECIALIZED COLLECTIONS AND MUSEUMS

A note on collections: The following appendix contains a selective list of the more specialized collections and museums, the majority in the United States and a few in England. Some of the more extensive public collections are located in major libraries and should be consulted along with those suggested here. It is important, also, to know that some of the largest and most significant collections, especially in areas such as the circus, magic, and burlesque, are in private collections and are virtually inaccessible or unknown. Among the well-known libraries, the following are especially rich in materials on virtually every form of popular entertainment: the Harvard Theatre Collection, the Library of Congress, the British Library (formerly the British Museum), the Bibliotheque Nationale in Paris, the Library and Museum of the Performing Arts (The New York Public Library at Lincoln Center), the main branch of the New York Public Library. Although not listed below, the State Circus Museum, Leningrad, USSR, holds some sixty thousand items on the circus. Several smaller libraries, although not holding major collections, are important sources. The Buffalo and Erie County Public Library is strong on minstrel songbooks, the Western History Department of the Denver Public Library is good for Buffalo Bill Wild West programs, and the Nebraska State Historical Society and the Arizona Pioneers Historical Society hold material on the Wild West Show as well. English pantomime manuscripts can be found in the Larpent Collection in the British Library and in the Larpent Collection in the Huntington Library (San Marino, California). Other pantomime holdings are to be found in the Victoria and Albert Museum, the Finsbury Public Library, the Bodleian Library, the Birmingham Reference Library, the University of Kent, and the University of Chicago. The Enthoven Collection (currently at the Victoria and Albert) has a good collection on Juvenile Drama (Toy Theatres), as does the University of Toronto Library and Harvard. For additional sources of isolated groups of material and related collections, consult Young (item 97) or Veinstein (item 87).

COLLECTIONS AND MUSEUMS

2411   American Museum of Magic. Address: 107 East Michigan, Marshall, Mich. 49068.

> As of this writing, not yet open to the public. See item 2230.

2412   American Museum of Public Recreation. Address: Coney Island,
        Brooklyn, N.Y.

>   Artifacts relating to amusement parks. Especially notable is
>   the Dentzel Collection.

2413   Barnum Institute of Science and History. The P.T. Barnum Museum.
        Address: 804 Main Street, Bridgeport, Conn. 06600.

>   Personal effects of P.T. Barnum; memorabilia of Tom Thumb,
>   Jenny Lind, and local history items of interest. Also consult
>   holdings in the Bridgeport Public Library.

2414   British Theatre Museum. Address: Room 132 of the Victoria and
        Albert Museum, London.

>   Note: in 1980 the Museum is scheduled to move to the
>   Flower Market in Covent Garden, along with the combined
>   collections from other repositories throughout the London area.

2415   Buffalo Bill Historical Center. Address: P.O. Box 1020, Cody, Wyo.
        82414.

>   The Buffalo Bill Historical Center includes the Plains Indian
>   Museum, the Buffalo Museum, and the Whitney Gallery of
>   Western Art.

2416   Circus World Museum. Address: 415 Lynn Street, Baraboo, Wis.
        53913.

>   In addition to exhibits located in many of the Ringling Brothers
>   Circus winter quarters buildings, plus thirty-three acres of live
>   shows, displays, and a wonderful collection of circus wagons,
>   an excellent research library is located in the area. The
>   collection contains circus artifacts, route books, motion pic-
>   tures, periodicals, and standard library materials. A detailed
>   brochure on the holdings will be sent on request. This col-
>   lection is especially rich in advertising materials, including
>   original poster art.

2417   Curtis Theatre Collection. Address: Hillman Library, University
        of Pittsburgh, Pittsburgh, Pa. 15260.

>   Useful collection of about one hundred burlesque skits and bits,
>   formerly belonging to Billy Hagan, Billy Fields, and Billy
>   Foster (comics), although the holdings have been depleted
>   since first assembled.

2418   Detroit Institute of Arts Reference Library. Address: 5200 Woodward
        Avenue, Detroit, Mich. 48202.

The puppet file at the institute contains the collection of the late Paul McPharlin, the most extensive collector in the United States.

2419   Egyptian Hall Museum of Magical History.   Address: 1954 Old Hickory Boulevard, Brentwood, Tenn. 37027

One of the world's largest museums of memorabilia of magic and magicians.   Holds a number of major collections.

2420   FLOSSO HORNMANN MAGIC COMPANY.   Address: 304 West 34th Street, New York, N.Y. 10001.

Small but choice display of magical apparatus and memorabilia in America's oldest magic shop.

2421   H. ADRIAN SMITH MAGIC COLLECTION.   Address: North Attleboro, Mass. 02761.

This is currently a private collection and possibly the largest single collection of magic books in North America. It also contains good holdings of periodicals and memorabilia. The collection is slated to be housed, in the future, in Special Collections, John Hay Library, Brown University, Providence, R.I. 02912.

2422   HARRIS COLLECTION OF AMERICAN POETRY AND DRAMA.   Address: Specials Collection, John Hay Library, Brown University, Providence, R.I. 02912.

In addition to its major collection of published and unpublished texts of American plays, the Harris Collections contains a large number of minstrel and vaudeville joke books, sheet music, songbooks, and playlets.

2423   HERTZBERG CIRCUS COLLECTION.   Address: 210 West Market Street, San Antonio Public Library, Main Library Annex, San Antonio, Tex. 78205.

This collection has fairly extensive holdings of late nineteenth-century material, including a number of rare route books, a large Tom Thumb collection, handbills and heralds, a fine miniature circus, and standard library materials (twenty thousand volumes). Descriptive brochure available on request.

2424   THE HOBLITZELLE THEATRE ARTS LIBRARY.   Address: Humanities Research Center, University of Texas at Austin, Austin, Tex. 78712.

In addition to good general holdings on most aspects of popular entertainment and theatre, the Hoblitzelle houses the G.C.

Howard Collection on productions of UNCLE TOM'S CABIN,
The Messmore Kendall Collection which contains materials
gathered by Harry Houdini, and the Joe E. Ward Collection
of circus memorabilia.

2425 HOUDINI MAGICAL HALL OF FAME. Address: 4983 Clifton Hall,
Niagara Falls, Ontario, Canada.

Displays of illusions, apparatus, and memorabilia associated
with Harry Houdini and other noted conjurers.

2426 ILLINOIS STATE UNIVERSITY CIRCUS AND RELATED ARTS COLLEC-
TION. Address: Illinois State University, Normal, Ill. 61761.

Possibly the best-balanced collection in the United States.
Four thousand book items and fifty thousand nonbook items.
International in scope. See item 77. The Scholl and Van
Doveran book collection is located here, as is a near com-
plete record of the Ringling Brothers Circus before the com-
bination with Barnum and Bailey in 1919.

2427 JONATHAN KING COLLECTION. Address: London Museum, London,
Engl.

Major collection of juvenile drama. For a summary of the
holdings (and those of the Rippon-Fagg Collection), see
Katherine Hudson, "The Jonathan King Collection at the
Museum of London." THEATRE NOTEBOOK 30 (1976): 132-
33.

2428 LIBRARY OF CONGRESS. Address: Washington, D.C. 20540.

Other than general information on most forms of popular entertainment and theatre, the Library of Congress houses the
following magic collections: John J. and Hanna M. McManus
Collection, Morris N. and Chesley V. Young Collection,
and the Harry Houdini Collection.

2429 THE MAGIC CASTLE. Address: 7001 Franklin Avenue, Hollywood,
Calif. 90028.

This private club houses a magic library and magic memorabilia. See item 2351.

2430 THE MAGIC CELLAR. Address: Earthquake McGoon's Saloon, 630
Clay Street, San Francisco, Calif. 94111.

Displays in the drinking establishment of magic memorabilia.

2431 THE MAGIC CIRCLE LIBRARY. Address: 84, Chenies Mews, London
W.C.1.

Private club with a reference library on magic. In 1952, CATALOGUE OF THE REFERENCE AND LENDING LIBRARY, compiled by Colin Donister, was published (vi, 95 p.). See item 2255.

2432 THE MARGARET WOODBURY STRONG MUSEUM. Address: 700 Allen Creek Road, Rochester, N.Y. 14618.

More than three hundred thousand items, most as yet uncataloged, touching many areas of popular entertainment, i.e., carousel figures, Toby jugs, broadsides and other printed advertising material, and many other items relating to virtually every form of popular entertainment. At present the museum is seeking a new facility to house and display this mammoth collection.

2433 THE MUSEUM OF BROADCASTING. Address: 1 East 53d Street, New York, N.Y. 10022.

Significant radio and television programs from the 1920s to the present, selected, cataloged, and indexed.

2434 MUSEUM OF REPERTOIRE AMERICANA. Address: Route 1, Mount Pleasant, Iowa 52641.

Museum established by the Midwest Old Settler and Threshers Association in order to preserve the memory and artifacts of the tent rep movement. The museum houses a display area, a research center with hundreds of play manuscripts, a small theatre with the walls hung with drops and front curtains from old opera houses of small towns, and other items of interest. The curator, Mrs. Neil Schaffner, was a performer with her husband in Toby shows.

2435 THE NATIONAL MUSEUM OF MUSIC HALL. Address: Tyne and Wear County Council Museums, Sunderland, Engl.

This collection is located in premises adjoining the Sunderland Empire Theatre and is a comprehensive collection of daybills of the Empire from 1907 to 1931. For a description, see Joe Ging, "The National Museum of Music Hall." THEATRE NOTEBOOK 31, no. 2 (1977): 36-37, and 31, no. 3 (1977): 38.

2436 NEW YORK HISTORICAL SOCIETY. Address: 170 Central Park West, New York, N.Y. 10024.

Contains the Westervelt Collection of Barnum material plus a few items on the circus.

2437 POLLOCK'S TOY (THEATRE) MUSEUM. Address: 1, Scala Street, London, W.1.

Pollock's Toy Museum and the associated Toy Theatre Shop was established in 1808. In addition to a superb collection and display of toy theatres, the shop sells toy theatre models (modern reconstructions), books on toy theatre and puppetry, and related items.

2438 PRINCETON UNIVERSITY LIBRARY. Address: Princeton, N.J. 08540.

In addition to general materials on popular entertainment, the Princeton Library contains two specialized collections of interest: the McCaddon Collection houses the working papers of the Barnum and Bailey Circus, circa 1890 to 1910. McCaddon was the brother-in-law of James A. Bailey and an officer of the enterprise. Included in the collection are route books, inventories, scrapbooks, posters, couriers, contracts, diaries, and other useful items. In addition, there is miscellaneous material relevant to spectacles and Wild West shows. Although no longer in a self-contained collection, Princeton also owns the Carl Waring Jones Collection on magic, most of which is housed in the Rare Book Department.

2439 RINGLING MUSEUM OF THE CIRCUS. Address: Sarasota, Fla. 33577.

Not a major collection but valuable for the Glasier photographs, over a thousand glass negatives taken in the late 1890s. Some clippings and permanent exhibits.

2440 SHUBERT ARCHIVES. Address: 234 West 44th Street, New York, N.Y. 10036.

This collection, not as yet accessible, should prove to be an extremely valuable collection on popular theatre in America. The holdings are enormous, especially rich on the revue and musical forms of theatre.

2441 SOCIETY OF AMERICAN MAGICIANS MAGICAL HALL OF FAME. Address: Sunset and Vine, Hollywood, Calif. (located in the Home Savings and Loan Building).

Galleries of photographs of famous magicians, a library, an auditorium, and museum of magic. Life-size figures of magicians are displayed performing their most famous effects; valuable apparatus and magic memorabilia are featured.

2442 SOMERS, NEW YORK, HISTORICAL SOCIETY. Address: Somers, N.Y. 10589.

Materials on the early American circus, mostly from the local area called the "cradle of the American circus."

2443 SONGWRITERS HALL OF FAME MUSEUM. Address: One Times Square, New York, N.Y. 10036.

New museum dedicated to the art of the American songwriter. Displays of memorabilia and other items of interest.

2444 STOCK COLLECTION. Address: Lilly Library, Indiana University, Bloomington, Ind. 47401.

The Keith L. Stock Collection is probably the major collection of Victorian English drama in the United States, containing more than ninety percent of the plays published in England during the nineteenth century, plus other collateral material. See item 2078.

2445 TOM THUMB COLLECTION. Address: Middleboro Historical Museum, Middleboro, Mass. 02346.

This small collection of memorabilia relating to Tom Thumb and his wife is not open on a regular basis. Interested parties should contact Mrs. Lawrence Romaine, P.O. Box 272, Middleboro, Mass. 02346.

2446 THE WALTER HAMPDEN-EDWIN BOOTH THEATRE COLLECTION AND LIBRARY. Address: The Players, 16 Gramercy Park, New York, N.Y. 10003.

In addition to general materials relating to popular theatre, the library houses two major collections. The John Mulholland Magic Collection is a large private collection rich in rare books and periodicals in many languages, plus playbills and other magic memorabilia. The Chuck Callahan Burlesque Collection contains nearly three hundred vaudeville and burlesque skits, music in manuscript, photographs, programs, a group of about two hundred wisecracks, a watercolor copy of a vaudeville scenic backdrop, a typed biography of Chuck Callahan (a well-known burlesque doctor or fix-it man for others' sketches), a rough index to the skits, and various other souvenirs of burlesque days.

Appendix C
CONCERNED ORGANIZATIONS

2447 American Puppet Arts Council. Address: 59 Barrow Street, New York, N.Y. 10014.

2448 American Society for Theatre Research. Address: Department of English, Queens College, Flushing, N.Y. 11367.

> Concerned with all aspects of the American theatre; publishes THEATRE SURVEY (see item 2405).

2449 British Music Hall Society. Address: 1 King Henry Street, London N 16. Membership inquiries should be addressed to 67 Russell Court, Woburn Place, London, W.C. 1.

> Aims and objects of the society are to preserve the history of the British Music Hall and the artistes who created it and to encourage and support the entertainers of the present day. Publishes THE CALL BOY (see item 2348).

2450 British Pantomime Association. Address: 170 Clarence Gate Gardens, London, N.W. 1.

> Interest in the history and tradition of English (Christmas) pantomime. Publishes PANTO! (see item 2384).

2451 British Theatre Association. Address: 9 Fitzroy Square, London, W. 1.

2452 Circus Fans of America. Address: 4931 Rosslyn, Indianapolis, Ind. 46205.

> Publishes WHITE TOPS MAGAZINE (see item 2408).

2453 Circus Historical Society. Address: 2515 Dorset Road, Columbus, Ohio 43221.

> Publishes BANDWAGON (see item 2345).

2454   Clowns of America. Address: 2300 Foster Avenue, Parkville, Md. 21234.

       Publishes CALLIOPE (see item 2349).

2455   Committee on Research in Dance (CORD). Address: Dance Department, Educ. 675 D, New York University, 35 West Fourth Street, New York, N.Y. 10003.

       Publishes DANCE RESEARCH JOURNAL (see item 2355).

2456   Friends of Old Time Music. Address: 321 Sixth Avenue, New York, N.Y. 10014.

2457   Hollywood Comedy Club. Address: 2567 South Armacost, West Los Angeles, Calif. 90064.

       This is a males only organization as of this writing.

2458   International Association of Amusement Parks and Attractions. Address: 7222 West Cermak Road, Suite 303, North Riverside, Ill. 60546.

2459   International Brotherhood of Magicians. Address: 114 North Detroit Street, Kenton, Ohio 43326.

       Publishes THE LINKING RING (see item 2367).

2460   International Centre for Research on Traditional Marionettes. Address: 10 Quai de Rome, Liege B-4000, Belgium.

2461   International Mimes and Pantomimists. Address: Route 3, Spring Green, Wis. 53588.

       Publishes MIME NEWS (see item 2375).

2462   The Lambs. Address: 5 East 66th Street, New York, N.Y. 10019.

       Social organization of men connected with various forms of entertainment.

2463   The League of Historic American Theatres. Address: 3208 North Monroe Street, Wilmington, Del. 19802.

       Concerned with the restoration and reclaiming of historic buildings used as places of live entertainment.

2464   The Magic Castle (Academy of Magical Arts & Sciences). Address: 7001 Franklin Avenue, Hollywood, Calif. 90028.

       A private club with memorabilia, library, and live performances.

Admission for nonmembers only with a member or with a guest card signed by a member.

2465 The Magic Circle. Address: 84, Chenies Mews, London, W.C. 1.

Private club with clubrooms, museum with fine exhibits of magical apparatus and memorabilia, magical library, and theatre. Admissions are limited. For information write: The Secretary, 12 Hampstead Way, London, N.W. 11.

2466 The Magic Collectors Association. Address: 5103 North Lincoln Avenue, Chicago. Ill. 60625.

Publishes MAGICOL (see item 2371).

2467 The Masquers. Address: 1765 North Sycamore Avenue, Hollywood, Calif. 90828.

2468 The National Society for the Preservation of Tent, Folk and Repertoire Theatre. Address: Route 1, Mount Pleasant, Iowa 52641.

Founded by the Midwest Old Settlers and Threshers Association.

2469 Outdoor Amusement Business Association. Address: 4600 West 77th Street, Minneapolis, Minn. 55435.

2470 The Players. Address: 16 Gramercy Park, New York, N.Y. 10003.

Private social organization for members and friends of the arts.

2471 Popular Culture Association. Address: University Hall, Bowling Green University, Bowling Green, Ohio 43404.

P.C.A. in association with Bowling Green University's Center for the Study of Popular Culture publishes three quarter journals: POPULAR CULTURE, POPULAR FILM, AND POPULAR MUSIC AND SOCIETY, as well as books in the area of popular culture.

2472 Puppeteers of America. Address: 5 Cricklewood Path, Pasadena, Calif. 93023.

Publishes PUPPETRY JOURNAL (see item 2391).

2473 The Society for Theatre Research. Address: 77 Kinnerton Street, London, S.W. 1. Membership information: 14 Woronzow Road, London NW8 6QE.

Publishes THEATRE NOTEBOOK (see item 2402).

2474　The Society for the Preservation of Variety Arts.　Address:　940
　　　　Figueroa Street, Los Angeles, Calif. 90015.

　　　　　　As of this writing, this organization is just getting underway.
　　　　　　Its aim is to save the past knowledge of the great variety
　　　　　　entertainers.　Part of the organization is The Variety Arts
　　　　　　Playhouse which features live performances; a museum–library
　　　　　　will house a major collection of materials relating to variety.
　　　　　　A private club similar to the Magic Castle (see item 2464).

2475　Society of American Magicians.　Address:　Aqueduct Road, RFD #2,
　　　　Peekskill, N.Y. 10566.

　　　　　　Publishes M.U.M. (see item 2368).

2476　The Sonneck Society.　Address:　69 Undine Road, Brighton, Mass.
　　　　02135.

　　　　　　Concerned with all aspects of music in America.

2477　Theatre Historical Society.　Address:　P.O. Box 2416, Alameda, Calif.
　　　　94501.

　　　　　　Principal concern is with the reclamation of old theatres, in
　　　　　　particular movie palaces.　Publishes MARQUEE (see item
　　　　　　2373).

2478　Theatre Library Association.　Address:　111 Amsterdam Avenue, New
　　　　York, N.Y.　10023.

　　　　　　Publishes PERFORMING ARTS RESOURCES (see item 2386) and
　　　　　　BROADSIDE (a newsletter).

INDEXES

AUTHOR INDEX

This index includes all authors, editors, compilers, and contributors cited in this text. It is alphabetized letter by letter. Numbers, except where preceded by "p.," refer to entry numbers.

A

Abbott, George 154, 1852
Abrams, Aleck 767
Adams, Allen J. 2202
Adams, Franklin P. 1051
Adams, Joey 201, 1052
Adams, William Davenport 2059
Adamson, Joe 1053
Addison, William 731
Aflalo, F.G. 1487
Agate, James 276-77
Albee, Edward F. 1054
Albert, Allen D. 1268
Albert, Frank L. 888
Alden, William Livingston 768
Aldridge, A. Owen 1224
Alexander, H.L. 1225
Alfredson, James B. 1307
Aline, Mackenzie Taylor 278
Allen, Edward 533
Allen, Fred 201
Allen, Frederick Lewis 98
Allen, Ralph G. 1226, 1427,
 1656-59
Altick, Richard D. 1, 279, 732,
 769
Amacher, Richard E. 2141
Amidon, C.H. 355

Anderson, Hugh Abercrombie 1485
Anderson, Jean 1727
Anderson, John 156, 1853
Anderson, John Murray 1485
Andrews, Herbert C. 1428
Angier, Roswell 1227
Angoff, Charles 1935
Anthony, Edward 539
Appel, Livia 157
Appelbaum, Stanley 1854-55
Apperson, G.L. 1429
Appignanesi, Lisa 2
Appleton, William W. 770, 1969
Apter, Andrew W. 2060
Archer, Stephen p. xv
Archer, William 1728, 1970
Ardizzone, Edward 35
Ardman, Harvey A. 771
Ardmore, Jane Kesner 1499
Armstrong, William A. 1971-72
Arnold, Richard L. 1430
Arnott, James Fullarton 3
Aronson, Arnold 889
Aronson, Boris 356
Aronson, Rudolph 1486
Arrington, Joseph Earl 1431-33
Arthur, Thomas 1660
Arundell, Dennis 280, 1973

Author Index

Asbury, Herbert 99
Astley, Philip 81
Atherton, Lewis 100
Atkinson, Brooks 158, 1856
Austin, E.L. 734
Austin, John 1142
Avery, Emmett L. 1661-62
Avery, S.P. 772
Aylward, William J. 2315

B

Bacon, Gertrude 773
Bader, Arno Lehman 4
Bailey, Olga 534
Baird, Bil 1384
Baker, H. Barton 281, 1974
Baker, Michael 1975
Baker, Roger 5
Baker, Seymour O. 2061
Bakner, Andrew J. 851
Bakshy, Alexander 1056-57
Balcom, William 1578
Baldwin, Raymond P. 1877
Ballantine, Bill 357, 535
Bamberger, Louis 1729
Bandelier, Adolf F. 159
Bank, Rosemarie Katherine 2142
Banks, George Linnaeus 536
Bantock, Granville 1487
Bapst, Germaine 1434
Baral, Robert 101, 1488
Barber, Rowland 1228
Barber, W. Charles 1058
Baring, Maurice 1385
Barker, Barbara M. 1489
Barker, Clive 1976, 2024
Barker, Kathleen 282-83
Barnabee, Henry Clay 1857
Barnard, Alfred 2361
Barnes, Clive 1571
Barnes, Djuna 1858
Barnum, Phineas T. 81, 774-76
Barrett, Marvin 102
Barrett, Richmond 890
Barrie, J.M. 1821
Barton, Bob 358, 928
Baskervill, Charles Read 6
Bason, Fred 1729a
Basso, Hamilton 2316

Batchelder, Marjorie 1386
Bateman, Dr. E.J. 360, 537
Batistell, Annabel ("Fanne Fox")
    1229
Baumann, Charly 538
Baxter, Alice 2203
Baxter, Sylvester 891
Bayes, Nora 1059
Baylis, Lilian 2002
Bayly, Charles, Jr. 359
Beal, George Brinton 361
Beard, Miriam 938
Beatty, Clyde 539
Beaumont, Charles 103
Beaumont, Cyril W. 1663
Beaver, Patrick 735
Beer, Thomas 104
Beerbohm, Max 284-87, 1730
Behrens, E. 589
Beitz, Lester U. 610
Belasco, David 1859, 2060
Belcher, Fannis S., Jr. 2143
Belcher, Horace G. 975
Bell, Archie 1060
Bell, Campton 2204
Bendiner, Robert 105
Benet, Laura 777
Bennett, Ernestine 2206
Bennett, Joan 160, 1860
Benny, Jack 201
Bentley, James M. 611
Benton, Joel 778-79
Bergainnier, Earl F. 2062
Berkeley, Philip 2205
Bernard, Charles 362
Bernheim, Alfred 1861
Berry, W.H. (Bill) 1490
Bertram, Charles 1318-19
Bertram, James Celass.
    See Paterson, Peter
Bestor, Arthur Eugene, Jr. 1269
Bettmann, Otto 141
Betts, John Rickards 780
Beuick, Marshall D. 1061
Bier, Jesse 106
Bigelow, Joseph 1230
Binder, Pearl 288
Bird, Anthony 736
Birdoff, Harry 2144
Birks, Reginald 289

Bishop, Conrad Joy 1977
Bishop, George 582
Blair, Walter 107, 2145
Blanchard, Edward Laman 1664
Blayney, Glenn H. 2063
Blegen, Theodore C. 1435
Blesh, Rudi 161, 976, 1062, 1491
Blind, Adolphe 1308
Bliven, Bruce 1270
Bloom, Ursula 1492
Blumenthal, George 162, 1862
Boardman, Fon W., Jr. 107a
Boardman, William H. ("Billy") 1731
Bode, Carl 108
Bodin, Walter 781
Boe, Roy A. 1436
Boles, Don 852
Bolitho, Hector 1493
Bolton, Guy 1653
Bond, Frederick W. 163, 1863
Bond, Jessie 1494
Bontemps, Arna 999
Booth, Charles 1732
Booth, John Bennion 290–96
Booth, Michael R. 1978–80, 2024, 2064–70
Born, Wolfgang 1437–38
Bostock, Edward Henry 363
Bostock, Frank 540
Botkin, B.A. 109
Bouissac, Paul A.R. 364, 541, 583
Bowen, Elbert R. 164, 365–66, 977
Bowen, Ezra 110
Bowman, Harry P. 367
Boxell, Paul J. 782
Boyak, Burt 1088
Boyar, Jane 1088
Boyer, Robert 1175
Boymer, Gunter 1387
Braathen, Faye O. 368
Braathen, Sverre O. 368
Bradbury, Joseph T. 369–73, 612–13
Bradford, Gamaliel 783
Bradley, John Lewis 1733
Bradna, Fred 374
Brady, Cyrus T. 1063
Brady, William A. 165
Braithwaite, David 737, 853, 892
Brand, Jean 929

Brandreth, Gyles 1665–66, 1736a
Brasmer, William 614, 2146
Bratton, Jacquelin S. 1734–35
Braugh, James 1593
Brayley, Arthur W. 784
Brazier, Marion Howard 1864
Breitenbach, Edgar 1865
Briggs, Harold Edward 166, 1064, 2206, 2317
Brininstool, E.A. 725
Bristol, Michael 7
Bristow, Eugene Kerr 1065–68, 1736, 1948
Britt, Albert 1271
Broadbent, R.J. 1667
Brock, H.I. 1069
Brooks, Van Wyck 145
Broun, Heywood 249
Brown, Daniel J. 167
Brown, David J. 1866
Brown, Henry Collins 167–69, 1867–68
Brown, Ivor 1737
Brown, John Mason 170, 1869
Brown, Maria Ward 584
Brown, T. Allston 978, 1070, 1870
Browne, Ray B. 139, 172, 979, 1071
Browne, Walter 8
Brownstein, Oscar 9
Bryan, Alfred 1766
Bryan, J. III 785
Bryant, Billy 2318
Bryant, Clifton D. 886
Buckland, F.T. 786
Buel, J.W. 615
Buley, R. Caryle 958
Bunn, George W. 2207
Burg, David F. 738
Burgess, C.F. 1668
Burgess, Hovey 542–43
Burke, Billie 1495–96
Burke, John 618
Burke, Peter 9a
Burke, Thomas 297
Burleigh, Henry T. 980
Burlingham, H.J. 1320–22
Burman, Ben Lucian 2319

Burnand, Sir Francis C. 298, 1738
Burnett, Frances Hodgson 2270
Burrows, Abe 226
Burt, William P. 930
Burton, Jack 173, 1497
Busby, Roy 1739
Byng, Douglas 1740
Byram, John 1498

C

Caffin, Caroline 1073
Cahn, William 174
Calkins, Earnest Elmo 111
Calthrop, Dion Clayton 1741
Camp, John 931
Campbell, Walter. See
 Vestal, Stanley
Canfield, Mary C. 1074
Cannell, John Clucas 1323
Cantor, Eddie 175-76, 201, 1075,
 1499, 1500-1502
Cantor, Norman I. 177
Carmichael, Bill 788
Carothers, Robert L. 1439
Carrillo, Leo 1076
Carrington, Hereward 854
Carrington, Richard 789
Carroll, Charles Michael 1440
Carson, Gerald 178, 932-33
Carson, Saul 1077
Carson, William G.B. 2208-11
Carter, Randolph 1503
Carver, Gordon M. 375
Case, Victoria 1272
Castaigne, Andre 10
Castle, Irene 1504
Castle, Marian Johnson 1273
Cautero, Gerard Salvatore 11
Cavanah, Frances 790
Cavin, Lee 791
Ceram, C.W. [Kurt W. Marek] 1441
Chambers, E.K. 12
Chancellor, Edwin Beresford 299,
 1981
Chaplin, Charles 300-301
Chapuis, Alfred 1442
Charles, Barbara F. 893
Charles, Lucille Horner 585

Burton, William 2072

Charters, Ann 1505
Charters, Samuel B. 180
Chase, Edwin T. 2212
Chase, Gilbert 181, 981
Cheney, Louise 619-20
Cheshire, David F. 302, 1742-43
Chevalier, Albert 1744-45
Chevalier, Florenz 1746
Chevalier, Maurice 22
Chindahl, George L. 376
Chipman, Bert J. 377
Chirgwin, G.H. 1747
Christensen, C.C.A. 1456
Christopher, Milbourne 1324-30,
 1376, 2368
Churchill, Allen 112, 182-83,
 1506, 1871-72
Claflin, Edward 13
Clair, Colin 792
Clancy, Foghorn 621
Clapp, William W., Jr. 184, 379,
 1873
Clark, Hyla M. 1331
Clark, Larry D. 2147-48
Clark, Neil M. 717
Clarke, John S. 380
Clarke, Norman 1507
Clarke, Sidney W. 1308, 1332
Clausen, Connie 544
Clemens, Samuel L. 622
Clement, Herb 381
Clifford, F.J. 934
Cline, Julia 2149
Clinton-Baddeley, V.C. 303,
 1669, 1982, 2071
Cloutman, John C. 444
Coborn, Charles 1748
Coburn, Charles 2213
Coburn, Walt 623-24
Cochran, Charles B. 14-15, 201,
 1426, 1814
Cockton, Henry 16
Coco the Clown [Nicholai Poliakoff]
 586
Cocroft, Thoda 2320
Cody, Louisa Frederici 625
Cody, William Frederick 81, 626,
 671
Coggin, Frederick Marsh 1670
Cohan, George M. 1508

Cohen, Octavus Roy 1078
Colby, Elbridge 1983
Cole, Richard J. 1671
Coleman, William S.E. 2150
Collier, Constance 1509
Collier, Edmund 627-28
Collier, Gaylan 2151
Collier, John Payne 1388
Collings, Ellsworth 629
Collins, Pete 793
Collins, Sewell 1079
Compardon, Emile 17
Compton-Rickett, Arthur 344, 1832
Coneys, Anthony. See
  Gorham, Maurice
Congdon, Don 113
Conklin, George 382
Conlin, James W. 1274
Conolly, L.W. 18, 1984
Conover, Richard E. 383-89
Conquest, Betty 1682
Conrad, Earl 1510
Cook, Doris E. 1874
Cook, Dutton 304, 1672, 1985
Cook, Gladys Emerson 587
Cook, Olive 739, 1333, 1441,
  1443
Cooke, Conrad William 1444
Cooper, Courtney Ryley 390-92,
  545-46, 625, 630
Cooper, Frank C. 631
Cooper, Tex 632
Coplan, Maxwell Frederick 393
Copley, Frank B. 1080
Corbett, Elizabeth F. 2152-53
Corbin, John 206
Corio, Ann 1231
Cosgrave, Luke 2214
Cotes, Peter 401, 1749
Cottrell, Leonard 794
Coup, William C. 394
Court, Alfred 547-48
Courtney, W.B. 633
Couse, E.P. 2329
Coward, Noel 1512-13, 1602
Cowell, Joseph 395
Cowen, John 1750
Cox, Harvey G. 19
Cox, Paul Ronald 2154
Coxe, Antony D. Hippisley 81,
  396-98
Crane, Warren E. 1081

Crane, William 2215
Crane, William H. 2216
Cranton, Heath. See
  Newton, Henry Chance
Crawford, Captain Jack 634
Crawford, Mary Caroline 1875
Cressy, Will M. 1082
Crews, Harry 855
Crichton, Kyle 1083-2321
Croce, Benedetto 20
Croft-Cooke, Rupert 399-402, 635
Croghan, Leland A. 2072
Cross, Gilbert B. 2073
Crothers, J. Frances 1389
Crouse, Russell 114
Crowder, Richard 115
Crowley, Alice Lewinsohn 1514
"Crowquill, Alfred" [Alfred Henry
  Forrester] 1673
Croxton, Arthur 1751
Croy, Homer 636, 1515
Cuber, John F. 894
Cummings, E.E. 895, 1232, 1516
Currell, David 1390
Curvin, Jonathan W. 2155
Cushing, Charles Phelps 403
Cutler, Jean Valjean 2074

D

Daam, Paul Alexander 1986
Daguerre, Louis J.M. 1445
Dahl, Curtis 1446-48
Daily, George L., Jr. 1307
Dale, Alan 1517
Dallas, Duncan 740
Dallas, Sandra 116
Daly, Brian 1745
Daly, John Jay 982
Daly, Joseph Francis 1876
Damase, Jacques 21
Damon, Foster S. 983
Daum, Paul Alexander 404, 2074a
Davenport, Francis Garvin 984
David, J. Frank 2156
Davis, John Russell 1084
Davidson, Frank C. 985
Davidson, Randall 896
Davies, Ayres 405
Davies, Thomas 1987
Davis, A.W. 185
Davis, Hartley 406, 1085-87

Author Index

Davis, Michael Marks, Jr. 186
Davis, Owen 2075-76
Davis, Ronald L. 2217-18
Davis, Sammy, Jr. 1088
Davison, Peter 1752
Davy, Kate 1089
Day, Charles H. 978, 986, 1070
Day, Donald 1518-19
Day, Susan Stockbridge 1520
Deahl, William E., Jr. 637-39
De Angelis, Jefferson 2219
DeBelle, Starr 857
Debus, Allen G. 68
Decastro, Jacob 407, 1674
De Courville, Albert 305
De Frece, Lady Vesta Tilley 1753
Degen, John Alden III 2077-78
Deghy, Guy 1521
Degitz, Dorothy M. 2220
Delavoye, Will [William Lambert]
    408
Delcourt, Marie 795
DeLeon, Walter 1092
Delgado, Alan 306
Demarest, Michael 987
Dembroski, Theodore M. 858
de Mille, Agnes 1522
Dempsey, David 1877
Denier, Tony 409
Denney, Reuel 117
Dent, Edward J. 1988
Derval, Paul 22
Desmond, Alice Curtis 796
Desprez, Frank 2361
De Tocqueville, Alexis 143
Detzer, Karl W. 1275, 1278
Devant, David [David Wighton]
    1334-35, 1367
De Wolff, J.H. 640
Dexter, T.F.G. 23, 741
Dhotre, Damoo G. 549
Dibdin, Charles 1989
Dibdin, Thomas 1422
Dickens, Charles 307, 1675, 1990,
    2071
Dillon, William A. 187
DiMeglio, John E. 1093-94
Dimmick, Ruth Crosby 188
DiMona, Joe 1231

Dingwall, Eric John 797
Dircks, Henry 1336, 1449
Dircks, P.T. 1523, 2079
Disher, Maurice Willson 24, 81,
    308-12, 410, 1676, 1754-56,
    1991, 2080-82
Distler, Paul A. 1095-96
Dithmar, Edward A. 1878
Dixson, Harry L. 2221
Dodd, Ken 1799
Dodd, William G. 411
Dodswell, Jack 856
Doenecke, Justus D. 742
Doerflinger, William 1337
Dolkey, Matthew 2083
Dondore, Dorothy 1450
Donohue, Joseph W. 2024, 2084-85
Donovan, Frank 2322
Donovan, Richard 935
Doran, John 25
Dormon, James H. 988
Dorn-Heft, Dolores 2157
Dorson, Richard M. 118-19, 2158-
    60
Douglas, W.A.S. 936, 1097
Downer, Alan S. 189, 413
Downing, Robert 2161-62
Draper, Walter Headen 1677-78
Dressler, Albert 412, 573
Drew, John 1879
Drimmer, Frederick 798
Droz, Edmund 1442
Drummond, A.M. 2180
Ducharte, Pierre Louis 26
Duffet, Thomas 2071
Duff-Gordon, Lady Lucile 1524
Dugger, Leonard P. 241
Duke, Vernon 1525
Dulles, Foster Rhea 120, 177
Dunbar, Willis Frederick 2222
Duncan, Bob 1504
Duncan, Wanda 1504
Dunleavy, Yvonne 1229
Dunn, Roy Sylvan 641
Dunville, T.E. 1757
Durang, John 189, 413, 1880
Durant, Alice 414
Durant, John 414
Dye, William Seddinger, Jr. 2086

E

Earle, Alice Morse 121
East, John M. 1992-94
Easto, Patrick C. 859-60, 886
Eaton, Julia 2087
Eaton, Walter Prichard 989, 1098, 1881, 2088-89, 2163, 2223-25
Edgar, Randolph 190
Edmonds, Walter D. 415
Edstrom, David 937
Edwall, Harry R. 990
Edwards, Frank 799
Edwards, Mrs. Gus 201
Edwards, Richard Henry 191
Edwards, Samuel 1882
Eich, Louis M. 2164
Eipper, Paul 416
Elbirn, William L. 417, 642
Elder, Mildred 667
Eliot, T.S. 1758
Elkin, Robert 1759-60
Ellerbe, Alma 1276
Ellerbe, Paul 1276
Elliott, Eugene Clinton 1100
Ellis, Edward Robb 122
Ellis, James 2085
Ellison, Ralph 991
Elsom, John 313
Emmett, Frank 2226
Engel, Lehman 1526-28
England, Alma Miller 629
Engle, Gary D. 992
Epstein, Dena J. 993
Epstein, Samuel 1383
Erenstein, Robert L. 28
Ericson, Robert Edward 2228
Ernst, Alice Henson 2229
Erskine, Gladys Shaw 643
Esslin, Martin 29
Estavan, Lawrence 192
Estill, Robin 2090
Eustis, Morton 743
Evans, Henry Ridgely 1309, 1338-42, 1460
Ewen, David 1529-34, 1596
Eytinge, Rose 2230

F

Fadner, Frederick 800

Fagg, Edwin 1995
Falk, Bernard 1883
Falk, Heinrich Richard 30
Faral, Edmond 31
Farelli, Victor 1379
Farmer, Peter 1679
Farnsworth, Marjorie 1535
Farson, Daniel 1761
Fause, Kenneth 898
Favorini, Attilio 1996
Fawcett, Claire H. 418
Fawcett, James Waldo 419
Fay, Arthur 1451
Feder, Sid 199
Felheim, Marvin 1884
Feller, John H. 1170
Fellows, Dexter W. 420, 644
Felstead, S. Theodore 1762
Fenner, Mildred S. 421
Fenner, Wolcott 421
Ferber, Edna 249, 2329
Fergusson, Sir Louis 1763
Ferris, Helen 801
Feuillet, R.A. 76
ffrench, Yvonne 744a
Fiedler, Leslie 802-3
Field, Alfred Griffith 422, 994
Fielder, Mildred 645
Fields, Ronald J. 193
Fields, W.C. 193
Finck, Herman 1764
Findlater, Richard 1675, 1680, 1997
Findlay, James B. 1310, 1343
Firmage, George J. 895, 1232, 1516
Fischer, Ottokar 1344
Fisher, John 1765
Fiske, Roger 314, 1681
Fitch, Clyde 2060
Fitzgerald, Percy 1766, 1998
FitzGerald, William G. 423, 804
Fitzsimons, Raymond 805
Flanagan, Bud 315
Fleetwood, Frances 1682
Fletcher, Ifan K. 1683
Fletcher, Tom 995
Flint, Richard W. 32, 194, 424
Flood, Priscilla 1536
Foley, Doris 1885

Foote, Stella Adelyne 646
Forbes, J. Malcolm 1842
Forbes-Winslow, D. 1536a, 1999
Ford, George D. 2231, 2323
Fordin, Hugh 1537
Foreman, Carolyn Thomas 647
Forrester, Alfred Henry. See
    Crowquill, Alfred
Forsyth, Gerald 1684
Foster, George 1767
Foster, J. Walter 2232
Foster, William Trufant 1102
Fowler, Gene 425, 648-49, 806
Fox, Charles Philip 378, 426-39
Foy, Eddie 1103
Foy, Peter 1538
Francesco, Grete de 938
Franco, Barbara 807
Freedland, Michael 1105, 1539
Freedley, George 1198
Freedman, David 226, 1075, 1500-
    1502
Freedman, Jill 431
Freeman, Andrew A. 420, 644
Freeman, Graydon La Verne 939,
    1540
Fried, Frederick A. 899
Friedman, Robert 1541
Frohman, Daniel 1886
Frost, Richard I. 678
Frost, Thomas 33, 432, 745, 1345
Fruth, Mary Ann 2165
Funke, Lewis 198
Funnell, Charles F. 900
Furnas, J.C. 2166
Furst, Arnold 1346
Futcher, Palmer Howard 808
Fyles, Franklin 195, 1887

G

Gaer, Joseph 2233
Gage, John 1452
Gagey, Edmond McAdoo 2234
Gallagher, Kent G. 1888-89
Gallegly, Joseph S. 2235
Gamble, George 1768
Gammond, Peter 1769-70
Ganson, Lewis 1347
Garnier, Jules 45

Garrett, John M. 1771
Garrett, Thomas M. 746
Gaul, Harvey B. 996
Geary, William Neville Montgomerie
    1772
Gehman, Richard B. 252, 1107
Gershwin, George 1542, 1544
Gershwin, Ira 1542-43
Gerson, Noel Bertram 1890
Gerson, Walter M. 433
Gibson, Walter Brown 861, 1348-51
Gilbert, Mrs. Anne Jane Hartley
    1891
Gilbert, Douglas 196, 1108
Gilbert, George 1378
Gilbert, Vedder M. 2236
Gilder, Rosamond 197
Giles, Dorothy 1214
Gilette, William 2270
Gill, Robert 1311
Gillette, Don Carle 588
Gipson, Fred 650
Girard, Chet Anthony 2091
Glasstone, Victor 316, 1773, 2000
Glenn, Frank Warren 2092
Glenn, Stanley L. 2093
Glenroy, John H. 550
Glover, Jimmy 317-19
Goewey, Edwin A. 1109
Goff, Lewin 2094
Goldberg, Isaac 1544
Golden, George Fuller 1110
Goldsmith, Robert 34
Gollmar, Robert H. 434
Goodlad, J.S. 2095
Goodman, Julia Cody 677
Goodwin, Nat C. 1112, 1892
Gordon, Cora 2324
Gordon, Jan 2324
Gordon, Lesley 1454
Gordon, Max 198
Gorham, Maurice [Anthony Coneys]
    35
Gotlieb, George A. 1113
Gould, George M. 810
Gould, Joseph E. 1277
Graham, Philip 2325-26
Granlund, Nils Thor 199

Grant, H. Roger 651
Grant, James 2001
Grau, Robert 200, 1114-20
Graves, Charles 320
Graves, George 1545
Green, Abel 201-2, 1121-22
Green, Alan W.C. 997
Green, Benny 901
Green, Elvena Marion 2237
Green, Gordon C. 1123
Green, Helen 1124
Green, Stanley 1546-48
Green, William 27, 1233-35, 1685
Greenberg, Clement 143
Greenwall, Harry James 1774
Greenwood, Isaac J. 437, 998
Gregori, Leon 628
Gresham, William Lindsay 862-65, 1352
Gressler, Thomas H. 1549
Griffin, Al 903
Griffin, Charles Eldridge 652
Grimsted, David 2096
Grinde, Nick 1123
Grock [Adrian Wettach] 589
Gronig, Kark 29
Grossmith, George 1550-52
Grossmith, George, Jr. 1553
Grossmith, Weedon 1552
Gunn, Archie 1127

H

Haberly, Loyd 811
Hackett, Frances 1554
Haddon, Archibald 1775
Hadfield, John 78, 789, 1410, 1729a, 1825
Hagen, Claude L. 200
Hagenbeck, Lorenz 551
Hagler, Nevis Ezelk, Jr. 1893
Haines, George W. 812
Haley, James L. 552
Hall, Ben M. 1126
Hall, Linda 2238
Hall, Roger Allan 1555-56
Hall, Stuart 123
Hall, Trevor H. 1312-13
Halliday, Andrew 1686
Halliday, E.M. 1894

Hallock, E.S. 438
Hamid, George A. 439
Hamid, George A., Jr. 439
Hamilton, Cicely 2002
Hamilton, Clayton 2097-98
Hammerstein, Oscar II 1557
Hammond, Percy 249
Hancock, Ralph 199
Handlin, Oscar 203
Handy, William Christopher 204, 999
Hanson, Frank Burton 2003
Hanson, Herman 1353
Hapgood, Norman 1127
Harlow, Alvin F. 440, 1103-4, 1895, 2219
Harper, Robert D. 205
Harriman, Karl Edwin 441
Harris, Neil 124, 155, 206, 813
Harrison, Gabriel 1896
Harrison, Harry P. 1278
Harrison, Shirley Madeline 2239
Hart, William S. 1897
Harting, L.P. 966
Hartley, Marsden 207, 1128
Hartnoll, Phyllis 36
Hartt, Rollin Lynde 208, 904
Harvey, R.M. 653
Haskins, Jim 1558
Hatch, Alden 472
Hatton, Joseph 2004
Hauser, Odell 734
Haverly, Jack 1000
Havighurst, Walter 654-55
Havoc, June 1129-30
Hay, Henry 1354
Haywood, Charles 1001-2
Heaps, Porter W. 1559
Heaps, Willard A. 1559
Heath, Eric 683
Heather, John Fry 1455
Hebberd, Mary Hardgrove 656, 940
Hecht, Ben 125, 221
Hechtlinger, Adelaide 941
Hedgbeth, Llewellyn Hubbard 1456
Hedges, R. Alan 1279
Hediger, Heinrich 553
Heilbron, Bertha L. 1457-58
Held, Anna 1560

Author Index

Henderson, J.Y. 554
Henderson, Jerry 1131
Henderson, Mary C. 209, 1898
Henderson, W.J. 980
Henning, Doug 1355
Hensey, Donald L. 442
Heppner, Sam 321
Herford, Oliver 919
Hershey, Burnet 781
Hibbert, H.G. 1776-77
Hicks, Seymour 322, 1490, 1561, 2005
High, Fred 1280-81
Higham, Charles 1562
Hill, Clare Maynard 1132
Hill, George H. 2167
Hill, Lucienne 22, 54
Hill, Lyn Stiefel 1391
Hill, West T. 2240
Hilliam, Bentley Colingwood 1778
Hilliard, John Northern 1356
Hillier, Mary 1459
Hingston, Edward P. 2241
Hinkle, Milt 657-67
Hodge, Francis 2168-70
Hodges, C. Walter 606
Hoffman, Arthur S. 1133
Hoffman, James William 677
Hoffman, Professor [Angelo John Lewis] 1357
Hogan, William Ransom 2242
Holbrook, Stewart H. 668, 942, 1236-37
Holdredge, Helen 1899
Hollingshead, John 1563-65
Hollister, Katharine Stevens 2243
Holloway, Stanley 1779
Holm, Don 669
Holm, Ed 670
Holtman, Jerry 822
Honour, Hugh 814
Honri, Peter 1780
Hood, Charles Newton 2244-45
Hopkin, John 2024
Hopkins, Albert A. 1460
Hopper, DeWolf 210
Horner, Charles F. 1282-83
Horowitz, I.L. 859
Horton, Judge William E. 211-12

Horwitt, Arnold B. 226
Hotson, Leslie 37
Houdini, Harry 1358
Howard, Cecil 1664
Howard, Diana 323, 1781
Howard, John Trasker 1003
Howard, Randall R. 1284
Hoyt, Harlowe 2246
Hubbard, Elbert 1134
Hubler, Richard 555
Hudd, Roy 1725, 1782, 1792
Huggins, Nathan 1004
Hughes, Gervase 1566
Hughes, Langston 213
Hughes, Leo 2006, 2099
Hume, Charles V. 2247-48
Hume, Ruth 815
Humphreys, Anne 345
Humphreys, R. 407
Hunt, Brampton 38
Hunt, Charles T., Sr. 444
Hunt, Douglas 1687
Hunt, Douglas L. 2171
Hunt, Gaillard 126
Hunt, Kari 1687
Hunter, John Marvin 2327
Hunter, Kay 816
Hunter, Ruth 1135
Hutchens, John K. 1136
Hutton, James S. 905
Hutton, Laurence 214, 1005, 1900
Hyman, Alan 1567

I

Inciardi, James A. 445
Inge, M. Thomas 126a
Inman, Henry 671
Ireland, Joseph N. 215, 1901
Irving, Gordon 1783
Irwin, Wallace 1138
Irwin, Will 868
Isaacs, Edith J.R. 216
Isman, Felix 1139

J

Jablonski, Edward 1568-69
Jackson, Alan S. 57, 1570, 2007

Jackson, Arthur 1571
Jackson, Sir Barry 1822
Jackson, Bruce 119, 1002
Jackson, Joseph 747
Jacob, Naomi 1784
Jacobs, Norman 203
Jacques-Charles 39
James, Reese D. 217, 1902
James, Theodore, Jr. 818
Jameson, Eric 943
Janis, Elsie 218
Janis, Harriet 161, 976, 1491
Jefferson, Joseph III 1903
Jeffrey, John B. 219, 1904
Jenkins, Stephen 220, 1905
Jenness, George A. 1359
Jennings, John J. 220a, 446, 1360
Jensen, Andrew F. 2249
Jensen, Dean 447
Jensen, Oliver 127
Jerningham, Charles Edward 1804
Jerome, Jerome K. 2100
Jerrard, Leigh 672
Jessel, George 201, 221, 1140-42, 1206
Joachin, Harold 1382
Johannsen, Albert 673
Johnson, Edgar 307
Johnson, Eleanor 307
Johnson, James Weldon 1006, 1573
Johnson, Raoul Fenton 1906
Johnson, Vance 2195, 2250
Johnston, Alva 1143-44
Johnston, Winifred 944
Jolson, Al 1572
Jones, Barbara 324
Jones, Howard Mumford 128
Jones, John Bush 674
Jones, LeRoi 222, 1007
Jones, Libby 1238
Jorgensen, Joseph G. 860
Joseph, Helen Haiman 1392
Joseph, Richard 1239
Judd, "Doctor" 2328
Juliani, Giovanni 819
Jump, John D. 2101
Jupp, James 1574

K

Kahan, Stanley 2102

Kahn, E.J., Jr. 1575, 2103
Kaplan, Max 129
Kaser, Arthur LeRoy 1145-46
Katigan, Madelon B. 675
Katkov, Norman 1576
Katz, Herbert 40, 820
Katz, Marjorie 40, 820
Kaufmann, Helen L. 1008
Kavanagh, Ted 1785
Kaye, Marvin 1361
Keaton, Buster 1147
Keats, John 130
Keegan, Marcia 1148
Keeler, Ralph 1009-10
Keese, William L. 1908
Keller, George 556
Kelley, Francis Beverly 393, 429, 448-50, 533, 590
Kelley, Thomas P., Jr. 945
Kellock, Harold 1362
Kelly, Emmett 590
Kelm, William E. 2251
Kemmerling, James D. 2252
Kendall, John Smith 1011
Kennard, Joseph Spencer 41
Kennedy, David 325
Kennedy, John B. 1149-50
Kernodle, George R. 2008
Kerr, Alex 557
Kilby, Quincy 1963
Kimball, Robert 1577-79
King, Donald C. 224, 1151
Kingsley, W.J. 1153
Kinnard, J. 1012
Kirby, E.T. 42
Kirk, Rhina 451
Kirstein, Lincoln 225
Klein, Charles 2060
Klein, Frederick C. 869
Kliess, Werner 29
Klussen, Robert Dean 2253
Kmen, Henry A. 1013
Knapp, Margaret M. 1580
Knight, Laura 452
Knowles, Richard George 1786
Knowlton, Dora 1909
Knox, Collie 1822
Knox, Rose B. 2329
Kober, A.H. 453
Kobler, J. 870
Koch, E. De Roy 8

Koford, William 454
Krassowski, Wittold 871
Kreps, Bonnie 676
Krows, Arthur E. 1910
Krueger, Miles 1581, 2330
Krutch, Joseph Wood 1582-84, 2104
Kummer, George 2105
Kunstadt, Leonard 180
Kunzog, John C. 455-56, 591
Kusell, Maurice L. 2254
Kyriazi, Gary 906

L

Lader, Lawrence 1153a
Lagerkvist, Par 43
Lahr, John 226
Lamb, Geoffrey Frederick 1363-64
Lambert, William. See Delavoye, Will
Langdon, Claude 1787
Langtry, Lillie [Lady de Bathe] 1911
Lano, David 558
Lanthrop, West 2331
Larer, Marian L. 982
Lasswell, Mary 890
Lathrop, West 457
Lauder, Harry 1788-91, 1812
Laüfe, Abe 1585, 1912
Laurie, Joe, Jr. 201-2, 1122, 1154-58
Lausanne, Edita 1461
Laver, James 326
Lawrence, Gertrude 1586
Lea, Kathleen 44
Leamy, Hugh 1159
Leavitt, Michael B. 227
Leavitt, Michael Bennett 1014, 1160, 2255
Lebel, Jean-Patrick 1688
LeBlanc, Thomas J. 946
Ledger, Edward 2361
Lee, Albert 458
Lee, Gypsy Rose 201, 249, 1240-41
Lee, Polly J. 821
Leighton, Isabel 131
Leman, Walter M. 1913
Lemmon, Sarah McCulloh 2256
Leno, Dan 1792
Leonard, Eddie [Lemuel Toney] 228, 1015

Leonard, Elizabeth Jane 677
Leonard, H. Steward 1476
Lerche, Frank Martin 1587
Le Roux, Hughes 45
Le Roy, George 1793
Lesser, Allen 1914
Leuchtenburg, William E. 132
Levant, Oscar 1588
Levy, Bert 1161
Lewes, John Lee 1689
Lewine, Richard 1589-90
Lewis, Arthur H. 872
Lewis, John Angelo. See Hoffman, Professor
Lewis, Paul [Noel B. Gerson] 1915
Lewis, Philip C. 2257
Lewiston, Harry 822
Liebling, Abbott J. 233-34
Liebman, Max 1591
Lillie, Beatrice 1593
Lindley, Kenneth 907
Lines, Harry 908
Lipnitski, Bernard 1242
Lippincott, Horace Mather 1916
Litto, Fredric M. 46
Litton, Glenn 1594
Locke, Alain 1016, 1595
Locke, Edwin 2060
Loeffler, Dr. Robert J. 592-93
Logan, Herschel C. 559, 1243
Logan, Olive 229, 1017, 1244-45, 1917
Lorch, Fred W. 1286
Lord, Walter 133
Loring, Janet 1918
Lowenthal, Leo 143
Lubbock, Mark 1596
Lucia, Ellis 1162
Luckhurst, Kenneth W. 823
Ludlow, Noah M. 1919
Ludwig, Jay F. 2258
Lukens, John 459
Lund, Ralph Eugene 2172
Luntley, John 609
Lupino, Stanley 1690
Lyman, George D. 2259
Lyon, Peter 909
Lyons, Jimmy 1163

M

McArdle, John 1365
McCabe, James D., Jr. 230
McCabe, John 1597
McCaghy, Charles H. 1246, 1257
McClung, Gale S. 824
McClung, Robert M. 824
McConachie, Bruce Alan 2106
McCracken, Harold 678, 726
McCreight, M.I. 679
McCullough, Edo 748, 910
McCullough, Jack W. 1920
McDaniel, Ruel 680
McDermott, Douglas 2260-61
McDermott, John Francis 1462-64
MacDonald, Cordelia Howard 2173
MacDonald, Dwight 143
McDonald, Jan 2024
McDowell, John H. 47, 2174-75
McGee, Thomas R., Jr. 1921
McGlinchee, Claire 1922, 2107
McGregor, Donald 1164
Machee, James T. 1649
MacInnes, Colin 1794
MacKay, Patricia 911, 1598
McKean, Gil 268-69
McKechnie, Samuel 48
McKennon, Joe 873
McKennon, Marian 2262
Mackenzie, Sir Compton 1815
MacKenzie, Shelton 1376
McLanathan, Richard 1465
MacLaren, Gay 1287
McLean, Albert F., Jr. 1165-67
MacMinn, George R. 2263
McNally, William 1168
McNamara, Brooks 49-50, 155, 825-26, 912, 947-49, 1169, 1393
McNeal, Violet 950
McPharlin, Paul 1394
Macqueen-Pope, Walter 327-28, 1599-1601, 1795-96, 2009-11
McVicker, James H. 2264
Madden, David 51
Magowan, David 725
Mahan, Bruce E. 2265
Malcolmson, Robert W. 329
Malin, James C. 2266

Maloney, Martin J. 2267
Maloney, Tom 460
Mammen, Edward W. 1923
Mander, Raymond 330-31, 1602-3, 1691, 1797, 2012
Mandeville, Gloria E. 2108
Maney, Richard 231
Mangels, William F. 913
Manley, Robert 914
Manley, Seon 914
Mann, E.B. 681
Manning-Sanders, Ruth 915
Mannix, Daniel 827, 874
Marcosson, Isaac F. 461, 594
Marcuse, Maxwell F. 232
Marek, Kurt W. See Ceram, C.W.
Marion, F. 1466
Mark, David 865
Mark, Frederick A. 682
Marker, Lise-Lone 2109
Marks, Edward Bennett 233-34, 1604-5, 1924
Marsden, Christopher 916
Marsh, John L. 1439, 1467-68, 2268-73
Marston, William 1170
Martens, Frederick H. 416
Martin, Pete 235, 2332
Martinek, Lt. Commander Frank 725
Marx, Groucho 201, 1171-72
Maskelyne, Jasper 1366
Maskelyne, Nevil 1367
Massett, Stephen C. 2274
Mates, Julian 1606-8
Matlaw, Myron 52, 236, 1173-74, 2110
Mattfeld, Julius 1609
Matthews, Brander 237, 595, 1018, 1395
Maupin, Will M. 725
Maurer, David W. 462, 875
Maurice, Arthur B. 1692
Mawer, Irene 1693
Mawson, Harry P. 2275
May, Earl Chapin 177, 463
Mayer, David III 28, 53, 71, 95, 283, 614, 1234, 1694-1700, 2013, 2030
Mayes, Stanley 332
Mayhew, Henry 333, 1701

Author Index

M'Clure, W. Frank 2333
Mead, David 1288
Meade, Edward Hoag 2276
Meadmore, W.S. 402, 635
Medary, Edgar F. 725
Meersman, Roger 1175
Meisel, Martin 2111
Meiselas, Susan 876, 1247
Meldon, Charles 94
Mellor, Geoffrey James 918, 1798-99
Meltzer, Milton 213
Mendelson, Andrew David 2112
Menken, Adah 81
Menkin, Arthur H. 162
Merchant, W. Moelwyn 2024
Meredyth, Bess 806
Merrill, Katherine 1176
Merritt, M.S. 2254
Meserve, Walter J. p. xv, 1946, 2176
Metcalf, Francis 919
Meyer, Bernard C. 1368
Meyer, Hazel 1610
Mickel, Jere C. 2177, 2277
Middleton, George 464
Middleton, William D. 920
Miesle, Frank Leland 1702
Milburn, George 465
Miles, Carlton 2278
Miles, Henry Downes 1703
Milford Haven, Marquess of 1787
Miller, Doc Art 951
Miller, H.E. 466
Miller, Kelly 1020
Miller, Melvin H. 1289
Miller, Ruby 1611
Millette, Ernest Schlee 560
Millingen, John 1401
Mills, Bernard 557
Mills, Steve 1248
Millstein, Gilbert 877
Minney, R.J. 334
Minnigerode, Meade 134
Mistinguett, Jeanne-Marie Bourgeois 54
Mitchell, Joseph 828
Mitchenson, Joe 330-31, 1602-3, 1691, 1797, 2012

Mix, Olive Stokes 683
Mix, Paul E. 684
Mockridge, Norton 878
Moffett, Cleveland 561
Monaghan, Jay 685, 2178
Money, John 829
Monson, William Neil 2279
Montagu, Ashley 830
Moody, Richard 238-39, 1021-23, 1925-26, 2113, 2179-80
Morath, Max 1612
Mordden, Ethan 1613
Morehouse, Ward 240, 1614-15, 1927
Moreley, Henry 749
Morell, Parker 1616
Morice, Gerald 1387, 1396-99
Morley, Christopher 596
Morley, Henry 55, 335, 2014
Morley, Malcolm 2015
Morosco, Helen M. 241
Morris, Joe Alex 2181
Morris, Lloyd 135-36, 1177
Morrison, Theodore 1290
Morrow, John Charles 1704, 2007, 2182
Morsberger, Robert E. 1928
Morton, A.P. 45
Morton, William H. 1801
Moses, John 750
Moses, Montrose J. 1178, 1929-30, 2114
Mossberger, Katherine M. 1928
Moy, James S. 467-68
Moynet, Georges 56
Moynet, Jean-Pierre 57
Mozart, George [David John Gillings] 1800
Mulholland, John 58, 1369-71, 2397
Mullens, W.H. 831
Muller, Dan 686
Mumford, Lewis 137
Muncey, R.W. 751
Mundis, Jerrold J. 687
Munro, John M. 1802-3
Murray, Charles Theodore 469-70
Murray, D.L. 81
Murray, Ken 1617
Murray, Marian 471

402

Murtagh, Mathews 1843
Mussey, Barrows 1382
Mussey, J.B. 1344
Musson, Bennett 1179

N

Nadeau, Albert Henry 2115
Naeseth, Henrietta C.K. 2280
Nanry, C. 859
Nardin, James T. 2116
Nast, Thomas 1456
Nathan, George Jean 242-46, 952,
   1180, 1618, 1931-35
Nathan, Hans 1024-25
Nathanson, Y.S. 1026
Nathe, Patricia A. 879
Naylor, Stanley 1619
Neafie, Nelle 832
Nebel, Long John 953
Nevill, Ralph Henry 1804
Nevin, R.P. 1027
Newquist, Roy 1250
Newton, Douglas 598
Newton, Henry Chance [Heath
   Cranton] 1801, 1805, 2117
Nichols, Beverley 1645
Nicholson, Watson 2017
Nicoll, Allardyce 59-60, 2018
Niklaus, Thelma 61
Nobles, Milton 2281
Noell, Mae 954
Nolan, Paul T. 2183-85
Nordin, Charles R. 688
North, Henry Ringling 472
Northall, William Knight 247, 833,
   1936, 2186
Norwood, Edwin P. 562-63
Nye, Russel B. 138-40

O

Obee, Harold B. 2187
O'Brien, Esse Forrester 473, 689
O'Brien, P.J. 1620
O'Conner, T.P. 1776
O'Connor, Lois 1251
O'Connor, Richard 2282
Odell, George C.D. 248, 1937-38
Olf, Julian M. 1372

Oliver, N.T. 955-56
O'Neil, Nance 2283
Onosko, Tim 921
Oppenheimer, George 249
Orchard, Hugh Anderson 1291
Ord-Hume, Arthur W.J.G. 1471
Oreglia, Giacomo 62
Ormond, Robert 1272
O'Rourke, Eva 1806
Orr, Lynn E. 2118
Otis, James 475
Oulton, W.C. 336, 1705
Oursler, Fulton 1344
Owens, Mrs. John E. 1939

P

Page, Brett 1181
Page, Will A. 1807
Palmer, John 1808, 2019
Pancoast, Chalmers L. 250
Papich, Stephen 63
Papp, John 476
Park, A.J. 1836
Parkinson, Bob 477-78
Parkinson, Tom 430
Parrott, Frederick J. 1940
Parry, Albert 834
Parry, Lee 1472
Parsons, Bill 1941
Partridge, Bellamy 141
Paskman, Dailey 1028
Paterson, Peter [James Glass
   Bertram] 2020
Patterson, Ada 1182
Patterson, Cecil L. 1029-30
Patterson, Lindsay 1031
Pearce, Charles E. 2021
Pearl, Cyril 337
Pearsall, Ronald 1809-10
Pecor, Charles 1373
Peers, Donald 1811
Pemberton, Madge 589
Perry, Hue 1262
Petersen, David M. 445
Petersen, William J. 957
Pettit, Paul Bruce 2188, 2334
Pfening, Fred D., Jr. 479-83,
   691-92

Author Index

Pfening, Fred D. III 484, 564
Phillabaum, Corliss E. 1473
Phillips, Cabell 142
Phillips, Julien 1621
Philpott, A.R. 1400
Pickard, Madge E. 958
Pilat, Oliver 922
Pitou, Augustus 1942
Pitzer, F.P. 599
Planche, James Robinson 2120
Plowden, Gene 485-86, 565
Poggi, Jack 1943
Polacsek, John F. 487
Poliakoff, Nicholai. See Coco the Clown
Poling, James 881
Pond, Irving K. 566-67
Popkin, Zelda F. 2284
Posey, Jake 568, 693
Potter, Jack 1314
Pouska, Frank J. 694
Powers, James T. 1944
Powledge, Fred 488
Prentis, Terence 1812
Preston, Lillian E. 1474
Price, Cecil 2022
Price, Harry 1315-16
Price, Lucien 1292
Price, Willard 2335
Priestley, J.B. 338-39
Prill, Arthur 1183
Pringle, Henry F. 1252, 1293
Proske, Roman 569
Provol, William Lee 251
Pulling, Christopher 1813
Pyke, E.J. 67, 835
Pyke, Elizabeth 1812
Pyle, Walter L. 810

Q

Quarnstorm, I. Blaine 2189
Quigley, Martin 1475
Quin, Charles W. 1466
Quinn, Arthur Hobson 1945-46, 2119

R

Rahill, Frank 2121-24, 2190
Ramshaw, Molly Niederlander 1032
Ranck, Edwin Carty 2285

Randall, Harry 1814
Randi, The Amazing 1374
Ranney, Omar 2191
Ranson, Jo 922
Rathbone, Perry T. 1476
Reardon, William R. 1947-48
Reed, Edward 1184, 1706
Reed, Ronald Michael 1949
Reeve, Ada 1815
Reeves, Dorothea D. 959
Rehin, George F. 1033-34
Reid, Alec 1442
Relph, Harry [Little Tich] 1816
Remington, Frederick 695
Remy, Tristan 600-601
Renevey, Monica J. 435
Rennert, Jack 489, 696
Renton, Edward 1185
Revell, Nellie 1186-92
Revett, Marion S. 2286
Reynolds, Chang 490, 697-98
Reynolds, Charles 1355, 1375
Reynolds, Ernest 2023, 2125
Reynolds, George F. 1822
Reynolds, Harry 1035
Reynolds, Regina 1375
Rice, Edward LeRoy 1036
Richards, Dick 1779
Richards, Kenneth 28, 53, 71, 95, 614, 1234, 1710, 2024, 2030, 2068
Richards, Sandra L. 1622
Richman, Harry 252
Richmond, Rebecca 1294
Riedel, Johannes 253
Riker, Ben 570
Rinear, David L. 1950
Ringling, Alfred T. 491, 594
Ritchey, David 752
Ritchie, James Ewing 340, 1817
Robert-Houdin, Jean Eugene 1376
Roberts, Arthur 1623, 1818-19
Robeson, Dave 492, 571
Robey, George 1820-21
Robinson, C.O. 493, 699
Robinson, Clyde 2287
Robinson, David 1193, 1839
Robinson, Gil 494-95
Robinson, John William 3
Robinson, Josephine DeMott 572

Robson, Joseph Philip 1707
Rodescape, Lois 2288
Rodgers, Richard 1624
Rogers, Will 1075, 1500
Rohrer, Mary Katherine 2289
Rohrig, Gladys M. 2025
Romaine, Mertie E. 836
Ronnie, Art 1377
Root, Harvey W. 837
Rosa, Joseph G. 700
Rose, Clarkson 1822-24
Rose, Will 960
Rosenberg, Bernard 143
Rosenberg, C.G. 838
Rosenberger, Francis Coleman 1175
Rosenfeld, Sybil 753, 1477-78, 2026-30
Ross, Woodburn 2063
Rossiter, Will 1194
Rourke, Constance 144-45, 839, 2193, 2290
Row, Arthur William 1295
Rowe, J.A. 573
Rowell, George 341, 2031-32
Rowland, Mabel 1625
Roy, Donald 2024
Royle, Edwin Milton 206, 1195
Ruben, Aaron 226
Rubin, Benny 201, 1196
Ruddick, William 2024
Ruggles, Eleanor 1951
Rulfs, Donald J. 2291-92
Russell, Don 701-5, 725
Rust, Brian 68
Ryan, Kate 1952
Ryan, Pat M. 2126, 2293-94
Ryan, Thomas Richard, Jr. 2033
Rydell, Wendy 1378

S

Salsbury, Milton S. 722
Salutin, Marilyn 1253
Samuels, Charles 270, 1147, 1197
Samuels, Louise 1197
Sand, Maurice 69
Sandberg, Trish 1254
Sands, Mollie 754
Sanger, "Lord" George 496
Sappington, Joe 961

Sardina, Maurice 1379
Sargent, Dr. Malcolm 1759
Savo, Jimmy 1198
Sawyer, E.T. 1037
Sawyer, Paul 1708-10
Saxe-Wyndham, Henry 1711
Saxon, A.H. 81, 497-99, 840-41, 1712, 2034-37, 2127
Sayers, Isabelle 706
Scala, Flaminio 70
Scarne, John 882
Schaal, David 1953
Schafer, William J. 253
Schaffner, Neil E. 2195
Schick, Joseph S. 2295, 2336
Schiffman, Jack 254
Schlesinger, Arthur M. 146
Schlicher, J.J. 500
Schmidt, Emile 1954
Schoener, Allon 147
Schultz, Charles Albert 2196
Schwartz, Charles 1626
Schwartz, Joseph 707
Scotson-Clark, G.F. 1768
Scott, Amoret 1825
Scott, Christopher 1825
Scott, Clement 342, 1664, 2038
Scott, Harold 1826-27
Scott, Marian 1296
Scott, Matthew 574
Scott, Virginia P. 71, 1713
Scott, Walter Sidney 755
Scott-Stewart, Dick 756
Scrimgeour, Gary 1955
Seago, Edward 501
Seaton-Reid, D. 1401-3
Secrest, William B. 708-9
Sedgwick, Ruth W. 2128
Segel, Sherman Louis 73
Selby, Paul 750
Seldes, Gilbert 72, 143, 255, 1255-56
Sell, Henry Blackman 710
Senelick, Laurence 602, 1200, 1714, 1828-30
Severn, Bill 1380
Shafer, Henry B. 962
Shafer, Yvonne B. 1956, 2297
Shank, Theodore J. 1957
Sharp, R. Farquharson 2039

Sharpe, James 725
Shaw, Arnold 148
Shaw, Mary 1958, 2298
Shayne, Eddie 1201
Sheaffer, Louis 1959
Sheean, Vincent 1628
Sheridan, Jeff 13
Sheridan, Paul 1831
Sherlock, Charles R. 575, 1202
Sherman, Jan 1629
Sherman, Robert L. 2299
Sherson, Erroll 343, 2040
Sherwood, Robert Edmund 603-4
Shiffman, Jack 1199
Shipp, Cameron 1495-96
Shirley, Glenn 711-12
Short, Ernest 344, 1630, 1832
Sichel, Pierre 1960
Sidenberg, Sid 883
Sieben, Pearl 1631
Sillman, Leonard 1632
Silverman, Kenneth 149
Silvers, Phil 201
Simmen, Rene 1404
Simon, Alfred 1579, 1589-90
Simond, Ike 1038
Simpich, Frederick 2337
Sims, George R. 1715
Sitton, Fred 2197
Skipper, James K., Jr. 1246, 1257
Slout, L. Verne 1297
Slout, William Lawrence 1633, 2300
Smith, Bill 1203
Smith, Cecil 1594, 1634-35
Smith, Charles Manby 345
Smith, Harry James 2129
Smith, Horatio 74
Smith, James L. 2130
Smith, Joe 201, 226
Smith, Matthew Hale 150
Smith, Winifred 75-76
Smoot, James S. 1298
Snook, Sidney 2338
Snow, Robert E. 923
Snyder, Frederick Edward 1204-5
Snyder, Sherwood III 2198
Sobel, Bernard 256, 1206, 1258-60,
    1636-38

Sobol, Louis 257
Sokan, Robert 77
Soldene, Emily 1833
Solomon, Laurence M. 830
Sondheim, Stephen 1537, 1590
Sonneck, Oscar G. 757, 1639
Sothern, Georgia 1261
Soutar, Robert 1834
Southern, H. 1479
Southern, Richard 346-47, 2041-44
Southworth, James Granville 758
Spaeth, Sigmund 258, 1028, 1640
Speaight, George 78, 502, 1399,
    1405-13, 1480, 1716, 1835,
    2045-46, 2131, 2394
Spears, Raymond S. 2339
Spence, Hartzell 374
Spencer, Charles 1641
Spencer, H.D. 1414-15
Spinney, Frank Oakman 1039
Spitzer, Marian 1208-9
Sprague, Arthur Colby 2024
Sprague, Rosemary 2047
Sprinchorn, Evert 62
Spring, Agnes Wright 713
Stagg, Jerry 1642, 1961
Stallings, Roy 2301
Stambler, Irwin 1643
Starr, Blaze 1262
Starsmore, Ian 759
Stead, Philip John 1416
Stearns, Jean 259
Stearns, Marshall 259
Stedman-Jones, Gareth 348
Steegmuller, Frances 1211
Steiner, Jesse Frederick 260
Stephens, John Russell 2048
Sterling, Sir Louis 1778
Stetis, Dr. H.R. 1896
Steven, John 1456
Stevens, Aston 249
Stevens, Henry Bailey 2302
Stevens, Leonard A. 538
Stewart, George R., Jr. 2303
Stewart, Lawrence D. 1569
Still, Bayrd 151
Stoddart, Dayton 261
Stone, Fred 262
Stone, M.W. 1417-20
Stout, Wesley Winans 210, 955-56,
    2199

Stoutamire, Albert 1040
Stow, Charles 503
Strang, Lewis Clinton 1644
Stratman, Carl J. 2341-42
Striker, Hopper 2340
Strutt, Joseph 349
Stuart, Charles Douglas 1836
Stump, Walter Ray 1837
Sturtevant, Col. C.G. 504-5, 576
Sugar, Bert Randolph 1374
Sullivan, Mark 152
Suthern, Orrin Clayton II 1041
Sutton, Felix 506, 605
Swain, Barbara 79
Swartwout, Annie Fern 714
Sweet, Robert C. 507-8
Swortzell, Lowell 606
Symons, Arthur 1838

T

Taber, Bob 509
Talley, Truman H. 1299
Tandy, Jennette 153
Taplinger, Richard 549, 554
Tarbell, Harlan 1381
Tarkington, Booth 1879
Taylor, Dwight 2132
Taylor, Justus Hurd 2304
Taylor, Robert Lewis 263-64, 510,
    577, 884, 963
Taylor, Vic 1421, 1839
Tedford, Harold C. 511
Telbin, William [the younger] 1481
Terriss, Ellaline 1645
Thackeray, William Makepeace 1840
Thaler, Alwin 2049
Thanet, Octave 760
Thayer, Stuart 512-16, 715
Thetard, Henry 27, 518, 578
Thomas, Augustus 2060
Thomas, G. Ernest 358
Thomas, Lowell 579
Thomas, Richard 519
Thomas, Russell B. 2050
Thompson, Alan Reynolds 2133
Thompson, Charles John Samuel 80,
    842, 964
Thompson, Edward Palmer 350
Thompson, William C. 520, 716

Thomson, Peter 1710, 2024, 2068
Thornton, Harrison J. 1300
Thorp, N. Howard (Jack) 717
Thorp, Raymond W. 718
Tich, Little. See Relph, Harry
Tilley, Vesta. See De Frece,
    Lady Vesta Tilley
Timberlake, Craig 1962
Timbs, John 351-53
Titterton, William Richard 1841
Tobias, Henry 1052
Toll, Robert C. 265, 1038, 1042-
    43
Tompkins, Charles H. 719
Tompkins, Eugene 1963
Toole-Stott, Raymond p. ix, 81-82,
    1317
Towne, Charles Wayland 720
Towsen, John H. 83-84, 607
Tozier, Roy Becker 1301
Traber, J. Milton 1213
Treadwell, Bill 266
Trevelyan, John 313
Treves, Frederick 830
Trotter, James Monroe 1044
Troubridge, St. Vincent 2051
Truman, Benjamin C. 761
Trussler, Simon 2134
Trux, J.J. 1045
Truzzi, Marcello 521-25, 843,
    859-60, 885-86
Truzzi, Massimiliano 525
Tsai, Andre Tii-Kang 2135
Tucker, Sophie 1214
Tulin, Miriam S. 1717
Tully, Jim 965
Turner, Darwin T. 1964
Turner, Willis L. 2200
Tussaud, John T. 844
Tuttle, George Palliser 526, 2052,
    2136
Twain, Mark. See Clemens, Samuel
Tyron, John 608
Tyrwhitt-Drake, Sir Garrard 527

U

Underwood, Peter 85
Unthan, Carl Hermann 1842
Uraneff, Vadim 1215
Urban, Joseph 267
Utley, Francis Lee 1038

Author Index

V

Vail, Robert William Glenroie 528–29

Vallee, Rudy 268–69

Van Lennep, William 1717a

van Ravenswaay, Charles 1476, 1482

Vardac, A. Nicholas 86

Varney, George Leon 1857

Veinstein, Andre 87

Venne, Bill 602

Verney, Peter 530

Vestal, Stanley [Walter S. Campbell] 721

Vincent, W.T. 1646

Visscher, Col. William Lightfoot 626

Volkmann, Kurt 1382

Von Hagen, Victor Wolfgang 1483

W

Wadleigh, Paul 2024

Wadlow, Harold F. 800

Wagner, Leopold 1718

Waitzkin, Leo 2053

Walford, Cornelius 762

Wallace, A. Doyle 2063

Wallace, Amy 846

Wallace, Irving 845–46

Wallett, William F. 609

Walsh, Richard J. 722

Walsh, Townsend 2054

Walton, Thomas 1422

Ward, Edward 1719

Warde, Frederick 1302

Warden, Ben W. 994

Ware, Helen 2306

Warner, Frederick Elliott 2137

Washington, Booker T. 1647

Waterman, Arthur E. 2201

Waters, Ethel 270

Waters, H.W. 763

Watson, Elmo Scott 723

Watson, Ernest Bradlee 2138

Watson, Margaret 2307

Watson, William R. 580

Watters, Eugene 1843

Wearing, J.P. 18

Webb, Harry E. 724

Webber, Malcolm 966

Wells, Helen 847

Wells, L. Jeanette 1303

Wells, Mitchell P. 1720

Wells, Stanley 2139

Wells, Staring 1721

Welsford, Enid 88

Werner, M.R. 848

Werthman, Michael S. 177

Westervelt, Leonidas 531, 849

Wetmore, Helen Cody 727

Wettach, Adrian. See Grock

Wewiora, G.E. 1844

Weybright, Victor 710

Whalon, Marion K. 89

Whannel, Paddy 123

White, David Manning 143

White, Newman 1046

White, Stanley 1047

White, William Allen 2308

Whitehill, Walter Muir 787

Whitman, Walt 143

Whitney, Dwight 935

Whitton, Joseph 1648

Wickham, Glynne 90

Wickman, Richard Carl 1484

Wighton, David. See Devant, David

Wilder, Alec 1649

Willeford, William 91

Willey, Day Allen 926

Williams, Bert 1650

Williams, Beryl 1383

Williams, Bransby 1845–47

Williams, Charles D. 1423–25

Williams, Clifford John 2055

Williams, Henry B. 1608

Williams, Mark 756

Willows, Maurice 1219

Wills, J. Robert 1965–66

Willson, Clair Eugene 1220, 2309

Wilmeth, Don B. 92–93

Wilson, Albert Edward 354, 1426, 1682, 1722–25, 1848, 2056–57

Wilson, Edmund 1265

Wilson, Edna Erle 1304

Wilson, Francis 271, 1651

Wilson, Graff B. 272

Wilson, Harry Leon 967

Wilson, John S. 1579

Wilson, M. Glen 57, 2024

Wilson, W.L. 2310

Wilstach, John 728
Winch, Frank 729
Winesanker, Michael 2140
Winks, Evert M. 1305
Winks, Robin W. 1305
Winslow, David 155
Winter, Marian Hannah 94-95, 532, 1048, 1726
Winter, William 1967-68
Wisely, Edward Burdock 2058
Wittke, Carl 1049
Wodehouse, P.G. 1653
Wood, Edward J. 850
Wood, George 1799
Wood, Georgie 1849-50
Wood, Jay Hickory 1851
Woods, Alan 2311-12
Woodworth, Samuel 74
Woolf, S.J. 1221
Wortley, Richard 1266
Wraxall, Lascelles 1376
Wright, David E. 923
Wright, Richardson 96
Wroth, Arthur Edgar 765
Wroth, Warwick 764-65
Wyndham, Francis 301
Wyndham, Robert 560

Y

Yates, Edmund 766
Yates, L.B. 2313
Yellow Rob, Chauncey 730
Yeo, Eileen 350
Y Gasset, Jose Ortega 143
Young, James Harvey 177, 968-74
Young, Miriam 273
Young, Morris N. 1350-51
Young, William C. 97, 274

Z

Zanger, Jules 1050
Zayas, Malins de 1073
Zeidman, Irving 1267
Zellers, Parker R. 1222-23
Ziegfeld, Florenz, Jr. 1654
Ziegfeld, Patricia 1655
Zilboorg, Gregory 1306, 2314
Zincser, William K. 887
Zolotow, Maurice 275
Zora, Lucia 581
Zweers, John U. 1353

TITLE INDEX

This index includes the titles of all books and plays cited in this text. Some titles have been shortened. It is alphabetized letter by letter. Except where preceded by "p.," references are to entry numbers.

A

About Stage Folks 211
Acrobats and Mountebanks 45
Actor's Story, An 1845
Ada Rehan 1967
Adventures in Magic 1340
Adventures in the Arts 207
Adventures of Arthur Roberts by Rail, Road and River, The 1818
Affairs of James A. Bailey, The 384
Albert Chevalier Comes Back 1746
Al G. Barnes, Master Showman, as Told by Al G. Barnes 492
All Right on the Night 303, 1982
Amazing Mississippi, The 2335
Amazing Oscar Hammerstein I, The 1628
American Learns to Play 120
American Burlesque Show, The 1267
American Culture, The 124
American Dissertations on the Drama and the Theatre 46
American Drama to 1900 p. xv
American Folklore and the Historian 118
American Humour 144, 2193
American Musical Stage before 1800, The 1606
American Medical Profession, 1783 to 1850, The 962

American Musical Theatre, The 1526
American Pastimes 155
American Popular Song, the Great Innovators 1900-1950 1649
Americans at Play 260
American Stage of Today, The 1881
American Stage to World War I, The 93
American Theatre, The 156, 1853
American Theatrical Arts 97
American Theatrical Periodicals, 1798-1967 2341
American Tradition in the Arts, The 1465
American Vaudeville 1108
American Vaudeville as Ritual 1166
America's Music 181
America's Music from the Pilgrims to the Present 981
America Takes the Stage 238, 1022, 1925
Among the Freaks 768
Anatomy of American Popular Culture, 1840-1861, The 108
Anderson and His Theatre 1343
And Where It Stops Nobody Knows 865
Animals Are My Life 551
Annal of Covent Garden Theatre from 1732 to 1897, The 1711

Annals of Conjuring, The 1332
Annals of the American Circus 1793–1829 516
Annals of the New York Stage 248, 1937
Annie Oakley, Woman at Arms 630
Annie Oakley of the Wild West 654
Annotated Bibliography of Pantomime and Guide to Study Sources 1700
Annual Editions: Readings in Sociology '72-'73 859
Anomalies and Curiosities of Medicine 810
Anthropology in American Life 860
Apropos of Women and Theatre 229
Archaeology of the Cinema 1441
Armless Fiddler, The 1842
Around Theatres 286
Artistic Guide to Chicago and the World's Columbian Exposition, The 733
Art of Mime, The 1693
Art of Moneygetting, or Hints and Helps to Make a Fortune, The 776
Art of Ragtime, The 253
Art of the Puppet, The 1384
As I Remember Them 176
Aspirin Age, 1919-1941, The 131
As Told on a Sunday Run 367
Astonished Muse, The 117
As We Were 141
As You Were, Reminiscences 1740
At Home and on Tour by Ma' Sel' 1788
Autobiography of a Clown 594
Autobiography of an Eccentric Comedian, The 1757
Autobiography of Joseph Jefferson, The 1903
Autobiography of Jumbo's Keeper and Jumbo's Biography 574
Autobiography of Mrs. Tom Thumb, The 841
Autobiography of Will Rogers, The 1518
Automata 1442
Automata and Mechanical Toys--An Illustrated History 1459
Automata Old and New 1444
Les Automates dan Les Ouevres d'Imagination 1442

B

Back Peddler, The 251
Banned! 1997
Bare Facts, The 1251
Barnum 848
Barnum, Showman of America 847
Barnum in London 805
Barnum Presents General Tom Thumb 796
Bawdy Songs of the Early Music Hall 1835
Beaches: Their Lives, Legends, and Lore 914
Before and behind the Curtain, or Fifteen Years' Observation among the Theatres of New York 247, 833, 1936
Before I Forget 1744
Before the Footlights and behind the Scenes 1244, 1917
Behind My Greasepaint 586
Bennett Playbill, The 160, 1860
Bert Williams: Son of Laughter 1625
Beside the Seaside 1823
Best Musicals from Show Boat to a Chorus Line, The 1571
Best Music Hall and Variety Songs 1770
Best Remaining Seats, the Story of the Golden Age of the Movie Palace, The 1126
Better Foot Forward 1613
Between Ourselves 2005
Between the Wars 326
Between You and Me 1790
Bibliography of Books on Conjuring in English from 1580 to 1850, A 1312
Bibliography of Conjuring and Kindred Deceptions, The 1308
Bibliography of English Conjuring, 1581-1876 1317
Bibliography of North American Folklore and Folksong, A 1001
Bibliography of the Books on the Circus in English from 1773 to 1964, A 82

Bibliotheque et Musees des Arts du Spectacle dans le Monde [Performing Arts Collections: An International Handbook] 87
Big Change, 1900-1950, The 98
Biggest, the Smallest, the Longest, the Shortest, The 447
Big River to Cross 2319
Big Show, The 506
Big Top, The 374
Big Top Rhythms 567
Billy Rose 1510
Biographical Dictionary of Wax Modellers, A 67, 835
Bioscope Shows and Their Engines 1451
Bishop of Broadway, The 1962
Black Crook, The 234, 1084
Blacking Up 1042
Black Magic, a Pictorial History of the Negro in American Entertainment 213
Black Manhattan 1006, 1573
Blaze Starr 1262
Blondes, Brunettes, and Bullets 199
Blondin, His Life and Performances 536
Blood and Thunder 2081, 2132
Blue Book of Broadway Musicals 1497
Blues People 222, 1007
Body Merchant 1617
Book about the Theatre, A 237
Book of Burlesque Sketches of English Stage Travestie and Parody, A 2059
Book of Clowns, The 605
Book of Marionettes, A 1392
Book of the Play, A 304, 1985
Book of Travels (and Wanderings), A 1816
Borscht Belt, The 1052
Bow Bell Memories 1729
Bring on the Girls 1653
Bristol at Play 282
Britain's Theatrical Periodicals, 1720-1967 2342
British Music Hall 1739, 1797
Broadway 158
Broadway Heartbeat 256, 1638
Broadway's Greatest Musicals 1585

Broncho Charlie, a Saga of the Saddle 643
Brothers Shubert, The 1642, 1961
Brown Decades, The 137
Buckstkin and Satin 559, 1243
Buckskin Joe 712
Buffalo Bill, King of the Old West 677
Buffalo Bill: The Legend, the Man of Action, the Showman 635
Buffalo Bill, the Noblest Whiteskin 618
Buffalo Bill and His Horses 713
Buffalo Bill and the Wild West 710
Buffalo Bill's Great Wild West Show 655
Buffalo Bill Story--A Brief Account, The 678
Buffalo Bill's Wild West 616
Buffalo Bill's Wild West and Congress of Rough Riders of the World 617
Bunco Book, The 861
Burlesque Tradition in the English Theatre after 1660, The 2071
Burleyque 1258
Business Man in the Amusement World, The 1117
Business of Pleasure, The 766
Business of the Theatre, The 1861
Buster Keaton (Lebel) 1688
Buster Keaton (Robinson) 1193
By the Beautiful Sea 900

C

Cabaret, The 2
Cabinet of Curiosities, A 787
Cagliostro 1342
California I Love, The 1076
California's Pioneer Circus 573
California's Pioneer Circus, Joseph Rowe, Founder 412
Career of Dion Boucicault, The 2054
Careers of Danger and Daring 561
Carnival 872
Carnival Strippers 876, 1247
Carriages at Eleven 327, 2009
Castles in the Air 1504

Cavalcade of Clowns 602
Cedar Chest, The 1405
Celebrated Comedians of Light Opera and Musical Comedy in America 1644
Censor and the Theatres, The 2019
Censorship of English Drama 1737-1824, The 1984
Cent ans de Music-Hall 39
Center Ring 577
Century of English Farce, A 2099
Chad Hanna 415
Champagne from My Slipper 1611
Changeable Scenery 346, 2043
Chautauqua 1290
Chautauqua, an American Place 1294
Chautauqua Caravan 1296
Chautauqua Movement, The 1277
Chautauqua Publications 1269
Chicago Stage, Its Records and Achievements 2299
Chicago's White City of 1893 738
Child of the Century, A 125
Children of Ol' Man River 2318
Chirgwin's Chirrup 1747
Christmas Pantomime 1722
Circus (Hamid) 439
Circus: A World History 401
Circus, Bigger and Better than Ever?, The 381
Circus: Cinders to Sawdust 473
Circus! From Rome to Ringling 471
Circus: Its Origin and Growth Prior to 1835, The 437, 998
Circus: Lure and Legend, The 421
Circus: Men, Beasts, and Joys of the Road 416
Circus, Wisconsin's Unique Heritage, The 388
Circus and Allied Arts, a World Bibliography, p. ix, 81
Circus & Culture 364
Circus Book, The 399
Circus Clowns on Parade 587
Circus Company 501
Circus Day 392
Circus Days 431
Circus Days and What Goes on Back of the Big Top 460
Circus Doctor 554
Circus Has No Home, The 400

Circus Heroes and Heroines 451
Circus in America 430
Circus in Literature, The 531, 849
Circus Kings, The 472
Circus Lady, The 572
Circus Life and Circus Celebrities 432
Circus Menagerie, The 563
Circus Nights and Circus Days 453
Circus Parade 380
Circus Parades 426
Circus Techniques 543
Le Cirque dans L'Univers 498
Cities and Sea Coasts and Island 1838
City and the Theatre, The 209, 1898
Civic Theatres and Entertainments Directory 289
Clockwork Music 1471
Clown 590
Clowning through Life 1104
Clowns (Newton) 598
Clowns (Towsen) 84, 607
Les Clowns 600
Clowns and Pantomimes 24, 308, 1676
Cochran Story, The 320
Cock-A-Doodle-Do 14
'Cockie' 321
Cole 1577
Cole Porter, a Biography 1626
Collectors Annuals 1310
Colonial Virginians at Play 179
Col. Tim McCoy's Real Wild West and Rough Riders of the World 691
Come Back on Tuesday 1135
Come Backstage with Me 1196
Comical Fellows 1686
Commedia Dell 'Arte, The (Oreglia) 62
Commedia Dell 'Arte, The (Smith) 75
Comparison between Two Stages, A 1721
Complete Book of Light Opera, The 1596
Complete Book of Puppets, The 1390
Complete Entertainment Discography from the Mid-1890s to 1942, The 68

Composers of Operetta 1566
Confessions of a Con Man, The 868
Continuous Vaudeville 1082
Cotton Club, The 1558
Cowells in America, The 1755
Crackerbox Philosophers in American Humor and Satire 153
Cradle of Culture, 1800-1810 217, 1902
Cremorne and the Later London Gardens 764
Crime and the Drama, or, Dark Deeds Dramatized 2117
Cristianis, The 555
Critical Idiom, The 2101
Crowded Nights and Days 1751
Crystal Palace 1851-1936, The 735
Cultural History of the American Revolution, A 149
Cultural Life in Nashville on the Eve of the Civil War 984
Cultural Life of the New Nation, 1776-1830, The 138
Culture under Canvas 1278
Curiosities of London 351
Curiosities of London Life 345
Curiosities of Natural History 786
Curiosities of the American Stage 214, 1900
Curtain Call for the Guv'nor 1492
Cyclopedia of Magic 1354

D

Daguerre 1453
Dai Vernon Book of Magic, The 1347
Daly's, the Biography of a Theatre 1536a, 1999
Dancing Devils, The 1719
Dan Emmett and the Rise of Early Negro Minstrelsy 1025
Daniel Frohman Presents 1886
Dan Leno 1851
David Belasco 2109
Days and Nights in London 1817
Days I Knew, The 1911
Days We Knew, The 296
Day under the Big Top, A 566
Delight Makers, The 159

Denver Brown and the Traveling Town 450
Descriptive and Bibliographic Catalog of the Circus & Related Arts Collection at Illinois State University, Normal, Illinois, The 77
Diary of a Daly Debutante 1909
Diary of a Nobody, The 1552
Dickens Theatrical Reader, The 307, 1990
Dictionary of Puppetry 1400
Discovering Pantomimes 1665
Discretions and Indiscretions 1524
Divine Eccentric, The 1885
Dollars and Sense, or How to Get On 776
Les Domteurs, ou la Menagerie des Origines a Nos Jours 578
Doubling Back, Autobiography of an Actor, Serio-Comical 2276
Down Front on the Aisle 1201
Drama of Yesterday and Today, The 342, 2038
Dramas from the American Theatre, 1762-1909 239, 1023, 1926
Drama's Patrons, The 2006
Dramatic Life as I Found It 1919
Drifting About 2274
Driftwood of the Stage 212
Duet for a Lifetime 816
Dwarf, The 43

E

Earl's Court 1787
Early Concert Life in America (1731-1800) 757
Early Doors--Origins of the Music Hall, The 1827
Early English Stages 1300 to 1600 90
Early Havoc 1129
Early Magic Shows, The 58, 1371
Early Opera in America 1639
Early Theatre in Eastern Iowa, The 2295
Early Victorian Drama (1830-1870) 2023, 2125
East End Entertainment 354, 2057
Edwardian Age, The 334
Edwardians, The 338
Elegy in Manhattan 221

Elephant Man 830
Elephant Man and Other Reminiscences 830
Elizabethan Jig and Related Song Drama, The 6
Enchanting Jenny Lind 777
Enchanting Rebel 1914
Enciclopedia Dello Spettacolo 27
Encyclopedia of Popular Music 1643
Encyclopedia of Stage Material 1163
Encyclopedia of Theatre Music 1589
Encyclopaedia of the Musical Theatre 1548
Encyclopaedia of the Theatre (Moses) 1934
Encyclopaedia of the Theatre (Nathan) 245
Encyclopedia of World Theatre, The 29
English at the Seaside, The 916
English Circus and Fair Ground, The 527
English Drama and Theatre, 1800–1900 18
English Eccentrics and Eccentricities 353
English Fairs 759
English Fairs and Markets 731
English Melodrama 2066
English Plays of the Nineteenth Century 2067, 2069
English Song Book, An 1826
English Theatre Music in the Eighteenth Century 314, 1681
English Theatrical Literature 1559–1900 3
Enter Foot and Horse 497, 1712, 2127
Entertainment 325
Entertainment of a Nation, The 1618
Entrees Clownesque 601
L'Envers du Theatre 57
Erotic Theatre 313
Erte 1641
Essai Sur l'Histoire des Panoramas et des Dioramas 1434
Every Other Inch a Lady 1593
Exploitation of Pleasure, The 186

F

Fabulous Empire 650
Fabulous Fanny, The 1576
Fabulous Forties, 1840–1850, a Presentation of Private Life, The 134
Fabulous Kelley, The 945
Fabulous Showman, The 845
Fairground Architecture 737, 853, 892
Fairs, Circuses and Music Halls 309
Fairground Snaps 756
Fairs, Past and Present 762
Famous Actors and Actresses on the American Stage 274
Famous Magicians of the World 1346
Fanfare 231
Father of the Blues 999
Feast of Fools, The 19
Festivals, Games and Amusements, Ancient and Modern 74
F.F. Proctor, Vaudeville Pioneer 1170
Fielding Band Chariots, The 389
Fifty Years in Theatrical Management, 1859–1909 227, 1014, 1160, 2255
Fifty Years of a Londoner's Life 1776
50 Years of American Comedy 266
Fifty Years of Chautauqua 1291
Fifty Years of Make Believe 1302
Fifty Years of Spoof 1623, 1819
Fifty Years of Vaudeville 1630
First Bulldogger, The 689
First Decade of the Boston Museum, The 1922
Flotsam's Follies 1778
Folies Bergere, The 22
Les Folies du Music-Hall 21
Fool, The 88
Fool and His Scepter, The 91
Fools and Folly during the Middle Ages and the Renaissance 79
Footlights Afloat 2329
Footlights Flickered, The 1601
Footlights on the Border 2235

Footlights on the Prairie 2277
Foreigner in Early American Drama, The 1888
For the Good of the Race and Other Stories 1161
Forty Years in the Limelight 1490
Forty Years of Observation of Music and the Drama 1114
Four White Horses and a Brass Band 950
Four Years in Europe with Buffalo Bill 652
Francis Wilson's Life of Himself 271, 1651
Freaks: A Collector's Edition of Nature's Human Oddities, Past and Present 819
Freaks: Myths & Images of the Secret Self 803
Freak Show Man 822
Frederick Catherwood, Architect 1483
French Theatrical Production in the Nineteenth Century 57
Friedrichs Theaterlexikon 29
From Jehovah to Jazz 1008
From Theatre to Music Hall 1841
From the Crash to the Blitz, 1929–1939 142
From the Stocks to the Stars 1690
Fun by the Ton 533
Fun in Black, or Sketches of Minstrel Life 986, 1070
Fun Land U.S.A. 921
Funniest Man on Earth, The 1736a
Funny Way to be a Hero 1765
Future Indefinite 1513
Future of the Theatre, The 1808

G

Gaieties and Gravities 1545
Gaiety, Theatre of Enchantment 1599
Gaiety and George Grossmith 1619
Gaiety Chronicles 1564
Gaiety Stage Door, The 1574
Gaiety Years, The 1567
Gangs of New York, The 99
Gargantua, Circus Star of the Century 565
General Tom Thumb and His Lady 836

Genial Showman and Pictures of a Showman's Career in the Western World, The 2241
Gentleman Giant, The 800
"Gentlemen, be Seated!" 1028
George and Ira Gershwin Songbook 1542
George M. Cohan: Prince of the American Theatre 1614
George M. Cohan: The Man Who Owned Broadway 1597
George Robey 1749
Georgia 1261
Gershwins, The 1579
Gershwin Years, The 1569
Getting to Know Him 1537
G.G. 1553
Ghost!, The 1336, 1449
Ghosts and Greasepaint 328, 2010
Giant: The Pictorial History of the Human Colossus 821
Giants and Dwarfs 850
Giants and Dwarfs: A Study of the Anterior Lobe of the Hypophysis 808
Girl with the Swansdown Seat, The 337
Give 'em a John Robinson 387
Glimpses of Real Life as Seen in the Theatrical World and in Bohemia 2020
Golden Age of Quackery, The 942
Golden Age of Toys, The 1461
Gold in Tin Pan Alley, The 1610
Goodbye to Uncle Tom 2166
Good Old Coney Island 909, 910
"Good Old Gaiety" 1565
Good Old Summer Days 890
Good Years, The 133
Grandin Opera House, or Theatre on the Kerosene Circuit, 1872–1904, The 2271
Le Grand Livre due Cirque 435
Grandmother and the Miller, The 502
Great American Amusement Parks, The 906
Great Belzoni, The 322
Great Book of Magic, The 1378
Great Chess Automation, The 1440
Great Circus Street Parade in Pictures, The 429

Great Days of the Circus 436
Greater Magic 1356
Greatest Show on Earth 410, 1991
Greatest Street in the World--Broadway, The 220, 1905
Great Exhibition, The 744a
Great Forepaugh Show, The 385
Great Houdini, The 1383
Great Men of American Popular Song 1534
Great Patent Medicine Era, The 941
Great Rascal, The 685
Great Salt Lake Trail, The 671
Great Scot, the Life Story of Sir Harry Lauder, Legendary Laird of the Music Hall 1783
Great White Way, The 182, 1871
Green Retreats, the Story of Vauxhall Gardens, 1661-1859 755
Green Room Book, The 38
Grimaldi, King of Clowns 1680
Groucho, Harpo, Chico--And Sometimes Zeppo 1053
Groucho and Me 1171
Grouchophile, The 1172
G-String Murders, The 1240
Gypsy: A Memoir 1241

H

Half Century Reviews and Red Wagon Stories 362
'Halls', The 1768
Handbook of American Popular Culture 126a
Harlem Renaissance 1004
Harlequin 61
Harlequinade 1509
Harlequin in His Element 1696
Harlequin Sorcerer 1662
Harlequin's Stock, Charlie's Cane 51
Harold Arlen 1568
Harry Randall, Old Time Comedian 1814
Hawkers and Walkers in Early America 96
Hell of a Life, A 252
He Made Lincoln Laugh 588
Here, Keller--Train This! 556

Here Comes Barnum 801
Here Comes the Circus 530
Here Comes the Clowns 606
Here We Are Again 603
Hermann the Magician 1321
Hermaphrodite 795
Heroes of the Plains 615
Hey Rube 377
Hey There Sucker 856
Hims Ancient and Modern 319
His Eye Is on the Sparrow 270
Hiss the Villain 2064
Historical and Descriptive Account of the Various Processes of the Daguerreotype and the Diorama, An 1445
History of Conjuring and Magic 1341
History of Court Fools, 1858, The 25
History of English Drama, 1660-1900, A 2018
History of Fairs and Expositions 763
History of Female Impersonation on the Stage, A 5
History of Harlequin, The 1663
History of Pantomime, A 1667
History of Popular Culture, The 177
History of Popular Music in America 258, 1640
History of Seattle Stock Companies, The 2289
History of the American Drama from the Beginning to the Civil War, A 1945
History of the American Drama from the Civil War to the Present Day [1936], A 1946
History of the Boston Theatre, 1854-1901, The 1963
History of the Circus in America 376
History of the English Puppet Theatre, The 1406
History of the English Toy Theatre, The 1409
History of the Harlequinade, The 69
History of the London Stage and Its Famous Players (1576-1903) 281, 1974
History of the Music Festival at the

Chautauqua Institution, 1874-1957, A 1303
History of the New York Stage, from the First Performance in 1732 to 1901 in Encyclopedic Form 171, 1870
History of the Progress of the Drama, Music and Fine Arts in the City of Brooklyn, A 1896
History of the Theatres of London, Containing an Annual Register of New Pieces, Revivals, Pantomimes, &C with Occasional Notes and Anecdotes, A 336, 1705
History of the World's Fair being a Complete and Authentic Description of the Columbian Exposition from Its Inception 761
History of Variety--Vaudeville in Seattle, A 1100
Hold Yer Hosses! 604
Houdini: A Man in Chains 1368
Houdini--a Pictorial Life 1329
Houdini, His Legend and His Magic 1355
Houdini: His Life Story 1362
Houdini: The Man Who Walked through Walls 1352
Houdini: The Untold Story 1327
Houdini's Fabulous Magic 1351
House of Beadle and Adams, The 673
How I Made Millions, the Life of P.T. Barnum, Written by Himself, to Which Is Added the Art of Money-Getting 776
How To Join a Circus 409
Human Curiosities 792
Humbug 813
Humbugs of the World, The 774
Hys Booke 1792

I

I Bow to the Stones 1198
Iche Lebergerni! 589
I'd Like to Do It Again 2076
Idols of the "Halls" 1805
I Had Almost Forgotten 15
I Had to be "Wee" 1849
Iliad 1405

Illustrated Catalogue and Guide Book to Barnum's American Museum, An 817
Illustrated History, An 1387
Illustrated History of Magic, The 1328
Illustrated Magic 1344
I Love You Honey, but the Season is Over 544
Il Teatro delle Favole Rappresentative 70
Immoment Toys 276
Immortal Jolson 1631
Incredible Collectors, Weird Antiques, and Odd Hobbies 788
Incredible New York 136, 1177
Indians Abroad 647
Infinite Variety 1843
In Memorium--Oldtime Show Biz 173
Ins & Outs of Circus Life 550
In the Golden Nineties 169, 1868
In the Spotlight 1134
Invitation to Ranelagh, 1742-1803 754
I Scream for Ice Cream 1666
Isn't It Wonderful 1318
Italian Comedy, The 26
Italian Popular Comedy 44
I Tell You 305
It's a Small World 781
It Seems Like Yesterday 114
I've Lost My Little Willie 901

J

Jazz: A History of the New York Scene 180
Jazz Age, The 102
Jazz Dance 259
Jenny Lind: Her Life, Her Struggles and Her Triumphs 838
Jenny Lind's America 790
Jersey Lily, The 1960
Jimmy Glover--His Book 317
Jimmy Glover and His Friends 318
Jno. B. Jeffrey's Guide and Directory to the Opera Houses, Theatres, Public Halls, Bill Posters, etc. of the Cities and Towns of America 219, 1904

Joe Taylor, Barnstormer, His Travels, Troubles and Triumphs, during Fifty Years in Footlight Flashes 2304

John Mulholland's Story of Magic 1370

John Ringling 519

Jolson 1105, 1539

Les Jongleurs en France au Moyen Age 31

Journal of a London Playgoer, from 1851 to 1866 335, 2014

Journey to Matecumb, A 963

Jubilee of Dramatic Life and Incident of Joseph A. Cave, A 1834

Julius Cahn's Official Theatrical Guide 223, 1907

Just a Little Bit of String 1645

Just Around the Corner 105

Juvenile Drama 1409

K

Kind of Life, A 1227

King Panto 1723

Klondike Kate 1162

L

Lambeth and Music Hall 1806

Land of Contrasts, The 206

Language of Show Biz, The 73

Last of the Forty Horse Drivers 568

Last of the Great Scouts 702, 727

Late and Early Joys at the Players' Theatre 1831

Late Joys at the Players' Theatre 1727

Late Nineteenth Century Drama, 1959 2018

Laugh Makers, The 174

Law of Theatres and Music-Halls, The 1772

Leaves from Conjurers' Scrap Books 1320

Leisure in America 129

Letters from a Theatrical Scene-Painter 1971

Letters from Buffalo Bill 646

Let the Chips Fall 269

Life and Adventure of Far-Famed Billy Purvis, The 1707

Life and Adventures of Billy Purvis, the Extraordinary, Witty, and Comical Showman, Containing Many Humorous Incidents and Anecdotes, Not Hitherto Published, The 1660

Life and Adventures of Buffalo Bill 626

Life and Adventures of Valentine Vox, the Ventriloquist, The 16

Life and Art of Andrew Ducrow & the Romantic Age of the English Circus, The 499

Life and Death of Tin Pan Alley, The 1531

Life and Genius of Jenny Lind, with Beautiful Engravings, The 772

Life and Labour of the People in London 1732

Life and Legend of Tom Mix, The 684

Life and Recollections of Yankee Hill 2186

Life and Reminiscences of E.L. Blanchard, The 1664

Life and Reminiscences of Jessie Bond, the Old Savoyard, The 1494

Life Doubles in Brass 187

Life in America One Hundred Years Ago 126

Life of Augustin Daly 1876

Life of Dan Rice, The 584

Life of David Belasco, The 1968

Life of James Redpath and the Development of the Modern Lyceum, The 1282

Life of Joseph Grimaldi, The 1703

Life of Oliver Morosco 241

Life of Phineas T. Barnum 778
Life's a Drag! 85
Life's a Lark 589
Life Story of the Ringling Bros. 491
Lights and Shadows of New York Life 230
Lillian Russell 1616
Lillie Langtry 1890
Limelight 1800
Lions, Tigers and Me 569
Lions 'n' Tigers 'n' Everything 545
Little Annie Oakley and Other Rugged People 668, 1237
Little Journey to B.F. Keith Palace, Cleveland, A 1060
Lives and Legends of Buffalo Bill, The 701
Lives of the Conjurers, The 1345
London in My Time 297
London Labour and the London Poor 333, 1701
London Pleasure Gardens in the Eighteenth Century, The 765
London's Lost Theatres of the Nineteenth Century with Notes on Plays and Players Seen There 343, 2040
London Stage, 1660-1800, The 1662
London Theatres and Music Halls 1850-1950 323, 1781
London Town 292
Longest Street, The 257
Looking Back on Life 1821
Lord Broadway 261
Lost Chords 196
Lost Panoramas of the Mississippi, The 1464
Lost Theatres of London, The 331, 2012
Louis Roth; Forty Years with Jungle Killers 571
Lyceum, The 2056
Lyrics 1557
Lyrics on Several Occasions 1543

M

McArdle's International Dictionary of Magitain 1365

La Machinerie Theatrale 56
Mack's Vaudeville Guide 1168
McSorley's Wonderful Saloon 828
Madame Tussaud 794
Madame Vestris, a Theatrical Biography 2055
Madame Vestris and Her Times 2021
Madame Vestris and the London Stage 1969
Magic: Stage Illusions and Scientific Diversions including Trick Photography 1460
Magic & Its Professors 1338
Magic and Magicians 1380
Magic as a Performing Art 1311
Magic Catalogue, The 1337
Magician in Many Lands, A 1319
Magician on the American Stage, 1752-1874, The 1373
Magician's Handbook 1322
Magic Man, The 1353
Magic Shadows 1475
Mainly on the Air 285
Mainstreet on the Middle Border 100
Making of Buffalo Bill, The 722
Managers in Distress 2210
"Man Who Broke the Bank, The" 1748
Marie Lloyd, Queen of the Music-Halls 1795
Marie Lloyd and the Music Hall 1761
Marquee Ballyhoo 2254
Marx Brothers, The 1083
Maskelyne and Cooke 1359
Masks, Mimes and Miracles 59
Masks and Marionettes 41
Mass Culture 143
"Master" and Men, Pink 'Un Yesterdays 291
Master Index to Magic in Print, The 1314
Master Magicians--Their Lives and Most Famous Tricks, The 1348
Masters of the Show 1942
Matinee Tomorrow 240, 1927

Title Index

Mauve Decade, The 104
Max Gordon Presents 198
Mazeppa 2259
Medical Messiahs, The 974
Medicine Show 966
Medicine Showman, The 939
Medieval Stage, The 12
Melodies Linger On, The 1540, 1796
Melodrama (Disher) 2082
Melodrama (Smith) 2130
Melodrama Unveiled 2096
Memoires, Une Etoile Francaise au Ciel de L'Amerique 1560
Memoir of John Durang (American Actor, 1785-1816), The 189, 413, 1880
Memoirs of an Amnesiac, The 1588
Memoirs of Bartholomew Fair 749
Memoirs of Charles Lee Lewes, The 1689
Memoirs of Joseph Grimaldi 1675
Memoirs of Robert-Houdin 1376
Memoirs of the Life of David Garrick 1987
Memoirs of the Life of J. Decastro, Comedian, The 407, 1674
Memories of an Old Actor 1913
Memories of Bartholomew Fair 55
Memories of Daly's Theatre 1878
Memories of Rose Eytinge 2230
Memories of the Professional and Social Life of John E. Owens, by His Wife 1939
Men, Beasts, and Gods 178
Menageries, Circuses and Theatres 363
Men of Daring 579
Merle Evans, Maestro of the Circus 486
Merry Partners, The 1575, 2103
La Merveilleuse Histoire du Cirque 518
Metamorphosis of a Sack, The 502
Midway Showman, The 852
Midwest Pioneer, His Ills, Cures, and Doctors, The 958
Mighty Barnum, The 806
Mighty Hippodrome, The 1507
Mimes and Miners 2309
Mimic World, and Public Exhibitions, The 1245

Minstrel in France, A 1789
Minstrel Memories 1035
Minstrel Town, A 2286
Mirror for Gotham 151
Mississippi Panorama 1476
Missie 714
Mister Abbott 154, 1852
Mistinguett 54
Modern Columbus, A 1786
Modern Magic 1357
Mollie Bailey, the Circus Queen of the Southwest 534
Monarchs of Minstrelsy from "Daddy" Rice to Date 1036
Monster Midway 864
Morally We Roll Along 1287
More 284
More Theatres 287
Mother Wore Tights 273
Movement in Two Dimensions 1443
Mud Show 488
Museums, U.S.A. 40, 820
Musical Comedy in America 1634
Musical Stages 1624
Music and Some Highly Musical People 1044
Music Hall 1782
Music Hall in Britain 1743
Music Hall Land, an Account of the Natives, Male and Female, Pastimes, Songs, Antics, and General Oddities of that Strange Country 1766
Music-Hall Memories 1812
Music-Hall Nights 1741
Music Hall Stars of the Nineties 1793
Music of the Old South 1040
My Autobiography 300
My Crazy Life 315
My Desire 580
My Father Owned a Circus 434
My Fifty Years in Rodeo 621
My Lady Vaudeville and Her White Rats 1110
My Life 1715
My Life East and West 1897
My Life in Pictures 301
My Life Is in Your Hands 1500
My Lifetime 1563

My Life Up to Now, a Naughtibiography 1820
My Life with Buffalo Bill 686
My Life with the Big Cats 548
My Magic Life 1335
My Melodies Memoirs 1764
My Sixty Years in Show Business 1862
Mystery and Lore of Monsters, The 842
My Theatrical and Musical Recollections 1833
My Time Is Your Time 268
My Wanderings 1857
My Wonderful World of Slapstick 1147
My Years on the Stage 1879

N

Naked Lady 1883
"Naked Truth!, The" 1648
Nat Goodwin's Book 1112, 1892
Nation in Torment, A 122
Native American Humor (1800-1900) 107, 2145
Natural History of Quackery, The 943
'Neath the Mask 1992
Negro and His Music & Negro Art, The 1016, 1595
Negro and the Drama, The 163, 1863
Negro Authors and Composers of the United States 204
Negro in Music and Art, The 1031
Negro in the American Theatre, The 216
Negro Minstrel Melodies 980
Negro Minstrels 1000
Neighborhood Playhouse, The 1514
Newcomes, The 1840
New Complete Book of the American Musical Theatre 1533
New York Stage, The 1854
Next Week--East Lynne 2073
Nightmare Alley 862
Night Side of London 340
Nights of Gladness 1600
Night They Raided Minsky's, The 1228

Nineteenth Century British Theatre 2024
Nineties, The 127
No Bar Between 557
Nobody 1505
No More than Five in a Bed 116
No People Like Show People 275, 793
Northern Music Hall, The 1799
Notes on a Cowardly Lion 226

O

Oil Paint and Grease Paint 452
Old and the New Magic, The 1339
Old Boston Museum Days 1952
Old Bowery Days 1895
Old Clown's History, The 608
Old Concert Rooms of London, The 1760
Old Conjuring Books 1313
Old Covered Wagon Show Days 358, 928
Old Drama and the New, The 1970
Oldest Deception, The 1382
Old "Old Vic", The 1995
Old Pink 'Un Days 290
Old Showmen and the Old London Fairs, The 33, 745
Old Slacks's Reminiscences and Pocket History of the Colored Profession from 1865 to 1891 1038
Old Stock Company School of Acting, The 1923
Old Time Actor and Penny Showman, The 1846
Old-Time Music Hall Comedians 1763
Old Vic, The 2002
Old Wagon Show Days 495
Once a Clown, Always a Clown 210
Once Upon a Stage 1197
One for a Man, Two for a Horse 932
One-Horse Show, The 591
100 Posters of Buffalo Bill's Wild West 696

100 Years of Circus Posters 489
100 Years of Magic Posters 1375
100 Years of the Negro in Show Business 995
O'Neill, Son and Playwright 1959
On the Road with a Circus 520, 716
On with the Show 265, 1043
Optical Instruments 1455
Original Houdini Scrapbook, The 1349
Other Side of the Circus, The 562
Our Magic 1367
Our Marie 1784
Our Old English Fairs 751
Our Times, the Turn of the Century 152
Our Will Rogers 1515
Outdoor Entertainment Business, The 913
Out Theatres To-Day and Yesterday 188
Out without My Rubbers 1485
Oxford Companion to the Theatre, The 36

P

Pagan Origin of Fairs, The 23, 741
Palace, The 1209
Panorama of Magic 1326
Panorama of Prestidigitation 1325
Pantomime 1687
Pantomime: A Story in Pictures 1691
Pantomime Budgets, and by Special Command a Tete-a-Tete between Sir John Barleycorn and the Old Lady of Threadneedle Street 1671
Pantomime Pageant 1724
Pantomimes, Extravaganzas, and Burlesques 2069
Pantomimes and All about Them, Their Origin, History, etc., The 1718
Paradise in the Strand 1521
Pardner of the Wind 717
Particular Pleasures 339
Passionate Playgoer, The 249
Passport to Paris 1525
Pathway 1811
Pawnee Bill 711

Pawnee Bill (Major Gordon W. Lillie) 640
Paxton's Palace 736
Pearlies, The 288
Peep at Buffalo Bill's Wild West, A 690
Peepshow into Paradise 1454
Pegasus Book of Magic and Magicians 1363
Penny Plain Twopence Coloured 1426
People at Play, The 208
Performing Arts Research 89
Perils of Prosperity, 1914-32, The 132
Pete Martin Calls On 235
Pharoah's Fool 312
Piano and I 1551
Piccadilly to Pall Mall 1804
Pictorial History of Burlesque, A 1260
Pictorial History of Performing Horses, A 428
Pictorial History of Striptease 1266
Pictorial History of the American Carnival, A 873
Pictorial History of the American Circus 414
Pictorial History of the Carousel 899
Pictorial History of Vaudeville, A 1206
Pillars of Drury Lane 2011
Pink Lemonade 393
Pink Parade 293
"Pink 'Un" Remembers, A 294
Pioneer Circuses of the West 490
Pipefuls 596
Playgoer's Memories, A 1777
Play Production in America 1910
Plays, Players & Playgoers! 812
Pleasure Haunts of London during Four Centuries, The 299, 1981
Pleasures of London 310
Poet Scout, The 634
Poms-Poms and Ruffles 918, 1798
Pony Wagon Town, along U.S. 1890 570
Popular Amusements 191
Popular Arts, The 123

Popular Culture in Early Modern Europe 9a
Popular Entertainments through the Ages 48
Popular Recreations in English Society, 1700-1850 329
Popular Theatre, The 242, 1931
Portal to America 147
Postscript to Yesterday 135
Power of the Charlatan, The 938
Pre-Romantic Ballet, The 1726
Present Indicative 1512
Presenting Houdini 1374
Prime Minister of Mirth 1848
Prince of Players 1951
Proceedings of the Conference on the History of American Popular Entertainment 52, 236
Professional & Literary Memoirs of Charles Dibdin the Younger 2045
Professional Life of Mr. Dibdin, The 1989
Professor How Could You? 967
P.T. Barnum Bibliography, A 832
Public Life of W.F. Wallett, the Queen's Jester, The 609
Punch and Judy 1411
Punch and Judy, with Illustrations Designed and Engraved by George Cruikshank 1388
Punch and Judy & Other Essays 1385
Puppeteer's Library Guide, The 1389
Puppet Theatre Handbook, The 1386
Puppet Theatre in America, The 1394
Pursuit of Happiness, The 128

Q

Quacks of Old London, The 80, 964
Queen of the Plaza 1915
Queen of the Plaza: A Biography of Adah Isaacs Menken 1882
Queen's Hall 1893-1941 1759
Quicker Than the Eye--the Magic & the Magicians of the World 1369

R

Recollection of Fred Leslie 1646
Recollections and Reflections of J.R. Planche, The 2120

Recollections of Vesta Tilley 1753
Record by Himself, A 1745
Record of the Boston Stage, A 184, 379, 1873
Records and Reminiscences, Personal and General 298, 1738
Records of the New York Stage from 1750 to 1860 215, 1901
Red Plush and Greasepaint, a Memory of the Music-Hall and Life and Times from the '90's to the '60's 1824
Remember? Remember? 103
Remembering Josephine 63
Remember When 112
Reminiscences of a Showman 1421, 1839
Reminiscences of J.L. Toole 2004
Reminiscing with Sissle and Blake 1578
Revue: A Story in Pictures 1603
Revue: The Great Broadway Period 1488
Rifle Queen, Annie Oakley 706
Right Red Hand, The 2183
Ring Bells! 1547
Ringlings--Wizards of the Circus, The 440
Ring Up the Curtain, Being a Pageant of English Entertainment Covering Half a Century 344, 1832
Rise and Fall of American Humor, The 106
Rise of the City, 1878-1898, The 146
Rise of the Victorian Actor, The 1975
Riverboats of America 2322
River Circus 457, 2331
Roamin' in the Gloamin' 1791
Rogue's Progress 1733
Rolling Stone 262
Romance of London, The 352
Romance of Madame Tussaud's, The 844
Romance of the American Theatre, The 1875
Roots of American Culture, The 145

Round the World with "A Gaiety Girl"
1487
Royal Aquarium, The 1803
Royalty, Religion and Rats! 1850
Running Pianist, The 264

S

Saga of the Comstock Lode, The
2259
San Francisco Stage, The 2234
Sanger Story, The 459
Sawdust and Solitude 581
Sawdust and Spangles 394
Sawdust Ring, The 402
Scenarios of the Commedia dell'Arte
70
Scenes from the Life of an Actor
2167
Scenes from the Nineteenth-Century
Stage 1855
Seaside Architecture 907
Seaside England 915
Seat at the Circus, A 396
Secrets of a Showman 15
Secrets of Houdini, The 1323
Selected Essays: 1917-32 1758
Sequi-Centennial International Expo-
sition, The 734
7 Lively Arts, The 72
Seventy Years a Showman 496
Sex Errors of the Body 829
Seymour Hicks 1561
Shakespeare's Motley 37
Sheridan to Robertson 2138
Sherlock Holmes and Much More
1874
Shores of Light, The 1265
Short History of Scene Design in
Great Britain, A 1478
Short Title Catalogue . . . from Circa
1450 A.D. to 1939 A.D. 1315
Short Title Check List of Conjuring
Periodicals in English, A 1307
Show Biz from Vaude to Video 202,
1122
Show Boat: The Story of a Classic
American Musical 1581, 2330
Showboats 2325
Showcase 1250

Show Life in America 408
Showman 165
Showman Looks On 15
Showmen and Suckers 35
Shows of London, The 1, 279,
732
Sideshow and Animal Tricks 854
Side Show Studies 919
Silver Theatre, Amusements of the
Mining Frontier in Early Nevada,
1850-1864 2307
Sinful Tunes and Spirituals 993
Singing Sixties, The 1559
Sitting Bull, Champion of the Sioux
721
Sixty Years of British Music Hall
1771
Sixty Years' Stage Service, Being a
Record of the Life of Charles
Morton, "The Father of the
Halls" 1801
Sketches by Boz 307
Snappy Vaudeville Jokes 1146
Society Clown, A 1550
Sociology of Popular Drama, A
2095
Sodom by the Sea 922
So Far, So Good 218
So Help Me 1140
Solo in Tom-Toms, A 649
Some Human Oddities 797
Some of These Days 1214
Some Pantomime Pedigrees 1669
Some Rare Old Books on Conjuring
and Magic of the 16th, the 17th,
and the 18th Century 1309
Song in His Heart, A 982
Songs of the American Theater 1590
Songs of the British Music Hall 1752
Speak to Me, Dance with Me 1522
Les Spectacles de la Foire 17
Spice of Life, The 1767
Spice of Variety, The 201
Spirit Gun of the West 718
Sporting Times, the "Pink 'Un"
World 295
Sports and Pastimes of the People of
England, The 349
Stage and Screen 1864
Stage and Screen: Theatrical
Method from Garrick to Griffith
86

Stage-Coach and Tavern Days 121
Stage in the Twentieth Century, The 200
Stage-Land 2100
Stage Reminiscences of Mrs. Gilbert 1891
Star Danced, A 1586
Stars of the Ziegfeld Follies 1621
Stars Who Made the Halls 1762
Stein & Day Handbook of Magic, The 1361
Stephen Foster 1003
Step Right Up 874
Step Right Up: An Illustrated History of the American Medicine Show 826, 949
"Step Right Up Folks!" 903
Stirring Lives of Buffalo Bill and Pawnee Bill 631
Story of America's Musical Theatre, The 1532
Story of Annie Oakley, The 628
Story of Buffalo Bill, The 627
Story of Exhibitions, The 823
Story of George Gershwin, The 1530
Story of Mr. Circus, The 444
Story of Pantomime, The 1725
Story of Sadler's Wells, 1683-1964, The 280
Story of Sadler's Wells, 1683-1977, The 280, 1973
Story of the Music Halls 1775
Strange Life of Willy Clarkson, The 1774
Strange People 799
Street Magic 13, 1330
Street That Never Slept, The 148
Strike the Tents, the Story of Chautauqua 1283
Striptease, the Vanished Art of Burlesque 1225
Strolling Players & Drama in the Provinces 1660-1765 2026
Struggle for a Free Stage, The 2138
Struggle for the Free Stage in London, The 2017
Struggles and Triumphs 775
Studies of the Psychology and Behavior of Captive Animals in Zoos and Circuses 553

Study of Melodrama in England from 1800 to 1840, A 2086
Sunshine and Shadow in New York 150
Sweet Saturday Night 1794
Supplement to Short Title Catalogue . . . from 1472 A.D. to the Present Day 1316

T

Tailor to Brentford, The 502
Take It for a Fact 1815
Take My Life 1499
Tambo and Bones 1049
Tanbark and Tinsel 456
Tarbell Course in Magic, The 1381
Tattoo: Secrets of a Strange Art 834
Telescoping Tableaux 383
Tent Show 2262
Testament of Caliban, The 937
Theater, The 2264
Theater in America 1943
Theater of Augustin Daly 1884
Theater of the Golden Era in California, The 2263
Theater of the Gold Rush Decade in San Francisco 2233
Theater Tonight 2214
Theatre, the Drama, the Girls, The 243, 1932
Theatre and Its People, The 195, 1887
Theatre for Everybody, A 1988
Theatre in a Tent 2300
Theatre in Early Kentucky, 1790-1820, The 2240
Theatre in the Age of Garrick 2022
Theatre of Marvels, The 94
Theatre of the London Fairs in the Eighteenth Century, The 753, 2027
Theatre on the Frontier, The 2208
Theatre Royal Drury Lane 2011
Theatres 267
Theatres of London, The 330
Theatre through Its Stage Door, The 1859
Theatrical and Circus Life 220a, 446, 1360

Title Index

Theatrical and Musical Memoirs   1486
Theatrical Entertainment in Rural
   Missouri before the Civil War   164
Theatrical Twenties, The   183, 1506,
   1872
There Were Giants on the Earth   791
These Were Actors   2231, 2323
They All Had Glamour   234, 1605,
   1924
They All Played Ragtime   161, 976,
   1491
They All Sang   233, 1604
They Broke the Prairie   111
They Called Him Wild Bill   700
They Were Singing and What They
   Sang About   1813
Thirties, The   107a
Thirties--A Time to Remember, The
   113
Thirty Years Passed among the Players
   in England and America   395
This Fabulous Century   110
This Grotesque Essence   992
This Was Burlesque   1231
This Way, Miss   1141
This Way to the Big Show   420, 644
Those Amazing Ringlings and Their
   Circus   485
Those Golden Years--The Circus   476
Those Innocent Years   115
Those Were the Nights   277
Three Hundred Years of American
   Drama and Theatre   272
Thrilling Lives of Buffalo Bill and
   Pawnee Bill   729
Through the Back Door of the Circus
   361
Ticket to the Circus, A   427
Tiger Tiger--My 25 Years with the
   Big Cats   538
Timber Line   648
Tin Pan Alley   1544
Tin Pan Alley in Gaslight   232
Toadstool Millionaires, a Social His-
   tory of Patent Medicines in
   America before Federal Regulation,
   The   972, 974
Toby Tyler   475
Tommy Handley   1785
Tony Pastor   1223

Town Hall Tonight   2246
Trail Blazers of Advertising   250
Training of Wild Animals, The   540
Travelling People, The   740
Treasury of American Folklore, A
   109
Triumphs and Trials of Lotta Crab-
   tree, The   1877
Trouble Begins at Eight, The   1286
Troupers of the Gold Coast, or the
   Rise of Lotta Crabtree   2290
Trouping   2257
Trouping the Oregon Country   2229
Trumpets of Jubilee   839
Turn of the Century   1271
Turn West on 23rd   101
Twenty Years on Broadway   1508
Twinkle Little Star   1944
Two, The   846
Two on the Aisle   170, 1869

U

Uncle Tom's Cabin   250, 2165,
   2166, 2172, 2174, 2182, 2190,
   2199
Under the Big Top   391
Unembarrassed Muse, The   140
Unknown Barnum, The   837
Unknown Mayhew, The   350
Unmasking of Robert-Houdin, The
   1358
Unsophisticated Arts, The   324
Uptown, the Story of Harlem's
   Apollo Theatre, The   254, 1199

V

Vagabond Adventures   1010
Vagabond Trouper   2219
Valentine's Manual, 1927   168,
   1867
Vanishing Village, The   960
Variety Music Cavalcade   1609
Variety Stage, a History of the
   Music Halls from the Earliest
   Period to the Present Time, The
   1836
Vaudeville   1073
Vaudeville: From the Honky-Tonks
   to the Palace   1106, 1158

Vaudeville and Motion Picture Shows 1102
Vaudeville Days 1731
Vaudeville Prompter, The 1194
Vaudeville Theatre--Building--Operation--Management, The 1185
Vaudeville Turns 1145
Vaudeville U.S.A. 1094
Vaudevillians, The 1203
Vauxhall Gardens--A Chapter in the Social History of England 758
Very Special People 798
Victorian & Edwardian Theatres 316, 1773, 2000
Victorian Dramatic Criticism 341, 2032
Victorian Entertainment 306
Victorian Magic 1364
Victorian Popular Ballad, The 1734
Victorian Popular Music 1810
Victorian Sheet Music Covers 1809
Victorian Song 311
Victorian Theatre, The (Rowell) 2031
Victorian Theatre, The (Southern) 347, 2044
Vintage Years When King Edward the Seventh Was Prince of Wales 322
Voyage to Brobdingnag, The 278

W

Wandering Showman, A 558
Watch Yourself Go By 422, 994
Way I See It, The 175
Ways of the Circus, Being the Memories and Adventures of George Conklin, Tamer of Lions, The 382
W.C. Fields, His Follies and Fortunes 263
W.C. Fields by Himself 193
Weber and Fields 1139
Webster Was a Sucker 857
We Called It Culture 1272
We Can Still Hear Them Clapping 1148
We Fell in Love with the Circus 418
Westerners Brand Book 1945-46, The 725
West of Buffalo Bill, The 726
We Who Are Not as Others 827

What a Life I'm Telling You 228, 1015
Where Houdini Was Wrong 1379
White City, The 750
White Magic 1366
Who's Who on the Stage, 1908 8
Wicked Stage, The 1912
Wild Animal Man 549
Wild Bill and Deadwood 645
Wild Circus Animals 547
Wild Tigers and Tame Fleas 357, 535
Wild West or, a History of the Wild West Shows, The 703
William E. Burton, Actor, Author, and Manager 1908
Will Rogers: A Biography 1519
Will Rogers: Ambassador of Good Will, Prince of Wit and Wisdom 1620
Wilton's Music Hall 1735
Winkles and Champagne 1756
Wise Fools in Shakespeare 34
Witch of Wych Street, The 2053
With a Feather on My Nose 1495
With a Twinkle in My Eyes 1822
With Powder on My Nose 1496
With the Circus 546
Wiv a Little Bit O' Luck 1779
Woes of a Wizard 1334
Woman in Black--The Life of Lola Montez, The 1899
Wonder of Optics, The 1466
Words Are Music, The 1528
Words with Music 1527
Working the Halls 1780
World behind the Scenes, The 1998
World I Lived in, The 1142
World in Falseface, The 244, 1933
World of Clowns, The 582
World of Flo Ziegfeld, The 1503
World of George Jean Nathan 246, 1935
World of Harlequin, The 60
World of Melodrama, The 2124
World of Musical Comedy, The 1546
World's Fair Midway 748
World's Greatest Hit--Uncle Tom's Cabin, The 2144

World's Greatest Magic, The 1331
World's Greatest Showman, The 785
Worlds of Music 1635
Writing for Vaudeville 1181

Y

Yankee Theatre 2170
Yes I Can 1088

You Might as Well Live 130
Your Own, Your Very Own 1769

Z

Ziegfeld 1562
Ziegfeld Follies, The 1535
Ziegfelds' Girl, The 1655
Ziegfeld the Great Glorifier 1502

SUBJECT INDEX

This index is alphabetized letter by letter. Numbers refer to entry numbers.

A

Abbott, George 1852
Aberle, Jac 1216
Academy of Magical Arts & Sciences 2464
Acrobats and acrobatics 207, 409, 521, 528, 560-61, 566, 579, 2042
  French 94
  See also Gymnastics and gymnasts
Actors and actresses 114
  American 160
  biographical directories of 8, 274, 1548
  discography of 68
  English 343, 1975, 1979, 1996
    compared to American 1517
  life of in chautauqua 1295
  makeup of 2073
  See also Entertainers
Adams, Joey 201
Adelphi (theater) 1490
Adler, Felix 587
Advertising
  circus 478-79, 504
  relationship to popular theater 95
  techniques in show business 250
Aerialists 358, 536, 561, 576.
    See also Wallenda family
Albee, E.F. 1060, 1080, 1098, 1121, 1151, 1159

Aldridge, Ira 213
Alhambra Theatre (London) 331, 1832
Allard Brothers 1721
Allen, Edward 533
Allen, Fred 201, 221, 275, 1136
Almanacs, patent medicine 973
Almar, George 1405
Alter, Lew 880
American Indians. See Indians
American Museum. See Barnum, P.T.
American Museum of Magic 2411
American Museum of Public Recreation 2412
American Puppet Arts Council 2447
American Society for Theatre Research 2448
Amusement parks 194, 208, 260, 879, 882, 888-927
  associations for 913, 2458, 2469
  guides to 903, 921
  importance of the trolley to 891, 920, 926
  live entertainment at 924
  museums devoted to 2412
  music at 898
  patrons of 894
  rural 891
  safety in 896
  social and moral investigation of 191

Subject Index

as a way of "acting out Utopia"
7
"Ancien Theatre Italien" (acting
company) 71
Anderson (Professor) 1343, 1348,
1364
Anderson, John Henry 1373
Anderson, John M. 1485
Andrews, Robert C. 2028
Animal acts 358, 423, 528, 535,
539, 541, 545-46, 551,
561-64, 570, 854
at amusement parks 924
bibliography on 531
elephants 533, 552, 574, 581,
771
in England 349, 527
gorillas 565
lions and tigers 538, 547, 556-57,
569, 579, 856
training and taming 382, 474,
521, 540, 571
in France 45, 94, 578
See also Equestrian amusements
Animals 178
baiting of in England 9, 74, 325
psychology of 553
See also Bull fights; Menageries
Apollo Theatre (Harlem) 254, 1248
"Aquadrama" 2007
Arcades 882
English 324
penny 186
Architecture
of English seaside resorts 907
fairground and exhibition 737, 744
of opera houses 267
of theaters 267
English 316, 1781
Arkansas
circus in antebellum 511
showboats in 2327
Arlen, Harold 1568, 1649
Art, popular, relationship to popular
theater 95
Arts, The, leisure and 129
Ashcroft, Billy 975
Ashley, Annie 1258
Asia, court fools of 25
Astaire, Fred 225

Astley, Philip 298, 352, 499
bibliography on 81
Astley's Royal Amphitheatre of Arts
343, 410, 526, 1994,
2035, 2045, 2127
Athenaeum (Cairo, Ill. theater)
2301
Atlantic, Iowa, theater of 2212
Atlantic City, N.J., as a resort
900, 914
Austin Brothers Circus 417
Austria, commedia dell' arte in 75
Authors, black 204. See also
Playwrights
Automata 94, 96, 324, 1365,
1440, 1442, 1444, 1454,
1459
Avant-garde, popular entertainment
and 65

B

Bailey (George F.) Circus 487
Bailey, James A. 368, 384
Bailey, M.B. 420
Bailey, Mollie 534, 2327
Baiting. See Animals, baiting of
in England
Baker, Gardiner 811, 824
Baker, Josephine 22, 63
Ballads and balladry 22
English 1734
history of 6
See also Opera, ballad
Ballet 39
costume and set design for 1641
in England 2071
in France 94
in San Francisco 2233
Balloon ascensions 477
Baltimore
pleasure gardens of 752
striptease in 1239
theater in 1913
Bamberg, Theodore 1340, 1354
Banker, Ed H. 1011
Bankhead, Tallulah 275
Banvard, John 1436, 1450, 1462,
1464, 1472
Banvard's Museum and Opera House
1489

432

Bar Harbor, Maine, as a resort 891
Barnabee, Henry Clay 1857
Barnell, Jane 828
Barnes (Al G.) Circus 492
Barnes, James 1680
Barnum, P.T. 134, 141, 178, 188,
    213, 220-21, 247, 363,
    368, 384, 451, 515, 770-
    72, 774-80, 782-83, 785-
    86, 790, 796, 801, 805,
    809, 811-13, 815, 817,
    824, 833, 837-39, 845-48
    advertising of 250
    archives pertaining to 2436
    bibliographies on 81, 531, 831
    motion picture about 806
Barnum and Bailey Circus 360, 384,
    568, 812
    archives pertaining to 2438
    See also Ringling Brothers Barnum
        and Bailey Circus
Barnum Institute of Science and
    History 2413
Barrymore, Ethel 234
Barrymore, William 1995
Bars. See Saloons and taverns
Bartholomew, Truman C. 1433
Bartholomew Fair 55, 279, 731,
    749, 842, 2027
Bates, Blanche 234
Bates, Martin Van Buren (Capt. and
    Mrs.) 791
Batistella, Annabel 1229
Batty, Thomas 578
Baumann, Charly 538
Baxter, Alice 2203
Baxter, Richard 1721
Bayes, Nora 276, 1059
Baylis, Lillian 1988, 1995, 2002
Beadle and Adams (publishers) 673
Bear baiting. See Animals, baiting
    of in England
Bearded ladies 828
Beatty, Clyde 451, 539
Beatty-Cole Circus 431, 533
Beck, Martin 1118
Bedini, Jean 1258
Beerbohm, Max 341, 2071
Belasco, David 86, 240, 1918,
    1921, 1929, 1962, 1968,
    2060, 2109

Bell ringing 349
Belzoni, Giovanni Battista 312,
    332
Benedict, Lew 975
Bennett, Billy 276
Bennett family 160
Benny, Jack 175-76, 201, 275
Bergen, Frank 863
Berle, Milton 176
Berlin, Irving 1534, 1649
Bernhardt, Sarah 1731
Berrell, George Barton 2211
Berry, W.H. 1490
Bertram, Charles 1318-19, 1364
Bidel, Francois 578
Biograph shows 208
Bird Cage Variety Theatre (Tomb-
    stone, Ariz.) 1220, 2309
Bismark, N.Dak., theater in 2206
"Bits, The" (burlesque act) 1258
BLACK CROOK, THE 264, 1084,
    1571, 1607, 1633, 1648,
    1912
Blacks
    attitudes toward in the 19th
        century 1029-30
    as authors 204
    as composers 204
    as dancers 259, 1048
    in early American songsters 983
    in the entertainment world 163,
        180, 213, 216, 995,
        1004-5, 1038, 1558
    musicals for 1573
    music and songs of 994, 1007,
        1016, 1031, 1044, 1047
    as singers 1013
    as stage characters 144, 988,
        991, 2141, 2149, 2188
    See also Minstrel shows and
        minstrels
Blackstone (magician) 1331, 1354,
    1378
Blake, Eubie 1578, 1612
Blake, William 1418
Blanchard, Edward Laman 1664
Bland, James A. 980, 982, 995,
    1020, 1534
Blondin (circus performer) 536, 786
Blossom, Violet 942

Blues 999, 1007
Blumenthal, George 162
Bolger, Ray 225
Bolivar, Tenn., theater in 2287
Bond, Jessie 1494
Bonfils, Frederick Gilmer 648
Bonheur, Rosa 672, 678
Booker Troupe (minstrel show) 1010
Books and reading. See Dime novels
Booth, Edwin 1951
Borough (London theater) 354
Bostock, Frank 578
Boston
    burlesque and striptease in 1227,
        1232, 1236, 1263
    circus in 379
    theater in 184, 224, 668
Boston Museum 1857, 1922-23,
    1952, 1958
Boston Museum (Wood's) 784, 820.
    See also Wood's Museum and
    Metropolitan Theatre
Boston Theatre 1857, 1963
Boucicault, Dion 2025, 2054, 2072,
    2118
Bourgeois, Jeanne. See Mistinguett
    (performer)
Bowery (New York City), popular
    theaters in 188, 1895,
    1954
Bowery Theatre 1895, 1954, 1957
Bradna, Fred 374
Brady, William A. 165, 1893
Brice, Fanny 176, 1258, 1499,
    1501, 1562, 1576, 1621
Bridgeport (Conn.) Public Library.
    Barnum Collection 832,
    2413
Bristol, Engl., popular entertainment
    in 282-83
Britannia Saloon (London) 354
Britannia Theatre 1976
British Music Hall Society 2449
British Pantomime Association 2450
British Theatre Association 2451
British Theatre Museum 2414
    Juvenile Drama Collection 1407
Broadway 182, 220, 241, 256-57,
    1488, 1497, 1508, 1547,
    1571, 1585, 1597

"dancing fools" of 225
history of 158
songs from 1589
Brooks, Van Wyck 1450
Broom, Charles H.H. 1068
Brougham, John 2072, 2105, 2126
Brown University. John Hay Library
    bibliography of black songsters
        found in 983
    Harris Collection of American
        Poetry and Drama 2422
Bryant, Dan 1017, 1037
Buchanan, Jack 225
Buck, Gene 1501
Buckley's Hall (N.Y. City) 220
Buffalo Bill. See Cody, William
Buffalo Bill Historical Center 678,
    726, 2415
Buffalo Bill Museum (Le Claire,
    Iowa) 611
Bull Fights, English 74
Bullock, William 769, 831
Bunker Hill, Battle of, panoramas
    of 1433
Buntline, Ned 668, 685
Buford, R. 1483
Burke, Billie 1495, 1501, 1562,
    1886
Burke, William Ethelbert 592
Burlesque 24, 27, 35, 39, 52,
    66, 146, 173, 208, 226,
    272, 1214, 1224-67, 1950
    Americanization of 2105, 2107
    archives pertaining to 2446
    audiences of 1235
    blacks in 163
    in Boston 224, 668, 1232,
        1236, 1263
    censorship of 1912
    in Chicago 1263
    comedy in 266
    dramatic 2101
    in England 314, 328, 335,
        343-44, 1715, 2004,
        2059, 2069, 2071, 2077,
        2099, 2101, 2111
    literary 335, 1900, 2072, 2105
    morality of 245, 1208
    musical 1570, 1633
    in New York City 186, 256-57,
        1228, 1235

pantomime in 1678
political satire in 2111
in San Francisco 192
skits and routines from 1226,
1248, 2059, 2417
terminology of 73
See also Striptease
Burlettas, English 2079, 2084, 2137
Burnand, Francis C. 298
Burnett, Frances Hodgson 2270
Burns, George 1089
Burton, Jack 173
Burton, William 2072, 2105
Burton, William E. 1908, 1938
Burton's (New York theater) 247
Busch Gardens 925
Busch's Old Country 924
Buskers 306, 345, 1393
Butler, Frank 676
Butler's Floating Theatre 2328
Byng, Douglas 1740
Byron, H.J. 2004

C

Cabarets 2, 39, 63, 260, 1593
comedy in 1765
in England 307, 344, 1553,
1740, 1765
in New York City 188, 922
Cafes, amusement features of 191
Cagliostro (Magician) 1342
Cagney, James 176
Caine, Hall 285
Cairo, Ill.
circus and steamboats in 166,
2317
theater in 2301
California
circus in 412
minstrel shows in 1039
theater in 1913, 1951, 2230,
2260, 2263, 2290, 2304
See also Los Angeles; Sacramento,
Calif.; San Francisco; Visalia,
Calif.
California Joe ("plains hero") 615
Callahan, Chuck 2446
Campbell-Bailey-Hutchinson Circus
371

Canada, guides to theaters in 223
Can Can 1243
Canning, George 2071
Canterbury Hall 340
Canterbury Theatre 1806, 1833
Cantor, Eddy 175-76, 201, 1075,
1258, 1499-1502, 1621
Capon, William 2037
Captain Charley's Private Museum
for Intelligent People. See
Castle, Charles Eugene
Cardini (magician) 1331
Carey, Henry 2071
Carney, George 276
Carney, Kate 276
Carnivals 100, 194, 213, 508,
524, 822, 851-87
blacks in 259, 1007
in England 740
in fiction 862, 865
of the Middle Ages and the
Renaissance 7
sociological studies of 860, 871
strippers in 876, 1247
terminology of 73, 855-57, 859,
875, 882, 910
See also Side shows
Carousel. See Merry-go-round
Carr, Alexander 1258
Carroll, Carl 1485
Carroll, Earl 221, 1499, 1485,
1516, 1617
Carroll (Earl) Vanities 183, 193,
252, 1582
Carson, Kit 615, 659-60
Carter, Billy 1011
Carter, James 578
Carver, William F. 638, 688, 718
Cassell, Charles Eugene 828
Castle, Irene 1504
Castle, Vernon 221
Castle Garden 188, 772, 815
Castleton, Kate 1216
Catherwood, Frederick 1483
Catskill Mountain area, vaudeville
in 1052
Cave, Joseph A. 1834
Cave of Harmony (London) 340
Censorship 186
of English theater and drama
1984, 1997, 2019, 2048

theater 1912
Chanfrau's National (N.Y. theater) 1895
Chang and Eng 816, 846
Chaplin, Charlie 175, 300-301, 1886, 1993
Chapman, William, Sr. 2231
Chapman family 2328
Characters and characterization 2188
  in American comedy 2093
  Indian 2141, 2154, 2197
  in melodrama 2100
  stereotypes in 144
  the Yankee 2151, 2155, 2158, 2164, 2167, 2169-70, 2186, 2196
  See also Toby shows
Charlatans. See Imposters and imposture; Quacks and quackery
Charlot, Andre 1586
Charlot's Revue 183, 1593
Chatham Garden Theatre (New York City) 1895
Chautauqua 100, 146, 260, 272, 1268-1306, 1365
  drama and theater in 1297-98, 1306
  management aspects of 1273
  in Michigan 1289
  in New York State 1271
  periodicals concerning 2351-52
  western expansion of 1284, 1300, 1305
  See also Redpath Chautauqua
Chautauqua Association (Merom, Ind.) 1274
Chautauqua Institution 1277, 1303
Chevalier, Albert 311, 1630, 1744-45, 1770
Chevalier, Florenz 1746
Chevalier, Maurice 22
Cheyenne, Wyo., theater in 2204, 2206
Chicago
  burlesque in 1263
  medicine shows in 936
  theater in 2258, 2264, 2299
  vaudeville in 1207
  See also World's Columbian Exposition (1893)

Children
  impact of the circus on 262
  in vaudeville 218
Children's drama. See Toy theater
Chinese shades. See Shadow pantomimes and plays
Chirgwin, G.H. 1747
Chorus girls 114
Christensen, C.C.A. 1456
Christy, George 1017
Cider Cellars 298, 340
  in fiction 1840
Cincinnati
  museums in 787
  theater in 2240
Cinema. See Motion pictures
Circus Bartok 381
Circuses 10, 27, 49, 66, 100, 110, 120, 146, 173, 178, 185, 194, 211-12, 220a, 237, 272, 662, 821, 859, 884-85, 994, 1151, 1280
  advance men for 454, 469
  advertising of 250, 478-79, 504
  in antebellum Arkansas 511
  in antebellum Missouri 164, 365-66
  association with minstrel shows 977
  bibliographies on 32, 81-82, 531
  blacks in 259, 1007
  in Boston 184, 379
  in California 412, 2279
  classification of techniques in 65
  in Connecticut 514
  dangers in 35
  directories to 219
  English 290, 306-7, 309-10, 325, 328, 339, 397-98, 499, 501, 527, 530, 2034
  European 364
  fiction about 415, 442, 450, 484, 531
  in Florida 411
  folklore of 521
  fools and jesters in 91
  French provincial 45
  gambling in 445, 879

histories and surveys of 355-532
impact on children 262
laws pertaining to 514
as a medium of communication 364
museums and collections of
    materials on 77, 476, 2416,
    2423-24, 2426, 2436,
    2438-39, 2442
in New Orleans 487
in New York City 169, 171,
    188, 230, 248
in Nineteenth-century Cairo, Ill.
    166
organizations and associations for
    1452-53
periodicals about 2353, 2378,
    2395
in Philadelphia 505
plays and films about 401
posters of 489
in rural areas 2152
sanitation in 466
on showboats 2336, 2339
social and moral investigations of
    191, 437, 441
in Sweden 416
tent repertoire 52
terminology of 73, 357, 377,
    401, 462, 465, 473, 521,
    604, 875
wages in 461
wagons of 383, 386, 389, 426
in Washington, D.C. 419
in Wisconsin 388, 405, 447
See also Animal acts; Clowns;
    Flea circuses; Menageries;
    Side shows; names of circuses
    (e.g. Rickett's [John B.]
    Circus)
Circus Fans of America 2452
Circus Historical Society 2453
Circus parades 383, 386, 426-27,
    429-30
Circus trains 427, 429, 443
Circus World Museum 2416
Cirque Olympique 2127
Cities, in drama 2063, 2200
City (London theater) 354
City of London (theater) 354
Civil War, in pantomime 1685

Clark, Bobby 264
Clark, William 787
Clark and McCullough (vaudeville
    team) 264
Clarke, H.G. 1423
Clarkson, Willy 1774
Clausen, Connie 544
Clemens, Samuel. See Twain, Mark
Clement, Herb 381
Cleveland, vaudeville in 1060
Clint, Luke 2028
Clowns 24, 84, 174, 189, 376,
    451, 474, 480, 582-609,
    1034, 1687
bibliography on 531
biographies of 592
dancing 225
English 80, 308, 527, 1660,
    1676, 1686, 1697-98,
    707
French 45
linguistic analysis of performances
    of 583
organizations and associations for
    2454
pantomime of 409, 1660, 1676,
    1686, 1698, 1707
periodicals about 2349
singing 599
See also names of clowns (e.g.
    Rice, Dan)
Clowns of America 2454
Clum, John P. 2294
Clyde, Vander 1211
Coborn, Charles 1748
Cochran, Charles B. 14-15, 201,
    321-21
Cock fights, in England 325
Coco (clown). See Poliakoff,
    Nicholai
Cocteau, Jean 1211
Cody, William 109-10, 384, 420,
    451, 611, 615, 618, 620,
    625-27, 632-35, 637-38,
    641, 648-49, 655-56,
    668-69, 671, 677-79,
    681-82, 685-86, 696,
    701-2, 708, 710-11, 713,
    718, 720, 722, 725-29,
    2150, 2183-85

Subject Index

advertising by 250
bibliography on 81
career in melodrama 614, 2150, 2178
correspondence of 646
fiction about 622
See also Wild West shows, Cody's
Coghlan, Rose 234
Cohan, George M. 175-76, 198, 221, 244, 1508, 1534, 1597, 1614, 1886, 2092
Cole, W.W. 384
Cole Brothers Circus 373, 533
Cole Brothers Wagon Show 358
Coleman, George Sanger 459
Colin, Peter 592
Collectors and collecting 788
Collier, Constance 1509
Coltman, Frank 2272
Columbia Circuit (burlesque) 1258
Columbia Exposition. Se World's Columbian Exposition (1893)
Columbia Garden 752
Columbine (pantomime character) 1686
Comedians 174, 1644, 1879, 1908, 1939, 1944
discography of 68
English 1545, 1745-7, 1749, 1757, 1763, 1765, 1786, 1788-92, 1800, 1814, 1848, 1851
music hall and show 24, 244, 1745-47, 1749, 1757, 1763, 1786, 1788-92, 1800, 1814, 1848, 1851
testing of 244
See also names of comedians (e.g. Jessel, George)
Comedy 197, 266
characterization in 2093
definition of 2097
English 2087
influence of commedia dell' arte on bourgeois 11
in opera 200
organizations and associations 2457
race in 1095-96, 1650, 1888
routines 226
slapstick 35
compared to commedia dell' arte 51

in vaudeville 266, 1095-96, 1167
See also Musical comedy; Wit and humor
Commedia dell' arte 20, 26, 41, 44, 47-49, 59-62, 65, 69, 75, 225, 1687, 1721
clowns in 595, 1676
comparison to silent slapstick comedy 51
in England 4
in France 71
influence on English drama 11
parallels with vaudeville 1215
satire in 28
scenarios of 70
Composers 1531, 1533-34, 1546, 1643
black 204
of operettas 1566
See also Lyricists; Tin Pan Alley; names of composers (e.g. Gershwin, George)
Concerts
in the colonial period 179
in Nashville 984
in New York City 230, 757
in Nineteenth-century saloons 116, 220a, 230, 1222
in pleasure gardens 757
troupes performing 96
Coney Island 169, 180, 902, 906, 908-10, 917, 919, 922-23, 927
Conference on Nineteenth-century British Theatre, papers of 2085
Conference on the History of American Popular Entertainment (1977) 52
Confidence men. See Hoaxes and swindlers
Conjurers. See Magic
Conklin, George 382
Connecticut, anti-circus laws of 514
Conquest family 1682
Cons, Emma 1988, 2002
Contortionists 423
Cook, Joe 1258

Cooke, Louis E. 729
Coop and Lent Circus 370
Cooper, James E. 384
Cord, Marie 1225
Corio, Ann 1225, 1250, 1254
Cosgrave, Luke 2214
Cosmetics. See Actors and actresses, makeup
Costermongers
    entertainment by 340
    songs of 311
Costume design 1511, 1524, 1536, 1641, 1921, 2073
Cotton, Ben 975, 1037
Cotton Club 1558
Coup, Wm. Cameron 368, 515, 812
Court, Alfred 547–48
Court fools. See Fools and jesters
Courtright, Billy 1037
Covent Garden (theater) 336, 1658, 1708, 1711, 2017
Coward, Noel 175, 198, 1512–13
Cowell, Sam 1736, 1755
Crabtree, Lotta 1260, 1877, 2290
Cranton, Heath. See Newton, H. Chance
Crawford, Jack 634
Crawford, John Wallace 2183–84
Cremorne (London garden) 298, 340, 764, 766
Crime, in melodrama 2117, 2122
Cripple Creek, Colo., theater in 2202
Cristianis family 555
Critics
    biographies of 341
    lists of 219
    melodrama and the 2096
Crockett, Charles James 578
Crockett, Davy, as a folk hero 119
Croxton, Arthur 1751
Crumbine, Samuel J. 264
Crystal Palace 298, 306, 735–36, 744a
Cuba, guide to theater in 223
Curtis Theatre Collection 2417

D

Daguerre, Louis Jacque 1445, 1453

Dale, Charles 201
Dalston (London theater) 354
Daly, Augustin 1876, 1878–79, 1891, 1938, 1949, 1953, 1967, 1999, 2074
Daly's (theater) 327, 344, 1490, 1509, 1652, 1878, 1909, 1958, 1999
Dance 52
    black 259
        influence on the minstrel show 1048
    in England 74, 1661, 1708
    history of dramatic 6
    organizations and associations 2455
    periodicals 2355
    See also Can Can; Marathon dancing; Morris dance; Rope dancing
Dance academies, in New York City 186
Dance halls 260
    in New York City 186, 230
Dancers 211, 252
    blacks as 163, 259
    as clowns 225
    in the Ziegfeld Follies 1629
Darton (Wells Gardner) & Co., Ltd. 1425
Davenport, Iowa, theater in 2295
Davenport, John 592
Davenport Brothers (magicians) 1364
Davis, Owen 2075–76, 2094
Davis, Richard Harding 1181
Davis, Sammy, Jr. 1088
Deagle's Variety Theatre (St. Louis) 1084
De Angellis, Jeff 2219
DeBar's Opera House (St. Louis) 2211
DeCastro, J. 407, 1674
De Courville, Albert 305
de Mille, Agnes 1522
Dentists, medicine shows of 935
Denvir, Arthur 1181
DePol, John 1489
Depression (1929), entertainment during 107a. See also U.S. Works Progress Administration

Deslys, Gabys 2005
Des Moines, Iowa, theater in 2232
Detroit Institute of Arts. Reference
    Library 2418
Devant, David 1334-35
DeVeny, William 669
DeWolf, Hopper 210
Dhotre, Damoo G. 549
Dibdin, Charles, Jr. 280, 2045
Dibdin, Charles, Sr. 280, 526,
    1989, 2028, 2058
Dibdin, Thomas 526, 1422, 2033,
    2071
Dickens, Charles 2071
Dickeson, Montroville W. 1456,
    1476
Dillon, William A. 187
Dime museums 208, 220a, 273,
    768, 787, 813, 821, 825-
    26, 834
    in Boston 224
    in Minnesota 190
    See also Hubert's Dime Museum
Dime novels 139, 673, 701
Dioramas 134, 1441, 1445, 1453,
    1470, 1478
    English 279, 299, 306, 1469
    as stage scenery 1484
    See also Panoramas
Dircks, Henry 1480
Discography
    of C. Porter 1626
    1890s-1942 68
    of the Gershwin songs 1579
    music hall 1752
    of the musical theater 1526,
    1528
    of Sissel and Blake songs 1578
Disguises 90
Disney Land and World 897, 906
Dixey, Henry E. 234
Dixon, George Washington 997,
    1011
Dixon, Henry P. 1258
Dockrill (Mme.) 503
Doctors, itinerant 96
Dr. Wait's Kickapoo Indian Medicine
    Show. See Medicine shows

Dodge City, Kans., theater in
    2267
Domestic drama 2073
Drake, Samuel 2231
Drama 126, 260, 272, 1926,
    1946-47, 1955, 2060,
    2078, 2142, 2176
    about the circus 401
    bibliography of dissertations on
    46
    in chautauqua and the lyceum
    movement 1297-98, 1306
    the city in 2063
    jazz-vaudeville in 1964
    museums and special collections
    pertaining to 2422
    periodicals and serials 2356,
    2363, 2380
    reviews of (1929-38) 170
    sociology of 2095
    in vaudeville 1079, 1087
    See also Shadow pantomime and
    plays; Theater
Drama, English 276, 1708, 1970,
    2018, 2023-24
    archives relating to 2444
    bibliography on 18
    in burlesque 2101
    burlesquing of serious 2110
    censorship of 1984
    criticism of 307
    influence of the commedia dell'
    arte on 11
    See also "Aquadrama"; Domestic
    drama; Nautical drama;
    Theater, English
Drew, John 1879, 1891
Drury Lane (London) 160, 336,
    1657, 1659, 1670, 1684,
    1690, 1717a, 1722, 2011,
    2017
Drury Lane Company 2056
DuBois (Madame) 933
Dubuque, Iowa 2251
Ducrow, Andrew 499, 1994,
    2035-36
Duffet, Thomas 2071
Duff-Gordon, Lucille 1424
Duke, Vernon 1525
Dunn, Roy Sylvan 641

Dunninger (magician) 1331
Dunville, T.E. 1757
Duprez, Charles H. 975, 1011
Durang, John 189, 355, 413, 1880
Durante, Jimmy 175-76, 275
Dwarfs 808, 842, 850
  sociological investigation of 843
  See also Midgets
Dyer Company 1419

E

Eagle, Nate 510, 884
Eagle Tavern (London) 340
Eagle Theatres 2247
Eagle Variety House 2215
East, John and Charles 1992
Ebsen, Buddy 225
Eden Musee 101
Edwardes, George 1487, 1490,
      1492, 1509, 1521, 1545,
      1561, 1567, 1599, 1630,
      1645, 1652, 2005
Edwards, Gus 176, 1075, 1140,
      1221, 1258, 1534
Edwards, Gus (Mrs.) 201
Effingham Saloon (London) 354
Egan, I.J. 1456, 1476
Egyptian Hall (London) 279, 767,
      769, 773, 814, 831, 1359,
      1366
Egyptian Hall Museum of Magical
      History 2419
Eidophusikon 279, 1427, 1452,
      1477
Elder, Ted 667
Elen, Gus 311
Ellar, Thomas 1680
Ellison, M. Roy 1291
Elmira, N.Y., vaudeville in 1058
Eltinge, Julian 5, 221
Emerson, Bill 1037
Emmett, Dan 1025, 1534
Emney, Fred 276
Empire Palace of Variety 1832
Empire Theatre 2435
Emporia, Kans., opera Houses in
      2252
Empress Theatre Brixton 1806
England, general sources on popular
      entertainment in 276-354,
      1656-1851. See also Drama,
      English; London; Theater,
      English; the subheading
      "English" or "in England"
      under types of entertain-
      ment (e.g. Circuses, Eng-
      lish)
English Opera House 336
Entertainers 135
  biographies of 234, 2409
      English 1739
  blacks as 163, 180, 213, 995,
      1004-5, 1038, 1558
  relationship with the "sucker" 35
  traveling 49, 58, 96, 164,
      173, 210, 262, 1697,
      1919, 2214, 2216, 2219,
      2223-24, 2226, 2228-29,
      2244-45, 2249, 2257,
      2260, 2262, 2266, 2272-
      73, 2276, 2282-85, 2298,
      2304-6, 2312, 2314
  See also actors and actresses;
      Street entertainment
Equestrian amusements 45, 428,
      498, 532, 708, 2034-35,
      2080, 2091
  bibliography of 81
  in circuses 376, 404, 410,
      499, 502, 528, 538, 550,
      555, 572-73
  in England 304, 306, 343,
      351-52, 502, 1994, 2127,
      2136
  in France 94, 2127
  pantomime in 1674
Errol, Leon 1258, 1260
Erte 1536, 1641
Europe
  circuses of 364
  court fools of 25
  popular culture of pre-industrial
      9a
Evans, Merle 451, 486
Exhibition halls. See names of ex-
      hibition halls (e.g. Egyp-
      tian Hall [London])
Exhibitions 134, 763, 824
  in the colonial period 179

Subject Index

English 279, 290, 328
See also names of exhibitions
(e.g. World's Columbian Exposition [1893])
Extravaganzas 2069, 2077, 2107, 2120
politics in 2111
references to Shakespeare in 2139
in San Francisco 2233
Eytinge, Rose 2230

F

Faimali, Upilio 578
Fairs 10, 48, 362, 508, 524, 739, 748, 763, 856, 882, 885
architecture of 737
in England 33, 35, 56, 160, 299, 306, 309-10, 312, 325, 351-52, 731, 737, 740, 745, 749, 751, 753, 756, 759, 762, 792, 2027, 2099
periodicals about 2410
in France 17, 45, 762, 1726
pagan origins of 23, 741
social and moral investigations of 191
theater of 2027
See also Carnivals; names of fairs (e.g. Bartholomew Fair)
Fakes and fakery 35
Falconi, Signior 1324
Fantasy, in the Middle Ages 19
Farce 2088, 2116
definition of 2097
English 1987, 2061, 2068, 2099
history of operatic 6
influence of commedia dell' arte on 11
Fargo, N. Dak., theater in 2206
Farjeon, Herbert 1630
Farren, Nellie 1630
Farrington, R. 682
Fay, Frank 275
Fellows, Dexter 420, 644
Female impersonation 85, 1211
history of 5
Ferber, Edna 2320, 2329-30

Festivals
in England 74, 325
of the Middle Ages 19
Fiction
Buffalo Bill in 622, 673-74, 701, 722
carnival in 862, 865
circus in 415, 442, 450, 457, 475, 484, 531
medicine shows in 960, 963, 966-67
music halls in 1840
showboats in 2320, 2329-30
the stage in 2254, 2308
vaudeville in 1078, 1099, 1124, 1160
ventriloquism in 6
See also Dime novels
Field, Alfred Griffith 994
Fielding, Henry 2071
Fields, Billy 2417
Fields, Gracie 276, 1630
Fields, W.C. 176, 193, 263, 1258, 1499, 1621
Film. See Motion pictures
Finck, Herman 1764
Fink, Mike, as a folk hero 119
Finnell, Carrie 1225
Fire-eating 786
Fitch, Clyde 240, 2060
Fitzball, Edward 2135
Flanagan, Bud 315
Flea circuses 856
Florida, circuses in 411
Flying Concellos (aerial-trapeze act) 264
Foghorn, Clancy 621
Folies Bergere 22, 63, 263, 1536
Folklore, American 109
of the circus 521
creation of heroes and demigods in 119
relationship to popular culture 118
Folk songs
blackface minstrel influence on negro 1046
of the circus 522
Follies 173, 1514. See also Ziegfeld Follies

Folly Theatre 208
Fools and jesters 25, 79, 84, 91
  in preindustrial Europe 9a
  in Shakespearean drama 34, 37
  social history of 88
Forepaugh (Adam) Show 384-85
Forepaugh Circus 520, 568
Formby, George 311
Forrest, Sam 1858
Foster, Billy 2417
Foster, George 1767
Foster, Stephen 980, 1003, 1027,
  1534
Foster family 996
Four Danubes (vaudeville performers)
  1128
Fox, Fannie. See Batistell, Annabel
Fox, George L. 220a, 234, 595,
  1677-78, 1692, 1714, 2072
Foy, Eddie, Sr. 198, 1103-4
France
  commedia dell' arte in 70-71, 75
  court fools of 25
  fairs and shows of 17, 45, 762
  influence of the dance of on
    English harlequin 76
  jugglers in medieval 31
  melodrama in 2081
  music halls in 39
  See also Cabarets; Paris; Theater,
    French
Frank, Joseph. See Keaton, Buster
Fratellini family 339, 518
Freaks 35, 96, 358, 528, 768,
  786, 788, 792-93, 797-99,
  802-3, 810, 819, 822, 827,
  829-30, 842, 852, 856,
  859
  bibliography on 531
  in England 279, 352-53
  in Vaudeville 176
  See also Dwarfs; Giants; Herma-
    phrodites; Midgets
Frere, John Hookham 2071
Friends of Old Time Music 2457
Frohman, Charles 327, 1879, 1886
Frohman, Daniel 234
Frontier
  opera houses on 2218
  theater on 2231, 2241, 2260-61,
    2267, 2279, 2303-4

  See also Mining towns
Frontiersmen, stage characterizations
  of 28, 2188
Fulton, James C. 1011
Fyffe, Will 276

G

Gaiety Theatre 322, 327, 344,
  331, 1492, 1509, 1521,
  1545, 1553, 1561, 1563-
  65, 1567, 1574, 1599,
  1619, 1646, 1804, 2004
Galesburg, Ill., history of 111
Galveston, Tex., theater in 2235
Gambling
  carnival 861, 866-69, 879,
    882
  circus 445
  tricks of 854
Games 74
  colonial 179
  See also Toys
Garbo, Greta 176
Garden amusements 134. See also
  Pleasure gardens
Garland, Judy 176, 1028, 1157
Gay, John 2071
Geddes, Norman Bel 743
Germany
  commedia dell' arte in 75
  court fools of 25
Gershwin, George 1530, 1534,
  1542, 1569, 1579, 1649
Gershwin, Ira 1535, 1542, 1569,
  1579
Ghosts. See Optical-mechanical
  entertainments
Giants 251, 312, 332, 786, 789,
  791-93, 799-800, 807-8,
  810, 821, 850
Gielgud, John 1250
Gilbert, Anne Jane Hartley 1891
Gilbert, W.S. 2005, 2071
Gilbert and Sullivan productions
  210, 344, 1494
Gillette, William 240, 1874,
  1886, 1930, 1966, 2270
Gillings, David John. See Mozart,
  George

Glenroy, John H. 537, 550
Glover, Jimmy 317-19
Goldoni, Carlo 41
Gollmar Brothers Circus 434
Goodman, Julia Cody 702
Goodwin, Nat 285, 1112, 1118
Gordon (panoramist) 1456
Gordon, Max 198
Gozzi, Carlo 41
Graham (Dr.) 352
Grandin Opera House (Tidioute, Pa.)
    2268-69, 2271
"Grand Street Follies" 1580
Grand Theater (New York City) 147
Granlund, Nils Thor 199
Granville, Taylor 1181
Grau, Robert 1114
Graves, George 1545
Gray, Billy 1217
Great Roman Hippodrome 812
Grecian Theatre (London) 343, 1682
Greece
    early mime and pantomime in 59
    festivals, games, and amusements
        of 74
"Greenwich Street Follies" 1582
Greenwich Village Follies 1485
Griebling, Otto 587
Grieve, John Henderson 2028
Griffin, Charles Eldridge 651-52
Griffiths Brothers 276
Grimaldi, Joseph 280, 353, 1667,
    1669, 1672, 1675, 1679-80,
    1688, 1692, 1694-95, 1703,
    1706, 1717, 1733
Grock (clown). See Wettach, Adrian
Grossinger's 176
Grossmith, George 1550-53, 1619
Guignol, Grand 65
Guilbert, Yvette 1731
Gwynne, Jack 1370
Gymnastics and gymnasts 45. See
    also Acrobats and acrobatics

H

Hackett, Charles H. 2171
Hagan, Billy 2417
Hagenbeck, Carl 578
Hagenbeck, Lorenz 551

Hall, Rhodolphus 1039
Hall, William P. 564
Hallam (theater company) 1373
Hamblin, Thomas S. 1957
Hamid, George A. 439
Hamilton (panoramist) 1479
Hamlin, John Austin 930
Hammerstein, Oscar 162, 221,
    1628
Hammerstein, Oscar, II 1537, 1557
Hanby, B.R. 980
Handley, Tommy 1785
Handy, William Christopher 999
Handy Brothers (publishers) 204
Hank, Harry 1037
Hanlon-Lee (acrobatic team) 2042
Hanson, Herman 1353
Hardeen (magician) 1348
Harlem Opera House. See Apollo
    Theatre (Harlem)
Harlequin 60-61, 69, 84, 88,
    2148
    dance in 76
    in England 1663, 1683, 1686,
        1689, 1696, 1721
    the spirit of Jim Crow in 1034
Harmount Company 2174-75, 2182,
    2189
Harnois Theatre (Missoula, Mont.)
    2236
Harrigan, Edward 272, 1217,
    2113-14
Harrigan and Hart (vaudeville team)
    220, 232, 1095, 1544,
    1575
Harris, Augustus 1670, 1722
Harris, Jed 275
Harrison, Harry P. 1278
Hart, Tony 975, 1217
Hart, William S. 1897
Harvard University. Library.
    Theatre Collection 1412
Havoc, June 1129-30
Haydon, Benjamin Robert 805
Haymarket (theater) 327, 336
Hays, Will S. 980
Healy, John E. See Medicine
    shows, Healy's Kickapoo
    Indian Medicine Show
Heath, William 1415

Hecht, Ben 125
Heilbron, Bertha L. 1457
Held, Anna 221, 1560, 1562, 1621
Henderson, J.Y. 554
Henning, Doug 1331
Henshaw, John E. 1258
Herbert, Victor 1534
Herk, I. 1258
Hermann (animal trainer) 578
Hermann, Alexander 1321-22, 1373, 1378, 1380
Hermann, Carl 1321-22, 1378, 1380
Hermaphrodites 795, 829
Heroes, folk
on the early American stage 119
humor and satire of 153
Hickok, James Butler ("Wild Bill") 109, 615, 645, 700
Hicks, Seymour 1561, 2005
Hill, George Handel 2151, 2167
Hilliam, Bentley Colingwood 1778-79
Hinkle, Milt 620, 659-60
Hippodrome 188, 249, 305, 498, 1498, 1507, 1529, 1832
Hoaxes and swindlers 774, 807, 1371, 1377
in carnivals 861, 866-69, 879-80
in medicine shows 950
See also Fakes and fakery; Quacks and quackery
Hobson, Frederick. See Leslie, Fred
Hoffman, Aaron 1181
Holborn Empire (London theater) 331
Holland, George 2072
Hollingshead, John 1563-65, 1599, 2004
Honky tonks 1258, 1260
Hope, Bob 1069
Hornmann (Flosso) Magic Company 2420
Hotels, entertainment in 19th century 116
Houdini 1323, 1327, 1329, 1331, 1348-52, 1354-55, 1362, 1368, 1373-74, 1377-80, 1383
Houston, theater in 2235
Howard (Boston theater) 224, 668, 1232, 1236
Howard, George C. 2173

Howard, May 1258, 1260
Howes Circus 487
Hoxie, Jack 692
Hoxie Brothers Circus 381, 489
Hoyt, Charles H. 232, 2171
Hoyt, Edward Jonathan 712
Hubbard, Elbert and Alice 1134
Hubert's Dime Museum 251
Hudson, Samuel 1436
Hudson River School, influence of panoramic painting on 1438
Hugard (magician) 1354
Hughes, Charles 526
Hughes, Charles Evans 1121
Hughes' Floating Enterprise 2333
Humor. See Comedy; Wit and humor
Hunt, Charles T., Sr. 444
Hunter, Ruth 1135

I

Iberson's Tent Show Attraction 2287
Illinois State University. Circus and Related Arts Collection 77, 2426
Illusion. See Optical-mechanical entertainments
Impersonation 218. See also Female impersonation; Male impersonation
Imposters and imposture, in pre-industrial Europe 9a
Indiana University. Lilly Library. Stock Collection 2078, 2444
Indian Museum (St. Louis) 787
Indians
as actors 2294
in the circus 528
medicine shows and 971
stage characterizations of 2141, 2154, 2197
Wild West shows and 647, 670, 721, 723, 730
See also Pueblo Indians
International Association of Amusement Parks and Attractions 2458
International Brotherhood of Magicians 2459

International Centre for Research on Traditional Marionettes 2460
International Mimes and Pantomimists 2461
Iola (Princess) 933
Iowa
  opera houses in 2265
  theater in 2295
  See also Davenport, Iowa; Des Moines, Iowa; Sioux City, Iowa
Iroquois Theatre 1103
Irving, Henry 87
Irving Place Theatre 1225, 1232
Isman, Felix 1118
Italy
  court fools of 25
  influence of the dance on English harlequin 76
  See also Commedia dell' arte

J

Jack, Sam T. 1258
Jackson, Mich., theater in 2253
Jackson, Miss., theater in 2243
Jacobs, Lou 587
James (Charles S.) Theatre (Shrevesprt, La.) 1941
Jameson, J.H. 1417
Janis, Elsie 218
Jazz 180, 213
  in drama 1964
Jefferson, Joseph 1903, 2201
Jefferson, Joseph II 2072
Jerrold, Douglas 2135
Jessel, George 175, 201, 1075, 1140-42, 1499
Jesters. See Fools and jesters
Jews, in vaudeville 52
Johnson, H.L. 465
Jolson, Al 175-76, 221, 1047, 1258, 1499, 1539, 1572, 1631
Jones, Buck 692. See also Wild West shows, Buck Jones
Joplin, Scott 1028
Judson, Edward Zane Carroll. See Buntline, Ned
Jugglers 84, 423, 854

circus 521, 525, 542
  in England 74
  in medieval France 31
  in preindustrial Europe 9a
Jung, Paul 587
Jupp, James 1574
Juvenile drama. See Toy theater

K

Kansas, theater in 2266. See also Dodge City, Kans.
Karno, Fred 1806, 1993
Kaye, Danny 1250
Keaton, Buster 1062, 1147, 1193, 1688
Keeler, Ralph 1009-10
Keene, Richard Wynne 1717a
Keith, B.F. 200, 1054, 1098, 1118-19, 1151, 1154, 1165
Keith (B.F.) Palace (Cleveland) 1060, 1181
Kellar, Harry 1319, 1378, 1380
Keller, George 556
Kelley (Doc) 945
Kelly, Emmett 587, 590, 602
Kelly, J.W. 1095
Kelly, John 1216
Kempner Theatre (Little Rock, Ark.) 2205
Kennedy, Robert E. 1377
Kentucky, theater in 2240
Kern, Jerome 198, 1534, 1649
Kerr, Alex 557
Kerstand, Billy 995
Kickapoo Indian Medicine Co. See Medicine shows
Kilanyi, Edward 1920
Kinescopes, blacks in 259
King Brothers (circus) 381
Kinsey (Madge) Players 2250
Kischko, Glenn 680
Klein, Charles 2060
Knight, Laura 452
Knowlton, Dora 1909
Knox College, history of 111
Kober, Arthur 201
Koster and Bial's Music Hall (New York City) 1475

L

Laboring classes, English 348
  theater of 1976, 1980, 2001,
    2070
Lafayette Theatre. See Apollo
    Theatre (Harlem)
Lahr, Bert 170, 226
Lake, Alice 503
Lake family 708
Lambs, The 2462
Lane, Lupino 1630
Lane, William Henry 1048
Langtry, Lillie 114, 1890, 1911,
    1960, 2005, 2238
Lansing, Mich., chautauqua in 1289
Lapierre, Auguste 1461
La Rue, Danny 85
Las Vegas, revues in 1511, 1538,
    1592, 1598, 1627
Lauder, Harry 276, 1118, 1149,
    1152, 1750, 1783, 1807
Laurel, Stan 1993
Laurie, Joe, Jr. 201
Lawrence, Gertrude 1586, 1806
Laylander, O.J. 1134
Leacock, Stephen 2071
Leadville, Colo., opera houses of
    2220, 2297
League of Historic American Theatres
    2463
LeBlanc, Dudley J. 968, 974
Lectures 230
  in Nineteenth-century St. Louis
    2209
Lee, Gypsy Rose 170, 201, 249,
    1129, 1241
Leicester Square (exhibition hall)
    1428, 1483
Leipzig, Nate 1370
Leisure 120
  the arts and 129
  of the 1930s 260
  See also Recreation
Leitzel, Lillian 451
Leman, Walter M. 1913
Leman Street (theater) 2051
Lemmon, Jack 1250
Leno, Dan 1722, 1736a, 1806,
    1851, 2005

Leonard, Ada 1225
Leonard, Eddie 228
Leslie, Fred 1646
Levant, Oscar 275, 1588
Levy, Bert 1161
Lewes, Charles Lee 1689
Lewis, Al 198
Lewis, Harry 1435-36
Lewis, Henry 1457, 1463-64,
    1482
Lewis, James 1891
Lewis, Minard 1433
Lewis, Ted 176
Lewiston, Harry 822
Library of Congress 2428
Librettists 1542
Lillie, Beatrice 170, 176, 1593,
    1630
Lillie, Gordon W. 711, 729. See
    also Wild West shows,
    Pawnee Bill's
Lincoln's Inn Fields Theatre 1708
Lind, Jenny 772, 777, 790, 812,
    815, 838
Litt, Jacob 200
Little Doc Robert's Tay-Joy Show.
    See Medicine shows
Little Rock, Ark., theater in 2205
Living statues. See Tableaux
    vivants
Lloyd, Alice 1118
Lloyd, Marie 276, 285, 1761,
    1784, 1795
Locke, Edwin 2060
Loew, Marcus 1118, 1183
Loftus, Cecilia 1886
Logan, Olive 1965-66
London
  burlettas in 2137
  entertainment in 281, 292, 297,
    299, 310, 340, 345, 351-
    52
  the East end 288
  the West side 328
  fairs of 745, 753, 2027
  melodrama in 2108
  mountebanks, clowns, quacks of
    80, 964
  musical theaters in 1552-53,
    1571

music halls in 1728-29, 1732-33, 1781
pantomime in 1702, 1720
striptease in 1266
theater in 330, 343, 354, 781, 1976, 1992, 2003, 2006, 2017, 2047, 2070, 2138
See also Drury Lane (London); names of theaters (e.g. Gaiety Theatre); names of exhibition halls (e.g. Egyptian Hall [London]); names of music halls (e.g. Wilton's Music Hall [London])
London Museum. Jonathan King Collection 2427
Long Branch, N.J., as a resort 890
Longfellow, Henry Wadsworth 1450
Lord (James A.) Chicago Dramatic Company 2266
Lorraine, Lillian 1501
Los Angeles, theater of 2311
Lotus Blossom, Little (medicine show performer) 933
Lotus Blossom (Princess) 950
Loutherbourg, Philippe Jacques de 1452, 1474, 1477, 1656-59
Lowlow, John 592
Lowrey, Dan 1843
Lucas, Sam 995
Ludlow, Noah M. 1919, 2210
Lupino, Stanley 1690
Lyceum (theater) 2029, 2056
Lyceum movement 272, 1282-83, 1286, 1299, 1302
drama presented in 1288
Lyricists 1528, 1531, 1541. See also Songs; names of Lyricists (e.g. Gershwin, Ira)

M

McCoy, Tim 691-92
Mack, J. Herbert 1258
MacKaye, Steele 86, 614
McKinley, Myrtle 273
McLean-Prescott Company 2256
McVicker, James H. 2258
Madison, James 1181
Magic 35, 39, 58, 220a, 237, 312, 332, 352, 1318-83, 1442, 1460
bibliographies on 1307-17
circus 358, 423
in England 307, 335, 1687, 1697
fictional accounts of 16
in France 94
history of street 13, 1330
museums and collections of materials about 2411, 2419-21, 2425, 2429-31, 2441, 2446
organizations and associations 2459, 2464-66
periodicals 2343, 2347, 2354, 2362, 2365, 2367-72, 2397
terminology 1365
Magic Circle 2465
Magic Collectors Association 2466
Magic lanterns 306, 325, 1333, 1441, 1443, 1455, 1461, 1466, 1475, 1480
Maguire, Tom 2288
Male impersonation 302, 1753
Malone, Edward G. 788
Maloney, Jonathan 965
"Man and His World" (Montreal) 7
Manchester, Engl., music hall audiences of 1844
Mander (Raymond) and Joe Mitchenson Theatre Collection 2056
Maney, Richard 231
Manhattan Beach 180
Mannix, Daniel 874
Marathon dancing 1129
Marble, Dan 2160
Mardi Gras, as a way of "acting out utopia" 7
Marionettes. See Puppets and puppetry
Market Museum. See Boston Museum (Wood's)
Marks, Edward Bennett 233
Marlowe, Julia 234
Marriott's Great America parks 925
Martin, Henri 578
Martin, Mary 240

Martin, Pete 235
Marx, Groucho 175-76, 201, 235, 1171-72
Marx Brothers 339, 1053, 1083, 1143, 1172
Mary, Adelaide. See Reeve, Ada
Maskeylne, John Nevil 1364, 1378
Maskeylne family 1366
Maskelyne's Theatre of Mystery 331
Masks 90
Masquers, The 2467
Massilia, Huguet de 578
Mass media, social and cultural aspects of 123
Maxwell, Barry 1011
May Fair 2027
Mayhew, Henry 350, 1399, 1698
Maynard, Ken 692
Meade, Edward Hoag 2276
Mechanical entertainments. See Automata; Optical-mechanical entertainments
Medicine shows 52, 96, 160, 187, 251, 358, 632, 656, 826, 928-74, 1062
    advertising for 250
    Bigelow's Kickapoo Medicine Show 942, 955
    blacks in 259
    caste system of 956
    dental 935
    Dr. Lamereux's Indian Medicine Show 937
    Dr. Watt's Kickapoo Indian Medicine Show 262
    fiction about 960, 963, 966-67
    Healy's Kickapoo Indian Medicine Show 933, 942, 955
    licensing of 929, 936
    Little Doc Robert's Tay-Joy Show 944
    in Missouri 929
    Oregon Indian Medicine Co. 942
    on showboats 2339
    terminology of 949, 953
Medieval period. See Middle Ages
Melodrama 35, 86, 208, 244, 246, 272, 1954, 1957, 2062, 2064, 2081-82, 2089, 2094, 2096, 2098, 2102,
    2119, 2121, 2124-25, 2128-30, 2132-34, 2150, 2178
    character types in 2100
    crime in 2117, 2121
    definition of 2097, 2104
    economic values expressed in 2106
    in England 290, 328, 343, 1977-78, 1992, 2013, 2031, 2066-67, 2070, 2108, 2112, 2117, 2135
    music of 2013
    posters for advertising of 1894
    as propaganda 2090
    sex in 2284
    sociological studies of 2112
    temperance expressed in 2065
    writing of 2075-76
Melville, "Big Dic" 975
Melville, Herman 1439
Melville, Rose 2192
Melville Brothers 2056
Melville family 503
Memphis
    minstrel shows in 990
    variety shows in 1065-68
Menageries 96, 363, 515, 528, 812, 1451
    advertising for 504
    in antebellum Missouri 365
    in England 527
    See also Animal acts
Menken, Adah Isaacs 234, 298, 1882-83, 1912, 1914-15, 1941, 2259
    bibliography on 81
Merman, Ethel 275
Merrick, John 830
Merry-go-rounds 899
    carvings 893
Metropolitan Hall (Raleigh, N.C.) 2256
Mexico, guides to theaters in 223
Michigan, opera houses in 2222. See also Jackson, Mich.
Middle Ages
    entertainment in 1687
    festivals and fantasies of 19
    fools and jesters of 79, 91

the juggler in France of 31
mime in 84
theater in 12, 59, 90
the traditional "carnival" in 7
Middleboro (Mass.) Historical Museum.
Tom Thumb Collection 2445
Middleton, George 464
Midgets 781, 799. See also Dwarfs
Midwestern states
chautauqua in 1300, 1305
theater in 2214, 2251, 2276-77
Miles City, Mont., theater in 2206
Military, sports of the English 349
Miller, Charlie 643
Miller, Lewis 1274
Miller, Marilyn 1621
Miller, Ruby 1611
Miller, Zack 650, 663
Miller Brothers 629, 675. See also
Wild West shows, 101
Ranch Show
Millette, Ernest Schlee 560
Millingen, John 1401
Mills (Bertram) Circus 557
Mills, Steve 1254
Mime 48
in England 2035-36
in Greece and Rome 59
medieval 84
organizations and associations 2461
periodicals about 2374-75
See also Pantomime
Mining towns, theater in 2202, 2217,
2247-48, 2259, 2293, 2307,
2309
Minneapolis, Nineteenth-century
theater in 157
Minnesota
early theaters of 190
panoramas of 1457
Minsky's 1228, 1235, 1248-49,
1252, 1255
Minstrel shows and minstrels 39, 52,
96, 100, 110, 114, 120,
134-35, 141, 146, 163,
173, 185, 187, 212, 220a,
228, 237, 259, 272, 437,
975-1050, 1070, 1226,
1260, 1556, 1612, 1634,
1925

association with the circus 977
in California 1039
clowns in 174, 595
in England 307, 311, 317,
1034-35
influence of Afro-American dance
on 1048
in Memphis 990
in Mississippi 2243
in Missouri 164, 977, 1019
in Nashville 984
in New Orleans 1011
in New York City 230, 248
in Pennsylvania 996
recordings of 68
routines, skits, etc. from 992,
1163, 1926
in San Francisco 192, 987,
1037, 2233
Shakespeare mentioned in 172,
1002
songs and music from 258, 311,
980-83, 993, 1008, 1544
bibliography of 1001
Mississippi, medicine shows in 944.
See also Jackson, Miss.
Mississippi River area
panoramas of 1431-32, 1435-36,
1450, 1456, 1462, 1464,
1476
traveling theater in 1919
See also Showboats
Missoula, Mont., theater in 2236
Missouri
circuses in antebellum 365-66
entertainment in antebellum 164
medicine shows in 929
minstrel shows in 977, 1019
See also St. Louis
Mistinguett (performer) 22, 54
Mitchell, William 1938, 1950,
2072, 2105
Mitchell's (New York theater) 247
Mitchells, The (minstrel troupe)
1010
Mix, Tom 624, 683, 687, 692
Mix (Tom) Circus 369, 699, 715
Montez, Lola 298, 1885, 1899

Montgomery, Dave 1258
Morality
  burlesque and 245
  entertainment and 186
  the music hall and 1750
  the theater and 229, 1244–45
  vaudeville and 1208
  See also Censorship
Morosco, Oliver 1499
Morris, William 1116
Morris dance 349
Morrison family 160
Morton, Charles 1833
Morton, William H. 1801
Motion pictures 49–50, 101, 142,
      155, 200, 210, 218, 226,
      242, 1151, 1214, 1441,
      1475, 1897
  about P.T. Barnum 806
  about the circus 401
  blacks in 163, 259
  compared to Punch and Judy shows
      1385
  contributions of vaudeville to
      1125
  costume and set design for 1641
  in England 315, 1553, 1992
  fools and jesters in 91
  matinee idols of 114
  in New York City 169, 186
  pantomime in 1687
  periodicals 2373
  songs from 1589–90
  transition of popular theater into
      86
Motion picture theaters 1126
  vaudeville in 1180
Mozart, George 1800
Mulhall, Lucile 619
Mummery. See Disguises; Masks
Murphy, Joe 1037
Museum of Broadcasting 2433
Museums 134, 787, 811, 820,
      2411–46
  in Boston 784
  broadcasting 2433
  circus 476, 2416, 2439, 2445
  in England 767
  magic 1337, 2411, 2419, 2421,
      2425, 2441

music hall 2435
  on songs and songwriters 2443
  theater 2414
  toy theater 2437
  See also Barnum, P.T.; Dime
      museums; names of museums
      (e.g. Museum of Repertoire
      Americana)
Music 145, 181, 212, 232, 1635
  amusement park 898
  black 163, 993, 1007, 1016
  circus 376, 401, 521
  dramatic 163
  in England 314, 2013
  mechanical 1442
  of melodrama 2013
  of minstrel shows 981–82, 985,
      993, 1008
  music hall 1810, 1825
  in New York City 1896
  organizations and associations
      2456, 2476
  of the popular theater 109
  in Richmond, Va. 1040
  See also Blues; Composers; Jazz;
      Lyricists; Ragtime music;
      Sheet music; Singers; Songs
Musical comedy 197, 244, 246,
      255, 262, 1487, 1546,
      1556, 1575, 1612, 1634,
      1636
  blacks in 163, 1016
  comedians of 1644
  in England 290, 344, 1599,
      1602, 1623, 1630, 2031
  music of 258
  stage design in 1587
  writing for 1653
Musicals 66, 140, 213, 240, 242,
      245, 271, 1485–1655
  archives pertaining to 2440
  blacks in 259, 1573
  burlesque in 1570, 1633
  in England 276, 1523, 1545,
      1553–54, 1600–1601, 1623,
      2140
  on the frontier 2279
  lyrics and scores from 1526,
      1528
  in Omaha, Nebr. 205

Subject Index

reviews of (1929-38) 170
vaudeville in 1180
See also Burlettas
Music halls 39, 49
  architecture of 316, 1781
  audiences of 1844
  biographical directory to performers
    in 1739
  comedy in 24, 1730, 1745, 1747,
    1757, 1763, 1786, 1788-92,
    1800, 1814, 1848, 1851
  discography of entertainers in 68
  English 276, 284-85, 287, 290,
    297, 300, 302, 306, 309-
    11, 313, 316-17, 322,
    325, 327-28, 334, 338-41,
    343-44, 349, 1727-1851,
    1975, 2002, 2005, 2031,
    2449
  fiction about 1848
  government control of 1728
  laws concerning 1772, 1837
  male impersonation in 302
  management of 1834
  morality of 1750
  museums pertaining to 2435
  in New York City 171
  organizations and associations per-
    taining to 2449
  of Paris 21
  periodicals and serials about 2358,
    2376
  sexual attitudes and 313
  sociological studies of 1794
  songs and music from 1734, 1752,
    1769-71, 1793, 1807, 1809-
    10, 1812-13, 1825-26,
    1829-30, 1835
  See also names of music halls (e.g.
    Southwark Music Hall)
Musicians
  black 1044
  street 230

N

Nadja (stripper) 1225
Narragansett Pier, R.I., as a resort
  890

Nashville
  concerts and minstrel shows in
    antebellum 984
  vaudeville in 1131
Nast, Thomas 1456
National Museum of Music Hall
  2435
National Society for the Preservation
  of Tent, Folk, and Reper-
  toire Theatre 2468
National Theatre (N.Y. City) 247
National Vaudeville Artists, Inc.
  Joint Complaint Bureau
  1164
National Winter Garden 1232,
  1265
Natural history, popularization of
  by P.T. Barnum 780
Nautical drama 2135
Nelson, John Young 709
Nervo and Knox (vaudeville team)
  276
Nevada, theater in 2228, 2230,
  2307. See also Las Vegas,
  Virginia City, Nev.
Nevada City, Nev., theater in
  2303
New Deal. See Depression (1929);
  U.S. Works Progress Adminis-
  tration
New Los Angeles Theatre 2311
New Opera House (Cairo, Ill.)
  2301
New Orleans
  circus in 487
  minstrel shows in 1011
  theater in 2239
  Wild West shows in 639
Newport, R.I., as a resort 890
New Theatre Comique 220
Newton, H. Chance 1805
New York Casino 1486
New York City 148, 150
  burlesque and striptease in 1228,
    1235, 1266, 2072
  circuses in 596
  jazz in 180
  pleasure gardens of 746, 757
  theatrical entertainment in 101,
    147, 151, 167-69, 171,
    186, 188, 206, 209, 230,

240, 247-48, 256-57, 1177,
1854, 1896, 1898, 1901,
1913, 1938
variety in 1218
vaudeville in 1077, 1153a,
1156-57, 1209-10
World's Fair in (1964) 744
See also Bowery (N.Y. City);
Broadway; Coney Island;
Manhattan Beach
New York Historical Society 2436
New York State, chautauqua in 1271
New York University. Dance Depart-
ment. Committee on Research
in Dance 2455
Niblo's Garden Theatre 220, 247,
1520, 1633
Night clubs 260
blacks as entertainers in 163
See also Honky tonks
Nivellon, Louis 1721
Noell, Mae 954
Northall, William Knight 833
Norton, Wash 1011
Noverre (pantomimist) 1726
Nudity. See Striptease; Theater,
nudity in
Nutt (Commodore) 792

O

Oakley, Annie 451, 628, 630, 654,
668, 676, 681, 706, 714
O'Connor, Lois 1251
Ohio River Valley, traveling theater
in 1919
Ohio Show-Shop (Cincinnati) 787
Okito (magician). See Bamberg,
Theodore
Oklahoma, medicine shows in 944
Oklahoma City, medicine shows in
936
Old Drury (theater) 327
Old Strand (London theater) 343
Old Vic (theater) 1806, 1988,
1995, 2002
Olympia (Dublin music hall) 1843
Olympic Theatre (N.Y. City) 247,
1950, 2021
Olympic Theatre (St. Louis) 2294

Omaha, Nebr.
musical and variety shows in 205
theater in 2281
Omohundro, J.B. 559, 636
O'Neill, Eugene 1959
O'Neill, James 1959
Opera 141, 162, 1639
ballad 11, 314, 1708, 1989
comic 200, 328, 344, 1630
costume and set design for 1641
in England 314, 328, 344,
1630, 1708, 1989
farce in 6
influence of commedia dell' arte
on 11
light 162, 1596, 1644
romantic 1630
in San Francisco 2233
See also Librettists
Opera houses 100, 1173
architecture and design of 267
in Colorado 2220
in fiction 2308
on the frontier 2218
guides to 219
in Illinois 2207, 2301
in Iowa 2265
in Kansas 2252
in Michigan 2222
in Minnesota 190
in New York City 171
in Pennsylvania 2268-69, 2271,
2273
in St. Louis 2211
See also names of opera houses
(e.g. English Opera House)
Operetta, composers of 1566
Opryland's Production Center 924
Optical-mechanical entertainments
852, 1441-43, 1449, 1451,
1455, 1460, 1471, 1480
in England 279
See also Automata; Dioramas;
Magic lanterns; Panoramas;
Solar microscope; Toys
Oregon, theater in 2229. See also
Portland
Oregon Indian Medicine Co. See
Medicine shows
Orpheum Circuit 218

Subject Index

Outdoor Amusement Business Association 2469
Owens, Buck 692
Owens, John E. 1939
Oxford (London theater) 331, 1801

P

Paganism, in the origin of fairs 23, 741
Pageants
English 325, 349
medieval 90
Palace Theatre 176, 1077, 1113, 1153a, 1156-57, 1203, 1764, 1797, 1832
Palladium (theater) 1832
Palmer, Albert M. 1938
Palmer, John 526
Panoramas 96, 134, 1434, 1441, 1443, 1446, 1456-57, 1465, 1468, 1470, 1473, 1478, 1482
of the Battle of Bunker Hill 1433
in England 279, 299-300, 302, 1428-29, 1479, 1481, 1483
influence on landscape painting 1438, 1472
of Minnesota 1457
of the Mississippi River area 1431-32, 1435-36, 1450, 1462, 1464, 1476
parodies and satirization of 1447-48
as theater scenery 1484
of whaling voyages 1439, 1467
See also Dioramas
Pantages, Alexander 200, 1081, 1162
Pantaloon (pantomime character) 1686
Pantomime 24, 48, 52, 56, 85-86, 220a, 237, 2120
bibliography on 81, 1700
in burlesque 1678
burlesques and extravaganzas as derivations of 2107
Christmas 311, 1659, 1679, 1685, 1722, 2107
clowns and 409, 1660, 1686, 1698, 1707

economics in the production of 1671
English 5, 35, 61, 160, 276, 287, 302-4, 306-8, 311-312, 314, 317, 328, 335-36, 341, 343-44, 1545, 1656-1726, 1733, 1814, 1821, 1851, 1975, 1987, 1989, 2011, 2031, 2056, 2069, 2099
equestrian 1674
French 94
in Greece and Rome 59
male impersonation in 302
in motion pictures 1687
organizations and associations 2450, 2461
periodicals about 2384
scenery and lighting for 1659
sexuality of 1699
songs, jokes, and routines from 1666, 1696
See also Harlequin; Pantaloon (pantomime character); Pierrot (pantomime character); Shadow pantomimes and plays
Paris
fairs of 17, 1726
music halls in 21
striptease in 1264, 1266
See also Folies Bergere
Parker, Dorothy 130
Park Theatre (N.Y. City) 1895
Parody, of Shakespearean plays 2039
Parrington, Caleb 1439, 1456
Pastor, Tony 1070, 1173-74, 1177-78, 1212, 1216, 1218, 1223, 2072
Patch, Sam 2160
as a folk hero 119
Patent medicines 932-33, 939, 941-43, 959, 962, 969-70, 972, 974
advertising of 957, 973
crusades against 264
Hadacol phenomenon 968, 974
Hamlin's Wizard Oil 930
Indian Sagwa 952
See also Medicine shows

Paterson, Peter 2020
Patterson, Johnny 593
Pavilion (London theater) 354
Pavlova (stage performer) 1731
Paxton, Joseph 736
Payne, Bill 1011
Payne, Noah D. 975
Peale, Charles Wilson 824
Pedlars, itinerant 96
Peep shows 96, 1437, 1443, 1454
    in England 325
Peers, Donald 1811
Pelissier (vaudeville performer) 276
Pennsylvania, minstrel shows in 996.
    See also Philadelphia; St.
    Petersburg, Pa.; Tidioute,
    Pa.; Warren, Pa.
Penny arcades. See Arcades
Pentland, Joe 593
Pepper, J.H. 1364, 1480
Pezon family 578
Phelps, Samuel 1473
Philadelphia
    circuses in 505
    entertainment in 1916
    theater in 217, 1902
Pickett, Bill 657, 687, 689
Pierrot (pantomime character) 84, 918
Pinkham, Lydia 933
Planche, James Robinson 344, 1410,
    1523, 1969, 2071, 2077,
    2079, 2115, 2120, 2139
Playbills, illustrations of 233
Players, The 2470
    Walter Hampden-Edwin Booth
        Theatre Collection and
        Library 2446
Players' Theatre (London) 1727, 1831
Playwrights, biographies and directories
    of 1548. See also names of
    playwrights (e.g. O'Neill,
    Eugene)
Pleasure gardens 299, 306, 314,
    325, 351-52, 397
    in Baltimore 752
    concerts in 756
    in England 298, 340, 747, 754-
        55, 758, 764-66
    in New York City 746, 757
    See also names of gardens (e.g.
        Renelagh Gardens)

Poli, S.Z. 1118
Poliakoff, Nicholai 586
Politics
    in burlesque-extravaganzas 2111
    of music hall songs 1830
    in the satire of American folk
        heroes 153
    in the theater 64
Pollock's Toy (Theatre) Museum
    2437
Pomarede, Leon D. 1431, 1435-
    36, 1464
Pond (Major) 1134
Poole (panoramist) 1479
Pope, Alexander 1405
Popular Culture Association 2471
Popular entertainment
    definition of 53
    general sources on 154-354
        American forms 154-275
        English forms 276-354
    museums devoted to 2411-46
    organizations and associations
        2447-78
    origins, early forms, major
        references, and surveys
        1-97
    periodicals 2341-2410
    social and cultural background of
        American 98-153
    See also Animal acts; Amusement
        parks; Burlesque; Cabarets;
        Carnivals; Chautauqua; Cir-
        cuses; Clowns; Dance; Dio-
        ramas; Drama; Fairs; Harle-
        quin; Lyceum movement;
        Magic; Medicine shows;
        Melodrama; Menageries;
        Mime; Minstrel shows and
        minstrels; Motion pictures;
        Music; Musical comedy;
        Musicals; Music halls; Opera;
        Panoramas; Pantomime; Pleas-
        ure gardens; Revues; Side
        shows; Striptease; Theater;
        Variety shows; Vaudeville;
        Wild West shows
Porter, Cole 1577, 1626, 1649
Portland, vaudeville in 1102
Posey, Jake 568

Powell, David Franklin 632, 656
Powers, James T. 1944
Preachers, itinerant 96
Press, Percy 1393
Press agents 199, 231, 256, 2305
    carnival 856
    circus 420
Princess Stock Company 2232
Princeton University. Library 2438
Proctor, F.F. 1118, 1170
Promptbooks 2025, 2187
Propaganda, melodrama as 2090
Pueblo Indians
    the delight makers of 84
    manners, customs, and rites of
        159
Punch and Judy shows 35, 48, 237,
        352, 1388, 1393, 1400,
        1404, 1406, 1411, 1416,
        1421
    clowns in 595
    compared with early motion
        pictures 1385
Puppeteers of America 2472
Puppets and puppetry 41, 96, 189,
        558, 1384-1426, 1451
    at amusement parks 924
    bibliography on 1389
    dictionaries on 1400
    in England 349, 351, 1406,
        1697
    organizations and associations
        2447, 2460, 2472
    outline of recent research on
        1408
    periodicals about 2374, 2390-91
Purvis, Billy 1697, 1707

Q

Quacks and quackery 45, 48, 352,
        931, 938, 942-43, 958,
        964, 970, 1370, 1376
    in England 80, 352-53, 931,
        964
Queen, John 1011
Queens Hall Music Hall 1759

R

Radio 103, 142, 260

blacks as entertainers on 163
museums devoted to 2433
Ragtime music 253, 976, 1016,
        1491
Raleigh, N.C., entertainment in
        2256
Randall, Harry 1814
Ranelagh Gardens 754, 765
Rasaire's (circus) 400
Rath Brothers 1128
Rattler, Lew 1037
Raymond (The Great) 1348
Read, Thomas 526
Realism. See Theater, realism in
Recordings, early music hall 1830.
        See also Discography
Recreation 120
    of the 1930s 260
    Seventeenth-century English 349
    See also Leisure
Redpath, James 1282, 1286
Redpath Chautauqua 1278
Reeve, Ada 1815
Reeves, Al 1258
Rehan, Ada 1891, 1967
Relph, Harry 1816
Renaissance
    fools and jesters of 79, 91
    stage of 1437
    the traditional "carnival" of 7
Rentz-Stanley Company 1258
Repertory theater 187, 2225-27,
        2250, 2253, 2284, 2300,
        2310
    fiction about 2254
    museums pertaining to 2434
    organizations and associations
        2468
Resorts, seaside 141, 890, 900,
        914
    English 324-25, 901, 915-16,
        918, 1798
    architecture of 907
Revolutionary War, entertainment
        during 149
Revues 15, 66, 85, 173, 198,
        240, 255-56, 263, 267,
        273, 1214, 1485-1655
    at amusement parks 924
    archives pertaining to 2440
    blacks in 259

censorship of 1912
comedy in 174, 197
comments on (1929-38) 170
in England 39, 276, 305, 315,
        328, 344, 1601, 1603, 1630
in France 39, 54, 63, 1516
in Las Vegas 1511, 1538, 1592,
        1598, 1627
in New York City 1488
staging and scenic design of 267,
        1538, 1627, 1641
vaudeville in 1180
See also Charlot's Revue
Rhoades, Charley 1037
Rhoda Royal Circus 372
Rhode Island, minstrel shows in 975.
        See also Narragansett Pier,
        R.I.; Newport, R.I.
Rice, Billy 587
Rice, Dan 451, 455, 480, 503,
        584, 588, 591, 604
Rice (Dan) Circus 487
Rice, Edward Everett 1570
Rice, J.D. 977, 997
Rice, John 1726
Rice, Thomas D. 1005, 1018, 1027,
        1032
Rich, John 1662, 1668, 1708-10
Richardson, John 343, 2030
Richman, Harry 252
Richmond, Va., history of music in
        1040
Rickett's (John B.) Circus 189, 355,
        412, 467-68
Rickey, Sam 1037, 1217
Riley, James Whitcomb 115
Ringling, August 500
Ringling, John 519
Ringling Brothers 368
Ringling Brothers and Barnum and
        Bailey Circus 264, 356,
        420, 538, 554, 594, 667,
        884. See also Barnum and
        Bailey Circus
Ringling Brothers Circus 427, 449,
        451, 485-86, 491, 509,
        544, 548, 560, 596, 648
museum and collections pertaining
        to 2416, 2426, 2439
Ringling family 472

Ritchie, James Ewing 1817
Roadhouses 260
Robert-Houdin (magician) 1338, 1348,
        1358, 1376, 1378-80
Roberts, Arthur 1623, 1818
Roberts (Little Doc) Tay-Joy Show.
        See Medicine shows
Robey, George 276, 339, 1749,
        1806, 1820-21, 1848
Robinson, Bill 221
Robinson, C.O. 699
Robinson, John 503
Robinson (John) Circus 387, 454,
        477a, 495
Robinson, Josephine DeMott 572
Rockwell, Kitty 1162
Rodeos 178, 428, 621, 623, 664,
        667, 687, 717
Rodgers, Richard 1624, 1649
Rogers, Will 175-76, 221, 620,
        687, 1499, 1515, 1518-19,
        1620-21, 1886
Romano's (London restaurant) 1521
Romanticism. See Theater, Romanti-
        cism in
Rome
festivals, games, and amusements
        of 74
mimes and pantomimes in 59
Roof Garden (theater) 188
Rooney, Mickey 1028
Rooney, Pat and Marion 1150
Rope dancing 349, 2035
Rose, Billy 1137, 1510
Rose, Clarkson 1822-24
Rose, Julian 1095
Rosier Players 2253
Ross, W.G. 1738
Rowe, J.A. 573
Rowe, Joseph 412
Rowland, Betty 1225
Roxy Theatre (N.Y. City) 1126
Royal, John F. 1144
Royal American Shows 870
Royal Aquarium Theatre (London)
        331, 1803
Royal Circus 404, 526, 2037,
        2045, 2136
Royal Coburg. See Old Vic (theater)
Royalty (theater) 2045

Rubin, Benny 201, 1196
Ruger (panoramist) 1456
Rural areas
  circus in 2152
  theater in 2202-2314
Russell, Benjamin 1439, 1456
Russell, Lillian 221, 240, 1616

S

Sacramento, Calif., theater in 2247
Sadler (Harley) Company 2250
Sadler's Wells Theatre 280, 312,
    1473, 1704, 1973, 1988,
    2007, 2028, 2045
St. Cyr, Lili 1249
St. George's Hall (London) 1366
St. Louis
  museums in 787
  theater in 1913, 2208-11, 2294
  variety in 1084
St. Petersburg, Pa., opera houses in
    2273
Salmon (Mrs.) 352
Saloon and taverns, entertainment in
    116, 121, 141, 179, 230,
    1177, 1222
  in England 325, 343
Salsbury, Nate 1555
Salt Lake City, theater in 1913
Sandow (strongman) 792, 1621
San Francisco
  minstrel shows in 987, 1037
  theater in 192, 2233-34, 2247,
    2274, 2288
Sanger, George 459, 496
Sankey, Ira D. 975
San Souci (London theater) 331
Saratoga, N.Y., as a resort 890
Satire
  of American folk heroes 153
  in the commedia dell' arte 28
  English 1830, 2099
  in music hall songs 1830
  on panoramas 1447-48
Savannah, Ga., theater in 2237
Savannah Theatre 2213
Savo, Jimmy 1198
Savoy (theater) 1494
Schaffner, Neil 2157, 2162, 2181,
    2194-95

Schaffner Players 2181, 2195,
    2250
Schieffelin Hall (Tombstone, Ariz.)
    2309
Schoolcraft, Luke 980, 1011
Scott, Marian 1296
Scott, Matthew 574
Scudder, John 811, 824
Seattle
  stock companies of 2289
  vaudeville in 1100, 1123
Sells and Gray (circus) 381
Sells Brothers 384
Sells Circus 481
Sells-Floto Circus 375, 454, 509,
    648
Sesqui-Centennial International Ex-
    position (1926) 734
Sex
  in melodrama 2284
  in pantomime 1699
Shadow pantomimes and plays 1443,
    1460
Shakespeare, William
  clowns in the plays of 595
  equestrian productions of 2034
  in extravaganzas 2139
  fools in the plays of 34, 37,
    91
  juvenile drama and 1420
  in minstrelsy and vaudeville
    172, 1002
  Nineteenth-century productions
    of 2024
  parodies of 2039
Shamanism, in the origin of popular
    entertainment 42, 65
Shapiro, Sam 869
Sharpley, Sam 975
Shaw, Bernard 341, 2071
Sheet music, illustrations of covers
    of 233
Sheridan, R.B. 2071
Sherman, Hal 225
Sherwood, Robert Edmund 603-4
Shields, Ella 1128
Short, Hassard 1485
"Show Boat" (Musical) 1581
Showboats 486, 2315-40
  audiences on 249

medicine shows on 963
in Nineteenth-century Cairo, III.
166
Showmen. See Entertainers
Shubert Archives 2440
Shubert family 183, 1642
Siamese twins. See Chang and Eng
Side shows 185, 213, 423, 428,
510, 530, 737, 821-22,
834, 851-52, 874, 919,
922
in England 527
See also Freaks
Silverman, Sime 261, 1122
Silvers, Phil 201, 235
Sims, George R. 1715
Simulacre 324. See also Wax
museums and figures
Singers 68, 211, 252
black 1013
music hall 1793
See also Songs
Sioux City, Iowa, theater in 2206
Sissle, Noble 1578
Sitting Bull 721, 723
Six Flags Over Texas (park) 889,
924
Skelton, Red 176
Skelt's Juvenile Drama 1395
Slapstick. See Comedy, slapstick
Slave songs, contrasted with white
minstrel imitations 1045
Smith, H. Adrian 2421
Smith, Henry Bache 1541
Smith, Joe 201
Smith, Joe R. 694
Smith, John Rowson 1435-36, 1464
Smith, Solomon 1919, 2210
Smith and Dale (burlesque team) 1260
Sobel, Bernard 256
Sobol, Louise 257
Society for Theatre Research, The
2473
Society for the Preservation of
Variety Arts, The 2474
Society of American Magicians 2475
Sohlke, Augusta 1489
Solar microscope 1455
Soldene, Emily 1833
Somers (N.Y.) Historical Society
2442

Song, dramatic, history of 6
Song books, Nineteenth-century,
attitudes toward blacks in
1029-30
Songs 126, 187, 1531, 1540,
1571, 1578-79, 1589-90,
1649
circus 521
lyrics and music of popular 233,
1542-43, 1557, 1559,
1577
minstrel show 980, 982-83
music hall and variety 1752,
1769-71, 1807, 1809,
1812-13, 1826, 1829-30,
1835
political satire in 1830
reference guides to 1548
vaudeville 196
Victorian 311
See also Ballads and balladry;
Composers; Discography;
Folk songs; Lyricists; Music;
Singers; Slave songs
Songwriters Hall of Fame Museum
2443
Sonneck Society, The 2476
Soo, Chung Ling 1348
Sothern, Georgia 1225, 1261
Southwark Fair 2027
Southwark Music Hall 340
Spain
commedia dell 'arte in 75
court fools of 25
Spas, English 325
Spaulding and Rogers Circus 487,
2336
Spaulding and Rogers Floating
Palace 1009-10
Spectral exhibits, English 279
Sports 110, 117, 141
colonial 179
in England 349
Springfield, Ill., opera houses of
2207
Stage. See Theater
Stage, Licensing Act (1737) 1984
Starr, Blaze 1239, 1262
Steele, S.S. 980
Stevens, John 1456-57

Stevenson, Robert Louis 1395
Stewart, James E. 980
Stock companies 240, 1858, 1922–23, 1938, 1942–43, 1948, 1958, 2275–76
Stockwell, Samuel B. 1432, 1435–36, 1464
Stodare ("Colonel") 1364
Stone, Fred 262, 1258
Stone, M.W. 1407
Stone and Montgomery (vaudeville team) 262
Stowe, Harriet Beecher. See UNCLE TOM'S CABIN
Strand (exhibition hall) 1428
Strand Music Hall. See Gaiety Theatre
Strates (James E.) Shows 877, 881, 887
Stratton, Charles Sherwood 781, 792, 796, 805, 812, 817–18, 842, 2423
Street entertainment 13, 49, 66, 78, 207, 230, 1393
    in England 325, 333
    French boulevard theater 65
    of the Middle Ages 90
    See also Costermongers
Strippers 1257
    morals of 1253
    psychological characteristics of 1256
    sexual and social behavior of 1246
    unsolved murders of 1240
Striptease 35, 246, 1224–67
    in Baltimore 1239
    in Boston 1227, 1232
    carnival 876, 1247
    in England 313, 1266
    how-to-books 1238, 1266
    in New York City 1228, 1266
    in Paris 1264, 1266
    protests against 229
    See also Burlesque
Strolling players 9a, 48, 160, 1983, 2020, 2026, 2049, 2099
Strong (Margaret Woodbury) Museum 2432

Strongmen and women 312, 332, 792–93
Surrey Theatre 1682, 2033
Sweden, circuses in 416
Swindlers. See Hoaxes and swindlers
Sword swallowers 793
Sydell, Rose 1258

T

Tableaux vivants 1920
Tabor Opera House (Leadville, Colo.) 2220, 2296
Tammany Museum. See Baker, Gardiner
Tammen, Harry Hege 648
Tanquay, Eva 221, 1118
Tate, Harry 339
Tattooing 324, 834
Taverns. See Saloons and taverns
Taylor, Charles A. 2132
Taylor, Joe 2304
Taylor, Vic 1421, 1839
Teague, Walter Dorwin 743
Television
    museums pertaining to 2433
    songs from 1590
Temperance
    expressed in melodrama 2065
Tempest, Marie 1493
Tent shows 936, 2148, 2191, 2221, 2226–27, 2250, 2253, 2262, 2277–78, 2282, 2284, 2287, 2300, 2310
    fiction about 2254
    lists of 367
    museums pertaining to 2434
    organizations and associations pertaining to 2468
    See also Chautauqua
Terriss, Ellaline 1645
Terriss, William 2005
Texas
    medicine shows in 944
    showboats in 2327
    theater in 2242
    See also Galveston, Tex.; Houston
Texas, University of (Austin). Humanities Research Center.

Hoblitzelle Theatre Arts
Library 2424
Thalia Theater (N.Y. City) 147,
2129
Theater 49, 57, 104, 113, 134–35,
138, 140–42, 156, 162,
183, 186, 194, 200, 203,
211, 218, 226, 231, 237,
242–43, 249, 255, 272,
1112, 1852–1968, 2078
bibliography of 46, 93
blacks in 163, 216, 2143, 2149
in Boston 184, 2114
censorship in 1912
chautauqua as a form of 1306
in the colonial period 179
death of certain forms in 86
economics of 1861, 1943, 1948
encyclopedias and biographies on
29, 36, 38
fiction about 2308
folk 66
folk heroes of 119
fools and jesters in 91
guides to 223
influence of the minstrel on 989
Italian-American 206
lighting in 1906, 1921
management in 8, 1160, 1563–
65, 1567, 1876, 1878,
1884, 1908, 1942, 1950,
1963, 2244–45, 2258
of the Middle Ages 12, 59
in Minnesota 157, 190
morality and 229, 1244–45
museums and collections pertaining
to 2414, 2417, 2428,
2446
music of 109
in New York City 147, 167–68,
171, 186, 188, 206, 209,
230, 240, 247–48, 1854,
1895–96, 1898, 1901, 1938
nudity in 1966
organizations and associations
2473, 1478
in Philadelphia 216, 1902
political 64
production and direction in 14–15,
241, 1510, 1548, 1852,

1859, 1910, 1920, 1940,
1953, 1968
realism in 1918, 1921, 2074
relationship to popular art 95
Romanticism in 1925
in San Francisco 192
slang of 211
small town and provincial 2202–
2314
stage setting and scenery of 94,
1474, 1906, 1921, 1949,
1962
See also Broadway; Drama;
Musical comedy; Musicals;
Repertory theater; Showboats;
Toy Theaters
Theaters
Theater, English 64, 74, 90, 276,
281, 286–87, 290, 299,
303–4, 306–7, 310, 325,
327, 335, 338, 341–42,
352, 397, 1808, 1969–
2058, 2085
bibliography on 3, 18
censorship in 1997, 2019, 2048
comedy in 1765
directory of civic 289
at fairs 2027
illustrations of minor 2046
laws concerning 1772, 1837,
2017
management in 2021–22, 2033,
2035, 2045
music of 2013
organizations and associations
2451
penny theaters 2001
political 2111
production and direction in 2024
reviews and essays on 277, 336
sexual attitudes and 313
stage setting and effects 346–47,
1478, 1484, 1971, 1998,
2008, 2041, 2138
See also Drama, English
Theater, French 94
booth 45
boulevard 65
effects used in 56
Theater audiences 249, 1219

Subject Index

burlesque 1235
in domestic drama 2073
English 303, 1844, 1980, 2003, 2006, 2073
in melodrama 2096, 2098, 2284
music hall 1844
in small towns 2283, 2302
vaudeville 1102
Theaters 1151
architecture and design of 267, 316
English 316, 330-31, 343, 354, 1718, 1971
outdoor 2138
fires in 1110
guides to 219
organizations for restoration of 2463, 2477
vaudeville 1185, 1195
See also Motion picture theaters
Theatre Historical Society 2477
Theatre Library Association 2478
Theatre of Astronomy 2015
Theatre Royal (Stratford East) 354
Theatres Regulation Act (1843) 2017
Theatrical posters 95, 489, 1865, 1894
Theme parks. See Amusement parks
Third Varieties Theatre (New Orleans) 2239
Thomas, Augustus 2060
Thompson, Lydia 298, 1258, 1260
Thurston, Howard 1348, 1354, 1378, 1380
Tich, Little. See Relph, Harry
Tidioute, Pa., theater in 2268-69, 2271
Tightrope walkers. See Aerialists
Tombstone, Ariz., theater in 2293, 2309
Tompkins, C. 1414
Tilley, Vesta 5, 276, 302, 1753
Tilyou, George 909
Tin Pan Alley 147, 232, 1531, 1554, 1610
Toby shows 2147-48, 2157, 2161-62, 2177, 2181, 2191-92, 2194-95, 2198, 2227, 2250, 2300
terminology of 73

Toledo, Ohio, entertainment in 2286
Tom shows 2156, 2282
Tom Thumb. See Stratton, Charles Sherwood
Toney, Lemuel. See Leonard, Eddie
Toole, J.L. 2004-5
Toto (vaudeville performer) 276
Tournaments and jousts, medieval 90, 325, 349
Toys 1454
mechanical 1459
optical 1461
See also Automata; Games
Toy theaters 237, 1391, 1395-99, 1401-3, 1405, 1407-10, 1412-13, 1415, 1417-20, 1422, 1426
collections of materials pertaining to 2427, 2437
lighting of 1424
See also Punch and Judy shows
Tragedy 2312
definition of 2097
Trans-Mississippi Exposition (1898) 760
Transsexuals 829
Trolleys, electric 891, 920, 926
Tucker, Sophie 276, 1214
Turnour, Jules 594
Tussaud's (Madame) Wax Museum 279, 284, 324, 794, 840, 844
Twain, Mark 1286, 1448

U

UNCLE TOM'S CABIN 213, 2144, 2152-53, 2164, 2166, 2172-73, 2179-80, 2182, 2189-90, 2199, 2424
advertising for 250
condemnation of 244
scenery and staging of 2165, 2174-75
U.S. Works Progress Administration
patronage of the arts by 105
theater project of 122
Unthan, Carl Hermann 1842
Urban, Joseph 1587
Urling, Serge 877

V

Valentine, William 1218
Vallee, Rudy 268-69
Van Amburgh, Isaac 578
Van Amburgh Menagerie Company 812
Vanderlyn, John 1472
Van Raalte, Joseph 1258
Van Winkle, Rip (character) 2201
  promptbooks for stage versions of
    2187
VARIETY (newspaper) 261
Variety shows 39, 49, 101, 120,
    135, 185, 237, 263, 1084,
    1112, 1177, 1200-1201,
    1216-18, 1556, 1783
  comedy in 1765
  in England 300, 305, 315, 340,
    1545, 1751, 1765, 1839,
    1842
  on the frontier 2279
  glamour girls in 5
  in Memphis 1065
  in New York City 248, 1218
  in Omaha, Nebr. 205
  organizations and associations per-
    taining to 2474
  in St. Louis 1084
  social history of 1065-68
Variety Theatre 220
Vaudeville 39, 52, 66, 101, 103,
    112, 135, 146, 162, 173,
    187, 194, 198, 200-203,
    206-7, 211-12, 226, 228,
    240, 243, 245-46, 255,
    262-63, 269, 272-73, 1051-
    1223, 1260, 1519, 1612,
    1783
  archives pertaining to 2446
  blacks in 213, 1007
  in Boston 224
  in Chicago 1207
  children in 218
  in Cleveland 1060
  comedy in 174, 197, 266, 1095-
    96, 1167
  contributions of to the movies
    1125
  discography of entertainers in 68
  drama and 1191, 1964

economics of 1943
effect on young audiences 1102,
    1219
English 276, 338-39
fashion in 1132
fiction about 1078, 1099, 1124,
    1160
fools and jesters in 91
"freak" acts in 176
glamour girls in 5
location of talent in 1072, 1159
in Mississippi 2243
music of 258
in Nashville 1131
in New York City 147, 180,
    186, 248, 256-57, 1077,
    1153a, 1156-57, 1209-10
in New York State 1052, 1058
parallels with commedia dell'
    arte 1215
patriotism in 1192
periodicals about 2378, 2388
in Portland 1102
psychology of 1113, 1166
racial aspects of 1095-96,
    1101, 1145-46
routines and scripts from 193,
    1139, 1145, 1158, 1163,
    1188, 1190, 1194, 1200
in Seattle 1100, 1123
Shakespeare mentioned in 172
social and moral investigations of
    191, 1166, 1207-8
songs for 196
tabloid dramas in 1087
terminology of 73
theaters for 1185, 1195
in the Trans-Mississippi West
    1064
in Washington, D.C. 1175
writers and writing for 1133
    1181,
Yiddish 52
Vaudeville Managers' Protective
    Association. Joint Complaint
    Bureau 1164
Vauxhall Gardens 298, 747, 755,
    758, 765
Vawter, Keith 1291
Ventriloquism 39, 423, 1460
  fiction about 16

Vereen, Ben 1028
Vernon, Dai 1331, 1347
Vestris, Lucia Elizabeth 298, 302, 344, 1630, 1969, 1972, 2021, 2053, 2055
Victor, Edward 1370
Victoria (Queen) 805
Vincent, John H. 1274
Virginia City, Nev., theater in 1913, 2259
Virginia Minstrels (band) 1024
Visalia, Calif., theater in 2279

W

Wadlow, Robert Pershing 800
Wagon shows 662
   in antebellum Missouri 164
   circus 358, 495
   medicine 928
Walker, George 1622
Walker, John 2090
Wallace, Lew 1928
Wallack, James and Lester 1938
Wallenda family 451
Wallett, William F. 609
Ward, Artemus 1447, 2241
Warde, Frederick B. 2312
Warren, Lavinia 818, 836, 841
Warren, Pa., theater in 2270
Washington, theater in 2229. See also Seattle
Washington, D.C.
   circuses in 419
   theater in 1175
Waters, Ethel 270
Watson, William R. 580
Watts, James 1128
Wax modellers, biographies of 67, 835
Wax museums and figures 1451
   advertising for 250
   in England 352
   See also Tussaud's (Mme.) Wax Museum
Weaver, John 1726
Webb, Harry E. 724
Weber and Fields (vaudeville team) 1097, 1139, 1182, 1217, 1285

Weber 1488
Weber, Lawrence 1258
Welch, Rufus 424
Weslyn, Louis 1181
West, Buster 225
West, Mae 1886
West, William 1399, 1403, 1414, 1418, 1426
Western states
   chautauqua in 1284
   theater in 2214, 2217, 2219, 2230, 2238, 2241, 2276
   See also Frontier; Mining towns
Wettach, Adrian 24, 327, 331, 589
Wheatley, William 1520
White, George 1485
Whitechapel (theater) 2051
White's (George) Scandals 183, 198, 226, 252, 268, 1536
Whitley Opera House (Emporia, Kans.) 2252
Whittier, John Greenleaf 1450
Wighton, David. See Devant, David
Wild, Johnny 1217
Wild West shows 52, 110, 146, 362, 376, 420, 428, 430, 530, 610-730, 1518
   archives pertaining to 2438
   Austin Brothers 417
   Buck Jones 613, 692
   Buckskin Joe's 419
   Carson's 659-60, 666
   Cody's 251, 610, 616-18, 630-31, 633, 635, 637, 639, 641, 643, 647-48, 651-53, 655, 665-66, 670, 672, 674, 678, 680, 685, 690, 693, 695-96, 701, 704, 709-11, 720-21, 723-24, 726-27, 750
   Gabriel Brothers 719
   Indians and 647, 670, 721, 723, 730
   Irwin Brothers 666
   McCoy's 691
   101 Ranch show 486, 629, 650, 657, 661, 663, 666, 675, 680, 687, 689, 697-98

Pawnee Bill's 520, 631, 640, 643, 648, 711, 716
Star Ten Ranch Show 663
Tomkins 612
Two Bills Show 666
Young Buffalo Show 694
Williams, Bert 175-76, 213, 1505, 1621-22, 1625, 1647
last interview of 249
Williams, Bransby 1806, 1845-47
Williams, E.C. 1468
Williamsburg, Va., entertainment in colonial 179
Wilmington, N.C., theater in 2291
Wilson, Francis 271
Wilton, Robb 339
Wilton's Music Hall (London) 1735
Winks, Evert M. 1305
Wirth, May 451
Wisconsin, circuses in 388, 405, 447
Wit and humor 106-7
of American folk heroes 153
music hall 1730
stereotype characters and 144
See also Comedy
Wombwell, George 578
Wood, Georgie 1849-50
Wood, John (Mrs.) 2072
Woods, Al 2094
Woods family 160
Wood's Museum and Metropolitan Theatre 812. See also Boston Museum (Wood's)
Woolf, Edgar Allan 1181
Wooten, C. Richard 740
Work, Henry C. 980
Works Progress Administration. See U.S. Works Progress Administration

"World of Mirth, The". See Bergen, Frank
"World of Tomorrow" Fair 743
World's Columbian Exposition (1893) 733, 738, 742, 750, 760-61, 873
World's Fair, New York City (1964) 744
World's Industrial and Cotton Exposition (1884) 639
Wynn, Ed 170, 175

Y

Yankee, The 1925, 1939, 2151, 2155, 2164, 2167, 2170, 2186, 2188, 2196
in English theater 2169
as a stereotyped character 144, 2158
Yankton, S. Dak., theater in 2206
Yukon Territory, theater in 2282

Z

Ziegfeld, Florenz 101, 176, 198, 221, 242, 246, 792, 1075, 1485, 1488, 1499, 1501-2, 1562, 1637
Ziegfeld, Patricia 1655
Ziegfeld Follies 183, 193, 218, 226, 244, 249, 1500-1503, 1505, 1516, 1518, 1524-25, 1535, 1554, 1560, 1615, 1621-22, 1629, 1654
Ziegfeld Theatre (N.Y. City) 267